JONES & BARTLETT LEARNING INFORMATION SYSTEMS SECURITY & ASSURANCE SERIES

Legal Issues in Information Security

JOANNA LYN GRAMA

JONES & BARTLETT
LEARNING

World Headquarters
Jones & Bartlett Learning
5 Wall Street
Burlington, MA 01803
978-443-5000
info@jblearning.com
www.jblearning.com

Jones & Bartlett Learning books and products are available through most bookstores and online booksellers. To contact Jones & Bartlett Learning directly, call 800-832-0034, fax 978-443-8000, or visit our website, www.jblearning.com.

Substantial discounts on bulk quantities of Jones & Bartlett Learning publications are available to corporations, professional associations, and other qualified organizations. For details and specific discount information, contact the special sales department at Jones & Bartlett Learning via the above contact information or send an email to specialsales@jblearning.com.

Production Credits
Chief Executive Officer: Ty Field
President: James Homer
SVP, Chief Operating Officer: Don Jones, Jr.
SVP, Chief Technology Officer: Dean Fossella
SVP, Chief Marketing Officer: Alison M. Pendergast
SVP, Chief Financial Officer: Ruth Siporin
SVP, Business Development: Christopher Will
VP, Design and Production: Anne Spencer
VP, Manufacturing and Inventory Control: Therese Connell
Editorial Management: High Stakes Writing, LLC, Editor and Publisher: Lawrence J. Goodrich
Reprints and Special Projects Manager: Susan Schultz
Associate Production Editor: Tina Chen
Director of Marketing: Alisha Weisman
Associate Marketing Manager: Meagan Norlund
Cover Design: Anne Spencer
Composition: Sara Arrand
Cover Image: © Julien Tromeur/ShutterStock, Inc.
Chapter Opener Image: © Rodolfo Clix/Dreamstime.com
Printing and Binding: Malloy, Inc.
Cover Printing: Malloy, Inc.

ISBN: 978-0-7637-9185-8

Library of Congress Cataloging-in-Publication Data
Unavailable at time of printing

6048
Printed in the United States of America
16 15 14 13 12 10 9 8 7 6 5

Contents

Contents

CHAPTER 10 Intellectual Property Law   262

CHAPTER 11 The Role of Contracts   300

Contents

To my son, A.J.,
and my husband, Ananth

Preface

Purpose of This Book

This book is part of the Information Systems Security & Assurance Series from Jones & Bartlett Learning (*www.jblearning.com*). Designed for courses and curriculums in IT Security, Cyber Security, Information Assurance, and Information Systems Security, this series features a comprehensive, consistent treatment of the most current thinking and trends in this critical subject area. These titles deliver fundamental information-security principles packed with real-world applications and examples. Authored by Certified Information Systems Security Professionals (CISSPs), they deliver comprehensive information on all aspects of information security. Reviewed word for word by leading technical experts in the field, these books are not just current, but forward-thinking— putting you in the position to solve the cyber security challenges not just of today, but of tomorrow, as well.

This book discusses information security and the law. Information security is the practice of protecting information to ensure the goals of confidentiality, integrity, and availability. Information security makes sure that accurate information is available to authorized individuals when it is needed. Governments, private organizations, and individuals all use information security to protect information. Sometimes these organizations do a very good job of protecting information. Sometimes they do not.

When governments, private organizations, and individuals do a poor job of protecting the information entrusted to them, legislatures respond with new laws that require a more structured approach to information security. The U.S. federal government has enacted a number of laws that focus on protecting different types of information. Since information security is a complex field, these laws are sometimes complicated as well. Finding out which law applies to a particular situation, or type of data, is often confusing.

This book tries to help eliminate that confusion. Part 1 of the book discusses common concepts in information security, privacy, and the law. These concepts are used throughout the book. Part 2 discusses the federal and state laws and legal concepts that affect how governments and organizations think about information security. This part uses laws and case studies to help explain these concepts. A quick-reference list of the federal laws and cases that are discussed in the book is included at the end of the book. Finally, Part 3 focuses on how to create an information security program that addresses the laws and compliance requirements discussed throughout the book.

Learning Features

The writing style of this book is practical and conversational. Each chapter begins with a statement of learning objectives. Illustrations are used both to clarify the material and to vary the presentation. The text is sprinkled with Notes, Tips, FYIs, Warnings, and sidebars to alert the reader to additional and helpful information related to the subject under discussion. Chapter Assessments appear at the end of each chapter, with solutions provided in the back of the book.

Chapter summaries are included in the text to provide a rapid review or preview of the material and to help students understand the relative importance of the concepts presented.

Audience

The material is suitable for undergraduate or graduate computer science majors or information science majors, students at a two-year technical college or community college who have a basic technical background, or readers who have a basic understanding of IT security and want to expand their knowledge.

Acknowledgments

Many talented people worked long hours to make this book a reality. I owe them a great debt of gratitude. I wish to thank Jones & Bartlett Learning for allowing me the opportunity to write a book on information security and the law. Editors Kim Lindros (Gracie Editorial), Cynthia Hansen (Galloping Hills Publishing), and Lawrence J. Goodrich (High Stakes Writing, LLC) were especially patient with this first-time author and took great care to make this project successful. Thanks to Carole Jelen, literary agent, for putting this deal together and answering my many questions. Talented attorneys Michael H. Goldner, JD, CISSP, CEH, CHFI, Chair of the School of Information Technology, ITT Technical Institute (Norfolk Campus), and David Massey, JD, MBA, CISSP, MCTS, provided many thoughtful insights, comments, and suggestions on drafts of this book. Thank you to author Darril Gibson for writing Chapter 5. Thank you to Kristen McVey, chief deputy prosecuting attorney, Tippecanoe County, Indiana, for providing extensive source materials and advice on Chapter 12.

I could not have written this book without the support of my mentors. Attorney Pamela Hermes has supported me throughout my legal career. Scott Ksander, Chief Information Security Officer at Purdue University, has supported me in my career as an information security professional. Thank you both for having faith in me even when I did not have it in myself. I also am fortunate enough to work with a dedicated group of information technology professionals at Purdue University. They make coming to work each day fun. This includes Vice President for Information Technology, Gerry McCartney; Scott Ksander; and the phenomenal professionals who work for IT Networks and Security. Everyone should be so lucky to work where the smart people are!

I am also fortunate to have wonderful friends and family members who provided extra special support to my family and me during this project. You took care of us and served as sounding boards for ideas and examples in the book. I would especially like to thank William Bormann, Julie Corron, Cherry Delaney, Faith and Darryl Graham, the Hallberg family, William Harshbarger, Gregory Hedrick, the Justice-Coulter family, the Lill family, Patricia and Arthur Rosen, David Seidl, Jeffrey Smith, and Robert Stanfield for their friendship. I also want to thank my parents for a love of learning that has sustained me well in many endeavors. Finally, my husband, Ananth, and son, A.J., deserve special thanks for enthusiastically encouraging me to write this book. You are the best. My love, always, to you both.

About the Author

Joanna Lyn Grama, (JD, CISSP, CIPP/IT) serves as the information security policy and compliance director for Purdue University, where she creates the university's IT security policy and is responsible for compliance governance and activities. She is a member of the Information Systems Audit and Control Association, the organization for IT governance professionals; the American Bar Association, Section of Science and Technology Law, Information Security Committee; EDUCAUSE; and the Indiana State Bar Association. Joanna graduated from the University of Illinois College of Law with honors, and was the editor-in-chief of *The Elder Law Journal*. She is a frequent speaker on a variety of IT security topics, including identity theft, personal information security, and university compliance issues.

PART ONE

Fundamental Concepts

Information Security Overview

ENSURING INFORMATION IS SECURE is not just the job of computer geeks in data centers. It concerns government, corporations, and individuals. The digital revolution greatly changed how people communicate and do business. Because information exchanges now take place instantly, and because almost everyone shares data of some kind, you should question how all organizations use and protect data.

This book is about information security and the law. Information security seeks to protect government, corporate, and individual information. It's a good business practice. Many organizations today want a reputation for properly protecting their own and their customers' data. A good reputation can make a company stand out from its competitors. It can increase sales. It also can make a government agency seem more trustworthy.

Laws also protect information, especially private personal information. They require that data be protected in certain ways. Laws aren't optional. If a law applies to an organization, it must follow the law. Laws make information security more than just a good business practice. They make it a business requirement.

Part 1 of this book reviews the concepts of information security, privacy, and the legal system in the United States. You should develop a broad understanding of these concepts. You will find them throughout this book. Part 2 introduces U.S. laws that influence information security and privacy issues. Finally, Part 3 discusses how to create an information security program.

This book doesn't provide legal advice. Many topics covered here could fill a book on their own. Additional resources listed at the end of the book will help you learn more about the topics that interest you.

Chapter 1 Topics

This chapter covers the following topics and concepts:

- Why information security is an issue
- What information security is
- What the basic information security concepts are
- What common information security concerns are
- How different types of information require different types of protection
- Which mechanisms protect information security
- How special kinds of data require special kinds of protection

Chapter 1 Goals

When you complete this chapter, you will be able to:

- Describe the key concepts and terms associated with information security
- Describe information security goals and give examples of each
- Describe common information security concerns
- Describe mechanisms used to protect information security

Why Is Information Security an Issue?

You see these kinds of stories in the news media every day:

- Someone attacks a university computer. They gain access to the records of over 30,000 students and staff members. These records include names, photographs, and Social Security numbers.
- A computer virus infects an organization's computer network. The virus uses up system resources and slows down the network. It takes the organization several days to remove the virus and repair the network.
- A bank loses a backup tape, potentially exposing more than 1 million customer records. It's never found.
- A company that processes credit cards stores unencrypted account information on its servers. Attackers gain access to the servers, exposing over 40 million accounts.

- An e-mail scam targets an organization. The scam asks employees to verify their account settings. When employees respond, they provide their computer user names and passwords. Attackers use them to access and compromise the organization's computer systems.

Organizations use and store a lot of data. For many, **information** is one of their most important assets. They use data to conduct their business operations. They use large and complex databases to keep track of customer product preferences. They use these same systems to manage the products and services that they offer customers. Organizations also transfer information to other businesses.

Organizations collect data for many reasons. Much of the data they collect is "personal information," which you can use to identify a person. Personally identifiable information includes the following:

- Social Security numbers
- Driver's license numbers
- Financial account data, such as account numbers or personal identification numbers (PINs)
- Health data and biometric data
- Authentication credentials, such as logon or user names and passwords

Based on media reports, security breaches appear to be growing in number. These breaches include data that is lost, stolen, or disclosed without permission. A security breach can damage an organization's reputation. Customers take their business elsewhere when organizations fail to protect their data. The organization may have to pay fines and/ or defend itself in court. If a security breach is particularly bad, an organization's leaders can face criminal charges.

An organization that fails to protect its information risks damaging its reputation— or worse. Information security is the term that generally describes the steps an organization should take to protect its information.

What Is Information Security?

Information security is the study and practice of protecting information. The main goal of information security is to protect its **confidentiality**, **integrity**, and **availability**. Professionals usually refer to this as the "CIA triad," or sometimes the "AIC triad." (A "triad" is a group of three things considered to be a single unit.) The CIA triad appears in Figure 1-1.

FIGURE 1-1

The CIA triad.

In some ways, securing information isn't new. For instance, Julius Caesar used a simple letter-substitution code to share secrets with his military commanders. This type of code is a "Caesar cipher." **Cryptography** is the practice of hiding information so that unauthorized persons can't read it. Using cryptography preserves confidentiality. Only those with the secret key are able to read an encoded note. Caesar used codes to ensure that his enemies could not read his messages.

Secret decoder badges were popular during the golden days of radio. Business sponsors often paid for decoders to market their products. Radio program fan clubs gave them to their members to promote specific radio shows. Secret decoder badges often used a Caesar cipher.

In other ways, information security is a relatively new area of study. Modern computing systems have only existed since the 1960s. The Internet didn't exist in its current form until almost 1983. The first well-known computer security incident was discovered in 1986. President Obama created the first "cybersecurity czar" in the federal government in 2009.

> **NOTE**
>
> Cliff Stoll described the first well-known computer security incident in his book *The Cuckoo's Egg: Tracking a Spy Through the Maze of Computer Espionage.* Stoll noticed an error in the records of systems connected to the Internet's predecessor— the Advanced Research Projects Agency Network. During the investigation, he exposed an international plot to steal information from U.S. computer systems.

The range of information security topics and the number of places to protect data may seem overwhelming. However, the main goal is to protect information's confidentiality, integrity, and availability.

What Is Confidentiality?

Confidentiality means that only people with the right permission can access and use information. It also means protecting it from unauthorized access at all stages of its life cycle. You must create, use, store, transmit, and destroy information in ways that protect its confidentiality.

Encryption is one way to make sure that information remains confidential while it's stored and transmitted. Encryption converts information into code that makes it unreadable. Only people authorized to view the information can decode and use it. Attackers who intercept an encrypted note can't read it because they don't have the decoding key. Encryption protects the note's confidentiality.

Access controls are another way to ensure confidentiality. They grant or deny access to information systems. An example of an access control is requiring a password to access a computer system. Passwords keep unauthorized individuals out of information systems. You also can use access controls to ensure that individuals view only information they have permission to see.

You can compromise information confidentiality on purpose or by accident. For example, **shoulder surfing** attacks are intentional. Such attacks occur when an attacker secretly looks "over the shoulder" of someone at a computer and tries to discover their sensitive information without permission. Shoulder surfing is a visual attack. The attacker must view the personal information. This term also describes attacks in which a person tries to learn sensitive information by viewing keystrokes on a monitor or keyboard. Attackers use the stolen data to access computer systems and commit identity theft.

Social engineering attacks are another intentional threat to confidentiality. They rely heavily on human interaction. This type of attack takes advantage of how people talk with one another and interact. It's not a technical attack. It involves tricking other people to break security procedures and share sensitive information. Social engineering attackers take advantage of human nature, such as kindness and trust. They are often charming. Their victims want to help them by providing information. The attacker uses the information obtained from the victim to try to learn additional sensitive information. An old-fashioned "con game" is an example of a social engineering attack.

FYI

The classic film *The Sting* is a great example of a social engineering scam. In the movie, two con artists, played by Paul Newman and Robert Redford, set up an elaborate plan to con a man out of his money. Their scam relies heavily on manipulating the victim and those around him. The scam takes advantage of human nature.

Kevin Mitnick is perhaps one of the most well-known computer hackers of all time. In his book *The Art of Deception,* he writes that he gained much of the information he used to compromise computer systems through social engineering activities. It was very easy to get information from people if he asked questions in the right way, he said.

Confidentiality compromises also take place by accident. An employee of the U.S. Transportation Security Administration (TSA) posted a redacted copy of a TSA manual on a federal Web site in December 2009. The manual described how TSA agents should screen airline passengers and luggage. It also contained the technical details of how airport screening machines work. The manual contained pictures of identification cards for average Americans, the Central Intelligence Agency, and U.S. legislators.

The TSA posted the manual by mistake, and the public could access the manual online for several months. TSA employees redacted some portions of the manual; however, the TSA improperly performed the redaction. Some people were able to uncover the original information with common software tools. They reposted the manual on a number of other non-governmental Web sites. Some of the other Web sites posted the document with all of the original text available.

This incident highlighted the increase in airport security requirements after the September 11, 2001, terrorist attacks. Lawmakers immediately questioned the TSA about the incident. They asked how it would mitigate the disclosure. They also asked what it would do to prevent future mistakes. Lawmakers wanted to know how the government could prevent other Web sites from reposting the unredacted manual. The TSA argued that posting the manual didn't compromise the safety of U.S. air travel.

The TSA example shows that compromises to confidentiality can have serious results, even to public safety.

What Is Integrity?

Integrity means that information systems and their data are accurate. Integrity ensures that changes can't be made to data without appropriate permission. If a system has integrity, it means that the data in the system is moved and processed in predictable ways. It doesn't change when it's processed.

Controls that ensure the correct entry of information protect integrity. In a computer system, this means that if a field contains a number, the system checks the values that a user enters to make sure that they are numbers. Making sure that only authorized users have the ability to move or delete files on information systems protects integrity. Antivirus software is an example of a control that protects integrity. This type of software checks to make sure that there are no viruses in the system that could harm it.

Information systems can be compromised in a number of ways. A compromise can be accidental or on purpose. For example, an employee accidentally mistypes a name or address during data entry. Integrity is compromised if the system doesn't prevent this type of error. Another common accidental compromise is an employee deleting a file by mistake.

Integrity compromises also can take place on purpose. Employees or external attackers are potential threats. For example, an employee deletes files that are critical to an organization's business. The employee might do this on purpose because they are upset with the organization. **External attackers** also are a concern. They can infect information systems with computer viruses or vandalize a Web page. External attackers who access systems without permission and deliberately change them harm confidentiality and integrity.

In 2007, three Florida A&M University students installed secret keystroke loggers on computers in the university registrar's office. A "keystroke logger" is a device or program that records keystrokes made on a keyboard or mouse. The students obtained the user names and passwords of registrar employees from the logger. For a fee, the hackers modified 650 grades in the computer system for other students. They changed many failing scores to an "A." The student hackers also changed the residency status of other students from "out-of-state" to "in-state." This resulted in the out-of-state students paying less tuition.

The university discovered the keystroke loggers during a routine audit. It then found the modified data. It fixed the incorrect data, but the student hackers accessed the system and changed grades again. The university discovered the hackers' identities through security measures such as logging and audit review.

Prosecutors charged the student hackers with breaking federal laws. The court sentenced two of them to 22 months in prison each. In September 2009, it sentenced the third student to seven years in prison.

The Florida A&M case illustrates how safeguards protect the integrity of computer systems. Routine security audits can detect unauthorized or harmful software on a system.

What Is Availability?

Availability is the security goal of making sure information systems are reliable. It makes sure data is accessible. It also helps to ensure that individuals with proper permission can use systems and retrieve data in a dependable and timely manner.

Organizations need to have information available to conduct their business. When systems work properly, an organization can make money. Information must be available during peak hours when customer demand is high. System maintenance should be scheduled for off hours when customer demand is low.

Availability can be protected in a number of ways. Information systems must recover quickly from disturbances or failures. Organizations create plans that describe how to repair or recover systems after an incident. They specify how long systems may be offline before an organization starts to lose money. In the worst case, an organization might go out of business if it can't repair its information systems quickly.

Organizations also can protect system availability by designing systems to have no single points of failure. A **single point of failure** is a piece of hardware or application that is key to the functioning of the entire system. If that single item fails, a critical portion of the system could fail. Single points of failure also can cause the whole system to fail.

An example of a single point of failure is a modem. A modem connects an organization to the Internet. If the modem fails, the organization can't connect to the Internet. If the organization does most of its business online, the modem failure can really hurt its business.

Organizations also can protect availability by using redundant equipment. This equipment has extra functional elements designed into it. In the event of a failure, the extra elements make sure that the piece of equipment is still able to operate for a certain period. Backing up systems also ensures their availability.

Attackers target availability in order to harm an organization's business. A **denial of service (DoS) attack** disrupts information systems so they're no longer available to users. These attacks also can disable Internet-based services by consuming large amounts of bandwidth or processing power. They can disable an organization's Web site. These services are critical for businesses that sell Web-based products and services or provide information via the Internet.

> **NOTE**
>
> In late December 2009, hackers attacked the Twitter.com Web site. Twitter is a social networking site that allows members to send short messages to each other. Hackers replaced the homepage for a short period with a political message allegedly sponsored by a foreign government. Twitter services were unavailable while it responded to the attack.

Not all DoS attacks directly target information systems and their data. Attackers also target physical infrastructures. For example, an organization can experience a loss of availability if an attacker cuts a network or power cable. The result is the same as a technical DoS attack. Customers and other audiences can't reach the needed services.

Unplanned outages can also negatively impact availability. An "outage" is an interruption of service. Natural disasters create outages, such as a power outage after an earthquake. Outages also take place if a technician accidentally cuts a service cable.

A Web site experiencing an increase in use can result in a loss of availability. When Michael Jackson died in 2009, the Internet experienced a massive increase in search queries. The rapid rise in search traffic caused Google to believe it was under a DoS attack. In response to this perceived attack, Google slowed down the processing of "Michael Jackson" queries. Users entering those queries received error messages until Google determined its services were not under attack.

The Michael Jackson/Google example shows that organizations can take actions to make sure their information systems are available to their customers. These actions can alert organizations to an issue. Then they can take steps to correct it.

The Seven Domains of a Typical Information Technology Infrastructure

There are seven domains in a typical information technology (IT) infrastructure.

- **User Domain**—This domain refers to any users of an organization's IT system. It includes employees, consultants, contractors, or any other third party. These users are called "end users."
- **Workstation Domain**—This area refers to the computing devices used by end users. This includes devices such as desktop or laptop computers.
- **LAN Domain**—This domain refers to the organization's local area network (LAN) technologies. A LAN is two or more computers connected together within a small area.
- **WAN Domain**—A wide area network (WAN) is a network that spans a large geographical area. The most common example of a WAN is the Internet. Organizations with remote locations use a WAN to connect those locations.
- **LAN-to-WAN Domain**—This domain refers to the infrastructure that connects the organization's LAN to a WAN.
- **Remote Access Domain**—This domain refers to the processes and procedures that end users use to remotely access the organization's IT infrastructure and data.
- **System/Application Domain**—This domain refers to the equipment and data an organization uses to support its IT infrastructure. It includes hardware, operating system software, database software, and client-server applications.

Figure 1-2 illustrates the seven domains and how they relate to one another.

Common Information Security Concepts

A number of different concepts are helpful in understanding information security and the laws that affect it. Laws that regulate information security often use risk management to justify them. Risk management is the process of listing the risks that an organization faces and then taking steps to control them. You will briefly learn about basic risk management concepts and terms here. Part 3 of this book fully explores these concepts.

Vulnerabilities

A **vulnerability** is a weakness or flaw in an information system. Vulnerabilities can be "exploited" (used in an unjust way) to harm information security. They may be construction or design mistakes. They also may be flaws in how an internal safeguard is used or not used. Not using antivirus software on a computer is a vulnerability.

There are many different types of vulnerabilities. You can classify them into the following broad categories:

- People
- Process
- Facility
- Technology

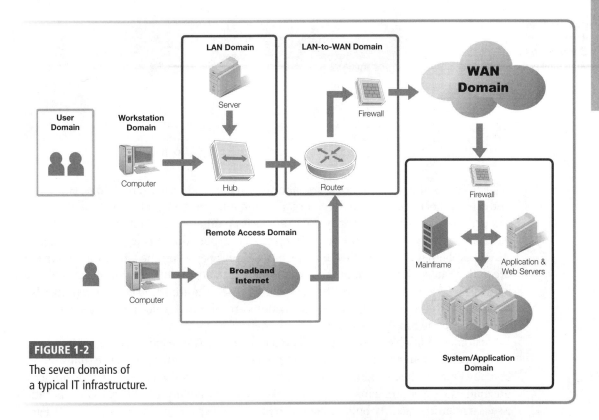

FIGURE 1-2

The seven domains of
a typical IT infrastructure.

People can cause a number of vulnerabilities. One
employee could know too much about a critical financial
function in an organization. This is a violation of the
separation of duties principle. This rule requires that two
or more employees must split critical task functions so
that no employee knows all of the steps of the critical
task. When only one employee knows all of the steps
of a critical task, they can use the information to harm
the organization. The harm may go unnoticed if other
employees can't access the same information.

> **NOTE**
>
> A common example of the separation
> of duties principle is a rule requiring
> two people to sign organization checks.
> This is so one person can't steal from the
> organization by writing and signing checks
> made out to himself or herself. Requiring
> two signatures protects the organization.

  Process-based vulnerabilities are flaws or weaknesses in an organization's procedures.
An attacker can exploit these weaknesses to harm security. Process-based vulnerabil-
ities include missing steps in a checklist. They also may include not having a checklist.
Another is the failure to apply hardware and software vendor patches in a timely manner.
A **patch** is a piece of software or code that updates a program to address security problems.
Patches are available for many types of software, including operating systems. Systems
may be open to attack if patches are not properly applied.

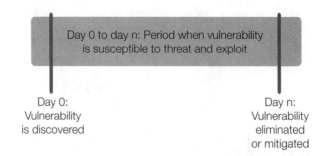

Day 0 to day n: Period when vulnerability
is susceptible to threat and exploit

Day 0:
Vulnerability
is discovered

Day n:
Vulnerability
eliminated
or mitigated

Facility-based vulnerabilities are weaknesses in physical security. Buildings, equipment, and other property are resources an organization must protect. Failing to protect these resources is poor physical security. An example is an organization that doesn't have a fence around its property. Another is an open server room that any employee can access.

Vulnerabilities also can be technology based. Improperly designed information systems are in this category. Some design flaws allow people to access information systems without permission. After gaining entry, the person may enter unauthorized code or commands that disrupt the system. Unpatched applications are technology vulnerabilities. So are improperly configured equipment, such as firewalls or routers.

Customers don't like flaws in products that they buy. They expect vendors to inform them quickly about product flaws. "Vulnerability management" makes sure that vendors find any flaws in their products and quickly correct them. It also ensures that customers are made aware of problems so they can take protective action. The Microsoft Corporation issues a monthly security bulletin for customers that lists known vulnerabilities in their products. The bulletins also explain how to address them.

Exploits are successful attacks against a vulnerability. They take place in a period known as the **window of vulnerability**, as shown in Figure 1-3. This window opens when someone discovers a vulnerability. It closes when someone reduces or eliminates it. Exploits take place while the window is open.

The window of vulnerability is a notable concept. In some ways, this window is shrinking fast because more people are interested in information security. Many people have developed the skills to find new vulnerabilities. Often they report them to the company that provides the product or service. Not all people act with good intentions: There are also more people with the skills needed to find and attack vulnerabilities. Many of these people attack them for financial gain.

Some vulnerabilities are exploited almost as soon as they are discovered. The term for this is a **zero-day vulnerability**. It's unique because it's exploited before a vendor provides a patch or some other fix. The SANS Institute has one of the largest collections of information security resources in the world. Every year it creates a list of Top Cyber Security Risks. Zero-day vulnerabilities are on the 2009 list at *http://www.sans.org/top-cyber-security-risks/*.

The number of vulnerabilities appears to be growing. The National Vulnerability Database recorded 350 new vulnerabilities between January 1 and January 15, 2010. One reason for this could be that information systems are becoming larger and more complex. Another possibility is that as more people work together to create new systems, the likelihood of introducing flaws increases. Poor programming practices may be another reason. Vulnerabilities also may be increasing due to a lack of checking to make sure that systems work as intended.

 NOTE

The U.S. government maintains the National Vulnerability Database (NVD), a searchable database of known security flaws and weaknesses. It also includes listings of known system problems. The National Cyber Security Division of the U.S. Department of Homeland Security sponsors the NVD. You can find it at *http://nvd.nist.gov/home.cfm*.

The number of known vulnerabilities also may be increasing because some developers use well-known programming codes and components to design systems. They also use well-known software in the systems they design. Using familiar components makes it easier for many people to work together on the same project. There are dangers, however. The more well known the code, hardware, or software, the greater the chance that an attacker has the necessary skills to find vulnerabilities in the final product.

Threats

Threats are anything that can cause harm to an information system. They are successful exploits against vulnerabilities. A threat source—which is a person or circumstance—carries out a threat or causes it to take place.

It's worth taking some time to understand how vulnerabilities and threats are related. For example, an organization may have few controls to prevent an employee from deleting critical computer files. This lack of controls is the vulnerability. A well-meaning employee could delete files by mistake. The employee is the threat source. The threat is the action of deleting the critical files. If the employee deletes the files, a successful exploit of the vulnerability has taken place. If the files are not recoverable, or recoverable only at great expense, the incident harms the organization and its security. In this example, availability is compromised.

Threats fall into broad categories:

- Human
- Natural
- Technology and Operational
- Physical and Environmental

People carry out human threats. Common examples are internal and external attackers. Even the loss of key personnel in some instances is a type of human threat. People threats include both good actors and bad actors. Good actors include well-meaning employees; bad actors are attackers who intend to harm an organization.

"Natural threats" are uncontrollable events such as earthquakes, tornadoes, fires, and flood. These types of threats aren't predictable. Organizations can't control these types of threats.

"Technology and operational threats" operate inside of information systems to harm information security goals. Malicious code is an example of these threats. Hardware and software failures are technology threats. Improperly running processes are also threats.

"Physical and environmental threats" can be facility based. These types of threats can include a facility breach due to lax physical security. Loss of heating or cooling within a facility also is an environmental threat.

Threats are either deliberate or accidental. Accidental threats are the results of either unintentional actions or inactions. You can think of accidental threats as mistakes or acts of God. Unintended equipment failure also is an accidental threat.

Mistakes most often are the result of well-meaning employees. The file deletion example at the beginning of this section is an accidental threat. The TSA employee improperly posting the manual to a Web site is an accidental threat. Organizational policy and security training and awareness can help mitigate such mistakes.

An act of God also can cause an accidental threat. "Act of God" is a legal term that describes a natural event or disaster for which no person is responsible. Acts of God that disrupt services or compromise information security are threats. Earthquakes, tornadoes, and floods are all examples of acts of God. It's hard for organizations to plan for these types of threats. They can take basic precautions against some types of natural disasters by building redundant systems. An organization also may choose not to build facilities in areas prone to environmental instability.

All organizations must plan for equipment failure. Sometimes equipment breaks through no fault of its operators. Sometimes it reaches the end of its life and stops working. Unfortunately, it's hard for organizations to plan for such failures. This is especially true if the equipment that fails is particularly specialized or expensive. Organizations can mitigate this type of threat by building redundant systems and keeping spare parts on hand.

"Deliberate threats" are intentional actions taken by attackers. Both internal and external attackers are deliberate threats. **Internal attackers** have current relationships with the organization that they are targeting. They can cause a lot of damage in computer systems. This is because they have special knowledge about those systems. They use their legitimate access to harm an organization. Upset employees are often the cause of internal attacks. They usually wish to harm the organization by causing a loss of productivity. They also may wish to embarrass the organization or hurt its reputation. These attackers may delete files or disclose information without permission. They also may intentionally disrupt the availability of information systems.

Internal attackers also can take advantage of lax physical security. They might do this to steal resources such as confidential information. Theft of resources is a problem for many organizations.

In 2007, a former Coca-Cola employee was sentenced to eight years in jail for stealing Coca-Cola trade secrets. She also was ordered to pay $40,000 in restitution. She stole Coca-Cola secrets and tried to sell them to rival Pepsi. Surveillance video showed the employee putting company documents into bags and leaving the building. The video also showed her putting a container of a Coca-Cola product sample into her bag and leaving the building. All of these actions were violations of Coca-Cola company policies. The theft was discovered when Pepsi informed Coca-Cola.

External attackers are another concern. They usually have no current relationship with the organization they're targeting. Some are former employees with special knowledge about the organization. External hackers include spies, saboteurs, and terrorists. Many seek financial gain. Others want to embarrass an organization, make a political statement, or exploit systems for a challenge.

In 1997, a former employee deleted the U.S. Coast Guard personnel database. She had helped to design the system. Once she left the Coast Guard, she used her knowledge of the system to access it and deleted the database. The media reported that she deleted the database because the Coast Guard had not taken her work-related complaints seriously. It cost the Coast Guard $40,000 and took 115 employees more than 1,800 hours to recover the data.

The former employee pleaded guilty to accessing a federal computer without authorization and intentionally causing damage. A court sentenced her to five months in jail followed by five months' house arrest. She also had to pay a $35,000 fine.

Organizations must take steps to avoid threats. When an employee leaves an organization, the organization should promptly remove his or her access to information systems. Good information security practices also help reduce threats posed by external attackers. These include patching known vulnerabilities in hardware and software. They also include monitoring access to systems and engaging in logging and audit review.

Risks

A **risk** is the likelihood that a threat will exploit a vulnerability and cause harm. The harm is the impact to the organization. Impacts from threats vary. An information security impact includes a loss of confidentiality, integrity, and availability. Other impacts include a loss of life, productivity or profit, property, and reputation. You can measure impact in terms of money costs or by perceived harm to the organization.

 NOTE

It is not possible to identify every security vulnerability, plan for every threat, or identify all risks. Even when you identify risks, you can't limit all risk of harm.

Not all risks receive the same level of attention from an organization. Organizations must engage in complex risk analysis and risk management programs to classify and respond to risks. A brief overview of some risk analysis and management terms is included here. Part 3 of this book discusses the risk analysis process.

Risk analysis is the process of reviewing known vulnerabilities and threats. Organizations generally classify the probability that a threat will exploit a vulnerability as low, medium, or high. They then attempt to assess the impact of a successful exploit. They should address risks that have large impacts on the organization and its information security.

Organizations have a number of options for responding to risk. Common responses include:

- Risk avoidance
- Risk mitigation
- Risk transfer
- Risk acceptance

All organizations must assess risk. They also must respond to risk. Organizations can apply safeguards to respond to vulnerabilities, threats, and ultimately, risk. A safeguard is any protective action that reduces exposure to vulnerabilities or threats. A risk response strategy determines how safeguards should be applied.

Organizations can try to get rid of risk by applying safeguards to fix vulnerabilities and control threats. **Risk avoidance** is the process of applying safeguards to avoid a negative impact. A risk avoidance strategy seeks to eliminate all risk.

Organizations also can mitigate risk to reduce a negative impact. They apply safeguards to vulnerabilities and threats. Safeguards lower risks to a level deemed acceptable, but do not eliminate it. This is **risk mitigation**. The leftover risk is **residual risk**.

Organizations also transfer risk. In a **risk transfer** strategy, an organization passes its risk to another entity. The risk impact is borne by the other entity. An organization might choose this type of strategy when the cost of mitigating risk is more expensive than transferring it. For example, organizations could purchase cyber liability insurance in response to a risk. They purchase these policies to transfer their risk to the insurance company. The insurance company bears the cost of any risk impact. These insurance policies can cover losses for a number of issues. A cyber liability insurance policy can cover organizational loss due to unauthorized access to information systems. It also can cover loss due to system interruption and crime. Cyber liability policies have grown popular in the last five years.

An organization also can decide to accept the assessed risk and take no action against it. An organization makes an intentional decision to do nothing about a risk in a **risk acceptance** strategy. This means that avoiding, mitigating, or transferring risk isn't part of the plan. Organizations don't take decisions to accept risk lightly. Organizations may choose to accept risk if the cost of the risk itself is less than the cost to avoid, mitigate, or transfer the risk.

Safeguards

A **safeguard** reduces the harm posed by information security vulnerabilities or threats. Safeguards may eliminate or reduce risk of harm. They are **controls** or countermeasures, and you can use these terms interchangeably.

Safeguards belong to different classifications according to how they work. These classification levels are:

- Administrative
- Technical
- Physical

Administrative safeguards are actions and rules implemented to protect information. Laws and regulations influence these safeguards. They usually take the form of organizational policies, which state the rules of the workplace. These documents are usually specific. They set forth the rules for running the workplace to protect information security. One administrative safeguard is the workplace rule of **need to know.**

Applying need to know, an employer gives employees access only to the data they need to do their jobs. An employee doesn't receive access to any other data even if they have appropriate clearance. Using need-to-know principles makes it harder for unauthorized access to occur and protects confidentiality. There eventually should be technical enforcement of these principles. However, the first step is specifying that a workplace will follow them.

Technical safeguards, also called "logical safeguards," are applied in the hardware and software of information systems. They are the rules that state how systems will operate. Technical safeguards include automated logging and access-control mechanisms, firewalls, and antivirus programs. Using automated methods to enforce password strength is also a technical control.

One technical safeguard that companies use to protect information security is the access control rule of **least privilege**. This rule is very similar to the need-to-know rule. It means that systems should always run with the least amount of permissions needed to complete tasks. For example, some operating systems allow administrators to set up different privilege levels for system users. This enforces least privilege. Users with administrative privileges can access all system functions. They can fully manipulate and modify the system and its resources.

"Local users," on the other hand, have fewer privileges. They are only able to use some programs or applications. They can't add, modify, delete, or manipulate the computer system. "Power users" have more privileges than local users but fewer privileges than administrators do. Power users may use and access many functions of the computer system. However, they may not modify critical functions of the operating system.

FYI

A strong password is easy for you to remember but difficult for others to guess. Strong passwords don't contain any dictionary words, references to your user logon, or your name. They often are longer than eight characters. These types of passwords use a combination of uppercase and lowercase letters, numbers, and special characters. It's important to use them to help keep your information safe. Password-cracking programs can easily break weak passwords.

Physical safeguards are actions that an organization takes to protect its actual, tangible resources. They keep unauthorized individuals out of controlled areas. They also keep people away from sensitive equipment. Key-card access to buildings, fences, doors, locks, security lighting, and video surveillance are physical safeguards. They also include security guards and guard dogs.

A more sophisticated example of a physical security control is a **mantrap**, as shown in Figure 1-4. A mantrap is a method of controlled entry into a facility and provides access to secure areas such as a research lab or data center. This method of entry has two sets of doors on either end of a small room. When a person enters a mantrap through one set of doors, the first set must close before the second set can open. This process effectively "traps" a person in the small room.

Often a person must provide different credentials at each set of mantrap doors. The first set of doors might allow access to the mantrap via a card reader. An employee scans an identification badge to gain entry. The second set of doors then may require a different method to open. For example, an employee may need to enter a personal identification number on a keypad. Technicians often configure mantraps so that both sets of doors lock if a person can't provide the appropriate credentials at the second set of doors. When locked in a mantrap, the person must await "rescue" by a security guard or another official.

Mantraps aren't just for highly sensitive data centers or labs. Some apartment buildings apply a modified mantrap concept to building entry. Any individual can access the lobby area of the apartment building. However, only people with keys or access cards may pass through a locked security door and enter the building's interior. Usually, only residents have the proper credentials to enter the interior. Guests to the building need to use the intercom system to phone the resident they want to visit. The apartment resident can then "buzz" guests through the locked door to allow access to the building's interior.

You also can classify safeguards based on how they act. These classification levels are:

- Preventative
- Detective
- Corrective

"Preventative controls" are safeguards used to prevent security incidents. These controls keep an incident from happening. Door locks are a preventative safeguard. This is because they help keep intruders out of the locked area. Fencing around a building is a similar

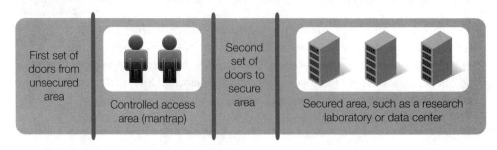

FIGURE 1-4

An example of a mantrap.

First set of doors from unsecured area

Controlled access area (mantrap)

Second set of doors to secure area

Secured area, such as a research laboratory or data center

TABLE 1-1	A safeguards matrix.		
SAFEGUARD TYPE	**PREVENTATIVE**	**DETECTIVE**	**CORRECTIVE**
Administrative	Organization hiring policy	Organization periodic background checks policy	Discipline policy
Technical (Logical)	Least privilege principle	Antivirus software	Updating firewall rules to block and attack
Physical	Locks on doors to critical areas	Burglar alarms	Locking a door that was inadvertently left unlocked

preventative control. Teaching employees how to avoid information security threats is also a preventative control.

"Detective controls" are safeguards put in place in order to detect a security incident while it's in progress. These controls then report that there's an incident in progress. Examples of detective controls include logging system activity and reviewing the logs. Log review can look for unauthorized access or other security anomalies that require attention. An "anomaly" is something strange or unusual—activity that isn't normal.

"Corrective safeguards" are controls put in place in order to limit the damage caused by a security incident. These types of controls are automated or manual. Some types of databases allow an administrator to "roll back" to the last known good copy of the database in the event of an incident. Corrective controls also can be quite simple: locking doors inadvertently left unlocked, for example.

Table 1-1 summarizes the safeguards described in this section.

Choosing Safeguards

Organizations may have difficulty choosing safeguards. Many organizations use reference guides to help with this task. Two of the most common guides are the "ISO/IEC 27002:2005, Information Technology—Security Techniques—Code of Practice for Information Security Management (2007)" and "NIST Special Publication 800-53 (Rev. 3), Recommended Security Controls for Federal Information Systems and Organizations (2009)."

The International Organization for Standardization (ISO) and the International Electrotechnical Commission (IEC) first published ISO/IEC 27002 in December 2000. These two groups work together to create standards for electronic technologies. ISO/IEC 27002 has 11 major sections. Each discusses a different category of information security safeguards, or controls. They explain why organizations should use the listed controls and how to use them. Security practitioners often use ISO/IEC 27002 as a practical guide for developing security standards and best practices.

"NIST Special Publication 800-53 (Rev. 3), Recommended Security Controls for Federal Information Systems and Organizations," was published in 2009 by the National Institute of Standards and Technology (NIST). This document states the minimum safeguards required in order to create an effective information security program. NIST developed this guidance specifically for federal agency use on federal information systems. Many non-governmental organizations also use the document to help guide their own information security programs.

What Are Common Information Security Concerns?

Information security practitioners have their hands full. This section describes some of the concerns that practitioners deal with daily.

Shoulder Surfing

Shoulder surfing occurs when an attacker looks over the shoulder of another person at a computer to discover sensitive information. This isn't a technical exploit. The attacker has no right to the information they are trying to see. The attacker could be attempting to learn user names and passwords or discover sensitive information. They do this by viewing keystrokes on a monitor or keyboard. Shoulder surfing is a concern at public places such as automated teller machines (ATMs) or self-service credit card terminals at grocery stores.

Shoulder surfing also can be a concern at airports, coffee shops, and other places with wireless access. Computer users may attempt to access e-mail accounts, bank accounts, and other sensitive information while in these public places. A person's guard is often down in these places. The coffee drinker at the next table really could be an attacker who is watching and recording sensitive information.

Social Engineering

Social engineering describes an attack that relies heavily on human relations. It's not a technical attack. This type of attack involves tricking other people to break normal security procedures to gain sensitive information. These attackers take advantage of human nature.

---

technical TIP

Individuals can guard against shoulder surfing attacks by shielding keypads with their hands. You also can hide an ATM screen by blocking it with your body so that attackers can't view the screen. Laptop privacy guards and privacy shields also work well. These shields are placed over a monitor when computing in public places. Organizations may wish to purchase these types of privacy guards for executives who frequently travel. That way the executive can work on business data in public places, such as an airport, while not worrying about shoulder surfing attacks.

These attacks are sometimes simple to carry out. For instance, an attacker telephones a large organization. The attacker identifies himself as a member of that same organization's technology group. He has a conversation with the person who answered the phone. The attacker might ask about that person's Internet connectivity or computing equipment. The person answering the call is inclined to participate in the conversation. They trust the attacker because he said that they both work for the same organization.

The attacker may ask for the person's user name, identification number, or logon name at the end of the call. He may claim that this is for verification purposes. The person answering the call might provide that information because it seems like a reasonable request. Without much effort, the attacker has gained information that could be used to access organizational resources. This is a social engineering attack.

Phishing and Targeted Phishing Scams

Phishing is a form of Internet fraud where attackers attempt to steal valuable information from their victims. Phishing attacks take place in electronic communications. These attacks can take place via e-mail or instant messages. Phishing attacks also can take place in Internet chat rooms.

These attackers are "phishing" for confidential information. This includes credit cards, Social Security numbers, user logon credentials, and passwords. Phishing attacks may attempt to look like a legitimate message from a known organization. They also may pretend to be from organizations familiar to the intended victim.

Phishing messages usually request that the recipients click on a uniform resource locator (URL) to verify their account details. When the victim clicks on the URL, a Web site opens that looks like a legitimate site. It prompts the victim to enter personal information to verify identity. In reality, the site that the victim navigated to is a fake Web site designed only to capture the victim's personal information. The fake Web site often is a copy of a trusted site.

"Spear phishing" is a targeted phishing scam. Attackers may target a particular organization. This is a more sophisticated form of attack where a message might look as if it's from a highly trusted and authentic source. Attackers often research the targeted organization to make their messages look authentic. This background research is easy due to the wealth of information on the Internet. Spear phishing messages may use an organization's logo or terms specific to it. Spear phishing attacks attempt to obtain information about the targeted organization. This can include logons and passwords.

"Whaling" is a new type of targeted phishing scam. In a whaling scam, attackers target corporate executives. The federal judiciary circulated an alert in 2008 that warned about a whaling scam. The alert stated that some corporate executives had received a scam e-mail that claimed to be a grand jury subpoena. The e-mail was not a real subpoena. Executives unintentionally downloaded malware onto their computer systems when they clicked on a link in the "subpoena" e-mail.

The Morris worm was one of the first Internet computer worms. Robert Morris Jr. was a student at Cornell University in 1988 when he created the worm. It was an experimental piece of code. It spread very quickly and infected some computers multiple times. Over 6,000 computers were infected. It overwhelmed government and university networked systems. Morris was charged with violating the 1986 Computer Fraud and Abuse Act. He was convicted and sentenced to a $10,000 fine, 400 hours of community service, and three years' probation.

Malware

Malware is a general term that refers to any type of software that performs some sort of harmful, unauthorized, or unknown activity. Malware includes computer viruses, worms, and Trojan horses. The term malware is a combination of the words malicious and software.

Computer viruses are programs that spread by infecting applications on a computer. These types of programs are called viruses because they resemble biological viruses. They copy themselves in order to infect a computer. Viruses can spread over a computer network or the Internet. They also can spread from computer to computer on infected disks, CDs, DVDs, or universal serial bus (USB) thumb drives. When the infected virus code is executed, it tries to place itself into uninfected software.

A computer worm is similar to a virus. Unlike a virus, a computer worm is a self-contained program that doesn't require external assistance to propagate. Some well-known Internet worms include the Morris worm, SQL Slammer, and Blackworm.

A Trojan horse is malware that pretends to be legitimate and desirable software. In reality, it's malicious. A Trojan horse can masquerade as an image or file that a user wants. It spreads when a user downloads the seemingly legitimate file. While the user believes a legitimate file is downloading, the Trojan horse is actually loading. This type of malware is especially prevalent on social networking sites. Accepting virtual "gifts" on these sites can often expose users to nasty surprises.

Spyware and Keystroke Loggers

Spyware and keystroke loggers are forms of malware. Spyware is any technology that secretly gathers information about a person or organization. Many users inadvertently download spyware with other programs from the Internet. Spyware hides on a system. It can collect information about individuals and their Internet browsing habits. Cookies set by Web sites can allow spyware to track the sites that a person visits. This is especially dangerous because some cookies can contain Web site logon and password information. Spyware can slow computer systems, hog resources, and use network bandwidth. Some spyware programs install other programs on a computer system. These activities can make a computer system open to other attacks.

A keystroke logger is a device or program that records keystrokes made on a keyboard or mouse. Attackers secretly install keystroke loggers. Attackers are able to recover computer keyboard entries and sometimes even mouse clicks from keystroke loggers. They can review the data retrieved from a keystroke logger to find sensitive information. This includes user names, passwords, and other confidential user information. The student hackers in the Florida A&M example discussed earlier in this chapter used a keystroke logger. They obtained computer access credentials from the keystroke logger data.

Logic Bombs

A logic bomb is harmful code intentionally left on a computer system. It lies dormant for a certain period. When specific conditions are met, it "explodes" and carries out its malicious function. Conditions that cause the logic bomb to explode vary. Programmers can create logic bombs that explode on a certain day or when a specific event occurs. Attackers also program logic bombs to explode in response to no action. A logic bomb may explode when the creator doesn't log onto the target computer system for a predetermined number of days.

Upset employees sometimes use logic bombs. In October 2008, Fannie Mae fired an employee from his Unix engineer position. Management didn't disable his computer access to Fannie Mae systems until nearly four hours after his firing. The engineer allegedly tried to hide a logic bomb in the computer system during that time. The logic bomb was set to activate the morning of January 31, 2009. It was designed to delete 4,000 Fannie Mae servers when activated.

Fannie Mae information technology professionals accidentally found the logon bomb five days after he planted the "explosive." He was indicted in January 2009 for unauthorized computer access. He is free on bail while awaiting trial at this writing.

Backdoors

A backdoor, also called a "trap door," is a way to access a computer program or system that bypasses normal mechanisms. Programmers sometimes install a backdoor to access a program quickly during development to troubleshoot problems. This is especially helpful in large and complex programs. Programmers usually remove backdoors when the programming process is over. However, they can easily forget about the backdoors if they don't follow good development practices.

A backdoor is a security vulnerability regardless of its initial purpose. Attackers search for system backdoors to exploit them. Sometimes attackers install backdoors on systems they want to visit again. Attackers can have virtually unhindered access to a system through a backdoor.

> **NOTE**
>
> The computer worm MyDoom installed backdoors on infected Microsoft Windows computers. Attackers could then send spam e-mail from the infected machines. It helped to spread the worm. Some versions of the MyDoom worm also blocked access to popular antivirus software vendor Web sites. This made it very hard to remove the worm.

Denial of Service Attacks

You learned about denial of service attacks earlier in the chapter. This type of attack disrupts information systems. Attackers do this so that the systems aren't available for legitimate users. These attacks can disable an organization's Web page or Internet-based services.

A "distributed denial of service" (DDoS) attack is another form of DoS attack. This type of attack occurs when attackers use multiple systems to attack a targeted system. These attacks really challenge the targeted system. It often can't ward off an attack coming from hundreds or thousands of different computers. A DDoS attack sends so many requests for services to a targeted system that the system or Web site is overwhelmed and can't respond.

In a DDoS attack, the attacker takes control of multiple systems to coordinate the attack. They call this type of attack "distributed" because it involves multiple systems to launch the attack. Usually the attacker exploits security vulnerabilities in many machines. The attacker then directs the compromised machines to attack the target. Another term for these compromised machines is "zombies." Major Web sites are often DDoS attack victims. These systems handle a lot of traffic by design. They pose an attractive target for DDoS attackers seeking to compromise a system's availability.

Information security deals with these types of issues every day. Organizations can implement safeguards to help decrease the impact of such attacks.

Do Different Types of Information Require Different Types of Protection?

There are many types of information. Public and private are two major categories, for example. Not all information has the same level of sensitivity. An organization must weigh the sensitivity of information against the way in which it wants to use that information. To do this easily, an organization might choose to create data protection models to classify the different types of information it uses.

To create a data protection model, an organization first creates data classification levels. These levels serve as the basis for specifying certain types of safeguards for different categories of data. Information that would not harm the organization with its disclosure might be labeled "public" information. This would be the lowest classification of data. It would typically have no special rules for its use.

> **NOTE**
>
> Businesses compete for customers and money. They must distinguish themselves from their competitors. A competitive edge is the designs, blueprints, or features that make one organization's products or services unique. Protecting competitive edge is one of the functions of information security.

Information that would harm the organization, its reputation, or its **competitive edge** if publicly disclosed might be called "confidential." Another term that is often used for this type of information is "restricted." Organizations take multiple steps to protect this type of information. They create rules that prevent unauthorized access to it. Other rules might address the sharing and storage of information and its disposal.

An organization must carefully review its data and put it in the proper classification level. For example, an organization has advertising materials that it freely gives to its customers. It would probably assign these materials to the "public" category. The organization has no special rules for how employees should protect this information. Employees are able to freely use, copy, and share this type of information. The organization also might have design blueprints for its products. These documents contain the secrets that make the organization's products special. This type of material is labeled "restricted." Employees are limited in how they can use, copy, or share this information.

Data classification is a common way to think about protecting data. The general rule for protecting information is that the more sensitive or confidential the information, the fewer people that should have access to it. Very sensitive information should have more safeguards. Information that isn't as sensitive doesn't need such extensive protection.

U.S. National Security Information

The U.S. government classifies its data. It also specifies rules for using classified information. President Barack Obama signed *Executive Order 13526* in December 2009, which describes a system for classifying national security information.

The Order establishes three classification levels. The difference between the levels is the amount of harm that could be caused to U.S. security if the data were disclosed to an unauthorized person. The levels are Confidential, Secret, and Top Secret:

- "Confidential" describes information that could cause damage to U.S. security if disclosed to an unauthorized person. This is the lowest data classification level.

- "Secret" describes information that could cause serious damage to U.S. security if disclosed to an unauthorized person.

- "Top Secret" is the highest classification level. This type of information could cause exceptionally grave damage to U.S. security if disclosed to an unauthorized person.

The Order also sets forth the rules to follow when using national security information. Among other rules, it states how the information must be marked and identified. It also gives instructions on how long it must remain classified. The Order also specifies when to release such information to the public.

Another part of protecting information involves reviewing security goals in the CIA triad. Organizations must decide which goals are most important to them. For some organizations, making sure their data is available and accurate is the most important goal. These organizations use controls that ensure that correct data is always available to their customers.

Military or government organizations may place a higher value on confidentiality and integrity goals. They value secrecy and accuracy. It's usually very important to them that sensitive data not fall into the wrong hands. It's equally important that their data be correct. This is because key personnel rely on it when making decisions. These organizations use controls that ensure that data is accurate and protected from unauthorized access.

What Are the Mechanisms That Ensure Information Security?

Protecting information isn't easy. It's often expensive and time consuming to do well. The security of a system relates to the time taken to implement safeguards and their cost. Highly secure information systems take significant time and expense to create. If an organization wants to implement secure systems quickly, it must be prepared to spend money. If it wants to keep time and money costs low, it must be prepared for lower security.

Laws and Legal Duties

Most organizations are subject to a number of laws. Although this book focuses on laws that affect information security, these are not the only types of laws organizations must follow. For example, they may have to follow workplace safety laws and fair labor standards. Other laws may include equal employment opportunity, hazardous materials disposal, and transportation. An organization must make sure that it follows all of the laws that apply to it.

"Industry sector" is a term that describes a group of organizations that share a similar industry type. They often do business in the same area of the economy. In the United States, Congress enacts laws by industry sector. These laws address the protection of data used by organizations in a particular industry, such as finance and health care. Even the federal government has laws that it must follow to secure certain types of information. Some of these laws have very specific requirements.

Organizations also must follow general legal duties. For example, executives must act reasonably and in the best interest of the organization. This means they must use good judgment when making decisions for it. Part 2 of this book will address the legal duties an organization must fulfill.

 NOTE

Data centers aren't inexpensive. In January 2010, Facebook announced plans to build its first data center. Facebook is a social networking application and Web site. It has 350 million users around the world. It has sizable server and data storage needs. Media reports estimate it will cost about $180 million to build the data center.

Contracts

The action of paying someone to do work on your behalf is called outsourcing. Many organizations outsource information technology functions to save money. Outsourced functions can include data center hosting, e-mail facilities, and data storage. It's very expensive for organizations to build their own data center. It's cheaper for some of them to rent equipment space in another organization's data center.

An organization can't avoid its legal duties by outsourcing functions. It must enter into a contract with the company to which it's outsourcing. A "contract" is a legal agreement between two or more parties that sets ground rules for their relationship. The parties use a contract to define their relationship and state their obligations. Organizations must include specific security clauses and safeguards in outsourcing contacts to make sure they meet their legal obligations.

Organizational Governance

An organization's governance documents form the basis for its information security program. These documents include policies, standards, guidelines, and procedures. They show the organization's vow to protect its own information and that which is entrusted to it. Policies are the first level of governance documents. A "policy" tells an organization how it must act and the consequences for failing to act properly. It's important for an organization's management team to support its policies. Policies often fail without that top-level support.

NOTE

As discussed earlier in the chapter, a policy is an administrative safeguard.

Standards state the activities and actions needed to meet policy goals. They state the safeguards necessary to reduce risks and meet policy requirements. Standards don't refer to particular technologies, operating systems, or types of hardware or software.

Guidelines are recommended actions and guides for employees. Guidelines tell users about information security concerns and suggest ways to deal with them. Guidelines should be flexible for use in many situations.

Procedures are step-by-step checklists. They explain how to meet security goals. Procedures are the lowest level of governance documents. They often are tailored to a certain type of technology. They also can be limited to the activities of specific departments, or even specific users in departments. Procedures are revised often as technology changes.

Voluntary Organizations

Individuals and organizations may belong to voluntary membership groups that seek to promote information security. Group members often have rules that they agree to follow. These rules usually set forth behavior expectations. These rules are usually ethical in nature. They sometimes are called a code of practice or code of ethics.

Individuals who hold the Certified Information Systems Security Professional (CISSP) certification agree to adhere to the (ISC)² code of ethics. These rules require that a CISSP must provide competent information security advice and maintain a certain knowledge level. The (ISC)² code of ethics also requires that a CISSP-certified individual work to keep the public infrastructure strong.

Whole organizations also participate in voluntary membership groups. They agree to follow the terms of codes of conduct. The Internet Commerce Association (ICA) adopted a code of conduct for its member organizations in 2007 to provide for fair practice in the domain name industry. Its rules require protection of intellectual property rights. The rules also require members to abide by Internet fraud laws, including laws to stop the spread of phishing scams. You can learn more about the code at: *www.internetcommerce.org/member_code_of_coduct*.

The Systems Security Certified Practitioner (SSCP) Certification

The International Information Systems Security Certification Consortium (ISC)[2] developed a Common Body of Knowledge (CBK) for information security. The CBK covers all areas of information security. These areas are called "domains." Individuals seeking certification must fully understand the CBK subject areas.

(ISC)[2] offers information security certifications. The Systems Security Certified Practitioner (SSCP) is one of its credentials. SSCP holders are IT professionals who are interested in security. They have one year of work experience. They must take a test to show their understanding of the SSCP CBK information security domains.

The CBK domains for the SSCP are:

- **Access Controls**—This domain explores granting or denying permission to use a resource. Access control mechanisms protect resources from use by unauthorized persons. They also ensure that only people with appropriate permissions can modify or change information.

- **Cryptography**—This domain explores the science of hiding information. You can disguise information to protect it from unauthorized persons by encrypting it. There are many different ways to encrypt information in order to protect it.

- **Malicious Code and Activity**—This domain explains how to identify malicious code and protect against it.

- **Monitoring and Analysis**—This domain discusses how to properly monitor information systems to keep them secure. It also discusses how to analyze logs and reports.

- **Networks and Communications**—This domain addresses how to secure communication networks, such as telephone and data systems. One way to design secure network communications is to make sure they are redundant and have no single points of failure.

- **Risk, Response, and Recovery**—This domain explores risk management concepts. Organizations use risk management to document the value of their information assets. It also describes the steps they must take to make sure they can continue to operate in the event of a disaster or incident.

- **Security Operations and Administration**—This domain describes how proper governance can help protect information systems. It explores the different types of processes organizations must use at an operational level to protect information systems.

You can learn more about the SSCP certification by visiting the (ISC)[2] Web site at *http://www.isc2.org*.

Do Special Kinds of Data Require Special Kinds of Protection?

The United States doesn't have one comprehensive data protection law. As a result, many laws focus on different types of data found in different industries. They also focus on how that data is used. A number of federal agencies regulate compliance with these types of laws.

The Health Insurance Portability and Accountability Act (HIPAA) regulates some kinds of health information. The Department of Health and Human Services (HHS) and Office of Civil Rights (OCR) oversee HIPAA compliance. The Gramm-Leach-Bliley Act (GLBA) protects some types of consumer financial information. The Federal Trade Commission (FTC) ensures compliance.

You will learn about these and other laws in detail in Part 2 of this book. Table 1-2 lists the laws discussed in Part 2, the type of data they address, and the authority that regulates compliance with them.

TABLE 1-2 Laws that influence information security.

NAME OF LAW	INFORMATION REGULATED	REGULATING AGENCY
Gramm-Leach-Bliley Act	Consumer financial information	FTC
Red Flags Rule	Consumer financial information	FTC
Payment Card Industry Standards*	Credit card information	Credit Card Issuers via Contract Provisions
Health Insurance Portability and Accountability Act	Protected health information	Department of Health and Human Services
Children's Online Privacy Protection Act	Information from children under the age of 13	FTC
Children's Internet Protection Act	Internet access in certain schools and libraries	FTC
Family Educational Rights and Privacy Act	Student educational records	U.S. Department of Education
Sarbanes-Oxley Act	Corporate financial information	Securities and Exchange Commission
Federal Information Systems Management Act	Federal information systems	Office of Management and Budget
State Breach Notification Acts	State information systems containing protected health information	Varies among states

*The Payment Card Industry (PCI) Standards are not a law. Organizations that wish to accept credit cards for payment of goods and services must follow these standards. The standards are enforced through contracts between organizations and the credit card issuing companies.

CHAPTER SUMMARY

Information security is the study and practice of protecting information. It's important because information is valuable. Organizations need data to conduct business. Governments need information to protect their citizens. Individuals need information to interact with businesses and government agencies. They also stay in touch with friends and family over the Web. Information is a critical resource that must be protected.

The main goals of information security are to protect the confidentiality, integrity, and availability of information. Basic information security concepts include vulnerabilities, threats, risks, and safeguards. These concepts appear in detail in Parts 2 and 3 of this book.

KEY CONCEPTS AND TERMS

Administrative safeguard	Internal attacker	Risk transfer
Availability	Least privilege	Safeguard
Competitive edge	Malware	Separation of duties
Confidentiality	Mantrap	Shoulder surfing
Control	Need to know	Single point of failure
Cryptography	Patch	Social engineering
Denial of service (DoS) attack	Physical safeguard	Technical safeguard
Exploit	Residual risk	Threat
External attacker	Risk	Vulnerability
Information	Risk acceptance	Window of vulnerability
Information security	Risk avoidance	Zero-day vulnerability
Integrity	Risk mitigation	

CHAPTER 1 ASSESSMENT

1. What are the goals of an information security program?

   A. Authorization, integrity, and confidentiality

   B. Availability, authorization, and integrity

   C. Availability, integrity, and confidentiality

   D. Availability, integrity, and safeguards

   E. Access control, confidentiality, and safeguards

2. An employee can add other employees to the payroll database. The same person also can change all employee salaries and print payroll checks for all employees. What safeguard should you implement to make sure that this employee doesn't engage in wrongdoing?

   A. Need to know

   B. Access control lists

   C. Technical safeguards

   D. Mandatory vacation

   E. Separation of duties

3. An organization obtains an insurance policy against cybercrime. What type of risk response is this?

   A. Risk mitigation

   B. Residual risk

   C. Risk elimination

   D. Risk transfer

   E. Risk management

4. Which of the following is an accidental threat?

   A. A backdoor into a computer system

   B. A hacker

   C. A well-meaning employee who inadvertently deletes a file

   D. An improperly redacted document

   E. A poorly written policy

5. What is the window of vulnerability?

   A. The period between the discovery of a vulnerability and mitigation of the vulnerability

   B. The period between the discovery of a vulnerability and exploiting the vulnerability

   C. The period between exploiting a vulnerability and mitigating the vulnerability

   D. The period between exploiting a vulnerability and eliminating the vulnerability

   E. A broken window

6. A technical safeguard is also known as a _____.

7. Which of the following isn't a threat classification?

   A. Human

   B. Natural

   C. Process

   D. Technology and Operational

   E. Physical and Environmental

8. What information security goal does a DoS attack harm?

   A. Confidentiality

   B. Integrity

   C. Authentication

   D. Availability

   E. Privacy

9. Which of the following is an example of a model for implementing safeguards?

   A. ISO/IEC 27002

   B. NIST SP 80-553

   C. NIST SP 800-3

   D. ISO/IEC 20072

   E. ISO/IEC 70022

10. Which of the following is not a type of security safeguard?

   A. Corrective

   B. Preventative

   C. Detective

   D. Physical

   E. Defective

11. It's hard to safeguard against which of the following types of vulnerabilities?

   A. Information leakage

   B. Flooding

   C. Buffer overflow

   D. Zero-day

   E. Hardware failure

12. What are the classification levels for U.S. national security information?

   A. Public, Sensitive, Restricted
   B. Confidential, Secret, Top Secret
   C. Confidential, Restricted, Top Secret
   D. Public, Secret, Top Secret
   E. Public, Sensitive, Secret

13. Which safeguard is most likely violated if a system administrator logs into an administrator user account in order to surf the Internet and download music files?

   A. Need to know
   B. Access control
   C. Least privilege principle
   D. Using best available path
   E. Separation of duties

14. Which of the following are vulnerability classifications?

   A. People
   B. Process
   C. Technology
   D. Facility
   E. All of the above

15. What is a mantrap?

   A. A method to control access to a secure area
   B. A removable cover that allows access to underground utilities
   C. A logical access control mechanism
   D. An administrative safeguard
   E. None of the above

Privacy Overview

PRIVACY IS AN AREA OF GROWING IMPORTANCE for people and organizations. This growth roughly corresponds with the growth of the Internet. The Internet has made it possible for people to share all types of information very quickly. Organizations collect and use information to conduct business. Governments collect and use information to provide for their own security. Individuals share information to get goods and services. People also share information to network for employment purposes and catch up with old friends. With this increased collection of information come questions about proper information use.

This chapter provides an overview of privacy issues. Privacy is a very large field. It's impossible to discuss all of the unique and interesting issues in the field of privacy. For the most part, this chapter is limited to the areas where information technology and privacy meet. This chapter also will address general privacy concepts.

Chapter 2 Topics

This chapter covers the following topics and concepts:

- Why privacy is an issue
- What privacy is
- How privacy is different from information security
- What sources of privacy law exist
- What threats to privacy exist in the Information Age
- What workplace privacy is
- What general principles for privacy protection exist in information systems

Chapter 2 Goals

When you complete this chapter, you will be able to:

- Describe basic privacy principles
- Explain the difference between information security and privacy
- Describe threats to privacy
- Explain the important issues regarding workplace privacy
- Describe the general principles for privacy protection in information systems

Why Is Privacy an Issue?

Advances in technology are forcing people to think about how their personal data is used.

- A chef enters her e-mail address on a Web site to buy a new blender. She then begins to receive junk e-mail from a number of different appliance companies.
- A school district fires an elementary school teacher after parents complain to the school principal about unprofessional pictures on the teacher's personal Web page.
- A professor gives students a homework assignment. The students must use the Internet to collect as much publicly available data as possible about a particular government official.
- An organization tracks how many users visit its Web site each day. It records the number of times users click on links on the homepage. It tracks each user's computer Internet Protocol (IP) address. It also tracks the Web page that each user was on immediately before visiting the organization's Web page.
- A person buys an MP3 player at a thrift shop. The person later discovers that the MP3 player contains files on U.S. military personnel. The files contain Social Security numbers.

Advances in technology change how people live. For example, the discovery of electricity led to huge societal advances. Today, electrical service is a utility that many take for granted. The creation of the telephone allowed people to communicate over greater distances. Today, it seems unusual to find an adult who doesn't carry a personal cell phone.

The rise in Internet use also has the potential to change how people live. According to U.S. Census Bureau data, in 2007, 62 percent of U.S. households reported that they had Internet access. You can expect that number to grow. The Internet and related technologies such as e-mail rapidly are becoming indispensable tools.

People use the Internet for almost everything. It's a tool for learning and entertainment. You can search the Internet for almost any type of data. You also can use it as a forum for sharing all types of information nearly instantaneously. The Internet allows media companies to report on world events immediately. Anyone can publish information to the world with just the click of a mouse.

This increased access to information has some complications. Anyone in the world can view information published on the Internet. Enemies of the government can view government information posted online. People can copy and use articles posted to the Internet without the author's permission. Blogs and pictures on personal Web pages for family and friends to view are sometimes available to anyone, anywhere.

 NOTE

The search engine Google is the most used Internet search engine.[1] A **search engine** is a program that retrieves files and data from a computer network. You use a search engine to search the Internet for information. Google use has become so popular that "to google"— meaning to search the Internet for information—was added to the Oxford English Dictionary in June 2006.[2]

NOTE

A **blog** is a personal, online journal. A blog author publishes comments and personal observations to a blog. The word "blog" comes from the words "Web" and "log."

The amount of information on the Internet is also a concern. Larger and more complex information systems allow businesses and governments to collect more and more individual data. Sophisticated applications review and analyze collected data, perhaps from many sources. The owners of these systems can accumulate large amounts of data about people. They can use the data for their own purposes. They can create highly detailed individual profiles by combining their data with that of other systems. They also can sell the data they collect to third parties.

People leave electronic footprints in many places on the Internet. "Internet service providers" (ISPs) maintain logs that track performance information. Web sites track the actions of visitors to the site. Organizations may track and record the Internet and e-mail activities of employees. Service providers of all types back up their logs and data for disaster recovery purposes. These backups contain personal information. Many people don't know that their activities are recorded, stored, and monitored in so many different ways.

Electronic monitoring also creates privacy concerns. Many people believe that they are anonymous on the Internet. When most people surf the Internet or post information, they believe their actions are private. They aren't.

Most people want certain types of data kept secret. They believe that if they must share their data, they should at least be able to control how the data is subsequently used. These beliefs form part of the basis of the concept of privacy.

What Is Privacy?

Privacy is a simple term that describes a number of different but related concepts. At its core, privacy means that a person has control of his or her personal data. "Control" means that a person can specify the collection, use, and sharing of their data. People also can decide whether they will provide personal data to third parties.

Most traditional views on privacy include the belief that the government's power to interfere in the privacy of its citizens is limited. This means that people and their information must be free from unreasonable government intrusion. The government must not investigate a person or their personal information without a good reason. Courts spend a lot of time defining the reasons to allow governments to investigate their citizens. This is a core privacy concept for most Americans.

The types of information that a person considers private are usually very personal. What is private information for one person may not be as private for others. Information that most people consider private includes the following:

- **Social Security or other identification numbers**—This includes driver's license and passport numbers.
- **Financial information**—This includes bank and credit card account numbers. This also includes investment and retirement account information. Most people also consider the amount of money in these accounts private information.
- **Health information**—This includes diagnoses and prescription drug information. Most people consider information regarding mental illness to be highly sensitive and private.
- **Biometric data**—This type of data includes fingerprints, DNA analysis, and iris scanning. It's data about a person's physical or behavioral traits. Security professionals and security equipment use biometric data to identify a particular person. **Biometric data** is unique because you can't change it.
- **Criminal history data**—This includes criminal charges, the outcome of a criminal case, and any punishment that a person may have received.
- **Other**—This includes any other information that may embarrass a person if released to the public.

> **NOTE**
>
> The U.S. Freedom of Information Act (FOIA) governs access to public records of the U.S. federal government. Most states have similar laws for the public records of state government and agencies. These types of laws often are called "sunshine" laws because they shine light onto the inner workings of government agencies.

Some types of information that people may consider private is actually publicly available information. **Public records** are records that the law states must be available to the public. Governmental entities create or file these types of records. Most public records are available to the public for free or for a small fee. Many government agencies make these records available to the public via the Internet. Putting public records on the Internet makes it easier for the government to meet its legal requirements to make them available to the public. It also makes it easier for almost anyone to access the records.

Laws determine whether a record is public or not. The law designates some records as public because there's a compelling interest in making them public. Common types of public records include birth and death certificates. The minutes of meetings of government agencies are usually public records. Real estate filings are often public records. Court records, including most types of criminal records, are usually available to the public. Sex offender registration lists are public records in most communities. Professional license records are also public records.

In most states, the professional license status of attorneys is public information. This allows potential clients to research attorneys before hiring them. A potential client can use this information to make sure that an attorney is properly licensed and has no disciplinary actions pending against him or her. The public has a compelling interest in making sure that attorneys have proper licenses to practice law. This is because attorneys guide their clients through the legal system.

Anyone can access public records. Law enforcement officials access public records routinely. So do private investigators, attorneys, government officials, and employers. Friends and family members can casually view public records. Marketing agencies access public records and compile lists of potential customers. People often have little control over the content of public records and how others use the data.

Another type of public record is the docket. A **docket** is the official schedule of a court and the events in the cases that are pending before a court. Many federal, state, and local court systems publish dockets online. Electronic dockets may even include the actual documents filed in a court case. These documents are called pleadings. **Pleadings** can contain data about civil lawsuits and criminal actions. They also can contain personal information.

Privacy rights are individual rights. They exist independent of any type of technology. Privacy is a large area of study. In this book, we will discuss how information technology affects individual privacy rights. In particular, this chapter discusses personal data privacy concerns created or heightened due to an increase in electronic information gathering, storage, monitoring, and transmission.

How Is Privacy Different from Information Security?

Information security and privacy are closely related. However, they're not the same. Privacy is an individual's right to control the use and disclosure of his or her own personal information. The individual has the opportunity to assess a situation and determine how their data is used. Information security is the process used to keep data private. Security is the process; privacy is the result.

Just because information is secure doesn't mean it's private. Information security is about protecting data to ensure confidentiality, access, and integrity. Privacy with respect to information systems means that people have control over and can make choices about how their information will be used. Security is used to carry out those choices. Privacy can't exist in information systems without security.

What Are the Sources of Privacy Law?

Most people consider the right to privacy to be a fundamental human right. A number of different sources define the scope of this right to privacy.

Constitutional Law

NOTE

The Constitutional Convention adopted the U.S. Constitution in 1787. It is the oldest written constitution still in use by any nation today. It's also the shortest constitution. The U.S. Constitution applies to all the states in the country.

The United States Constitution is the source of legal authority for the U.S. government. It states the relationship between the federal government and the states. It also provides some authority for certain individual rights retained by all U.S. citizens. Constitutional rights are basic individual rights recognized in the U.S. Constitution.

Most people consider privacy to be a basic constitutional right. Yet, the U.S. Constitution does not use the word "privacy" anywhere. You can piece together the constitutional right to privacy from a number of different provisions. U.S. Supreme Court cases have interpreted the scope of the right.

The following amendments to the U.S. Constitution contribute to the right to privacy:

- First Amendment, which reads, "Congress shall make no law respecting an establishment of religion, or prohibiting the free exercise thereof; or abridging the freedom of speech, or of the press; or the right of the people peaceably to assemble, and to petition the government for a redress of grievances." U.S. Constitution, amend. 1.

  This amendment sets forth the right to freedom of religion, speech, the press, and assembly. Within these rights is the implicit right of freedom of thought, which has a privacy component.

- Third Amendment, which reads, "No soldier shall, in time of peace be quartered in any house, without the consent of the owner, nor in time of war, but in a manner to be prescribed by law." U.S. Constitution, amend. 3.

  This amendment means that the government can't force people to house government soldiers in their homes. This gives people a limited right of privacy in their homes.

- Fourth Amendment, which reads, "The right of the people to be secure in their persons, houses, papers, and effects, against unreasonable searches and seizures, shall not be violated, and no warrants shall issue, but upon probable cause...." U.S. Constitution, amend. 4.

  This amendment truly forms the basis for many of the privacy rights that Americans enjoy today. This amendment protects against unreasonable government searches and seizures.

- Fifth Amendment, which reads, "No person shall be … compelled in any criminal case to be a witness against himself. . . ." U.S. Constitution, amend. 5.

  This amendment provides a number of protections. Many people know it for its "right to remain silent." One interpretation is that it protects the privacy of one's thoughts.

You can see a high-resolution image of the U.S. Constitution online. Visit the National Archives and Records Administration Web site at *http://www.archives.gov/exhibits/charters/*.

Each of these amendments sets forth general elements that are part of an overall right to privacy. The U.S. Supreme Court first acknowledged that a person has an interest in being "let alone" in 1834 in a case called *Wheaten v. Peters* (1834). In 1890, Samuel Warren and Louis Brandeis more fully explained this right to privacy in their article "The Right to Privacy." This article referred to a right they called "the right to be let alone." Legal cases today still refer to the phrase "the right to be let alone." The phrase now includes the idea that people have the right to be free from intrusions by the government.

The first U.S. Supreme Court decision to state a constitutional right to privacy was *Griswold v. Connecticut* (1965). In this case, the Supreme Court found that the right to privacy was a fundamental right that was present in the Constitution. Subsequent Supreme Court cases have further defined the scope of this right.

In *Katz v. United States* (1967), the U.S. Supreme Court held that the Fourth Amendment of the U.S. Constitution protects a person's right to privacy. The holding meant that the right of privacy belongs to the individual and not just locations (such as a person's home). In the case, Charles Katz was convicted of illegal gambling. He had used a public pay phone to place his bets. The government listened to his telephone conversations through a listening device attached to the phone booth. The government did not have a warrant to listen to the conversations. The conversations were used as evidence to convict Katz. The U.S. Supreme Court held that Katz's right to privacy was not diminished just because he used a public pay phone booth. Justice Harlan, in his concurring opinion in this case, used the famous term "a reasonable expectation of privacy."

"A reasonable expectation of privacy" is a belief regarding private places that society recognizes as valid. Courts use the idea of a reasonable expectation of privacy to determine whether an ordinary person would believe he or she was in a private place. For instance, people have a reasonable expectation of privacy in their homes. They don't have one when they are out in public.

In U.S. Supreme Court cases, the court writes a "majority opinion." This opinion explains the decision of the court. It also explains how the judges arrived at their decision. A "concurring opinion" is one that agrees with the court's majority decision. The judge or judges writing the concurring opinion may have a different explanation for how they reached that decision. A "dissenting opinion" disagrees with the majority opinion. The judge or judges writing the dissenting opinion explain why they disagree with the majority.

 NOTE

Case law refers to the decisions courts make in the cases they decide. Most high-level courts, such as the U.S. Supreme Court and the highest-level state courts, publish their opinions on cases. These opinions contribute to the body of case law. Case law is a part of common law.

In *Whalen v. Roe* (1977), the U.S. Supreme Court specifically recognized a right of "informational privacy." This right focuses on a right to control information. This case reviewed a New York law that created a state database of the names and addresses of patients who were prescribed narcotic drugs. Doctors had to share the names of their patients who were prescribed narcotic drugs with the state. The New York law was challenged on the basis that it unconstitutionally infringed on a right to privacy.

The Court upheld the validity of the New York law. It found that the law included procedures that properly protected the privacy of information included in the database. However, the Court didn't reject the possibility that some types of government data collection would be improper. The Court wrote, "We are not unaware of the threat to privacy implicit in the accumulation of vast amounts of personal information in computerized data banks or other massive government files."

Other Supreme Court cases have continued to define the scope of the constitutional right to privacy. *United States v. White* (1971) found that there is no right of privacy in information voluntarily shared with another person. In *Smith v. Maryland* (1979), the Court found that there is no right of privacy in electronic communications routing information.

Federal Laws

Federal laws are the laws that a country's federal government creates. No comprehensive data privacy law exists in the United States. Like the laws that regulate information security, U.S. federal laws that address information privacy are also industry based. These laws put limits on the use of personal information based on the nature of the underlying data. Congress has enacted laws to protect various types of data. Descriptions of those laws appear in this section.

The United States Code outlines the laws of the United States. It's the official record of U.S. laws. It's published every six years. The United States Code is available online at *http://www.gpoaccess.gov/uscode/*.

Census Confidentiality (1952)

This law requires the U.S. Census Bureau to keep census responses confidential. The statute also forbids the Bureau from disclosing any data allowing a person to be individually identified. The law states that census responses can be used only for statistical purposes that don't show individual or household personal data.

A "census" is a count of the population of a country. The U.S. Census Bureau 2010 census form is one of the shortest forms in history. It has only 10 questions. You can't complete the form electronically.

Freedom of Information Act (1966)

This Act establishes the public's right to request information from federal agencies. Information that can be requested includes paper documents and electronic records. The law applies to federal executive branch agencies and offices. Federal agencies must comply with the law and provide requested information. There are nine FOIA exemptions. Data in these categories doesn't have to be provided to the requester. Agencies are required to provide information to the public about how to make a FOIA request. Anyone can file a FOIA request.

The U.S. Department of Justice maintains a Web page of links to the FOIA Web sites for federal agencies. That list is available at *http://www.justice.gov/oip/other_age.htm*.

Wiretap Act (1968, amended)

These statutes forbid the use of eavesdropping technologies without a court order. The law protects all e-mail, radio communications, data transmission, and telephone calls. Amendments to the original Wiretap Act include protection for electronic communications.

Mail Privacy Statute (1971)

This law protects U.S. postal mail from being opened without the recipient's consent. Domestic mail can be opened without consent only if there's a valid search warrant for that mail. This law only applies to postal mail.

Privacy Act (1974)

This Act applies to records created and used by federal agencies. It states the rules for the collection, use, and transfer of personally identifiable information. It requires federal agencies to tell people why they're collecting personal information. Federal agencies also must provide an annual public notice. The notice must describe their record-keeping systems and the data in them. The Act also requires federal agencies to have appropriate administrative, technical, and physical safeguards to protect the security of the records they maintain.

Cable Communications Policy Act (1984)

This Act states that cable companies must provide a yearly written privacy notice to each customer. The notice must inform the customers about the cable company's data collection and disclosure practices. Cable providers also must ask their customers for permission before using the cable system to collect personal information.

Electronic Communications Privacy Act (1986)

This Act sets out the provisions for access, use, disclosure, and interception of electronic communications. Electronic communications include telephone, cell phones, computers, e-mail, faxes, and texting. The government cannot access these types of communications without a search warrant. This Act is an amendment to the original Wiretap Act.

U.S.A. PATRIOT Act (2001)

Congress passed the Uniting and Strengthening America by Providing Appropriate Tools Required to Intercept and Obstruct Terrorism Act (U.S.A. PATRIOT Act) in 2001. Congress passed this law in six weeks. Congress introduced the Act in response to the September 11, 2001, terrorist attacks.

The Patriot Act made three major changes to the Electronic Communications Privacy Act (ECPA). The Homeland Security Act (2002) modified the ECPA again. These changes weakened the ECPA. Today these amendments allow the following:

- The government may easily intercept electronic communications that may be related to national security. The government has to meet a very low proof standard to get this information.

- A service provider may disclose the contents of communications to law enforcement or government agencies. The provider must have a good-faith belief that a life-threatening emergency requires the disclosure.

- Service providers may ask for government help to intercept the communications of a computer trespasser. The government can help track and intercept the communications when asked.

These changes give the federal government the power to intercept communications easily in situations that may affect national security. As a result, electronic communications privacy has fewer government protections.

Driver's Privacy Protection Act (1994)

This Act requires states to protect the privacy of personal information contained in motor vehicle records. Protected information includes any personal data in the record. This includes the driver's name, address, phone number, Social Security number, driver's license identification number, photograph, height, weight, sex, and date of birth.

Congress passed the Driver's Privacy Protection Act in 1994. Senator Barbara Boxer, from California, introduced the Act to the U.S. Senate. One of Senator Boxer's reasons for introducing the Act was the 1989 murder of a California actor. A stalker obtained the actor's address from the California Department of Motor Vehicles. The stalker later went to the actor's home and killed her.

E-Government Act (2002)

This Act requires the federal government to use information technologies that protect privacy. The Act requires federal agencies to conduct Privacy Impact Assessments (PIAs). A PIA is done when an agency develops information technology systems to collect and process individually identifiable information. A PIA makes sure that systems are evaluated for privacy risks. The law also requires privacy protection measures to secure the data in the systems. Federal agencies also must post their privacy policies to their Web sites.

Many other federal laws also have privacy protections. Some also have information security provisions. These laws include the Gramm-Leach-Bliley Act and the Health Insurance Portability and Accountability Act (HIPAA). Further discussion of these laws takes place in Part 2 of this book.

State Laws

State constitutions are the documents that form the individual state governments. State constitutions apply to the people who live in a particular state. State constitutions are the highest form of law for state governments.

Ten state constitutions recognize a right to privacy. They are Alaska, Arizona, California, Florida, Hawaii, Illinois, Louisiana, Montana, South Carolina, and Washington. These state constitutions provide clear privacy guarantees. The Montana state constitution reads, "The right of individual privacy is essential to the well-being of a free society and shall not be infringed without the showing of a compelling state interest."[3]

The California state constitution states, "All people are by nature free and independent and have inalienable rights. Among these are enjoying and defending life and liberty, acquiring, possessing, and protecting property, and pursuing and obtaining safety, happiness, and privacy."[4]

The State of New York was the first state to write a right of privacy into its statutes after Warren and Brandeis published their article "The Right to Privacy."[5] Many states have written a right of privacy into their laws.

Other states have recognized a right of privacy through their case law. In 1905, the Georgia Supreme Court recognized a right to privacy. Georgia was the first state to recognize, through case law, a right to privacy in its own Constitution.

> **NOTE**
>
> The California Office of Privacy Protection was created in 2000. It protects the privacy rights of state residents. California was the first state to create this type of agency. The agency has an extensive Web site that includes privacy tips and consumer information. The Web site is *http://www.privacyprotection.ca.gov.*

State governments also create laws to protect data. At the time this book was written, 45 states, including the District of Columbia, had enacted breach notification laws. These laws require an organization to notify state residents if it experiences a security breach that involves the personal information of the residents. Breach notification laws are discussed in Chapter 9.

At least 19 states have laws requiring proper disposal of paper and electronic information that contains personal data. States also have industry-specific laws that protect certain types of data, such as financial, health, and motor vehicle information.

> **NOTE**
>
> States that do not currently have a breach notification law are Alabama, Kentucky, New Mexico, and South Dakota.

Common Laws

The U.S. Supreme Court didn't specifically recognize a constitutional right to privacy until 1965. However, U.S. common law recognized certain privacy torts as early as 1902. A **tort** is some sort of wrongful act or harm that hurts a person. In a tort, the injured party may sue the wrongdoer for damages. Tort law governs disputes between individuals.

The **common law** is a body of law developed because of legal tradition and court cases. The U.S. common law is a body of law and legal principles inherited from England. Common law changes very slowly. It develops as judges decide court cases.

Four privacy torts still exist today. Most states give either common law or statutory recognition to these torts. Statutory recognition means that the state has included the tort in the written laws of the state. The four privacy torts are:

- Intrusion into seclusion
- Portrayal in a false light
- Appropriation of likeness or identity
- Public disclosure of private facts

Intrusion into Seclusion

> **NOTE**
>
> The **reasonable person standard** is a legal concept used to describe an ordinary person. This fictitious ordinary person represents how an average person would think and act. Courts use this standard to determine if conduct that is complained about in a lawsuit is offensive to an ordinary person. Conduct is wrongful if a reasonable person finds it offensive.

The "intrusion into seclusion" privacy tort is the act of invading a person's private space. The intrusion into private space takes a number of forms. It can be a physical intrusion. It also can be an intrusion through electronic means, such as using an eavesdropping device. The intrusion must be highly offensive to a reasonable person. In this tort, the legal wrong occurs as soon as the private space is invaded.

In 2009, the Supreme Court of Ohio found that people have a reasonable expectation of privacy in their cell phones. This is because cell phones have the ability to hold large amounts of personal data. Other courts have held that people have a reasonable expectation of privacy in the data stored on their personal computers. This is especially true if they take steps to protect the data. These steps can include encrypting the data or using a password to protect the computer.

Portrayal in a False Light

The "portrayal in a false light" privacy tort involves publishing highly offensive private information about an individual to create a bad impression. The information published is true, but it's published in an offensive way. This tort often is confused with defamation. **Defamation** is another type of tort that involves maliciously saying false things about another person.

The portrayal in a false light privacy tort occurs when a person's photograph or image is used to create a bad impression. For example, taking a picture for a magazine of a person standing outside of a bar might create the impression that the person is a customer. The impression might be offensive if the person held a position of high respect in the community. The person photographed could sue for invasion of privacy based on portrayal in a false light.

In 1993, the Alabama Supreme Court reviewed a false light case. In that case, a greyhound racetrack took a picture of a group of men sitting together. That picture was later used in advertising materials. The men sued for false light. The Alabama court held that the men did not state a claim for false light because they were in a public place. The court said there was nothing offensive about sitting at the track. It also said that the men consented to the taking of the photograph because they didn't move or object when the photographer appeared and began taking pictures.

Appropriation of Likeness or Identity

The "appropriation of likeness or identity" privacy tort is the oldest privacy tort. It involves appropriating, or taking, an individual's name or likeness without their consent. The taking of the likeness must be for financial gain. This tort often occurs with public figures if their likeness is used without their permission to sell a product or service. Court cases have held that likeness includes identifiable characteristics about a person. This would include a person's voice or mannerisms.

In 1992, a Samsung advertisement featured a robot dressed in a blond wig and evening gown. The robot was hosting a futuristic version of a popular game show. Vanna White, a game show host, sued Samsung for appropriating her identity for commercial gain. She successfully argued that being a game show host on a popular game show was her identity. She won the case.

Public Disclosure of Private Facts

The "public disclosure of private facts" privacy tort involves the publication of embarrassing private facts. The facts publicized must be so embarrassing that a reasonable person would be offended by their publication. The disclosures must be true. In addition, they must be truly private. Facts published as part of the public record are not private. Many courts have applied a "newsworthy" defense to this tort. This defense allows the media to report on newsworthy incidents without fearing a lawsuit for public disclosure of private facts.

The Maryland Court of Appeals has held that the publication of a criminal "mug" shot is not a privacy violation based on the public disclosure of private facts privacy tort. This is because the mug shot is originally published as part of the public record. The mug shot was not a private fact because it was a public record.

 NOTE

All of the privacy torts can be waived by consent. A person may not bring a tort action against an alleged wrongdoer if he or she gives permission for the privacy invasion. Those who give permission for use of their likeness, intrusion into their private space, or publication of facts about them can't claim harm.

Voluntary Agreements

Protecting personal data privacy grows harder as technology advances. People must understand their privacy choices in order to protect their data. Governments and organizations must understand the information that they need to provide. Organizations use **fair information practices principles** to help specify how they collect and use data. Organizations are not legally required to follow these principles. Instead, they use them to make sure they are properly informing people about their data collection practices.

The U.S. Department of Health, Education, and Welfare developed the "Code of Fair Information Practice Principles" in 1973. They created the principles because there was no federal law that protected personal data. These principles stated that there should be no secret record keeping systems. The principles also required that individuals have a way to find out if information is collected about them. Individuals must have a way to correct inaccurate data. These practices eventually formed the basis for the 1974 federal Privacy Act.

> **NOTE**
>
> The Organization for Economic Cooperation and Development was established in 1961 to promote a market economy. There are 31 members. The United States has been a member since 1961.

In 1980, the Organization for Economic Cooperation and Development (OECD) adopted guidelines to protect personal data. These guidelines are the "OECD Guidelines on the Protection of Privacy and Transborder Flows of Personal Data." They are an extension of the 1973 U.S. fair information practices. The U.S. was actively involved in creating the OECD guidelines. The guidelines help guide privacy legislation for OECD members.

The OECD guidelines contain eight privacy principles:

- **The Collection Limitation Principle**—Individuals must know about and consent to the collection of their data.
- **The Data Quality Principle**—Any data collected must be correct.
- **The Purpose Specification Principle**—The purpose for data collection should be stated to individuals before their data is collected.
- **The Use Limitation Principle**—Data should only be used for the purposes stated when it was collected.
- **The Security Safeguards Principle**—The collected data must be protected from unauthorized access.
- **The Openness Principle**—People can contact the entity collecting their data. People can discover where their personal data is collected and stored.
- **The Individual Principle**—People must know if data about them has been collected. People also must have access to their collected information.
- **The Accountability Principle**—The entity collecting data must be held accountable for following the privacy principles.

Compliance with fair information practice principles is encouraged through voluntary membership in self-regulating organizations. Organizations often choose to regulate themselves. They do this to keep governments from making laws that would limit their behavior.

The Network Advertising Initiative (NAI) is an organization of online advertising companies. NAI members want to make sure that consumers understand how online marketing works. The group has created self-regulatory standards to promote responsible online marketing. It also has created standards that address the proper use of marketing tools.

The Online Privacy Alliance (OPA) is an organization of companies dedicated to protecting online privacy. OPA members agree to meet certain requirements for protecting personal information online. These members also agree to create a privacy policy for their customers that's easy to read and understand. The policy must include the following provisions:

- Types of data collected
- How data is used
- How collected data is shared
- How collected data is secured

OPA members must post their privacy policy online in a place that's easy to find.

Organizations can participate in a **seal program** to show their compliance with fair information practice principles. A seal program is run by a trusted third-party organization. The seal program verifies that an organization meets industry-recognized privacy practices. If the organization meets the required standards, then it's allowed to display a privacy seal on its Web site. The seal is an image that customers recognize. It's used to signify a trustworthy organization. Common seal programs in the U.S. are WebTrust, TRUSTe, and BBBOnline.

What Are Threats to Personal Data Privacy in the Information Age?

Privacy issues existed before technology became an issue. It seems, however, that privacy issues became more urgent due to advances in technology. People often have very little control over how their data is collected, used, and shared in an electronic manner. They're concerned about how their data will be used later. The rise in electronic communications makes people wonder how private their lives truly are. This section discusses some of today's privacy concerns.

Technology-Based Privacy Concerns

Technology-based privacy concerns are caused by advances in technology. These concerns arise because of the types of data that can be collected with various technologies.

Spyware, Keystroke Loggers, and Adware

Spyware and keystroke loggers are discussed in Chapter 1. Spyware is any technology that secretly gathers information about a person or system. A keystroke logger is a device or program that records keystrokes made on a keyboard or mouse. Spyware and keystroke loggers are designed to gather information secretly.

Spyware and keystroke loggers pose a threat to personal data privacy. This is because of the nature of the information and the secret manner in which they collect that data. They can easily record very personal information such as account numbers, user names, and passwords. These programs also can record Internet search queries and other personal data.

Utah was the first state to enact an anti-spyware law. The law was quickly challenged by an advertising company. The company argued that the law unconstitutionally limited its right to advertise. A court granted an injunction in the case. An "injunction" is a formal order for someone to stop doing something. In this case, Utah was prohibited from enforcing its new anti-spyware law.

> **NOTE**
>
> Spyware, keystroke loggers, and adware raise privacy concerns because they are secretly downloaded onto a user's computer. People have no control over the software or data it collects. Some users unknowingly agree to download this type of software onto their computers. Sometimes these programs are part of a legitimate software application that a user wants to download.

Utah legislators then worked to revise the state anti-spyware law. The current Utah law prohibits pop-up advertising that uses spyware to target the ads that the user sees on their computer. The law authorizes the Utah attorney general to prosecute violations.[6]

Adware is software that displays advertising to a user. It can display banner advertisements or redirect a person to other Web sites. It also can display **pop-up advertisements** on a person's computer. These types of advertisements open a new Web browser window to display ads. Some types of adware are also spyware. This adware displays targeted advertisements based on secretly collected user information.

In 2006, the U.S. Federal Trade Commission (FTC) settled a case with Zango, Inc. Zango was an Internet marketing company. The FTC alleged that Zango had used unfair and deceptive methods to download adware onto computers. The adware was bundled with other software that users willingly downloaded onto their computers. There was no disclosure that the desired software included the Zango adware. The FTC also alleged that Zango made it very difficult for users to remove their adware. As part of the agreement with the FTC, Zango had to pay $3 million and provide users with a way to remove the adware.

Cookies, Web Beacons, and Clickstreams

Cookies are a small string of text that a Web site stores on a user's computer. Cookies contain text—you can't execute them like a program file. Cookies aren't considered spyware because they're not executable. A cookie by itself isn't dangerous or a privacy threat. However, other individuals and companies can use cookies in ways that invade your privacy.

There are two kinds of cookies: First-party cookies and third-party cookies. "First-party cookies" are exchanged between a user's browser and the Web site the user is visiting. "Third-party cookies" are set by one Web site but can be read by another site. Third-party cookies are set when the Web page a user visits has content on it that is hosted by another server.

Cookies are used for many things that most computer users consider beneficial. For example, they can be used by a Web site to remember information about visitors to the site. They also can save your settings if you "personalize" a Web application that you regularly use.

However, advertising companies that sell content and advertising to companies with a Web presence often use third-party cookies. Advertisers can track their cookies over a number of Web sites. They use the tracked information to create a profile about each user's browsing habits. They then direct targeted advertisements to the users. This is a privacy concern.

A **Web beacon** is a small, invisible electronic file that is placed on a Web page or in an e-mail message. It counts users who visit a Web page. A Web beacon also can tell if a user opened an e-mail message and took some action with it. It also can monitor user behavior. A Web beacon also is called a Web bug.

Web beacons recognize a number of different types of data. When you retrieve a Web beacon, it recognizes your computer's IP address, your browser, and the time you retrieved the beacon. Web beacons usually track users by a random identification number. This number contains no personally identifiable data.

Spammers sometimes use Web beacons to verify whether an e-mail address is valid. If a recipient opens a spam message with a Web beacon, information is returned to the spammer, which shows that the message was opened. An opened e-mail message generally indicates a valid e-mail address.

Web beacons cause privacy concerns because they secretly monitor user behavior. They monitor Internet browsing patterns. Web beacons let Web site operators know which pages a user looks at. They also disclose the order in which the pages are viewed. Information tracked by Web beacons and cookies, when combined, can potentially identify a computer user. This is a privacy concern.

A **clickstream** is the data trail that an Internet user leaves while browsing. Movements are recorded as a user moves through a Web site. Users click on links to request information from the Web site. A clickstream is essentially a set of digital footprints that track an Internet user's steps.

2

Privacy Overview

> ▶ **TIP**
>
> Most modern Internet browsers have privacy settings that allow you to choose whether to accept cookies from the Web sites you visit. You also can configure browsers to warn you before a cookie is accepted, and to block third-party cookies automatically.

> ▶ **TIP**
>
> You can try to avoid Web beacons in e-mail messages by not down-loading messages that contain images. That's why many e-mail programs prevent pictures from downloading automatically. The e-mail program lets you decide whether to download images.

Clickstream data can be recorded by Web sites and Internet service providers. A clicksteam helps webmasters learn how computer users are using their sites. Clickstream data can be used to determine the order in which users click on Web pages or links on Web pages. Clickstream data can be collected and stored. It can act as the basis for modifying Web sites for a better user experience. Clickstream data also can make online advertising more effective.

Many of the technologies described so far are used to create an online profile for a user. **Online profiling** is the practice of tracking a user's actions on the Internet in order to create a user profile. The profile contains information about the user's online habits and preferences. It can be used to direct targeted advertising toward a specific user.

A profile can contain very detailed information about the user's online habits. One concern with online profiles is that they might contain personally identifiable information. Many people believe their online actions should be private. Data for online profiles is often gathered without the user's knowledge or consent. This is a privacy concern.

RFID and GPS Technologies

Radio Frequency Identification (RFID) is a technology that uses radio waves to transmit data to a receiver. RFID technology is wireless. It's a way to identify unique items using radio waves. The main purpose of RFID technology is to allow "tagged" items to be identified and tracked. Sometimes you will hear devices that use this technology called a RFID tag or chip.

You can incorporate RFID tags into almost any product. You can even use them to track animals. A vet simply inserts a small tag under the skin of a household pet. You can then identify and track the pet if it becomes lost.

The anti-theft tags attached to clothing in department stores are RFID tags. These tags can be used to catch and deter shoplifters. Some proximity card readers use RFID tags to "unlock" doors to allow the person carrying the card to enter secure areas. E-ZPasses used by many states to collect tolls on roads and bridges use this technology. A librarian can place RFID tags in books to ensure that they don't leave the library without proper checkout. Individuals have very little control over the information contained on an RFID tag.

FYI

Since 2007, the U.S. federal government has been issuing the U.S. Electronic Passport. It's also known as E-Passport. This passport is the same as a regular U.S. passport, but it has an RFID tag placed in the back cover. The chip stores the passport holder's personal information and a digital photograph. It also contains a digital signature to protect the chip from being altered. The government has taken several steps to help protect the personal information on the E-passport. You can read about those steps at *http://travel.state.gov/passport/eppt/eppt_2498.html*.

Most RFID tags do not contain a battery. The tags are activated when a receiver is within range and sending out radio waves. The receiver initiates communication with the tag. The tag responds with self-identifying data. It's possible for unauthorized persons to read the information that the tag sends if transmission between the receiver and tag isn't secured or protected.

RFID technology poses privacy concerns in that it can track a person's movements and daily habits. You don't need an RFID tag inserted under your skin to be tracked by RFID technology. Cell phones, purses and briefcases, and driver's licenses or credit cards can be equipped with RFID tags. This tracking can be completely secret if you don't know that the items you're carrying contain an RFID tag.

Information exposure is also a concern. Information contained on an RFID tag can be exposed to unauthorized individuals if the communication channel between the tag and receiver is not secure. Individuals usually have no control over these channels.

Global positioning system (GPS) technology uses satellites above the earth to compute the location of a GPS receiver. GPS receivers use a number of different satellites to calculate time and location. GPS receivers can be incorporated into a number of devices. They are used in automobile navigation units. Runners use GPS receivers built into heart rate monitors to help measure the distances that they have run. GPS units are built into many cell phones to help locate cell phone users in an emergency. Cell phone applications also use GPS technology to track other users and family members.

Courts are struggling with the privacy implications of GPS tracking. In 2009, New York's highest court held that police officers must have a warrant in order to place a GPS tracking device on a suspect's car. The court said that the GPS device's intrusion into the suspect's privacy was too great to violate without first getting a warrant.

Also in 2009, a Wisconsin court held that police didn't need a warrant to attach a GPS unit to a suspect's car. That court was bothered by the amount of data a GPS could return. However, it held that the GPS device returned the same information that could be obtained by other techniques that didn't require a warrant, such as following the suspect around all day.

GPS technology raises many of the same issues as RFID technology. GPS technology precisely tracks a receiver's every step. A person with GPS technology enabled on a cell phone can be tracked every minute of every day. GPS units also are placed in cars. Individuals may not know that their cars or cell phones have GPS units that track their every move. People have very little control over the location information that a GPS unit can track and provide.

> ▶ **NOTE**
>
> The Federal Communications Commission (FCC) Enhanced 911 (E911) initiative requires cell phone carriers to be able to pinpoint their customers' locations within 100 meters. This allows emergency responders to reach cell phone users more quickly in a crisis.

Security Breaches

The Privacy Rights Clearinghouse maintains a list of U.S. security breaches that involve records that contain personal information. The clearinghouse began collecting this data in January 2005. As of February 2010, the site reports that 345,124,400 records have been involved in security breaches. The list is available at *http://www.privacyrights.org/ar/ChronDataBreaches.htm.*

A **security breach** is a compromise of a computer system that results in the loss of personally identifiable information. After a breach, unauthorized individuals potentially can access data in the system. Any organization can experience a security breach. Security breaches can be due to direct external attacks, poor internal safeguards, or both.

Security breaches are a large privacy concern. Organizations store vast amounts of personal information. One security breach has the potential to expose the personal information of a large number of people. This data can be used to commit identity theft. Many people are upset when organizations entrusted with their personal information experience a security breach. Many states have breach notification laws that require organizations to notify customers in the event of a breach. Customers can then monitor their financial accounts and personal data to protect them from misuse.

People-Based Privacy Concerns

People-based privacy concerns are caused by people's actions. These concerns are raised when people compromise others' privacy. They also are caused when people take actions that compromise their own data privacy.

Phishing

Phishing attacks are described in Chapter 1. Phishing is a form of Internet fraud where attackers attempt to steal valuable information. Phishing attacks usually take place via e-mail. Phishers usually try to steal confidential information such as user names and passwords, or financial account information.

Phishing scams are a privacy concern. However, people can protect themselves from phishing scams. They should not respond to unsolicited e-mails that request personal information. Phishing scams are also a concern if an employee in an organization that stores lots of personal information falls for the scam. If an employee responds to a scam with user name and password information, the organization can experience a large data breach. That breach can involve customers' personal information.

Social Engineering, Shoulder Surfing, and Dumpster Diving

Social engineering and shoulder surfing are introduced in Chapter 1. Social engineering attacks rely on human interaction. They involve tricking people to gain sensitive information. Shoulder surfing occurs when an attacker looks over the shoulder of another person to discover sensitive information. In each type of attack, attackers are trying to get data they do not have permission to have. Often attackers are trying to get personally identifiable information.

Dumpster diving is another threat to data privacy. Dumpster diving is sifting through trash to discover personal information. It's an issue because individuals and organizations dispose of personal information in unsecure ways. Thieves steal personally identifiable information to commit identity theft. Shredding documents before placing them in the trash is a safe disposal method.

In May 2009, a New York law firm was preparing to move. The firm hired a document destruction company to help it dispose of old client files. Many of those files contained personally identifiable information on clients. The personal information included medical records, Social Security numbers, and other personal data. Six dumpsters full of intact, old client files ended up on the street. Media outlets reported that several people were noticed rummaging through the bins and looking at documents.

Social Networking Sites

Personal data privacy is not compromised just by the actions of third parties. People can harm their own privacy by participating in online social networks. They have the potential to expose a lot of personal information. **Social networking sites** are Web site applications that allow users to post information about themselves. These sites promote interaction between people.

Some social networking sites are employment based. These sites promote professional networking. They allow users to post their work history and information and connect with other users in the same industry or across industries. Some social networking sites are purely social. They allow users to share snapshots of their lives with family and friends. Users often share large amounts of highly personal data on social networking sites.

Social networking has two main privacy concerns:

- Information sharing
- Security

Information Sharing.   On social networking sites, users share lots of information about themselves in a virtually unlimited forum. Many people engage in online behaviors that put them at risk. People share details about their daily schedules, finances, and family members. Thieves can use this information to steal from a person's home or target them for identity theft.

Most social networking sites allow users to control some privacy settings. However, users may not be knowledgeable about all of the settings. Sometimes the privacy settings on social networking sites are difficult to understand. If they are hard to understand, users may not use them. People often don't realize how much information is available on the Internet and that other users have access to it.

A fugitive from New York State was caught in Terre Haute, Indiana, in February 2010. Police tracked him down because he posted his workplace on his social networking profiles. Police arrested him at his job. The police then posted this message on his Facebook account: "It was due to your diligence in keeping us informed that now you are under arrest."

Security.   Another privacy concern about social networking sites is their security. Many sites allow users to add applications and other third-party software to their profiles. These applications enhance the social networking experience. If these applications don't use proper security practices, personal information can be exposed. A compromise in an application can disclose data stored on a user's profile. Social networking users often have little control over information used or shared by these types of applications.

RockYou, Inc., is a provider of social networking applications. In 2009, RockYou notified its customers that their sensitive information might have been compromised in a security breach. Information disclosed included user name and password information. An Indiana man has sued RockYou. He claimed that it stored personal data in an unencrypted database and failed to take reasonable steps to secure it.

The lawsuit is seeking class action status. Class action status means that the lawsuit proceeds on behalf of all RockYou account holders who were impacted by the breach. At the time the case was filed, the breach may have affected the personal information of 32 million account holders.

Online Data Gathering

The Internet has made it much easier to learn personal details about people. People can search the Internet for data on their neighbors, co-workers, family members, prospective dates, and public figures. Almost every person has some sort of digital presence. Social networking sites, personal Web pages, media Web sites, and government public records databases can be easily reviewed for personal information. While there are legitimate uses for viewing online personal data, it also can be used to harass and threaten victims.

NOTE

Up to 9 million Americans are victims of identity theft each year, according to the Federal Trade Commission.

Many of the privacy concerns discussed in this section existed before the Internet. They just didn't exist on the same level as they do now. It's easy to discover personal information about other people. **Identity theft** is one of the fastest growing crimes. It's becoming easy to find and misuse others' personal information. Identity theft occurs when a person's personally identifiable information is used without permission to commit other crimes.

What Is Workplace Privacy?

Workplace privacy is a term that describes privacy issues in the workplace. Privacy can be implicated in a number of ways in the workplace. Hiring, firing, performance reviews all have potential privacy concerns. How employers interact with employees in these matters can have privacy implications.

As a rule, most U.S. employees have very little expectation of privacy in their workplaces. Very few states have enacted laws about workplace privacy issues. Some states may have laws relating to general issues, such as telephone wiretapping. Not all states have considered the impact of those laws in the workplace.

Employers can use technology, such as electronic communications, to make workers more productive. Employers provide employees with equipment to use at work. This equipment includes desktop and laptop computers, cell phones, telephones, voice mail, e-mail, and Internet access. These technologies allow employers greater opportunity to monitor how their employees are working each day. This is called workplace monitoring.

This section will discuss the following types of monitoring:

- Telephone and voice mail monitoring
- Video surveillance monitoring
- Computer use monitoring (including Internet access)
- E-mail monitoring

For the most part, workplace monitoring is permissible in the United States. Courts are just beginning to address the limits of an employer's ability to monitor employees. Employers usually are permitted to monitor their employees so long as the employer has a legitimate business reason to do so. Employers have great discretion in determining legitimate business reasons for monitoring.

Workplace monitoring is legitimate when used to measure employee productivity and workplace safety. It's also legitimate when used to protect assets and prevent theft. Monitoring can be used to ensure that employees are properly using the organization's sensitive data. It also can be used to verify that employees aren't violating other policies (such as acceptable use policies). Some organizations may use various types of monitoring to protect themselves from liability for bad acts committed by employees.

Telephone and Voice Mail Monitoring

Some organizations monitor employee telephone conversations as a part of routine activities. One reason to do this is to make sure the employees are providing good customer service. Employees have few protections from this type of monitoring.

An employer's right to monitor telephone conversations must be reviewed under federal and state law. Federal protection for electronic communications is found in the Electronic Communication Privacy Act (ECPA). It also protects telephone calls. Under this law, the use of eavesdropping technologies to record a telephone conversation requires a court order.

NOTE

A 2007 study conducted by the American Management Association and ePolicy Institute reported that 45 percent of employers monitor the amount of time employees spend on telephone calls. They also make note of the phone numbers dialed. The same study reported that 16 percent of employers record telephone conversations.

Telephone conversation monitoring in the ordinary course of business may be allowed without a court order. To use this exception, the employer must state a legitimate business interest in monitoring telephone calls. Employers also must show that the monitoring occurred on equipment provided by a communications service provider.

Courts tend to give employers deference when reviewing their legitimate business reason for monitoring. In most cases, the reason is met if a call is even slightly related to business matters. Telephone calls with customers about services or products that the employer provides clearly relate to business matters. Monitoring telephone calls for quality control purposes also is a legitimate business purpose.

For monitoring to stand up in court, an employer must show that the monitoring took place on equipment supplied by its phone system service provider. The equipment used to monitor calls must be more than a simple tape recorder. In *Deal v. Spears* (1992), the Eighth Circuit Court of Appeals found that a recorder purchased at a consumer electronics store didn't qualify as ordinary telephone equipment. The court held that even though the employer's reason for monitoring was legitimate (the prevention of theft), the exception wasn't met. The monitoring was a violation of federal law.

Federal law allows monitoring only when the conversation clearly relates to the employer's business. Employers must immediately stop monitoring a call once they determine that it's personal. Personal calls are outside of the ordinary course of business.

Employers may always monitor employee telephone calls when the employee gives consent. An employer must provide notice of the monitoring. It also must show that its employees consented to the monitoring. Employers can prove that they gave notice by putting the monitoring policy in the employee handbook. An employer can prove that an employee consented to monitoring by having employees sign an acknowledgment form. There's no violation if an employee gives the employer permission to monitor the call.

Most state laws have wiretap statutes that are based on federal law. There may be subtle differences. In California, state law requires that residents be notified in advance that a call is being monitored. A recorded message or tone at the beginning of the call satisfies this requirement. In Delaware, employers must provide written notice before monitoring calls. In Connecticut, all parties to the conversation must give consent.

There is far less regulation with employer monitoring of stored voice mail messages. Under federal law, employers that provide electronic communication services may access messages once they are stored in their computer or telephone systems. They can do this without notifying employees. If an employer owns the telephone system, then it may legally access stored voice mails.

Video Surveillance Monitoring

Employers may want to use video surveillance to monitor their employees. They can use it to protect against workplace theft. Video surveillance also can be used to protect workplace safety and monitor productivity.

Workplace video surveillance monitoring generally is allowed if employees are given notice. Employers must have a legitimate business reason for the surveillance. Employers must not use video surveillance to monitor places where employees have a reasonable expectation of privacy. Areas considered private include restrooms, employee lounges, or private offices. Employers must be careful when using hidden video surveillance.

It can be a privacy violation if the person under hidden surveillance has a reasonable expectation of privacy in the area under surveillance.

Some states have laws that set limits on what employers may videotape, and employers can run into complications with federal and state wiretapping laws if the video surveillance also includes audio recording. Audio recording can trigger the wiretap acts.

Computer Use Monitoring

Employers may monitor employee computer and Internet use for a number of reasons. In addition to those already mentioned, employers may monitor it to discourage inappropriate online conduct at work. This could include online shopping during work hours or viewing adults-only Web sites.

NOTE

The 2007 American Management Association and ePolicy Institute study reported that 66 percent of employers monitor Internet connections. Forty-five percent of employers monitor keystrokes.

Employees generally don't have any reasonable expectation of privacy in their use of employer-provided resources. An employer generally is allowed to monitor an employee's use of work-provided computers and Internet access. This monitoring includes reviewing files and software on the computer. It also includes tracking Internet use and the Web pages that an employee visits.

An employer can monitor computer or Internet use in a number of ways. A keystroke logger can be used to monitor keystrokes made in a certain period, or the number of Web sites visited. Employers also can monitor how much time employees spend in software applications provided for work purposes. Employers might do this to measure productivity. Employers also can use software programs to measure time spent on the Internet. They also can block employee access to some Web pages to limit the types of sites that employees access from work.

There's no federal prohibition against employer computer or Internet-use monitoring when the employer provides the equipment to the employee. Computer and Internet monitoring is permitted in most states. Connecticut and Delaware are notable exceptions. These states require employers to give notice prior to monitoring computer use.

Many questions are unanswered with respect to the limits of employer computer use and Internet monitoring. Court opinions provide little guidance. Employees that challenge employer computer monitoring claim that the monitoring infringed upon their reasonable expectation of privacy in the use of the work computer. Different courts in different areas have come to different conclusions.

Some courts have ruled that an employee never has any privacy in employer-provided computers. Other courts have decided that an employee may have a reasonable expectation of privacy in employer-provided computers. Other facts are needed to support that expectation. For instance, if an employee keeps the computer in his or her locked office and uses a password to protect the machine, they might have a reasonable expectation of privacy in the work computer. Courts also look at whether the employer had a written policy that gave employees notice of monitoring.

A potential question also arises when employers allow employees to use their own personal equipment at work. In *United States v. Barrows* (2007), an employee brought his personally owned laptop computer to work. He connected the computer to his employer's network. He used the computer at work in an open workspace area. He did not password-protect his computer. While he was away from his desk, another employee accessed his computer and found illegal materials.

The Tenth Circuit Court of Appeals held that the employee did not have a reasonable expectation of privacy in his personal computer. There was no expectation of privacy because he had connected the computer to his employer's computer network. The court also said the employee had no expectation of privacy in the machine because he used it in an open area. He also left it on when he was not using it and took no steps to password-protect the machine.

Computer use and Internet monitoring create individual privacy concerns. Internet monitoring can be invasive. People use the Internet to research many things, sometimes very sensitive things. An employer who monitors Internet use might inadvertently learn very personal things about an employee.

> **NOTE**
>
> A few states limit the ability of an employer to fire an employee for off-duty activity. Most of these laws deal with activities such as alcohol or cigarette use. These laws state that an employer can't fire an employee for use that was both off-duty and away from the employer's premises.

Another privacy concern is the monitoring of an employee's off-duty Internet activity. Employers can easily search the Internet for information related to potential and current employees. They can view employee postings on blogs, Web pages, or online listservs, and comments made in response to media articles. Many large employers have fired employees for online comments made on their own time.

In 2004, Delta Airlines fired a flight attendant for pictures that she posted on her personal Web site. The flight attendant was wearing her Delta Airlines uniform in the posted pictures. The flight attendant later sued Delta for firing her. The case was stayed while Delta Airlines was in bankruptcy. A "stay" in a bankruptcy case means that a lawsuit can't continue.

E-mail Monitoring

E-mail monitoring is very similar to telephone conversation monitoring. The federal wiretap laws in place for monitoring telephone conversations also apply to intercepting e-mail conversations. Like telephone conversations, real-time e-mail monitoring may be permitted in some instances. An employer may intercept employee e-mail using equipment furnished by the provider of electronic communication services. An employer must have a legitimate business purpose for intercepting e-mail.

E-mail monitoring does raise some questions that are different from telephone conversation monitoring. For instance, e-mail is different because it can be stored indefinitely on the employer's equipment. Under federal law, stored electronic communications can be accessed by the organization that provides the electronic communications service.

This "stored communication" exception is very broad. If the employer provides the e-mail service, then it may properly access stored e-mails from that service.

Under federal law, employee consent always permits an employer to monitor an employee's e-mail. State laws generally permit e-mail monitoring in a manner that is similar to telephone monitoring. There may be occasional variations among the states. In Delaware, employers must provide written notice before monitoring e-mail communications.

Court cases generally have found that employers are free to read employer-provided employee e-mail messages. These courts sometimes, but not always, consider whether the e-mail was intercepted for a legitimate business reason or if it was viewed from its storage location.

Sometimes employees access their private, Web-based e-mail accounts from employer-provided equipment. This is a different issue from employers' monitoring work-provided e-mail. Employers who access private e-mail accounts may run into problems with the federal law, even if the employee has accessed that private account from a work-provided computer. The Electronic Communications Privacy Act prohibits employers from accessing an employee's personal e-mail account. Court's have found that employers act inappropriately if they use computer-monitoring equipment to obtain user names and passwords to employee personal accounts. If the employer then accesses those private e-mail accounts without permission, it's considered an ECPA violation.

Public Employees

Some special rules exist for workplace monitoring of public employees. **Public employees** are employees that work for the federal or state government. Individuals in public employment have some extra privacy protections. The federal constitution protects individuals from interference by the government. Public employees receive extra protections because their employer is the government. State employees have similar extra protections because of rights provided in state constitutions.

The Fourth Amendment protects federal employees from unreasonable government search and seizure. The federal government must provide employees with notice if it intends to monitor the electronic communications of its employees. Even though the government might have to take additional steps to make sure that employee monitoring is legal, courts have recognized the government's right to engage in workplace surveillance for legitimate business reasons.

Workplace monitoring continues to be a sensitive issue for both employers and employees. Employers typically win legal challenges against workplace monitoring practices. To protect their own personal privacy, employees must assume that equipment provided by their employers is for work activities only. Employees should not engage in personal computer and Internet activities on an employer's computer if they wish to protect their privacy.

Workplace Monitoring and Employee Privacy

In December 2009, the U.S. Supreme Court agreed to hear a case about employee privacy rights on employer-provided equipment. The Court agreed to review a ruling by a federal appeals court. The appeals court had held that an employee's privacy rights are violated if his employer reads personal text messages sent on an employer-provided device. In the case, a California police officer was provided with an employer-issued pager. The police department had a general computer, Internet, and e-mail use policy. The policy stated that the use of the equipment was limited to city business. The police department didn't have a formal policy about text messaging. Officers were told that text messages sent on the pager would not be reviewed so long as the officers reimbursed the department for charges that went above the service contract amount.

The police officer in this case was a heavy user of the pager. He always paid the police department for the excess use amounts. Eventually the police department decided to audit pager use to determine whether the basic service contract amount needed to be increased.

The police department requested transcripts of the text messages sent from the pagers. The pager service provider gave the police department the requested transcripts. The department reviewed the transcripts of the police officer's text messages. The police officer sued, stating that reading the messages violated various federal laws and his right to privacy.

The Ninth Circuit Court of Appeals said that the police officer had a reasonable expectation of privacy in the text messages sent from his pager. The court based its decision on the fact that the department said there would be no review of pager text messages. The police department appealed that ruling.

In June 2010, the U.S. Supreme Court ruled that reviewing the police officer's text messages didn't violate federal law and the police officer's privacy rights. The Court held that the police department's audit of pager use wasn't intrusive and was for a legitimate purpose. The Court also found that the police officer didn't have a reasonable expectation of privacy in the text messages.

While this case deals with a public employee, it does help provide clarity for all employers on the acceptable limits of electronic communications monitoring. One thing that the case does help highlight is that all employers must have very clear policies on the use of electronic communication devices. You can read the Supreme Court's decision in this case at http://www.supremecourt.gov/opinions/09pdf/08-1332.pdf.

What Are General Principles for Privacy Protection in Information Systems?

Designing information systems in ways that protect data privacy is very important. Customers will be loyal to organizations that protect privacy. Organizations must understand how their customers feel about data privacy. Even though people are sharing more information than ever before, some feel that their privacy is under attack. Organizations must keep in mind that people want to control their personal data.

Organizations can use the fair information practice principles discussed earlier
in this chapter to help define the best way to approach privacy. A number of information
system activities impact personal data privacy. Data collection, storage, use, retention,
and destruction practices must be reviewed to make sure that privacy is ensured at each
stage in the data life cycle. The steps in the data life cycle are:

- Data collection
- Data use
- Data storage
- Data retention
- Data destruction

In the data collection phase, organizations must clearly state the types of data that
they need to collect. They also must determine how they are going to collect data from
their customers. "Active data collection" practices should be used. These data collection
practices are obvious to the customer. Customers are aware of active data collection
practices. The use of Web-based forms clearly indicates to a customer that data collection
activities are taking place. Customers understand what data is being collected because
they are providing the information.

Organizations should avoid passive collection methods. "Passive data collection"
happens secretly. An organization collects data in a passive manner by using devices such
as cookies and Web beacons. Customers may not know that data collection is occurring
with these collection methods.

Organizations must make sure that they use the data that they collect in ways that
the customer has approved. It should use the data for no purpose other than what was
specified when the data was collected. Information systems will need configuration so
that the collected data is available only for its approved use. Organizations also must make
sure that only authorized individuals have access to the data. Data must not be disclosed
to employees who have no business need for the data.

Organizations also must ensure that they know how the collected data is used within
the system. Data must not change when processed in the system. Organizations also
will want to include system checks that verify that the personal data collected remains
accurate.

Systems sometimes allow customers to create "accounts" that hold their personal data.
The organization must ensure that it uses appropriate access control measures for those
accounts. These measures protect accounts from unauthorized access. Organizations
should also verify that records are updated accurately.

FIGURE 2-1

The data life cycle.

Data Collection → Data Use → Data Storage → Data Retention → Data Destruction

Organizations must keep track of where collected personal data is stored in their systems. Appropriate safeguards are needed to protect the stored data. Organizations may choose to encrypt the collected personal data to protect it from disclosures or security breaches. Employers also should use safeguards to make sure that employees don't store the data on removable media. Personal data must be stored securely to protect it from disclosure.

Organizations should retain personal data for only as long as it's needed. Laws and organizational policy specify the appropriate retention periods. An organization must dispose of the data when the retention period expires. They must use a method that destroys old data in both primary and backup storage systems.

Privacy Policies and Data Privacy Laws

Organizations that collect personal data from customers should develop a privacy policy. This policy clearly explains all the protections the organization uses at each state in the data life cycle. It should inform customers about personal data collection practices. It should explain how the organization uses the data that it collects. The policy manages the privacy expectations of customers and the security obligations of the organization.

The United States does not have a comprehensive data privacy law. Many other nations that conduct business with the United States do have such laws. This difference can make business transactions hard at times.

European nations recognize privacy as a basic human right. The European Union's comprehensive data privacy law is called the European Union Data Protection Directive (95/45/EC). This directive sets limits on the collection and use of personal data. It states the minimum level of privacy protections that must be granted to European Union (E.U.) citizens. The directive has rules that look like the fair information practices principles. Nations that belong to the European Union can make additional laws that provide more protections for personal data.

The directive forbids most transfers of personal data to non-E.U. countries and organizations. This is so that the privacy protections granted to E.U. citizens are not weakened. Transfers are allowed when privacy protections can be promised. A non-E.U. country or organization that receives personal data from the European Union must show that it adequately protects that data.

FYI

The privacy settings that organizations use are very important to consumers. In late 2009, Facebook made changes to how its users could protect their privacy. It also made changes to its privacy policy at the same time.

The changes were made to give Facebook users more control over information in their Facebook profiles. The changes allowed users to specify who was allowed to see information posted to a user's profile. Facebook's privacy policy is available at *http://www.facebook.com/policy.php*.

The U.S. Department of Commerce runs a "Safe Harbor" program for U.S. organizations. This program helps show an adequate level of protection for E.U. personal data. U.S. organizations that participate in this program may receive transfers of personal data from the European Union. U.S. organizations can voluntarily participate in the Safe Harbor program. They must meet seven safe harbor principles. These principles are similar to the fair information practices principles.

The U.S. Department of Commerce requires organizations to certify that they meet the safe harbor principles in writing. They must do this each year. The Department of Commerce maintains a public list of all organizations that participate in the Safe Harbor program.

More information on the E.U. Safe Harbor program is available at *http://www.export.gov/safeharbor/index.asp.*

CHAPTER SUMMARY

Privacy is a "right" that people no longer are taking for granted. People want to have control over their personal information. They want to be able to choose how third parties collect, use, and store their information. The growth in electronic communication and data transfer has changed how individuals view privacy and how organizations must protect it. Organizations must use information security principles to make sure they respect a person's individual privacy choices.

KEY CONCEPTS AND TERMS

Adware	Fair information practice principles	Radio Frequency Identification (RFID)
Biometric data	Global positioning system (GPS)	Reasonable person standard
Blog	Identity theft	Seal program
Clickstream	Online profiling	Search engine
Common law	Pleadings	Security breach
Cookie	Pop-up advertisements	Social networking sites
Defamation	Privacy	Tort
Docket	Public employees	Web beacon
Dumpster diving	Public records	Workplace privacy

CHAPTER 2 ASSESSMENT

1. What does a seal program verify?

   A. That an organization meets recognized privacy principles
   B. That an organization misfits recognized security principles
   C. That a third party is trusted
   D. That a Web site does not use cookies

2. What techniques are used to create a list of the Web pages that a computer user visits?

   A. Adware, malware, and phishing
   B. Malware, cookies, and Web beacons
   C. Web beacons, clickstreams, and spyware
   D. Malware, spyware, and cookies
   E. Clickstreams, cookies, and Web beacons

3. Which amendment protects against unreasonable searches and seizures?

   A. First
   B. Third
   C. Fourth
   D. Fifth
   E. Seventh

4. Privacy refers to a person's right to control personal data.

   A. True
   B. False

5. What is the source of legal authority for the U.S. government?

   A. The United States Code
   B. The common law
   C. Supreme Court decisions
   D. The U.S. Constitution
   E. The Declaration of Independence

6. Which of the following is *not* a privacy tort?

   A. Intrusion into seclusion
   B. Portrayal in a false light
   C. Appropriation of likeness or identity
   D. Defamation
   E. Public disclosure of private facts

7. The OECD privacy protection guidelines contain _____ privacy principles.

8. Which principle means that an individual should be told the reason for data collection before the data is collected?

   A. The collection limitation principle
   B. The purpose specification principle
   C. The use limitation principle
   D. The openness principle
   E. The accountability principle

9. What are the two types of cookies?

   A. First-party and third-party cookies
   B. Active and passive cookies
   C. First party and second party cookies
   D. Rational and irrational cookies

10. What is a Web beacon?

   A. Text stored on a computer user's hard drive
   B. A small, invisible electronic file
   C. A pop-up advertisement
   D. Executable code
   E. A data trail left by a computer user

11. Employer monitoring of employees in the workplace is generally allowed.

   A. True
   B. False

12. To monitor telephone conversations, an employer must use equipment provided by a phone system service provider and have _____.

13. Why is biometric data unique?

   A. It can be used to identify a person.
   B. It is data about a person's physical traits.
   C. It can be used to commit identity theft.
   D. It cannot be changed.
   E. None of the above

14. Which of the following is *not* a people-based privacy threat?

   A. Social engineering
   B. Web beacons
   C. Shoulder surfing
   D. Dumpster diving
   E. Social networks

15. What is used to ensure privacy?

   A. Biometric data
   B. Encryption
   C. Information security
   D. Monitoring
   E. Online profiling

ENDNOTES

1. CNN.com. "New search engines aspire to supplement Google," May 12, 2009, http://www.cnn.com/2009/TECH/05/12/future.search.engine/index.html (accessed February 4, 2010).

2. Searchenginewatch.com. "Google Now a Verb in the Oxford English Dictionary," June 29, 2006, http://blog.searchenginewatch.com/060629-105413 (accessed February 4, 2010).

3. Montana Constitution, art. II, sec. 10.

4. California Constitution, art. 1, sec. 1.

5. New York Civil Rights Law, art. 5. sec. 50-52 (1903).

6. *Spyware Control Act*, Utah Code, title 13. ch. 40 sec. 13-40-101 to 401 (2004).

The American Legal System

FOR OVER TWO DECADES, the shows in the *Law and Order* franchise have been popular with television viewers. Each episode transports viewers into the world of American criminal law and process; from the dramatic opening theme song with its scene changing "clang" sound, to the final scene when justice is served. A crime, investigation, and judicial process are neatly wrapped in a one-hour episode. *Law and Order* episodes focus on criminal law, which is one aspect of the American legal system.

This chapter briefly reviews the American legal system. It's important for Americans to have a general understanding of this system. It affects us every day. We are bound by a system of laws that regulate our behavior and contribute to an ordered society. Laws are a reflection of our values, and they evolve over time.

The American legal system, its history, and its processes are a fascinating area of study. Many talented judges, attorneys, and law scholars have written excellent books about it. This chapter provides only an overview, but it will outline a framework that can enable you to do further reading and research on this topic.

Chapter 3 Topics

This chapter covers the following topics and concepts:

- How the American legal system is organized
- What the sources of American law are
- What the types of law are
- What the role of precedent is
- What regulatory authorities are
- What the difference is between compliance and audit
- How security, privacy, and compliance fit together

Chapter 3 Goals

When you complete this chapter, you will be able to:

- Describe the American legal system
- Explain sources of law
- Distinguish between different types of law
- Explain the role of precedent
- Describe the role of regulatory authorities
- Explain the different between compliance and audit
- Describe how security, privacy, and compliance fit together

The American Legal System

The American legal system comprises many distinct parts: federal and state governments, laws, and courts. Federal law exclusively governs some areas of law; other areas depend on the subtle nuances of state law. Some parts of the law are based on written laws, called "statutes" or "codes," which are developed by governments. Yet other areas of the law depend on principles developed from years of legal tradition and court decisions. Civil law provides for the resolution of disputes between private individuals, organizations, or governments. Criminal law governs the prosecution of those charged with serious offenses against public order, such as murder.

The basis for the American system of government, and the American legal system, is the U.S. Constitution. The U.S. Constitution is reprinted in Appendix D at the end of this book.

Federal Government

▶ **NOTE**

Rhode Island was the only original state that did not send representatives to the Constitutional Convention.

The U.S. Constitution was ratified in 1789 and sets forth the structure of the U.S. federal government. Representatives from almost all of the states in existence at the time worked together to draft the Constitution. The state representatives realized that there were some areas in which a strong federal government was needed in order to keep the states united. However, the state representatives didn't want a federal government that was too strong, nor did they want any one portion of the federal government to have too much power. These considerations help explain the current structure of the federal government.

The U.S. Constitution calls itself "the supreme Law of the Land."[1] It's the fundamental authority for the American federal system of government. The Constitution defines three co-equal roles in the federal government: legislative, executive, and judicial. The legislative branch makes the laws, the executive branch enforces the laws, and the judicial branch reviews the laws to make sure they are constitutional. This is the "checks and balances" system that describes the relationship between the three branches of the federal government. Each branch of government has a separate sphere of authority (balances). The actions of each branch of government are subject to review by the other branches (checks).

▶ **NOTE**

"Federalism" is a term that describes the relationship between the states and the U.S. federal government.

The U.S. Constitution also defines the relationship between the federal government and the states. At the time that the Constitution was drafted and ratified, debate raged on about the appropriate relationship between the federal and state governments. The previous legal document that established the federal government, the Articles of Confederation, proved to be too weak to keep the states joined together. However, an overly strong federal government was seen as an obstacle that would prevent states and individuals from controlling their own affairs. The states wanted to make sure that they retained general authority to regulate their own affairs. The Constitution contains specific provisions to reflect this divided authority.

The Constitution also provides some of the fundamental rights of individuals. Individual rights are located primarily in the Bill of Rights, which was ratified in 1791. The term "Bill of Rights" refers collectively to the first 10 amendments to the Constitution. These amendments are the basis for some of the rights that Americans hold most dear. The right to free speech, freedom from government-established religion, and the right against self-incrimination are all contained in the Bill of Rights.

Eligibility Requirements for the President and Members of Congress

The Constitution provides eligibility requirements for the president and members of Congress. The president must be a natural-born U.S. citizen and must be at least 35 years old. The president must have been a resident of the United States for at least 14 years at the time of election.[2]

Senators must be at least 30 years old. They must have been citizens of the United States for at least nine years. They must also be residents of the state from which they are elected.[3]

House members must be at least 25 years old. They must have been citizens of the United States for at least seven years. They must also be residents of the congressional district from which they are elected.[4]

Legislative Branch

Article I, section 8 of the Constitution sets out the lawmaking authority of the legislative branch of the federal government. Collectively, the legislative branch is called Congress. The federal government has limited lawmaking power. Congress can't make any laws outside the scope that the Constitution specifically delegates to it.

The U.S. Congress consists of two chambers: the U.S. Senate and the U.S. House of Representatives. The Senate has 100 members, two senators from each state. The Senate represents all states equally. The House of Representatives has 435 members. The House represents the population. Each Representative represents a congressional district. Congressional districts all have roughly the same amount of people. In March 2010, that number was about 650,000. The congressional districts are redrawn every 10 years after the U.S. Census is completed. Each state gets at least one representative no matter its total population size.

Article I, section 8 of the Constitution lists the powers delegated to Congress. Congress has the power to declare war, establish the post office, maintain armed forces, and make money. In addition to these very specific powers, Congress has the power to regulate commerce and make other laws necessary for carrying out its constitutional duties. These powers are very broad.

The Commerce Clause grants Congress the power to regulate commerce between the states.[5] Congress uses this provision as justification to regulate trade, or any other commercial activity, between the states. Many Supreme Court Cases have reviewed the limits of this power. In general, if an activity has the potential to affect the trade relations between the states, then Congress is able to legislate it.

> **NOTE**
>
> **Preemption** refers to the legal concept that means that a higher-ranking law will exclude or preempt a lower-ranking law on the same subject. This rule especially holds in the federal legislative context with respect to the Commerce Clause. States are preempted from making laws that may affect the trade relations between the states.

3

The American Legal System

Congress also has the power to enact laws that are "necessary and proper" for carrying out its duties.[6] Congress can use the power implied in this section to legislate in a number of different areas.

The Constitution specifies the basic lawmaking process. A "bill" is the initial draft of a potential law. Both chambers of Congress must approve the same bill, and the president must sign it before it becomes a law.

The procedural documents of both chambers describe the process for moving bills through each chamber. Once a bill is introduced, it's generally assigned to a specialty committee. The bill is revised during the committee process, which usually includes hearings to determine why a law is needed in the first place. After the hearings the committee votes on whether the bill should be sent to the full chamber for consideration. When a bill passes one chamber, it's forwarded to the other chamber for consideration.

Once a bill passes both chambers, it goes to a "conference committee" made up of both senators and representatives. This committee reviews both the Senate and House of Representatives' versions of the bill. This committee can't substantially change the bills being compared. The committee tries to reach a compromise on both versions of the bill. When the committee reaches a resolution on the bill, they report back to their respective chambers. Each chamber votes on the bill again. If the original conference committee can't reach an agreement, the bill may be assigned to a new conference committee or go back into committees of each chamber for additional revisions.

The speaker of the House of Representatives and the president of the Senate sign all bills that pass in Congress before delivering them to the president. The president has 10 days to sign the bill. If the president does not sign it within 10 days, then it becomes law just as if the president had signed it.

Executive Branch

Article II establishes the power of the executive branch of government. The president of the United States leads the executive branch of government. The president is a nationally elected official. The president is also the commander-in-chief of the U.S. armed forces. The president is often considered the "face" of the United States.

NOTE

Federal laws are published in the United States Code. The federal government publishes the Code every six years.

The president has the power to enforce the laws of the United States and the responsibility for maintaining the day-to-day operations of the U.S. government. The president has the power to sign or veto any legislation that Congress passes. (Congress can override a presidential veto with a two-thirds vote of both the House and the Senate.) Once the president signs the legislation, it becomes an Act of Congress. An "Act of Congress" is a law passed by the Congress and signed by the president. An Act of Congress is federal law.

The president also appoints federal judicial, executive, and administrative officials. The Senate must approve some of the president's appointees, such as Cabinet members or federal judicial appointees. The president also has the power to negotiate and enter into treaties with other countries. The U.S. Senate must ratify treaties.

The role of the U.S. Cabinet is to advise the president. The Cabinet includes the U.S. vice president and the heads of 15 executive departments. President George Washington established the first Cabinet. The Constitution recognizes that the president should have advisers in executive departments, but it does not specify the type or number of executive departments. Congress creates the executive departments.

Judicial Branch

Article III of the Constitution establishes the judicial branch of the federal government. This Article vests the judicial power of the United States in one supreme court. The U.S. Supreme Court is the highest court in the country.

The U.S. Supreme Court is the only court specifically required by the U.S. Constitution. Currently, there are nine Supreme Court justices. Congress has the authority to determine the actual number of Supreme Court justices. The president nominates the justices when there's a vacancy on the Court. The Senate must confirm the nomination. Supreme Court nominees are usually highly respected state or federal judges or highly respected attorneys.

Supreme Court justices, like all federal judges, are appointed for life. They serve until their retirement, death, or removal. Supreme Court justices can be removed only if they are impeached and convicted by Congress. The Constitution requires that all federal court judges be appointed for life for a reason: to help promote an independent judiciary. The drafters of the Constitution did not want the review of law to be dependent upon popular political ideas. Instead, they wanted federal judges appointed for life so that they could not be fired if their decisions were unpopular or not favorable to a particular political party. Table 3-1 lists the members of the U.S. Supreme Court as of February 2010.

Structure of the Federal Judiciary.   It's important to understand how the different courts in the federal system relate to one another. Once this structure is understood, it can be applied generally to state judicial systems.

TABLE 3-1   Members of the U.S. Supreme Court as of February 2010.

NAME	POSITION	APPOINTING PRESIDENT	DATE TERM BEGAN
John G. Roberts	Chief Justice	George W. Bush	September 2005
Antonin Scalia	Associate Justice	Ronald Reagan	September 1986
Anthony Kennedy	Associate Justice	Ronald Reagan	February 1988
Clarence Thomas	Associate Justice	George H.W. Bush	October 1991
Ruth Bader Ginsburg	Associate Justice	Bill Clinton	August 1993
Stephen Breyer	Associate Justice	Bill Clinton	August 1994
Samuel Alito	Associate Justice	George W. Bush	January 2006
Sonia Sotomayor	Associate Justice	Barack Obama	August 2009
Elena Kagan	Associate Justice	Barack Obama	August 2010

Courts have the ability to hear only "cases," or disputes, that are within their jurisdiction. **Jurisdiction** describes the types of cases that a court has the authority to hear. There are three main types of jurisdiction used to describe the function of a court:

- **Original jurisdiction**—The power of a court to hear the initial dispute between parties. These courts conduct trials. Usually trial courts have **original jurisdiction**.
- **Concurrent jurisdiction**—Jurisdiction that is shared by several different courts.
- **Appellate jurisdiction**—The power of a court to review a decision made by a lower court.

> **NOTE**
>
> **Federal question jurisdiction** refers to the power of federal courts to hear only disputes about federal laws or constitutional issues. **Diversity of citizenship jurisdiction** refers to the power of federal courts to hear only disputes between citizens of different states that are above a certain dollar amount.

In the federal court system, federal courts have "limited jurisdiction." That means that they can hear only certain types of cases that fall within a limited subject matter. The jurisdiction of the federal courts is determined by the Constitution and laws made by Congress. Federal courts can hear only the following kinds of cases:

- Disputes regarding federal laws or constitutional issues
- Disputes between residents of different states where the amount of money in controversy is greater than $75,000

A court cannot hear cases that fall outside its functional or subject matter jurisdiction.

In addition to establishing the Supreme Court, Article III of the Constitution also gives Congress the power to make as many lower-level federal courts as needed. Congress has established district courts, appellate courts, and some specialized courts.

District courts are the lowest level of courts in the federal court system. There are 94 judicial districts in the United States. Each state has at least one judicial district. Some states may be divided into many judicial districts, and each district may have more than one judge. The number of judges in a district is determined by the number of cases, or caseload, in the district. Usually only one judge hears a case at the trial court level.

The district courts are the "workhorses" of the federal judicial system. They are courts of original jurisdiction. They might hear disputes between parties or conduct criminal trials for violations of federal law. Each federal district court also has its own bankruptcy court. The Constitution gives the federal government the sole power over bankruptcy law.

The next level of courts is the intermediate appellate courts. In the federal system, these courts are called the U.S. Courts of Appeals. There are 13 Courts of Appeals. The 94 district courts are grouped into 12 geographical circuits. There is also one circuit, called the Federal Circuit, which hears cases from specialized courts. The Courts of Appeals hear appeals from the district courts in their circuit. For example, the Seventh Circuit Court of Appeals hears cases from Illinois, Indiana, and Wisconsin. The home for the Seventh Circuit is in Chicago, Illinois. The number of judges in each circuit is determined by Congress. These courts usually hear cases in three-judge panels.

The Court of Appeals is a court of **appellate jurisdiction**. Courts of Appeals do not review the facts of a case; they also do not accept any additional evidence for the case. Instead, they review the record of the trial court for only mistakes of law.

The highest court in the U.S. federal system is the U.S. Supreme Court. The highest level of court in any judicial system, state or federal, is often called a "court of last resort." The Supreme Court is a court of appellate jurisdiction. For the most part the Supreme Court decides cases on appeal from the U.S. Court of Appeals. The Supreme Court reviews the decisions of the lower court to make sure that it complies with the law.

The Supreme Court is under no obligation to review a decision from the U.S. Court of Appeals. A party has to ask the Supreme Court to review the case by using a petition known as a *writ of certiorari*. The Supreme Court justices review the *writs of certiorari*. The Court usually approves the petition if four of the nine justices decide that the Court should look at the case. The Court might decide to hear a case if it presents a question of whether a federal law is unconstitutional. It also might decide to hear a case if two or more of the federal appellate courts have ruled differently on the same question of federal or U.S. Constitutional law.

The Supreme Court has exclusive original jurisdiction to decide cases about disputes between state governments. It exercises **concurrent jurisdiction** with federal district courts in some cases. It exercises this original jurisdiction very rarely. Most of the cases heard before the Supreme Court are appeals cases.

The Supreme Court has the power to decide cases that involve questions about the federal Constitution and other federal laws. It can review both state and federal laws to make sure that those laws do not conflict with the U.S. Constitution. The authority to review laws in this way is called judicial review. The Supreme Court is the final authority on cases heard in the federal court system. The decisions of the U.S. Supreme Court cannot be appealed. Figure 3-1 shows the structure of the U.S. federal court system.

> **NOTE**
>
> In the law, an "appeal" is a formal request for a higher authority to review the decision of a lower court. Any party who is unhappy with the judgment received in a district court can appeal to the Court of Appeals for that district. The unhappy party must be able to show that the trial court made a legal error that affected the "holding," or decision, in the case.

3

The American
Legal System

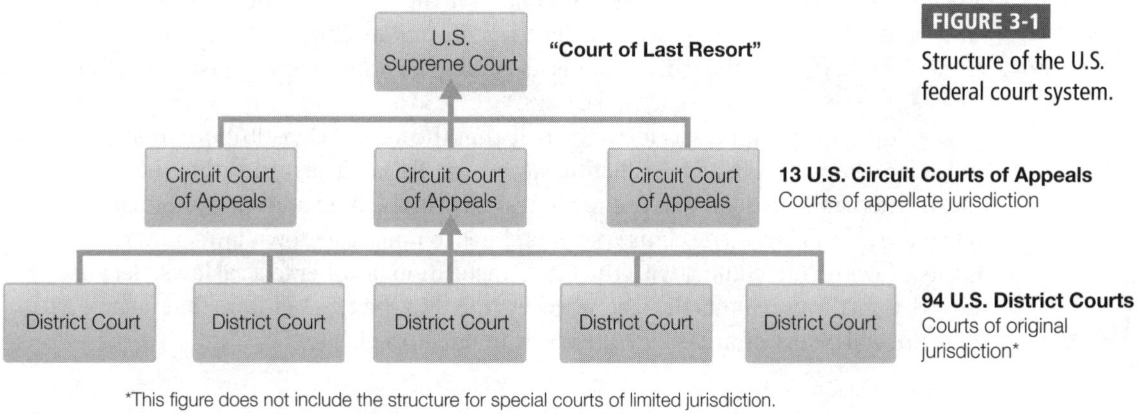

FIGURE 3-1

Structure of the U.S. federal court system.

U.S. Supreme Court — **"Court of Last Resort"**

Circuit Court of Appeals / Circuit Court of Appeals / Circuit Court of Appeals — **13 U.S. Circuit Courts of Appeals** Courts of appellate jurisdiction

District Court / District Court / District Court / District Court / District Court — **94 U.S. District Courts** Courts of original jurisdiction*

*This figure does not include the structure for special courts of limited jurisdiction.

State Government

In negotiating and drafting the U.S. Constitution, state governments gave up some of their own power in order to create the federal government. They did this because the first system of government after the American Revolution that was organized under the Articles of Confederation didn't work. That document didn't create a national government that could require unity on subjects of common interest. The U.S. Constitution changed that relationship.

Under the Constitution, the federal government has certain stated powers and responsibilities. Powers that are not specifically granted to the federal government in the Constitution remain with the states. The Tenth Amendment to the Constitution formalized this relationship. The Tenth Amendment says, "The powers not delegated to the United States by the Constitution, nor prohibited by it to the States, are reserved to the States respectively, or to the people."[7]

> **NOTE**
>
> The State of Alabama is widely recognized as having the longest state constitution. It has 799 amendments. The current constitution was adopted in 1901, and it's the state's sixth constitution.

State governments existed before the federal government as we know it today. Like the federal government, most states are organized under a constitution. State constitutions may vary widely from the U.S. Constitution. Although the federal Constitution primarily describes the relationship between the federal government and the states, state constitutions primarily describe the relationship between a state and its citizens. For this reason, state constitutions often list many more individual rights than are listed in the federal Constitution. State constitutions also tend to be longer than the federal Constitution. Finally, state constitutions are generally easier to change than the federal Constitution.

> **NOTE**
>
> Only the state of Nebraska has a "unicameral legislature." It has only one legislative chamber. All other states have a "bicameral legislature." Bicameral legislatures have two chambers. The U.S. Congress is a bicameral legislature.

There are typically three branches to most state governments, roughly aligned in the same manner as the federal government. Most state legislatures look like the legislative branch of the federal government and have two different legislative chambers. A governor leads the state executive branch.

State governments have the general authority to govern and make laws for the state and its citizens. That is not to say that this power is absolute. The Supremacy Clause limits this broad power to make laws.[8]

The Supremacy Clause sets forth the rule that the federal Constitution, treaties, and federal law outrank any conflicting state laws. This clause means that the U.S. Constitution and federal laws are the highest laws in the land and state judges must follow the federal laws. The clause permits states to make their own laws only so long as those laws do not conflict with the U.S. Constitution or other federal laws. Because the U.S. Constitution limits the federal government in the types of laws that it can enact, there are still plenty of areas for state governments to legislate.

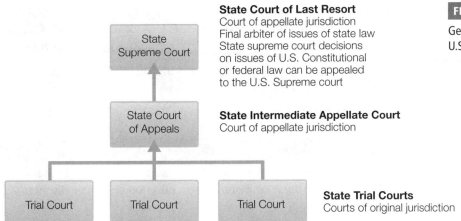

State Court of Last Resort
Court of appellate jurisdiction
Final arbiter of issues of state law
State supreme court decisions
on issues of U.S. Constitutional
or federal law can be appealed
to the U.S. Supreme court

State Intermediate Appellate Court
Court of appellate jurisdiction

State Trial Courts
Courts of original jurisdiction

FIGURE 3-2

General structure of the
U.S. state court system.

Most states have a judicial system that looks similar to the federal system, with a system of trial courts, appellate courts, and courts of last resort. The trial courts are the original jurisdiction courts for a state. These courts are organized by geographical location, with county-level courts being the typical entry-level courts for hearing most disputes. Trial courts have the general authority to hear all sorts of cases, but they are limited to hearing disputes between citizens of the state.

States usually have two appellate courts: a state intermediate appellate court and a state supreme court. States usually only have one type of each court. The intermediate appellate courts hear appeals from the trial courts. The State Supreme Court hears appeals from the appellate court. It's important to remember that not all states have the exact same structure, even though you can draw parallels when discussing structure in general. These courts may go by different names in different states. For example, the highest court in New York is called the New York Court of Appeals. In many states, the "court of appeals" is the intermediate appellate court. Figure 3-2 shows the general structure of a state court system.

The relationship between the state and federal court systems is very interesting. The U.S. Supreme Court has complete authority over courts in the federal system. It also has complete authority over interpretations of federal law and the U.S. Constitution. However, the Supreme Court has no authority over the organization or procedures used by state courts. The Supreme Court may not interpret issues that rely solely on state law or issues arising under state constitutions. Only the highest court in a state is allowed to make interpretations about that state's law.

Federal and state courts don't exist in separate spheres. State courts do have the power and authority to review cases that concern issues of constitutional or federal law.

3

The American
Legal System

TABLE 3-2   A comparison of the federal and state judicial systems.

	STATE JUDICIAL SYSTEM	FEDERAL JUDICIAL SYSTEM
Courts of Original Jurisdiction	Trial courts	U.S. District Courts
Courts of Appellate Jurisdiction	Intermediate appellate courts	Circuit Courts of Appeal
Courts of Last Resort	State supreme court	U.S. Supreme Court
Scope of Authority	General authority to hear all disputes; authority is limited to disputes involving state citizens	Cases must involve a federal question or involve disputes between citizens of different states and be over $75,000
Authority of Court of Last Resort	Final, unless the case involves a federal question; if so, case can be appealed to U.S. Supreme Court	Final

However, the state courts must yield to the superiority and previous decisions of the Supreme Court when doing so. The U.S. Supreme Court can review a state court case in the event that the case concerns a question of federal law or a federal constitutional issue. Table 3-2 compares the federal judicial system to a general state judicial system.

Sources of Law

The law is not secret, but it's complicated. Many of the processes and procedures in the law have evolved over time. They are a combination of the will of the federal and state governments, longstanding traditions about right and wrong, and society's values. It's no wonder that finding out what law applies to a particular situation is sometimes puzzling.

This chapter has already discussed several sources of law: U.S. Constitutional law, U.S. federal law, state constitutional law, and state laws. Now it is time to put these sources in context for the American legal system. This next section discusses the general sources of law and how they relate to one another.

Common Law

As discussed in Chapter 2, the common law is a body of law that's developed through legal tradition and court cases. The U.S. common law is a body of law and legal principles inherited from England. Common law changes very slowly—it develops as judges decide court cases. Therefore, it's sometimes also known as "case law" or "judge made law."

In the common law, courts decide cases by referring to established legal principles and the customs and values of society. They also look at decisions made in earlier cases to see if the cases are similar. If the cases are similar, a new case should reach a similar result. Finally, formal principles of logic and reason are used to help reach a decision when the result is unclear.

Parties arguing a common law case use a similar approach. Attorneys may argue that the customs and values of society have changed such that a new result is appropriate. Attorneys also may attempt to distinguish the facts of the current case from the facts of earlier cases. In all instances, attorneys must use logic and reason to form the basis for their arguments.

The American legal system generally follows the common law tradition. Many countries colonized by the English have adopted similar systems. After the Revolutionary War, common law grew in America and was heavily influenced by "new" American social and economic values. The common law has continued to evolve, and judicial decisions continue to influence it. The development of the common law continues so long as its decisions and conclusions are not in conflict with other laws, such as constitutional documents or state and federal statutes.

Common law principles are often included within the code law of the federal or state government. An example of this is the torts of privacy that were discussed in Chapter 2. The four privacy torts came to be recognized as torts through the evolution of common law. Courts gradually heard cases regarding issues related to the subject matter area of these torts. As they heard the cases, some courts would recognize the tort and allow the cause of action. Some would not. Gradually many states adopted the four privacy torts and some states have even written the torts into their statutes.

In the United States, the common law continues to be very influential in civil law areas such as torts, contract law, and property law.

Code Law

Code law is law that is enacted by legislatures. It's also sometimes called "statutory law." This is the written law that is adopted by governments. In its truest form, code law attempts to state the complete system of law for a state or federal government. Citizens and members of the legal profession are all bound by the terms of the written law.

In the United States, in most states the common law and code law work together to form the laws that society must follow. There has been a strong movement within the law to codify the common law. Many states have codified their common law criminal principles into written law. Some states also have codified parts of their civil (non-criminal) laws. Once a code or statute provision is made that addresses the common law, it supersedes the common law in that area. The principles and traditions of common law are transformed into a code of laws.

NOTE

No discussion of the law would be complete without a Latin phrase or two. Code law is called *lex scripta*, meaning law that is written down. Common law is called *lex non scripta*, meaning law that is not written down.

NOTE

Louisiana is the only state that doesn't base its law on common law principles. Instead, the laws of the state are based upon the Napoleonic Code, which is the French civil code.

Constitutional Law

The U.S. Constitution is the final source of authority for issues involving U.S. federal laws. When federal laws are disputed, they are subject to scrutiny to determine whether the law is constitutional. If the law isn't constitutional, it's invalid. If the law is constitutional, then it's the source of authority for its particular subject matter.

Similarly, state constitutions are the final source of authority for issues involving state law. So long as the state constitutional provision itself is not in conflict with the U.S. Constitution or federal law, then it will be the final decision on state laws. If a state law is constitutional (under both the state and, if challenged, U.S. Constitution), then it's the source of state authority for its particular subject matter.

How Does It All Fit Together?

The American legal system contains many different levels of codified and uncodified laws. This is why it's sometimes hard to figure out what the "law" is with respect to a new situation. When an attorney or judge has to analyze the law that applies to a certain situation, he or she applies the rules of statutory construction for looking at an issue. The rules of statutory construction generally mean that the laws of the legislature (code law) are given greater deference than the laws of the courts (common law). If codes are in conflict with the common law, then the text of the code should control the outcome of the case. The problem in analysis occurs when a code has ambiguous terms.

> **NOTE**
>
> Legal issues are rarely resolved simply by looking at statutes. If they were, there would be little need for attorneys or courts. Often times a statute is poorly written. For example, its terms and provisions could be ambiguous or open to interpretation. Sometimes statute writers simply don't anticipate the legal issue that's being considered.

When reviewing a legal issue, an attorney or court might start by first reviewing whether the issue involves a question that can be answered by the U.S. Constitution or a state constitution. If the legal issue involves a question of federal law, the U.S. Constitution is the first authority that should be consulted. The same principle applies for questions of state law.

Assuming that the legal issue can't be resolved by looking at constitutional laws, the next step is to look at the code law. For federal issues, federal statutes would be reviewed. For state issues, state statutes would be reviewed. The attorney or court will look to see that the issue fits clearly within the scope of the code law. If the issue is clearly resolved by looking at code, then the analysis is complete.

When the issue can't be resolved by looking at the code, attorneys and lawyers turn to the common law to find the guidance needed to resolve the case. For federal issues, federal common law doctrine and federal court cases need to be reviewed. For state issues, state common law doctrines and court cases need to be reviewed. Key in the review of common law is the influential role of precedent, which is discussed later in this chapter.

Types of Law

The legal system usually distinguishes between **procedural law** and **substantive law**. Substantive law is also known as subject matter law. Subject matter areas of law are areas in which an attorney might specialize. For instance, contract law, tort law, elder law, and intellectual property law are just some of the many different subject matter areas within the study of law. Attorneys often choose to specialize in a particular area of law simply because there are so many areas of study within the law.

This section discusses the different types of procedural law. Procedural law deals with the processes that courts use to decide cases. Procedural areas of the law are designated to ensure **due process**. Due process means that all parties in a case are entitled to a fair and consistent process within the courts. There are three types of procedural law: criminal, civil, and administrative.

Civil

Civil procedure deals with the procedures and processes that courts use to conduct civil trials. Civil trials concern claims between individuals. Substantive areas of law such as contract law and property law are civil law areas. The parties in these types of cases must follow civil procedure rules when bringing disputes to court.

In the federal courts, a case begins when a complaint is filed with the court. A "complaint" is a court document that sets forth the names of the parties and the facts and legal claims. This is how a lawsuit begins.

In the federal system, the rules outlining the civil trial process are found in the Federal Rules of Civil Procedure. These rules are made by the Supreme Court and approved by Congress. State courts also have rules for how civil trials are conducted. Often state rules are based upon the Federal Rules of Civil Procedure.

> **NOTE**
>
> The rules for civil procedure can be complicated. The Federal Rules of Civil Procedure has 86 regular rules (not including special rules for admiralty or maritime claims). By contrast, the rules of civil procedure for the state of Indiana number 117 (including subparts of rules).

Most civil trial cases must be proven by a **preponderance of the evidence**. This is the lowest level of proof in a civil case. Preponderance of the evidence means that it's more probable than not that an action (or wrong) took place. While it's simplistic to express this standard as a percentage, preponderance of the evidence means the probability of an action taking place is greater than 50 percent. Some civil cases, such as actions to terminate parental rights, use the "clear and convincing evidence" standard. To meet this standard, a party must convince a court that it's more likely than not that an action (or wrong) took place.

Criminal

Criminal procedure deals with the rules that courts follow in criminal law cases. It also includes the processes for investigating and punishing crimes. The federal and state governments have criminal codes. These codes specify the actions that constitute a "crime." Crimes are wrongs against society. Crimes are prosecuted by the government against an alleged wrongdoer. The federal or state official with the power to pursue criminal cases is called a prosecutor.

In the federal system, the rules outlining the criminal trial process are called the Federal Rules of Criminal Procedure. State courts also have rules for how criminal trials are conducted. Most states have rules that are modeled after the federal rules. Most criminal law cases are tried in front of a jury. The jury decides questions of fact. The judge's role is to watch over the proceedings and decide questions of law.

The standard of proof for most criminal cases is **beyond a reasonable doubt**. This is the highest level of persuasion that a prosecutor must meet. This burden is met when a prosecutor proves to a jury that there can be no reasonable doubt in the mind of a reasonable person that a defendant is guilty. The reasonable doubt standard does not mean that the reasonable person is 100 percent convinced that a defendant is guilty. It does mean, however, that a juror must be fully satisfied that reasonable doubt has been eliminated.

A government has such a high burden of proof to meet in criminal cases because a criminal penalty usually requires a jail time, financial penalties, or even a death sentence. These penalties infringe on fundamental rights to liberty, property, and life. Therefore, these penalties may be imposed only with very strong proof that a person has committed the crime.

Burdens of Proof in the O.J. Simpson Trials

The different burdens of proof for different types of cases can be confusing. The O.J. Simpson criminal and civil trials illustrate the basic difference between criminal and civil law.

In June 1994, Nicole Brown Simpson and Ronald Goldman were murdered. Five days later O.J. Simpson was arrested for those murders. Simpson pleaded "not guilty" to the charges in late July 1994. In October 1995, a criminal jury announced that it found O.J. Simpson "not guilty" of the murders.

In May 1995, the Goldman family and Nicole Brown Simpson's estate filed civil wrongful death actions against O.J. Simpson. In February 1997, the civil jury found Simpson liable for the deaths of Ronald Goldman and Nicole Brown Simpson. Finding a defendant liable in a civil case is the rough equivalent of a guilty finding in a criminal case. It means that the defendant is held responsible for the action that is complained about.

O.J. Simpson was found "not guilty" of murder in the criminal case, but he was found liable in the civil case. The reason for the apparently inconsistent results is that the murder case was in the criminal system and the wrongful death case was a civil action. There are different burdens of proof in each system.

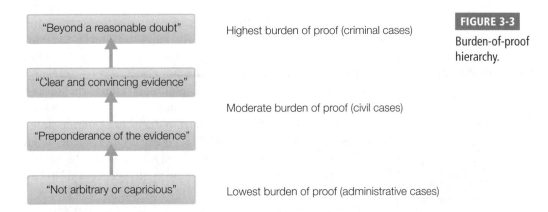

FIGURE 3-3
Burden-of-proof
hierarchy.

Administrative

Administrative procedure sets forth the process under which administrative agencies make and enforce rules. The federal government and most states delegate some regulatory and enforcement functions to administrative agencies. Governments delegate some of these functions in very detailed ways and for very specific reasons. When governments delegate power in this way, it's possible to have an agency that creates rules (a legislative function), enforces rules (an executive function), and reviews rules (a judicial power). Agency power is a combination of the power of all three branches of government.

The actions of these agencies are the focus of administrative procedure. Because these agencies are carrying out a function of the government, there must be processes put in place to ensure that all persons appearing before agencies are dealt with in a fair and consistent manner. At the federal government level, the Administrative Procedure Act (1946) helps define the federal administrative process. This act states the procedures for agency rulemaking, enforcement, and review.

The Administrative Procedure Act also allows U.S. federal courts to review agency decisions. There's a different burden of proof for administrative cases. In these cases, an administrative decision is valid so long as it's not "arbitrary and capricious" or an abuse of the law. An arbitrary and capricious decision is one made without a reasonable connection between the facts of the case and the administrative outcome.

Figure 3-3 shows the burden-of-proof hierarchy in administrative, civil, and criminal cases.

The Role of Precedent

The doctrine of **precedent** is one of the most important traditions in the American legal system. This doctrine means that courts will look at the decisions made in prior cases to determine the appropriate resolution for new cases. The basic concept of precedent has already been discussed in this chapter.

For example, the U.S. Supreme Court has the power to decide cases that involve questions about the federal Constitution and other federal laws. The Supreme Court is the final authority on cases heard in the federal court system. If other, lower courts in the federal system have a new case that concerns an issue that the Supreme Court has already addressed, those lower courts are required to follow the law as it was interpreted by the Supreme Court. State courts also must follow the decisions of the U.S. Supreme Court to the extent that the state court is reviewing issues that include U.S. constitutional or federal law.

> **NOTE**
>
> A "case of first impression" is a case for which there's no precedent. These cases raise a legal issue that has never before been decided.

The doctrine of precedent also is referred to as the doctrine of *stare decisis*, which means "to stand by things decided" in Latin. *Stare decisis* means that lower courts must follow the decisions of the court above it so long as those decisions are relevant to the case that the lower court is deciding.

Without precedent and its related concepts, there can be no predictability in the law. Precedent makes the law stable. The U.S. Supreme Court has recognized the value of precedent numerous times. In 1932, Justice Louis Brandeis stressed the importance of precedent when he wrote, "*Stare decisis* is usually the wise policy, because in most matters it is more important that the applicable rule of law be settled than that it be settled right."[9] Precedent is used to ensure that laws are fairly and consistently applied.

The doctrine of precedent is not absolute. Precedent can change when it's apparent that society's values on a particular issue have changed in such a way that precedent no longer reflects those values. Precedent also can change when a high court finds that the application of precedent is unreasonable. In *Payne v. Tennessee* (1991), Chief Justice William Rehnquist wrote, "Adhering to precedent is usually the wise policy, because, in most matters, it is more important that the applicable rule of law be settled than it be settled right. Nevertheless, when governing decisions are unworkable or are badly reasoned, this Court has never felt constrained to follow precedent. *Stare decisis* is not an inexorable command; rather, it is a principle of policy and not a mechanical formula of adherence to the latest decision."[10]

Overturning precedent is a milestone event for the law because it changes established legal principles. In essence, it changes the rules that judges and lawyers follow. *Plessy v. Ferguson* (1896) and *Brown v. Board of Education* (1954) are two cases that dramatically illustrate how precedent can change and how changing precedent can have a significant impact on society.

In *Plessy v. Ferguson*, the U.S. Supreme Court legalized racial segregation practices. These practices also were known as "separate but equal" practices. In this case, Homer Plessy boarded a train in Louisiana. Plessy was seven-eighths white and one-eighth black. He sat in the whites-only train car. Louisiana law considered Plessy to be black and required him to sit in the blacks-only train car. Plessy refused and was subsequently arrested.

In *Plessy*, the plaintiff argued that these separate but equal practices violated the Fourteenth Amendment of the U.S. Constitution. The Fourteenth Amendment requires that all citizens be provided equal protection under law. In its decision, the Court held that separate but equal practices, such as having train cars segregated based upon race, were not inherently unequal. The Court stated that these practices did not violate the U.S. Constitution.

For almost 60 years, "separate but equal" was the law. The court's ruling was used to justify a number of "Jim Crow" segregation laws used throughout the United States. These laws segregated blacks and whites in schools, restaurants, restrooms, and public transportation. These laws were challenged again in the 1954 case, *Brown v. Board of Education.*

The *Brown* case was a consolidation of five different cases from four different states that all addressed the same issue: racial segregation in public schools. In *Brown,* the plaintiffs argued that "separate but equal" practices were inherently unfair. They argued that in reality these practices perpetuated the inferior treatment of blacks and had a negative impact on black Americans. Plaintiffs challenged the Court to overrule the precedent set in *Plessy v. Ferguson.*

In *Brown,* a unanimous U.S. Supreme Court reversed its holding in *Plessy.* In *Brown,* Chief Justice Warren wrote, "We conclude that, in the field of public education, the doctrine of 'separate but equal' has no place. Separate educational facilities are inherently unequal. Therefore, we hold that the plaintiffs and others similarly situated for whom the actions have been brought are, by reason of the segregation complained of, deprived of the equal protection of the laws guaranteed by the Fourteenth Amendment."[11]

The *Brown* decision was remarkable because the Court departed from the precedent set in *Plessy.* In fact, the Court specifically rejected the reasoning that it had used to support its decision in *Plessy. Brown* established new legal precedent, that separate but equal laws are unconstitutional.

 NOTE

A "landmark court decision" is a decision that establishes new precedent. Landmark cases can significantly change how the legal system views and interprets law.

Regulatory Authorities

As discussed in the administrative procedure section, the federal government delegates some regulatory and enforcement functions to administrative agencies. The delegations are usually to subject matter expert agencies. These delegations are made because it would be impossible for Congress to make timely laws in some of the many different areas that are regulated by the federal government.

According to the federal Administrative Procedure Act, an "agency" is any governmental authority besides Congress and the courts. Federal agencies fall under the executive branch of the government. They are used to help carry out the day-to-day activities of the government. Agencies may have many different functions. Many of the laws described in Part 2 of this book are actually administered by regulatory agencies. These agencies create rules, enforce compliance, and hand out sanctions within their specified area.

The president usually has the responsibility for overseeing the federal agencies. Federal agencies also can be created under other federal agencies. For instance, the U.S. Department of Agriculture oversees a number of different federal agencies.

NOTE

The oldest federal law enforcement agency is typically recognized as the U.S. Marshals Service. The Marshals Service was formed in 1789.

Congress also can create independent agencies that report directly to it. One of the agencies discussed in this book is the Federal Trade Commission (FTC). The FTC is an independent federal agency. Its mission is to promote consumer protection and eliminate practices that are harmful to competitive business in many areas of the economy. The FTC was created in 1914 under the Federal Trade Commission Act. The FTC is one of the most important regulatory authorities for consumer and some business practices issues.

The FTC reports to Congress on its actions. The FTC is led by five commissioners, who each serve a seven-year term. The commissioners are nominated by the president and confirmed by the Senate. The president also chooses one commissioner to act as chairman. To maintain the independence of the Commission, no more than three commissioners can belong to the same political party. The FTC has seven regional offices across the United States.

Most federal agencies have the ability to make rules. The rulemaking authority of the FTC is described in the Federal Trade Commission Act. The Act states that the FTC can make "rules which define with specificity acts or practices which are unfair or deceptive acts or practices in or affecting commerce."[12] The Act states the process for how the rules are made. After the FTC makes a rule, anyone who violates the rule can be sanctioned by the FTC.

Regulatory authorities provide another type of law that must be considered when thinking about the American legal system. These administrative agencies have the power to create and enforce regulations that must be considered equal to the law passed by the federal government. Individuals and organizations can be subject to penalties for violating the rules of these agencies.

What Is the Difference Between Compliance and Audit?

People often get compliance and audit confused. It's helpful to understand these terms because they will be used throughout this book. These terms are often associated with legal activities, which is why they are included in this chapter.

In the legal system, **compliance** is the action of following applicable laws and rules and regulations. Generally speaking, for an organization compliance involves not only following laws and regulations, but also following the organization's own policies and procedures. Compliance must be documented. With respect to law, it's not enough to say that an organization is compliant. The organization must prove that it's compliant.

Processes that might be used to demonstrate compliance include:

- Creating policies or other governance documents to comply with legal or regulatory requirements
- Comparing compliance requirements against an organization's daily practices, and modifying those practices as needed

- Developing and implementing monitoring systems in computer systems to alert the organization if security measures required by law or regulation are compromised
- Creating training and awareness activities that educate employees about compliance requirements

Compliance not only includes the actual state of being compliant, it also includes the steps and processes taken to become compliant. Compliance usually asks the questions: What are the rules? How must the rules be followed? Compliance is demonstrated daily through processes and procedures.

Audit is separate from compliance. An **audit** is an evaluation and verification that certain objectives are met. An audit can review laws, rules, regulations, policies, and procedures to ensure that an organization is complying with stated requirements. Audit looks at the processes that are put in place to meet compliance objectives and makes sure that those processes are accurate.

Audits may occasionally be performed by independent organizations. An organization also can have an internal audit function that ensures that organizations are following its internal policies and procedures.

An audit is an inspection at a fixed point in time. In the truest sense of the word, audits don't take place daily. An audit usually asks the questions: Are the rules being followed? How are the rules being followed?

Sometimes it's helpful to consider an example. Under the FTC's Red Flags Rule, discussed in Chapter 5, a covered organization is required to have a written identity theft prevention program. The program that is developed must provide for the identification, detection, and response to activities that could indicate identity theft.

The compliance functions that must be met include:

- Identify activities that could indicate identity theft.
- Determine how the organization will detect such activities.
- Determine how the organization will respond to such activities.
- Create a written identity theft prevention program.
- Educate employees about their responsibilities in the identity theft prevention program.

The questions that would be verified in an audit include:

- Did the organization properly identify activities that could indicate identity theft?
- Did the organization properly determine how it will detect such activities?
- Are the organization's responses to activities appropriate to prevent identity theft?
- Did the organization create a written identity theft program?
- Was the identity theft program approved by management?
- Are employees meeting their responsibilities under the identity theft prevention program?

Compliance is demonstrated by the processes and procedures that an organization uses to meet the law. Audit verifies that those processes and procedures actually do satisfy the legal requirements.

How Do Security, Privacy, and Compliance Fit Together?

Security, privacy, and compliance issues form a complicated web. The differences between security and privacy are addressed in Chapter 2. Information security is the practice of protecting information to ensure the goals of confidentiality, integrity, and availability. Information security makes sure that accurate information is available to authorized individuals when it's needed.

In contrast, privacy encompasses a person's right to have control of their personal data. Privacy means that a person has the right to specify how that data is collected, used, and shared. Information security practices are used to make sure that a person's privacy decisions are respected.

Organizations don't always do a good job of either information security or protecting privacy. For that reason, laws are enacted that force organizations to take a more structured approach to information security. To date, there have been no laws enacted in the United States that are comprehensive. There is no national data security or data privacy law that applies to private organizations. Instead, laws are made to protect certain types of information. Organizations that hold or process those types of information must follow the relevant laws. Many of the laws that impact information security and privacy practices are addressed in Part 2 of this textbook.

Once the laws are enacted, organizations impacted by the law must take actions to meet it. If an organization fails to meet its obligations, it can be subject to sanctions. Compliance is the action of following the applicable laws and rules and regulations. Compliance efforts are supported by documenting organizational controls and enhancing the capabilities of information systems to ensure information security.

CHAPTER SUMMARY

The American legal system, its history, and its processes regulate our behavior and contribute to an ordered society. Laws evolve over time. They are a reflection of the laws imposed by federal and state governments, longstanding traditions about right and wrong, and society's values.

Individuals and organizations must follow laws, rules, and regulations. Regulatory compliance is influencing security and privacy practices. Organizations must take a more structured approach to addressing information security and privacy issues in order to meet their compliance requirements.

KEY CONCEPTS AND TERMS

Administrative procedure
Appellate jurisdiction
Audit
Beyond a reasonable doubt
Civil procedure
Code law
Compliance

Concurrent jurisdiction
Criminal procedure
Diversity of citizenship
   jurisdiction
Due process
Federal question jurisdiction
Judicial review

Jurisdiction
Original jurisdiction
Precedent
Preemption
Preponderance of the evidence
Procedural law
Substantive law

CHAPTER 3 ASSESSMENT

1. What is the U.S. federal court of last resort?

A. The U.S. Supremacy Court

B The U.S. District Court

C. The Ninth Circuit Court of Appeals

D. The Federal Court of Appeals

E. The U.S. Supreme Court

2. What is judicial review?

A. The power of courts to review the decisions of other courts

B. The power of courts to review laws

C. The power of the president to review the decisions of the courts

D. The power of Congress to review the decisions of the courts

E. A variety show featuring people in wigs and black robes

3. What is appellate jurisdiction?

A. The power of some courts to review the decisions of others

B. The power of courts to resolve disputes between individuals

C. The process by which courts conduct civil trials

D. The process by which courts conduct criminal trials

E. The power of courts to declare a law unconstitutional

4. What article of the U.S. Constitution sets forth the powers of the president?

A. Article V

B. Article IV

C. Article III

D. Article II

E. Article I

5. What is a case of first impression?

A. The first case that court hears when it's in session

B. A case that changes established precedent

C. A case for which there's no established precedent

D. A case that's appealed

E. None of the above

6. The Federal Trade Commission is which type of federal agency?

A. Independent

B. Subordinate

C. Coordinate

D. Executive

E. Congressional

7. The doctrine of precedent is also known as
_____.

8. What is procedural law?

   A. Branches of law that deal with property cases

   B. Branches of law that set forth the structure of the judiciary system

   C. Branches of law that deal with following precedent

   D. Branches of law that deal with processes that courts use to decide cases

   E. None of the above

9. What is common law?

   A. A system of law inherited from England

   B. A system of law inherited from France

   C. A system of law that relies upon established legal principles and traditions

   D. Answers B and C

   E. Answers A and C

10. Compliance is _____, audit is _____.

   A. Following the rules, verifying that the rules were followed

   B. Verifying that the rules were followed, following the rules

   C. Making the rules, enforcing the rules

   D. Forcing the rules, making the rules

   E. None of the above

11. A federal agency is granted its authority by _____.

12. Which U.S. Constitution clause describes Congress' authority to regulate trade between states?

   A. The Supremacy Clause

   B. The Necessary and Proper Clause

   C. The Limitation of Powers Clause

   D. The Commerce Clause

   E. The Impeachment Clause

13. The U.S. Supreme Court has _____ justices.

14. How many representatives are in the U.S. House of Representatives?

   A. 100

   B. 1,000

   C. 435

   D. 400

   E. 50

15. There are _____ federal district courts.

ENDNOTES

1. U.S. Constitution, article VI.

2. U.S. Constitution, article II, sec. 1.

3. U.S. Constitution, article I, sec. 3.

4. U.S. Constitution, article I, sec. 2.

5. U.S. Constitution, article I, sec. 8, cl. 3.

6. U.S. Constitution, article I, sec. 8, cl. 18.

7. U.S. Constitution, amendment X.

8. U.S. Constitution, article VI, sec. 2.

9. *Burnet v. Coronado Oil & Gas Co.*, 285 U.S. 393, 406 (1932) (Justice Louis Brandeis dissenting).

10. *Payne v. Tennessee*, 501 U.S. 808, 809 (1991) (Internal citations and punctuation omitted).

11. *Brown v. Board of Education*, 347 U.S. 483, 495 (1954).

12. Federal Trade Commission Act (1914), U.S. Code Vol. 15, sec. 57a (2006).

PART TWO

Laws Influencing Information Security

Security and Privacy of Consumer Financial Information

IDENTITY THEFT IS A RAPIDLY GROWING CRIME. Consumer financial information is a gold mine for an identity thief. An identity thief can use this information to establish a new identity. Identity theft victims spend time and money repairing damage caused by identity thieves. Victims must repair their good name and their credit. Identity theft is a crime that can have a large impact on a person's financial situation.

Consumer information is valuable and must be protected. In 2008, 285 million records were compromised in data breaches. Credit card data and personally identifiable information were the top two types of compromised records. The financial industry was the source for 93 percent of the compromised records. Organized crime rings were involved in 91 percent of the breaches.[1]

Individuals take many steps to protect their financial information. Banks and other financial institutions use this data when they conduct business with us. We expect these companies to protect our data as well. This chapter focuses on the laws and regulations that financial institutions must follow to protect the security and privacy of consumer financial information.

Chapter 4 Topics

This chapter covers the following topics and concepts:

- What the business challenges facing financial institutions are
- What the different types of financial institutions are
- What consumer financial information is
- Who regulates financial institutions
- What the Federal Financial Institutions Examination Council is
- What the Gramm-Leach-Bliley Act is
- What the Federal Trade Commission Red Flags Rule is
- What the Payment Card Industry Standards are
- What some case studies and examples are

When you complete this chapter, you will be able to:

- Describe the business challenges facing financial institutions
- Define a financial institution and consumer financial information
- Explain the main parts of the Gramm-Leach-Bliley Act
- Explain the role of the Federal Financial Institutions Examination Council
- Describe the Federal Trade Commission Red Flags Rule
- Describe the Payment Card Industry Standards

Business Challenges Facing Financial Institutions

Media reports about financial institutions experiencing a data breach are not unusual:

- Bank of America reported that it lost a number of data backup tapes in 2005. The missing tapes contained the personal information of up to 1.2 million federal employees.

- Citigroup informed its customers in 2005 that backup tapes were lost during shipment to another business. The tapes contained the personal information of 3.9 million customers.

- RBS WorldPay reported that hackers accessed its computer systems in 2008. RBS WorldPay is the U.S. payment-processing arm of the Royal Bank of Scotland group. Thieves used the data they stole to withdraw over $9 million from ATMs around the world.

- Heartland Payment Systems reported that hackers accessed its computer systems in late 2008. This company processes payroll and credit card payments for more than 250,000 businesses. It processes 100 million transactions per month. The hackers might have had access to the system for a couple of weeks.

- A Wyoming bank employee sent an electronic file to an incorrect e-mail address in 2009. The file contained the personal information of 1,300 bank customers.

Financial institutions collect and use sensitive consumer financial information. They face many challenges in protecting this data. Consumers demand that financial institutions protect this data. They also want financial institutions to protect them from financial harm if this data is disclosed or stolen.

Consumers are not the only victims of identity theft. Financial institutions become identity theft victims when thieves use a consumer's financial information to do business with the institution. Identity thieves can open bank accounts in the victim's name and write bad checks. Thieves also can create counterfeit checks to use on a victim's account. They can take out loans in the victim's name. Many bank rules and regulations force financial institutions to bear the cost of many of these actions. A recent study estimated that these institutions paid $11 billion in identity theft costs in 2008.

Financial institutions often get entangled in phishing scams designed to steal customer financial information. Many of these e-mail scams appear as if they came from a well-known bank. These scams use the bank name and logos or other graphics to look like legitimate e-mail. These scams cost financial institutions money to investigate and respond to consumer complaints.

Most large national banks and even regional financial institutions have had their names and logos used in phishing scams. Many post information on their Web sites regarding phishing scams. They post information consumers can use to tell the difference between real e-mails from the bank and phishing scams.

Financial institutions are often the targets of hackers. The famous 1930s bank robber Willie Sutton said that he robbed banks "because that was where the money was." Banks and financial institutions still have plenty of money, but thieves no longer have to leave their own homes to steal. In 2009, hacker Ehud Tenenbaum pleaded guilty to fraud charges. He hacked into the computer systems of banks in California, Florida, Indiana, and Texas. Some reports indicate that up to $10 million was lost because of his attacks.

The financial industry is highly regulated. These institutions must follow regulations designed to protect the security and privacy of data that they collect and use. These rules place a compliance burden on financial institutions.

The Different Types of Financial Institutions

The National Bank Act of 1864 established the national banking system in the United States. The Act still governs U.S. national banks even though Congress has updated it many times since 1864. Many laws define the different types of financial institutions that are regulated in the United States.

Most people know that financial institutions include banks and credit unions. These are organizations that provide financial services to customers. They include:

- Savings and loan associations
- Finance companies
- Insurance companies
- Investment companies

Laws also define the types of organizations that are considered financial institutions. Different laws may use the term in different ways. For example, the Fair Credit Reporting Act of 1970 defines financial institutions as banks, savings associations, and credit unions. It also includes any organization that holds a transaction account on behalf of a customer as a financial institution. This law has a very specific definition.

Not all laws are that precise. The Bank Secrecy Act of 1970 has a long list of organizations that are financial institutions for the purposes of that law. The list includes banks, securities brokers, insurance companies, and pawnbrokers.[2]

The Bank Secrecy Act of 1970 also is known as the Currency and Foreign Transactions Reporting Act. Congress created this law to fight drug trafficking, money laundering, and other crimes. The Act keeps banks and other financial institutions from being used by criminals to hide or transfer money. It tries to keep criminals from profiting from illegal acts. The definition of financial institution is broad for this reason.

The Gramm-Leach-Bliley Act defines financial institution as any institution that conducts financial activities. This law is discussed later in this chapter. This law then points to the Bank Holding Company Act of 1956 for a list of actions that are considered financial activities. Financial activities under this law include lending, exchanging, or investing money. They also include insurance and other financial advising services.[3]

You must read laws carefully since different laws may define the same term in different ways. It's always important to make sure that you understand how terms are used in each law.

Consumer Financial Information

A consumer is a person who buys goods or services. Consumer information is the personally identifiable information that a person provides to get a good or service. In the financial industry, customers provide it to get services from banks or other financial institutions. People use it to get home or car loans, apply for credit cards, or open checking accounts.

Items that a person buys for personal, family, or household use are called **consumer goods**. Services that a person buys for personal, family, or household use are called **consumer services**. These terms are not used to refer to goods or services purchased by a business.

Consumer financial information includes many items other than a person's name. It can include:

- Social Security numbers
- Driver's license numbers
- Address and telephone numbers

> **technical TIP**
>
> Many people access their banking accounts though online bank Web sites. A 2009 survey from the American Bankers Association showed that most bank customers prefer to bank online. Some people also have multiple accounts at multiple banks. To protect your financial information, use different strong passwords for each online account. You also can protect these accounts better by using different user names and passwords for each online banking account.

It can include work history if a person needs to provide it in order to get a loan. Consumer financial information also can include a spouse's employment and income history. It's all information that a consumer provides to a financial institution in order to get a product or service.

Who Regulates Financial Institutions?

A number of different federal agencies regulate the different kinds of financial institutions. This section focuses on those agencies. These agencies enforce the consumer protection laws discussed later in this chapter. State governments may also regulate financial institutions. This chapter doesn't discuss that type of regulation.

There are five federal regulatory agencies for U.S. financial institutions. These agencies make sure that U.S. financial institutions are "sound." An institution is sound if it's financially healthy and safe. These agencies also make sure that their institutions follow federal law. The federal bank regulatory agencies are:

- The Federal Reserve System
- The Federal Deposit Insurance Corporation
- The National Credit Union Administration
- The Office of the Comptroller of the Currency
- The Office of Thrift Supervision

The Federal Reserve System

NOTE

The Federal Reserve System also is known as "the Fed."

Congress created the Federal Reserve System in 1913. The Federal Reserve Act of 1913 was passed to address financial uncertainty. Bank and business failures were having a tremendous impact on the U.S. economy. The Federal Reserve Act was intended to provide the nation with a more stable economy.

The Federal Reserve System is the central bank of the United States. Essentially, it's a bank for other banks. It's also a bank for the federal government. The Fed is an independent federal agency. It reports directly to Congress. The Fed is responsible for directing the nation's monetary policy and maintaining the stability of the U.S. financial system.

FIGURE 4-1

The structure of the U.S.
Federal Reserve System.

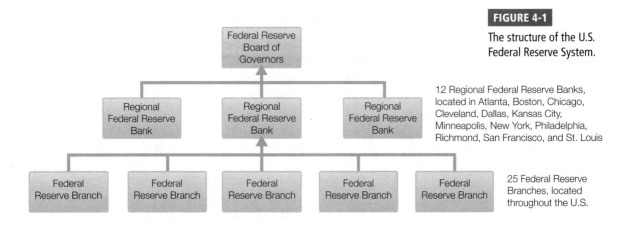

12 Regional Federal Reserve Banks,
located in Atlanta, Boston, Chicago,
Cleveland, Dallas, Kansas City,
Minneapolis, New York, Philadelphia,
Richmond, San Francisco, and St. Louis

25 Federal Reserve
Branches, located
throughout the U.S.

The Fed includes a Board of Governors and 12 regional Federal Reserve banks. The Board of Governors is located in Washington, D.C. The Board has seven members. Members are nominated by the president and must be confirmed by the Senate. Each member serves for one 14-year term. The terms of each member are staggered so that only one term expires at a time. The chair and vice chair of the Board of Governors are also nominated by the president and confirmed by the Senate. These positions are filled by current members of the Board of Governors. These positions serve for a four-year term.

There are 12 regional Federal Reserve Banks. These banks are located throughout the United States. These Reserve Banks have 25 other branches. Each of the Reserve Banks has a 12-member board of directors. They carry out a variety of banking functions. The main customers of the Reserve Banks are other banks. The Reserve Banks hold the cash reserves of other institutions. They distribute U.S. currency and coin within their region. They also supervise and review member banks to make sure that they are sound. Figure 4-1 illustrates the structure of the Federal Reserve System.

In addition to serving as the bank for the U.S. government, the Fed is the main regulatory authority for state-chartered banks that are members of the Federal Reserve System. State-chartered banks are not required to become Fed members. State-chartered banks that are not Fed members are regulated by the Federal Deposit Insurance Corporation (FDIC). The Fed also supervises companies that control banks (called bank holding companies), foreign banks that operate in the United States, and foreign activities of member banks.

There are approximately 900 state banks in the Fed. The Fed supervises approximately 5,000 bank holding companies. National banks, which are regulated primarily by other agencies, also are required by law to join the Fed. There are about 2,000 national banks in the Federal Reserve System.

The Fed supervises and examines the financial institutions that it regulates to make sure that those institutions are complying with the law. Since a number of different agencies regulate banks, the Fed's enforcement authority extends to state member banks of the Fed and some foreign banks that operate in the United States.

4

Consumer
Information

Federal Deposit Insurance Corporation

The Federal Deposit Insurance Corporation (FDIC) was formed in 1933 to provide deposit insurance to banks. Congress formed the FDIC originally as a temporary government corporation under the Banking Act of 1933. The FDIC was formed in response to bank failures during the Great Depression. From 1929 to 1933, bank failures resulted in about $1.3 billion in losses to depositors.

No depositor has lost any money on insured funds because of a bank failure since FDIC insurance began on January 1, 1934. Congress made the FDIC a permanent federal agency in 1935 under the Banking Act of 1935.

The FDIC has a five-member board of directors. Three of the directors are appointed by the president and confirmed by the Senate. These members each serve six-year terms. The other two members of the board are the government officials who serve as the comptroller of the currency and the director of the Office of Thrift Supervision. No more than three of the members of the FDIC board may be from the same political party. The chair and vice chair of the board of directors are also nominated by the president and confirmed by the Senate. These positions are filled by current members of the board and have five-year terms. The FDIC has eight regional offices.

The FDIC insures deposits made in banks and savings associations. The FDIC ensures deposit accounts only. It doesn't insure securities or mutual funds. When the FDIC was formed in 1933, the original deposit insurance limit was $2,500. In 2010, the deposit insurance limit was 100 times that amount, or $250,000.

The FDIC insures deposit accounts in the event of bank failure. If a bank fails, the FDIC returns the money that a customer put in the bank, up to the deposit insurance limit. The FDIC works to prevent bank failures by monitoring the economy. It also enforces regulations that require banks to act in a sound manner. All national banks are required by law to be insured by the FDIC. The FDIC insures deposits in almost every bank in the United States.

The FDIC examines and supervises over 5,000 banks. The FDIC is the primary federal regulator for state-chartered banks that don't join the Federal Reserve System. The FDIC reviews the banks that it regulates to make sure that those institutions are complying with the law.

National Credit Union Administration

Congress enacted the Federal Credit Union Act in 1934. That law allowed federally chartered credit unions to form. The National Credit Union Administration (NCUA) was formed in 1970. Its role is to charter and supervise federal credit unions. The NCUA is an independent federal agency.

A "credit union" is a cooperative financial organization. A credit union can have federal, state, or corporate affiliations. Members of a credit union share the same affiliation. They might live in the same city or work for the same employer. A credit union is a nonprofit institution that is run by its members. Members pool their money together at a credit union to save and make loans to one another.

NOTE

Federal credit unions often use the word "federal" in their name. They may also use the initials F.C.U., or "federal credit union."

The NCUA has a three-member board of directors. The president nominates board members, who then must be confirmed by the Senate. Board members serve for six-year terms. Their terms are staggered so that only one term expires at a time. No more than two board members can be from the same political party. The NCUA has six regional offices across the United States. These regional offices charter and supervise federal credit unions in their regions.

The NCUA operates the National Credit Union Share Insurance Fund (NCUSIF). Congress created this fund in 1970. All federal credit unions must be insured by NCUSIF. This fund also insures deposits in state-chartered credit unions that qualify for the fund. The NCUSIF operates in a manner similar to the deposit insurance provided by the FDIC. It protects almost 90 million federal credit union account holders. It also insures a majority of state-chartered credit unions.

NOTE

No credit union member has lost any money on deposit accounts because of failure of credit unions insured by the NCUSIF.

The NCUA supervises all federal credit unions and NCUSIF-insured state credit unions. It issues guidance and enforces the provisions of the Federal Credit Union Act. The NCUA is the regulatory enforcement authority for federal credit unions. It shares enforcement authority for some laws with other federal agencies. The NCUA enforces Gramm-Leach-Bliley Act consumer privacy provisions for federal credit unions. The FTC enforces those provisions for federally insured, state-chartered credit unions.

Office of the Comptroller of the Currency

The Office of the Comptroller of the Currency (OCC) was originally established in 1863. The National Bank Act of 1864 is the law that authorizes the OCC today. The OCC is a bureau of the U.S. Department of the Treasury. The OCC charters and supervises national banks. National banks receive their charters from the OCC. National banks are members of the Federal Reserve System. They are required to be insured by the FDIC.

NOTE

National banks often use the word "national" or "national association" in their name. They also may use the initials "N.A."

The OCC is led by a comptroller. This position is appointed by the president and confirmed by the Senate. The comptroller serves a five-year term. The comptroller serves as a member of the board of directors of the FDIC.

The OCC supervises and regulates about 1,900 national banks. It has the authority to enforce laws and regulations against national banks and some affiliated parties of national banks.

FYI

Federal savings banks and savings and loan associations often use the words "federal," "federal association," "federal savings bank," or "federal savings and loan association" in their name. They also may include initials for those terms, such as "F.A.," "F.S.B.," or "F.S.L.A."

Office of Thrift Supervision

Congress formed the Office of Thrift Supervision (OTS) in 1989 in the Financial Institutions Reform, Recovery, and Enforcement Act of 1989. This law restructured the U.S. banking business. The predecessor to the OTS was the Federal Home Loan Bank Board. That Board was established in 1933. The Federal Home Loan Bank Board was dissolved and the OTS was formed in response to the savings and loan crisis of the late 1980s. The OTS was formed to charter, supervise, and regulate the thrift industry.

A "thrift" is an organization that accepts savings account deposits and then invests the proceeds of those deposits in home mortgages. These types of organizations were created in the early 1800s. Many of these savings associations failed during the Great Depression in the 1930s. They grew in popularity again after World War II. This growth was because veterans were returning to the United States and buying homes.

Commercial banks may lend money for a number of different purposes. Thrifts tend to lend money primarily for home buying.

The OTS is led by a director. The OTS director is appointed by the president and confirmed by the Senate for a five-year term. The OTS director also serves as a member of the board of directors of the FDIC. The OTS has four regional offices located in Atlanta, Chicago, Dallas, and Jersey City.

The OTS is the primary federal regulator for both state and federally chartered thrifts. OTS also supervises thrift holding companies. A thrift holding company is a company that owns or controls a savings association.

Each federal bank regulatory agency can review only the financial institutions that are under its scope of authority. Congress specifies the scope of authority in the law creating the agency. An agency can't review a bank outside of its authority. Table 4-1 summarizes the federal agencies and their scope of regulatory authority discussed in this section.

Special Role of the Federal Trade Commission

The Federal Trade Commission (FTC) is an independent federal agency. Congress created it in 1914 under the Federal Trade Commission Act. The FTC is the most important regulatory authority for consumer protection issues.

The FTC is led by five commissioners. Each commissioner serves a seven-year term. Each is nominated by the president and confirmed by the Senate. The president also chooses one commissioner to act as the chair. To maintain the independence of the FTC, no more than three commissioners can belong to the same political party. The FTC has seven regional offices across the United States.

TABLE 4-1   Federal banking regulatory agencies.

AGENCY NAME	PRIMARY REGULATORY RESPONSIBILITY
Federal Reserve System (The Fed)	State-chartered member banks Bank holding companies
Federal Deposit Insurance Corporation (FDIC)	State-chartered banks that are not members of the Fed
National Credit Union Administration (NCUA)	Federally insured credit unions
Office of the Comptroller of the Currency (OCC)	Nationally chartered banks
Office of Thrift Supervision (OTS)	All nationally chartered and some state-chartered thrifts Thrift holding companies

The mission of the FTC is to protect consumers and make sure that business is competitive. It tries to eliminate practices that are harmful to business. The FTC has responsibilities under 46 different federal laws. Most of these laws include consumer protection elements.

Under the Federal Trade Commission Act, the FTC can investigate "the organization, business, conduct, practices, and management of any person, partnership, or corporation engaged in or whose business affects commerce."[4] It also can stop unfair and deceptive acts or trade practices.[5] Most of the FTC's authority comes from this law.

> **NOTE**
>
> **Unfair trade practices** are business practices that a consumer can't avoid and that cause injury. **Deceptive trade practices** are any business practices that include false or misleading claims.

The FTC makes and enforces rules for some parts of the financial industry. The FTC can't regulate banks, thrifts, or federal credit unions. The federal banking regulatory agencies already regulate them. The FTC does enforce laws at non-banking institutions such as consumer finance companies, debt counseling companies, and credit bureaus.

The FTC works closely with the federal banking regulatory agencies when making rules under the Gramm-Leach-Bliley Act and the Fair and Accurate Credit Transactions Act. Each of these laws includes provisions that protect consumer financial information. Both of these acts are discussed in this chapter.

Federal Financial Institutions Examination Council (FFIEC)

Congress established the Federal Financial Institutions Examination Council (FFIEC) in 1979. It was created by the Financial Institutions Regulatory and Interest Rate Control Act of 1978 (FIRA). The FFIEC promotes uniform practices among the federal financial institutions. Its purpose is to:

4

Consumer Financial Information

> **NOTE**
>
> "Examination" is the periodic evaluation of a bank. It includes a review of the health of the bank and its compliance with banking regulations. An examination might include a review of management and operations, as well as the bank's policies. A "bank examiner" is the person who conducts this review.

- Establish principles and standards for the examination of federal financial institutions.
- Develop a uniform reporting system for federal financial institutions.
- Conduct training for federal bank examiners.
- Make recommendations regarding bank supervision matters.
- Encourage the adoption of uniform principles and standards by federal and state banks.[6]

The council has six members. They are:

- The chair of the FDIC
- The chair of the NCUA
- The comptroller from the OCC
- The director of the OTS
- A member of the Board of Governors of the Fed
- The chair of the FFIEC State Liaison Committee

The chair of the FFIEC serves for two years. The chair position rotates among members of the council. The member agencies fund the FFIEC.

The FFIEC has six task forces. Representatives from each agency serve on each task force. Each task force includes at least one senior official from each of the member agencies:

- **Consumer Compliance**—This task force promotes a uniform approach to consumer protection laws and regulations. It develops proposed policies and procedures for the agencies to use in their regulatory activities.
- **Examiner Education**—This task force oversees the FFIEC's intra-agency examiner education programs. The task force also develops specific programs in response to requests from the FFIEC or its members.
- **Information Sharing**—This task force promotes sharing electronic information among FFIEC members to help them meet their regulatory responsibilities.
- **Reports**—This task force establishes uniform financial reports for FFIEC members.
- **Supervision**—This task force establishes supervision and examination procedures for FFIEC members. Its purpose is to help reduce regulatory burden by promoting effective supervision and examination practices.
- **Surveillance Systems**—This task force develops systems to monitor the financial condition and performance of financial institutions.

The FFIEC is required to submit an annual report to Congress on its activities. The FFIEC doesn't regulate financial institutions. It has no authority to do so. The federal agencies carry out their own enforcement actions against banks in their jurisdiction.

U.S. Bancorp and Customer Information

In June 1999, the Minnesota Attorney General sued U.S. Bancorp. The Attorney General alleged that U.S. Bancorp sold customer information to a telemarketing group in violation of the bank's own privacy policies. The telemarketing group then charged bank customers for goods and services that the customers didn't authorize. U.S. Bancorp settled the Minnesota case almost three weeks later and ended its contracts with the telemarketing group. State attorneys general in 39 other states also sued U.S. Bancorp. U.S. Bancorp ended up settling all of the cases.

The Gramm-Leach-Bliley Act

Congress passed the Gramm-Leach-Bliley Act (GLBA) in 1999. It's also known as the Financial Services Modernization Act of 1999. The law made great changes in the banking industry. It allowed banks, securities, and insurance companies to merge together. This wasn't allowed before the law. The financial industry urged Congress to pass the law so that customers could use one company for all their financial needs.

GLBA allowed large companies to merge. These new, larger corporations would have access to sizable amounts of consumer financial information. People feared that their privacy would suffer as a result. This fear wasn't unreasonable. Financial institutions often sold customer banking information to other companies. To help alleviate this fear, Congress included privacy protections in the Gramm-Leach-Bliley Act.

Purpose, Scope, and Main Requirements

GLBA applies to financial institutions. It defines financial institution as any institution that engages in financial activities. The definition of financial activities is very broad. It includes borrowing, lending, providing credit counseling, debt collection, and other activities.

The law requires financial institutions to protect a customer's nonpublic financial information. It states that "each financial institution has an affirmative and continuing obligation to respect the privacy of its customers."[7] This means institutions must provide privacy and security protections to its customers.

Nonpublic personal information (NPI) is personally identifiable financial information that a consumer gives to a financial institution. NPI also includes private information that an institution gets from other sources. It includes lists or descriptions of consumers that are prepared by using this kind of information. NPI can be in paper or electronic form. NPI includes:

- Social Security number
- Financial account numbers
- Credit card numbers

- Date of birth
- Name, address, and phone numbers when collected with financial data
- Details of any transactions or the fact that an individual is a customer of a financial institution

NPI doesn't include publicly available information about a consumer. Publicly available personal information is available to the general public. It can be made public through

NOTE

A person's address in a phone book is publicly available.

state or federal records or disclosures that are required by law. Information can be made public in different ways, such as records filed in a county recorder's office. Financial institutions can't assume that certain types of personally identifiable information are publicly available. They must take reasonable steps to make sure that information is publicly available if they want to claim that it's publicly available.

GLBA requires financial institutions to follow three main rules to protect consumer financial information:

- Privacy Rule
- Safeguard Rule
- Pretexting Rule

GLBA applies to consumer financial transactions. These are transactions made for personal, family, or household services. GLBA doesn't apply to business transactions.

The Privacy Rule

Under the GLBA Privacy Rule,[8] a financial institution may not share NPI with non-affiliated third parties unless the institution gives notice to the consumer. The notice must tell consumers about the types of data that the institution collects and how it uses that information. This is called a notice of privacy practices. GLBA also requires that consumers have a chance to opt out of some data sharing. The GLBA Privacy Rule went into effect July 1, 2001.

Congress gave the federal bank regulatory agencies, the Securities and Exchange Commission (SEC), and the FTC the authority to enforce the Privacy Rule. They also must make regulations that support the rule. Congress required them to issue consistent regulations.[9] All of the agencies created and issued similar regulations.

GLBA distinguishes between customers and consumers for its notice requirements. A "consumer" is any individual who obtains a consumer financial product or service from a financial institution. A "customer" is a consumer who has a continuing relationship with the institution.

A person is a customer of a financial institution if he or she has an ongoing relationship with the institution. A person with a checking or savings account at a bank has an ongoing relationship with that bank. An example of a consumer without a customer relationship is a person who withdraws cash from an ATM machine that doesn't belong to his or her personal bank.

An institution must give a customer notice of its privacy practices as soon as the customer relationship begins. Customers also must receive a copy of the privacy notice annually for as long as the customer relationship continues. The notice must be provided in writing. A financial institution does not have to give a consumer notice of its privacy practices if it doesn't share their NPI with nonaffiliated parties.

GLBA requires that certain information be included in the privacy notice. Some of these requirements are similar to the fair information practices principles discussed in Chapter 2. For example, the financial institution must describe the types of NPI that it collects. It must disclose how it shares NPI with affiliated and nonaffiliated third parties. Finally, it must state how it protects a consumer's NPI.

> **NOTE**
> A "nonaffiliated party" is an entity that isn't legally related to a financial institution. Affiliated parties have a legal relationship of some kind. An "affiliated party" is any entity that controls, is controlled by, or is under the common control of another entity. Affiliates are businesses that are within the same corporate family.

The privacy notice also must provide a consumer with an opportunity to stop a financial institution from sharing the consumer's NPI with nonaffiliated third parties. This is called an "opt-out" provision. The privacy notice must tell consumers how to opt out. If a consumer doesn't opt out, then the financial institution can share NPI in the ways described by its privacy notice.

GLBA doesn't give consumers the right to opt out of situations where a financial institution shares NPI with its affiliates. There are also some instances where consumers don't have the ability to opt out at all. For example, consumers can't opt out of a disclosure that is required by law.

The Fair Credit Reporting Act of 1970 (FCRA) allows consumers to opt out of some types of information sharing. Under that law, consumers can stop financial institutions from sharing their credit report or credit applications with affiliates. GLBA privacy notices must include this disclosure.

GLBA doesn't specify how a financial institution should write its notice of privacy practices. Many of these notices are hard to read. That makes it difficult for consumers to understand their rights. It's also very hard for consumers to compare the privacy policies of different financial institutions.

> **NOTE**
> In 2001, the Privacy Rights Clearinghouse studied the privacy notices of 60 financial institutions. That study found that most notices were written at a third- or fourth-year college reading level.

Consumers complained about the hard-to-read notices. Congress responded quickly. The Financial Services Regulatory Relief Act of 2006 amended the GLBA Privacy Rule. It required the agencies responsible for enforcing the Privacy Rule to propose a model form for privacy notices. Congress directed that this model form should be easy to read and understand.

On November 17, 2009, the federal bank regulatory agencies, the SEC, and the FTC announced that they had completed the model form. All of the agencies amended their privacy regulations to include it. The agencies hope to make an online form builder available in late 2010. The Model Privacy Notice Form is shown in Figure 4-2.

4

Consumer Financial Information

FACTS	**WHAT DOES [NAME OF FINANCIAL INSTITUTION] DO WITH YOUR PERSONAL INFORMATION?**
Why?	Financial companies choose how they share your personal information. Federal law gives consumers the right to limit some but not all sharing. Federal law also requires us to tell you how we collect, share, and protect your personal information. Please read this notice carefully to understand what we do.
What?	The types of personal information we collect and share depend on the product or service you have with us. This information can include: ■ Social Security number and [income] ■ [account balances] and [payment history] ■ [credit history] and [credit scores]
How?	All financial companies need to share customers' personal information to run their everyday business. In the section below, we list the reasons financial companies can share their customers' personal information; the reasons [name of financial institution] chooses to share; and whether you can limit this sharing.

Reasons we can share your personal information	Does [name of financial institution] share?	Can you limit this sharing?
For our everyday business purposes— such as to process your transactions, maintain your account(s), respond to court orders and legal investigations, or report to credit bureaus		
For our marketing purposes— to offer our products and services to you		
For joint marketing with other financial companies		
For our affiliates' everyday business purposes— information about your transactions and experiences		
For our affiliates' everyday business purposes— information about your creditworthiness		
For our affiliates to market to you		
For nonaffiliates to market to you		

To limit our sharing	■ Call **[phone number]**—our menu will prompt you through your choice(s) ■ Visit us online: **[website] or** ■ Mail the **form** below **Please note:** If you are a *new* customer, we can begin sharing your information [30] days from the date we sent this notice. When you are *no longer* our customer, we continue to share your information as described in this notice. However, you can contact us at any time to limit our sharing.
Questions?	Call [phone number] or go to [website]

✂- -

Mail-in Form		
Leave Blank OR [If you have a joint account, your choice(s) will apply to everyone on your account unless you mark below. ❑ Apply my choices only to me]	Mark any/all you want to limit: ❑ Do not share information about my creditworthiness with your affiliates for their everyday business purposes. ❑ Do not allow your affiliates to use my personal information to market to me. ❑ Do not share my personal information with nonaffiliates to market their products and services to me.	
	Name	**Mail to:**
	Address	[Name of Financial Institution] [Address1] [Address2] [City], [ST] [ZIP]
	City, State, Zip	
	[Account #]	

Page 2	
Who we are	
Who is providing this notice?	[insert]
What we do	
How does [name of financial institution] protect my personal information?	To protect your personal information from unauthorized access and use, we use security measures that comply with federal law. These measures include computer safeguards and secured files and buildings. [insert]
How does [name of financial institution] collect my personal information?	We collect your personal information, for example, when you ■ [open an account] or [deposit money] ■ [pay your bills] or [apply for a loan] ■ [use your credit or debit card] [We also collect your personal information from other companies.] **OR** [We also collect your personal information from others, such as credit bureaus, affiliates, or other companies.]
Why can't I limit all sharing?	Federal law gives you the right to limit only ■ sharing for affiliates' everyday business purposes—information about your creditworthiness ■ affiliates from using your information to market to you ■ sharing for nonaffiliates to market to you State laws and individual companies may give you additional rights to limit sharing. [See below for more on your rights under state law.]
What happens when I limit sharing for an account I hold jointly with someone else?	[Your choices will apply to everyone on your account.] **OR** [Your choices will apply to everyone on your account—unless you tell us otherwise.]
Definitions	
Affiliates	Companies related by common ownership or control. They can be financial and nonfinancial companies. ■ *[affiliate information]*
Nonaffiliates	Companies not related by common ownership or control. They can be financial and nonfinancial companies. ■ *[nonaffiliate information]*
Joint marketing	A formal agreement between nonaffiliated financial companies that together market financial products or services to you. ■ *[joint marketing information]*
Other important information	
[insert other important information]	

FIGURE 4-2b

The Model Privacy Notice Form, page 2.

4

Consumer Financial Information

The Safeguards Rule

GLBA requires the federal bank regulatory agencies, the SEC, and the FTC to issue security standards for the institutions that they regulate. This is commonly referred to as the Safeguards Rule. The law requires that each agency establish standards that:

- Protect the security and confidentiality of customer information.
- Protect against threats to the security or integrity of customer information.
- Protect against unauthorized access to or use of customer information that could result in harm to a customer.[10]

Congress didn't require the regulatory agencies to work together to create these standards, as it did for the privacy provisions. [11] The federal bank regulatory agencies worked through the FFIEC to create joint guidelines. Those guidelines were issued in early 2001. The SEC issued its standards in June 2000. The FTC issued its Safeguards Rule in May 2002. Financial institutions regulated by the FTC had to comply with its rule by May 2003. This section will refer to the FTC Safeguards Rule.

NOTE

Administrative, technical, and physical safeguards were discussed in Chapter 1.

The FTC Safeguards Rule[12] requires financial institutions to create a written "information security program." The program must state how the institution collects and uses customer information. It must also describe the administrative, technical, or physical controls used to protect that information. The program must protect information in paper and electronic form.

The FTC rule requires that a financial institution's information security program be a good fit for its size and complexity. The program also must be suitable for the sensitivity of the customer information that the institution uses. As part of its program, an institution must:

- Assign an employee to coordinate the program.
- Conduct a risk assessment to identify risks to the security, confidentiality, and integrity of customer information. Assess current safeguards to make sure that they are effective.
- Design and implement safeguards to control the identified risks.
- Select service providers and make sure that any contract includes terms to protect customer information.
- Review the information security program on an ongoing basis to account for changes in business.

The Safeguards Rule allows financial institutions to pick the controls that best protect its customer information. It specifies three areas that institutions must review:

- Employee management and training
- Information systems design
- Detecting and responding to attacks and system failures

Institutions must be sure to address these areas when conducting their risk assessments. They also must make sure that these areas are included in their information security program.

A financial institution must make sure that its service providers protect customer information as well. A "service provider" is an entity that provides services to a financial institution. A business that handles outsourced tasks is a service provider. These providers may access customer information when they provide services to an institution. Institutions must require their affiliates and service providers to protect customer information.

FYI

The FTC launched "Operation Detect Pretext" in January 2001. FTC staff reviewed Web sites and print advertisements. They were looking for businesses that offered to get and then sell customer financial information. The FTC filed lawsuits against three businesses for violating the GLBA pretexting provisions. As part of their settlements with the FTC, these businesses were barred from violating the GLBA pretexting provisions.

The Pretexting Rule

GLBA's final consumer protection is the Pretexting Rule.[13] **Pretexting** is when someone tries to gain access to customer information without proper authority to do so. Pretexting also is known as social engineering. Social engineering attacks were discussed in Chapter 1.

Under the law, it's illegal to make false, fictitious, or fraudulent statements to a financial institution or its customers in order to get customer information. It's also illegal to use forged, counterfeit, lost, or stolen documents to do the same thing. These rules try to stop identity theft before a crime is committed. Courts can impose criminal penalties if these rules are violated.

Most financial institutions address pretexting in their information security programs. It's covered as part of security awareness and training activities. Employees are trained to recognize and report pretexting.

Oversight

GLBA compliance oversight falls to different federal agencies. Oversight is based on the type of financial institution under review. The federal bank regulatory agencies (the Fed, FDIC, OTS, OCC, and NCUA) enforce GLBA for the institutions that they regulate. The SEC oversees GLBA for securities brokers and dealers. Each agency can bring an action against the institutions that they regulate for not complying with GLBA.

The FTC enforces GLBA for any financial institution that isn't regulated by one of the other agencies. Like the other agencies, the FTC may bring an action against any financial institution that doesn't comply with GLBA. The FTC has been quite active in pursuing GLBA enforcement actions.

Federal Trade Commission Red Flags Rule

Congress passed the Fair and Accurate Credit Transaction Act of 2003 (FACTA) in response to growth in identity theft crimes. FACTA made it harder for consumer financial information to be used to commit these crimes. FACTA made changes to the Fair Credit Reporting Act of 1970 (FCRA).

Congress recognized that the financial industry has a role in protecting customers from identity theft. FACTA required the federal bank regulatory agencies (the Fed, FDIC, OTS, OCC, and NCUA) and FTC to work together to create rules that would identify and respond to possible instances of identity theft.

These agencies issued a joint rule on November 9, 2007. The joint rule is known as the Identity Theft Red Flags Rule.[14]

> **NOTE**
>
> A **Red Flag** is any "pattern, practice, or specific activity that indicates the possible existence of identity theft."[15]

Purpose

The purpose of the Red Flags Rule is to fight identity theft. The rule requires covered financial institutions to be on the lookout for certain warning signs. Certain types of warning signs might indicate that identity theft is taking place in consumer financial transactions.

The Red Flags Rule isn't a data security rule. It doesn't require institutions to protect data in a certain way. Instead, it requires them to be flexible and responsive to different business situations where identity theft could be possible.[16]

> **NOTE**
>
> "Payment in arrears" describes payments that are made after a business provides goods or services. Many businesses bill in arrears. They include utility companies, medical providers, and cell phone service providers.

Scope

The Red Flags Rule applies to financial institutions and creditors that have covered accounts. Financial institutions are state and federal banks, credit unions, and savings and loan associations. They are regulated by the Fed, FDIC, OTS, OCC, and NCUA.

The Red Flags Rule defines creditor broadly. A "creditor" is any person or organization that grants customer credit, continues credit, or renews credit.[17] It also includes any organization that provides goods and services in advance and bills customers later. Retailers that offer financing are also creditors.

The definition of "covered account" is also broad. There are two types of covered accounts. The first type is any account that's used "primarily for personal, family, or household purposes, that involves or is designed to permit multiple payments or transactions."[18] Examples of this type of account include:

- Credit card accounts
- Car loan accounts
- Utility accounts
- Cell phone carrier accounts

The second type of covered account is any account for which identity theft is a reasonably foreseeable risk due to the use of the account. The risk includes harm to a customer. It also could be harm to the soundness of the financial institution or creditor. These types of accounts are considered covered accounts if the potential for identity theft is "reasonably foreseeable."

Organizations fall within the scope of the Red Flags Rule because of their actions. They may not rely on just the definitions of "financial institution," "creditor," or "covered account" to determine if they must comply with the Rule. Organizations must comply with the Red Flags Rule if they act like financial institutions or creditors and use accounts that look like covered accounts.

Main Requirements

Under the Red Flags Rule, covered entities must develop a written "Identity Theft Prevention Program." These programs must detect, prevent, and mitigate identity theft in covered accounts. The written program must address both new and existing covered accounts.

Organizations can take the size and complexity of their operations into account when preparing their plan. Larger companies that handle more accounts may need a more detailed plan. Smaller companies with fewer accounts may not need a very detailed plan. The written program must be appropriate for the organization.

An organization's board of directors must approve the program. If an organization doesn't have a board of directors, then a senior official must approve the program. The Rule requires organizations to train their employees about their written programs. Organizations also must review their relationships with third-party service providers. Organizations must make sure that those activities don't raise any Red Flags.

A written program must have the following components:

- Identify Red Flags that apply to the organization.
- Determine how the Red Flags will be detected during business processes.
- Determine how to respond to Red Flags that are detected.
- Review the written program periodically.

The agencies that worked together to create the Red Flags Rule realized that it may be difficult for organizations to determine activities that might raise a Red Flag. They created five different Red Flag categories. The agencies also provided 26 examples that might be considered a Red Flag. The categories of Red Flags and some of the examples that fall in each category are provided in Table 4-2.

Once an organization identifies an action that might raise a Red Flag, it must take steps to detect that activity in its normal business practices. For example, an organization decides that forged or altered documents are a potential Red Flag. It must then detect when documents are forged or altered. Other ways to detect Red Flags could include asking customers to provide additional identification.

The proper response to a Red Flag depends on the situation. An organization could contact the customer or monitor accounts as a potential response. An organization also can investigate a potential Red Flag and determine that a response isn't needed depending upon the circumstances.

Oversight

Each agency that worked together to create the Red Flags Rule enforces it within their authority. The Federal Reserve System, FDIC, OCC, OTS, and NCUA regulate most financial institutions. Since financial institutions are highly regulated, it makes sense for Red Flags Rule enforcement to stem from one of these regulatory agencies. The FTC enforces the Red Flags Rule for all other organizations.

4

Consumer Financial
Information

TABLE 4-2 Red Flag categories and examples.	
RED FLAG CATEGORY	**RED FLAG EXAMPLES**
Alerts, Notifications, and Warnings from a Credit Reporting Company	A fraud alert placed on a consumer report
	A credit freeze placed on a consumer report
	A consumer report indicating a pattern of activity that does not match the customer's historical activity
Suspicious Documents	Identification documents that look altered or forged
	A signature on a document doesn't match the signature in the customer's file
	A photograph on an identification document that doesn't look like the person presenting the identification document
Suspicious Personal Identifying Information	Personal information provided that doesn't match external information sources, for example, an address that doesn't match the customer's consumer report
	Incomplete personal information provided when opening an account
	Personal information provided that doesn't match the information in the customer's file
Unusual or Suspicious Activity on a Covered Account	A covered account used in a manner that doesn't match the customer's historical activity
	An unpaid account with no history of non-payment on that account
	Frequent new use of a covered account that was unused for a long period
Notice from Customers or Others about Identity Theft	Customer notification to the covered organization about suspected identity theft
	Law enforcement notification to the financial institution or creditor about fraudulent activity

> **NOTE**
>
> States also have limited ability to enforce the Red Flags Rule. States can impose civil fines of up to $1,000.

Federal civil fines of up to $2,500 are possible for violations of the Red Flags Rule. Only the government can impose sanctions for violating the Red Flags Rule. The Red Flags Rule doesn't permit a "private right of action." This means that individuals can't sue financial institutions or creditors if they violate the Red Flags Rule.

Implementation Concerns

The Red Flags Rule was intended to take effect on November 1, 2008. The FTC delayed enforcement of the rule four times. The delays allowed covered organizations more time to comply with the Rule.

Many types of organizations are confused about whether the Red Flags Rules really apply to them. Traditional service providers who ask for payment in arrears are pulled into the scope of the rule. These include doctors, lawyers, and similar professional services providers. These service providers argue that Congress didn't intend for them to be covered by the rule.

In August 2009, the American Bar Association (ABA) asked the U.S. District Court for the District of Columbia to stop the FTC from enforcing the Red Flags Rule against lawyers. The ABA argued that Congress didn't intend that attorneys and similar service providers be considered "creditors" under the Rule. The ABA won its argument. In October 2009, the District Court stopped the FTC from enforcing the Red Flags Rule against practicing attorneys. In February 2010, the FTC filed notice that it intends to appeal the court's ruling.

The American Institute of Certified Public Accountants filed a similar action in November 2009. The American Medical Association, American Dental Association, American Osteopathic Association, and American Veterinary Medical Association sent a letter to the FTC in January 2010. These groups also asked to be excluded from the Red Flags Rule. They said that they provide services in the same manner as attorneys. As such, they argued that the Red Flags Rule shouldn't apply to them.

In October 2009, the FTC delayed enforcement of the Red Flags Rule until June 1, 2010. Several members of Congress requested the delay. They did this because Congress is considering a bill that would exempt certain types of organizations from the Red Flags Rule. The pending legislation would exempt any health care, accounting, or law practice with 20 or fewer employees from the rule. The bill had passed the House of Representatives and had moved to the Senate at the time this book was written.

Payment Card Industry Standards

The Payment Card Industry Security Standards Council (PCI Council) is made up of representatives of the major credit card companies. They are:

- MasterCard
- Visa
- American Express
- JCB International
- Discover

The PCI Council is not a governmental agency. It's a private industry organization. The PCI Council was formed in 2005. It creates safeguards designed to protect credit card data. Any merchant or service provider who accepts credit cards must follow the safeguards. This list of security measures is called the Payment Card Industry (PCI)

Data Security Standard (DSS). The most recent version of the DSS was released in October 2008 and updated in July 2009. The PCI Council expects another update to the DSS sometime in late 2010.

> **NOTE**
>
> Cardholder data is the data available from a credit card. It includes cardholder name, expiration date, account number, and verification numbers. The data is printed on the card and can be contained in the magnetic stripe on the back of the card.

Purpose

Before the PCI Council was formed, each credit card company made up their own security requirements that applied to the credit cards that they issued. Merchants who accepted credit cards for payment had to follow these standards. Most merchants wanted to accept more than one type of credit card. It was hard for the merchants to follow so many different standards. The first DSS combined the standards of the founding credit card companies into one standard.

The DSS offers a single approach to safeguarding sensitive cardholder data for all credit card issuers. It identifies 12 basic categories of security requirements that must be followed in order to protect credit card data.

> **NOTE**
>
> A "merchant" is a businessperson who sells goods or services to earn a profit. A merchant can be a large, well-known store or the small corner grocery store. For the PCI DSS, a merchant is any entity that accepts credit cards for payment.

Scope

All merchants who accept credit cards must comply with the PCI DSS. PCI has different compliance requirements for different merchants. The compliance levels are based upon the size of the merchant's credit card operations. The credit card companies set the merchant levels individually. There are four levels of merchant compliance validation with the PCI DSS.

For example, Visa merchant Level 1 includes merchants that process over 6 million Visa transactions per year. MasterCard Level 1 includes any merchant that processes 6 million MasterCard transactions per year or meets Visa's Level 1 criteria. MasterCard Level 1 also includes merchants that have suffered a data breach that compromised account data, or any merchant that MasterCard feels should be a Level 1 merchant to minimize risk.

The different merchant levels have different compliance requirements. The credit card companies set these requirements. Visa requires its Level 1 merchants to have an independent evaluation each year. They also must have a quarterly network scan by an approved vendor. A Level 3 merchant must complete an annual self-assessment form and have a quarterly network scan.

> **NOTE**
>
> The complete list of PCI DSS requirements is available at *https://www.pcisecuritystandards.org/index.htm*.

Main Requirements

The DSS has specific requirements that each merchant must follow to protect cardholder data. The DSS applies only to the systems that process, store, or transmit credit card data. The DSS requirements use preventative, detective, and corrective controls to secure credit card data. The DSS has six high-level categories and 12 major rules. The main categories of controls and rules are listed in Table 4-3.

TABLE 4-3 PCI DSS categories of controls and rules.

DSS CONTROL CATEGORY	MAIN RULES
Build and Maintain a Secure Network	Merchants must install and maintain firewall and router configurations to protect cardholder data. Merchants may not use vendor-supplied defaults for passwords and other security measures.
Protect Cardholder Data	Merchants must take actions to protect stored cardholder data. Merchants must encrypt cardholder data while it is transmitted across public networks.
Maintain a Vulnerability Management Program	Merchants must use antivirus software that is updated regularly. Merchants must develop and use secure systems and applications.
Implement Strong Access Control Measures	Merchants must use need-to-know principles to restrict access to credit card data. Merchants must assign unique logons to each person with computer access. Merchants must restrict physical access to cardholder data.
Regularly Monitor and Test Networks	Merchants must monitor access to network resources and cardholder data. Merchants must test their security systems and processes regularly.
Maintain an Information Security Policy	Merchants must create an information security policy.

Each DSS rule has several sub-requirements that explain how the rule should be met. Merchants must understand how their information systems work in order to implement the DSS. They also must understand their business processes and be aware of how credit card data is used within their systems.

Oversight

The PCI Security Standards Council doesn't manage compliance programs. It also doesn't force any penalties for non-compliance. The Council only creates the DSS and provides merchants with resources to comply with those standards. Each of the individual credit card companies enforces the DSS for their own cards. Most credit card companies use the threat of financial penalties to compel DSS compliance.

For example, Visa requires its merchants to notify it immediately if they experience a breach involving credit card data. Visa may impose a penalty of up to $100,000 per event if it's not notified immediately. Visa also has the right to impose penalties of up to $500,000 per data loss incident if the merchant was not compliant with the DSS at the time of the breach. Credit card companies can reduce fines if the merchant can show that they were compliant with the DSS at the time of the breach.

Case Studies and Examples

The following case studies show how the laws discussed in this chapter are used. These case studies are real-world examples of how regulatory agencies apply laws and rules to protect consumer information.

FTC Privacy and Safeguards Rule Enforcement

The Federal Trade Commission enforces the GLBA Privacy and Safeguards Rule against some types of financial institutions. The FTC can begin an investigation on its own or in response to a consumer complaint. The FTC can file a complaint against organizations that don't follow the law. The FTC is called the petitioning party when it files a complaint. A "respondent" is the organization that must respond to the complaint.

NOTE

The FTC documents related to its Nationwide investigation are available at *http://www.ftc.gov/os/adjpro/d9319l*.

In November 2004, the FTC filed a complaint against Nationwide Mortgage Group, Inc. The FTC claimed that Nationwide violated the GLBA Privacy and Safeguards Rule. The FTC had just finished an industry-wide review of automobile dealers and mortgage companies to assess their levels of GLBA compliance. This was one of the very first FTC Safeguards Rule enforcement actions.

In its complaint, the FTC alleged that Nationwide violated the Safeguards Rule. It stated that Nationwide collected sensitive customer information, but that it had no policies and procedures in place to protect that information. It also stated that Nationwide failed to monitor its computer network for vulnerabilities that would expose stored customer information to attack. (Complaint paragraph 6).

The FTC also alleged that Nationwide failed to provide its customers with privacy practices notices as required by the privacy rule. (Complaint paragraph 10).

Nationwide worked quickly with the FTC to resolve the complaint. The FTC withdrew its complaint in December 2004 as the parties worked together to reach a consent agreement. A "consent agreement" is an agreement made between the FTC and a respondent. In a consent agreement, the respondent agrees to comply with the law but doesn't admit any wrongdoing. A consent agreement states the corrective measures that respondent must take to comply with the law. Once the consent decree is approved, it's treated like a court order.

In March 2005, Nationwide and the FTC entered into a consent agreement. Nationwide agreed to:

* Comply with the GLBA Safeguards Rule and Privacy Rule.
* Obtain an independent assessment of its information security program every two years. This assessment must certify that the program is reasonable and appropriate. They must do this for 10 years.
* Deliver a copy of the consent agreement to all current and future Nationwide officers, directors, managers, and employees.

The FTC's consent agreement with Nationwide ends on April 12, 2025. Nationwide must follow the terms in the consent agreement until it expires, such as delivering a copy of the consent agreement to employees.

> **NOTE**
> The consent agreement between the FTC and Nationwide can be viewed at *http://www.ftc.gov/os/adjpro/ d9319/050415dod9319.pdf.*

PCI DSS Example

The TJX Companies, Inc. (TJX) is a retailer of apparel and home fashion. The company operates several discount stores, including A.J. Wright, Bob's Stores, HomeGoods, T.J.Maxx, and Marshalls in the United States; HomeSense and Winners in Canada; and T.K.Maxx in the United Kingdom, Ireland, and Germany.

In January 2007, TJX disclosed that hackers had breached its credit card systems. The company reported that the attackers might have accessed credit card data going back to 2002. It reported that 45.7 million credit and debit card numbers might have been disclosed. At the time, the breach was believed to be the largest ever. Banks and customers sued TJX in connection with the breach. State governments also sued the company for failing to protect the credit card information of state residents. In addition, credit card companies and the FTC investigated TJX's data security practices.

In December 2007, TJX reached a settlement with Visa. It agreed to pay $40.9 million to fund payments to banks that issued Visa cards. TJX also agreed to serve as a spokesperson in support of the PCI Data Security Standards. In early 2008, TJX entered into a similar settlement agreement with MasterCard. In that agreement, it agreed to pay $24 million.

The FTC also investigated the TJX breach. The FTC determined that it had violated the Federal Trade Commission Act. In 2008, the company entered into a consent agreement with the FTC. As part of the agreement, TJX agreed to establish an information security program. The requirements for the information security program closely mirror the requirements of the FTC Safeguards Rule. The company also agreed to every-other-year evaluations of its information security program for 20 years. It also must provide certain types of employees a copy of the consent decree. The consent agreement terminates on July 29, 2028.

> **NOTE**
> The FTC documents related to its TJX investigation are available at *http://www.ftc. gov/os/caselist/0723055/.*

In June 2009, TJX settled lawsuits with 41 states. Under the terms of the settlement, it agreed to pay $9.75 million to the states. Some $5.5 million of that amount was directed toward state consumer and data protection efforts. It also agreed to establish a comprehensive information security program.

In 2008, the U.S. Department of Justice charged 11 people with participating in the attack on TJX. The ringleader pleaded guilty in September 2009. He was ordered to pay $2.7 million in restitution. As part of his plea, he had to forfeit a home and personal property. In March 2010, he was sentenced to 20 years in prison. This same person pleaded guilty in December 2009 in the Heartland Payment Systems breach. He was sentenced to 20 years in prison in March 2010 for the Heartland crime, as well as another 20-year sentence for a third hacking crime. The three 20-year sentences are to run all at the same time. They are the harshest sentences ever for a hacking case.

CHAPTER SUMMARY

Consumer financial information is valuable. In the wrong hands, it can be used to commit identity theft. The U.S. federal government regulates how this information can be used. Private industry also takes steps to guard this information. These laws and standards work together to protect consumers from identity theft.

KEY CONCEPTS AND TERMS

Consumer goods
Consumer services
Deceptive trade practices

Nonpublic personal information (NPI)
Pretexting

Red Flag
Unfair trade practices

CHAPTER 4 ASSESSMENT

1. What are consumer goods?

A. Items purchased for personal use
B. Items purchased for family use
C. Items purchased for household use
D. All of the above
E. None of the above

2. Which rule is not a GLBA consumer protection provision?

A. The Safeguards Rule
B. The Red Flags Rule
C. The Privacy Rule
D. The Pretexting Rule
E. None of the above

3. Which federal agency regulates national banks?

A. The Office of the Comptroller of the Currency
B. The Federal Reserve System
C. The Federal Deposit Insurance Corporation
D. The Office of Thrift Supervision
E. The Federal Trade Commission

4. What is the organization that promotes uniform reports among federal banking institutions?

A. The Fed
B. The FFIEC
C. The FTC
D. The NCUA
E. The SEC

5. What is a Red Flag?

A. A crime
B. An activity that prevents identity theft
C. An activity that might indicate identity theft
D. An activity that mitigates identity theft
E. None of the above

6. Pretexting is also called _____.

7. Which of the following is nonpublic personal information?

A. Personally identifiable financial information provided by a customer to a financial institution
B. Personally identifiable financial information provided by a financial institution to a customer
C. Personally identifiable financial information provided by a financial institution to an affiliate
D. Personally identifiable financial information provided by an affiliate to a financial institution
E. Personally identifiable financial information provided by an affiliate to a customer

8. A written information security program under the Safeguards Rule must include _____.

A. Technical safeguards
B. Physical safeguards
C. Administrative safeguards
D. A designated employee to run the program
E. All of the above

9. The _____ established the national banking system in the United States.

10. What is the central bank of the United States?

A. The FDIC
B. The Fed
C. The NCUA
D. The OCC
E. The OTS

11. Which of the following is not a federal bank regulatory agency?

A. The FDIC
B. The NCUA
C. The FTC
D. The OCC
E. The Fed

12. What customer option must be included in a privacy practices notice?

   A. Disclosure
   B. Opt-out
   C. Opt-in
   D. Notice
   E. None of the above

13. The Payment Card Industry Standard includes _____ categories of security requirements.

14. The Payment Card Industry Standards are enforced by the Federal Trade Commission.

   A. True
   B. False

15. What is a customer?

   A. A consumer with a past relationship with a financial institution
   B. A consumer with no relationship with a financial institution
   C. A consumer with a continuing relationship with a financial institution
   D. A consumer who wants to enter into a relationship with a financial institution
   E. None of the above

ENDNOTES

1. Verizon Business, *2009 Data Breach Investigations Report,* April 15, 2009, *http://www.verizonbusiness.com/resources/security/reports/2009_databreach_rp.pdf* (accessed March 1, 2010).

2. U.S. Code Vol. 31, sec. 5312.

3. U.S. Code Vol. 12, sec. 1843(k)(4).

4. U.S. Code Vol. 15, sec. 46(a).

5. U.S. Code Vol. 15, sec. 45(a)(1).

6. U.S. Code Vol. 12, sec. 3305.

7. U.S. Code Vol. 15, sec. 6801(a).

8. U.S. Code Vol. 15, sec. 6801-6803.

9. U.S. Code Vol. 15, sec. 6805(b)(1).

10. U.S. Code Vol. 15, sec. 6801(b).

11. U.S. Code Vol. 15, sec. 6805(b)(2).

12. *Standards for Insuring the Security Confidentiality, Integrity and Protection of Customer Records and Information* ("Safeguards Rule"), Code of Federal Regulations, Title 16, sec. 314.

13. U.S. Code Vol. 15, sec. 6821.

14. *Identity Theft Red Flags Rule,* Code of Federal Regulations, Title 16, sec. 681.2. See also Federal Register 72, No. 217 at 63,772 (Nov. 9, 2007).

15. Code of Federal Regulations, Title 16, sec. 681.1(b)(9).

16. Federal Register 72, No. 217 at 63,719, background information.

17. U.S. Code Vol. 15, sec. 1681a(r)(5).

18. Code of Federal Regulations, Title 16, sec. 681.1(b)(3)(i).

Security and Privacy of Information Belonging to Children and Educational Records

EVERAL LAWS ARE IN PLACE to protect children. The Children's Online Privacy Protection Act (COPPA) protects the information of children. If you host a Web site that collects information from children, COPPA applies to you. The Children's Internet Protection Act (CIPA) ensures that minors can't view obscene or objectionable material from certain school or library computers. These computers must implement technology to ensure the content is filtered. The Family Educational Rights and Privacy Act (FERPA) protects the rights of students. FERPA requires schools to protect student records. Schools cannot release records without the written consent of a student or parent. Additionally, students or parents have the right to review these records.

This chapter begins with a discussion of children and the Internet, and the unique challenges Web site operators face in protecting children. The chapter then provides details about COPPA, CIPA, and FERPA.

Chapter 5 Topics

This chapter covers the following topics and concepts:

- What the challenges are in protecting children on the Internet
- What the Children's Online Privacy Protection Act (COPPA) is
- What the Children's Internet Protection Act (CIPA) is
- What the Family Educational Rights and Privacy Act (FERPA) is
- What some case studies and examples are

Challenges in Protecting Children on the Internet

Although most people agree that children should be protected, they don't always agree on how that should be accomplished. For example, some people suggest that a parent should monitor a child's Internet access and decide if the child's Internet activities are acceptable. Others suggest that laws should be in place to protect the child. As you will see in this chapter, several laws have been enacted to protect children.

However, even when enacting laws, challenges still exist. These include:

- Identification of children
- First Amendment and censorship
- Defining obscenity

Identification of Children

To protect children, you must first be able to identify them. This means you must differentiate between adults and children. Some laws define a child as anyone under the age of 13. However, most Web sites are anonymous. Although you can require an ID from restaurant customers to ensure they're old enough to purchase alcohol, it isn't as easy to require identification when users access a Web site.

Web site operators can use several methods to distinguish children from adults. These include:

- **Require user input**—A Web site can require users to identify if they are children or adults. For example, users can select a check box indicating they are over a certain age. They can be required to enter an age or a birth date. This isn't a foolproof method, however, because a person can simply enter or select an incorrect age. If a child accesses an age-restricted Web site under false pretenses, the Web site operator can still be liable. For example, if a Web site operator targets children, but then requires them to identify themselves as older, the operator can be charged with engaging in deceptive tactics.

- **Require payment**—If a Web site has material that should be restricted from children, it can require a payment. Payment can be made using a credit card, a PayPal account, or another method that a child is unlikely to have. The payment may be a nominal fee, such as 99 cents. It could also be a larger fee designed to generate revenue. A payment requirement can be effective because children generally don't have access to payment sources.

- **Use parental controls**—Some operating systems such as Windows Vista and Windows 7 include **parental controls**. Additionally, many applications use parental controls. These allow a parent to restrict their children's access to objectionable material based on different ratings.

 NOTE

The Entertainment Software Rating Board (ESRB) is a self-regulating nonprofit that assigns independent ratings to computer and video game content. This includes games available online. The ratings help parents select appropriate games and other content for their children. Web site operators can rate their Web sites according to ESRB so that parental controls work properly.

- **Require parental permission**—All access can be blocked until a parent provides permission. However, parental permission should be verifiable. A Web site operator needs to ensure that a parent is providing the permission rather than someone posing as the parent.

First Amendment and Censorship

As discussed in Chapter 3, the First Amendment is a part of the Bill of Rights. The First Amendment grants certain rights related to freedom of speech, freedom of the press, and free exercise of religion. First Amendment issues sometimes come into play on the Internet. The First Amendment guarantees certain rights, including freedom of speech without censorship. If a Web site operator must censor material because a child may view it, does this violate the First Amendment? Some argue that any restrictions on Internet access also restrict freedom of speech.

Similarly, if individuals are required to identify themselves before they can use a Web site, does that restrict free speech? Does it infringe on the First Amendment rights to communicate anonymously? Some believe these are constitutional issues yet to be addressed by the Children's Online Privacy Protection Act. You'll learn about the act later in this chapter.

Defining Obscenity

Most people agree that children should be protected from obscene material. However, the definition of "obscene material" is complex. According to the 1973 U.S. Supreme Court ruling in *Miller v. California,* for material to be identified as "obscene," it must meet three conditions. The conditions are based on the average person applying contemporary community standards. The three conditions are that the material:

 NOTE

The three conditions of obscenity are commonly known as the "Miller test."

- Appeals predominantly to prurient interests; "prurient" indicates a morbid, degrading, and unhealthy interest in sex
- Depicts or describes sexual conduct in a patently offensive way
- Lacks serious literary, artistic, political, or scientific value

Although a legal definition for obscenity exists, it isn't easy to apply. One may consider another person's healthy interest in sex unhealthy. Material that is offensive to one person may be viewed as valuable artwork by another person. For example, some consider Gustave Caillebotte's painting titled *Naked Woman Lying on a Couch* a master-piece. Others consider it pornography. Additionally, various communities can interpret this definition differently. The values of a tightly knit religious community may be considerably different from those of a large urban community.

I Know It When I See It

A 1964 U.S. Supreme Court case helps show the difficulty of defining obscenity. The case was *Jacobellis v. Ohio,* 378 U.S. 184 (1964). A manager of a motion picture theater was convicted under a state obscenity law of illegally possessing and exhibiting an allegedly obscene film. Although the state supreme court in Ohio upheld the conviction, the U.S. Supreme Court later reversed the decision.

In the decision, U.S. Supreme Court Justice Potter Stewart expressed the difficulty of defining obscenity and pornography. He then wrote "But I know it when I see it, and the motion picture involved with this case is not that."

In this case, the U.S. Supreme Court agreed that the First Amendment does not protect pornography or obscenity. The court only disagreed that the motion picture in this case was obscene. Although this case was settled over 50 years ago, the challenge of formally identifying obscenity exists today.

Children's Online Privacy Protection Act

The Children's Online Privacy Protection Act (COPPA)[1] passed in November 1998. It went into effect 18 months later in 2000. It covers any Web sites that collect information from children under the age of 13. These Web sites must follow specific rules under COPPA.

Several important definitions are included in COPPA. A "child" is any person under the age of 13. A "parent" is a legal guardian of a child. An "operator" is a Web site operator who collects or maintains personal information about users.

 NOTE

COPPA is not the same as the Child Online Protection Act (COPA). COPA passed in 1998 with the purpose of protecting minors from access to harmful material on the Internet. However, courts ruled that COPA violates free speech. CIPA is similar to COPA and is discussed later in this chapter.

Purpose of COPPA

The primary purpose of COPPA is to protect children's privacy on the Internet. Web sites must follow specific rules if they collect or use a child's personal information. They must obtain a parent's consent before doing so. They must also post a privacy policy explaining their practices.

Personal information includes:

- A child's first and last name
- A child's e-mail address
- A child's telephone number
- A child's Social Security number
- Any other information that permits someone to contact the child
- Any other information that can be used to identify the child

Online contact information primarily refers to an e-mail address. However, it could mean other identifiers that allow online contact. For example, some forums and chat rooms allow users to communicate with each other privately. This can only be done after information is shared between the users. COPPA doesn't prevent the users from communicating privately. However, COPPA restricts the Web site from allowing this information to be shared publicly.

Any personal information that's collected needs to be protected. Web site operators are required to ensure the information is not made publicly available to others on the Internet. This includes ensuring it isn't displayed on a home page of a Web site, in a pen-pal service, in an e-mail service, on a message board, or in a chat room.

Scope of the Regulation

COPPA is primarily for Web sites or online services that collect or use information for children age 13 or under. This includes operators of Web sites or online services targeted for children. General-audience Web sites or online services, and those that have a separate area for children, must also adhere to COPPA. Essentially, COPPA applies to any online activities that collect or use information about children.

Main Requirements

COPPA includes two main requirements. The first requirement relates to gaining consent from parents to collect or use the information. The second requirement relates to the creation and posting of a privacy policy.

Gaining Parent's Consent

In general, a Web site must not collect or use any information about children without gaining permission from the child's parent. COPPA has several specific rules related to gaining a parent's consent. For example, Web site operators must obtain parental consent to collect information on children. Consent must be obtained before collecting, using, or disclosing information about a child. If the Web site changes how it uses the information, consent must be obtained again.

Parents must be allowed to review information collected from their children. Web site operators are required to verify the identity of the requesting parent before releasing this information. Parents must also be allowed to revoke their consent. Web site operators must stop collecting, using, or disclosing information when requested by the parent. Parents also can request that a Web site operator delete data held on their children.

Consent is not required in some instances. Web sites don't need parental consent if they're collecting an e-mail address to respond to a one-time request from a child, or to provide notice to the parent. Nor is consent required to ensure the safety of the child or the site, or when sending recurring e-mails as long as the site notifies the parent and allows unsubscribe requests.

In addition, parental consent must be verifiable. Only a parent can give consent. The Web site operator must verify it is truly the parent giving consent. This becomes especially important if the parent requests to see the information held about his or her child. Web site operators must have measures in place to prevent the information from being released to the wrong party.

Obtaining parental consent represents several challenges. The Web site needs to implement technology that can verify the parent. This can be costly and time consuming. It also can affect First Amendment rights. Some argue that requiring identification affects the right to communicate anonymously.

Privacy Policy

Under COPPA, Web sites must post a privacy policy. The privacy policy provides details as to what kind of information the site collects about children. It also identifies how the site will use the information. In general, a privacy policy must meet several specific requirements. The requirements fall into two primary categories: location and content.

COPPA doesn't explicitly use the phrase "privacy policy." It requires Web site operators to provide a notice on their Web sites that identifies the collected information. However, the COPPA Rule created by the Federal Trade Commission (FTC) calls this a privacy policy. You'll learn about the COPPA Rule in the upcoming "Oversight" section.

Verifying Parental Consent

A Web site operator can use one of several methods to verify a person is a parent of a child. These include:

- **Sending signed printed forms**—These may be sent via mail, fax, or e-mail.
- **Using credit cards**—The credit card can verify details about the parent.
- **Using toll-free numbers**—Parents can call and provide details to verify their identities.

Some operators suggest that these methods are too costly to be practical. As a result, many Web sites avoid the law. They don't collect information on children, and their privacy statement reflects this. Users are required to indicate they are at least 13 years old before information is collected. Users must enter their age or check a box indicating they're at least 13 years old. However, it's possible for children to indicate they're over 13 years old when they are not.

Privacy Policy Location

The privacy policy should be easily visible and accessible. At the very least, it should be included on the home page of the Web site and on every area of the Web site where personal information is requested.

A COPPA-compliant privacy policy must be accessible from a clear and prominent link. This means the link needs to stand out and be noticeable. A Web site designer can achieve this in a variety of ways. For example, the designer can use different type sizes, different fonts, different colors, or contrasting backgrounds. In addition, the privacy policy must be clearly labeled to indicate it's a privacy policy. The most common label is "Privacy Policy." Other examples of clear labels are "Privacy Statement" and "Information Practices Statement."

Privacy Policy Content

The privacy policy needs to contain specific information to be COPPA-compliant. The format isn't as important as the content. At a minimum, the policy must contain:

- **Operator contact information**—This includes the name, mailing address, telephone number, and e-mail address of all operators collecting or maintaining the information. If several operators are collecting information, you can list the details of only one operator as long as you meet two conditions. First, you must list the names of all operators either in the privacy policy or in a link accessible from the privacy policy. Second, the listed operator must respond to all inquiries from parents about the policy and the uses of children's information.

- **What information is collected**—The policy should specifically identify what information is collected. For example, you can use terms such as name, address, telephone number, gender, age, and e-mail address to identify what you're collecting. A generic term such as "contact information" isn't acceptable.

- **How information is collected**—A Web site can collect information passively or actively. Active collection is by the user entering the information using a form of some type. Passive collection includes the use of cookies or other methods when personal information is included.

- **How the information will be used**—Web sites must state how the information will be used. For example, a Web site could collect e-mail addresses for newsletter subscriptions. It could collect mailing addresses for prizes. It could also collect the information for sales and marketing purposes.

- **If the information is disclosed to third parties**—The Web site must also disclose if collected information is shared with a third party. A "third party" is any entity that's not an operator of the Web site or doesn't provide internal support for the Web site. Parents must have the option to refuse the sharing of information with third parties.

- **Include the ban on conditioning participation on information collection**— This ban prevents the Web site from collecting information that's not reasonably necessary. For example, a Web site may collect an e-mail address for an e-mail newsletter subscription. However, collecting a mailing address for an e-mail newsletter is not reasonable. The privacy policy should explicitly state this prohibition.

- **Parental rights**—The policy must indicate that a parent can review information collected on his or her child. It also should indicate the parent could refuse further collection, and have the collected information deleted.

Oversight

The FTC provides oversight for COPPA. The FTC can bring enforcement actions and impose civil penalties for COPAA violations. The FTC provides many tools to help Web site operators comply with COPPA. This includes a guide that explains each component of a COPPA-compliant privacy policy. Additionally, the FTC investigates complaints of Web sites that violate COPPA.

 NOTE

The FTC summarizes the rule at *http://www.ftc.gov/privacy/ privacyinitiatives/childrens. html.*

COPPA required the FTC to create a rule implementing COPPA. The FTC implemented the COPPA Rule in 1999. It reiterates and clarifies COPPA. In addition to the requirements already discussed in this section, the rule requires that Web sites specifically provide parents access to their child's personal information. Web sites must allow parents the opportunity to delete the child's personal information. They also must give parents the ability to opt out of future collection or use of the information.

COPPA Checklist for Privacy Policy

The FTC provides a checklist you can use for COPPA compliance. It includes a list of simple yes-and-no questions. The following list of questions illustrates the wide range of issues a Web site developer must consider for COPPA compliance. Answering "No" may indicate areas in which a Web site is not in compliance with COPPA. This list is representative of the types of issues that the FTC asks Web site developers to consider for COPPA compliance:

- Is there a link to your privacy policy on the home page of your Web site or on the home page of the children's area of your Web site?
- Are the links to your privacy policy near each place on your Web site where you collect personal information from children?
- Does the link to your privacy policy stand out so that the Web site visitor can locate it easily? Is the link in a different color, a different font, or a larger type size?
- Does your privacy policy include the names of all the Web site operators who collect or maintain children's personal information?
- Does your privacy policy provide the telephone numbers for all Web site operators who collect or maintain personal information through your site? Does your privacy policy provide the e-mail addresses of all Web site operators who collect or maintain personal information through your site?
- Does your privacy policy state each type of personal information that you collect from children?
- Does your privacy policy tell parents how your Web site will use the personal information that it collects?
- Does your privacy policy let parents know that they can review the personal information that your Web site has collected from their child?
- Does your privacy policy tell parents how they can review their child's personal information?
- Does your privacy policy tell parents they can have their child's personal information deleted from your site?
- Does your privacy policy tell parents how they can have their children's personal information deleted from your site?
- Does your privacy policy tell parents that they can stop your Web site from further collecting or using the personal information from your child?
- Does your privacy policy tell parents how they can stop the further collection and use of their child's personal information?
- Is your privacy policy clear and understandable? Is it easy to read?
- Does your privacy policy give a complete description of your information practices? Does it explain all the personal information you collect? Does it spell out how you will use the information?
- Are you sure your practices reflect the promises you make in your privacy policy?

You can view the full checklist here:
http://www.ftc.gov/bcp/edu/microsites/coppa/checklist.htm.

The FTC is required to review its COPPA Rule every five years. It made no changes to the rule after its review in 2005. In 2010, the FTC began collecting comments on possible changes to the rule. The FTC said it may consider changes to its COPPA Rule due to rapidly changing Internet technologies.

Children's Internet Protection Act (CIPA)

NOTE

Note the differences in ages between CIPA and COPPA. COPPA defines a child as anyone under the age of 13. CIPA defines a minor as anyone under the age of 17.

The Children's Internet Protection Act (CIPA)[2] passed in 2000. It requires certain schools and libraries to filter offensive content. These schools and libraries had until July 1, 2004, to comply. The goal is to ensure that minors don't accidentally access offensive content. CIPA defines a minor as anyone under the age of 17.

CIPA was quickly challenged. The American Library Association and the American Civil Liberties Union claimed CIPA violated free speech rights of adults. They also claimed the law could prevent minors from getting information about topics such as breast cancer. The law was temporarily overturned in 2002. The U.S. District Court for the Eastern District of Pennsylvania agreed that CIPA violated First Amendment rights.

The suit went to the U.S. Supreme Court. In *United States et al. v. American Library Association, Inc. et al.* in 2003, the U.S. Supreme Court overturned the District Court and upheld the law. Only schools and libraries that receive E-Rate funding for Internet access must comply with the law. A school or library can choose not to accept the funding, if desired.

E-Rate funding provides discounts to schools and libraries for Internet access and telecommunications services. The goal is to help all schools and libraries have affordable Internet access. Discounts range from 20 percent to 90 percent of the service costs depending on the need of the school or library. Part of the E-Rate application requires verification that the school or library is complying with CIPA.

NOTE

A "visual depiction" is any picture, image, or graphic image file.

Purpose

The primary purpose of CIPA is to protect minors from accidentally seeing offensive content. Offensive content includes any visual depictions that are obscene, child pornography, or harmful to minors (if the computers are accessed by minors).

CIPA doesn't attempt to define obscenity or child pornography. Most laws use the Miller test mentioned earlier in this chapter from the 1973 U. S. Supreme Court ruling in *Miller v. California*. Although CIPA doesn't define child pornography, child pornography is illegal in the United States. Other state and federal laws also ban child pornography.

CIPA defines the phrase "harmful to minors." This includes any visual depiction that:

- Taken as a whole and with respect to minors, appeals to a prurient interest in nudity, sex, or excretion
- Depicts, describes, or represents, in a patently offensive way with respect to what is suitable for minors, an actual or simulated sexual act or sexual contact, actual or simulated normal or perverted sexual acts, or a lewd exhibition of the genitals
- Taken as a whole, lacks serious literary, artistic, political, or scientific value as to minors

This definition closely resembles the Miller test.

Scope of the Regulation

Any school or library that receives federal funding from the E-Rate program must comply with CIPA. The E-Rate program is funded by the federal government. The Federal Communications Commission manages it. The E-Rate program provides discounts to most schools and libraries for Internet access. Discounts range from 20 percent to 90 percent of the actual costs. Schools and libraries don't have to accept these funds. They can either pay for the Internet access with other funds, or choose not to use the Internet.

Main Requirements

The primary requirements of CIPA mandate the filtering of content. Offensive content must be filtered so that minors don't see it. Although this may seem difficult, there are tools to make the job easier. CIPA identifies these tools as a **technology protection measure (TPM)**. A TPM is any technology that can block or filter the objectionable content.

Consider Figure 5-1. This figure shows a proxy server used to filter content. A **proxy server** accepts Internet requests from clients, retrieves the pages, and serves them to the client. Content filters filter out objectionable content. As shown, you'd configure the internal clients to access the Internet through a proxy server.

The proxy server has a content filter. This content filter blocks all content marked as unacceptable. Similarly, it allows all content marked as acceptable. The proxy server identifies what's acceptable based on filter lists.

Third-party companies sell subscriptions to filter lists. These companies constantly search the Internet identifying restricted materials and adding them to the list. When a network administrator adds the filter to an organization's proxy server, the server blocks prohibited material.

The Federal Communications Commission (FCC) recognizes that a TPM cannot be 100 percent effective. However, neither CIPA nor the FCC defines what level is acceptable. A third-party company may claim its filter is CIPA compliant. However, there is no certification process to verify a filter is CIPA compliant. The FCC has stated that local authorities should determine which measures are most effective for their community.

Although a proxy server is a common method of filtering, CIPA doesn't specify where to filter the content. An Internet service provider (ISP) may be able to filter it. You may be able to purchase software to install on individual computers for filtering purposes. CIPA states what must be filtered but not how to filter it.

In addition to the TPM, the school or library must also create an Internet safety policy and identify a method to address exceptions.

Internet Safety Policy

School and libraries must adopt and enforce an Internet safety policy to comply with CIPA. Provisions in this policy must be able to monitor the online activity of monitors and restrict the objectionable content. An Internet safety policy addresses access by minors to inappropriate content on the Internet. It also addresses the safety and security of minors when using e-mail, chat rooms, or other electronic communications. Provisions must cover any unauthorized access or unlawful activities by minors online, and unauthorized use of minors' personal information. The policy also includes measures that restrict minors' access to harmful materials.

Exceptions

According to CIPA, you should be able to disable the TPM for any adult. As a reminder, content must be filtered for minors, not adults. A minor is anyone under the age of 17. If an adult needs to use a computer, you can disable the TPM for this person. This is an important point. If you can't disable the TPM for an adult, you run the risk of violating First Amendment rights. Adults should be able to use the system without any filtering.

Proxy Servers in Any Company

Many companies use proxy servers. Their use isn't restricted to CIPA compliance. Many companies choose to restrict employee's access to different Internet Web sites. For example, your company may want to prevent employees from accessing gambling sites. You can purchase a subscription to gambling sites from one of the third-party sites. You can then install this filter on your proxy server. When an employee accesses a Web site, the proxy server can block their access.

When the user tries to access the prohibited site, the proxy server can instead show a different page. For example, you could redirect the user to a Web page that states "access is restricted." This page also could show the company's acceptable usage policy. Additionally, many proxy servers log all activities. Administrators are able to view the logs to determine which employees are trying to access restricted sites.

Some third-party companies that sell these subscriptions estimate that CIPA lists are less than 5 percent of their sales. The majority of these sales are from companies.

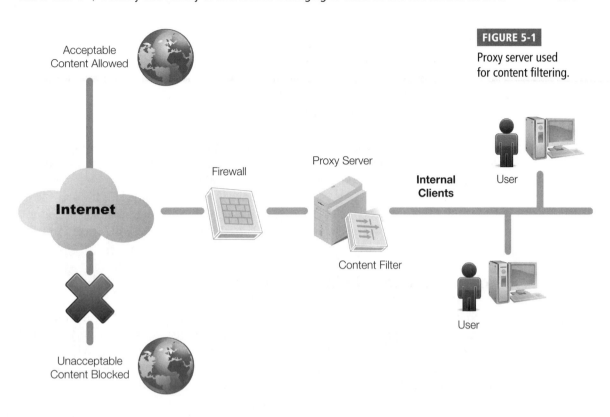

FIGURE 5-1

Proxy server used
for content filtering.

The *United States et al. v. American Library Association, Inc. et al.* Supreme Court ruling
in 2003 explicitly mentioned this point.

For example, if an adult asks to have the TPM disabled but the request is not honored,
the library places itself at risk. Supreme Court Justice Anthony Kennedy wrote that a
library could risk a possible "as applied" challenge. In other words, a patron could charge
the library with deliberate censorship while using CIPA as the shield. The library will
find itself on the wrong side of the law. Additionally, patrons don't have to state why
they want the TPM disabled. CIPA applies to minors. Any adult should be able to ask
for the TPM to be disabled.

Libraries can use any method to disable the TPM that works best for their location.
For example, library personnel could label some computers as "adult only." Librarians
would prevent minors from using these computers. Librarians also could log onto
a program designed to disable the TPM. Only personnel with the proper credentials
could disable the TPM. Another method is to require an administrator to disable the
TPM. Upon request by a patron, the librarian could contact an administrator to disable
the TPM for the patron. This method may be more difficult and time-consuming than
other methods, however.

Oversight

The FCC has oversight for CIPA. However, little oversight action is required. When a public school or library requests E-Rate funding, they must certify that they comply with CIPA. This certification is usually all that's required.

If a TPM fails, the school or library is expected to take steps to resolve the failure. As mentioned previously, a TPM isn't expected to be 100 percent effective. Patrons may complain to the library for specific instances. If the library doesn't resolve them, the patron can file a complaint with the FCC. If the FCC receives complaints that too many objectionable images are getting through, it may investigate.

The FCC presumes that Congress never intended libraries to be fined if they don't comply with CIPA. At most, the FCC may require a library to refund the E-Rate discount for the period of time it wasn't in compliance. The FCC states that it "will rarely, if ever" take such action.

Family Educational Rights and Privacy

The Family Educational Rights and Privacy Act (FERPA)[3] passed in 1974. The primary goal is to protect the privacy of student records. A "student record" includes any personal and education data on the student. Students or their parents have the right to inspect and review their educational records. FERPA grants these rights to parents of students under 18 years old. When the student reaches 18, these rights pass to the student.

FERPA includes several definitions. These include:

 NOTE

FERPA formally defines PII. Several other laws and regulations also define PII. In general, laws mandate the protection of any PII. PII can be a name, a Social Security number, biometric data, or any data used to identify a person. Several laws and regulations specify that PII must be protected.

- **Student**—Any individual that has ever been in attendance at the agency or institution. This includes current and past students.

- **Attendance**—This includes a student's physical attendance, and attendance in other ways. Other methods of attendance include through the Internet, video conference, satellite, correspondence, or other methods used by the school.

- **Personally identifiable information (PII)**—Direct identifiers such as a student's name, Social Security number, and student number. PII also includes indirect identifiers when matched with a student name. "Indirect identifiers" are any personal characteristics that can be used to easily identify the student.

- **Directory information**—Information that is publically available about all students. The school can release directory information about a student without consent.

- **Disclosure**—Any release of PII information by the school to a third party. This includes any type of access, release, or transfer of the information. Consent is required before the disclosure of any PII.

FERPA and Peer-Grading

Many professors use peer-grading techniques. Students may be required to work in a project together and grade each other at the completion of the project. Additionally, students may be required to exchange assignments or tests and grade each other. Some professors require students to call out other students' grades in class. This is acceptable under FERPA.

Under FERPA, a school can't publish students' grades on a bulletin board, for instance. However, this doesn't extend to peer-grading. The U.S. Supreme Court decided this in 2002 in *Owasso Independent School District No. I-011 v. Falvo*. The court decided that peer grades are not maintained as education records and are not covered by FERPA.

* **Educational records**—Any records related to a student maintained by an educational agency or institution. It can include written documents, computer media, video, film, or photographs. This also includes any records maintained by any outside party acting for the agency or institution.

The official phrase used by FERPA is "any educational agency or institution." For readability, this is often shortened to "school" in this section.

Although FERPA defines what educational records are, it's also important to understand what they are not. Items such as medical records, campus law enforcement records, statistical data that doesn't identify the student, and private notes of faculty or staff are not considered educational records. However, if the faculty or staff notes are kept in a student record or student advising folder, they are considered part of the educational record.

Purpose and Scope

The purpose of FERPA is to protect the privacy of student records. FERPA applies to any education agencies or institutions that receive funding under any program administered by the U.S. Department of Education. This includes community colleges, institutions of higher education, state and local educational agencies, schools or agencies offering a preschool program, and any other educational institution.

Although the wording of the law is specific, the meaning is general. Any type of school or training institution that receives federal funds falls under FERPA. Notice that the funding can be indirect. For example, if a student receives a federal grant or federal aid and uses this as payment, the school is receiving federal funding.

If any educational agency or institution chooses not to comply with FERPA, it can't receive any federal funds. This includes federal funds for any program. Because federal funding is so valuable, almost all schools comply with FERPA. It's possible some small private schools don't receive public funds. They don't have to comply with FERPA.

Main Requirements

Students have a right to know what's in their student records. This includes the purpose and content of the records. They also have a right to expect the school to maintain confidentiality of their records. The school is responsible for protecting the records. They also must inform students of different exceptions.

Parent and Student Rights

The parent or student has several rights under FERPA. The parent or student has the right to inspect and review any records maintained by the school. The school doesn't have to make copies of the records. It only needs to make them available for review. If any of the data is incorrect, the parent or student has the right to request the correction of any errors in the record. If the school doesn't believe the record is inaccurate, it doesn't have to make the change. However, the school is required to inform the student of the decision.

> **NOTE**
>
> It's important to remember that the parent has these rights until the student reaches the age of 18. After that point, the parent no longer has the rights. Only the child has the rights. In other words, a parent may be paying for a 20-year-old son or daughter's college education, but the parent doesn't have the right to inspect the records.

Parents and students can refuse to give consent to have their data released. The school can still release data to certain entities. The next section explains these exceptions.

If a parent or student believes that the school is not complying with FERPA, he or she can file a complaint with the **Family Policy Compliance Office (FPCO)**. FPCO provides oversight for FERPA.

Protection of Records

The school has a requirement to protect students' records. With this in mind, it's important to know what information must be protected. This is referred to as PII. It's also called "non-directory information."

Information covered by FERPA includes personal identifiers such as the student's name, Social Security number, and student number. It can include any information that can be used to identify the student as long as it's not directory information. Demographic information such as race and gender can't be given out if it's directly connected with the student name. It's acceptable to give general statistics such as "50 percent of the school population is female." It's not acceptable to state that "Shannon Smith is female."

Grades or transcripts of grades are protected under FERPA. Students that want transcripts transferred to another college or university must submit a written consent.

Any disciplinary records are considered a part of the student record. This includes behavioral notes on the student if the notes are kept in the student record. Notes kept privately by a teacher or professor are not protected by FERPA.

It's possible for a student record to contain additional information outside the scope of FERPA. FERPA doesn't require schools to reveal this data. For example, a school doesn't have to reveal financial records of the parents of a student, confidential letters of recommendation, or statements of recommendation.

The school must obtain written consent to release the record. Most schools have forms for this purpose. Prior written consent must include:

- Which records will be disclosed
- The purpose of the disclosure
- Who will receive the record
- The date the consent is granted
- Signature of the student or parent
- Signature of the school official releasing the data

Annual Notification

FERPA requires schools to provide an annual disclosure notification to students and parents. This disclosure lets the parents and students know what their rights are related to FERPA. Additionally, it identifies school officials that will have access to records without consent. For example, FERPA allows any school official that has legitimate educational interest in the school record to view it without consent. The school can identify who these personnel are. They could be teachers, instructors, professors, administrative personnel such as principals or provosts, or Board of Education personnel.

Exceptions

There are some exceptions when a school can release student records without prior consent. School officials, such as principals or teachers, can view records in the performance of their jobs. These officials must have a legitimate educational interest. When a student transfers from one school to another, the school can transfer the student's record to the new school without consent. Data also can be transferred when some types of financial aid are used.

An accrediting organization may need to view student records to verify the school is performing to the standards of the organization. If so, the student information does not require prior consent. In addition, schools must comply with any court order or lawful subpoena for student records. For health and safety reasons, FERPA should not stand in the way of releasing data that can aid personnel in an emergency.

Schools may disclose some directory information on students without consent. Students and parents must be able to opt out of this directory information disclosure. Directory information includes:

- Student's name
- Photograph
- Address and telephone number
- E-mail address
- Date and place of birth
- Honors and awards
- Dates of attendance

How to Respond to Requests

A school may face several real-life situations. Any personnel that have access to records should have training on how to respond. Put yourself in the situation of the person answering the phone. How would you respond?

An employer calls and asks about a student that graduated last year. Specifically, the employer asks if the student graduated. Does FERPA restrict the release of this information? How do you respond?

- FERPA covers this information. You may need to explain this to the employer.
- You can give the information to the employer if the student signs a consent form.

A student needs a copy of his transcript. He asks a friend to pick it up for him. What should you tell the friend when he shows up?

- FERPA restricts the school from giving him this information.
- You may check the student's record to see if it has a signed consent form for this friend. If not, the transcript shouldn't be given out.
- The student must sign a consent form.

A mother calls about her 17-year-old son, who is in college. She wants to know if her son will be graduating with his class. Does the parent have rights to this information? What do you tell her?

- FERPA rights transferred to the son when he began his studies at a post-secondary institution. The parent doesn't have rights to this information. You may want to explain the FERPA requirements to the mother.
- Encourage the mother to talk with her son. In other words, ask her son if he will be graduating. You can provide information on how someone can reenroll in classes.

The mayor recently made a speech and mentioned a student at your school. The mayor talked about how the student had earned a specific degree and was now working on a higher level degree. You know that the student never completed any degree at your school. What should you do?

- FERPA protects this information. You shouldn't take any action.
- If the mayor or the mayor's office requests the information, you can't release it without a consent form.

Under no circumstances should the directory information include PII information such as a student's Social Security number or student ID number. You can release information on awards or honors that a student obtained. Honors and awards are directory information. However, you can't release information on the actual degrees earned.

Oversight

The Family Policy Compliance Office (FPCO) provides oversight for FERPA. FPCO also provides oversight for the Protection of Pupil Rights-Amendment (PPRA). FPCO is in Washington, D.C., and includes a 1-800 number for assistance. Students or parents that wish to make a complaint about FERPA are encouraged to do so in writing.

Case Studies and Examples

The following case studies provide some real-world background on COPPA and FERPA. These examples provide insight into how the laws are challenged and viewed.

Liberty Financial and Children's Privacy

In 1999, the FTC charged Liberty Financial Companies, Inc. (Liberty Financial) with making false promises. These false promises were related to the collection of personal information from children and teens. In this complaint, children were identified as anyone under 13. Teens were identified as anyone aged 13 to 17.

Liberty Financial hosted a Web site at *younginvestor.com*. It targeted children using contests and prizes. At one point, Liberty Financial created a survey called The Young Investor Measure Up. The survey's introduction stated, "All of your answers will be totally anonymous." The survey then collected information such as:

- Amount of allowance
- Gifts of stocks, bonds, or cash
- Spending habits
- Part-time work
- Plans for college
- Family finances

The survey ended with a request for name, address, and e-mail. It stated this information would be used to send a newsletter and award a prize every three months. Clearly, this information removed the child's anonymity. Additionally, Liberty Financial didn't send any newsletters. Neither did they award any prizes.

Liberty Financial was required to post a clear and prominent privacy policy on its Web sites directed to children under 13. The FTC also required Liberty Financial to obtain verifiable parental consent before collecting or using information for children under 13. These requirements were directly related to compliance with COPPA. The case occurred between the time when COPPA was passed and when compliance was required 18 months later.

The FTC documents related to the Liberty Financial case are available at *http://www.ftc.gov/os/1999/05/index.shtm#6.*

Iconix Brand Group, Inc.

In *United States of America v. Iconix Brand Group, Inc.*, the FTC alleged that the site falsely represented that personal information would be maintained anonymously. Instead, the data was collected and maintained in such a way that the child could be identified.

In 2006, the FTC charged Iconix Brand Group, Inc. (Iconix) with failing to comply with COPPA and for engaging in deceptive tactics. Specifically, the FTC charged that Iconix was deliberately collecting information on children. However, the Iconix Web site's privacy policy specifically stated it was not. Part of the privacy policy stated:

> We do not seek to collect personally identifiable information from persons under
> the age of 13 without prior verifiable parental consent. If we become aware that
> we have inadvertently received such information online from a child under the
> age of 13, we will delete it from our records.

Although the policy was sound, the company didn't follow it. The Iconix Web sites clearly targeted children. Iconix had domain names such as MuddGirls.com and Candies.com. Web site graphics included cartoon characters and photos of young girls. Over 1,000 girls under the age of 13 allegedly registered on Iconix Web sites between 2006 and 2009. This was determined based on birthdates given by the registrants.

The FTC concluded that the Iconix sites were targeted for children. The FTC based the conclusion on the activity of the Web site, not just the privacy policy. Further, the FTC concluded that Iconix was deliberately trying to avoid the requirements of COPPA. Iconix ultimately paid a fine of $250,000 to settle the case.

The FTC documents related to the Iconix Brand Group case are available at *http://www.ftc.gov/os/caselist/0923032/index.shtm.*

Gonzaga University Student

Gonzaga Univ. v. Doe involves a graduate who was denied the ability to become a public school teacher because of information released by the school. The student sued and won. Monetary damages were awarded to the student. However, the U.S. Supreme Court overturned the case, stating that the student can't sue the university for damages based on violating FERPA.

The student graduated from Gonzaga University in Washington State and planned to become a public elementary school teacher. The student needed to provide an affidavit of good moral character from her college. The teacher certification specialist at Gonzaga University contacted the state certification agency and provided damaging information. This specialist indicated that the student was engaged in sexual misconduct and identified the student by name. The student didn't receive the affidavit from the school and didn't get the job.

A jury ultimately awarded the student compensatory and punitive damages. The school contested this to the Washington State Supreme Court. The state supreme court upheld the verdict. However, the U.S. Supreme Court reversed the decision. In a 7–2 decision, the U.S. Supreme Court said that FERPA does not give the student personal

---

FYI

Gonzaga Univ. v. Doe doesn't address whether the school did the right thing related to FERPA. Instead, the focus is on the ability of the student to sue a school for a violation of FERPA. This is known as a "private cause of action" and was presented in Chapter 6. The Washington State Supreme Court agreed that the student could sue. The U.S. Supreme Court overturned this and stated that FERPA doesn't create any individual rights that can be enforced.

rights that can be enforced. In other words, the U.S. Department of Education could bring a lawsuit against the school. However, the student doesn't have the right to sue.

The documents related to the Gonzaga University case are available at *http://www.law. cornell.edu/supct/html/01-679.ZS.html.*

Release of Disciplinary Records

Disciplinary records are a part of student records. FERPA protects student records, which include disciplinary records. A student's consent is required prior to releasing any of these records.

A U.S. district court in the Southern District of Ohio decided this in 2000. The U.S. Court of Appeals affirmed the decision in 2002. However, the case actually started in 1995 and has a colorful history.

In 1995, the Miami University student newspaper asked Miami University to provide disciplinary records on students. This was to track crime trends on campus. The university refused to release the records. The paper then made a request using the Ohio Public Records Act. Miami University released the records but removed all personally identifiable information. They also removed information such as the date, time, and location of the incidents.

Editors of the paper thought that the university removed too much information from the records. They went to the Ohio Supreme Court seeking full disclosure of the records. In a divided decision, the Ohio Supreme Court agreed and ruled that FERPA doesn't cover the disciplinary records. Miami University tried to take the case to the U.S. Supreme Court, but the court chose not to hear the case in 1997.

Miami University notified the U.S. Department of Education (ED) that it didn't think it was able to comply with FERPA based on the decision. The university also adopted a policy of releasing disciplinary records to any third-party requestor. Ohio State University also released records and notified ED that it planned to honor future requests. ED disagreed and thought that the Ohio Supreme Court had made a mistake.

ED filed a motion to stop both universities from releasing these records. The U.S. district in the Southern District of Ohio heard the case. The universities didn't dispute the facts and were willing to allow the court to rule. However, the school newspaper filed a motion to intervene. Although the newspaper wasn't named in the suit, it wanted its voice heard.

The newspaper claimed that ED didn't have authority in the case. Instead, ED could take action only after the release of records, not before. However, the circuit court disagreed. It determined that ED did have authority. Additionally, the circuit court determined that disciplinary records are education records and covered by FERPA. The court ordered the universities not to release the information.

The newspaper appealed this decision to the U.S. Court of Appeals. The newspaper argued that FERPA violates the First Amendment and the district court didn't recognize this violation. However, the U.S. Court of Appeals upheld the district court's decision in 2002. Even today, schools must not release student disciplinary records without student consent.

ED documents related to the Miami University case are available at *http://www2. ed.gov/policy/gen/guid/fpco/ferpa/library/unofmiami.html* and *http://www2.ed.gov/policy/ gen/guid/fpco/courtcases/miami.html.*

CHAPTER SUMMARY

This chapter covered several laws designed to protect the rights of children and students. The Children's Online Privacy Protection Act (COPPA) protects the information of children. It prohibits Web sites from collecting information about children without a parent's consent. COPPA defines a child as anyone under the age of 13. The Children's Internet Protection Act (CIPA) requires schools and libraries to filter Web site traffic. CIPA ensures that children don't view objectionable material from these publicly funded locations. CIPA defines a child as anyone under the age of 17.

The Family Educational Rights and Privacy Act (FERPA) requires schools to protect educational records. Schools need written consent prior to releasing educational records. The student or parent has the right to review these records. FERPA grants these rights to the parent until the child reaches the age of 18. At that point, the right passes to the student.

KEY CONCEPTS AND TERMS

Parental control   **Technology protection measure**
Proxy server   **(TPM)**

CHAPTER 5 ASSESSMENT

1. Obscenity is easy to define.

A. True
B. False

2. Web operators who attempt to restrict access for children may be accused of violating basic rights. What amendment concerns these rights?

A. First amendment
B. Fifth amendment
C. Ninth amendment
D. Tenth amendment

3. Which law is designed to protect children's personal information?

A. CIPA
B. COPPA
C. FERPA
D. Bill of rights

4. COPPA defines "child" as anyone under the age of _____ .

5. How can a Web site operator verify parental consent to comply with COPPA?

A. Using signed, printed forms
B. Using toll-free numbers
C. Using e-mail
D. A and B only
E. None of the above

6. A Web site is collecting information on children. What must be included on the Web site?

    A. Parental consent forms
    B. Privacy policy
    C. Definition of children
    D. A Contact Us page

7. Libraries and schools that accept E-Rate funds must comply with _____ .

8. Libraries and schools that accept E-Rate funds must implement a _____ to filter objectionable content.

9. CIPA requires certain content to be restricted for minors. How old is a minor?

    A. Anyone under the age of 13
    B. Anyone under the age of 17
    C. Anyone under the age of 18
    D. Anyone under the age of 21

10. CIPA requires a library to be able to disable the TPM for some situations.

    A. True
    B. False

11. What law governs the release of student information?

    A. CIPA
    B. COPPA
    C. FERPA
    D. Department of Education

12. What type of information can a school release about a student without the student's consent?

    A. Directory information
    B. Personally identifiable information (PII)
    C. Name and student ID number
    D. None

13. A parent believes a school is not following FERPA requirements. After trying to resolve it with the school, where can they file a formal complaint?

    A. FERPA compliance office
    B. Family Policy Compliance Office
    C. Federal Communications Commission
    D. Federal Trade Commission

14. What must a school obtain prior to releasing information about a student to a third party?

    A. Verbal consent
    B. Written consent
    C. Signed affidavit
    D. Notarized consent

15. Disciplinary records are a part of educational records.

    A. True
    B. False

ENDNOTES

1. United States Code, Title 15, sec. 6501.
2. Pub. L. No. 106-554, 114 Stat. 2763A-335, codified in scattered sections of U.S. Code.
3. United States Code, Title 20, sec. 1232g.

Security and Privacy of Health Information

HEALTH INFORMATION CAN BE USED in a number of different ways. Doctors and other health care professionals use and share it to provide medical care. Insurance companies and employers share it for insurance coverage and payment. Many people worry that, in addition to valid uses, this type of information could be used improperly. Insurance companies could use it to deny health care coverage. Employers could use it to make employment decisions. Thieves could steal medical information and use it to commit medical identity theft.

Health care providers no longer store health information just in paper files. Many providers use computer systems to create and store electronic health records. When information is stored electronically, data may be combined from a number of different sources. It's possible to create comprehensive medical records that contain a lot of data about a person. The health care industry must take steps to secure these types of records.

This chapter focuses on laws that protect the privacy and security of health information. For the most part this chapter focuses on the unique challenges presented by growing amounts of electronic health information. This chapter also discusses how federal and state laws work together to protect this information.

Chapter 6 Topics

This chapter covers the following topics and concepts:

- What business challenges facing the health care industry are
- Why health care information is sensitive
- What the Health Insurance Portability and Accountability Act is
- What the HITECH Act provisions are
- What the role of state law in protecting medical records is
- What some case studies and examples are

When you complete this chapter, you will be able to:

- Describe the business challenges facing the health care industry
- Explain why health care information is sensitive
- Explain the main parts of the Health Insurance Portability and Accountability Act
- Describe the requirements of the HITECH Act
- Describe the role of state law in protecting the confidentiality of medical records

Business Challenges Facing the Health Care Industry

The health care industry faces many of the same privacy and security challenges as other industries. The difference is the type of data that is used. The health care industry collects consumer financial and personal health information. Providers collect consumer financial information to make sure that consumers pay for medical goods and services. They collect health information to provide these goods and services. Many people consider health information to be very sensitive.

The health care industry often collects and stores this data in electronic form. It's collected from a number of sources. Hospital computer systems contain notes from hospital employees and primary care physicians. Health insurance companies collect and combine patient data from different providers. It's important for organizations to maintain the security of computer systems that hold health data. Patients demand that this data be protected. Unfortunately, health information often is compromised in data breaches. This can cause problems for health care consumers.

 NOTE

In November 2009, Health Net of the Northeast, Inc. reported that 1.5 million patient records were affected when it lost an external hard drive. The hard drive also contained the personal information of physicians who participated in its network. The data was not encrypted.

Health information can be exploited and used improperly. A relatively new crime is medical identity theft. **Medical identity theft** is a specialized type of identity theft. In medical identity theft, thieves steal a person's name and other parts of his or her medical identity. They use this information to get medical services or goods. When the thief gets health care, providers could add treatment notes about the thief on the victim's medical record. A thief can use personal information obtained from health records to steal health insurance information and make a false claim for health care services. Unpaid medical charges could end up on the victim's credit report.

FYI

In November 2007, the Federal Trade Commission estimated that medical identity theft accounted for 3 percent of all identity theft crimes. A February 2010 study by the Ponemon Institute estimated that these victims pay almost $20,000 in costs linked to the theft.

Medical identity thieves are not only computer hackers or members of organized crime rings. Health care providers such as doctors, dentists, and hospital employees also can be identity thieves. In 2003, an employee at a cancer center stole the identity of a center patient. The identity thief was sentenced to 16 months in prison and ordered to pay restitution.

> **NOTE**
> A judge orders defendants to pay restitution. It's paid to victims to compensate them for damages related to a crime.

In 2006, a desk clerk at a Florida clinic stole the health information of over 1,000 patients. The clerk sold the data to another person. That person used the data to submit almost $2.8 million in fraudulent Medicare claims to the U.S. government. After trial, the court sentenced the person who submitted the fraudulent claims to seven years in prison. The court ordered the person to pay $2.5 million in restitution. The court sentenced the desk clerk to three years of probation for her part in the crime. She also had to pay $2.5 million in restitution.

Medical theft is very serious. It can damage a victim's finances with false insurance claims for services. Like regular identity theft, victims must spend time and money resolving payment disputes and credit issues. It also can affect a victim's future medical care. If a thief's medical information becomes a part of the victim's medical record, the victim may not qualify for medical insurance benefits.

Medical identity theft also can harm a person's physical safety. In this crime, health care providers enter diagnoses and treatment notes about the identity thief onto a victim's medical record. If doctors rely on those false notes later, they could give a victim an erroneous diagnosis. If false health information concerns life-threatening conditions, a victim could even be killed by an incorrect course of treatment.

Medical identity theft is a problem because it can be hard to correct false information in a medical record. Since health information is shared electronically for a number of purposes such as treatment and payment, it can be hard to determine all of the places where false information must be corrected.

Why Is Health Care Information So Sensitive?

Most people consider their medical information to be among the most sensitive types of personal information. It's because this information can be full of private details that people don't want to share. People must share these details with health care providers to receive treatment. Providers include this information in medical records.

These records contain information on diagnoses, lab results, and treatment options. They also contain information about chronic conditions or mental health counseling. They also hold private details about a person's lifestyle.

Doctor/patient confidentiality is a long-held tradition. The Hippocratic Oath, which dates back to the 4th century B.C.E., recognizes this belief. The Hippocratic Oath is a pledge that many medical school students recite upon their graduation. The traditional version of the oath states: "Whatever I see or hear in the lives of my patients, whether in connection with my professional practice or not, which ought not to be spoken of outside, I will keep secret, as considering all such things to be private."[1] The statement means that a doctor will keep the patient's health secrets.

Health records often contain intimate details about a person. People fear that they will be embarrassed if their health information isn't kept secret. Some people may even fear for their lives if particularly intimate facts, such as reasons for health counseling, are disclosed. People fear that others may discriminate against them. They fear that insurance companies or employers could reject them because of information in their health records. For instance, a person who has been treated for anxiety or high blood pressure in the past might fear that their application for private life insurance will be denied. People with a genetic predisposition for certain types of diseases might fear that they will be denied health insurance.

The U.S. government recognizes the special sensitivity of some medical records. The Drug Abuse Prevention, Treatment, and Rehabilitation Act of 1980 protects patient information about alcohol or drug abuse. This law applies to any federally assisted alcohol or drug abuse treatment program. It states that these programs may not disclose patient information without consent. There are very few exceptions to this rule. Patient information can be disclosed without consent only in limited situations. A treatment program may disclose patient information in a medical emergency or to report child abuse.

People often feel as if they have little control over where their health information is shared. This is a privacy concern. Providers share health information for treatment purposes. It's also shared with government agencies if payment is made through

---

FYI

The MIB Group, Inc. is an industry group that helps protect against fraud. Members of the group are U.S. and Canadian insurance companies. Group members share information about life, health, and long-term care insurance applicants. They share this information to make sure that applicants don't conceal or hide certain types of health information. Insurance companies need some of this information to determine whether a person is insurable. This helps avoid fraudulent insurance applications and claims. MIB members share this information in a coded format to protect privacy. The MIB is subject to a number of U.S. security and privacy laws. These include the Gramm-Leach-Bliley Act, the Health Insurance Portability and Accountability Act, and Canadian privacy legislation. To learn more about the MIB, visit *http://www.mib.com/html/consumer_guide.html*.

government programs such as Medicaid or Medicare. It's also shared with insurance companies. Insurance companies sometimes ask for health insurance records to make decisions about whether a person is a suitable risk for life or health insurance. These records are shared in court cases, particularly if a plaintiff claims an injury in a lawsuit. They are used to prove that a defendant caused the plaintiff's injury and is liable for that injury.

People can do very little to mitigate an improper disclosure of their health information. They may feel a social stigma if certain facts are shared indiscriminately or exposed in a data breach. There are few ways to correct that stigma. For instance, people recovering from substance abuse might not want other people to know. They may be concerned that society will judge them unfairly for their past substance abuse. They may be concerned about being denied employment or other opportunities. They may worry that they could be prosecuted for using illegal substances. No amount of money or fines assessed against a provider who improperly discloses this information can compensate a patient for such embarrassment or fear. People can't be instructed to "forget" this type of information once they hear it.

The federal government recognizes that health information is highly sensitive. The Health Insurance Portability and Accountability Act is the most well-known U.S. law protecting the security and privacy of health information.

The Health Insurance Portability and Accountability Act

Congress passed the Health Insurance Portability and Accountability Act (HIPAA) in 1996. It created the law to help make health insurance portable. HIPAA is used to fight health insurance fraud and eliminate waste. It also simplifies how health insurance is administered.

Purpose

HIPAA is best known for its rules that protect the privacy and security of personally identifiable health information. These terms are part of the law's "Administrative Simplification" requirements. While these rules are the focus of this chapter, it's important that you know that HIPAA has other provisions as well. They were enacted so that health insurance could be portable. Prior to HIPAA, some workers felt that they were "stuck" in a job because they feared they would lose their health insurance if they changed jobs.

"Job lock" refers to situations where workers feel locked into their jobs. They're afraid they will lose their employer-provided benefits if they leave.

HIPAA protects health care coverage when workers change jobs. It protects both workers and their families. It forbids a new employer's health plan from denying coverage for some reasons. It prohibits employers from discriminating against workers based on certain conditions, such as pregnancy. It also limits employer-provided health plans from using pre-existing conditions as reasons for excluding workers from the plan.

The Difference between COBRA and HIPAA

Often the words COBRA and HIPAA are used when discussing continuing health benefits following job loss or resignation. While both laws work together to help protect employees and their health benefits, they have different functions.

COBRA is the Consolidated Omnibus Budget Reconciliation Act of 1986. COBRA allows some types of employees (and their families) to continue their health coverage when they change or lose a job. COBRA is usually more expensive than health coverage under the employer's plan. It is usually less expensive than individual coverage through a private health insurance company.

COBRA covers employer-provided health plans that have 20 or more employees. It also applies to health coverage offered by federal, state, and local governments. Former employees qualify for COBRA if they leave a job voluntarily. They also are eligible for COBRA if they are terminated for any reason other than gross misconduct. To be eligible for COBRA, a former employee must have been enrolled in an employer's health plan at the time of leaving the job.

When employees leave their job, they must receive a notice from their employer about COBRA eligibility. Former employees who qualify are entitled to health coverage that is the same as they had while they were employed. Under COBRA, former employees must pay their own health insurance premiums. This includes any amount a former employer might have previously paid on the employees' behalf. COBRA benefits usually last for a maximum of 18 months.

COBRA lets employees continue to get health coverage that they had through an employer for a certain period of time. HIPAA, on the other hand, makes sure that an employee is not discriminated against in new health coverage because of health history and pre-existing conditions.

A "pre-existing condition" is a health condition that existed before a person applies for a medical or other insurance policy. Insurance companies have different ways of dealing with these types of conditions. Some may provide only partial coverage for them. Others may not cover them at all. Some companies may only cover the condition after a certain period of time has passed.

HIPAA protects workers in group health plans. Employers that offer health insurance coverage typically offer these types of plans. HIPAA doesn't require that employers offer health coverage. If they do, however, HIPAA applies. Most of HIPAA's rules apply to situations when workers change jobs or move from one group health plan to another. This is the "portability" portion of the law. HIPAA doesn't apply to situations where a worker had no health coverage at all and then gets a job with health care coverage.

HIPAA's pre-existing condition rules are very important. They help prevent job lock. They also promote mobility. HIPAA limits pre-existing condition exclusions in two ways. First, it allows employer-provided health plans to look back only six months for pre-existing conditions. A condition counts as pre-existing only if a worker received treatment for it sometime over the six months prior to enrolling in a health plan. If a worker didn't receive treatment for the condition in those six months, then the condition isn't pre-existing.

The second limitation applies to conditions that are determined to be pre-existing. HIPAA limits the amount of time that employer-provided health plans can force a worker to "sit out" of coverage because of these conditions. Prior to HIPAA, health plans could force workers with pre-existing conditions to do without coverage for those conditions for a very long time. In most instances, HIPAA limits this waiting period to 12 months. That period can be shortened in many situations.

HIPAA also provides some protection against discrimination based upon genetic testing results. HIPAA states that the results of these types of tests alone can't be considered a pre-existing condition. There must be an illness diagnosis to trigger a pre-existing condition. This rule is very important as more people become aware of their genetic histories. Genetic testing is used to determine if a person is more likely to have some illnesses or diseases. This information is very sensitive. Under HIPAA, a woman who has been genetically tested and has the breast cancer gene can't be denied coverage in an employer-provided health plan if she hasn't been diagnosed with breast cancer. Just having the gene can't be considered a pre-existing condition.

Other HIPAA provisions were aimed at improving U.S. health care. These provisions are called the "Administrative Simplification" provisions. They were designed to encourage "the development of a health information system through the establishment of standards and requirements for the electronic transmission of certain health information."[2] As part of these provisions, HIPAA required the Department of Health and Human Services (HHS) to make rules regarding the privacy of individually identifiable health information. HHS was also required to create security standards to protect this information. This chapter addresses the Privacy and Security rules.

FYI

The Genetic Information Nondiscrimination Act of 2008 protects against some types of genetic testing discrimination. It states that health insurance companies can't use genetic testing results to make eligibility decisions about a healthy person. They also can't use that information to determine the cost of premiums. The law also states that employers can't use genetic information when making hiring, firing, or other job decisions. It bars employers or health insurance plans from requiring genetic testing.

Scope

HIPAA's Privacy and Security Rules apply to **covered entities.** The rules tell covered entities how they may use protected health information. Under HIPAA, **protected health information (PHI)** is any individually identifiable information about the health of a person. This includes mental and physical health data. PHI includes past, present, or future information.[3] It also includes information about paying for health care. PHI can be in any form. It's commonly considered to be all information that is put in a person's medical record.

> **NOTE**
>
> PHI includes notes that your doctor puts in your medical record. It also includes any conversations your doctor has with anyone else about your health care. Billing information for health care goods and services provided to you is PHI. Information that your health insurance company has about your health care may also be PHI.

HIPAA requires covered entities to handle PHI in certain ways. The law defines covered entities. They include health plans, health care clearinghouses, and any health care provider that transmits certain types of health information in electronic form.[4]

A "health plan" is an individual or group plan that pays for medical care. It includes group health plans of more than 50 people, a health insurance issuer, and health maintenance organizations (HMOs). The government's Medicare and Medicaid programs are health plans. Military health care programs are also health plans. All health plans must follow HIPAA.

Many workers receive health insurance through their employers. These plans help provide medical care for workers and their families through insurance or reimbursement. These are group plans. The workers and their families are the "group" that is being insured.

A "health care clearinghouse" is an organization that processes health information that is in a nonstandard format. HIPAA requires that some health care electronic transactions be conducted in electronic format. HHS specifies these formats. Some health care providers may not conduct these transactions electronically. If they don't, they might enter into contracts with other organizations called clearinghouses. Clearinghouses handle the electronic transactions on the provider's behalf. They include billing services or repricing companies. They facilitate business operations between health care providers and insurers. A clearinghouse is covered by HIPAA because it conducts electronic health care transactions.

A "health care provider" is a covered entity under HIPAA. It's covered if it provides health care and if it shares certain types of information electronically. This is a two-part test. A health care provider is a person or organization that provides health care services. This includes preventative and diagnostic physical care. It also includes mental health counseling and services. In short, a provider performs all activities traditionally associated with health care. Providers include doctors and clinics, dental practices, and pharmacies.

Even if an entity provides health care, it may not be a covered entity. A health care provider is only a covered entity under HIPAA if it shares certain types of information electronically. HHS calls the information that is shared a "standard transaction." A standard transaction is an electronic exchange of information for health care activities that falls within defined categories. If a health care provider electronically shares information that falls within a category, then it must share it in a particular way.

FYI

The Department of Health and Human Services provides tools to help entities determine whether they are covered by HIPAA. Those tools are available at *http://www.hhs.gov/ocr/privacy/hipaa/understanding/coveredentities/index.html*.

HHS has defined some standard transactions. It also determines the format requirements for each standard. These formats provide efficiency in processing health care data. Some HHS standard transactions include information related to:

- Billing and claims payment
- Health plan eligibility
- Enrollment and disenrollment in a health plan
- Health plan premium payments

NOTE

Covered entities must make sure that their business associates protect PHI. They do this by entering into a "business associate's agreement." The agreement states the requirements that the associate agrees to follow to protect PHI. A business associate's agreement is a contract.

HIPAA also applies to the **business associates** of covered entities. A business associate is an organization that performs a health care activity for a covered entity. Covered entities may outsource some health care functions to other organizations. If these functions include using PHI, then they are business associate functions. Common business associate functions include claims and billing processing. They also can include quality assurance review if it involves the use of PHI. Legal services can even be business associate activities when those services require the use of PHI.

When outsourced functions involve the use of PHI, a covered entity must make sure that the business associate protects it. Prior to 2010, covered entities entered into contracts with their associates to do this. The contracts required the business associates to follow the HIPAA Privacy and Security Rules. The HHS could hold a covered entity responsible for its business associates' failure to protect PHI. HHS could not pursue the business associate directly. A covered entity would have to sue a business associate to recover damages.

This changed when Congress passed the Health Information Technology for Economic and Clinical Health Act (HITECH) of 2009. Under the HITECH Act, business associates must specifically follow the HIPAA Security Rule. HHS may now directly require business associates to comply with HIPAA. It can impose penalties on noncompliant business associates. Business associates are now held to the same standard as covered entities. The HITECH Act, and the changes that it made to HIPAA, are discussed in this chapter.

Covered entities that use PHI must follow the HIPAA Privacy and Security Rules. The Privacy Rule dictates how covered entities must protect the privacy of PHI. The Security Rule states how they must protect the confidentiality, integrity, and availability of electronic PHI.

Main Requirements of the Privacy Rule

HHS published the final Privacy Rule in December 2000. It was modified in August 2002. Compliance with the Privacy Rule was required in April 2003. The Privacy Rule is the first time the U.S. government has specified federal privacy protections for PHI. The HHS said that the Privacy Rule had three main purposes:

- To allow consumers to control the use of their health information. This includes providing consumers with a way to access their health information.
- To improve health care in the U.S. by restoring consumer trust in the health care system
- To create a national framework for health privacy protection.[5]

Under the Privacy Rule, covered entities may not use or disclose people's PHI without their permission. The Rule specifies situations where use or disclosure is allowed. The term **use** refers to how a covered entity shares or handles PHI within its organization. Use refers to how employees of a covered entity might handle PHI to provide health care. **Disclosure** refers to how a covered entity shares PHI with other organizations that may not be affiliated with it. A person must specifically consent to a use or disclosure that isn't permitted by the Privacy Rule.

The Rule also requires covered entities to put safeguards in place to protect a person's PHI. Covered entities must also limit how their employees use and access PHI. They also must create training programs for their employees on how to protect PHI.

Required Disclosures

Under the Privacy Rule, there are only two situations where a covered entity must disclose PHI. The first is when a person requests access to his or her PHI. Under the Privacy Rule, people have the right to access, review, and get a copy of their PHI. This right to access PHI extends to records held by a covered entity that are used to make decisions about that person. It includes PHI held in medical records, billing information, and insurance claim information.

The Privacy Rule recognizes that people may not be able to request their own PHI for some reason. The rule allows people who are legally authorized to act for another to request PHI on that person's behalf. For instance, parents can request the PHI of their minor children. A "minor" child is one who is under the age of legal adulthood. The age of legal adulthood is determined on a state-by-state basis. For most situations in the U.S., a minor is a person under the age of 18.

> **NOTE**
>
> A covered entity may not charge people requesting access to their PHI a handling and storage retrieval fee. The Privacy Rule specifically doesn't allow these fees.

Covered entities must respond to a person's request to access PHI within a specific period. The rule requires covered entities to respond in 30 days. This period can be extended to another 30 days if the PHI that a person is requesting is stored in an off-site location. Additional extensions of time are allowed in some instances. A covered entity may charge a reasonable fee for copying the records and sending them to the requestor.

There are some types of PHI that a covered entity doesn't have to provide. They don't have to provide it even if a person specifically requests it. If a covered entity chooses to deny access to PHI, then it must specify in writing why it's denying access. It should explain the reason for the denial and how to appeal the denial.

Some types of PHI access denials are not appealable. People can't challenge a covered entity's decision to deny access to PHI in some of the following situations:

- Information that is compiled in anticipation of a lawsuit
- Psychotherapy notes
- Any information release that would be denied under the Privacy Act of 1974
- Any information that prisons compile on inmates. The covered entity must conduct a risk assessment about the risks of providing access prior to issuing a denial.

A covered entity may choose to deny a person access to his or her PHI. It may do this if it believes that the PHI requested is reasonably likely to endanger the life or physical safety of the person requesting the PHI. They may also deny access if they believe that the access could cause substantial harm to another person. A person may appeal this decision. A licensed health care professional who didn't participate in the original decision to deny access will review the appeal.

The second type of situation where a covered entity must disclose PHI is when HHS is investigating the covered entity. HHS investigates covered entities to make sure that they are following the Privacy Rule. A person may file a complaint with HHS if they believe that a covered entity isn't properly handling PHI. HHS is allowed to access PHI if it's necessary to review compliance with the Privacy Rule.

FYI

HHS provides a Health Information Privacy Complaint for consumer use. The complaint is available at *http://www.hhs.gov/ocr/privacy/hipaa/complaints/hipcomplaint.pdf.*

Permitted Uses and Disclosures

A covered entity is permitted to use and disclose a person's PHI, without written consent, in a number of situations. A use or disclosure that doesn't fall within the situations described by the rule isn't permitted unless a person specifically allows it.[6] HHS allows the following uses and disclosures of PHI without consent:

- Made to a person about his or her own PHI
- Made for treatment, payment, and health care operations
- Made after giving a person an opportunity to opt out of the use
- Made for public health and safety activities
- Limited data sets of PHI used or disclosed for specified activities

A covered entity may always disclose a person's PHI to him or her without written consent. This makes sense because health care providers must communicate with people about their own care. It would not facilitate efficient health care if people had to specifically authorize covered entities to discuss their health care with them. Providing a person's PHI to them when they ask for it also is a required disclosure under the Privacy Rule.

Treatment, Payment, and Health Care Operations.   A covered entity may use a person's PHI for its own treatment, payment, or health care operations.[7] These are the most common covered entity activities. The Privacy Rule defines each of these terms. A covered entity is engaging in "treatment activities" when it's giving health care or services to a person. These activities include managing a patient's health care among several providers. They also include referring a patient to another provider. A covered entity also can disclose PHI for the treatment activities of another covered entity. For example, a dentist can send a copy of a patient's dental records to an orthodontist who needs that information to treat the patient.

"Payment activities" are actions to get payment for health care goods and services. A covered entity may disclose PHI without consent for these activities. They include billing and collection functions. They also include submitting claims for services to health insurance companies. Covered entities also may disclose PHI to another covered entity for the payment activities of the other entity. For instance, a doctor can share a person's health insurance coverage with a laboratory that it uses to process patient blood work. The lab needs the information in order to bill the patient for the services that it provides to the doctor.

> **NOTE**
> Covered entities may disclose PHI to other health care providers for treatment and payment purposes. These providers don't have to be covered by the Privacy Rule.

"Health care operations" are actions that support the covered entity's business. A covered entity may use a person's PHI for these activities without consent. These activities are the administrative and financial functions needed to run the business. They include review processes to make sure that a covered entity is compliant with the laws that it must follow. Health care operations include quality assessment and improvement actions. A covered entity may not usually share any PHI used for these purposes with another covered entity. The only time it's allowed is when both entities have a relationship with the person.

Covered entities may choose to get a person's consent to use PHI for treatment, payment, and health care operations. It isn't required under the Privacy Rule. Even when a covered entity gets consent to share PHI for these purposes, it should always make sure that it uses and discloses PHI in a way that is consistent with its notice of privacy practices. These notices are discussed in this chapter.

Uses and Disclosures Made After an Opportunity to Opt Out.   There are some situations where a covered entity may use or disclose a person's PHI only after they've had an opportunity to opt out of the use or disclosure.[8] An opt-out is a more informal type of consent. It applies only in limited situations. A written consent isn't needed so long as a person was advised of the right to opt out. These situations include publishing a patient's name and condition in a facility directory, and sharing PHI with a person's family and friends.

Some covered entities, like hospitals, maintain a directory of patient information. Nursing homes do this too. They use this directory to list the person's name, facility room number, and general condition. The directory contains a limited amount of PHI. A common example of a facility directory is a list of people who are patients at a hospital. Nursing homes often make a similar list. The covered entity must ask patients if they want their data included in the directory. Many covered entities ask patients this question when they enter the facility for treatment. It's part of a pre-admission checklist.

Covered entities also may disclose a person's PHI to their family, friends, and caregivers without written consent. The person must be given an opportunity to opt out of the disclosure. So long as a person doesn't object, a covered entity can share PHI with friends, family, and caregivers. Covered entities can share information for treatment or payment purposes.

A person may place limits on these types of disclosures. They may specify that some, but not all, family members can receive PHI from a covered entity. For instance, a doctor may not discuss a patient's health information with his or her mother if the patient says not to.

A covered entity must use professional judgment in sharing PHI in this manner if a patient isn't present or unable to object to a disclosure. A patient can't object to a disclosure if unconscious. In these cases, the covered entity must decide that sharing the PHI is in the patient's best interest. For instance, an emergency room doctor may share information about a person's condition with his or her family and friends if the person is in surgery.

Just because a covered entity is allowed to share PHI under the rule doesn't mean that it has to do so. It isn't required to share PHI if the patient isn't present or unable to object to the disclosure. It can choose not to disclose any PHI until someone can talk to the patient.

FYI

HHS has created guidance for patients to help them understand when health care providers may share their PHI. That guidance is available at *http://www.hhs.gov/ocr/privacy/hipaa/ understanding/consumers/consumer_ffg.pdf.*

Made for Public Health and Safety Activities.   HHS recognized that there are some situations where a covered entity should disclose a person's PHI. Sometimes it's necessary for the good of society.[9] A covered entity doesn't need a person's consent to disclose PHI in these situations. Generally, these situations involve public safety and welfare. HHS felt that requiring a person's consent to disclose PHI in these situations could negatively affect society.

A covered entity may disclose a person's PHI without consent to report births, deaths, and other vital statistics. It must report these events to public health authorities. It may also disclose PHI to these authorities to prevent or control disease, injury, or disability. These types of disclosures of PHI don't require consent. For instance, New York health care providers must report certain diseases to their local health departments. They must report diseases that are highly contagious. They also must immediately report diseases that might indicate bioterrorism. Diseases that must be reported immediately include smallpox, anthrax, botulism, and typhoid. These diseases are serious public health threats.

 NOTE

Public health is the branch of medicine that is concerned with the health of a community of people. A public health authority is a state or federal agency that is responsible for public health matters. A state or local health department is a public health authority. The federal Centers for Disease Control and Prevention (CDC) is a public health authority.

A covered entity may disclose PHI about victims of child abuse or neglect without consent. The covered entity may disclose the PHI only to government agencies that have the legal authority to receive these reports. Child welfare and social services agencies are allowed by state law to receive reports about child abuse and neglect. Law enforcement agencies also are allowed to receive these types of reports.

All U.S. states have laws that require health care providers to report evidence of child abuse and neglect. Other professionals that work with children, such as teachers, have similar requirements. They must report information either to state social services agencies or to local law enforcement. States make these laws because it's important to the public welfare to protect children.

The Privacy Rule contains slightly different provisions for adult victims of abuse, neglect, or domestic violence. A covered entity may disclose PHI about adult victims of these crimes if the disclosure is required by law and if the patient allows it. They may still disclose PHI if a patient doesn't allow the disclosure, or can't agree to the disclosure. In that case, the covered entity must use professional judgment to determine that the disclosure is necessary. A disclosure is necessary if it must be made to prevent serious harm to the person.

A covered entity must promptly notify a person or his or her personal representative if it makes a disclosure of PHI in these cases. There are some exceptions to this general rule. The covered entity doesn't have to notify adult victims if it believes that informing them would place them at risk of harm. It also doesn't have to notify the individual's personal representative if it believes that the representative is responsible for the victim's injuries.

FYI

Attorneys are allowed to issue subpoenas for information as part of lawsuits. These are often issued as part of the discovery process. **Discovery** is the legal process used to gather evidence in a lawsuit. A discovery request is a request for information from one party in a lawsuit to the other party. These requests also can be made to witnesses. Subpoenas issued by attorneys as part of the discovery process don't require court approval. When a subpoena issued as part of discovery requests PHI, the individual involved must be notified.

A covered entity may use or disclose PHI to the extent that it's required by law. It may disclose PHI in response to a court order or court-ordered warrant. It may also disclose PHI in response to a subpoena issued by a grand jury. If the covered entity is providing PHI in response to a discovery request generated as part of a lawsuit, then it must notify the person who is the subject of the PHI. That person must have a chance to object to the discovery request.

Covered entities may also disclose PHI without consent for some law enforcement activities. They may provide some types of PHI to help identify or locate a suspect, witness, or missing person. Information that a covered entity can provide in these situations is limited to identifying information. This includes name and address. It also includes distinguishing physical characteristics that could be used to identify the person that the police are looking for.

Covered entities may also provide PHI without consent if it's requested by law enforcement and it's about a victim of crime. They can also disclose PHI as needed to identify or apprehend a violent criminal. Covered entities may alert law enforcement about a person's death if they believe that the death was caused by criminal activity. They also may disclose PHI to law enforcement or government officials if they believe there's a serious threat to health or safety.

Limited Data Sets Used or Disclosed for Specified Activities.   A "limited data set" is PHI that doesn't contain any data that identifies a person. It is PHI that is stripped of certain identifiers. These identifiers must be redacted from the PHI. Information is redacted when it is removed or obscured in a document before sharing that document with other individuals or groups.

A covered entity may share limited data sets for research, health care operations, and public health activities. It doesn't need a person's permission to share them. Identifiers that must be removed from PHI in order to create a limited data set are:[10]

- Name
- Street address (except that some geographical information may remain if certain conditions are met)
- Telephone and fax numbers
- E-mail addresses
- Social Security numbers

- Medical record numbers
- Health plan beneficiary numbers
- Account numbers
- Certificate/license numbers
- Vehicle identifiers and serial numbers, including license plate numbers
- Device identifiers and serial numbers
- Web Universal Resource Locators (URLs)
- Internet Protocol (IP) address numbers
- Biometric identifiers, including finger and voice prints
- Full face photographic images and any similar images
- Any other unique identifying number, characteristic, or code that identifies a person or their PHI

A limited data set is still PHI. A covered entity must enter into a data use agreement with the organization that receives it. The data use agreement specifies how the PHI in the limited data set will be protected.

Uses and Disclosures that Require Authorization.   A covered entity must get people's written consent in order to use or disclose their PHI in ways that are not expressly allowed under the Privacy Rule.[11] Under the Rule, written consent is called an **authorization**. These are very specific documents that allow PHI to be shared. A written authorization is required for many purposes. They are required to disclose psychotherapy notes and to use PHI in marketing materials.

A covered entity must get an authorization before it discloses PHI if a permitted use or disclosure doesn't apply. This comes into play in many ways. A covered entity needs an authorization to share a person's PHI with an employer for employment purposes. Even if a person asks the covered entity to provide this information to an employer, he or she must sign an authorization. A parent will need to sign an authorization on behalf of his or her minor child to have the covered entity disclose PHI to the child's school. This might be required to allow children to participate in some school activities like sporting events.

FYI

HIPAA uses the term authorization to distinguish between consent to use or disclose PHI and other types of consent that are used in the health care industry. For example, "informed consent" is a basic rule in health care. This is written consent from a patient to undergo a medical treatment. These types of consent explain the risks and benefits of treatment. When patients sign these informed consent documents, they are agreeing to undergo the treatments specified. These forms are very different from a Privacy Rule authorization that allows PHI to be shared. When people must consent to sharing their PHI, they show their consent by signing an authorization. This eliminates confusion among different types of documents used in the health care industry.

The Privacy Rule forbids a covered entity from requiring a person to sign an authorization in order to receive health care treatment. They can't condition benefit eligibility on signing an authorization. This is so that covered entities can't force people to sign authorizations under pressure by withholding needed care.

The Privacy Rule requires authorizations to contain specific terms. It also states situations in which an authorization is defective. A defective authorization isn't valid. Authorizations are defective if the expiration date stated in the authorization has passed. They're also invalid if they aren't filled out completely. They're also invalid if a person has revoked them.

An authorization must be in plain language. This means that it should not contain any legal terms or other terms that are hard for a person to understand. A valid authorization must contain the following elements:[12]

- A specific and meaningful description of the PHI that will be used or disclosed
- Identification of the people who are allowed to make the requested use or disclosure
- Identification of the people who will receive the use or disclosure
- A clear description of the reason for the requested use or disclosure
- The date that the authorization will expire
- The signature of the person and the date

The Privacy Rule requires that covered entities provide people with a copy of any authorizations that they sign.

Minimum Necessary Rule

A covered entity is permitted to use and disclose some types of PHI without an authorization. This doesn't mean that it should always disclose the entire allowable PHI. Covered entities must follow the **minimum necessary rule**.[13] They may disclose only the amount of PHI absolutely necessary. The amount disclosed must be able to satisfy the reason why the information is being used or disclosed, but no more.

A covered entity must use professional judgment and make reasonable efforts to limit its use or disclosure of PHI. For instance, a health care provider shouldn't disclose a person's entire medical record if only a portion of it is responsive to a request.

> **NOTE**
>
> The Privacy Rule minimum necessary rule is similar to the general information security principle of need to know. Only the information needed to carry out a function or activity should be disclosed.

There are some exceptions to this rule. Uses or disclosures of PHI made by a health care provider for treatment purposes are not subject to the minimum necessary rule. It also doesn't apply to disclosures made to people about their own PHI. The rule also doesn't apply to uses or disclosures made when a person specifically authorizes the use or disclosure. It also doesn't apply to uses or disclosures required by law or made to HHS for its complaint investigation function.

Other Individual Rights under the Privacy Rule

The Privacy Rule gives people additional rights regarding their PHI. These rights help people make sure that their PHI is used properly.

Amendments of PHI.   A person has the right to ask that a covered entity amend the person's PHI.[14] A covered entity doesn't have to correct data in the record. Instead, it can include the amendment in the record. That way the integrity of the record is maintained. If a covered entity amends the PHI, then it must inform others about the amendment. Other entities that might rely on the unamended PHI to the person's detriment must be notified of the amendment. The covered entity also must notify any other person or organization that the individual has specified as needing the amended PHI.

A covered entity must respond to a request to amend PHI within 60 days. That time can be extended for 30 days if the covered entity notifies the requestor in writing. A covered entity may choose not to amend PHI for some reason. A covered entity doesn't have to amend PHI if it didn't create the PHI that is in question. It also doesn't have to amend PHI if it determines that the PHI in the record is accurate and complete.

If an entity chooses to deny a request to amend PHI, then it must issue a written denial notice to the person who requested the amendment. The denial notice must contain the basis for the denial. It also must contain a statement of the person's right to disagree with the denial. A person may submit a statement of disagreement to the covered entity. The covered entity may prepare a rebuttal to the person's statement of disagreement. If a request for amendment is denied, the covered entity must include the following in the person's record:

- Identification of the PHI that is under dispute
- A copy of the person's request to amend the PHI
- A copy of the covered entity's denial of the request
- A copy of the person's statement of disagreement
- A copy of the covered entity's rebuttal statement

All of this information must be included in future uses or disclosures of the PHI that is under dispute.

Accounting of Disclosures.   Covered entities must keep records of how they disclose a person's PHI. Under the Privacy Rule, a person has the right to receive an accounting of how the covered entity has used or disclosed the person's PHI.[15] People have the right to get an accounting of disclosures of PHI made in the six years prior to the date of their request. They also can request accountings for shorter periods.

A covered entity doesn't have to account for every PHI disclosure that it makes. The Privacy Rule states that some kinds of disclosures don't have to be included in an accounting. Any disclosure not specifically excluded must be included and tracked. Table 6-1 compares different types of disclosures.

TABLE 6-1 Different types of disclosures.	
DISCLOSURES THAT ARE NOT TRACKED	**DISCLOSURES THAT MUST BE TRACKED**
Disclosures made to carry out treatment, payment, and health care activities	Disclosures to HHS for its compliance functions
Disclosures to individuals	Disclosures required by law
Disclosures made after an authorization is received	Disclosures required for public health activities
Incidental disclosures	Disclosures made to report abuse
Disclosures where the person had the opportunity to opt out	Disclosures for judicial and administrative proceedings (in response to subpoenas and court orders)
Disclosures for national security or intelligence purposes	Disclosures for law enforcement purposes
Disclosures to correctional institutions or to law enforcement officials having custody of an inmate	Disclosures for research purposes (unless authorized or made via a limited data set)
Disclosures that are part of a limited data set	Disclosures to the public health agencies
Disclosures made more than six years before the date of the person's request for an accounting	Disclosures to avert a threat of serious injury
	Disclosures made by mistake (inadvertent disclosures)
	Any other disclosures not specifically excluded by the Privacy Rule

A covered entity must provide a person a first accounting in a 12-month period at no charge. If he or she requests more than one accounting in that period, then the covered entity can charge a reasonable fee for each subsequent request. The covered entity must inform the person that it intends to charge a fee for an extra accounting. It must give the person a chance to withdraw or change the request in order to avoid the fee.

A covered entity must respond to a request for an accounting in writing. It must respond within 60 days. This period can be extended 30 days with notice to the person who has requested the accounting. When it responds, the covered entity must include the following information:

- Date of disclosure
- Name of recipient
- Description of the PHI disclosed
- Reason for the disclosure, or a copy of the request for the disclosure

The HITECH Act made changes to the accounting of disclosures requirement for electronic PHI. These changes are discussed later in this chapter.

Incidental and Inadvertent Disclosures

The difference between incidental and inadvertent disclosures of PHI is important to understand. Even though they sound similar, they are very different.

"Incidental disclosures" are permitted disclosures under the Privacy Rule. Covered entities don't have to track these types of disclosures. An incidental disclosure can result from any use or disclosure that is allowed under the Privacy Rule. They are allowed so long as a covered entity implements safeguards to limit the amount of PHI exposed though an incidental disclosure.

Examples of incidental disclosures include:

- A customer at a pharmacy hears the pharmacist quietly discussing a medication with another customer. This is an incidental disclosure because it's made as a result of an activity that is allowed under the Privacy Rule. The permitted activity is the covered entity's treatment activities.
- A patient going to a hospital to pay a bill briefly views another patient's payment information on the billing clerk's computer monitor. The first patient can see this information only briefly before the clerk accesses the patient's own record. This is an incidental disclosure because it's a result of the covered entity's permitted payment activities.

Covered entities must take steps to limit incidental disclosures. This includes speaking quietly when discussing conditions with patients and their families. It also includes shielding monitors from view as much as possible.

Inadvertent disclosures are different. "Inadvertent disclosures" are not permitted under the Privacy Rule. Covered entities must track inadvertent disclosures. They also must provide an accounting of these types of disclosures if a person requests it. These disclosures happen by mistake. An example would be if a covered entity discloses PHI without a valid authorization when one was needed. Under the HITECH Act, some types of inadvertent disclosures could even be considered an impermissible data breach that requires further action.

Privacy Notices

Covered entities must inform people about their privacy practices.[16] The Privacy Rule requires covered entities to let people know how they use and disclose their PHI. It does this in a privacy policy. A covered entity must use and disclose PHI only in the ways described by their privacy policy.

A covered entity must use plain language to draft its notice. An average person must be able to understand the notice. The Privacy Rule requires the notice to include specific parts:

- A title that reads: "THIS NOTICE DESCRIBES HOW MEDICAL INFORMATION ABOUT YOU MAY BE USED AND DISCLOSED AND HOW YOU CAN GET ACCESS TO THIS INFORMATION. PLEASE REVIEW IT CAREFULLY." The covered entity must display this header in prominent type.

- A description of how the covered entity may use and disclose a person's PHI. It should include examples of disclosures that the entity makes for treatment, payment, and health care operations.

- A description of the person's rights with respect to his or her PHI. This section should also include information on how a person can exercise these rights. The covered entity must include information about its complaint processes. It must also include information about the person's right to complain to HHS.

- A statement that the covered entity is required by law to maintain the privacy of PHI. This statement must include the entity's legal duties with respect to PHI.

- The contact information of a person the individual can contact to ask additional questions about the covered entity's privacy notice.

> **NOTE**
>
> Many of the elements that are required in the Notice of Privacy Practices contain portions of the fair information practices principles. These principles are covered in Chapter 2.

> **NOTE**
>
> A "material change" is a change in an organization's operating practices that's significant. Material changes can affect how people understand their rights or interact with an organization.

A covered entity's privacy policy must contain an effective date. The covered entity must revise and redistribute its notice any time it makes a material change to the notice. Covered entities must make the notice available to anyone who asks for it. It also must make the notice available on any Web site that it maintains.

Different types of covered entities have additional rules to follow when giving their privacy notices to individuals. Health plans must distribute their privacy notices to people when they enroll in the health plan. They also must make sure that plan participants receive a copy of the notice at least once every three years.

In some cases, the Privacy Rule doesn't require health care clearinghouses to develop a notice of privacy practices. They are not required to develop a notice if the only PHI that they create or receive is as a business associate of another covered entity.

Health care providers have additional rules to follow for distributing their notices to individuals. Providers must give the notice to a person no later than when they first provide services to that person. They also must make a good-faith effort to get the person's written acknowledgement of receipt of the notice. A provider must document a person's receipt of the notice if it can't gain a receipt from the person.

In emergencies, the health care provider must provide its notice of privacy practices to a patient as soon as it's reasonable. A health care provider must also post its notice in a clear and prominent location where patients can read the notice. Covered entities must retain copies of privacy notices that they distribute. They must also retain written acknowledgments.

Administrative Requirements

A covered entity has administrative duties under the Privacy Rule.[17] It must designate a privacy official. This official is responsible for developing the covered entity's privacy policies and procedures. HHS allows a covered entity to scope its privacy policies and programs to its size and structure. This allows covered entities some discretion when they create their programs. Covered entities that are large with complex structures must develop policies appropriate for that structure. Smaller entities are not held to the same standard. They must develop their own policies.

The covered entity must also designate a person to receive consumer privacy complaints. This person handles complaints about the entity's own privacy policies. They also handle consumer complaints about the Privacy Rule. This person also answers questions about the entity's privacy notice. The privacy official often serves as this contact person.

Covered entities must train their employees on the Privacy Rule and its privacy policies and procedures. It must train all employees—even part-time employees, volunteers, and interns. A covered entity also must have a discipline policy for workers who violate the Privacy Rule. This is called a sanctions policy.

Main Requirements of the Security Rule

HHS published the Security Rule in February 2003. It's an information security rule. It requires covered entities to use security safeguards. These safeguards must protect the confidentiality, integrity, and availability of **electronic protected health information (EPHI)**. EPHI is patient health information that is computer based. Covered entities were required to comply with the Rule by April 20, 2005.

Like the Privacy Rule, the Security Rule was the first time the U.S. government stated federal protections for EPHI. Under the Rule, covered entities must protect all EPHI that they create, receive, maintain, or transmit.[18] They must protect it from reasonably anticipated threats. They also must guard against uses or disclosures of EPHI that aren't allowed by the Privacy Rule.

> **NOTE**
>
> The Security Rule contains document retention requirements. Covered entities must maintain their Security Rule documentation for six years after it's created. They also must maintain old documents for six years after they're retired. The six-year time limit starts to run on whichever date (creation or retirement) is later.

Covered entities must create policies and procedures to comply with the Security Rule.[19] They must review their documents on a regular basis and update them as needed. They must provide training to their employees. They also must make security program documents available to employees in printed manuals or on Web sites. A covered entity also must have a sanctions policy to discipline workers who violate the Security Rule.

The Security Rule allows covered entities flexibility in creating their overall security program. The Rule doesn't require covered entities to use specific types of technology. In creating their program, covered entities may think about:

- The size and complexity of the entity
- Its technical infrastructure, hardware, and software security resources
- The costs of security measures
- The potential risks to EPHI[20]

Safeguards and Implementation Specifications

The Security Rule requires covered entities to use information security principles to protect EPHI. They must use administrative, physical, and technical safeguards. The Rule contains instructions on each safeguard. It also includes standards that must be implemented for each safeguard. These standards include a list of items that a covered entity must put into practice. These lists are called "implementation specifications."

There are some implementation specifications that a covered entity must implement. These are called "required" specifications. Other specifications are "addressable." Covered entities have more discretion when considering addressable specifications. For these specifications, it must assess whether that control is reasonable and appropriate in its environment.[21] If it is, then the covered entity must use it.

If an addressable specification isn't reasonable and appropriate, the covered entity doesn't have to use it. However, it must document why the specification was not appropriate. It also must implement an equivalent control. The equivalent control should accomplish the goal of the addressable specification.

Administrative Safeguards.   Half of the safeguards required by the Security Rule are administrative in nature. These safeguards are actions, policies, and procedures that a covered entity must implement in order to follow the Security Rule. There are nine different administrative requirements. A covered entity must implement the following standards:

- Security management process
- Assigned security responsibility
- Workforce security
- Information access management

- Security awareness and training
- Security incident procedures
- Contingency plan
- Evaluation
- Business associate contracts

The "security management process" standard guides a covered entity in creating its security program. It has four required implementation specifications. To comply with this standard, a covered entity must conduct a risk analysis and engage in risk management. It must also create a sanction policy and review information system activity.

 NOTE

Risk analysis and risk management are standard information security concepts. They are discussed in Part 3 of this book.

Risk analysis is used to assess the vulnerabilities, threats, and risks that could harm EPHI. Risk management is the process of implementing controls to reduce risk. Information system activity review is the process of reviewing system logs and records. Covered entities must review them to make sure that EPHI is being used properly.

Covered entities are required to name an official responsible for Security Rule compliance. The "assigned security responsibility" standard requires this. This standard is similar to the Privacy Rule provision that requires covered entities to designate a privacy official. The privacy and security officials don't have to be the same person.

Under the "workforce security" standard, covered entities must implement need-to-know policies for EPHI access. They must make sure that all employees have appropriate access to EPHI. They also must ensure that employees without proper authority aren't able to access EPHI. There are three addressable specifications in this standard. To the extent that it's appropriate for its operations, the covered entity must implement authorization and supervision procedures. They must also implement workforce clearance and termination procedures.

Each of these specifications helps to ensure proper access to EPHI. The authorization and supervision procedures are used to make sure that an individual user has the authority to use EPHI in certain ways. Under the workforce clearance specification, a covered entity must create procedures to confirm that an employee's access to EPHI is correct. The termination procedures specification requires covered components to terminate employee access to EPHI when an employee leaves a covered entity.

The "information access management" standard is closely related to the workforce security standard. It requires covered entities to create policies to access EPHI. These policies must be consistent with the Privacy Rule. The standard has one required and two addressable implementation specifications.

The "security awareness and training" standard requires covered entities to create training and awareness programs. These programs must be for all members of its workforce. This standard has four addressable specifications. Where appropriate, the covered entity must implement password management procedures. It must also create log-in monitoring procedures. Other procedures must protect against malicious software. The entity also should provide security updates to its workforce.

▷ **NOTE**

Under the Security Rule, a security incident is unauthorized access or use of information. It can be successful unauthorized access or just attempted unauthorized access. Incidents also include interference with the operation of information systems.[22]

▷ **NOTE**

Incident response, business continuity, and disaster recovery plans are discussed in Chapter 14.

Under the "security incident procedures" standard, covered entities must implement policies to respond to security incidents. This standard has one required implementation specification. The covered entity must identify security incidents and respond to them. It also must attempt to mitigate the harm caused by security incidents. It also must document security incidents and their outcomes.

The "contingency plan" standard requires covered entities to develop policies to recover access to EPHI in the event of an outage or disaster. This standard contains three required and two addressable specifications. It requires covered entities to prepare data backup, disaster recovery, and emergency operation plans. Together the plans state how an organization backs up and restores its EPHI. The emergency operations plan requires covered entities to protect EPHI when it's operating in emergency mode. Where reasonable, the covered entity must also create procedures to test and review its contingency plans.

The "evaluation" standard requires the covered entity to review its security safeguards program. It must regularly review changes to its information systems and practices. It must make sure that its safeguards still protect EPHI. The covered entity can perform this evaluation on its own. It also can hire external organizations to conduct this review.

The "business associate contracts" standard requires covered entities make sure that their business associates protect EPHI. Covered entities must enter into written contracts with any organizations that use EPHI on their behalf. These are called business associates agreements. Business associates agreements are required under both the Privacy and Security Rules. A covered entity must identify all of its business associates. It also must make sure that it has contracts will all of them.

Table 6-2 summarizes the administrative safeguards required by the Security Rule. It also includes a summary of required and addressable implementation specifications.

▷ **TIP**

Remember that under the Security Rule, a covered entity must apply an addressable implementation specification if it's reasonable. It must also be appropriate. A covered entity must document why it doesn't implement one of these types of specifications. It must then implement an equivalent control if possible.

Physical Safeguards.   Physical safeguards are controls put in place to protect a covered entity's physical resources. These measures protect information systems, equipment, and buildings from environmental threats. The Security Rule contains four physical security standards. A covered entity must put into practice the following standards:

- Facility access controls
- Workstation use
- Workstation security
- Device and media controls

TABLE 6-2 Administrative safeguards.		
SAFEGUARD	**REQUIRED SPECIFICATIONS**	**ADDRESSABLE SPECIFICATIONS**
Security Management Process	Risk Analysis Risk Management Sanction Policy Information System Activity Review	
Assigned Security Responsibility	Required	
Workforce Security		Authorization and/or Supervision Workforce Clearance Procedure Termination Procedures
Information Access Management	Isolating Health Care Clearinghouse Function	Access Authorization Access Establishment and Modification
Security Awareness and Training		Security Reminders Protection from Malicious Software Log-in Monitoring Password Management
Security Incident Procedures	Response and Reporting	
Contingency Plan	Data Backup Plan Disaster Recovery Plan Emergency Mode Operation Plan	Testing and Revision Procedure Applications and Data Criticality Analysis
Evaluation	Required	
Business Associate Contracts and Other Arrangements	Written Contracts or Other Arrangements	

Under the "facility access controls" standard, covered entities must implement policies that limit physical access to their computer systems. They must limit access to the buildings where these systems are located. Only authorized individuals should be allowed to access these systems and facilities. This standard has four addressable implementation specifications.

Where appropriate, the covered entity must create access contingency plans. These plans allow access to facilities and systems during emergencies. A covered entity also must create a facility security plan. This plan is designed to protect systems and buildings from unauthorized access, tampering, and theft. When it seems appropriate, covered entities must create access control and validation procedures. They should include measures to manage visitor access. They also should document repairs and modifications to a facility.

The Security Rule contains two standards related to workstation security. Both standards are required. Neither standard has implementation specifications. In the "workstation use" standard, a covered entity must make sure that employees use workstations properly. This means that it should review the applications used on workstations. It must review whether those applications introduce security risks that could harm EPHI. For example, a covered entity might decide that it's too risky to allow workstations used to access EPHI to connect to the Internet. The covered entity must look at workstation use for both on-site and off-site locations.

> **NOTE**
>
> Under the Security Rule, a workstation is a computing device and any electronic media used by or around the device. Examples include a laptop or desktop computer or any similar device.[23]

According to the "workstation security standard" covered entities must implement physical safeguards for workstations that access EPHI. The covered entity must make sure that access to the workstation is restricted to authorized users. A covered entity might protect workstations by keeping them in areas that only employees are allowed to access.

Under the "device and media controls" standard, a covered entity must track information systems containing EPHI. They must track these systems in and out of a facility. They also must track system movement within a facility. This standard has two required and two addressable implementation specifications.

Under this standard, a covered entity is required to create media disposal and media re-use policies. Covered entities must make sure that EPHI is destroyed or made unusable before the covered entity disposes of electronic media. The process for accomplishing this is described in a media disposal policy. A covered entity must also create media re-use policies. These policies state that EPHI must be removed from electronic media that is going to be made available for re-use. These policies must take into account media re-use within a covered entity. They also should address media re-use outside of a covered entity.

Table 6-3 summarizes the physical safeguards required by the Security Rule. It also includes a summary of required and addressable implementation specifications.

TABLE 6-3 Physical safeguards.

SAFEGUARD	REQUIRED SPECIFICATIONS	ADDRESSABLE SPECIFICATIONS
Facility Access Controls		Contingency Operations
		Facility Security Plan
		Access Control and Validation Procedures
		Maintenance Records
Workstation Use	Required	
Workstation Security	Required	
Device and Media Controls	Disposal Media Re-use	Data Backup and Storage

Technical Safeguards . Technical safeguards are applied in the hardware and software of an information system. The Security Rule contains five technical security standards. It doesn't require that any specific type of technology be used to follow the rule. A covered entity must implement the following standards:

- Access controls
- Audit controls
- Integrity controls
- Person or entity authentication
- Transmission security

The "access control" standard requires covered entities to use access control rules to limit authorized access to systems that store EPHI. The implementation specifications require covered entities to assign unique user names to anyone who uses its systems. They also must create procedures to access EPHI in an emergency. Addressable specifications include using automatic logoff processes. These processes end an electronic session after a period of inactivity. A covered entity also should encrypt EPHI. Together these controls limit access to EPHI.

The "audit controls" standard requires covered entities to review activity in information systems that store or use EPHI. The entity must decide what audit controls it needs to implement to protect its EPHI. Audit controls are used to look for unauthorized access.

The "integrity controls" standard requires covered entities to create policies to protect EPHI from improper modification or destruction. This is an important control to protect EPHI. Health care providers rely on EPHI to treat patients. EPHI that has been improperly modified can put a patient in danger. This standard has one addressable specification.

TABLE 6-4	Technical safeguards.	
SAFEGUARD	**REQUIRED SPECIFICATIONS**	**ADDRESSABLE SPECIFICATIONS**
Access Control	Unique User Identification Emergency Access Procedure	Automatic Logoff Encryption and Decryption
Audit Controls	Required	
Integrity		Mechanism to Authenticate Electronic Protected Health Information
Person or Entity Authentication	Required	
Transmission Security		Integrity Controls Encryption

When it's appropriate, covered entities must authenticate EPHI. These are electronic mechanisms that are used to make sure that EPHI hasn't been improperly changed or destroyed.

Covered entities are required to create procedures to verify that a person or entity trying to access EPHI is who they claim to be. This is the "person or entity authentication" standard. People and entities must prove their identities. Authentication credentials are used to ensure that a person is who they claim to be. These credentials include passwords, tokens, smart cards, and biometric credentials.

The "transmission security" standard requires covered entities to guard against unauthorized access to EPHI during transmission. A covered entity must review how it transmits EPHI. It must determine if there is a risk of unauthorized access. This standard includes two addressable specifications. Where appropriate, the covered entity must implement security measures that protect EPHI from being modified during transmission. It also must encrypt EPHI during transmission if appropriate.

Table 6-4 summarizes the technical safeguards required by the Security Rule. It also includes a summary of required and addressable implementation specifications.

Oversight

The U.S. Department of Health and Human Services oversees compliance with the HIPAA Privacy and Security Rules. It delegated this function to the Office for Civil Rights (OCR). The OCR enforces both rules. It's also responsible for protecting people from discrimination in social services programs.

FYI

Since 2003, the OCR has received over 49,588 Privacy Rule complaints. As of January 31, 2010, it has received 28 Security Rule complaints.

A flowchart of the OCR complaint process is available at *http://www.hhs.gov/ocr/privacy/hipaa/ enforcement/process/index.html.*

OCR has enforced the Privacy Rule since the 2003 compliance date. It began enforcing the Security Rule in July 2009. Before that, the Centers for Medicare and Medicaid Services (CMS) enforced the Security Rule. CMS is also a part of HHS.

The HITECH Act changed many of the oversight and enforcement functions for HIPAA. It required HHS to improve how it enforced the Privacy and Security Rules. To do this, the HHS Secretary delegated Security Rule enforcement to the OCR. This change eliminated duplicate rule enforcement. HHS hopes to be more efficient by having one office enforce both rules.

The OCR can fine covered entities that don't comply with the Privacy and Security Rules. Prior to the HITECH Act, the maximum fine for a violation was $25,000. Only one fine can be assessed for all violations of the same type in the same year. This meant that if a covered entity continued to violate one provision of the Privacy Rule, its fine could be limited to $25,000 in a year. Its fine could be larger if it violated multiple provisions of the rule.

The HITECH Act changed the penalty structure. The new penalty structure went into effect February 17, 2009. Under the new structure, the maximum fine for a Security or Privacy Rule violation is $1.5 million per year. Minimum fines range from $100 to $50,000 per violation. The penalty amount is determined by reviewing the nature of the violation. OCR also will weigh how the covered entity responded to the violation when it determines a fine.

> **NOTE**
> HHS must bring an enforcement action against a noncompliant covered entity within six years of the date of the violation.[24]

A person may be subject to criminal liability if they obtain or disclose PHI in violation of HIPAA. The HITECH Act clarifies that any person who wrongfully obtains or discloses PHI can be held criminally responsible. This includes a covered entity, its employees, or any other person. A person must know that their conduct is wrongful under HIPAA. The U.S. Department of Justice handles HIPAA criminal violations.

The HITECH Act

The HITECH Act is part of the American Recovery and Reinvestment Act (ARRA) of 2009. ARRA is a $787 billion stimulus package. President Obama signed it into law on February 17, 2009. ARRA contains incentives that encourage the adoption of health care information technologies. It anticipates an increase in the use and exchange of EPHI. Because of this, the HITECH Act strengthens HIPAA privacy and security protections for PHI. It increases fines for noncompliance. It also changes how compliance is enforced. The HITECH Act also introduces a federal breach notification rule.

Electronic Health Records and Personal Health Records

In January 2005, President Bush called for the creation of a nationwide network of electronic health records. He wanted this network to be created within 10 years. "Electronic health record" (EHR) refers to government-endorsed technologies that allow health care providers to store, retrieve, and share medical information. The goal of an EHR is to make paper medical records obsolete.

The HITECH Act allocates $19.2 billon to promote the adoption of EHRs. Beginning in 2011, health care professionals who use approved EHR technologies will be eligible for some types of incentives. These incentives are to help cover the cost of adopting EHR technologies. Health care providers that move too slowly to adopt EHR will not receive the incentives.

An EHR is different from a "personal health record" (PHR). PHRs are health records that are compiled and maintained by a person. EHRs are compiled and maintained by health care providers. A PHR typically refers to individual-compiled health records in an electronic format. People can compile and store this information on their computers. They also can use applications and tools offered by third parties. Many health insurance companies give their members access to tools that allow them to compile PHRs. These tools and PHRs are specific to the health insurance plan.

Google Health is an example of a PHR service. It isn't affiliated with a health insurance plan. Google Health allows users to build health profiles. They also can import medical records from hospitals and pharmacies. The tool also allows users to share their health records with health care providers. You can learn more about Google Health at *http://www.google.com/intl/en-US/health/about/*.

The California Office of Privacy Protection has prepared an excellent paper explaining PHRs. You can read it at *http://www.privacy.ca.gov/res/docs/pdf/cis13phrs.pdf*.

Compliance and Enforcement

The HITECH Act substantially changed HIPAA compliance and enforcement. As discussed earlier in this chapter, it increased fines for violations of the HIPAA Security and Privacy Rules. It also requires HHS to audit covered entities and business associates to make sure they comply with HIPAA.[25]

The HITECH Act allows states to enforce HIPAA compliance. States did not have this authority before. State attorneys general can stop covered entities from engaging in practices that negatively affect state residents and their PHI. They also can recover damages on behalf of state residents who are harmed by a covered entity's conduct.[26]

As mentioned earlier, the HITECH Act also allows HHS to directly enforce the Security and Privacy Rules against business associates. This was not possible before the HITECH Act.

FYI

HHS relies on National Institute of Standards and Technology (NIST) guidelines to specify how PHI should be secured during storage and transmission. PHI is considered secured if a covered entity encrypts it according to these guidelines. The HHS guidance can be found at *http://www.hhs.gov/ocr/privacy/hipaa/administrative/breachnotificationrule/brguidance.html.*

Breach Notification Provisions

The Privacy Rule requires covered entities to mitigate an unauthorized use or disclosure of PHI.[27] Prior to the HITECH Act, a covered entity didn't have to notify individuals that their PHI was used or disclosed in an unauthorized manner. The HITECH Act now requires them to do so. It creates notification requirements that covered entities must follow in the event of a breach of unsecured PHI.[28] Both covered entities and business associates must follow these rules.

A "breach" is any impermissible use or disclosure of unsecured PHI that harms the security or privacy of the PHI. The use or disclosure must cause a significant risk of harm to the affected person. The harm can be financial or reputational.[29]

The HITECH breach notification provisions apply to unsecured PHI. Unsecured PHI is PHI that isn't protected by a technology that renders it unusable or unreadable. Unsecured PHI is PHI that isn't encrypted or properly destroyed. PHI must be encrypted through a process that is approved by HHS to be considered secure. In April 2009, HHS issued guidance on what technologies were acceptable to encrypt PHI. It will update this guidance yearly.

Unsecured PHI includes PHI that isn't disposed of properly. PHI is considered unsecured during destruction if it's still readable or recoverable after disposal. PHI that is shredded or destroyed is disposed of properly.

Covered entities must provide notice to people who are affected by a breach of unsecured PHI. These are the people whose PHI was disclosed, or potentially disclosed, because of the breach. The covered entity must notify them no later than 60 days after it discovers the breach. A breach is "discovered" on the first day that the covered entity knows about the breach. Individuals must be notified without "unreasonable delay." A covered entity may delay notification if a law enforcement official requests it.

> **NOTE**
> Neither HIPAA nor the HITECH Act provides a **private cause of action**. This means that people don't have the right to sue a covered entity that uses their PHI in a wrongful way.

The HITECH Act also specifies the method for notifying people of a breach of their unsecured PHI. The default way to provide notice is via first-class mail. There are other ways to provide notice in some circumstances. If the breach involves more than 500 people, then the covered entity must also immediately notify HHS about the breach. All covered entities must submit annual reports to the HHS about breaches involving less than 500 people.

Under the breach notification rules, business associates are required to notify covered entities following their discovery of a breach of unsecured PHI. The business associate must provide notice to the covered entity no later than 60 days after it discovers the breach. The business associate must help the covered entity notify people affected by the breach.

Changes to the Privacy and Security Rules

The HITECH Act made other changes to the Privacy and Security rules. These changes strengthen the protections provided by each rule. These changes include:[30]

- Provides a person with the right to receive a copy of his or her electronic health record if the covered entity maintains one.

- Clarifies the scope of the minimum necessary rule. The HITECH Act requires HHS to issue new guidance on the minimum necessary rule by August 2010.

- A covered entity must account for PHI disclosures made for treatment, payment, and health care operations if the disclosures are made from an electronic health record.

- A covered entity may not sell or market PHI unless a person specifically consents to the marketing activities. The person must be made aware that the covered entity is selling PHI.

The Role of State Laws Protecting Medical Records

HIPAA sets the floor for PHI security and privacy protections. This means that states are free to create laws and rules that provide more protections than HIPAA. Covered entities have to comply with both laws. Generally speaking, the controlling law is whichever law is stricter, or provides greater patient rights.

Any state law that is contrary to HIPAA isn't allowed. A state law is contrary if it's impossible for the covered entity to comply with both the state law and HIPAA. In these situations, the state laws are preempted by HIPAA. They are not allowed. Preemption is discussed in Chapter 3.

States enact many laws that may affect personal health information. These laws can provide more rights than allowed by HIPAA. For instance, in 2008 California enacted some of the strictest patient privacy protections in the country. California's laws specify harsh penalties for providers caught snooping in patient medical records. California health care providers must report privacy breaches more quickly than is specified in HIPAA. The California law requires health care providers to notify people within five days of a breach of a patient's medical information.[31] It also gives people the right to sue their health care providers for violations of the law.

It's important to review both state law and federal law when reviewing questions about the security and privacy of personal health information. You must review both types of laws to make sure that covered entities are appropriately protecting this information.

Case Studies and Examples

The following case studies show how the laws discussed in this chapter are used. These case studies are real-world examples of how regulatory agencies apply laws and rules to protect personal health information.

OCR Enforcement Information

The OCR posts HIPAA Privacy and Security Rule enforcement news on its Web page. It posts summaries of enforcement activities. It also posts monthly statistics about its activities. It also posts case examples and resolution agreements for HIPAA violations.

The OCR enforcement activities Web page can be found at *http://www.hhs.gov/ocr/privacy/hipaa/enforcement/index.html*.

HIPAA and Federal Trade Communications Act

Sometimes an act can touch several compliance laws. In 2006, an Indianapolis, Indiana, television news station conducted an investigative report on prescription privacy. As part of its report, the news station looked at the contents of pharmacy dumpsters. It was checking to see if pharmacies properly disposed of patient information. It checked the contents of unsecured dumpsters. These dumpsters were unlocked. There was nothing stopping the public from sifting through these dumpsters.

The news station reported that CVS pharmacies were throwing sensitive personal information in the trash. CVS is one of the largest pharmacy retailers in the United States. It has more than 6,000 stores. The investigation found that CVS was throwing away unredacted pill bottles. Information on the bottles included patient names, addresses, physician names, and the names of medication. CVS also threw away medication instruction sheets containing personal information. It threw away pharmacy receipts with credit card and health insurance account numbers. All of this information was PHI. All of it was unredacted. Other media outlets reported that CVS stores across the United States also were improperly disposing of PHI.

Information about the "Prescription Privacy" investigative report can be found at *http://www.wthr.com/global/Category.asp?c=83157*.

At the time, CVS's privacy policy stated: "CVS/pharmacy wants you to know that nothing is more central to our operations than maintaining the privacy of your health information ('Protected Health Information' or 'PHI'). PHI is information about you, including basic information that may identify you and relates to your past, present, or future health or condition and the dispensing of pharmaceutical products to you. We take this responsibility very seriously."

CVS disposal practices were investigated by the HHS and the Federal Trade Commission. It was the first time that HHS and the FTC worked together on an investigation. HHS, through the OCR, investigated CVS for violations of the HIPAA Privacy Rule. It found that CVS violated the Privacy Rule in a number of ways. Its review indicated that CVS didn't properly safeguard PHI during the media disposal process. It also found that CVS didn't properly train its employees on how to dispose of PHI. CVS also didn't have a sanctions policy.

The FTC investigated CVS for violations of the FTC Act. It alleged that CVS made false and deceptive statements about its privacy policies. It alleged that CVS promised customers that it would protect unauthorized access to personal information. It also alleged that CVS didn't actually do this. These misleading types of statements are illegal under the FTC Act.

CVS responded that there was no verification of the media reports. However, it settled charges with the FTC and HHS to resolve the cases. The FTC consent agreement requires CVS to create a comprehensive information security program. This program must protect the personal information that CVS collects from consumers and employees. The order also requires CVS to get an independent audit of its security program every two years. It must do this until 2029. CVS may not make any misrepresentations about the company's security practices.

The FTC complaint and consent agreement can be found at *http://www.ftc.gov/os/ caselist/0723119/index.shtm.* (Look for the February 18, 2009, entries.)

 NOTE

An HHS resolution agreement is similar to an FTC consent order. Both are settlement agreements.

Under the HHS resolution agreement, CVS agreed to pay $2.25 million to settle all claims. It also agreed to follow a corrective action plan. That plan requires it to create policies to comply with the HIPAA Privacy Rule. It must create policies and procedures to safeguard PHI during disposal. It also must establish an employee training program. CVS also must create an employee sanctions policy to discipline employees who fail to follow the Privacy Rule.

The HHS resolution agreement also requires independent review of CVS compliance. CVS must be reviewed each year. The agreement requires three years of monitoring.

The HHS resolution agreement and corrective action plan can be found at *http://www.hhs.gov/ocr/privacy/hipaa/enforcement/examples/cvsresolutionagreement.html.*

CVS's statement on the cases can be read at *http://info.cvscaremark.com/newsroom/ press-releases/cvs-caremark-issues-statement-settlement-concerning-disposal-patient-informa.*

Health Informat on

6

CHAPTER SUMMARY

Personal health information is one of the most sensitive types of confidential information. Personal health information is no longer limited to paper files. This type of information is often stored in electronic form. No matter what its form, this information must be protected.

Health care providers must take steps to ensure its privacy and security. They are required to do so by both federal and state laws. They face fines and other penalties for failing to protect this information.

KEY CONCEPTS AND TERMS

Authorization

Business associates

Covered entity

Disclosure

Discovery

Electronic protected health
    information (EPHI)

Medical identity theft

Minimum necessary rule

Private cause of action

Protected health
    information (PHI)

Use

CHAPTER 6 ASSESSMENT

1. An addressable implementation specification must be used if it is _____ .

2. What is the maximum fine for a single violation of the HIPAA Privacy or Security Rule?

    A. $100
    B. $1,500
    C. $1 million
    D. $1.5 million
    E. It's unlimited

3. Covered entities must notify affected individuals of a breach within _____ days.

4. HIPAA limits the pre-existing condition waiting period to _____ months.

5. What conditions must be met to be considered a health care provider under HIPAA?

    A. Provide health care services to a person.
    B. Conduct standard transactions electronically.
    C. Handle electronic transactions on a clearinghouse's behalf.
    D. A and B only
    E. None of the above

6. A business associate is _____ .

7. What term refers to how a covered entity shares PHI within the organization?

    A. Disclosure
    B. Discuss
    C. Use
    D. Handle
    E. None of the above

8. A covered entity must disclose PHI to a person's family and friends in an emergency.

    A. True
    B. False

9. A covered entity must respond to a person's request to access PHI within _____ days.

10. Which uses and disclosures of PHI are allowed without a person's consent?

    A. Made to a person about their own PHI
    B. Made for treatment, payment, and health care operations
    C. Made for public safety and health activities
    D. All of the above
    E. None of the above

11. What term refers to how a covered entity shares PHI with other organizations?

    A. Disclosure
    B. Discuss
    C. Use
    D. Handle
    E. None of the above

12. What is the legal process used to gather evidence in a lawsuit?

    A. Disclosure
    B. Discovery
    C. Forensics
    D. Trial
    E. None of the above

13. Which entity enforces the HIPAA Privacy Rule?

    A. FDIC
    B. FTC
    C. OCR
    D. CDC
    E. None of the above

14. Which rule is similar to the information security concept of need to know?

    A. Use rule
    B. Clearinghouse rule
    C. Operations rule
    D. Absolute rule
    E. Minimum necessary rule

15. A HIPAA breach is a beach of _____ PHI.

ENDNOTES

1. National Library of Medicine, "Greek Medicine: The Hippocratic Oath," Translated by Michael North, 2002, *http://www.nlm.nih.gov/hmd/greek/greek_oath.html* (accessed March 6, 2010).

2. Health Insurance Portability and Accountability Act (1996), Pub. L. No. 104-191, sec. 261.

3. Code of Federal Regulations, Title 45, sec. 160.103.

4. U.S. Code Vol. 42, sec. 1320d (2006).

5. Federal Register 65, No. 250 at 82463 (background information.).

6. Code of Federal Regulations, Title 45, sec. 164.502.

7. Code of Federal Regulations, Title 45, sec. 164.506(c).

8. Code of Federal Regulations, Title 45, sec. 164.510.

9. Code of Federal Regulations, Title 45, sec. 164.512.

10. Code of Federal Regulations, Title 45, sec. 164.514.

11. Code of Federal Regulations, Title 45, sec. 164.508.

12. Code of Federal Regulations, Title 45, sec. 164.508(c)(1).

13. Code of Federal Regulations, Title 45, sec. 165-502(b).

14. Code of Federal Regulations, Title 45, sec. 164.526.

15. Code of Federal Regulations, Title 45, sec. 164.528.

16. Code of Federal Regulations, Title 45, sec. 164.520.

17. Code of Federal Regulations, Title 45, sec. 164.530.

18. Code of Federal Regulations, Title 45, sec. 164.306.

19. Code of Federal Regulations, Title 45, sec. 164.316.

20. Code of Federal Regulations, Title 45, sec. 164.306.

21. Code of Federal Regulations, Title 45, sec. 164.306.

22. Code of Federal Regulations, Title 45, sec. 164.304.

23. Code of Federal Regulations, Title 45, sec. 164.304.

24. Code of Federal Regulations, Title 45, sec. 160.414[0].

25. Health Information Technology for Economic and Clinical Health Act (2009), Pub. L. No. 111-5, sec. 13411.

26. Health Information Technology for Economic and Clinical Health Act (2009), Pub. L. No. 111-5, sec. 13410(e).

27. Code of Federal Regulations, Title 45, sec. 164.530(f).

28. Health Information Technology for Economic and Clinical Health Act (2009), Pub. L. No. 111-5, sec. 13402.

29. Health Information Technology for Economic and Clinical Health Act (2009), Pub. L. No. 111-5, sec. 13402.

30. Health Information Technology for Economic and Clinical Health Act (2009), Pub. L. No. 111-5, sec. 13405.

31. Health Facilities Data Breach, California Health and Safety Code Sec. 1280.15.

Corporate Information Security and Privacy Regulation

THIS CHAPTER FOCUSES ON SPECIAL SECURITY ISSUES faced by publicly traded companies. Public companies must comply with a law that tries to improve corporate responsibility and stop fraudulent financial reporting. Rules and regulations created in response to the law impact information systems that process financial data. The rules require that these systems be reviewed to make sure that they appropriately control information security risks and threats to financial data.

This chapter reviews why Congress created this law. It also reviews how the law influences information security practices. Finally, it discusses how this law affects other kinds of organizations.

Chapter 7 Topics

This chapter covers the following topics and concepts:

- How the Enron scandal led to securities-law reform
- Why accurate financial reporting is important
- What the Sarbanes-Oxley Act (SOX) is
- What compliance and security controls are
- How SOX influences other types of companies
- What some corporate privacy issues are
- What some case studies and examples are

When you complete this chapter, you will be able to:

- Describe the difference between public and private companies
- Explain the history behind the Sarbanes-Oxley Act
- Discuss the main requirements of the Sarbanes-Oxley Act
- Explain the role of the Public Company Accounting Oversight Board
- Describe how Section 404 internal control requirements impact information security
- Discuss frameworks used to guide Sarbanes-Oxley internal control requirements

The Enron Scandal and Securities-Law Reform

Enron. WorldCom. Tyco. Adelphia. These companies have come to represent a wave of corporate scandal that plagued America in the early 2000s. Each company engaged in varying levels of mismanagement, questionable financial deals, and accounting fraud. The activities at these companies shook investor confidence in U.S. corporations. They also tarnished the reputations of financial services professionals such as analysts, accountants, and auditors. Consider the following:

- Once called the "Most Innovative Company in America," energy company Enron filed for bankruptcy in December 2001. It used a number of different fraudulent accounting methods to hide billions of dollars of debt from its investors and lenders.
- Cable company Adelphia filed for bankruptcy in June 2002. In 2004, a federal jury convicted Adelphia's founder of bank and securities fraud. He was sentenced to 15 years in prison.
- Telecommunications company WorldCom filed for bankruptcy in July 2002. At the time, it was the largest bankruptcy in U.S. history. In July 2005, a federal court sentenced the chief executive officer (CEO) of WorldCom to 25 years in prison for corporate fraud.
- In June 2005, a jury convicted a former Tyco CEO of theft, conspiracy, securities fraud, and falsifying business records. A court in New York sentenced him to between eight and 25 years in prison. He was ordered to pay restitution and fines of more $200 million.

The financial mismanagement at these companies contributed to the largest reform in U.S. securities laws since the Great Depression. The Enron bankruptcy is the case that spurred Congress to act. It's important to understand the Enron scandal to appreciate how significant the reform was.

Public Versus Private Companies

A **public company** also is called a publicly traded company. Many investors own a public company. The investors own a portion of the company in the form of stock. A stock represents a share of a corporation's profits or assets. A person's percentage of ownership in the corporation depends on how many shares of stock he or she owns.

Shareholders are entitled to portions of a public company's profits. Their share is called a **dividend**. A dividend represents the shareholder's portion of the company's earnings. People who own more shares of stock receive larger dividends.

Public corporations are allowed to sell stocks and bonds. A bond represents a loan to the corporation for a specified period. The corporation must pay bondholders back the full value of the bond, plus interest. A person who owns a corporate bond doesn't have any ownership in a corporation. Only stocks represent an ownership interest. Stocks and bonds together are called **securities**.

In the U.S., the stock of a public company is traded on a stock exchange. The two most popular U.S. stock exchanges are the New York Stock Exchange (NYSE) and the NASDAQ Stock Market. National securities exchanges are registered with the U.S. Securities and Exchange Commission (SEC). You can learn more at *http://www.sec.gov/divisions/marketreg/mrexchanges.shtml*.

Almost all securities sold in the United States must be registered with the SEC. To register its securities, a company must file documents about its financial condition with the SEC. It must file these documents with the SEC on a regular basis. Investors review these documents to make informed investment decisions.

A public company is different from a **privately held company**. A small group of private investors owns a privately held company. In some cases, the investors all might be members of the same family. A private company doesn't have to answer to shareholders in the same way that a public company does. A private company distributes its profits to its owners.

Private companies don't have to register with the SEC. They also don't have to file documents with the SEC that show their financial position. The largest private companies in the United States include Cargill, Chrysler, Mars, and PricewaterhouseCoopers.[1]

Corporate Fraud at Enron

The Enron case has become a part of American pop culture. Its name is synonymous with corporate greed and scandal. Almost 10 years after the scandal, it continues to hold our attention. CNBC aired a documentary in April 2010 called "Enron: The Smartest Guys in the Room."[2] The Enron scandal inspired a musical called "Enron: The Musical." At the time this book was written, a play about Enron was showing on Broadway.[3]

Enron formed in 1985 through the merger of two natural gas companies. It was based in Houston, Texas. Kenneth Lay was the CEO of the company. By the mid 1990s, Enron was the leading U.S. natural gas company.

Enron grew quickly because it took advantage of energy market deregulation in the late 1980s. It bought and sold gas and electricity. It did this through futures contracts. These investments were initially very successful. As it grew, Enron expanded into other markets. It purchased steel mills, water utilities, and even tried to enter the Internet broadband market. It also expanded internationally, pursuing opportunities in England, Mexico, and India.

From 1997 to 2001, *Fortune* magazine put Enron on its "Most Innovative Companies in America" list.[4] In 2000, it named Enron to its "World's Most Admired Companies" list.[5] Enron grew from 7,500 employees in 1996 to more than 20,000 employees in 2001. Its stock was valuable. Enron encouraged its employees to include Enron stock in their retirement portfolios.

To the outside world, Enron was a very successful company. Its required SEC filings showed that it was making money. It appeared to be able to translate its success in the energy markets to other markets. Financial analysts continued to recommend Enron stock. Investors continued to buy it.

In reality, Enron was struggling. It lost billions of dollars on its international investments. Enron also started to face increased competition in the energy business. It began to lose its market share in energy futures contracts. This is because other energy companies started to use Enron's own strategies to become profitable.

By the late 1990s, Enron was in financial trouble. It needed to raise money to meet its operating expenses. However, it couldn't do this in a way that would alarm its investors. It didn't want to alert investors to potential trouble. This could cause its stock price to fall. Maintaining a high stock price was important to bring in new investors. It also was critical to being able to maintain credit lines with banks.

FYI

A "futures contract" is a contract for the sale of a good. One party agrees to sell the other party an asset at some point in the future. The two parties agree on the future quantity and price for the asset at the time the contract is made. Companies use futures contracts as an investment tool rather than as an actual contract to supply goods.

Enron executives engaged in a number of complicated financial transactions to hide its losses. Its chief financial officer (CFO), Andrew Fastow, created a number of affiliated companies. He hid Enron's losses in the financial records of these companies. The Enron CFO and other employees who worked with him owned many of these affiliated companies. They profited from the transactions between Enron and the affiliated companies.

These transactions were very complex. They were complicated to understand because Enron often changed the names of its different divisions. It also moved assets back and forth between divisions. Many of these transactions violated traditional accounting principles. These principles are called generally accepted accounting principles (GAAP). They are the rules for the accounting process. Accountants prepare financial statements according to these rules. These rules are designed to promote accurate accounting records.

Enron also mislabeled loans that it received from banks. It did this to hide the transactions on its own financial statements so that its investors would not know about them. By some reports, Enron borrowed about $8.6 billion from 1992 to 2001.[6] It hid this information from its investors. During this time, Enron filed earnings statements with the SEC that misstated its financial position. The SEC filings were hard to understand. They also showed that Enron appeared to be making money.

In February 2001, CEO Kenneth Lay retired. The new CEO was Jeffrey Skilling. Skilling had been instrumental in taking Enron into new trading markets in the 1990s. He and CFO Andrew Fastow oversaw most of Enron's business practices.

In April 2001, many financial analysts began to question Enron's complicated financial statements.[7] Enron continued to portray the image of a successful company. Jeffrey Skilling unexpectedly resigned from the CEO post in August 2001. The Board of Directors asked Kenneth Lay to return to Enron as its CEO. Lay resumed his old post.

In October 2001, Enron announced its first ever loss. The SEC noticed this announcement and began to review Enron's financial statements. Enron also began its own investigation. In late October, the Enron Board of Directors established a special committee to investigate the affiliated companies created by Fastow. Director William C. Powers led this committee. The report that the committee issued is known as the "Powers Report."[8]

In November 2001, Enron announced that it was amending its 1997–2001 financial statements because of accounting errors. This announcement shook investor confidence in Enron. Its stock price began to drop. Banks would no longer issue it credit to meet its operating expenses. At the end of November 2001, Enron stock was worth less than a dollar per share.[9]

FYI

The Powers Report was released in February 2002. It noted that Enron's executive officers mismanaged many aspects of the company's business. It also placed blame on Enron's board of directors for failing in its corporate oversight duties. It blamed Enron's accounting advisor, Arthur Andersen, for failing to provide objective accounting advice. You can read a copy of the report at *http://i.cnn.net/cnn/2002/LAW/02/02/enron.report/powers.report.pdf*.

On December 2, 2001, Enron filed for bankruptcy. At the time, it was the largest bankruptcy ever. (The WorldCom bankruptcy surpassed it only six months later.[10]) In January 2002, Enron removed its stock from the New York Stock Exchange.[11]

The fallout from the Enron case was enormous. Employees who had invested their retirement savings in Enron stock lost $1.3 billion.[12] Accounting company Arthur Andersen, who was Enron's auditor, closed down. The U.S. government prosecuted many of Enron's top executives for their involvement in its business dealings. Some of these prosecutions were difficult because it was hard to determine which executives were involved in the fraud, and which executives weren't. The complexity of Enron's financial dealings contributed to this difficulty.

CFO Andrew Fastow entered into a plea agreement with the U.S. government. He agreed to testify against Jeffrey Skilling and Kenneth Lay in exchange for a sentence of no more than 10 years in prison. In September 2006, a federal court sentenced him to six years in prison. He also paid more than $30 million in restitution.

Enron founder and CEO Kenneth Lay was convicted in May 2006 for fraud and conspiracy. He died of a heart attack in July 2006. The court vacated his conviction after his death. His conviction was erased because he died before he could appeal his conviction.

Former CEO Jeffrey Skilling was convicted in 2006 on federal fraud charges. A federal court sentenced him to 24 years in prison. He appealed his conviction to the U.S. Supreme Court. The Supreme Court heard oral arguments in March 2010. A transcript of the oral argument can be read at *http://www.supremecourt.gov/oral_arguments/argument _transcripts/08-1394.pdf.* On June 24, 2010, the U.S. Supreme Court ruled that the government had improperly applied a law used to convict Skilling. It sent the case back to a lower court.

Why Is Accurate Financial Reporting Important?

Enron was one of many large corporate scandals in the early 2000s. These scandals shook investor confidence in the U.S. economy. The U.S. Congress held numerous hearings and committee meetings related to the aftermath of the scandal.[13] It got involved because of the scope of the fraud and the damage to Enron investors. Enron significantly misstated its financial condition in the financial statements that it filed with the SEC. Its investors lost money because of these fraudulent financial statements.

The Enron scandal showed why accurate financial information is important. Enron was able to sustain itself for at least five years due to inaccurate financial reporting. During this period, financial analysts continued to recommend its stock as a good investment. The public and Enron employees invested in it. These people had significant losses when Enron's troubles became public and the company finally declared bankruptcy. Enron duped its investors. By the time everyone knew the truth, it was too late to recover investment losses. Investors lost confidence in large public companies.

> **NOTE**
>
> The decade from 2000 to 2009 had some of the worst stock market performance ever.[14]

The financial statements that a company files with the SEC are one of the main sources of information that investors use to research that company. These documents help investors determine the true financial condition of a company. After the Enron scandal, the SEC required more information to be reported on these forms. It also required that the accuracy of these forms be certified in a number of different ways.

Public companies are required to file a number of financial disclosure statements with the SEC. These forms help investors understand the financial stability of a company. The most commonly filed forms are:

- **Form 10-K**—Annual report
- **Form 10-Q**—Quarterly report
- **Form 8-K**—Current report

A company uses **Form 10-K** to file its annual report. Federal law requires that publicly traded companies submit these reports each year. Depending on their size, companies must file this report within 60 to 90 days after the end of their fiscal year. The larger a company is, the faster it has to file its report.

Form 10-K is a very detailed disclosure of a company's financial condition. A company must fully describe its business in its 10-K disclosure. It must explain how it's organized and how it operates. It must provide its financial statements. These statements include balance sheets, statements of income and cash flows, and statements of shareholder equity. An independent auditor must audit the company's financial statements. The auditor's report also must be included in the Form 10-K filing.

The CEO and CFO of a company must sign the company's Form 10-K. A majority of the company's board of directors also must sign the form. The SEC estimates that it will take a company 2,102.90 hours to prepare its annual 10-K filing.[15]

Form 10-Q is a company's quarterly report. Federal law requires companies to file these reports. They must file these reports after the end of each of their first three quarters in a fiscal year. These reports are usually less detailed than the end-of-the year 10-K filing. Depending on their size, companies must file this report within 40 to 45 days after the end of each fiscal quarter.

Companies must file **Form 8-K** if they experience a major event that could affect their financial condition. Shareholders and investors should know about these events. Companies must file a Form 8-K with the SEC within four days of a major event. This period is shortened in some instances. For example, a company must file Form 8-K with the SEC immediately if it becomes aware of insider trading activities.

FYI

A company's two main financial documents are its "balance sheet" and "profit and loss" statements. The balance sheet provides a summary of the company's financial condition at a certain period. They're commonly prepared on a monthly basis. A profit and loss statement is used to determine whether a company made a profit during a certain period.

General events that trigger a Form 8-K disclosure requirement include:

- Filing for bankruptcy
- Selling off significant assets
- Acquiring another company
- Getting a loan
- Board member resignation
- Board member elections
- Any changes to board governance documents

Accurate information is the "investor's best tool."[16] People need accurate financial information so that they can invest wisely and make money. The SEC recommends that potential investors carefully review a company's prospectus and financial reports. You can read the SEC's list of information that investors should review before investing at *http://www.sec.gov/answers/infomatters .htm.* The benefit of reviewing information from a number of different sources is that an investor can get a better picture of a company's financial condition.

 NOTE

A company uses a "prospectus" to describe the securities that it offers for sale. The prospectus describes the company's business plan.

It can be very hard for investors to detect fraud. This was the case in the Enron scandal. As a result, the SEC recommends that investors look for potential red flags as they review a company's financial condition. Red flags include companies that have high-value assets, but low revenues. It also includes odd items listed in the footnotes of the company's financial statements. Both of these red flags were present in the Enron scandal.

The Sarbanes-Oxley Act of 2002

Congress passed the Public Company Accounting Reform and Investor Protection Act in 2002.[17] It's more commonly known as the Sarbanes-Oxley Act of 2002. It's called SOX or Sarbox in many resources. The Act was named after its sponsors, Senator Paul Sarbanes of Maryland and Representative Michael Oxley of Ohio. It was passed in response to corporate scandals like Enron, WorldCom, and Adelphia.

SOX moved through both the U.S. House of Representatives and Senate at a quick pace. It was originally introduced in the U.S. House of Representatives in February 2002. This was just months after the Enron scandal became public. On July 25, 2002, both the House and Senate voted on the final version of SOX. President George W. Bush signed SOX into law on July 30, 2002. As he signed it, he called SOX "the most far-reaching reforms of American business practices since the time of Franklin Delano Roosevelt."[18]

Purpose and Scope

Congress hoped that SOX reforms would prevent another Enron scandal. The main goal of SOX is to protect shareholders and investors from financial fraud. SOX increased corporate disclosure requirements. It also created strict penalties for violations of its provisions. SOX has 11 different titles. They are:

- **Public Company Accounting Oversight Board (Title I)**—Establishes the Public Company Accounting Oversight Board (PCAOB). The PCAOB oversees the firms that audit public companies.

- **Auditor Independence (Title II)**—Forbids auditors from providing some types of non-audit services to their clients.

- **Corporate Responsibility (Title III)**—Requires corporations to create audit committees on their board of directors. The audit committee is responsible for hiring the corporation's outside auditors.

- **Enhanced Financial Disclosures (Title IV)**—Enhances the amount of information that public companies must provide on their SEC filings. This section requires companies to report on internal controls that affect their financial reports.

- **Analyst Conflicts of Interest (Title V)**—Establishes rules to make sure that securities analysts can give independent opinions about a public company's stock risk.

- **Commission Resources and Authority (Title VI)**—Gives the SEC authority to discipline investment firms for unprofessional conduct. This section also gives the SEC additional funding to support its programs.

- **Studies and Reports (Title VII)**—Requires the SEC to review public accounting firms. The SEC must do this at least every three years. This section also requires the SEC to issue reports about how the securities market operates.

- **Corporate and Criminal Fraud Accountability (Title VIII)**—Imposes document retention requirements on companies and auditors. It protects whistleblowers. It also bans retaliation against employees who participate in fraud investigations. This section also imposes criminal penalties for violating SOX.

- **White-Collar Crime Penalty Enhancements (Title IX)**—Requires CEO and CFOs to certify that the company's financial reports fairly represent its financial condition. It creates criminal penalties for signing fraudulent statements.

- **Corporate Tax Returns (Title X)**—Is a statement from Congress that strongly suggests that a CEO sign the federal income tax return of a corporation.

- **Corporate Fraud and Accountability (Title XI)**—Establishes criminal liability for certain types of fraud committed by corporate officers. It also increases penalties for some types of corporate crime.

SOX supplements current federal securities laws. It applies to publicly traded companies that must register with the SEC. This includes international companies who trade stock on U.S. stock exchanges. SOX doesn't apply to privately held companies.

 NOTE

A small public company is a company with less than $75 million of public stock.

Large public companies had to comply with all portions of SOX beginning in 2004. The SEC extended the deadline for smaller public companies several times for some of the more complicated portions of the law. It extended the deadline for the company's report on internal controls that is required by Title IV. All compliance extensions have now expired. All public companies must comply with all SOX provisions.

Main Requirements

SOX is a very detailed act. It has many provisions. This chapter focuses on the parts of the act that have had the most impact on information technology (IT) functions. When SOX was first enacted, many companies assumed that it didn't have any IT components. Congress didn't mention IT anywhere within the act.

This opinion changed as companies began to review their SOX compliance requirements. Many SOX provisions require companies to verify the accuracy of their financial information. Since IT systems hold many types of financial information, companies and auditors quickly realized that these systems were in scope for SOX compliance. That meant that how those systems are used and the controls used to safeguard those systems had to be reviewed.

The relationship between IT and SOX compliance continues to evolve. This section reviews the SOX provisions that have an IT impact. First, this section reviews the PCAOB. The PCAOB creates standards that auditors must follow when reviewing the activities of public companies. These standards help auditors determine the IT controls that they must review. The creation of the PCAOB is one of the most notable SOX reforms.

Second, this section reviews SOX provisions that impact records management functions. These provisions have an impact on IT operations because of the vast amount of data that is stored electronically. These provisions are important because they affect how IT systems are configured.

Finally, SOX requires the executive management of a company to certify that there are controls in place to protect the accuracy of company information. This is the area where SOX compliance has caused the biggest challenge for companies and IT professionals.

Public Company Accounting Oversight Board

Prior to the creation of SOX, auditors and accountants belonged to a self-regulating profession. A profession is self-regulating when it creates and enforces its own rules of conduct. Federal and state laws place few oversight requirements on members of self-regulating professions.

A common example of a member of a self-regulating profession is an attorney. Attorneys must meet minimum state law requirements to become licensed. After that, their professional behavior is largely judged by commissions made up of other attorneys who enforce rules of professional conduct. The profession itself determines what these rules of professional conduct should be.

FYI

Information security professionals belong to a largely self-regulating profession. This is especially true when information security professionals obtain certifications that require the certificate holders to follow a code of conduct. This concept is discussed more in Chapter 12.

The Enron scandal proved that self-regulation does have some drawbacks. Enron's accounting firm, Arthur Andersen, provided it with accounting, auditing, and consulting services. Enron was a large Andersen client. It paid Andersen $52 million for auditing and consulting services in 2001.[19] Even the Powers Report noted that there was a lack of critical advice from its auditors at Arthur Andersen in reviewing Enron's publicly filed financial statements.[20] This may have been because Arthur Andersen was reluctant to challenge such an important client.

Congress created the PCAOB to provide a layer of government oversight on auditing activities. The PCAOB oversees auditors that audit public companies. It was created in order to ensure that audit reports for public companies are fair and independent. Under SOX, the PCAOB has several duties.[21] It must:

- Register accounting firms that prepare audit reports for public companies.
- Establish standards for the preparation of audit reports.
- Conduct inspections of registered public accounting firms.
- Conduct investigations and disciplinary proceedings against registered public accounting firms.
- Perform other duties or functions necessary to carry out SOX.
- Enforce SOX compliance.
- Set a budget for the PCAOB, and manage its operations.

 NOTE

You can learn more about the role of the PCAOB by visiting its Web page at *http://pcaobus.org.*

The PCAOB has five members. The SEC selects these members and appoints them to staggered terms. The SEC can remove PCAOB members only for good cause. PCAOB members are to be "individuals of integrity and reputation who have a demonstrated commitment to the interests of investors and the public."[22] They must be financially literate. This means that they must be able to understand financial statements. Only two members of the PCAOB are allowed to be certified public accountants (CPAs). The remaining three members can't be CPAs. Members of the PCAOB aren't allowed to have any financial interest in an accounting firm. Figure 7-1 shows the structure of the PCAOB.

FIGURE 7-1

PCAOB structure.

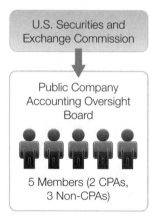

The SEC believes that a single set of globally accepted accounting principles will benefit U.S. companies. It's evaluating whether it should adopt the International Financial Reporting Standards (IFRS). The International Accounting Standards Board has created the IFRS. You can learn about IFRS at *http://www.ifrs.com/ifrs_faqs.html*. The SEC expects to make a decision on whether to adopt these standards in 2011.

One of the main functions of the PCAOB is to set standards for how auditors review public companies. It has created standards related to auditing, ethics, independence, and quality control. The SEC must approve its standards. The PCAOB bases many of its standards on GAAP. The Financial Accounting Standards Board (FASB) establishes these principles. The SEC has recognized GAAP as authoritative and requires financial statements to be prepared in accordance with GAAP.

The PCAOB's "Auditing Standard No. 5" provides guidance on how an auditor performs an audit of a company's internal controls over financial reporting. Auditing Standard No. 5 wasn't the PCAOB's first guidance on internal controls. Its first standard was "Auditing Standard No. 2." Auditors followed this standard for the first wave of audits under SOX. Companies complained that the standard was too broad. Following it led to greater than expected costs. An Ernst & Young survey found that 85 percent of companies with revenues greater than $20 billion spent more than $10 million for SOX compliance in the first year.[23]

The PCAOB created Auditing Standard No. 5 to respond to criticisms about Auditing Standard No. 2.[24] Auditing Standard No. 5 is important for audits of IT systems and processes that impact a company's financial reports. It's important because it specifies a top-down approach that might limit the scope of review of IT systems. Auditing Standard No. 5 also recommends that auditors focus their review on areas of the highest risk.

Document Retention

SOX contains some records retention provisions. It's important to know about them because companies store many of their records electronically. Some studies estimate that 93 percent of all business documents are created and stored electronically.[25] Companies must understand how their IT systems work in order to meet SOX retention requirements.

SOX requires auditors and public companies to maintain audit papers for seven years.[26] Audit papers are most documents used in an audit. They're the materials that support the conclusions made in an audit report. SOX takes a very broad view of the type of records that must be saved. This includes work papers, memoranda, and correspondence. It also includes any other records created, sent, or received in connection with the audit. SOX also includes electronic records.

Is the PCAOB Constitutional?

The constitutionality of SOX was challenged soon after it was enacted into law. The case is called *Free Enterprise Fund and Beckstead and Watts v. Public Company Accounting Oversight Board*.

The Free Enterprise Fund and Beckstead & Watts LLP filed the case in 2006. The Free Enterprise Fund is a public interest organization. Beckstead & Watts LLP is an accounting firm. The plaintiffs argued that SOX is unconstitutional. In particular, they argued that the PCAOB is unconstitutional because its creation and operation violates the constitutional separation of powers doctrine.

The plaintiffs argued that separation of powers is violated because the PCAOB is an executive branch agency that the president has virtually no control over. Under SOX, the SEC alone has the power to appoint PCAOB members. PCAOB members can be fired only for cause. Only the SEC can fire them. The president, and even the SEC, has little authority to control PCAOB members once they are appointed.

The plaintiffs argued that it violates the section of the Constitution that gives the president the power to appoint and remove officers of the executive branch. They also argued that under the Constitution, Congress isn't permitted to set up a structure that bypasses the president's authority.

The case was filed in the U.S. District Court for the District of Columbia. The District Court granted summary judgment for the PCAOB and upheld the constitutionality of SOX. In August 2008, the Circuit Court for the D.C. Court affirmed the decision of the lower court. The U.S. Supreme Court heard arguments in the case on December 7, 2009 and issued its decision in June 2010.

In its decision, the Court found that the way that the PCAOB is created does indeed violate the separation of powers doctrine. Even though the portions of SOX that creates the PCAOB is unconstitutional, however, the Court said that SOX is still good law. The Court's decision means that the SEC can now fire PCAOB members at will (or for any reason at all), instead of just for good cause.

You can view the Supreme Court's docket on the *Free Enterprise* case at: *http://www.supremecourt.gov/Search.aspx?FileName=/docketfiles/08-861.htm*.

SOX also requires that a public company retain the records and documentation that it uses to assess its internal controls over financial reporting.[27] These controls are discussed in the next section. Guidance issued by the SEC recognizes that this documentation takes a number of different forms. It also includes electronic data. Companies must permanently retain this information.

The penalties for failing to retain records for the right amount of time can be severe. SOX makes it a crime for a person or company to knowingly and willfully violate its records retention provisions. A person who violates this provision can face fines and up to 10 years in prison.

FYI

Many federal and state laws contain records retention requirements. SOX is another law to add to that list. Organizations should develop document retention policies to help them track their different obligations. Chapter 13 reviews these types of policies.

SOX also makes it a crime for any person to tamper with or destroy any record in an attempt to interfere with a federal investigation.[28] This section was created to respond to Arthur Andersen's involvement in the Enron scandal. As soon as Enron's financial difficulties became public, partners at Arthur Andersen instructed employees to follow its document destruction policies. The company shredded thousands of Enron documents. The government later charged the company with obstructing justice. It alleged that Arthur Andersen shredded Enron documents even after it was aware that the SEC would investigate Enron. In 2005, the U.S. Supreme Court overturned Arthur Andersen's obstruction of justice conviction.

Unlike other parts of SOX, this provision applies to any organization. Private companies also must follow it. People who violate this section can face fines of up to $10 million. They also face up to 20 years in prison.

A former Ernst & Young accountant was one of the first people to be charged with violating this provision. In that case, the government alleged that the accountant altered and destroyed client audit records during a federal investigation. The Office of the Comptroller of the Currency was investigating the accountant's client at the time that he altered the documents. In October 2004, the accountant pleaded guilty. In January 2005, a federal judge sentenced him to 12 months in prison. He also received a $5,000 fine.

Companies must make sure that electronic records are stored properly so that they can satisfy SOX retention requirements. They must store the records for the right amount of time. They also must make sure that those records are destroyed properly when the retention period expires.

Certification

SOX requires companies to report accurate financial data. They must do this to protect their investors from harm. To encourage a company to report accurate data, SOX requires its CEO and CFO to certify the company's SEC filings. SOX certification provisions require executives to establish, maintain, and review certain types of internal controls for their company.

Disclosure Controls.   SOX Section 302 requires CEOs and CFOs to certify a company's SEC reports. The purpose of the certifications is to put executive management on notice of the company's financial condition. The SEC can hold a CEO or CFO liable for submitting inaccurate financial reports. It makes sense that both the CEO and CFO would have to make these certifications. They're the officers who are most knowledgeable about the company's finances and overall condition.

A certification attests to the truth of certain facts. The SEC requires a certification to be included on a number of different forms. It must be included on a company's Form 10-Q and Form 10-K reports. (These certifications don't need to be included on Form 8-K.) Under the law,[29] a CEO and CFO each must certify that:

- They have reviewed the report.
- The report doesn't contain untrue or misleading statements about the company.
- The financial statements fairly represent the company's financial condition.
- The executive is responsible for creating disclosure controls and procedures that are designed to bring material information about the company to the executive's attention, and the controls are reviewed 90 days prior to filing the report.
- The executive has disclosed all significant deficiencies in its internal controls to their auditor.
- Whether any significant changes in the internal controls have occurred since they were last evaluated.

The controls required under Section 302 are called **disclosure controls**. They are very broad. They're the processes and procedures that a company puts in place to make sure that it makes timely disclosures to the SEC. They're how management stays informed about the company's operations. These controls must address any change in information that affects company resources. They bring events to the executive's attention so that they can be reported to the SEC.

Disclosure controls are different from SOX **internal controls.** Internal controls are the processes and procedures that a company uses to provide reasonable assurance that its financial reports are reliable. The next section reviews these controls. Internal controls address only processes that protect the reliability of financial reports. Disclosure controls are broader. They include internal controls.[30] Figure 7-2 shows the relationship between disclosure controls and internal controls.

FIGURE 7-2

Relationship between disclosure controls and internal controls.

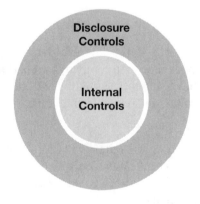

SOX Section 906 imposes criminal liability for fraudulent certifications. Under this section, CEOs and CFOs that knowingly certify fraudulent reports may be fined up to $1 million. They also could be imprisoned for up to 10 years. An officer who willfully makes a fraudulent certification may be fined up to $5 million. They could be imprisoned up to 20 years.

> **NOTE**
> SOX sections 302 and 906 were created in response to the Enron scandal. Would Enron's executives have acted differently if they had been required to make these certifications on SEC filings?

Internal Controls.   SOX Section 404 requires a company's executive management to report on the effectiveness of the company's internal controls over financial reporting (ICFR). They must make this report each year on their Form 10-K filing. Under this section, management must create, document, and test ICFR. After management makes its yearly report on its ICFR, outside auditors must review the report and verify that the ICFR work. This section has caused compliance headaches for IT professionals.

Under SEC rules, ICFR are processes that provide reasonable assurance that financial reports are reliable.[31] ICFR provide management with reasonable assurance that:

- Financial reports, records, and data are accurately maintained
- Transactions are prepared according to GAAP rules and are properly recorded
- Unauthorized acquisition or use of data or assets that could affect financial statements will be prevented or detected in a timely manner

SOX doesn't define reasonable assurance. The SEC and PCAOB recognize that reasonable assurance doesn't mean absolute assurance.[32] However, it's a high level of assurance that satisfies management that ICFR are effective. Management must be confident that these controls protect financial reporting mechanisms.

The SEC requires that management use evaluation criteria established by recognized experts to review the company's ICFR. The evaluation criteria helps to ensure that ICFR are effective. The SEC has recognized only one specific framework that meets its requirements: the COSO Framework. The Committee of Sponsoring Organizations (COSO) of the Treadway Commission created its "Internal Control—Integrated Framework" in 1992. It's commonly called the "COSO Framework." Many U.S. businesses use this framework to assess their internal control systems.[33] One thing to keep in mind is that the COSO Framework doesn't directly address IT or information security controls.

Companies trying to comply with Section 404 quickly learned that they needed to review their IT systems. Specifically, they needed to review the ICFR on their IT systems. An Ernst & Young survey found that public companies spent 70 percent of their time addressing IT controls in their first year of SOX compliance.[34] Companies spent a lot of time on IT controls because information systems contain financial data. An error in these systems could cause financial statements to contain errors or mistakes. To comply with Section 404, companies had to make sure that system data was accurate. They had to make sure that they had processes in place to detect inaccurate data.

What Is COSO?

COSO was established in 1985 to indentify factors that contributed to fraudulent financial reporting. Five U.S. financial organizations sponsored COSO. They are the American Accounting Association, the American Institute of Certified Public Accountants, Financial Executives International, the Institute of Internal Auditors, and the Institute of Management Accountants. COSO is a nonprofit organization.

In 1987, COSO issued a report on the factors that contribute to fraudulent financial reporting. Its report contained 49 recommendations to prevent and detect fraudulent financial reports. You can read the 1987 report at *http://www.coso.org/publications/ NCFFR.pdf*. Many SOX provisions mirror the report's recommendations. One of these recommendations called for the creation of effective ICFR.

In 1992, COSO issued guidance on internal controls. The COSO framework says that internal controls are effective when they give the management of a company reasonable assurance that:

- It understands how the entity's operational objectives are being achieved
- Its published financial statements are being prepared reliably
- It's complying with applicable laws and regulations

The COSO Framework has five components. They are:

- **Control environment**—This is the organization's culture. Control environment factors include management philosophy and the competence of the organization's people. The control environment sets the foundation for the other components of the framework.
- **Risk assessment**—This refers to the identification and review of risks that are internal and external to the organization.
- **Control activities**—This refers to how policies and procedures are followed throughout the organization.
- **Information and communication**—This addresses how an organization communicates information to employees. This component also addresses how information systems store and generate data.
- **Monitoring**—This refers to how the organization monitors its internal control systems.

You can learn more about COSO's "Internal Control—Integrated Framework" by visiting *http://www.coso.org/IC-IntegratedFramework-summary.htm*.

SOX Section 404 compliance isn't easy. Section 404 is very general about the types of ICFR that companies must implement. It doesn't give a good definition for ICFR generally. It doesn't address IT controls at all. In 2007, the SEC issued additional guidance to help companies assess ICFR during their Section 404 review. It did this in response to many complaints about the large scope of a Section 404 review. Many of these complaints focused on how to address IT controls.

The SEC stated two broad principles in its guidance:

- Management should assess how its internal controls prevent or detect significant deficiencies in financial statements

- Management should perform a risk-based review of the effectiveness of these controls

The SEC also said that management must exercise its professional judgment to limit the scope of a Section 404 review. It reminded companies that SOX applies to internal controls, including IT controls, that affect financial reporting only.[35]

 NOTE

SOX doesn't specify the IT controls that companies need to implement. Instead, companies must determine the best controls for their systems.

Management must review general IT controls to make sure that IT systems operate properly and consistently. The controls must provide management with reasonable assurance that IT systems operate properly to protect financial reporting. Table 7-1 shows how the goals of ICFR match up with information security goals.

It's clear that management's review of an organization's ICFR must include a review of IT controls as well. The COSO Framework doesn't specifically address IT controls. Organizations use many approaches to evaluating their IT controls. Some organizations follow the Guide to Assessment of IT Risk (GAIT) framework. Others use COBIT. Both of these frameworks appear to meet the SECs requirements for a suitable evaluation framework. They're discussed again later in this chapter.

TABLE 7-1 Internal controls and information security goals.

STEPS TAKEN TO MEET INTERNAL CONTROLS	INFORMATION SECURITY GOALS
Financial reports, records, and data are accurately maintained.	Integrity
Transactions are prepared according to GAAP rules and properly recorded.	Integrity, availability
Unauthorized acquisition or use of data or assets that could affect financial statements will be prevented or detected in a timely manner.	Confidentiality, integrity, availability

Some companies outsource functions. A company can't escape SOX Section 404 liability by outsourcing financial functions. SOX requires companies to monitor ICFR for outsourced operations as well. Many companies do this by asking their outsourcing companies to provide them with a SAS 70.

The American Institute of Certified Public Accountants (AICPA) created the Statement on Auditing Standards (SAS) No. 70, "Service Organizations." It's a widely recognized auditing standard for service organizations. Service organizations are those organizations that provide services to others. A SAS 70 audit reviews the service organization's control activities related to the outsourced service. It includes a review of IT controls on the outsourced service. A SAS 70 audit helps a service organization show that they have proper safeguards in place to protect their customer's data.

Many companies may ask a service provider to share their SAS 70 audit before entering into an outsourcing relationship. Many service organizations have their own auditors prepare an SAS 70 audit so that they can share it with potential customers. They do this because most customers will request a SAS 70. It's more efficient to prepare it in advance.

There are two types of SAS 70 audits. A "type I" audit focuses on controls at a specific point in time. It doesn't involve ongoing tests. A "type II" audit includes detailed tests on a service organization's controls over a certain period. For example, a type II audit can review the organization's controls over a six-month period.

A public company can review the SAS 70 to make sure that the service provider's controls are effective if the outsourced activity affects financial reporting.

Oversight

The Securities and Exchange Commission oversees most SOX provisions. The SEC was created under the Securities and Exchange Act of 1934. Its mission is to protect investors and maintain the integrity of the securities industry.

The SEC has five commissioners. The U.S. President must appoint them. They serve for five-year terms. No more than three of the commissioners may belong to the same political party. The SEC has 11 regional offices in the United States.

SOX gives the SEC specific duties. The SEC is required to designate the members of the PCAOB. It's also required to review various operations of public companies to make sure that they're following SOX.

SOX requires the SEC to review a public company's Form 10-K and Form 10-Q reports at least once every three years.[36] It must do this to try to detect fraud and inaccurate financial statements that could harm the investing public. The SEC has discretion in deciding how often to review companies. SOX states the factors that the SEC should consider when deciding to conduct a review. Under SOX, the SEC must consider:

- Whether a company has amended its financial reports
- Whether a company's stock price fluctuates significantly when compared to other companies
- How much stock the company has issued

- The difference between a company's stock price and its earnings
- Whether a company is large and affects a particular sector of the economy
- Any other factor that the SEC considers relevant

The SEC enforces SOX compliance. It has the power to investigate and sanction public companies that don't comply with SOX.

Compliance and Security Controls

Assessing ICFR in IT systems can be difficult. IT professionals have a number of different frameworks that they can use for reviewing IT controls. You are already familiar with some of these frameworks. Many of these frameworks help companies decide which controls to implement.

COBIT

In 1996, the Information Systems Audit and Control Association (ISACA) released the first version of "Control Objects for Information and related Technology" (COBIT). COBIT is a framework for IT management. The fourth edition of COBIT was released in 2005. ISACA has already started to plan for COBIT 5.0.

COBIT groups IT management into four areas:

- **Plan and Organize**—IT professionals determine the IT strategies needed to support business goals. The business also must understand and assess its IT risks.

- **Acquire and Implement**—IT professionals identify and implement technology solutions. Project management is required to make sure that technology solutions work and are delivered on time and within budget.

- **Deliver and Support**—IT professionals run the IT systems. They make sure that system use supports business objectives. Information security controls are reviewed to make sure that confidentiality, integrity, and availability are maintained.

- **Monitor and Evaluate**—IT professionals continue to monitor and evaluate strategy. They also review technology solutions.

COBIT has 34 high-level control objectives. Most of them are located in the "acquire and implement" and "deliver and support" domains. COBIT objectives are best practices and management measures. They provide organizations with a method for making their own decisions about technology. It's technology neutral. Information security objectives are specifically included within the COBIT framework.

COBIT is closely aligned with the COSO Framework. Both of them can be used together to review ICFR and IT controls for SOX compliance.

You can learn more about COBIT at *http://www.isaca.org.*

GAIT

The Institute of Internal Auditors (IIA) created the "Guide to the Assessment of IT Risk" (GAIT) series in January 2007. IIA updated it in August 2007 to reflect the PCAOB's Auditing Standard No. 5. The IIA created the GAIT framework to help auditors and companies comply with SOX Section 404.

The GAIT framework helps auditors and companies scope Section 404 reviews of IT controls. It realizes that companies must implement ICFR in IT systems. Like the SEC and PCAOB, GAIT advocates a top-down, risk-based approach to review IT controls.

GAIT has four main principles:

- A top-down approach should be used to review risks and IT controls
- The review of risks and IT controls should be limited to financially significant systems, applications, or data
- IT controls and risks exist at various layers in an IT system (application, database, operating system, and network infrastructure)
- IT processes should be mitigated by IT control objectives, not individual controls

Like COBIT, GAIT doesn't recommend individual controls. Instead, it specifies a series of control objectives. Companies are free to choose the individual controls that meet the control objectives. Information security objectives are included in the GAIT guidance to the extent that they scope to systems that impact a company's financial reports.

You can learn more about GAIT at *http://www.theiia.org/guidance/standards-and -guidance/ippf/practice-guides/gait/*.

ISO/IEC Standards

The International Organization for Standardization (ISO) and International Electrotechnical Commission (IEC) has created two standards that companies can use to implement information security controls. The two standards work together. One guides information security governance. The other reviews how to implement security controls. The standards are:

- ISO/IEC 27001:2005, "Information Technology—Security Techniques— Information Security Management Systems—Requirements"
- ISO/IEC 27002:2005, "Information Technology—Security Techniques— Code of Practice for Information Security Management"

ISO/IEC 27001 provides a framework for creating an information security management system. It uses a risk-based approach to review how information security is managed within an organization. It reviews the processes that management teams must consider to operate, monitor, review, and maintain IT systems.

ISO/IEC 27002 lists information security safeguards. Unlike COBIT and GAIT, ISO/IEC 27002 does describe specific controls. It has 11 major sections. Each section reviews a different category of information security controls. The standard explains why organizations should use the listed controls. It also explains how to use the controls. The 11 sections are:

- Security policy
- Organizing information security
- Asset management
- Human resources security
- Physical and environmental security
- Communications and operations management
- Access control
- Information systems acquisition, development, and maintenance
- Information security incident management
- Business continuity management
- Compliance

The ISO/IEC standards are specific to information security. Companies can use these standards to make sure that their information security practices provide reasonable assurance that ICFR are effective. See Table 7-1 for the relationship between SOX internal controls and information security goals.

NIST Computer Security Guidance

Finally, some organizations turn to the National Institute of Standards and Technology (NIST) for information security control guidance. NIST creates information security guidance for federal agencies. These agencies must comply with the Federal Information Security Management Act (FISMA). FISMA and NIST are discussed in Chapter 8.

Many non-governmental organizations also use NIST publications to guide their own information security programs. "NIST Special Publication 800-53 (Rev. 3), Recommended Security Controls for Federal Information Systems and Organizations" is discussed in Chapter 1. It states the minimum security controls that organizations should use to create an effective information security program.

You can learn more about NIST computer security resources at *http://csrc.nist.gov/index.html.*

SOX doesn't provide public companies with specific advice on how to use IT controls. Many organizations use the frameworks reviewed in this section to guide their SOX Section 404 compliance activities.

SOX Influence in Other Types of Companies

With few exceptions, SOX applies only to public companies. However, many different types of organizations have been affected by SOX. This is because SOX promotes good corporate governance practices. Many of these principles make sense for other organizations as well.

In addition to the certification provisions discussed earlier, SOX governance provisions include:

- **Independent directors**—SOX requires a public company to create an independent board of directors. Directors are independent when they don't have financial ties to the company. In some cases, the independence rules extend to members of the director's immediate family.

- **Audit committee**—SOX requires public companies to have an audit committee on their board of directors. This committee works with outside auditors to make sure that financial reports are accurate.

- **Conflicts of interest**—SOX requires executives to disclose certain types of conflicts of interest

A private company might implement SOX controls because it hopes to become a public company someday. Following SOX principles will make the transition from private to public easier. If a private company follows SOX principles, it might be in a better position to attract investors. It will have processes in place that allow investors to review the company's financial condition. Investors will be more likely to invest in companies that show financial transparency.

 NOTE

A nonprofit organization doesn't distribute its profits to owners or shareholders. Instead, it puts its profits back into the organization to help pursue its goals. Many charities are nonprofit organizations.

Nonprofit organizations also have an incentive to follow SOX. Good governance in a nonprofit organization is very important. Nonprofits depend on grants from other entities to support their operations. They also depend on individual donations. People won't contribute to nonprofits that aren't managed well. Nonprofits that adopt SOX governance principles can prove that they have controls in place to properly manage the organization and its finances. A reputation for good governance also will encourage more donations.

In some ways, SOX truly has become a best practice for good governance. Companies that follow SOX practices prove that they have controls in place to prevent and detect wrongdoing. This can be important if a company is involved in litigation about bad governance practices. A plaintiff's lawyer will surely point out if a board didn't follow SOX good governance practices. It won't matter whether the company was required by law to follow SOX or not. Since SOX is a best practice that many companies follow, the implication that a company didn't follow SOX can be damaging.

Corporate Privacy Issues

Corporate information privacy covers a number of issues. Many of them are covered in other chapters of this book. Since companies have a number of different kinds of records, they must approach privacy from many angles. The three major corporate privacy concerns are:

- Privacy of employee data
- Privacy of customer data
- Privacy of corporate data

Employee privacy issues are discussed in Chapters 2 and 13. In general, employees have no expectation of privacy in their workplaces. In most cases, this means that employers can monitor an employee's work activities. It includes monitoring telephone and e-mail conversations. Employers can also monitor employee Internet access and computer use. In most cases, it's best if employers give their employees notice that they're monitoring employees in this way. Chapter 2 reviews the limits of workplace monitoring.

Employers also can monitor employee workspaces and offices. They can use closed circuit television (CCTV) or other video tools to do this. Like other types of monitoring, it's best if the employer gives notice about the monitoring. While the ability to monitor is broad, employers usually can't monitor locations like bathrooms, locker rooms, and employee lounges. Some courts have held that employees do have a reasonable expectation of privacy in these areas.

Companies must protect certain types of information belonging to their employees. For example, if a company provides an employee health plan, it must keep some information private. The Health Insurance Portability and Accountability Act (HIPAA) requires companies to protect some information about employee health plans. A company with an on-site health clinic must protect employee medical records under HIPAA and state laws.

Companies also must protect customer data. Some companies must protect consumer information in special ways. These laws are discussed in Chapter 4. For example, the Gramm-Leach-Bliley Act (GLBA) requires companies to protect consumer financial information. Some states also have laws that require companies to protect the personally identifiable information of their customers. If the company suffers a security breach that compromises this data, then they have to inform their customers about the breach. These laws are called data breach notification laws. These laws are discussed in Chapter 9. The purpose of these laws is to help protect people from identity theft.

Finally, companies have their own internal records to protect. These records may contain data about the company's organization, finances, human resources, and legal matters. In general, a company's directors and officers always have the ability to see all company records. In a small company, the owner has this right. They also can enter employee offices to review records. They have the ability to do this in the regular course of business. This is because they are responsible for the business and its successful operation.

In corporations, the directors of a company have an absolute right to be able to inspect the company's records. Shareholders also have a right to inspect corporate records. However, the shareholder's inspection right is not as broad as a director's right. In most states, shareholders have a right to inspect some records during regular business hours. They must make a written request to inspect corporate records. The request must include the shareholders' reason for wanting to review the records.

Companies also have records regarding their products and services that they must protect. Some of these records might be trade secrets. Trade secrets are information about company products or services that helps one company compete against another company. Trade secrets are a form of intellectual property. A company must protect its trade secret information. If it properly protects this kind of information, it's entitled to legal protection. Trade secrets and intellectual property law issues are discussed in Chapter 10.

Case Studies and Examples

Investors can learn about a company's financial information from many different places. One place to learn information is from the SEC's Electronic Data Gathering and Retrieval (EDGAR) database. All public companies that are required to register with the SEC file their required reports through EDGAR.

You can search for a public company's filings on EDGAR. The URL is *http://www.sec.gov/edgar/searchedgar/webusers.htm.*

Pick a public company and try to search for them on EDGAR. Good companies to search include Microsoft Corp., Apple Inc., Starbucks Corp., and Dell, Inc. Look at the company's most recent Form 10-K report. Item 9 is the SOX Section 404 report on internal controls. What do these sections tell you? What can you learn about the company that you have searched?

CHAPTER SUMMARY

Congress created the Sarbanes-Oxley Act in response to scandal. It passed SOX to help improve investor confidence in publicly traded companies. SOX places rules on public companies and other organizations. These rules promote trustworthy financial reports. The scope of SOX extends to any public company functions or processes that impact financial reporting. The scope of SOX within a company is very broad. SOX requires that companies review many information technology processes to make sure that they're trustworthy.

The scope of SOX is broad. Its influence extends even to organizations that aren't required to follow it. For example, private companies and nonprofit organizations may choose to follow SOX to show their commitment to good governance.

KEY CONCEPTS AND TERMS

Disclosure controls	Internal controls
Dividend	Privately held company
Form 8-K	Public company
Form 10-K	Securities
Form 10-Q	

CHAPTER 7 ASSESSMENT

1. What types of companies must follow all Sarbanes-Oxley Act provisions?

A. Public
B. Private
C. Nonprofit
D. Governmental
E. None of the above

2. A dividend is a shareholder's earnings in a company.

A. True
B. False

3. What is the main goal of the Sarbanes-Oxley Act?

4. How many days after a major event must a company file Form 8-K?

A. Two
B. Three
C. Four
D. Five
E. None of the above

5. Which corporate scandals lead to the creation of the Sarbanes-Oxley Act?

A. Enron
B. WorldCom
C. Adelphia
D. Tyco
E. All of the above

6. What are internal controls over financial reporting (ICFR)?

7. How many members of the Public Company Accounting Oversight Board may be certified public accountants?

A. Five
B. Four
C. Three
D. Two
E. None of the above

8. Which standard replaced "Auditing Standard No. 2?"

A. "Auditing Standard No. 3"
B "Auditing Standard No. 4"
C. "Auditing Standard No. 5"
D. "Auditing Standard No. 6"
E. None of the above

9. Which framework has the U.S. Securities and Exchange Commission official approved as suitable evaluation criteria for internal controls?

A. COBIT
B. COSO
C. GAIT
D. ISO/IEC
E. None of the above

10. Which Sarbanes-Oxley Act provision causes the most concern for information technology professionals?

A. Section 302
B. Section 309
C. Section 404
D. Section 906
E. None of the above

11. A company's chief information security office and chief financial officer must sign a Section 302 certification.

A. True

B. False

12. How often must the U.S. Securities and Exchange Commission review a public company's Form 10-K and Form 10-Q reports?

A. Twice a year

B. Every year

C. Every other year

D. Every three years

E. Every five years

13. What does an internal control over financial reporting (ICFR) do?

14. Under the Sarbanes-Oxley Act, how many years must public companies keep audit papers?

A. Five

B. Six

C. Seven

D. Eight

E. None of the above

15. A public company must file a Form 10-K at the end of each quarter.

A. True

B. False

ENDNOTES

1. Forbes, "Special Report: America's Largest Private Companies," October 28, 2009, *http://www.forbes.com/2009/10/28/largest-private-companies-business-private-companies-09_land.html* (accessed April 16, 2010).

2. CNBC, "Enron: The Smartest Guys in the Room," April 2010, *http://classic.cnbc.com/id/35836210* (accessed April 16, 2010).

3. Entrepreneur, "Enron: A Hot Ticket Again," April 15, 2010, *http://www.entrepreneur.com/startingabusiness/successstories/article206090.html* (accessed April 16, 2010). See also *http://www.broadwaysbestshows.com/enronbroadway/home* (accessed April 16, 2010).

4. CNN, The Guiltiest Guys in the Room," July 5, 2006, *http://money.cnn.com/2006/05/29/news/enron_guiltyest/index.htm* (accessed April 16, 2010).

5. *Fortune* Magazine, "The World's Most Admired Companies," October 2, 2000, *http://money.cnn.com/magazines/fortune/fortune_archive/2000/10/02/288448/index.htm* (accessed April 12, 2010).

6. John Kroger, "Enron, Fraud, and Securities Reform," *Colorado Law Review*, Vol. 76, Issue 1 (2005): 57.

7. *Houston Chronicle*, "Jury Hears Ex-Enron CEO Curse in Wall Street Call," February 2, 2006, *http://www.chron.com/disp/story.mpl/front/3630836.html* (accessed April 16, 2010).

8. Powers, William C., "Special Investigative Committee of the Board of Directors of Enron Corp.," February 1, 2002, *http://i.cnn.net/cnn/2002/LAW/02/02/enron.report/powers.report.pdf* (accessed April 16, 2010).

9. *New York Times*, "An Implosion on Wall Street, "November 29, 2001, *http://www.nytimes.com/2001/11/29/opinion/an-implosion-on-wall-street.html* (accessed April 16, 2010).

10. *Fortune*, "The Ten Largest U.S. Bankruptcies," November 1, 2009, *http://money.cnn.com/galleries/2009/fortune/0905/gallery.largest_bankruptcies.fortune/index.html* (accessed April 16, 2010).

11. *Houston Business Journal*, "Enron Delists Stock as Financial Woes Continue," January 18, 2002, *http://www.bizjournals.com/houston/stories/2002/01/21/story3.html* (accessed April 16, 2010).

12. CNN, "401(k) Investors Sue Enron," November 26, 2001, *http://money.cnn.com/2001/11/26/401k/q_retire_enron_re/* (accessed April 16, 2010).

13. Congressional Research Service, "Enron: A Select Chronology of Congressional, Corporate, and Government Activities," April 9, 2002, *http://fpc.state.gov/documents/organization/9659.pdf* (accessed April 16, 2010).

14. *The Wall Street Journal,* "Investors Hope the '10s Beat the '00s," December 20, 2009, *http://online.wsj. com/article/SB1000142405274870478620457460 7993448916718.html* (accessed April 16, 2010).

15. U.S. Securities and Exchange Commission, "Form 10-K, Annual Report Pursuant to Section 13 or 15(d) of the Securities Exchange Act of 1934, General Instructions," *http://www.sec.gov/about/ forms/form10-k.pdf* (accessed April 16, 2010).

16. U.S. Security and Exchange Commission, "Information Matters," February 22, 2006, *http:// www.sec.gov/answers/infomatters.htm* (accessed April 16, 2010).

17. Sarbanes-Oxley Act of 2002, Pub. L. No. 107-204, 116 Stat. 745 (codified as amended in scattered sections of U.S. Code Vol. 15).

18. *The New York Times,* "Bush Signs Bill Aimed at Fraud in Corporations," July 30, 2002,*http:// www.nytimes.com/2002/07/31/business/corporate -conduct-the-president-bush-signs-bill-aimed-at-fraud -in-corporations.html?pagewanted=1* (accessed April 16, 2010).

19. *Time,* "Enron: Who's Accountable?" January 13, 2002, *http://www.time.com/time/business/ article/0,8599,193520,00.html* (accessed April 16, 2010).

20. Powers Report, see note 8, at page 24-25.

21. U.S. Code Vol. 15, sec. 7211.

22. Ibid.

23. Ernst & Young, "Emerging Trends in Internal Controls: Fourth Survey and Industry Insights," September 2005, *http://www.sarbanes-oxley.be/aabs_ emerging_trends_survey4.pdf* (accessed April 16, 2010).

24. U.S. Securities and Exchange Commission, "SEC Approves PCAOB Auditing Standard No. 5 Regarding Audits of Internal Control Over Financial Reporting," July 25, 2007, *http://www.sec.gov/ news/press/2007/2007-144.htm* (accessed April 16, 2010).

25. Marcella, Albert J., "Electronically Stored Information and Cyberforensics," *Information Systems Control Journal,* Vol. 5 (2008), Available at *http:// www.isaca.org/Template.cfm?Section=Home&CONTE NTID=52106&TEMPLATE=/ContentManagement/ ContentDisplay.cfm#4* (accessed April 16, 2010).

26. U.S. Code Vol. 15, sec. 7213m.

27. *Commission Guidance Regarding Management's Report on Internal Controls Over Financial Reporting,* Code of Federal Regulations, Title 17, sec. 241.

28. U.S. Code Vol. 18, sec. 1519.

29. U.S. Code Vol. 15, sec. 7241.

30. U.S. Securities and Exchange Commission, "Final Rule: Management's Report on Internal Control Over Financial Reporting and Certification of Disclosure in Exchange Act Periodic Reports," June 5, 2003, *http://www.sec.gov/rules/final/ 33-8238.htm#iib3a* (accessed April 15, 2010).

31. Ibid.

32. U.S. Securities and Exchange Commission, "Staff Statement on Management's Report on Internal Control Over Financial Reporting," May 16, 2005, *http://www.sec.gov/info/accountants/ stafficreporting.htm* (accessed April 16, 2010). *See also* Public Company Accounting Oversight Board, "AU Section 230: Due Professional Care in the Performance of Work," June 12, 2007 amendments, *http://pcaobus.org/Standards/Auditing/Pages/ AU230.aspx#ps-pcaob_8b4d2389-b14e-4358-a4b2 -93e6360eb378* (accessed April 15, 2010).

33. Committee of Sponsoring Organizations of the Treadway Commission, "Guidance on Internal Control," no date, *http://www.coso.org/IC.htm* (accessed on April 15, 2010).

34. Ernst & Young Survey, *http://www.sarbanes -oxley.be/aabs_emerging_trends_survey4.pdf.*

35. *Commission Guidance Regarding Management's Report on Internal Controls Over Financial Reporting,* Code of Federal Regulations, Title 17, sec. 241.

36. U.S. Code Vol. 15, 7266.

Federal Government Information Security and Privacy Regulations

I N A 2009 SPEECH, U.S. PRESIDENT BARACK OBAMA said that America's digital infrastructure is a "strategic national asset."[1] He urged a broad plan to protect the security and privacy of federal information systems. He said that we must better protect the nation's digital infrastructure. Both the federal government and private organizations have a role to play.

This chapter reviews how the federal government protects its information systems. These systems hold personal data about U.S. residents. They conduct the business of running the country. They also hold sensitive security data. They are used for the nation's defense. This chapter reviews the security and privacy laws that protect these systems.

Chapter 8 Topics

This chapter covers the following topics and concepts:

- What the information security challenges facing the federal government are
- What the Federal Information Security Management Act does
- How the federal government protects privacy in information systems
- What import and export control laws are
- What some case studies and examples are

Chapter 8 Goals

When you complete this chapter, you will be able to:

- Describe federal government information security challenges
- Explain the main requirements under the Federal Information Security Management Act
- Describe the role of the National Institute of Standards and Technology in creating information security standards
- Discuss approaches to protecting national security systems
- Describe how the U.S. federal government protects privacy in information systems
- Review import and export control laws

Information Security Challenges Facing the Federal Government

In 2010, federal chief information officer (CIO) Vivek Kundra said that the government's computers are attacked millions of times each day.[2] This statistic isn't very surprising. The federal government is the largest producer and user of information in the United States.[3] Government computer systems hold data that's critical for government operations. They hold data on people living in the United States. This includes employment, tax, and citizenship data. They hold data on businesses operating in the United States. They also hold data that's used to protect the United States from threats.

The government faces many of the same information security challenges that private entities face. Federal information technology (IT) systems and the data in them are attractive targets for criminals:

- Thieves stole a laptop that belonged to the National Institutes of Health (NIH). They stole it from a researcher's car. The laptop held the personal information of 2,500 people in a NIH study.

- Hackers gained entry to Federal Aviation Administration (FAA) computers. They stole the personal information of more than 45,000 FAA employees and retirees.

- Attackers illegally accessed the USAJOBS database. USAJOBS is the federal government's employment Web site. They stole account and contact information. The government said that the thieves didn't access sensitive personal information.

- The U.S. State Department warned 400 people about a computer security breach. The attackers stole passport application information. The stolen data included Social Security numbers (SSNs). The thieves used the data to open credit card accounts.

- Spies broke into the U.S. Pentagon's computer systems. They stole data on the Department of Defense's Joint Strike Fighter aircraft.

The U.S. government has a history of protecting its computers. In 1987, Congress passed the Computer Security Act (CSA).[4] This was the first law to address federal computer security. Under the CSA, every federal agency had to inventory its IT systems. They also had to create security plans for those systems. Agencies had to review their plans every year.

NOTE

FISMA initially gave the Office of Management and Budget (OMB) the authority to oversee FISMA compliance. The OMB is part of the President's Executive Office. In July 2010 the Department of Homeland Security (DHS) was made responsible for many aspects of FISMA compliance.

In 2002, Congress created the Federal Information Security Management Act (FISMA).[5] It created FISMA, part, because of the September 11, 2001, terrorist attacks. The attacks highlighted the need for better information security. FISMA recognizes that information security is crucial. It superseded most of the CSA. It's now the main law that states how federal agencies must secure their IT systems. It doesn't address **national security systems**, or NSSs. National security systems are IT systems that hold military, defense, and intelligence information.

In 2009, President Barack Obama ordered a review of cyberspace policy, which resulted in the document titled "Cyberspace Policy Review." This review looked at U.S. policies to secure government IT systems. It identified cybersecurity weaknesses. It also proposed solutions to them. After the review, President Obama identified cybersecurity as a national challenge. He said that both the federal government and private entities must focus on these issues.[6] You can read the "Cyberspace Policy Review" at *http://www.whitehouse.gov/administration/eop/nsc/cybersecurity.*

The review recommended that the president appoint a government cybersecurity official. This position is responsible for coordinating federal cybersecurity policies and activities. Some people call this official the "cybersecurity czar."

In March 2010, the federal CIO spoke at a House of Representatives subcommittee meeting. He talked about federal information security challenges.[7] He said the government faces the following challenges:

- Lack of coordination within the federal government
- Lack of coordination between the federal government and the private sector
- A culture within the federal government of merely complying with reporting requirements
- Lack of an enterprise approach to information technology
- Lack of focused research and development activities to enhance cybersecurity

This chapter focuses on how the federal government protects its IT systems and discusses many of FISMA's provisions. You should be aware that this area of law is changing. In early 2010, the OMB introduced new FISMA compliance tools. Now federal agencies can report on FISMA activities in near real time. Agencies with FISMA responsibilities are starting to work together to create a government-wide information security risk management structure. More changes in this area are expected.

In July 2010, the Departent of Homeland Security became responsible for many aspects of FISMA compliance. As of this writing, this change in compliance structure is new. It is unknown how these changes will ultimately affect how federal agencies comply with FISMA. Many references in this book refer to how the OMB approached FISMA compliance. You can expect some of the requirements described in this chapter to change as the DHS becomes more involved in compliance issues. As the government's approach to federal information security evolves, you can expect even more changes in this area.

The Federal Information Security Management Act

President George W. Bush signed the Federal Information Security Management Act in 2002. It's part of the E-Government Act of 2002. FISMA is Title III of the E-Government Act.

FISMA merges a number of different laws.[8] All of these laws addressed different information security issues. Since no law was comprehensive, Congress heard many reports that information security efforts at the federal level were not effective. Congress intended FISMA to be a strong law to fix this problem. It would guide federal agencies in making sure that their IT systems are secure.

Purpose and Scope

Congress created FISMA to protect federal IT systems and the data in those systems. FISMA defines "information security" as protecting IT systems in order to provide confidentiality, integrity, and availability.[9] IT systems must be protected from unauthorized use, access, disruption, modification, and destruction.

FISMA has six main provisions. The law:

- Sets forth agency information security responsibilities
- Requires a yearly independent review of agency information security programs
- Authorizes the National Institute of Standards and Technology (NIST) to develop information security standards
- Gives the OMB specific oversight responsibilities, some of which were transferred to the DHS in July 2010
- Clarifies that national security systems (NSSs) must be secured using a risk-based approach
- Provides for a central federal security incident response center

FISMA applies to federal agencies. These agencies fall under the executive branch of the U.S. government. They report to the president. Examples of federal agencies include the Federal Aviation Administration, the Social Security Administration, and the Department of Education.

Main Requirements

FISMA has many requirements. This section will review most of them. First, this section reviews what federal agencies must do to comply with FISMA. Second, it reviews how NIST helps agencies shape their information security programs. Third, it reviews the federal central incident response center. Finally, it reviews how FISMA applies to national security systems.

Agency Information Security Programs

FISMA requires each federal agency to create an agency-wide information security program. Even agencies with NSSs must create these programs. An agency's information security program must include:

- **Risk assessments**—Agencies must perform risk assessments. They must measure the harm that could result from unauthorized access to or use of agency IT systems. Agencies must base their information security programs on the results of these risk assessments.

- **Annual inventory**—Agencies must inventory their IT systems. They must update it each year.

- **Policies and procedures**—Agencies must create policies and procedures to reduce risk to an acceptable level. The policies must protect IT systems throughout their life cycle. Agencies also must create configuration management policies.

- **Subordinate plans**—Agencies must make sure that they have plans for securing networks, facilities, and systems or groups of IT systems. These plans are for technologies or system components that are a part of the larger information security program.

- **Security awareness training**—Agencies must give training to employees and any other users of their IT systems. This includes contractors. This training must make people aware of potential risks to the agency's IT systems. It also must make people aware of their duties to protect these systems.

- **Testing and evaluation**—Agencies must test their security controls at least once a year. They must test management, operational, and technical controls for each IT system.

- **Remedial actions**—Agencies must have a plan to fix weaknesses in its information security program.

- **Incident response**—Agencies must have an incident response procedure. They must state how the agency detects and mitigates incidents. The procedure must include reporting incidents to the Department of Homeland Security United States Computer Emergency Readiness Team (US-CERT) as needed.

- **Continuity of operations**—Agencies must have business continuity plans as part of their information security programs.

An agency's information security program applies to any other organization that uses the agency's IT systems or data. An agency must protect the IT systems that support the agency's operations. It must protect them even if another agency or contractor provides the systems. This can broaden the scope of FISMA, especially since IT systems and functions are often outsourced.

FISMA applies to contractors who perform services on behalf of a federal agency. For example, researchers at universities who work with federal agencies may have to follow FISMA requirements on their own IT systems. That's because those systems could store federal data. The OMB has required that FISMA security requirements be included in research grants where applicable.[10]

In January 2008, the NIH said that FISMA applies to NIH grants when a researcher collects, stores, processes, or uses data on behalf of the Department of Health and Human Services (HHS). The NIH is a part of HHS. You can read the notice at *http://grants.nih.gov/grants/guide/notice-files/not-od-08-032.html*.

One of the most important parts of a FISMA information security program is that agencies test and evaluate it. FISMA requires each agency to perform "periodic testing and evaluation of the effectiveness of information security policies, procedures, and practices."[11] Agencies must test every IT system at least once a year. They must test IT systems with greater risk more often.

Agencies also must review their security controls. Some kinds of security controls are required under FISMA. NIST specifies some minimum security controls. An agency must make sure that they implement these controls properly. They also must make sure that the controls work. The yearly testing requirement recognizes that security is an ongoing process. Agencies must always monitor their information security risk. They also must monitor the controls put in place to mitigate that risk.

Agencies must follow NIST guidance in performing their annual reviews. If an agency uses a different model to perform its review, that model must include the same elements that NIST does. The role of NIST is discussed later in this chapter.

Under FISMA, agencies must name a senior official to be in charge of information security. In most agencies, this is the chief information security officer (CISO). The CISO is responsible for FISMA compliance. The CISO's main job duties must focus on information security. Under FISMA, a CISO must have the resources necessary to make sure that the agency can comply with FISMA.

Each agency must report yearly to the OMB on its FISMA compliance activities. An agency also must send a copy of their report to:

 NOTE

CISOs must be information security professionals. They must have the "professional qualifications, including training and experience, required to administer" FISMA requirements.[12]

- House of Representatives Committee on Oversight and Government Reform
- House of Representatives Committee on Science and Technology
- Senate Committee on Governmental Affairs
- Senate Committee on Commerce, Science, and Transportation
- U.S. Government Accountability Office (GAO)
- The agency's congressional authorization and appropriations committee

An agency's FISMA report is shared widely. The OMB has said that agencies shouldn't include too much information about actual IT system operations in their reports. It's possible that criminals could learn about weaknesses in IT systems by reading the reports.

What Is an Inspector General?

An inspector general (IG) is an official who reviews the actions of a federal agency. An IG examines the agency's activities to make sure that it's operating efficiently and following good governance practices. IGs are independent officials by law. The agency that an IG reports to can't prevent the IG from performing an audit or investigation.

The Inspector General Act of 1978 defined an IG's role. An IG is responsible for:

- Conducting independent and objective audits, investigations, and inspections
- Preventing and detecting waste, fraud, and abuse
- Promoting economy, effectiveness, and efficiency
- Reviewing pending legislation and regulations
- Keeping the agency head and Congress informed about agency activities

IGs are appointed to their positions. Their appointment is based on their experience in accounting, auditing, law, and investigations. They're not political officials. Some agency heads may appoint and remove their own IGs.

The president nominates IGs for major federal agencies. The Senate approves them. Only the president can remove these IGs. The president nominates IGs in the Department of Commerce, Department of Justice, and OMB, as well as in some other agencies.

An agency's yearly report must review its information security program. It also must assess the agency's progress on correcting any weaknesses in the program or security controls.

The yearly report also must include the results of an independent evaluation of the agency's information security program. Some agencies have an **inspector general (IG)**. If an agency has an IG, then the IG may carry out this evaluation. Some agencies don't have an IG. If they don't, the head of the agency must hire an external auditor to perform the evaluation.

The FISMA reporting process is time consuming. Agencies spend a lot of time creating their reports. The OMB spends a lot of time reviewing them. It reports that it takes almost three full-time employees over a month to review agency reports.[13] The process also is very paper-intensive. For example, in six years, the Department of State produced 95,000 pages of paper to meet its FISMA reporting requirements. It spent $133 million to create these reports.[14]

The OMB recognized that the FISMA reporting process took up too much time. In 2010, it announced major changes to this process. It wanted to make FISMA reporting more efficient. The OMB is now requiring all federal agencies to file their annual FISMA reports electronically. Agencies will use the CyberScope data collection tool to do this. This is a tool created by the DHS. The tool allows a real-time data feed that helps agencies and the OMB quickly assess the agency's information security posture.[15]

The OMB also said that it will interview agency officials about their FISMA reports. It will ask them about their reports and information security programs. It also will conduct a government-wide review of federal information security posture. You can read the OMB's 2010 FISMA report instructions at *http://www.whitehouse.gov/omb/assets/memoranda_2010/m10-15.pdf.*

The Role of NIST

FISMA requires the Department of Commerce to create information security standards and guidelines. The Commerce Department delegated this responsibility to NIST. NIST is an agency of the Department of Commerce. Under FISMA, NIST must create:

- Standards that all federal agencies use to categorize their data and IT systems
- Guidelines recommending the types of data and IT systems to be included in each category
- Minimum information security controls for IT systems

The OMB has stated that agencies must follow NIST standards and guidelines for non-national security systems. These standards and guidelines help agencies meet their FISMA obligations. NIST creates two different types of documents. They are Federal Information Processing Standards (FIPSs) and Special Publications (SPs). FIPS are standards. SPs are guidelines.

> **NOTE**
> In general, a standard states mandatory actions that an organization must take to protect its IT systems. A guideline states recommended actions that an organization should follow. These terms are discussed in Chapter 1.

Federal agencies must follow FIPS. They must comply with new FIPS within one year of their publication date. FIPS don't apply to national security systems.

NIST creates FIPS when there's a compelling reason to do so. It creates FIPS if there's no acceptable industry standard or solution for the underlying information security issue. At the time this book was written, there were 17 FIPS for information security. You can view them at *http://csrc.nist.gov/publications/PubsFIPS.html.*

NIST uses procedures described in the Administrative Procedures Act (APA) to create FIPS. The APA states formal procedures for creating rules and regulations. This formal process ensures due process. It makes sure that all interested agencies have a chance to comment on draft FIPS. NIST publishes a proposed FIPS in the "Federal Register." A proposed FIPS is available for public review for 30 to 90 days. The Department of Commerce must approve FIPS before they can be finalized.

Special Publications are computer security guidelines. They are more general than FIPS. NIST creates SPs in collaboration with industry, government, and academic information security experts. NIST doesn't use the very formal FIPS drafting process to create these documents.

> **NOTE**
> You can view SPs at *http://csrc.nist.gov/publications/PubsSPs.html.*

FISMA Implementation Project

NIST has created a FISMA Implementation Project to help it meet its FISMA duties. The project helps it create FISMA-related standards and guidelines in a timely manner. The project has two phases. In the first phase, NIST is developing standards and guidelines to help agencies meet basic FISMA requirements. The documents developed in this phase help agencies create their information security programs. Phase I is expected to last from 2003 to 2012.[16]

In Phase II of the project, NIST will create additional guidance materials. These materials will help organizations fine-tune their information security programs. This phase lasts from 2007 to 2012.

It takes time to create thoughtful guidance and standards. NIST consults with many different sources when it creates guidance. You can learn more about the FISMA Implementation Project at *http://csrc.nist.gov/groups/SMA/fisma/overview.html*.

Federal agencies have some flexibility in using the SPs for guidance. They help guide federal agencies in strengthening their IT systems. The OMB understands that this may lead to different results among federal agencies. It acknowledges that different results are expected. Agencies have no flexibility in implementing FIPS, as they are mandatory.

NIST uses a risk management framework (RMF) approach to FISMA compliance. This framework is outlined in "SP 800-37, Guide for Applying the Risk Management Framework to Federal Information Systems: A Security Life Cycle Approach." This approach helps protect IT systems during their whole life cycle. The NIST RMF outlines six steps to protect federal IT systems. They are:

- Categorize IT systems
- Select minimum security controls
- Implement security controls in IT systems
- Assess security controls for effectiveness
- Authorize the IT system for processing
- Continuously monitor security controls

NIST's RMF recommends a continuous process of categorization, assessment, and monitoring. Figure 8-1 shows this process.

NIST guides agencies at each RMF step. "FIPS 199, Standards for Security Categorization of Federal Information and Information Systems" helps them categorize their IT systems. It serves as the starting point for an agency's information security program. It helps them separate their IT systems into categories based on risk. Agencies then apply security controls to their IT system based upon their category.

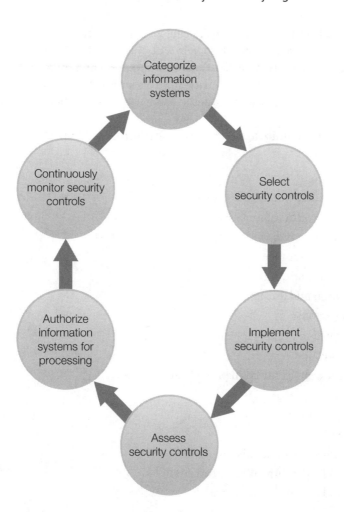

FIGURE 8-1

Risk management framework process.

Under FIPS 199, agencies must first assess the impact to IT systems due to a loss of confidentiality, integrity, or availability. The "security category" expresses that impact. FIPS defines three security categories. They are:

- **Low**—The loss of confidentiality, integrity, or availability has a limited adverse effect on the agency, its information assets, or people. A low impact event results in minor damage to assets.
- **Moderate**—The loss of confidentiality, integrity, or availability has a serious adverse effect on the agency, its information assets, or people. A moderate impact event results in significant damage to assets.
- **High**—The loss of confidentiality, integrity, or availability has a severe or catastrophic adverse effect on the agency, its information assets, or people. A high impact event results in major damage to assets.

8

Federal Government
Information

After the agency determines the security category, it must decide which controls to use. NIST created two documents to help with this task. They are "FIPS 200, Minimum Security Requirements for Federal Information and Information Systems" and "SP 800-53, Recommended Security Controls for Federal Information Systems." The OMB requires that agencies use these documents to make their security control decisions.

These documents require agencies to specify controls in 17 areas. FIPS 200 lists these areas. They are:

- Access control
- Awareness and training
- Audit and accountability
- Certification, accreditation, and security assessments
- Configuration management
- Contingency planning
- Identification and authentication
- Incident response
- Maintenance
- Media protection
- Physical and environmental protection
- Planning
- Personnel security
- Risk assessment
- System and services acquisition
- System and communications protection
- System and information integrity

Agencies must apply the right security controls. They must tailor controls to the level of impact. SP 800-53 defines the minimum thresholds, or baselines, for each category. For example, agencies must use low-impact security controls in IT systems where an adverse event has a low impact. It must follow a similar practice for moderate and high impacts.

Table 8-1 shows an example of how FIPS 200 and SP 800-53 work together. The example shows the different baselines for wireless access in the access control area.

TABLE 8-1 SP 800-53 access control baselines for wireless access.

SECURITY CONTROL AREA (FIPS 200)	LOW-IMPACT SYSTEM CONTROLS (SP 800-53)	MODERATE-IMPACT CONTROLS (SP 800-53)	HIGH-IMPACT SYSTEM CONTROLS (SP 800-53)
Access control (wireless access controls)	The agency must: • Establish use restrictions for wireless access • Monitor for unauthorized wireless access • Authorize wireless access to an information system prior to access • Enforce wireless access connection requirements	Low impact controls, and the agency must: • Protect wireless access to the system using authentication and encryption	Low and moderate impact controls, and the agency must: • Monitor for unauthorized wireless connections to the information system and scan for unauthorized wireless access points • Not allow users to independently configure wireless networking capabilities • Limit wireless communications to organization-controlled boundaries

Agencies can use other NIST guidelines to help them improve their security controls. For example, NIST has created a SP for wireless network access authentication.[17] An agency could use this SP to strengthen its access control baseline. Once it has implemented security controls, it must test them.

The OMB requires federal agencies to test their security controls. "NIST SP 800-53A, Guide for Assessing the Security Controls in Federal Information Systems" walks agencies through security control assessments. These assessments are performed throughout the RMF stages.

NIST's RMF requires agencies to authorize their IT system for processing. This means that an agency must test their systems and approve their operation. This process is based on a review of the risk of operating the system. An agency must specifically accept the risks of operation prior to allowing an IT system to operate.

Finally, agencies must continuously monitor their security controls. They must make sure that they're effective. They also must document any changes to their IT systems. They must assess changes for new risks.

The RMF and NIST supporting documents for each step are listed in Table 8-2.

NIST's Risk Management Framework

You should note that the RMF in SP 800-37 is relatively new. NIST updated this document in February 2010. This SP used to be called "Guide for Security Certification and Accreditation."

The OMB requires federal agencies to certify their IT systems. They also must accept the risk of running the systems. This process used to be known as "Certification and Accreditation," or C&A. Agencies used the old version of NIST SP 800-37 to complete a C&A. Some FISMA references still refer to the C&A process. This process is now called "security authorization."

NIST and the OMB realized that the C&A process had some problems. Some agencies thought that it was merely a compliance exercise. They didn't review their IT systems in a comprehensive manner. The new RMF and security authorization process shows that C&A is more than just planning for IT systems. It also includes continuous testing and monitoring of those systems. C&A is now one part of the RMF process.

The new RMF also is notable because NIST worked on it with many other federal agencies. This group was called the Joint Task Force Transformation Initiative Interagency Working Group. NIST and members of the intelligence, military, and national security communities were part of the group. The group created a common framework for information security management throughout the federal government.

The new RMF signals changes in FISMA compliance. It's becoming more thorough. It makes information security an ongoing and evolving process, rather than a documentation exercise.

TABLE 8-2   Risk management framework and NIST supporting documents.

RISK MANAGEMENT FRAMEWORK STEP	NIST SUPPORTING DOCUMENTATION
Categorize IT systems	FIPS 199, Security categorization SP 800-60, Security category mapping
Select minimum security controls	FIPS 200, Minimum security controls SP 800-53, Recommended security controls
Implement security controls in IT systems	SP 800-70, Checklist for IT products
Assess security controls for effectiveness	SP 800-53A, Guide to assessing controls
Authorize the IT system for processing	SP 800-37, Risk management framework
Continuously monitor security controls	SP 800-37, Risk management framework SP 800-53A, Guide to assessing controls

Central Incident Response Center

Under FISMA, the government must have a federal incident response (IR) center. The OMB is responsible for this. Under FISMA, the IR center must:

- Give technical support to agencies about information security incidents.
- Share information about security incidents.
- Inform agencies about current and potential threats and vulnerabilities.
- Consult with NIST and agencies with national security systems about information security incidents.

NIST created a national IR center in 1996. It was called the Federal Computer Incident Response Capability (FedCIRC). In 2003, the DHS was given the responsibility to run a federal IR center. The FedCIRC was absorbed into the DHS center. It's now called the US-CERT.

Agencies must report all incidents to the US-CERT. This includes NSS incidents. An incident is a violation of computer security policies or practices. It also includes an imminent threat of violation of policies or practices. The government's incident categories are:

- **Category 0, Exercise/Network Testing**—This category is for internal testing activities. These incidents aren't reported. This category is only for internal agency use.
- **Category 1: Unauthorized Access**—Agencies must report unauthorized access to their IT systems in this category. Unauthorized access is technical or physical access to an IT system. An agency must report these incidents even if data isn't compromised.
- **Category 2: Denial of Service (DoS)**—An agency must report successful DoS attacks that harm its IT systems.
- **Category 3: Malicious Code**—An agency must report successful installation of malicious software on its IT systems. They don't have to report attempted attacks stopped by antivirus software.
- **Category 4: Improper Use**—Agencies must report violations of their acceptable use policies.
- **Category 5: Scans, Probes, and Attempted Access**—Agencies must report any activities that seek to access or identify its IT systems. These activities aren't compromises or DoS attacks.
- **Category 6: Investigation**—This category is for unusual events. These incidents require more review because they're odd or potentially harmful. These incidents aren't reported. This category is only for internal agency use.

> ▶ **NOTE**
>
> From October to December 2008, agencies reported Category 5 incidents most often. They were 74 percent of all reported incidents to the US-CERT. You can read the report at *http://www.us-cert.gov/ press_room/trendsanalysisQ109.pdf*.

Agencies must report incidents within certain timeframes. Table 8-3 lists when agencies must report incidents to the US-CERT.

TABLE 8-3	Federal agency incident reporting timeframe.
CATEGORY	**REPORTING TIMEFRAME**
Category 0—Exercise/Network Defense Testing	None
Category 1—Unauthorized Access	Within one hour of discovery
Category 2—DoS	Within two hours of discovery if the attack is ongoing and the agency isn't able to stop it
Category 3—Malicious Code	Daily; must be reported within one hour of discovery if widespread across an agency
Category 4—Improper Use	Weekly
Category 5—Scans, Probes, and Attempted Access	Monthly; must be reported within one hour of discovery if an IT system contains classified information
Category 6—Investigation	None

The US-CERT coordinates IR across the government. It shares information to help the government respond to threats. It also provides information security tips to the public. You can learn more about US-CERT at *http://www.us-cert.gov.*

National Security Systems

FISMA requires federal agencies to secure national security systems using a risk-based approach. A NSS includes systems that are for:

- Intelligence activities
- Command and control of military forces
- Weapons or weapons-control equipment
- Use cryptography to protect national security
- Critical to military or intelligence missions
- Must be kept classified for national defense or foreign policy

FYI

FISMA doesn't apply to classified information. Classified information is protected by Presidential executive order. It's information that's labeled Confidential, Secret, or Top Secret. Its label is based upon its National Security importance. This data must be protected to meet national security goals. This type of data is discussed in Chapter 1.

The Committee on National Security Systems (CNSS) oversees FISMA activities for NSSs. "National Security Directive 42" (NSD-42) gives the CNSS this authority. NSD-42 defines the roles and responsibilities for securing national security systems. President George H. W. Bush signed it in 1990. The CNSS reports to the President on the security status of these systems.

The CNSS has 21 voting members. They include officials from the National Security Administration (NSA), Central Intelligence Agency (CIA), and Department of Defense (DoD). A DoD member leads the committee. You can learn about the CNSS at *www.cnss.gov*.

Federal agencies with NSSs must follow CNSS policies. In February 2009, the CNSS issued "Policy No. 22, Information Assurance Risk Management Policy for National Security Systems."[18] It outlines a six-step process for protecting NSSs. All agencies with a NSS must follow it. This framework is the same as the NIST RMF. They're similar because NIST and the CNSS worked together to create them.

NIST and CNSS also worked together to standardize how agencies categorize IT systems. They created similar processes for choosing information security controls. CNSS "Instruction No. 1253, Security Categorization and Control Selection for National Security Systems" lists security controls for NSSs.[19] This document is a companion to NIST "SP 800-53, Recommended Security Controls For Federal Information Systems."

Access Control Models

An access control model is an information security control. Security controls are built into operating systems and applications. They're used to control how people access files and data in an IT system. They're automated controls. There are three main types of access control models:

- **Discretionary access control (DAC)**—In this model, a data owner decides which subjects can access certain resources. DAC models are based on the identity of the subject seeking access to a resource. In this model, data owners have a lot of freedom to decide who can access files or data.

- **Mandatory access control (MAC)**—In this model, data owners don't have the ability to decide who can access certain files or data. This model is based on a security label system. Users of the system have a security label. Data and files in the system also have a security label. A user can access only data with the same (or lower) security label.

- **Role-based access control (RBAC)**—In this model, users are assigned roles in a system. They can access only data that is associated with their role. A person can't access data that isn't associated with his or her role.

DAC and RBAC models are usually found in industry. RBAC models, in particular, allow businesses flexibility in allowing access to data. MAC systems usually are associated with the military and classified data. This is because these systems place a high value on confidentiality.

FISMA permits the directors of the DoD and CIA to develop additional information security policies for NSSs within their own agencies. The OMB must report to Congress on FISMA compliance for NSSs. It also makes sure that agencies with a NSS are meeting FISMA's legal requirements. The OMB makes sure that agencies with a NSS create an information security program and test it each year.

Oversight

Prior to July 2010, the OMB was responsible for overseeing FISMA compliance. Some of this responsibility was transferred to the DHS at that time. The OMB will still oversee FISMA-related budgetary issues. The OMB can also withhold funding from agencies that fail to follow FISMA. In addition, the OMB must continue to issue a report to Congress each year on the government's FISMA compliance. This report details how federal agencies are complying with FISMA. It also identifies problem areas.

After July 2010, the DHS has the power to ensure that agencies are meeting their FISMA obligations. It can also create rules and other guidance that these agencies must follow. It retains its prior responsibilities with respect to incident response. The OMB and DHS share some FISMA oversight with other agencies, particularly with respect to national security systems. The Directors of the DoD and CIA also have some FISMA oversight responsibilities. The DoD has responsibility for NSSs that hold military information. The CIA has responsibility for NSSs with intelligence information.

Protecting Privacy in Federal Information Systems

Data privacy is an important issue for the federal government. There are a number of federal laws designed to protect data privacy. Many of these laws are discussed in Chapter 2. The two major laws protecting the privacy of data that the government uses in the course of business are:

- The Privacy Act of 1974
- The E-Government Act of 2002

The Privacy Act of 1974

> **NOTE**
>
> The Privacy Act applies only to data collected about U.S. citizens and permanent residents.

Congress created the Privacy Act of 1974[20] to protect data collected by the government. It applies to records created and used by federal agencies in the executive branch.

Under the Privacy Act, a **record** is any information about a person that an agency maintains. It includes a person's educational, financial, medical, and criminal history information. The act requires agencies to keep accurate and complete records. It also states that an agency should store only the data that it needs to conduct business. It shouldn't store any extra or unnecessary data.

The Privacy Act states the rules that an agency must follow to collect, use, and transfer personally identifiable information. An agency can't disclose a person's records without his or her written consent. There are 12 exceptions to this general rule.

If a situation falls within an exception, then the agency can disclose records without consent. An agency doesn't need written consent to disclose a record if the disclosure is:

- Made to a federal agency employee who needs the record to perform his or her job duties
- Required under the Freedom of Information Act
- Made for an agency's routine use
- Made to the U.S. Census Bureau to perform a survey
- Made for statistical research or reporting, and all personally identifiable data has been removed
- To the National Archives and Records Administration because the record has historical value
- Made in response to a written request from a law enforcement or regulatory agency for civil or criminal law purposes
- Made to protect a person's health or safety
- Made to Congress
- Made to the U.S. Comptroller General in the course of the performance of the duties of the U.S. Government Accountability Office
- Made in response to a court order
- Made to a consumer reporting agency for certain permitted purposes

Under the Privacy Act, a person may ask for a copy of any records that an agency has about that person. The person can ask only for records that are retrievable by the person's name, SSN, or some other type of unique identifier. A person also may ask an agency to amend any incorrect records. If an agency refuses to amend a person's record, then that person may sue the agency to have the record amended. A person also can sue the agency if it denies access to his or her records.

Federal agencies must protect the data that they collect. The act requires them to implement administrative, technical, and physical safeguards to protect the records that they maintain. They must protect their records against any anticipated threats that could harm the people indentified in the records. Under the act, harm includes embarrassment.

The law requires agencies to give the public notice about their record-keeping systems. This notice is called a **system of records notice (SORN)**. An agency must publish a SORN for any system that holds records on an individual. It must publish SORNs only for systems that retrieve records either by a person's name or some other personal identifier. An agency must publish its SORNs in the Federal Register.

8

Federal Government
Information

FYI

Every agency is required to post its SORNs on its Web page. You can find the SORNs for the National Aeronautics and Space Administration (NASA) at *http://www.nasa.gov/privacy/nasa_sorn_index.html*.

An agency that violates the Privacy Act can be subject to both civil and criminal penalties. A person can sue a federal agency for any Privacy Act violation. For example, people can sue if an agency denies them access to their records. They also can sue if an agency refuses to amend a record. If a court finds that an agency has intentionally or willfully violated the act, it can award a plaintiff the actual damages that he or she suffered due to the violation. Under the law, a person is entitled to recover at least $1,000. A court also can order the agency to pay the plaintiff's attorney fees.

A federal agency employee can be criminally responsible for violating the Privacy Act. If an employee improperly discloses information, he or she can be charged with a misdemeanor. The employee also could be fined up to $5,000. An agency employee who keeps records without filing a SORN can be fined up to $5,000.

The OMB oversees Privacy Act compliance. It can publish rules for federal agencies to follow to meet their Privacy Act responsibilities.

The E-Government Act of 2002

The E-Government Act of 2002 has privacy provisions that compliment the Privacy Act. Under the E-Government Act, federal agencies must:

- Review their IT systems for privacy risks
- Post privacy policies on their Web sites
- Post machine-readable privacy policies on their Web sites
- Report privacy activities to the OMB

A **privacy impact assessment (PIA)** is an agency's review of how its IT systems use personal information.[21] An agency conducts a PIA to make sure that it uses personal information in a way that follows the law. The PIA also helps an agency determine the risks of collecting personal information. It also examines the types of controls that an agency must put in place to reduce privacy risks.

 NOTE

A PIA is not the same as a SORN. An agency must perform a PIA any time it collects personally identifiable information. It must post a SORN whenever that data can be retrieved using a personal identifier.

An agency must conduct a PIA before it develops or buys any IT system that will collect personal information. It also must perform a PIA anytime its IT systems change in such a way that new privacy risks are introduced. This includes situations where an agency changes from paper to electronic systems. An agency must conduct a PIA if it chooses to outsource an IT system or function that uses personal data.

An agency's PIA must include information about its data collection practices. This information is similar to the fair information practice principles discussed in Chapter 2. The PIA must contain the following information:

- What data the agency will collect
- Why the agency is collecting the data
- How the agency will use the data
- How the agency will share the data
- Whether people have the opportunity to consent to specific uses of the data
- How the agency will secure the data
- Whether the data collected will be a system of records defined by the Privacy Act

An agency must submit its PIAs to the OMB. They also must make them available to the public. The only time an agency doesn't have to make a PIA available to the public is when doing so might compromise the security of an IT system.

The E-Government Act requires agencies to post privacy policies on their Web sites. The privacy policies must contain the same types of information that are in a PIA. They make the public aware of how the agency collects information. They also state how the agency uses that information.

Agencies must post a link to their privacy policies on their main Web site home page. They must write them in language that is easy to understand.

The E-Government Act also requires agencies to adopt machine-readable privacy policies. Agencies had to implement them by the end of 2004. These technologies alert users about the agency's Web site privacy practices. A machine-readable privacy policy lets users know if the agency's privacy practices match the user's browser privacy preferences. The machine-readable privacy policy standard is called P3P. You can read about it at *http://www.usa.gov/webcontent/reqs _bestpractices/laws_regs/privacy_p3p.shtml.*

> **NOTE**
> The Web site for the U.S. Department of Justice is at *www.justice.gov.* Can you find the agency's privacy policy link on that page?

OMB Breach Notification Policy

Some states have laws that require businesses and other entities to notify their customers if they suffer a security breach that discloses personal information. These laws are called breach notification laws or data breach laws. Many states have them. Some of these state laws apply to businesses operating within the state. Some also apply to state governments. State breach notification laws are discussed in Chapter 9.

Some federal laws have breach notification provisions. For instance, recent amendments to the Health Insurance Portability and Accountability Act (HIPAA) include notification requirements. These amendments are discussed in Chapter 6. There's no government-wide federal breach notification law.

In May 2007, the OMB required all federal agencies to create a breach notification plan. The OMB issued this instruction in response to a large data breach at the Department of Veterans Affairs. It stated that agencies must consider the following items when creating a breach notification plan:

- **Whether breach notification is required**—Agencies must review the data disclosed in a breach. They must determine the number of individuals affected by the breach. They must consider the likelihood that the data is usable by unauthorized individuals. They must assess the risk of harm to the people whose data is disclosed.

- **Time for notification**—Agencies must notify the people affected by the breach without delay. An agency may delay notice only for law enforcement or national security reasons.

- **Source of the notification**—The highest-ranking agency official should notify people who are affected by the breach.

- **Contents of the notice**—The notice should include a description of the breach and the type of data disclosed. It should include information on how people can protect themselves from having their data used by unauthorized individuals. It also should describe what the agency is doing to mitigate the breach.

- **Means of providing the notice**—The agency must consider how to give notice to the people affected by the breach. Telephone, first-class mail, e-mail, Web site postings, and release to national media outlets may all be appropriate ways to provide notice. The agency must consider the best method for a given situation.

- **Who gets the notice**—The agency must consider who must be notified. The people affected by the breach must be notified. In addition, the agency also must consider whether it should notify the media or other people who might be affected by the breach or the notification.

The OMB memo was very clear that agencies must report breaches of both paper and electronic information. You can read it at *http://www.whitehouse.gov/omb/assets/omb/ memoranda/fy2007/m07-16.pdf.*

The OMB also wanted agencies to take steps to limit the amount of data that they collect. It wanted them to limit data collection so that there's less chance that personal data could be compromised in a breach. The OMB breach notification memo also required federal agencies to:

- Review and reduce the volume of personally identifiable information that they store

- Eliminate unnecessary use of SSNs and explore alternatives to using SSN as a personal identifier

- Develop policies and procedures for individuals who are authorized to access personally identifiable information

Import and Export Control Laws

This chapter has discussed the laws that federal agencies must follow to protect the security and privacy of information. This section talks briefly about other laws that are in place to protect the export of certain kinds of data. The United States has export control laws that limit the export of materials, data, and technical information to foreign countries. The export of some of these items is limited based on U.S. security interests. It's important to be aware that these types of laws exist. These laws are very complicated and are reviewed briefly here.

Export means the shipment of items or transmission of technology outside of the United States. It also means the transmission of technology to a non-U.S. citizen or non-permanent resident who is located in the United States. Import and export laws are reciprocal. An export from the United States is an import to another country. A person who is bound by U.S. export control laws can't import controlled items somewhere else. Much as the United States forbids certain products from being exported, some other countries forbid certain products from being imported.

There are three different types of export control regulations. They restrict the export of certain items overseas. They also restrict the transmission of certain types of information to foreign nationals who are living in the United States. The three main regulations are:

- International Traffic in Arms Regulations (ITAR)
- Export Administration Regulations (EAR)
- Regulations from the Office of Foreign Asset Control (OFAC)

The U.S. Department of State issues the ITAR.[22] They apply to military or defense applications and technology that doesn't have civil (non-military or defense) uses. Any export of applications and technology covered by ITAR requires an export license. The Department of State issues the export license.

Items that are covered by ITAR are listed on the U.S. Munitions List. This list is published in the Code of Federal Regulations. The list has 21 categories of different items. If an item falls within one of these categories, then it's covered by ITAR.

The penalties for violating ITAR are severe. Civil fines up to $500,000 are possible. The Department of State determines civil penalties. ITAR violators also can be subject to criminal penalties. A person who willfully violates ITAR can be fined up to $1 million per offense. He or she also can be sentenced to up to 10 years in jail.

FYI

The U.S. Department of State is serious about enforcing ITAR. In 2006, the Boeing Company agreed to pay a $15 million fine to settle allegations that it violated ITAR. You can read about that case at *http://www.pmddtc.state.gov/compliance/consent_agreements/BoeingCompany.html*.

8

Federal Government
Information

FYI

The BIS prepares a report about export control violations. You can read the July 2008 report at *http://www.bis.doc.gov/complianceandenforcement/dontletthishappentoyou-2008.pdf.*

The U.S. Department of Commerce handles the EAR.[23] This responsibility is delegated to the Bureau of Industry and Security (BIS). The EAR apply to dual-use technologies. These technologies have both a military and a commercial use. They may be covered under export control laws because of national security concerns.

Under the EAR, an exporter must have an export license for items and technologies that are on the Commerce Control List (CCL). The CCL has 10 categories. They include electronics, computers, telecommunications, and information security technologies. Some items on the CCL can't be exported even if a person tries to get a license to do so. For example, the United States has a comprehensive trade embargo against Iran. An embargo is a ban against trade with another country. The government forbids almost all exports to Iran.

A person who violates the EAR can be subject to both criminal and civil penalties. Violators can be fined either up to $250,000 or up to twice value of the transaction. A person who willfully violates the EAR can be fined up to $1 million per offense. They also can be sentenced to up to 20 years in jail.

The Treasury Department also oversees some export laws. The Office of Foreign Assets Control (OFAC) enforces trade sanctions and embargoes. It is part of the Treasury Department. The OFAC administers trade sanctions and embargoes as part of United States foreign policy goals. It has the power to forbid some types of transactions based upon these goals. You can learn about the OFAC's sanctions programs at *http://www .ustreas.gov/offices/enforcement/ofac/index.shtml.*

OFAC regulations may forbid people in the United States from engaging in any trade or financial transactions with other countries. People in the United States are prohibited from engaging in trade with certain people in other countries. For example, the government prohibits trade with known terrorists or drug traffickers.

The OFAC publishes a list of individuals and companies that people in the United States are generally forbidden from dealing with. The people on this list are called "Specially Designated Nationals" (SDNs). You can view the OFAC's SDN list at *http://www.ustreas .gov/offices/enforcement/ofac/sdn/index.shtml.*

Penalties for violating OFAC regulations are generally the same as for EAR violations.

Case Studies and Examples

The following case studies and examples show how the concepts discussed in this chapter are used. These case studies are real-world examples of information security issues in the federal government.

Missing Hard Drives

In March 2009, the National Archives and Records Administration (NARA) learned that an external hard drive was missing. The hard drive held data from President William Clinton's administration. The data included the personal information of people who visited or worked at the White House during this time. The hard drive held two terabytes of data.

NARA discovered that the hard drive was missing on about March 24, 2009. On April 2, 2009, NARA notified its Inspector General that the hard drive was missing. It also reported it to US-CERT. NARA's Inspector General, the U.S. Secret Service, and the FBI are investigating the missing hard drive. It's not known if the hard drive was misplaced or stolen. NARA has offered an award of up to $50,000 for information about the case.

NARA had a backup copy of the hard drive. The NARA IG analyzed the hard drive. The IG determined that the hard drive held personal data. The IG also said that NARA needed to notify the people whose personal information was on the hard drive. As of January 4, 2010, NARA had notified over 175,000 people about the potential breach. You can read a NARA fact sheet about the breach at *http://www.archives.gov/press/press-releases/2010/nara-breach-notification-faq-2010-01-12.pdf.*

Social Networking Sites

The military must balance competing interests when thinking about information security. Most important, the DoD must make sure that it protects the lives of service members. In early 2010, the DoD issued a policy on using social media sites. Social media sites can be a potential danger. This is because of the amount of data that people sometimes post on these sites. Information posted on a social networking site could disclose where troops are stationed. The sites also are important ways for troops to communicate with family members.

In its policy, the DoD recognized that the Internet is critical to its operations. It helps people stay connected. The Internet also helps the DoD advertise the services that it provides to the country. The policy allows DoD employees to use its non-classified Internet system to access social media sites such as Facebook and Twitter. The policy also allows DoD components to maintain official DoD communications on social media sites. The DoD component must receive approval to do this.

You can read more about the DoD social media policy at *http://socialmedia.defense.gov/index.php/2010/02/26/dod-official-policy-on-newsocial-media/.*

The Future of FISMA

It's clear that FISMA is changing. The government is trying to change FISMA from a compliance exercise to an information protection philosophy. Many government agencies are working together to create an information security strategy that can be used for all federal IT systems. Having a common approach helps eliminate confusion.

8

Federal Government
Information

The Joint Task Force Transformation Initiative Interagency Working Group is working on this common approach. The group includes members from civilian, military, and intelligence agencies. It created a government-wide information security risk management framework. A government-wide RMF helps create consistency.

You can expect the law itself to change as well. A subcommittee of the U.S. House of Representatives Committee on Oversight and Government Reform held a hearing on FISMA in March 2010. The hearing focused on federal information security challenges. Witnesses who testified said that FISMA improved the federal government's approach to information security. They also said that more work must be done to protect the government's IT systems.

At the time this book was written, Congress is considering possible FISMA amendments. Both the House of Representatives and the Senate introduced bills in early 2010 to amend it.

CHAPTER SUMMARY

This chapter reviews the laws that protect the security and privacy of data that the federal government uses. FISMA is the main law protecting the security of federal government IT systems. It requires federal agencies to create information security programs. Agencies also must review their information security risks. The law requires them to implement controls to mitigate those risks.

The Privacy Act of 1974 and the E-Government Act of 2002 are the main laws protecting data privacy at the federal level. These laws govern how federal agencies use personally identifiable data. Under the E-Government Act, federal agencies must review their IT systems for any privacy impacts. Both laws require federal agencies to notify the public about their data collection practices.

KEY CONCEPTS AND TERMS

Inspector general (IG)   Record
National security systems   System of records notice (SORN)
Privacy impact assessment (PIA)

CHAPTER 8 ASSESSMENT

1. Which regulation controls the export of military or defense applications and technology?

  A. ITAR
  B. EAR
  C. OFAC
  D. FDIC
  E. None of the above

2. What information must a federal agency include in a privacy impact assessment?

3. The information collected in a PIA and a SORN is based upon what principles?

  A. NIST standards
  B. OMB standards
  C. Fair information privacy practices
  D. ITAR regulations
  E. None of the above

4. Which assessment must be completed any time a federal agency collects personal information that can be retrieved via a personal identifier?

  A. PIA
  B. SORN
  C. ACORN
  D. OFAC
  E. None of the above

5. Which agency has primary oversight responsibilities under FISMA?

  A. DoD
  B. CIA
  C. NIST
  D. CNSS
  E. None of the above

6. Federal agencies must report information security incidents to _____.

7. Federal agencies must test their information security controls every six months.

  A. True
  B. False

8. What are federal information security challenges?

  A. A culture of merely complying with reporting requirements
  B. Lack of an enterprise approach to information security
  C. Lack of coordination within the federal government
  D. All of the above
  E. None of the above

9. What is the name of the FISMA data-collection tool?

10. Which type of NIST guidance follows a formal creation process?

  A. Special Publications
  B. Federal Information Processing Standards
  C. Guidelines for Information Security
  D. Fair information practice principles
  E. None of the above

11. How many steps are there in the NIST Risk Management Framework?

  A. Six
  B. Five
  C. Four
  D. Three
  E. None of the above

8

Federal Government Information

12. Which level of impact for a FIPS security category best describes significant damage to organizational assets?

   A. Low

   B. Moderate

   C. High

   D. Severe

   E. None of the above

13. FedCIRC is the federal information security incident center.

   A. True

   B. False

14. How quickly must a federal agency report an unauthorized access incident?

   A. Monthly

   B. Weekly

   C. Daily

   D. Within two hours of discovery

   E. Within one hour of discovery

15. How many categories of security controls are designated in FIPS 200?

   A. 20

   B. 19

   C. 18

   D. 17

   E. None of the above

ENDNOTES

1. Remarks by the President, "On Securing Our Nation's Cyber Infrastructure," May 29, 2009, *http://www.whitehouse.gov/the_press_office/Remarks-by-the-President-on-Securing-Our-Nations-Cyber-Infrastructure/* (accessed April 21, 2010).

2. Committee on Oversight and Government Reform, "Federal Information Security: Current Challenges and Future Policy Considerations," March 24, 2010, *http://oversight.house.gov/index.php?option=com_content&task=view&id=4855&Itemid=28* (accessed April 21, 2010). See prepared testimony of Mr. Vivek Kundra.

3. U.S. Office of Management and Budget, Circular No. A-130, "Management of Federal Information Resources," December 2000, *http://www.whitehouse.gov/omb/circulars_a130_a130trans4/* (accessed April 21, 2010).

4. Computer Security Act of 1987, P.L. 100-235, 101 Stat. 1724.

5. Federal Information Security Management Act, Title III of the E-Government Act of 2002, P.L. 107-347; U.S. Code Vol. 44, sec. 3541 et seq.

6. Remarks by the President, "On Securing Our Nation's Cyber Infrastructure," May 29, 2009.

7. Committee on Oversight and Reform, "Federal Information Security: Current Challenges and Future Policy Considerations," March 24, 2010. See prepared testimony of Mr. Vivek Kundra.

8. H.R. Rep. No. 107-787, pt.1, at 54 (2002), *as reprinted in* 2002 U.S.C.C.A.N. 1880, 1889., available at *http://frwebgate.access.gpo.gov/cgi-bin/getdoc.cgi?dbname=107_cong_reports&docid=f:hr787p1.107.pdf* (accessed April 21, 2010).

9. U.S. Code Vol. 44, sec. 3542(b)(1).

10. U.S. Office of Management and Budget, "Memo M-10-15: FY 2010 Reporting Instructions for the Federal Information Security Management Act and Agency Privacy Management, April 21, 2010, *http://www.whitehouse.gov/omb/assets/memoranda_2010/m10-15.pdf* (accessed April 23, 2010).

11. U.S. Code Vol. 44, sec. 3544(b)(5).

12. U.S. Code Vol. 44, sec. 3544(a)(3)(A)(ii).

13. GovInfoSecurity.com, "Automated FISMA Reporting Tool Unveiled," October 30, 2009, *http://www.govinfosecurity.com/articles.php?art_id=1894* (accessed April 24, 2010).

14. Committee on Oversight and Reform, "Federal Information Security: Current Challenges and Future Policy Considerations," March 24, 2010. See prepared testimony of Mr. Vivek Kundra.

15. The White House Blog, Vivek Kundra, "Faster, Smarter Cybersecurity," April 21, 2010, *http://www.whitehouse.gov/blog/2010/04/21/faster-smarter-cybersecurity* (accessed April 23, 2010).

16. National Institute of Standards and Technology, Computer Security Division, "FISMA: Detailed Overview," last revised April 13, 2010, *http://csrc.nist.gov/groups/SMA/fisma/overview.html* (accessed April 24, 2010).

17. National Institute of Standards and Technology, SP 800-12, "Recommendation for EAP Methods Used in Wireless Network Access Authentication," September 2009, *http://csrc.nist. gov/publications/PubsSPs.html* (accessed April 21, 2010).

18. Committee on National Security Systems, CNSS Policy No. 22, "Information Assurance Risk Management Policy for National Security Systems," February 2009, *http://www.cnss.gov/Assets/pdf/ CNSSP-22.pdf* (accessed April 24, 2010).

19. Committee on National Security Systems, CNSS Instruction No. 1253, "Security Categorization and Control Selection for National Security Systems," October 2009, *http://www.cnss.gov/Assets/pdf/CNSSI-1253.pdf* (accessed April 24, 2010).

20. Privacy Act of 1974, U.S. Code Vol. 5, sec. 552a (2006).

21. U.S. Office of Management and Budget, "Memo M-03-22: OMB Guidance for Implementing the Privacy Protections of the E-Government Act of 2002," September 26, 2003, *http://www.whitehouse. gov/omb/memoranda_m03-22/#15* (accessed April 25, 2010).

22. *International Traffic in Arms Regulations*, Code of Federal Regulations, Title 22, sec. 120-130.

23. *Export Administration Regulations*, Code of Federal Regulations, Title 15, sec. 700-799.

8

Federal Government
Information

State Laws Protecting Citizen Information and Breach Notification Laws

A S DISCUSSED IN THIS BOOK, in the United States, there is no single comprehensive federal data privacy or security law. Instead, the United States has enacted industry-specific laws about security and privacy. These laws limit the use of personal information based on the nature of the data.

State governments also have entered this regulatory arena. States create data protection laws that are data specific. Many states have created laws to protect health and financial information. They also might try to protect data in certain types of records, such as motor vehicle records. In some ways, states are more aggressive in trying to protect personal information than the federal government.

This chapter focuses on state data protection laws. It includes laws from different states to give you an overview of the types of laws being passed to protect data. As you encounter issues regarding the law, security, and privacy, you must consider the impact of state laws and rules.

Chapter 9 Topics

This chapter covers the following topics and concepts:

- What the history is of state actions to protect personal information
- What state breach notification laws are
- What state data-specific security and privacy regulations are
- What encryption regulations are
- What data-disposal regulations are
- What some case studies and examples are

History of State Actions to Protect Personal Information

States have created many laws to protect personal information. California has worked hard to make laws that protect the security and privacy of its residents' data. It was this state's breach notification laws and a breach at a large corporation that led to the growth of data protection laws in many states.

ChoicePoint Data Breach

ChoicePoint is a data broker. It merges public records, credit reports, and demographic data to create individual consumer profiles. It sells these profiles to the government and private companies. People can use the profiles to conduct background checks. ChoicePoint also sells profiles to insurance companies. It collects many different types of personal information. It has names, addresses, and Social Security numbers. Its databases also can include credit history and DNA information.

In February 2005, ChoicePoint notified 35,000 California residents that their personal data was exposed in a data breach. California was the only state at that time with a **breach notification law.** The law applied to any business that stored the personal data of California residents. The law required them to notify state residents of any security breach involving their unencrypted personal information.

ChoicePoint said that it discovered the breach in late 2004. Law enforcement officials contacted the company about an identity theft ring. ChoicePoint learned that the criminals pretended to be its customers. In order to become a ChoicePoint customer, applicants had to provide proof of a lawful reason for buying consumer data. At the time of the breach, ChoicePoint had over 50,000 customers. They ranged from insurance companies to debt collectors.

> **NOTE**
> At the time of the data breach, news media reported that ChoicePoint had collected over 9 billion public records on U.S. residents. They reported that it had stored 250 terabytes of data.

9

State Laws and Breach Notification Laws

ChoicePoint's validation processes didn't find the fake customers. Some of them provided suspect documents to ChoicePoint. For example, multiple businesses submitted documents with the same information. This should have raised red flags for more review. ChoicePoint later found over 50 fake accounts. These accounts had access to ChoicePoint's databases.

At first ChoicePoint notified only California residents affected by the breach. This is because it was the only state requiring such notification. Nineteen other states were outraged. The state attorneys general wrote a letter to ChoicePoint. They demanded that it alert all people affected by the breach. ChoicePoint later sent notification letters to over 160,000 people.

In January 2006, the Federal Trade Commission (FTC) investigated ChoicePoint. It alleged that ChoicePoint violated consumer privacy rights. It also charged the company with violating federal laws. ChoicePoint settled with the FTC in December of that year. It paid $10 million in civil fines.

> **NOTE**
>
> ChoicePoint reported that it had many external audits after the 2005 breach. It was audited 80 times in the 24 months after the breach.

ChoicePoint also agreed to pay $5 million to fund a consumer relief program. The program would pay people who were victims of identity theft due to the breach. The agreement with the FTC also required ChoicePoint to create an information security program. It's required to get independent audits every year until 2026. At the time, the ChoicePoint settlement was the largest in the FTC's history.

> **NOTE**
>
> To help protect consumer information, ChoicePoint will give you a copy of your consumer file. You can request only your own file. You must provide proof of identify to get a copy of the file. You also must provide proof of address. To learn more about this service, you can visit *www.ChoiceTrust.com*.

In May 2007, ChoicePoint settled a multi-state lawsuit over the breach. Forty-three states entered the settlement agreement. As part of that agreement, ChoicePoint promised to improve its process for verifying customers. It also agreed to strengthen how it protects the data that it collects. ChoicePoint also agreed to pay $500,000 to the states involved in the lawsuit.

ChoicePoint was on the FTC's radar again in 2009. This time it was due to a 2008 security incident. ChoicePoint had changed some internal security controls. The changed controls failed to alert it that someone had unauthorized access to its data. The wrongful access continued for about 30 days. During this time, the data of about 13,750 people may have been disclosed. The data included Social Security numbers.

The FTC alleged that the 2008 incident was a violation of the 2006 agreement. As a result, ChoicePoint agreed to additional security requirements. It agreed to strengthen its information security program again. It's also required to report to the FTC on its security efforts every two months until 2011.

The ChoicePoint data breach is unique because it spurred the creation of data breach notification laws in many states. If it weren't for the California breach notification law, ChoicePoint might not have notified any consumers at all about the data breach. Other states realized that their residents might not be able to protect themselves from identity theft in similar situations without these laws. Thirty-five states considered breach notification laws in 2005. The ChoicePoint case is widely seen as the reason why other states have these laws.

You can read FTC documents about the ChoicePoint case at *http://www.ftc.gov/os/caselist/choicepoint/choicepoint.shtm*.

> **NOTE**
> Illinois Governor Rod Blagojevich proposed the Personal Information Protection Act just days after the ChoicePoint breach went public. The ChoicePoint breach affected about 5,000 Illinois residents. The act is Illinois's breach notification law. It was effective January 1, 2006.

Breach Notification Regulations

California was the first state to have a breach notification law. It required businesses to notify their customers if they suffered a data breach that disclosed personal data. Many states have modeled their own breach notification laws on the California law. This section discusses the California breach notification law. It also discusses the laws in other states.

California Breach Notification Act

California's Database Security Breach Notification Act law went into effect on July 1, 2003. The California legislature created the law after a security breach at a state-operated data facility. The legislature recognized that identity theft was one of the fastest growing crimes in California. It stated that people must act quickly to limit the harm caused by identity theft. The purpose of the law was to give California residents timely information so that they can protect themselves.

> **NOTE**
> California's breach notification law is Senate Bill 1386. This bill created the law.

The law applies to anyone who owns or uses computerized data that contains the unencrypted personal information of a California resident.[1] It applies to:

- State agencies
- Non-profit organizations
- Private organizations
- Businesses

It also can apply to businesses that aren't actually located in California. It covers any entity that stores the personal information of a California resident. Under the law, an entity must notify California residents of a breach of its computer systems. They must give notice if unauthorized individuals access and take the resident's unencrypted data.

FYI

Under California law, a security breach means unauthorized acquisition of computerized data. It must "compromise the security, confidentiality, or integrity of personal information" held by an entity.[2] This definition is confusing from an information security perspective because it refers to security and separately to confidentiality and integrity. Confidentiality and integrity are part of the standard definition of security. This type of imprecise definition is why information security professionals and lawmakers must work together in creating laws that impact information security.

The law defines personal information very broadly. It's information that allows a person to be identified. "Personal information" is a person's first name (or first initial) and last name. The person's name is combined with any of the following:

NOTE

California amended the law in 2008. The changes included adding medical and health insurance information to the law. They were not included as part of the original law.

- Social Security number
- Driver's license number or California Identification Card number
- Account number, or credit or debit card number, along with any security code, access code, or password that would allow access to a person's account
- Medical information
- Health insurance information

Under the law, personal information is unencrypted data. If any of the data is unencrypted, then all of the information is considered "personal information." Information that's available to the public through government records isn't personal information.

The law requires entities to notify California residents whenever a security breach occurs. They must also notify residents if they reasonably believe that a breach has occurred. They must notify people as quickly as possible. Under the law, there are two reasons to delay notification. The first is to figure out the scope of the security breach. An entity must do this so that it can notify the right people.

The second reason to delay notification is if law enforcement requires it. Law enforcement can allow entities to delay notification to conduct a criminal investigation. The entity must make the required notification as soon as possible after it's determined that it won't hurt the investigation.

The law requires entities to give written notice to California residents. It doesn't require the notice to have certain elements. The law allows "substitute notice" if the entity can prove that:

- The cost of giving written notice is greater than $250,000
- The number of people to be notified is greater than 500,000
- It doesn't have sufficient contact information

If an entity can prove one of these situations, it doesn't have to give individual written notices. Instead, it must do all of the following:

- Notify affected people by e-mail if the entity has an e-mail address for the person
- Post notice of the security breach on its Web site (if it has one)
- Notify major statewide media outlets about the breach

The California law provides a safe harbor for entities that encrypt personal information. A **safe harbor** is a legal concept. It protects an entity from legal liability. It's written into the law. Entities that encrypt the personal information that they own or maintain don't have to follow the notification requirements if they have a data breach.

Finally, the law gives California residents a limited private cause of action against entities who don't follow the law. Residents who are harmed when an entity doesn't follow the law can sue for damages.

> **NOTE**
>
> One major drawback of the California law is that it doesn't define an acceptable level of encryption. Other states have defined what type of encryption is sufficient to use as a safe harbor in their breach notification laws.

> **NOTE**
>
> In the law, a plaintiff can generally recover only damages in the amount that he or she has actually lost because of harm or injury.

Other Breach Notification Laws

After the ChoicePoint breach, many other states created breach notification laws. As of January 2010, 45 states, including the District of Columbia, have these laws. Many of them are based on the California law. Even though most states used the California law as a model, there are some differences. They include:

- Activities that constitute a breach
- Entities covered by the law
- The time for notifying residents
- Requirements that a notification contain certain types of information
- Minimum requirements for encryption
- Civil or criminal penalties for failing to notify affected people

Additionally, other state laws typically do not allow a private cause of action for failure to give notification.

Activities That Constitute a Breach

The California law applies to unauthorized acquisition of unencrypted personal information. If attackers access the data, that's enough to trigger the law's notification requirements. Some other states require a showing of harm before notification is required. This means that attackers must not only access the data, but do something with it. For instance, the attackers must steal, copy, or change the data before notification is required. In addition, some sort of harm must be anticipated as a result. Stealing data is an anticipated harm under these laws. You must review the definition of "breach" carefully to see what triggers the notification requirements.

> **NOTE**
>
> Other states that employ some sort of harm standard include Hawaii, Massachusetts, and Virginia.

In Arizona, there's a two-part test to see if notification is required. First, a breach is an unauthorized acquisition of personal information. This means that data must actually be taken. Second, the acquisition must cause, or be likely to cause, substantial economic loss to a person.[3] The harm caused must be substantial and economic. The law doesn't define the term "substantial." Notice isn't required if the acquisition isn't reasonably likely to cause this type of harm.

Ohio law also requires more than unauthorized acquisition to trigger notification. Under Ohio law, it also must be reasonably believed to have caused a material risk of identity theft or other fraud to an Ohio resident.[4] The risk of harm can also be a future risk of harm. In this law, the material risk of identity theft is enough to require notification.

Entities Covered by the Law

> **NOTE**
>
> Why might a government exclude itself from its breach notification laws? Should it? Some states do hold themselves responsible for security breaches. In fact, Oklahoma's notification law applies only to state agencies.[5]

The California law applies to any entity that owns or uses the personal information of California residents. It includes businesses, non-profit organizations, and government agencies. Not all states have laws this broad. Some states specifically exclude state agencies from notification requirements.

Georgia's notification law doesn't apply to state agencies. Instead, it applies to information brokers. "Information brokers" are entities that sell personal data to other entities. The law states that it doesn't cover government agencies.[6] If a government agency experiences a breach, it doesn't have to notify affected residents under this law.

The Maine notification law as it was originally created was similar to the Georgia law. It also applied only to information brokers. It excluded state agencies. It was amended about a year after it was first enacted in order to include state agencies.[7]

Time for Notification

> **NOTE**
>
> A business day is an official workday. Business days are the days of the week that include Monday through Friday. Saturday and Sunday are not business days. Public holidays also are not business days.

Under the California law, entities must give notice in the most expedient time possible. They must do so without unreasonable delay. A majority of states follow the California approach. However, some states require that entities give notice within a certain period.

Ohio law requires that notification be given to state residents in the most expedient time possible. However, that law states that entities must give this notice no later than 45 days after the discovery of the breach.[8] Florida has a similar requirement.[9] Wisconsin law requires entities to notify residents within 45 business days after learning about the breach.[10]

Entities Excluded from Breach Notification Laws

Some states exclude some kinds of entities from their breach notification laws. They do this because these entities are already subject to other laws with specific data security requirements. Many of these other laws have security and privacy obligations that are stricter than the states' own laws. If the entities are following these other laws, then a security breach may be less likely. In some cases, state lawmakers determined that making entities follow both the state breach notification law and the other laws would be too hard. It might hurt businesses operating in the state.

Some states exempt financial institutions covered by the Gramm-Leach-Bliley Act (GLBA). GLBA is discussed in Chapter 4. GLBA requires these institutions to protect a customer's nonpublic financial information. They must use security safeguards. They also must follow privacy rules. Breaches may be less likely if an institution follows GLBA. Many states exempt these entities from notification laws. They include Connecticut, Indiana, and Minnesota.

Some states also exempt entities that are covered by the Health Insurance Portability and Accountability Act (HIPAA). HIPAA is discussed in Chapter 6. HIPAA covered entities must follow rules designed to protect personally identifiable health information. They must follow the HIPAA Privacy and Security rules. Recent amendments also impose breach notification rules on HIPAA covered entities. These rules may be even stricter than some state notification laws. States that exempt HIPAA covered entities from their laws include Arizona, Rhode Island, and Wisconsin.

In Maine, an entity may delay notification if requested by law enforcement.[11] An entity can only delay notification to help a criminal investigation. An entity must give notice once law enforcement determines that the notification will not hurt the investigation. At that point, the entity must provide notice within seven days.

Contents of Notification

Some states require that entities give notice in a certain way. The California law has no specific rules, other than that notice should be in writing. Many states follow the California model. There's a growing trend, however, to specify the types of information that should be included in a notice. States do this to make sure that residents get enough information to protect themselves.

 TIP

Remember, the reason for notification is to let people protect themselves from identity theft. Any delay in notifying people should be as short as possible.

NOTE

In October 2009, the Governor of California vetoed a bill that would have required notices to include certain types of information. Gov. Arnold Schwarzenegger said that there was no proof that including additional information would help state residents.

9

State Laws and Breach Notification Laws

North Carolina law requires that notice be given in a "clear and conspicuous" form.[12] This means that it needs to be easily understandable. The notice also must:

- Describe the incident in general terms.
- Describe the type of personal information that was involved in the breach.
- Describe how the entity is going to protect the personal information from additional unauthorized access.
- Provide a telephone number for the entity, if one exists, that a person may call for more information.
- Advise the person being notified to review his or her account statements and get a free credit report.
- Provide the toll-free telephone numbers and addresses for the major consumer reporting agencies.
- Provide the contact information for the FTC and the North Carolina Attorney General's Office, along with a statement that these sources have additional information about preventing identity theft.

North Carolina also allows entities to notify residents by telephone. The law allows this only if the entity makes direct contact with the people whose data was accessed in the breach. Colorado law allows notice to be given in written and electronic form.[13] It also allows notice by telephone.

TIP

Remember, a safe harbor is a legal concept that protects an entity from liability for violating a law.

NOTE

Algorithms are mathematical computations used to solve a problem. They encrypt data.

Encryption Requirements

The California law provides an encryption safe harbor. Entities don't need to give notice of a breach if the personal information in their computer system was encrypted. California law doesn't specify the lowest level of encryption needed to use the safe harbor. It also doesn't reference any industry standards.

Most other states also provide an encryption safe harbor. Some states also specify the encryption standards required to take advantage of the safe harbor. For instance, Indiana provides an encryption safe harbor. Its law says that data is encrypted if it's changed by an algorithmic process. It must be changed into a form that is unreadable without the use of a confidential process or key.[14]

The Indiana law also addresses key management. For portable electronic devices, like laptop computers, the data must be protected by encryption and the encryption key can't be stored on the device. Indiana law also says that data is considered encrypted if it's secured by any other method that makes the data unreadable or unusable.

Penalties for Failure to Notify

California law doesn't impose any civil or criminal penalties if an entity doesn't notify state residents of a security breach. Other states do have penalties. In Texas, for example, the state can assess a fine against an entity that doesn't notify affected people.[15] The law states that an entity can be fined at least $2,000 for a violation. The fine can't be larger than $50,000 for a single violation.

> **NOTE**
>
> In Indiana, the failure to give notice is a deceptive act. The state attorney general's office has the power to prosecute deceptive acts. The fine for each act can be up to $150,000.[16]

Other states have more complicated penalty structures. Under Florida law, an entity that doesn't provide notification within 45 days of a breach faces potentially large fines.[17] It faces a $1,000-per-day fine for every day that the entity fails to give notice after the 45-day limit. This penalty is in effect for the first 30 days after the 45-day mark. After that, the fine increases to $50,000 for each additional 30-day period that the entity fails to give notice. This extends up to 180 days (about six months) after the 45-day mark. If entities don't give notification within 225 days after a breach, the state may fine them up to $500,000. Figure 9-1 illustrates the Florida fine structure.

Private Cause of Action

California law doesn't assess any penalties against an entity that doesn't follow the notification law. However, it does allow a person a private cause of action against those entities. A person can sue the private entity for any damages they have because they didn't receive notification in a timely manner. Many states allow a private cause of action. They include Alaska, Hawaii, and Louisiana.

Some states don't allow a private cause of action. They do this to protect the entity's business. They also do this to protect the court system. It could be burdensome to the court system to process many individual cases. Instead, most of these states allow the state attorney general to pursue an action against the entity for failure to give notification. These states include Iowa, Michigan, and Oklahoma.

Almost every state now has a breach notification law to protect its residents. The laws have some similarities. Some laws also have unique requirements. These laws can be very confusing to businesses that operate in a number of states. Breaches at these entities are

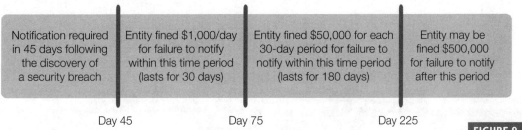

| Notification required in 45 days following the discovery of a security breach | Entity fined $1,000/day for failure to notify within this time period (lasts for 30 days) | Entity fined $50,000 for each 30-day period for failure to notify within this time period (lasts for 180 days) | Entity may be fined $500,000 for failure to notify after this period |

Day 45   Day 75   Day 225

FIGURE 9-1

Florida fine structure for failure to give notification.

almost certainly going to affect people in many states. If this happens, an entity will have to review the laws of several states to properly notify people about the breach.

Breach notification is hard for entities because states have different laws about what constitutes a breach. An incident can be a breach in one state, but not another. It also can be hard if entities must give notice in a certain way or within a certain time. Differing penalties for noncompliance may also be a problem. Since the laws all have different nuances, it may not be enough for an entity to comply with the laws of its own state. Figure 9-2 provides a general decision tree that entities can follow in reviewing a security breach to see if notice is required.

The lack of uniformity among states may place additional burdens on businesses that experience a security breach. People also may be confused if they get notices that don't

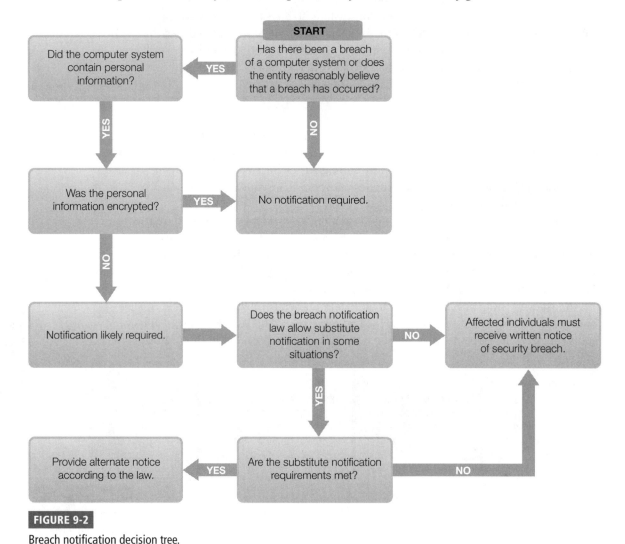

FIGURE 9-2

Breach notification decision tree.

When Is Federal Legislation Appropriate?

The federal government has limited law-making power. The U.S. Congress can't make any laws outside of the scope granted to it in the U.S. Constitution. This means that Congress can't usually interfere in state matters. It can't create a uniform federal law in areas legislated by the states unless there's a compelling reason to do so.

Congress can create laws in areas where the U.S. Constitution allows it. For instance, the Constitution grants the federal government the power to regulate commerce between the states. If an activity has the potential to affect the trade relations between the states, then Congress may address it under its Commerce Clause power.

Sometimes states enact laws that extend beyond their borders. If these laws affect trade between the states, then it's possible that they start to infringe upon an area where the federal government alone has the power to create laws. When this happens, the question rises whether that area has become "ripe" for federal legislation.

When deciding if an area is ripe for federal legislation, Congress looks at whether differing state laws affect activities that it traditionally regulates. It considers how many states have created laws addressing the specific topic. It reviews whether there's state confusion or complexity on activities that might affect relationships between the states. Congress also looks at whether the differing state laws create an undue burden or economic cost on businesses operating in several states.

Congress may use its legislative power to enact federal laws if there is confusion among the states. It does this to eliminate confusion for businesses that operate in several states. If it creates a national law in an area where there are many different state laws, the federal law will preempt the state laws. The state laws will no longer be valid.

The Congressional Research Service has compiled a report on various federal laws that may create breach notification requirements. The report notes that breach notification laws are complicated and often confusing. You can read the report at *http://www.fas.org/sgp/crs/secrecy/RL34120.pdf.*

9

State Laws and Breach
Notification Laws

look similar. Notices might look different depending upon the law that the entity followed in creating the notice. A federal breach notification law might eliminate the complexity in this area. A federal breach notification law would create uniform requirements that any entity should follow to notify people of a security breach.

Data-Specific Security and Privacy Regulations

Many states have created laws to protect the use of certain types of information. Like the federal government, they create laws by data type. This section discusses some of the data-specific laws that states have created to protect personal information.

> **NOTE**
>
> Businesses that wish to accept credit cards for payment must follow the PCI DSS. The major credit card companies require it. It isn't a law. Credit card companies like Visa and MasterCard enforce PCI DSS.

Minnesota and Nevada: Requiring Businesses to Comply with Payment Card Industry Standards

Some states have started to create laws that require entities in the state to comply with industry security standards. Minnesota and Nevada have created laws that require businesses operating in those states to comply with parts of the Payment Card Industry (PCI) Data Security Standard (DSS). The PCI DSS is discussed in Chapter 4.

Minnesota created the first state law that attempted to codify parts of the PCI DSS. This law is called the Plastic Card Security Act. It was effective August 2007. It forbids businesses from storing cardholder information for more than 48 hours after the credit card transaction is approved.[18] Information that can't be stored includes:

- Card verification number
- PIN number
- Contents of the card magnetic stripe

The PCI DSS also states that businesses may not retain this information. The Minnesota law has turned this part of the PCI DSS industry standard into a law.

The Minnesota law shifts the cost of a breach to a business that violates the law. If a business suffers a breach, and is found to have violated the storage requirements, then it can be held responsible for costs related to the breach. For instance, a bank or other financial institutions can sue the business to recover their costs in responding to the breach. These costs include issuing new cards or refunding unauthorized charges.[19]

The Minnesota Plastic Card Security Act Supported by Financial Institutions

One of the reasons the Minnesota Plastic Card Security Act was introduced was the 2007 TJX data breach. Financial institutions often paid the cost for notifying people that their credit and debit card information was disclosed in a breach. There were other costs as well. If another organization suffered a breach that included card data, financial institutions had to reissue the cards to their customers. Reissuing the cards cost money. They had to refund unauthorized changes. They also suffered reputation damage when customers asked whether the financial institution was also involved in the breach.

The Minnesota Credit Union Network was tired of paying for another organization's weak security practices. The network is an association of more than 160 credit unions in Minnesota. It engages in political advocacy, education, and awareness activities. It pushed for the creation of the Plastic Card Security Act. It wanted this law to help reduce its costs for another organization's security breach.

Nevada is the first state to make following the entire PCI DSS a state law requirement. In 2009, the Nevada legislature modified the state's Security of Personal Information Law. The law had been in effect since 2005. The law requires protection of personal information in a number of ways. The 2009 changes to the law added PCI DSS language. These changes were proposed in Nevada Senate Bill 227.[20] The law now requires businesses to follow the PCI DSS. It went into effect January 1, 2010.

NOTE

The Nevada law states that "personal information" is a person's name combined with Social Security number, financial account number, and driver's license or other identification number.[21]

The Nevada law applies to "data collectors."[22] Data collectors are:

- State agencies
- Financial institutions
- Businesses that handle personal information

The law requires any data collector who accepts credit cards for the sale of goods or services to comply with the current version of PCI DSS. It also states that a data collector isn't liable for damages from a data breach if it complies with the law. Entities that comply with the law will likely not expose credit card information in a security breach. The only exception to the law's safe harbor is if the data collector's own gross negligence caused the breach.

The Nevada law is novel because it's the first time that following the entire PCI DSS is required by law. Some commentators think that the new Nevada law will encourage other states to adopt similar laws. Others believe that the law is problematic. This is because businesses that accept credit cards already have to comply with the PCI DSS under their contracts with credit card companies. If they violate the PCI DSS, they can be subject to large fines from those companies. These commentators believe that the Nevada law's safe harbor terms may be confusing to businesses that accept credit cards. This is because the law will not protect them from fines from the credit card companies.

Indiana: Limiting SSN Use and Disclosure

Some states have created laws protecting Social Security numbers (SSN). These laws recognize that SSNs are highly sensitive pieces of information. A SSN can be very valuable to an identity thief. Thieves can use the number to easily establish new identities to commit identity theft crimes.

Indiana has laws designed to protect SSNs. Its laws forbid SSNs from appearing in public documents. It also has laws that forbid state agencies from disclosing a person's SSN to any other person or entity.

NOTE

The Social Security Administration created the Social Security number in 1936. It created the SSN to track worker earnings. This was necessary to administer the Social Security program.

The Importance of Legislative History

All laws have a **legislative history**. This history documents the number of times that a law is modified during the period from introduction to signing. It includes any materials generated in the course of creating legislation. It includes committee reports and hearings. It also includes transcripts of debate and reports issued by legislatures. The legislative history can be reviewed to help determine what a legislature intended when it created a law. The Nevada law requiring data collectors to follow PCI DSS went through many changes. You can read the law's legislative history at *http://www.leg.state.nv.us/75th2009/Reports/history.cfm?ID=629.*

When Senate Bill 227 was first introduced, it contained no language requiring data collectors to follow PCI DSS. Instead, it required data collectors to use certain types of approved encryption technologies. After the bill was introduced, industry groups contacted the bill's author. They expressed concerns about the bill. They opposed it because it was not technology neutral. You can read the letter submitted by industry groups at *http://www.leg.state.nv.us/75th2009/Exhibits/Assembly/CMC/ACMC1140C.pdf.*

After negotiation, the bill was amended to include the PCI language. Little information was included in the legislative history to indicate why the PCI language was added. A question that remains is whether the businesses that objected to the bill's original language are happy with the final law that requires PCI compliance.

Since 2006, Indiana law states that county recorders' offices may not accept any document for recording that contains a SSN.[23] The only time that they can accept a document containing a SSN is when another law requires that the document contain a SSN. Some types of federal laws, such as releases of federal tax liens, require the use of a SSN.

The state also was concerned that public records recorded before 2006 could contain SSNs. Identity thieves could use these documents to get SSNs. Since 2008, Indiana law states that county recorders can't provide a recorded document to a member of the public unless they first search the document for SSNs. If they find a document with a SSN, they

FYI

A county recorder's office keeps public records about certain types of transactions. These offices usually handle legal documents regarding real estate ownership. These documents are filed, or "recorded," with a county recorder's office. This is done to give public notice of the transaction. Certain types of records also can be filed with a county recorder for future reference or safekeeping.

must redact it before allowing public inspection. It's a civil violation for a county recorder or any employee to disclose a recorded document containing a SSN without first searching the document for a SSN. The law doesn't cover disclosure of the last four digits of a SSN.

Other states have laws designed to protect SSNs. Arizona law prohibits printing a SSN on government or private identification cards.[24] California law forbids companies from requiring people to transmit a SSN over the Internet unless the connection is secure or the SSN is encrypted.[25]

Indiana law also provides that a state agency may not disclose a person's SSN to anyone.[26] This law went into effect on July 1, 2006. State agencies include an elected official's office and state educational institutions.

There are limited exceptions to this law. A state agency is allowed to disclose an SSN if:

- A person gives explicit written consent for the disclosure of their SSN
- The disclosure is required by state or federal law
- The disclosure is required by a court order

The law lists very specific penalties for an inappropriate disclosure of a person's SSN. The state agency is not responsible for these penalties. Instead, they are directed at the state agency employee who disclosed the SSN. For instance, a state agency employee who "knowingly, intentionally, or recklessly" discloses a SSN in violation of the law commits a Class D felony. This is a criminal sanction. In Indiana, a Class D felony can result in a prison term between six months and three years. In addition, a person can be fined up to $10,000.

NOTE

One of the biggest differences between civil law and criminal law is punishment. In civil law, a defendant isn't sent to jail as a punishment. Instead, civil law imposes fines. Civil law also requires a defendant to reimburse a plaintiff for damages. In criminal law, punishment usually involves fines or prison sentences, or both.

If a state agency employee negligently discloses an SSN, the person commits a Class A infraction. In Indiana, an infraction is a civil sanction. A person can't be imprisoned for an infraction. However, they can receive a fine. Fines up to $10,000 are possible.

Under the law, if a state agency impermissibly discloses a SSN, it must notify the affected person. It also must notify the state attorney general's office. Under the law, the state attorney general has the authority to investigate an improper disclosure of a SSN. The state attorney general also can make additional rules to carry out the non-disclosure law. Individuals don't have a private cause of action under the law. They can't sue a state agency for wrongfully disclosing a SSN.

Encryption Regulations

Some states require entities doing business within the state to follow basic information security practices. These practices protect the security and privacy of data. Other states are more aggressive. They require entities to use specific security practices, such as encryption.

> **FYI**
>
> The Massachusetts Office of Consumer Affairs and Business Regulation held a public hearing on the data protection standards in January 2009. The hearing showed that businesses were worried about meeting the standards. You can read a transcript from the hearing and written comments at *http://www.mass.gov/?pageID=ocatopic&L=3&L0=Home&L1=Business&L2 =Identity+Theft&sid=Eoca*.

Massachusetts: Protecting Personal Information

Massachusetts has created some of the nation's most rigorous data protection laws. It created its breach notification law in 2007.[27] That law also required the state's consumer affairs department to issue standards for the protection of personal information. The law stated that the standards should:

- Protect the security and confidentiality of personal information consistent with industry standards.
- Protect against anticipated threats to the security or integrity of personal information.
- Protect against unauthorized access to or use of personal information that could harm a person.

The Massachusetts "Standards for the Protection of Personal Information of Residents of the Commonwealth" was released in September 2008. It originally was scheduled to take effect January 1, 2009. The state pushed back compliance to March 1, 2010. It did this in response to public comments on the regulation. The state released the final version of the standard in August 2009.

Entities must follow the data protection standard to safeguard personal information. They must protect data in paper and electronic form. The standard has broad application. Any person that uses and stores personal information about Massachusetts residents as part of the sale of goods and services must comply with it. It also applies to anyone who keeps this type of information for employment purposes. It doesn't apply to state agencies.

The standard applies to personal information about Massachusetts residents. The definition is similar to the definitions used in breach notification laws. Those laws are discussed at the beginning of this chapter. Under the data protection standard, personal information is a person's first and last name, or first initial and last name, and any of the following:

- Social Security number
- Driver's license number or state identification card number
- Financial account number, or credit or debit card number, with or without password or PIN

The standard requires entities to create an information security program. It states that an entity's information security program must be a good fit for its size and scope. It also must fit the entity's type of business. It must describe the administrative, technical, and physical controls that protect the personal information used by the entity. The program requirements are similar to those stated in the GLBA Safeguards Rule. GLBA is discussed in Chapter 4.

The standard uses a risk-based approach to information security. It allows the entity to review its resources and data use. It also can review its needs for security and confidentiality. The entity can use the results of this review to determine the safeguards it should use. As part of its program, an entity must:

- Assign an employee to manage the program
- Conduct a risk assessment to identify risks to the security, confidentiality, and integrity of information. Review current safeguards to make sure that they are effective
- Develop policies for use of personal information off business premises
- Develop disciplinary policies for failure to follow the information security program
- Develop policies to keep terminated employees from accessing personal information
- Select service providers and make sure that any contract includes terms to protect personal information
- Develop policies to physically safeguard personal information
- Monitor and review the program to make sure it's effective
- Document actions taken in response to any security breach

The standard also includes computer system security requirements. This part of the standard directs entities to implement the security requirements. They must do this as long as the requirements are technically feasible. An entity doesn't have to apply requirements that aren't technically feasible.

The standard states that an information security program must include specific security requirements. They are:

> **NOTE**
>
> Under the standard, "technically feasible" means that if there's a reasonable way to accomplish a required technology result, then an entity must do so.

- Secure user authentication
- Secure access control measures
- Encryption of all transmitted personal information that travels across public networks, and encryption of information to be transmitted wirelessly
- Reasonable monitoring of systems
- Encryption of all personal information stored on laptops or portable devices
- Up-to-date firewall protection and operating system security patches on computers containing personal information
- Virus and malware protection
- Security awareness and training activities

FYI

Massachusetts has released frequently asked questions (FAQs) about its data protection standard. You can read them at *http://www.mass.gov/Eoca/docs/idtheft/201CMR17faqs.pdf.*

The encryption requirements have received a lot of attention. They require businesses to encrypt the personal information of Massachusetts residents while it's stored on their systems. They also must encrypt it when it's transmitted. The standard doesn't define a preferred method of encryption. Encryption is defined in a technology-neutral way. Under the standard, encryption is changing data into an unreadable form. The encrypted data can't be read or understood without an encryption key. Encryption keys are used to encrypt and decrypt data.

The Massachusetts attorney general has the authority to enforce the data protection standard. The law allows civil penalties of up to $5,000 for each violation. The attorney general can also make an entity pay for the costs of an investigation into any violations. Entities can also be charged attorneys' fees.

The Massachusetts data protection standard is unique. It attempts to regulate businesses outside of Massachusetts by requiring businesses to encrypt the personal data of Massachusetts residents. This may be hard since businesses typically must follow only the laws of the state where they are located. Under the law, this is a jurisdiction issue. Only revisions to the standard, or a court case, will help clarify how widely the state may enforce this standard.

Nevada Law: Standards-Based Encryption

Nevada law also has encryption requirements. Its law has had encryption rules since 2008. They were strengthened in 2009 as part of Nevada Senate Bill 227. This same bill required data collectors in the state to follow PCI DSS. The PCI DSS portion of the bill was discussed earlier in this chapter. Senate Bill 227 went into effect January 1, 2010.

The Nevada law requires data collectors to use encryption if they are transmitting personal information outside of their business network. They must encrypt the data if it's sent externally via e-mail or any other electronic transmission. This requirement helps protect data while it's being transferred from one entity to another. The Nevada law excludes facsimiles from the transmission encryption requirements.

 NOTE

Nevada law defines data storage devices as computers, cell phones, and external computer hard drives. It also includes backup storage media.

The law also requires data collectors to encrypt personal information on any data storage device that is moved beyond the technical or physical controls of their business. This means that they must encrypt any storage device that leaves the business location. They must encrypt backup tapes containing personal information that they send to an off-site storage facility. This portion of the law helps protect data if the storage media is lost or stolen.

The encryption rule is novel because of its breadth. It covers data when it's stored and when it's transmitted. The law is also interesting because of how it defines encryption. This is one area where the Nevada law varies greatly from the Massachusetts encryption law. The Massachusetts law defines encryption in a technology-neutral way. It doesn't reference any industry standards. The Nevada law, however, references industry standards.

Under the law, data collectors must use encryption technologies adopted by a standards-setting body. The law references the Federal Information Processing Standards. These standards were issued by the National Institute of Standards and Technology (NIST). Under the law, the technology used must make the personal information unreadable.

You can read the Federal Information Processing Standards at *http://csrc.nist.gov/publications/PubsFIPS.html.*

The law also requires that data collectors use good cryptographic key management practices. These practices protect encryption keys. Encryption keys encrypt and decrypt data. They must be carefully guarded. These keys protect the confidentiality of data. They also protect the integrity of the whole encryption process. The law requires data collectors to use key management practices created by a standards setting body. Again, the law specifically refers to NIST standards.

A data collector that complies with the law isn't liable for damages resulting from a security breach. This protection extends to a breach so long as the data collector's own gross negligence didn't cause the breach.

The Nevada law gives guidance to data collectors on what is considered an acceptable level of encryption. This helps bring clarity to the law. It also gives information security practitioners help in advising businesses on encryption strategies.

The law does create some other ambiguities. For instance, Nevada's breach notification law provides a safe harbor for the unauthorized access of personal information. If an entity encrypts this information, then notification isn't required. The breach notification law doesn't define encryption with the same detail as the encryption law. It's possible that the new law might become the default standard used to specify a minimum level of encryption. This standard could then be applied to entities seeking the breach notification law safe harbor. It isn't known if the Nevada legislature intended this.

Data Disposal Regulations

Many states have created data disposal laws. They have created these laws to make sure that personal information is properly disposed of. Personal data must be protected throughout its lifecycle. This includes disposing of the information in an appropriate way.

Washington: Everyone Has an Obligation

Washington State created its personal data disposal law in 2002.[28] In creating the law, the state legislature made comments about how important the law was. It said that:

NOTE

The only entity specifically excluded by the Washington law is the federal government. The law also states that entities that comply with the GLBA Safeguards Rule are considered compliant with the state law.

- Careless disposal of personal information causes a significant risk of identity theft
- Improper disposal threatens a person's privacy and financial security
- Everyone in the state has a duty to dispose properly of personal information

The Washington disposal law applies to any person or entity in the state. It requires an entity to take reasonable steps to destroy records that contain health and financial data when it determines that it no longer needs those records.

The law requires entities to properly destroy information held in their records. "Records" are defined as any material that holds information. It includes paper or electronic materials. Entities must make sure that they destroy any personal financial or health information in their records. Personal financial and health information is data that identifies a person and is commonly used for financial or health care reasons.

The law states that an entity must destroy information in records so that it's no longer readable or decipherable. The law states that proper destruction includes shredding, erasing, or modifying records so that they're no longer readable.

The Washington law allows a person harmed by a violation of the law to sue the entity that violated it. The law provides the plaintiff with several remedies. The remedies vary depending on the type of violation. If the entity's failure to comply with the law was due to negligence, a court may award a penalty of $200 or actual damages. The court must award a plaintiff whichever amount is greater.

NOTE

Treble damages are damages that punish a defendant for intentional conduct.

If an entity's failure to comply with the law was intentional, then the court can award a penalty of $600 or actual damages. Again, the court must award whichever amount is greater. The law also allows the court to award "treble" damages. Treble damages are three times the amount of the actual damages awarded. The law states that treble damages may not be more than $10,000.

The law also allows the state attorney general to prosecute an entity that violates the law. In that instance, a court must award damages the same way that it awards damages to an individual plaintiff. The court may also grant injunctive relief. This means that it can order the entity to stop violating the law.

New York: Any Physical Record

On the other side of the country, New York State also has a data disposal law.[29] Its law states that no person or business may dispose of a record containing "personal identifying information" without shredding, destroying, or modifying it so that the infor-

NOTE

The New York law specifically excludes state agencies.

mation is no longer readable. The law requires that any person or business destroying the records must take action that is consistent with commonly accepted industry practices. They must use these practices to make sure that no unauthorized person has access to information in the record.

Confidential Documents Used as Confetti

If you are a Yankees fan, 2009 was a very good year. It was their first World Series win since 2000. They celebrated their 27th World Series win with a ticker tape parade in New York City on November 4, 2009.

The term "ticker tape parade" originated in New York City. These parades are rare now; real ticker tape hasn't been used since the 1960s. They are traditionally reserved for large celebrations, such as sports victories.

The 2009 parade for the Yankees was the first ticker tape parade in New York City since the Giants won the Super Bowl in 2008. Sports fans were very excited. When they ran out of confetti, they dumped any type of paper that they could find from skyscraper windows. This included documents containing personal information. News media reported that after the parade, law firm memos, banking records, and court files were recovered from the debris in the street.

One financial firm had to discipline an employee who threw documents marked for destruction instead of confetti. The documents contained financial information and Social Security numbers.

Under the New York law, "records" are any information held in any physical form. They can be paper or electronic. They include reports, letters, and computer tapes. Any type of data storage medium is a record. Personal identifying information is information in a record that identifies a person by name and includes any of the following:

- Social Security number
- Driver's license number or identification card number
- Mother's maiden name, financial account numbers or code, or any other identification number

The law allows for penalties of up to $5,000 for improper disposal. The attorney general alone has the authority to pursue violations of the law. There is no private cause of action.

Case Studies and Examples

The following case highlights unclear federal policies about data breach notification. At the time of this incident, federal law did not require agencies to have breach notification policies. There's still no federal law that requires this. Due to this incident, many federal agencies now have notification policies.

NOTE

The U.S. Department of Veterans Affairs is also called the Veterans Administration (VA).

In 2006, an employee of the U.S. Department of Veterans Affairs (VA) took home a laptop computer and external hard drive. The hard drive held the personal information of every veteran discharged since 1975. It was not encrypted. On May 3, 2006, the employee's home was burglarized. Thieves stole the laptop and hard drive. The local police department investigated the burglary.

The employee immediately informed his supervisors about the theft. They didn't take the matter seriously. The secretary of the VA didn't learn about it until almost two weeks later. The VA secretary notified the Federal Bureau of Investigations (FBI) about the theft. The FBI began to investigate the theft with the local police department.

The VA issued a statement about the theft on May 22, 2006. It reported the facts about the theft. It also said that the data stolen included names, Social Security numbers, and dates of birth for 26.5 million veterans. It included data on some of their spouses. At the time, the VA reported that the hard drive didn't contain any health or financial information.

Congress was outraged that the VA waited so long to make a public statement. On May 25, 2006, the secretary of the VA appeared at hearings before the U.S. House and Senate to discuss the issue. In his Senate testimony, he stated that he was furious that he was not notified in a timely manner. He also stated that the VA was planning to notify all people affected by the theft. He said that it would take time to prepare the mailing because the VA had to verify addresses. He also said that 26 million envelopes "were not immediately available." The VA began mailing the notification letters on June 9, 2006.

As it carried out its investigation, the VA learned that the hard drive held some health information for 2.6 million people. It also learned that the hard drive contained the personal information of active-duty military personnel.

On June 6, 2006, the VA reported that the hard drive held the data of 1.1 million active-duty troops. It also had information on 430,000 members of the National Guard and 645,000 members of the Reserves.

The police recovered the stolen laptop and hard drive in late June 2006. The FBI reported that a forensic review of the equipment showed that the database containing the personal information hadn't been accessed. In August 2006, the VA mailed a follow-up letter to people affected by the event.

The VA Inspector General investigated the incident. It found that the VA employee wasn't permitted to take the laptop or hard drive home. The report faulted the employee for using poor judgment in taking the data home. It also faulted the employee for not properly protecting it. The report also criticized VA supervisors for not taking initial reports about the data loss seriously.

In August 2006, police arrested two adults for the theft. Both men pleaded guilty in December of that year. In March 2007, each man was sentenced to six months in prison for stealing the computer equipment. They also were sentenced to three years of probation.

FYI

You can read the VA press release on the incident at *http://www1.va.gov/opa/pressrel/ pressrelease.cfm?id=1123.*

You can read the Senate Hearing testimony at *http://frwebgate.access.gpo.gov/cgi-bin/ getdoc.cgi?dbname=109_senate_hearings&docid=f:28754.pdf.*

You can read the VA Inspector General report at *http://www4.va.gov/oig/51/FY2006rpts/ VAOIG-06-02238-163.pdf.*

You can read the settlement agreement at *http://www.veteransclass.com/Documents/ SettlementAgreement.pdf.*

In January 2009, the VA agreed to pay $20 million to veterans whose information was potentially exposed in the incident. It paid this amount to settle lawsuits brought by five veterans groups. The money was used to create a compensation fund. Veterans who wished to make a claim against the fund needed to file claims by November 27, 2009.

Congress created the Veterans Affairs Information Security Act of 2006 in response to the breach. The law requires the VA to create a comprehensive information security program. It also requires it to create breach notification regulations. The VA issued those regulations in April 2008. They require the VA to notify people in the event of a security breach if there's a reasonable risk for the potential misuse of their personal information.[30]

> **NOTE**
>
> The U.S. Government Accountability Office released a report on lessons learned from the 2006 VA incident. You can read the report at *http://www .gao.gov/new.items/d07657.pdf.*

CHAPTER SUMMARY

This chapter reviewed state laws that protect data. States have been very active in trying to protect the personal data of their residents. They have created many different laws to protect the security and privacy of this information. They have created these laws because there's no one comprehensive federal data privacy or security law. When reviewing state laws that protect certain types of data, it's important for you to think about what other state or federal laws might also protect the data.

9

State Laws and Breach Notification Laws

KEY CONCEPTS AND TERMS

Breach notification law
Legislative history
Safe harbor

CHAPTER 9 ASSESSMENT

1. The ChoicePoint data breach was the triggering event that caused many states to create data protection laws.

   A. True
   B. False

2. California's breach notification law went into effect in _____.

3. Most states define personal information as *name* and which of the following elements?

   A. Date of birth
   B. Address
   C. Phone number
   D. Social Security number
   E. None of the above

4. An encryption safe harbor is _____.

5. What is a state breach notification law?

   A. A law that requires that residents be notified if a dam breaks
   B. A law that requires that residents be notified if a business has a security breach that compromises their personal data
   C. A law that requires that residents be notified if a business has a security breach that compromises the business's confidential data
   D. A law that requires that businesses be notified if a government has a security breach that compromises the business's confidential data
   E. None of the above

6. Which types of entities are sometimes excluded from breach notification laws?

   A. GLBA financial institutions
   B. HIPAA covered entities
   C. Out-of-state businesses
   D. A and B only
   E. A, B, and C

7. What is *not* a business day?

   A. An official workday
   B. A day of the week that includes Monday through Friday
   C. Memorial Day
   D. Tuesday
   E. None of the above

8. "Clear and conspicuous" notice means that _____.

9. Which states allow data breach notification to be given by telephone?

   A. California
   B. Colorado
   C. North Carolina
   D. A and B only
   E. B and C only

10. What technology standards are permitted under the Nevada encryption law?

    A. PCI DSS
    B. SO 1799
    C. NIST
    D. FTC
    E. HIPAA

11. Which states have required businesses to follow all, or part, of the PCI DSS?

A. Minnesota

B. Nevada

C. California

D. A and B only

E. A and C only

12. A private cause of action is _____.

13. If the U.S. Congress creates a federal breach notification law, what happens to state laws?

A. They are no longer valid.

B. They are still valid as long as they are stricter than federal law.

C. They are still valid in their original form.

D. They are still valid so long as they are weaker than federal law.

E. None of the above

14. What is the purpose of legislative history?

A. To help determine which laws to abolish

B. To help decide how to create new laws

C. To help determine how old a law is

D. To help determine what a legislature intended when it created a law

E. None of the above

15. What is one of the biggest differences between civil and criminal law?

A. The amount of fines

B. Whether a person can be sentenced to prison

C. How long the offense stays on your criminal record

D. The type of judge that hears the case

E. The color of the prison jumpsuits

ENDNOTES

1. California Civil Code, sec. 1798.29, and sec. 1798.82.

2. Ibid.

3. Arizona Revised Statues, sec. 44-7501.

4. Ohio Revised Code, sec. 1347.12.

5. Oklahoma Statutes, sec. 4-3113.1.

6. Georgia Code, sec. 10-1-910.

7. Maine Revised Statutes Annotated, title 10, sec 1346.

8. Ohio Revised Code, sec. 1347.12, and sec. 1349.19

9. Florida Statutes, sec. 817.5681.

10. Wisconsin Statutes, sec. 895.507.

11. Maine Revised Statutes, title 10, sec. 1348.

12. North Carolina General Statutes, sec. 75-65.

13. Colorado Revised Statutes, sec. 6-1-716.

14. Indiana Code, sec. 24-4.9-2-4.

15. Texas Business and Commercial Code Annotated, sec. 48.103.

16. Indiana Code, sec. 24-4.9-4-1.

17. Florida Statutes, sec. 817.5681.

18. Minnesota Statutes, sec. 325E.64.

19. Minnesota Statutes, sec. 325E.64(3), and sec. 325E.64 (4).

20. State of Nevada, Senate Bill 227, 2009 Statutes of Nevada, Page 1603-04.

21. Nevada Revised Statutes, sec. 603A.040.

22. Nevada Revised Statutes, sec. 603A.030

23. Indiana Code, sec. 36-2-7.5-4.

24. Arizona Revised Statutes, sec. 44-1373.

25. California Civil Code, sec. 1798.85.

26. Indiana Code, sec. 4-1-10-3(b).

27. Massachusetts General Law, chapter 93H.

28. Revised Code of Washington, title 19, sec. 19.215.005 to 19.215.030.

29. New York's General Business Law, sec. 399-h.

30. Department of Veterans Affairs, *Data Breach Fine Rule*, Code of Federal Regulations, Title 38, sec. 75.117 (April 2008).

9

State Laws and Breach Notification Laws

Intellectual Property Law

INTELLECTUAL PROPERTY IS THE AREA OF LAW that protects a person's creative ideas, inventions, and innovations. It protects people's ownership rights in their creative ideas. It gives you the right to control the use of your creative ideas. It protects your ability to profit from your ideas. It also prevents other people from exploiting your creative ideas.

Intellectual property protection in the United States has a long history. The U.S. Constitution recognizes the importance of protecting intellectual property. This chapter reviews the major ways you can protect intellectual property. It also reviews the role of information technology in intellectual property issues.

Chapter 10 Topics

This chapter covers the following topics and concepts:

- Why intellectual property law is important
- What the concept of legal ownership is
- What the basics of patent protection are
- What the basics of trademark protection are
- What the basics of copyright protection are
- What the basics of the Digital Millennium Copyright Act are
- What some case studies and examples are

Chapter 10 Goals

When you complete this chapter, you will be able to:

- Describe the importance of intellectual property law
- Explain the basic concept of legal ownership
- Explain how patents are used and what they protect
- Explain how trademarks are used and what they protect
- Explain how copyrights are used and what they protect
- Describe intellectual property concerns with respect to Internet use
- Describe the Digital Millennium Copyright Act and what it protects

The Digital Wild West and the Importance of Intellectual Property Law

It's hard to know who coined the term "Digital Wild West." It's clear, however, that the term is a good description for the state of the World Wide Web (WWW, or "Web") today. Like the American "Wild West" in the latter half of the 19th Century, the Web still has a frontier. Its outer limits are unknown.

The Web and our use of it are still changing and evolving. More people are accessing the Internet and using the Web than ever before. World Internet usage grew over 380 percent between the years 2000 and 2009.[1] Many different devices can access the Web. Cell phones, smart phones, netbooks, and televisions all access it. People can access the Web anytime, and from anywhere.

People are still exploring how to use the Web. They're joining social networking groups and taking many aspects of their lives "online." Organizations are learning how to conduct business online. Many people share novel ideas and champion social causes online. You can publish almost anything on the Web. The privacy implications about the collection and use of information on the Web are discussed in Chapter 2.

 NOTE

The World Wide Web is a system of linked hypertext documents and other media that are connected through the Internet. The Internet and the World Wide Web aren't the same. The Internet is the infrastructure. The Web resides on the infrastructure.

 NOTE

The U.S. Census Bureau has a Web site that attempts to measure the electronic economy. Their reports show that e-commerce continues to grow. The latest "E-Stats" report was issued on May 28, 2009. You can read the report at *http://www.census.gov/econ/estats/index.html*.

Like those of the American Wild West of the 19th century, the Web's boundaries are undefined. The landscape changes daily. Since the Web is always changing and growing, it's hard for the law to keep up. During the actual Wild West, settlers relied more on the federal government for protection. They did this because local governments were often weak. In the digital West, federal and state laws impose order in a patchwork manner. Laws that attempt to regulate content, like the Children's Internet Protection Act (CIPA), are discussed in Chapter 5. Laws that attempt to regulate behavior, such as the Health Insurance Portability and Accountability Act (HIPAA) and state breach notification laws, are the focus of other chapters.

It's hard for the law to keep up with technology. The pace of the law is slow. It relies on the actions of legislatures and decisions in court cases. These bodies move slowly. Technology moves much more quickly. To compensate, the law attempts to apply traditional legal principles to online activities.

The Web facilitates the exchange of ideas in a fixed form. All types of people and organizations use it to communicate. They create Web sites and blogs to share information. Online newspapers and journals publish content every day. Content drives the Web. Because people can easily share information over the Web, they also can easily copy and reproduce materials without an original author's permission.

One traditional area of law that is adapting to new issues raised through technology is intellectual property law. **Intellectual property (IP)** is the area of law that protects a person's creative ideas, inventions, and innovations. Intellectual property law protects ideas once they're in a physical form. When materials are published on the Web, they're in a physical form. Traditional legal concepts about IP ownership and how to protect it are applied to content on the World Wide Web.

Legal Ownership and the Importance of Protecting Intellectual Property

> **NOTE**
>
> Corporations and businesses also can own property. So can governments. In the context of property law, a "person" is a real person or other legal entity. Legal entities include corporations, businesses, private organizations, and governments.

A legal owner of property has the right to use it in any way he or she wants to, and the power to give those rights to another. This is a "property interest." It means that the owner has certain rights to property, and a court will enforce those rights if necessary. There are a number of different types of property ownership. A person can have a real property interest. This means that he or she owns land. A person also can have a personal property interest. This means that he or she owns physical possessions. Physical possessions are items like cars, books, and silverware. Owners of property have the ability to control how it's used.

Ownership is an important concept for intellectual property. An IP owner has certain exclusive rights. An owner is the person who created new works or inventions. That person is the only one that has these rights. Courts will enforce these rights. A court can punish people who violate these rights.

The federal government determines many intellectual property law rules in the United States. The U.S. Constitution specifically grants the power to do this. The Constitution grants Congress the power to "promote the progress of science and useful arts, by securing for limited times to authors and inventors the exclusive right to their respective writings and discoveries."[2] The drafters of the Constitution wanted to encourage innovation and discovery. To do this, they specifically said that authors and inventors must have the exclusive right to control their creations and inventions for a certain period.

The exclusive right to control how creations and inventions are used is the main purpose of IP law. Creators have a right to control how their creations are used for a certain period of time depending upon the underlying nature of the creation. Different laws protect inventions and literary works for different periods.

NOTE

Trademarks have the longest protection period. They're protected as long as an owner continues to use it in commerce.

During the protected period, the creator or author of a work or invention is the only person who can use or reproduce it. This allows authors and inventors to profit from their creative efforts. People would not be encouraged to write new books or create new inventions if they didn't earn money for their efforts. Intellectual property law protects their efforts. It also encourages them to continue to create. Ultimately, this helps the economy.

The federal law recognizes the following types of intellectual property:

- **Patents**—Used to protect inventions like machines, processes, designs, and specialized plants.
- **Trademarks**—Used to protect words, logos, symbols, or slogans that identify a product or service.
- **Copyrights**—Used to protect books, art, music, videos, computer programs, and other creative works.

Each type of intellectual property right is demonstrated in a different way. Each applies to different types of creations and inventions. They give protection for different lengths of times. They also have different requirements for establishing and enforcing IP rights.

Patents

A **patent** is an intellectual property right. It's granted by the federal government. Congress enacted the most recent version of U.S. patent law in the Patent Act of 1952.[3] Congress has amended this law several times. The U.S. Patent and Trademark Office (USPTO) grants patents. The USPTO is an agency located in the Department of Commerce.

NOTE

The National Inventors Hall of Fame and Museum is located at the U.S. Patent and Trademark Office in Alexandria, Va.

10

Intellectual
Property Law

NOTE

The USPTO granted 190,121 patents in 2009.

Patents are granted to encourage new and useful inventions. A patent owner has the right to keep others from making or using the patented invention. They also have the power to stop others from selling their invention. The United States follows a "first to invent" rule. This means that the first person to invent something and show that it works may patent it.

There are three types of patents:

- Utility patents
- Plant patents
- Design patents

Utility patents are the most common type of patents. They're issued for inventions and discoveries. There are four main categories of utility patents. They are:

- Machines
- Manufactured products
- Processes
- Compositions of matter

Utility patents are granted for a 20-year term. This term runs from the date of the filing of the patent. The USPTO often has a long backlog of patent applications. In 1999, the American Inventor's Protection Act was enacted to restore a minimum term of patent protection. It was created in part to compensate for USPTO delays. The law allows patent terms to be extended in certain circumstances:

- If the USPTO doesn't process a new patent application within 14 months of the date of filing
- If the USPTO doesn't issue a patent within three years from the date of filing
- If the USPTO doesn't take certain administrative actions for more than four months

The patent term is extended one day for each day of delay caused by the USPTO. The result of these rules is that patents are guaranteed a validity period of 17 years.

Under patent law, a "machine" is an instrument or tool that completes a task by using moving parts. These parts interact with each other to accomplish a function. Machines are things like lawn mowers, elevators, and automatic can openers. Devices that work because of an electrical process, such as computers, also fall into this category.

NOTE

Manufactured products are called "an article of manufacture" in patent law.

"Manufactured products" are products without moving parts. A milk carton is an example of a manufactured product. A manufactured product may have moving parts. However, the moving parts don't act together to accomplish a task. A folding table, even though it has moving parts, is a manufactured product. It's not a machine.

A "process" is a way of completing a task through a series of steps or actions. It's also called a method. A process can be patented as a utility patent. A recipe might be patentable as a process. Some types of computer software may be patentable as a process.

A "composition of matter" is a chemical compound. It's two or more substances combined together to make something new. Manufacturers patent new drugs under this subcategory of utility patents. Naturally occurring chemical compounds aren't patentable. For instance, air isn't patentable.

The second type of patents is plant patents. **Plant patents** are granted to an inventor who invents or discovers a new variety of plant. The inventor must prove that he or she can asexually reproduce the new plant. Asexual reproduction means that the plant is reproduced through cutting or grafting. Plants that grow from seeds don't reproduce asexually. Plants that are found in nature aren't patentable. A plant patent can protect special kinds of hybridized plants or food crops. Plant patents last for 20 years.

 NOTE

A different federal law governs plants that grow from seeds. The Plant Variety Protection Act of 1970 protects these types of plants.

The last type of patents is design patents. **Design patents** are granted for new and original ornamental designs for manufactured objects. A design is apparent in appearance. They're used to protect the visual appearance of an object. A design patent could protect the design for china or silverware. A design must be new and different from other designs in order to be patentable in this way. Design patents are granted for 14 years.

A design patent is different from a utility patent. Design patents protect only the appearance of an article. A utility patent protects how the article works. Unless otherwise noted, this chapter discusses utility patents.

Patent Basics

Inventions or discoveries must be "patentable" in order to be protected. They must meet certain requirements. An inventor must meet all of the requirements in a patent application.

Patent Requirements

In order to be patentable, an invention or discovery must be:

- Novel
- Useful
- Non-obvious

NOTE

In order to be patentable, the subject matter of an invention or discovery also must be patentable. The U.S. Supreme Court held in *Diamond v. Chakrabarty* (1980) that patentable subject matter is "anything under the sun that is made by man."[4] Some types of items aren't patentable—including objects found in nature.

To be patentable, an invention or discovery must be novel. This means that it must be a new invention or discovery. The USPTO won't issue a patent for an item that isn't new. To be considered new, an invention must be different from the **prior art**. Prior art is public knowledge about an invention that existed prior to a claimed invention date. An invention or discovery must include elements that make it different from prior art. An invention or discovery that merely contains prior art isn't new and isn't patentable.

The USPTO also looks at whether the invention was used in the United States or other countries prior to the date of invention claimed by the owners. It also reviews whether the invention was patented or published in other countries. If people know about the invention or discovery in other places, then it's not new.

Under the laws of many countries, if an inventor announces or sells an invention to the public before it's patented, it automatically becomes not patentable. The United States doesn't follow this rule.

U.S. patent law does allow an exception to this general rule. It allows a "one-year grace period" for inventions made available to the public. It means that a person must file for a patent within one year of announcing the invention to the public. In some cases, an inventor may want to announce an invention or discovery prior to applying for a patent. Inventors do this to see if there's commercial interest in the invention. An invention or discovery is still patentable in the United States if the inventor files a patent application within one year of announcing it. The USPTO won't consider a patent application if it's submitted more than one year after the invention is announced.

How Do You Protect Inventions Internationally?

In the United States, inventors register their patents with the U.S. Patent and Trademark Office. The USPTO patent grants apply only to the United States. They don't protect patents in foreign countries. If a person or business wishes to protect an invention in other countries, a foreign patent is needed.

Different countries have very different patent laws. Many foreign countries require that inventors file their patent applications before an invention is announced or sold. They won't grant a patent if the inventor announces or sells the invention prior to the application. The United States allows a one-year grace period for an invention that's announced or sold before a patent application. Since countries have different patent laws, they enter into international treaties to try to put all inventors on an even playing field for protecting their inventions internationally.

The Paris Convention for the Protection of Industrial Property (1883) was the first treaty to try to address patents on an international level. This treaty is important because it fixes the filing date of patent applications to the date that the inventor first files a patent application in their home country.

Most other nations follow a "first to file" rule. This means that the first person to file a patent application in that country is considered the patent owner. The United States follows a "first to invent" rule. It means that the first person to create an invention is the owner, regardless of when he or she files for a patent. The conflict in rules could place an inventor at a disadvantage in another country.

The Paris Convention says that a person that files for a patent in their home country can use that filing date with other member nations to establish his or her patent's priority in those nations. This protects an inventor's "place in line" in countries that follow a first-to-file rule. This priority right is available for only 12 months after the very first patent application. If an inventor wants to protect an invention in other countries, he or she must file patent applications in those countries within 12 months of first filing for a patent in the home country. Inventors who don't file within 12 months lose their place in line for determining patent ownership under the first-to-file rule.

The second patentability requirement is that an invention or discovery be useful. An inventor can meet this requirement by showing that the invention or discovery is beneficial to society. The inventor also must show that the invention actually works. The USPTO may reject patent applications that don't show that an invention or discovery is useful. It also can reject patent applications where the claimed usefulness seems implausible.

The final patentability requirement is that the invention or discovery must be non-obvious. This requirement is closely related to the "novel" requirement. If an invention or discovery isn't obvious, then it's patentable. Obvious inventions or discoveries aren't patentable.

Sometimes this requirement is hard to understand. Many inventions or discoveries seem "obvious" once they're publicly announced or offered for sale. People often say

The United States joined the Paris Convention in 1887. The Paris Convention only establishes the priority filing date. It doesn't confer other benefits to member nations. Inventors still must follow all the other provisions of patent laws in other countries in order to protect their inventions internationally.

It can be a very long and expensive process to file multiple patent applications within one year. The Patent Cooperation Treaty of 1970 (PCT) attempts to streamline the application process. The World Intellectual Property Organization (WIPO) administers the PCT. The WIPO is part of the United Nations.

The PCT was created to make international protection of patents easier. The treaty allows an inventor to file for patent protection simultaneously in a number of member countries. The PCT allows inventors to file one international patent application.

Inventors submit the international patent application to their national patent office or to the WIPO in some situations. This application then has the same effect filing for a patent in member countries. Like the Paris Convention, the filing date for the international application is fixed in priority as soon as the application is submitted.

Under the PCT process, an international patent application is subject to an international search. Examiners review the published documents in all member countries to see if there's any information that might affect the patentability of the invention. The search is very comprehensive.

The PCT gives other benefits as well. Under the PCT, inventors have up to 18 months after they submit their international patent applications to decide whether they'll pursue patents in other countries that are PCT members. If they do, the patent process is shortened because other countries will reply on the results of the international search in conducting their own review of the patent application. In addition, the inventor is guaranteed patent protection as of the date of the original international application. This is important because many foreign countries grant patent protection only to the first inventor who files for a patent application.

The United States joined the PCT in 1978. Over 140 countries have signed the treaty.

FYI

Judge Learned Hand was a U.S. federal court judge. He served as a judge for the United States District Court for the Southern District of New York. He also served as a judge on the Second Circuit Court of Appeals. Courts and attorneys often quote his opinions on patent and copyright law. Judge Hand wrote very clearly on a complicated topic.

"Why didn't I think of that?" when they see these types of products. Courts have recognized that an invention that seems obvious after it's created may actually meet the non-obvious requirement. That's the nature of some types of inventions. Judge Learned Hand even said, "It certainly cannot be necessary to repeat the well-known principle that it is no indication of noninvention that the device should seem so obvious after it is discovered."[5]

The USPTO looks at prior art and how an invention is used in order to determine if it's non-obvious. An invention is non-obvious if a person with ordinary skill in the kind of technology used in the invention wouldn't have discovered or invented it. The invention also must be sufficiently different from prior art.

Figure 10-1 shows how the three patentability requirements work together.

The Patent Process

An inventor must submit a patent application to the USPTO to patent an invention or discovery. **Patent prosecution** refers to the actions the USPTO must complete in order to grant a patent. It takes the USPTO almost 35 months to prosecute a patent application.[6] This is the period from submitting a patent application to receiving a decision on it. Some types of patent applications take even longer to prosecute. In 2009, the USPTO took almost 41 months to make decisions on patents related to computer architecture and information security.[7]

FIGURE 10-1

Patentability requirements.

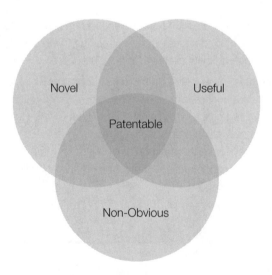

A patent application contains the following basic parts:

- **Specification**—The written technical description of the invention. The specification also contains information about how to make and use the invention. The specification must include enough information that a person with ordinary skill in the relevant area could make the invention based on the specification.
- **Drawings**—The pictorial description of the invention. The drawings must completely describe the invention or discovery. They help the USPTO understand the invention or discovery.
- **Oath**—The inventor must sign an oath that he or she is the first inventor of the item described in the patent application.
- **Filing fees**—There are different filing fees based upon the type of patent. There are also additional fees for large patent applications, search fees, and examination fees.

A patent application specification must include at least one claim. A "claim" defines the part of the invention that's to be protected by the patent. A patent specification may have a number of different claims.

Once the USPTO receives a patent application, it reviews it to make sure that it meets the patentability requirements. Patent office "examiners" conduct this review. U.S. law requires patent examiners to have sufficient "legal knowledge and scientific ability" to conduct this review.[8] After review, an examiner either rejects the application or issues a patent.

An inventor must pay patent maintenance fees once the USPTO issues a patent. This keeps the patent in force. If an inventor doesn't maintain a patent, then other people can take advantage of it. Patent maintenance fees are due at 3.5, 7.5, and 11.5 years after the original patent issue date.

Infringement and Remedies

When an inventor receives a patent for an invention or discovery, he or she has the exclusive right to keep others from using that invention. The inventor is the only one who can make, sell, or use it. This protection begins when the patent is issued. It lasts for as long as the patent is valid. The federal government doesn't enforce patents. Instead, inventors must enforce their own rights. They must sue people who violate their patent rights. They may sue people who make, use, or sell the patented invention during the patent period. They also may sue a person who makes, uses, or sells a substantially similar product.

 NOTE

USPTO employees aren't allowed to apply for patents of their own. This is because they see so many different ideas in the course of their work.

NOTE

The U.S. Patent and Trademark office estimates that the cost of patent application, issue, and maintenance fees can run over $4,000 for the life of a patent.[9]

NOTE

A "patent troll" is a person who owns a patent but doesn't intend to make, use, or sell the invention. Instead, patent trolls enforce their patent rights and file lawsuits against alleged infringers. The term "patent troll" isn't complimentary. It refers to a person who is overly aggressive and opportunistic.

A person who violates the IP rights of another is called an infringer. It doesn't matter if the infringer intended to violate the inventor's patent. An inventor can hold an infringer liable for violating a patent even if the infringer acted unwittingly. This is called **strict liability**. Strict liability means that people can be held responsible for their actions even if they didn't intend to cause harm.

Inventors must sue patent infringers in federal court. This is because patents are governed by federal law. Federal district courts have original jurisdiction for patent infringement cases. Jurisdiction is discussed in Chapter 3.

Infringers have two basic defenses to an inventor's claim of patent infringement. The first defense is that the inventor's patent is invalid for some reason. For example, a patent is invalid if an invention was publicly announced or sold for more than one year prior to the patent application. The infringer would argue that the patent isn't valid because the inventor violated the one-year grace period rule. An infringer also could argue that a patent is invalid if the inventor violated certain federal laws. It could also be argued that a patent isn't valid if the inventor misleads the USPTO during the patent application process.

Under patent law, an issued patent is presumed to be valid.[10] This means infringers can't merely assert that a patent is invalid to defend themselves in a lawsuit. Instead, they must prove that the patent is invalid for some reason. This is called the burden of proof. The infringer has the burden of proving that an issued patent is invalid.

Infringers also can argue that even if an inventor's patent is valid, they didn't violate it. They can claim that their products or inventions don't infringe upon the inventor's patent. These cases can become very technical. Courts and jurors must review the technical specifications of products and patents to decide whether infringement occurred.

Remedies in an infringement case include injunctive relief and damages. Inventors want the court to issue an injunction that orders the infringer to stop violating the inventor's patent. This type of order means that the infringer can no longer make, use, or sell a product that infringes on the inventor's patent.

> **NOTE**
>
> In the United States, the general rule is that each party in litigation will pay its own attorney's fees. In some cases, courts can order the losing party to pay the winning party's attorney's fees. Courts usually award attorney's fees as a penalty for bad behavior or frivolous lawsuits.

Inventors also are entitled to money damages in an infringement case. Damages compensate the inventor for profits that they may have lost because of the infringer's actions. In some cases, an inventor may be entitled to treble damages if the infringer willfully violated the inventor's patent.[11] They may also be entitled to recover their attorney's fees in some cases.[12]

What Is the Difference Between Patents and Trade Secrets?

Patents are intellectual property rights that are granted under federal law. They grant exclusive rights to an inventor of an item for a certain period of time. A patent owner has the right to keep others from making or using the patented invention. He or she also has the power to stop others from selling their invention.

A **trade secret** is similar. Trade secrets protect the formulas, processes, methods, and information that give a business a competitive edge. Trade secrets must have value to a person or business. Otherwise, there's no reason to protect it. A trade secret is a common law concept. It's been codified under federal law and by many states. To establish a trade secret, the information that's to be protected must:

- **Have value**—The information must have economic value. This means that it's valuable to the business that protects it. It also means that it would be valuable to competitors of the business. This also takes into account the money, time, and resources that the business put into developing the information. The more valuable the information, the more likely that it's a trade secret.

- **Be unknown**—The information must not be known outside of the business. If other companies or people know about the information, then it's not a secret. Any public awareness of the information can end its protected status.

- **Be unascertainable**—The information must not be easy to duplicate or even reverse engineer. If little effort is needed to ascertain the information, then it's unlikely to be considered a trade secret.

- **Be protected**—The information must be protected. This means that the business must take steps to make sure that it doesn't become accessible or known to the public. To protect the information, a business should use confidentiality and non-disclosure contracts when they share the information with others. The more a business protects the information, the more likely it's a trade secret.

> **NOTE**
>
> Unlike patents, trade secrets aren't registered. A person or business doesn't have to meet any registration or procedural formalities to protect their trade secrets.

Because they're kept secret, trade secrets can be protected for an unlimited period of time. In order to enforce their trade secrets, a person or business must take actions that protect them and keep them secret. A recent Alabama Court of Appeals case dealt with the protection of trade secrets. In that case, documents that contained trade secret information were left in an unmarked box on the back seat of a company vehicle. The keys to the vehicle were not safeguarded. Other company employees potentially had access to the vehicle. In determining that the company didn't take proper steps to protect its trade secrets, the Alabama Court of Appeals said, "we aren't convinced that leaving allegedly confidential and sensitive documents in a cardboard box in a company vehicle for over one week . . . amounts to a reasonable step to ensure the secrecy of the information contained therein."[13]

If a trade secret is stolen, then a person can pursue remedies allowed under law against the thief. A person who violates a trade secret can be held responsible under civil and criminal law.

How Should an Invention or Process Be Protected?

A person or business has to weigh many factors when considering whether to protect an invention through a patent or as a trade secret. They include:

- Reviewing whether the invention currently protected by trade secret is patentable. If it is, the person must review whether a patent provides better intellectual property protection.
- What processes and controls can be used to make sure that only a limited number of people know about the invention. A person must make sure that everyone knows that an invention protected as a trade secret must be kept extremely confidential.
- How long the person wishes to protect the invention and the type of protection required.

Trade secrets can be used to protect almost everything. One of the most popular examples of a trade secret is the Coca-Cola secret formula. Trade secrets also can be used to protect special ways to manufacture products, or a process for conducting business.

Patents are limited to protecting only certain types of inventions or discoveries. To be patentable, an invention or discovery must meet all patentability requirements. If an inventor fails to meet any one of the requirements, then the USPTO can deny the patent application.

Advantage goes to: Trade secrets. Trade secrets can protect more types of inventions and discoveries.

The owner of a patent has the exclusive right to use the invention or discovery that is patented. That means that the owner can stop anyone else from using it. It's a violation of a patent to reverse engineer a product and recreate it. Only the patent owner can make the patented product.

Under trade secret law, it's not a violation to reverse engineer a product. This means that a person can analyze products to try to determine their secrets. For instance, chemists have tried to figure out the Coca-Cola secret formula. So long as a person lawfully obtains the product, analyzing it to figure out its trade secrets is legal.

Advantage goes to: Patents. Patents give greater protection against use than trade secrets.

A patent's exclusive protection lasts only for the period of the patent. In most instances, this is 20 years. During this time, the inventor has the sole right to make, use, or sell the product. After the patented period is up, anyone may make the underlying product.

Trade secret protection can last forever. It lasts as long as the trade secret is kept confidential. Businesses implement many different types of policies to keep trade secrets confidential. They use access-control mechanisms in computer systems. They limit physical access based on need-to-know principles. They may even use separation-of-duty principles to make sure that no one person knows an entire trade secret.

Advantage goes to: Trade secrets. Trade secrets can be protected longer.

If a company patents a process, invention, or method, it may lose trade secret rights in it. Patent applications are made available to the public 18 months after they're filed. The only exception to this rule is if the inventor states that he or she is not filing for a patent abroad. The USPTO makes patent information available when a patent is issued. Once information is made available to the public, it no longer can be protected as a trade secret.

Trademarks

A **trademark** is an intellectual property right. It's used to protect words, logos, and symbols that identify a product or service. Businesses spend a lot of money developing their trademarks. A trademark is used to distinguish between different products. A mark used to identify services is called a **servicemark**.

The laws for trademarks and servicemarks are the same. Trademarks and servicemarks are collectively called "trademarks" in many texts, including this one. Even the U.S. Patent and Trademark Office uses the term "trademark" to describe both types of marks.

Trademarks represent a business's commercial identity. Some marks are well recognized by the public. For example, the distinctive red bull's-eye design of the Target Corporation identifies a retail department store. The bull's-eye design is its registered trademark. The New York Times Company has used the trademarked slogan "All the news that's fit to print" since 1896. It registered the slogan in 1958. The slogan still appears on the front page of *The New York Times* today.

Trademarks encourage brand loyalty. They also make it easy for customers to recognize products made by a particular manufacturer. They represent goodwill. Goodwill is the image and reputation a business has with its customers. Entities protect their trademarks from misuse because they want to protect their business and reputation.

Both federal and state laws govern trademarks. Federal trademark protection is the most well-known. The federal government regulates trademark registration under the Commerce Clause powers granted by the U.S. Constitution. Congress enacted the first trademark law in the late 1800s. Today the main federal law protecting trademarks is the Lanham Act (1946).[14] The Lanham Act allows for federal registration of trademarks. It also defines how trademarks can be protected. This chapter discusses federal trademark protection.

 NOTE

The U.S. Patent and Trademark Office says the oldest U.S. trademark still in use was registered in 1884. The design is the word SAMSON with a picture of a man wresting a lion. Samson Rope Technologies uses the trademark on its products. You can see the trademark at *www.samsonrope.com*.

NOTE

The Lanham Act also is known as the Trademark Act of 1946.

Trademark Basics

Trademark protection rights belong to the first person who uses the trademark in commerce. This is different from patent and copyright laws, which award rights to the inventor or author. The first person or business to use the trademark in commerce will have certain common law rights to use the trademark. This is true under common law and state and federal trademark statutes. Entities that use trademarks in U.S. interstate commerce often register them with the U.S. Patent and Trademark Office. Entities that use trademarks only in one state may choose to register only in that particular state.

The rise in Internet e-commerce may mean that more businesses will pursue federal registration for their trademarks. This is because business conducted over the Internet can't really be limited to customers of only one state. If an entity wants to conduct business over the Internet, it may want to register its trademarks with the federal government.

There are several benefits to federally registering a trademark. They are:

- **Notice of the date of first use**—The filing date of the registration application gives the public notice about use of the trademark. It establishes a priority date for determining who the first to use a trademark was. It establishes evidence of ownership of the trademark.

- **Right to sue in federal court**—A person or entity who registers a trademark with the USPTO has the right to sue infringers in federal court. They also have the right to recover damages and costs associated with an infringement lawsuit. In some cases, they may be able to recover attorney's fees.

- **Limited ways to challenge the trademark**—After five years of registration, a trademark can be contested only in limited ways. There are very few exceptions to this rule.

- **Right to use the federal registration symbol**—Only a federally registered trademark can use the federal registration symbol. The symbol is an uppercase R in an enclosed circle, or ®. A person violates federal law if he or she uses this symbol on a trademark that isn't federally registered.

> **NOTE**
>
> Trademarks that aren't federally registered often carry the raised "TM" symbol, or ™, to show that a person or business claims the underlying trademark as its own. Trademarks registered under state laws may use this notation.

A person must meet two basic requirements to register a trademark with the USPTO. They are:

- Use of the trademark in interstate commerce
- Distinctiveness of the trademark

Use in Commerce

> **NOTE**
>
> The federal government can regulate interstate commerce only under its Commerce Clause authority. That's why a trademark must be used in interstate commerce in order to be federally registered. A trademark that's used only in one state can be registered under state law.

First, the trademark must be used in interstate commerce.[15] A person uses a trademark in interstate commerce when it's placed on goods or services and sold to the public in a number of different states. The registration application must state when the trademark was first used in commerce.

A person may still register the trademark even if it's not used in interstate commerce at the time that the registration is filed. In this case, the person registering the trademark must show good faith intent to use the trademark in commerce in the future. "Good faith" means that a person honestly intends to use the trademark in interstate commerce.

Under the law, the person must begin using the trademark within six months after the USPTO approves it. The USPTO can extend this period up to 2.5 years. A person must notify the USPTO once it begins to use the trademark. At this point, the USPTO will issue the trademark registration.

Distinctive

The second basic requirement is that a trademark must be distinctive. Almost anything can be a trademark. It's anything used by a person to distinguish their goods and services from another person's goods and services. Words, numbers, logos, and pictures can all serve as trademarks.

The USPTO has two methods of registering trademarks. They're the "Principal Register" and the "Supplemental Register." Strong trademarks are registered right away on the "Principal Register." These trademarks are inherently distinctive. This is a term of art in trademark law. Registration on the "Principal Register" is the main way of registering trademarks. It gives a trademark owner the greatest amount of rights under federal law.

Weaker trademarks can be registered on the "Supplemental Register." These trademarks meet all of the registration requirements except that they're not inherently distinctive. The only federal right granted by registering on the "Supplemental Register" is that the trademark owner may sue in federal court for trademark infringement. After five years of using the trademark, the owner may submit proof of trademark use and evidence that it has achieved a secondary meaning. The USPTO will then move the trademark from the "Supplemental Register" to the "Principal Register."

The Registration Process

A person must submit a trademark registration application to the USPTO in order to register a trademark. It takes the USPTO almost 14 months to review trademark applications.[16] The USPTO encourages trademark applications to be filed electronically. The USPTO processes electronic applications faster than paper applications. In 2009, the USPTO reported that 97.8 percent of the trademark applications that it received were filed electronically.[17]

> **NOTE**
> You can learn more about the USPTO's Trademark Electronic Application System (TEAS) at *http://www.uspto.gov/teas/ e-TEAS/index.html.*

A trademark application must contain the following:

* Name and contact information for the owner of the trademark
* A drawing of the trademark
* A technical listing of the goods or services that the trademark represents
* Filing fee

After the application is filed, it's forwarded to an examiner. The examiner reviews the application to determine whether it's complete. They also review proof that the trademark is used in commerce. They review the trademark to make sure that it's inherently distinctive. Finally, they review other trademarks to search for conflicts.

Strong Versus Weak Trademarks

The USPTO "Principal Register" is for trademarks that are "inherently distinctive." These are strong trademarks. Traditionally, trademarks are inherently distinctive if they do more than describe a good or service. Trademarks that are unrelated to a good or service and are fanciful, arbitrary, or suggestive are considered strong trademarks.

The USPTO's oldest registered trademark is a good example of a strong trademark. That trademark is the name SAMSON with a picture of a man wrestling a lion. It has nothing to do with the company's product, which is rope. It's a strong trademark because it's inherently distinctive. Customers who see the trademark will immediately associate it with the Samson Rope Corporation.

One of the best examples of an inherently distinctive trademark is the Apple Corporation's rainbow-colored apple. It's their registered trademark. The trademark is inherently distinctive because it has nothing at all to do with the company's product. When customers see the rainbow-colored apple with a bite taken out of it, they immediately think of Apple computers. This trademark wouldn't have been inherently distinctive if an apple grower or a grocery store used it.

Weak trademarks aren't inherently distinctive. The most common type of weak trademark is a descriptive trademark. A trademark is descriptive when it describes the underlying product that it represents.

Descriptive trademarks get protection when they achieve secondary meaning. A trademark has "secondary meaning" when the public associates it with a particular good or service. Once a person can show that a trademark has a secondary meaning, it's entitled to full trademark protection.

For example, the trademark Kellogg's Raisin Bran is a descriptive trademark. It describes a kind of breakfast cereal. It has achieved secondary meaning as a particular type of cereal. It's a registered trademark of the Kellogg Company. The trademark Carpetland, USA for a flooring store is also descriptive. It also has acquired secondary meaning as a particular type of flooring store. It's a registered trademark of the Carpetland, USA Corporation.

If the USPTO determines that a trademark is descriptive and it hasn't achieved a secondary meaning, that trademark is listed on the "Supplemental Register." The only federal right granted by registering on the "Supplemental Register" is that the trademark owner may sue in federal court for trademark infringement. After five years of using a trademark, the owner can submit paperwork to move the trademark from the "Supplemental Register" to the "Principal Register."

Some types of trademarks can never be registered. For example, generic trademarks can't be registered. They aren't eligible because they describe a class of products and aren't unique. For example, the word "butter" can't be trademarked because it describes a class of dairy products.

An examiner can reject a trademark for a number of reasons. They include:

- The proposed trademark is a generic name for goods or services.
- The proposed trademark is descriptive of the applicant's goods or services and there's no secondary meaning.
- The proposed trademark is similar to another trademark already registered, and use of it on the applicant's goods or services is likely to cause customer confusion.
- The proposed trademark contains immoral, deceptive, or scandalous matter.
- The proposed trademark may disparage or falsely suggest a connection with persons (living or dead), institutions, beliefs, or national symbols.

When the USPTO approves a trademark, it publishes the trademark in the *Official Gazette*. The *Official Gazette* is the USPTO's official publication. It publishes the *Official Gazette* every week. It includes a listing for trademarks and a listing for patents.

The *Official Gazette* gives the public notice of new trademarks. Once the trademark is published, any party who has concerns about the trademark may contest it. They have 30 days from the date of publication in the "Official Gazette" to file an "opposition" to the registration. An "opposition" is a proceeding before the Trademark Trial and Appeal Board. This Board hears trademark disputes.

 NOTE
You can see entries in the "Official Gazette" online at *http://www.uspto.gov/news/og/index.jsp*.

If no one opposes the trademark, the USPTO issues a Certificate of Registration for trademarks already used in interstate commerce. If the person registering the trademark hasn't used it in commerce, he or she must begin using it within six months after the USPTO approves it. A person must notify the USPTO once it begins to use the trademark. The USPTO will then register the trademark.

The registration period for a trademark is 10 years for new registered trademarks. Some registrations issued before November 16, 1989, have different renewal periods. Between the fifth and sixth year after a person first registers a trademark, he or she must submit an "Affidavit of Use." This document shows that the person or business is still using the trademark. After that, the Affidavit of Use must be filed before the end of the 10-year registration period. The person or business also must pay a maintenance fee.

NOTE
An **affidavit** is a written statement. A person signing an affidavit swears that it's true. The person signs the affidavit in front of a notary public or other official allowed by law to administer oaths and witness signatures.

Infringement and Remedies

Trademark infringement is a violation of a person's trademark rights. A trademark owner has the right to use the trademark in commerce in association with certain goods and services. This protection begins as soon as the owner begins using the trademark in commerce. If a trademark is registered under either federal or state law, then the owner of the trademark has certain other rights as well. Federal and state governments don't enforce trademarks. Instead, owners must enforce their own rights. They must sue people who violate their trademarks.

> **FYI**
>
> While this section discusses federal law, you should remember that many of these same types of trademark infringement actions also could be pursued in state court. A trademark owner may have additional types of tort actions that they can pursue in state court.

There are two main types of infringement cases. The first type of infringement case occurs when there's an infringing use of a similar trademark that's confusing or deceptive to the customer.[18] The second type of case occurs when use of a similar trademark dilutes the value of a famous trademark.[19]

In the first type of case, a trademark owner can sue another person who uses a similar trademark in a way that is "likely to cause confusion, or to cause mistake, or to deceive."[20] The owner can bring this infringement action for innocent infringement and for willful infringement. The plaintiff, who is the trademark owner, has the burden of proof. The plaintiff must prove the following elements:

- The plaintiff owns a valid trademark.
- The defendant used a similar trademark in commerce.
- The defendant's use of a similar trademark is likely to confuse consumers.

If a trademark owner has registered their trademark with the USPTO, that registration is proof of ownership of the trademark. A plaintiff can use the defendant's own advertising materials to show that the defendant used the trademark in commerce. A plaintiff also can use these materials to show that the defendant's use of the trademark was confusing in some way. The confusion created could exploit the plaintiff's goodwill in his or her trademarks and products. That is, the defendant is using a similar trademark in the hopes of selling more products because of the plaintiff's good commercial reputation.

 NOTE

Examples of famous trademarks include the Apple Computers, Coca-Cola, and Kleenex trademarks. They are all registered. They're used extensively across the United States. Most people recognize these trademarks and the associated brand of products.

In reviewing whether a trademark is confusing, courts will compare the plaintiff and defendants' trademarks. They will look at how similar the marks are. They'll also look at the similarities between the goods and services that each trademark represents. They might also look at the defendant's intent in using a similar trademark. If the court finds the defendant's use of the trademark confusing, it can order the defendant to stop using the trademark.

The second type of trademark infringement case is for trademark dilution. This type of infringement case specifically applies to "famous" trademarks. Only holders of famous trademarks can file a lawsuit for trademark dilution. A famous trademark is one that is very well-known.

In a dilution case, the trademark owner can sue for any use of a similar trademark that dilutes or tarnishes their trademark. Dilution occurs when a trademark is used to promote different goods. An example would be Coca-Cola minivan or a Kleenex motorcycle. Customers wouldn't be confused by the different use of the famous trademark. However, the value of the famous trademark is diluted when it's used with dissimilar products.

The trademark owner also has a dilution case if the use of a similar trademark tarnishes a famous trademark. A trademark is tarnished when it's used in an unflattering light. For example, in 1996 the children's toy store, Toys "R" Us, sued an adult Web site with the domain name "adultsrus." The court held that the defendant's use of "adultsrus" to sell adult products diluted the "family" image and goodwill that Toys "R" Us had built in its products. The court ordered the defendants to stop using the "adultsrus" name.[21]

Remedies in an infringement case include injunctive relief and damages. Trademark owners want the court to stop infringers from using their trademarks in a confusing or diluting way.[22] Trademark owners also may be able to get damages for the defendant's profits in using the trademark, their own damages, and costs of the litigation.[23]

> **▶ NOTE**
>
> In some instances, treble damages can be awarded if a defendant intentionally used the plaintiff's trademark.[24]

Relationship of Trademarks on Domain Names

The rise of e-commerce has created some interesting questions about trademark use. Today, people take it almost as a given that *www.coca-cola.com* will take you to the Coca-Cola Company's Web site. Their domain name serves as their Internet business address. Many companies try to use their business name or trademark as their domain name.

A domain name includes a top-level domain. This is the *.com, .net,* or *.gov* at the end of the domain name. The second level is the information that comes directly to the left of *.com, .net,* or *.gov*. This is usually the place where a business or entity might want use its name or trademark. To do this, the entity must register their domain name.

A domain name is different from a uniform resource locator (URL). The domain name is only part of a URL. The complete URL is the actual Internet address. A URL goes into much more detail than a domain name, providing much more information, including the specific page address, folder name, machine name, and protocol language, such as *http://*.

Companies register their domain names and create Web sites. They do this to advertise and sell their products. They want their domain name to be recognizable to their customers. The first company to register a domain name has the right to use that name. Domain name registrars don't review a domain name to make sure that it doesn't infringe on a trademark. If a domain name is available for use, then they will accept a registration for that name.

In the mid to late 1990s, domain names were registered at a fast pace. Not all of these registrations were legitimate. "Cybersquatting" is the bad-faith registration of a domain name that's a registered trademark or trade name of another entity. A trade name is the

> ### Registering a Domain Name
>
> A domain name is the common name that people use to refer to their Web sites. It's the information after *www.* People register these names to grow their businesses and help others find their businesses on the Internet. Domain names are simply addresses on the Internet.
>
> Domain names must be registered with the Internet Corporation for Assigned Names and Numbers (ICANN). ICANN coordinates the Internet's naming system. You can't directly register a domain name with ICANN. Instead, you must register it with a "domain name registrar." ICANN authorizes these registrars to accept domain name registrations. It creates policies for how these registrations should be handled.
>
> ICANN and domain name registrars don't review whether a new domain name registration infringes upon a business or entity's trademark. Instead, they accept registrations for domain names on a first-come, first-served basis. Trademark laws and ICANN's Uniform Domain Name Dispute Resolution Policy are used to resolve domain name disputes regarding trademarks. You can view ICANN's dispute resolution materials at *http://www.icann.org/en/udrp/.*

business name of an organization. Cybersquatters tried to register these names before the legitimate owners of the trademark or trade name. They also registered domain names based on these famous trademarks or trade names but used a common misspelling of those names.

NOTE

"Bad faith" means that a person has a malicious or harmful motive for taking a certain action.

A cybersquatter registers trademarks or trade names to profit off of the other person's trademark or trade name. They also register them in the hopes of selling the domain name to the trademark owner for large amounts of money. They also may register the trademark or trade name in order to attract customers who were looking for a specific product or business. The cybersquatter then redirects the customer to other Web sites.

Trademark owners have a legal right to protect their trademark. This includes protecting their trademarks from cybersquatters. Many people, businesses, and organizations were harmed by cybersquatters. They had to pay large amounts of money to get ownership of their trademarks. They sued cybersquatters to stop them from engaging in trademark infringement. This was a time-consuming and expensive process.

Congress created the Anti-Cybersquatting Consumer Protection Act (ACPA) in 1999.[25] It was designed to stop people from registering domain names that were the trademarks of other entities. It allows entities to sue others for cybersquatting. To prove their case, the plaintiff must show that the cybersquatter registered the trademark in bad faith with intent to profit from the registration. Under the law, a plaintiff can recover damages and ask the court to issue an injunction that stops the cyber-squatter from using the contested domain name. Courts also can award the contested domain name to the winning party.

Trademark owners also can pursue a domain name dispute under the Internet Corporation for Assigned Names and Numbers (ICANN) Uniform Domain Name Dispute Resolution Policy (UDRP). This process may be faster than pursuing an action under the ACPA. Under the UDRP, a contended domain name may be disconnected or transferred to a winning plaintiff.

NOTE

The World Intellectual Property Organization (WIPO) is an arbitrator under the UDRP. The WIPO reported that it heard a record number of domain name disputes in 2008.

Copyright

A **copyright** is an intellectual property right. The U.S. Constitution establishes federal copyright protection. The first federal copyright law was established in 1790. The most recent version of federal copyright law is the 1976 Copyright Act. Copyright is protected under federal law. States are preempted from creating their own copyright laws.

NOTE

Federal law governs patent and copyright issues. State laws are preempted. This is because the Constitution granted the federal government the specific power to make laws to protect authors and inventors.

The holder of a copyright has the exclusive right to do anything with the copyrighted work. The holder is the only one who can reproduce, perform, or sell the work. Copyright holders also have the power to keep others from using their copyrighted material.

Almost anything can be copyrighted. In the digital realm, it's important for you to remember that most materials posted to the Internet are protected by copyright. Most informational and advertising materials posted on Web sites by businesses and organizations are subject to copyright. Blog posts and personal Web sites also are protected. When reposting information that you find on the Internet, you need to make sure that you don't violate the owner's copyright.

Sometimes copyrighted materials are marked with an uppercase "C" in an enclosed circle, or ©. The law doesn't require this. Even if material isn't marked, it may be copyrighted.

Copyright Basics

A copyright is used to protect almost any creative endeavor (called "a work"). It can be used to protect books, art, music, videos, computer programs, and any other creative work. Works that can be copyrighted include:

- **Literary works**—This includes novels, newspapers, textbooks, and computer software.
- **Musical works**—This includes songs, scores for musicals, and jingles.
- **Dramatic works**—This includes plays, skits, monologues. It can also include any music that might be included in the dramatic work.

- **Pantomimes and choreographic works**—This includes ballets or other expressions of dance. It also includes mime shows.
- **Pictorial, graphic, and sculptural works**—This includes photographs, sculptures, fine art, and cartoons.
- **Motion picture and audiovisual works**—This includes movies and television shows.
- **Sound recordings**—This includes recordings of music, sound, and words.
- **Architectural works**—This includes building designs, blueprints, and drawings.

> **NOTE**
>
> Copyright protection isn't available for names. You can read more about it at *http://www.copyright.gov/circs/circ34.pdf.*

The categories are very broad. A work of authorship might be properly copyrighted in a number of different categories. For example, the advertising and information material that an organization posts on its Web site can be copyrighted as a literary work. Pictures on the Web site can be copyrighted as a pictorial or graphic work.

Federal law grants copyright protection to "an original work of authorship fixed in any tangible medium of expression."[26] To be eligible for copyright protection, a work must be both original and in a fixed form.

A work is original if it's not copied from another source. If a work isn't original, it's not eligible for copyright. Works that are created completely from publicly known facts, with no other original material, aren't copyrightable.

Unlike an invention or discovery that's patentable, copyrighted works don't have to be new or novel. They also don't have to be good or aesthetically pleasing. They simply have to be an author's original expression of an idea.

Copyright protection doesn't extend to mere ideas. Instead, these ideas must be written down or put in a fixed format. This is why books are entitled to copyright protection, but ideas that are simply in the head of the author aren't. Copyright also isn't available for useful articles. Patents may protect these types of articles, which can include clothing, furniture, machinery, and other items. Works that are in the public domain also aren't copyrightable.

The **public domain** refers to the body of works that are free for public use. This includes works where the copyright has expired. It also includes works of the U.S. Government such as the United States Code. It's important for you to remember that information that's available on the Internet isn't necessarily in the public domain.

Copyright protection arises as soon as an original work is created in a fixed form. An author doesn't have to do anything to gain this protection. Instead, it arises as a matter of law. An author isn't required to register a work in order to get copyright protection. Writers don't have to mark their work to get copyright protection.

The owner of a copyright has the exclusive right to do anything with the copyrighted work. Only the copyright owner can reproduce, perform, or sell the work. Copyright owners also have the power to keep others from using their copyrighted material. The law gives copyright holders the following broad rights:

- To reproduce the copyrighted work
- To prepare derivative works based upon the copyrighted work
- To distribute copies or phonorecords of the copyrighted work to the public
- To publicly perform the copyrighted work
- To publicly display the copyrighted work

> **NOTE**
> A "derivative work" is a work derived from an original work. A movie based on a best-selling novel is a derivative work.

It's important to understand who the owner of a copyright is. Often the owner of a copyright is the person who created the original work. This isn't always the case, however. For example, when an employee creates work for his or her employer, the employer typically is the owner of the copyright. Copyright law calls this situation a "work made for hire" (WFH).

Other than in the employer/employee context, a WFH must be reflected in a written document. This document shows that a person has specifically commissioned a WFH. The document also reflects that the author agrees to work on a WFH, and that copyright belongs to the person who commissioned the work. The following items are common works for hire:[27]

- A contribution to a collective work
- A part of a motion picture or other audiovisual work
- A translation
- A supplementary work
- A compilation
- An instructional text
- A test and answer material for a test
- An atlas

> **NOTE**
> A WFH situation is created via a contract.

The length of copyright protection is determined through ownership. For original works created after January 1, 1978, a copyright lasts for the length of the author's life plus 70 years after the author's death. For WFH, a copyright lasts for 95 years from publication of the work. Protection also could extend for 120 years from creation of the work. Whichever period is shorter is the proper term.[28] If two or more authors prepare a work, the 70-year period doesn't begin to run out until after the last author's death.

There are special rules for unpublished works. These rules depend on when the work was created. Unpublished works created after January 1, 1978, follow the regular rules of term of life for the creator plus 70 years. A work created before January 1, 1978, and published between January 1, 1978 and January 1, 2003, has copyright protection until at least December 31, 2047. To read about the laws for unpublished and unregistered works, you can visit *http://www.copyright.gov/circs/circ1.pdf.*

NOTE

The U.S. Copyright Office has prepared a number of documents to help people better understand copyright. You can see a list of those documents at *http://www.copyright.gov/circs/*.

Copyright Registration

Copyright protection arises automatically as soon as an original work of authorship is fixed. An author isn't required to register a work in order to get protection. There are many reasons why an author may choose to register for copyright protection. The main reason for a person to register a copyright is so that the copyright can be enforced. An author who created a work in the United States may not file a lawsuit for copyright infringement without first registering the copyright with the U.S. Copyright Office.[29]

The U.S. Copyright Office is a unit of the Library of Congress.

The law creates a number of other reasons to register a copyright. Registration creates a public record of the copyright. In addition, if a copyright is registered within five years of publication, it creates a presumption of valid ownership. This means a copyright is presumed to be valid, and the person challenging it must present proof that it's invalid.

An author must submit copyright registration to the U.S. Copyright Office. The Copyright Office accepts both paper and electronic registration applications. It reports that it takes approximately nine months to process electronic applications. It takes approximately 22 months to process paper-based applications.[30]

A person registers a work by submitting an application and a copy of the work. The applicant also must pay a fee.

How Do You Protect Copyrights Internationally?

The Berne Convention for the Protection of Literary and Artistic Works (1886) is the main treaty regarding international copyright protection. The World Intellectual Property Organization administers it. The Berne Convention also states that any party to the convention agrees to protect the copyrighted works of foreign citizens at least as much as it protects the copyrighted works of its own citizens.

Over 160 countries are members of the Berne Convention. The United States became a member of the Berne Convention in 1989. It took a long time for the United States to join the Berne Convention because the convention requires member countries to provide a minimum level of copyright protection. The United States had to rewrite its copyright laws in order to give these protections. The Berne Convention requires each member nation to recognize the following:

- A minimum term of copyright protection that is the life of the author plus 50 years.

- Freedom from formalities such as notice or registration to recognize a copyright. Copyright protection arises automatically.

- Protection for certain moral rights of the author.

The only way to register a copyright is with the U.S. Copyright Office. Some people believe that mailing a copy of their work to themselves via U.S. mail is copyright registration or proof of ownership in the work. It is not. The only way to register a copyright in the United States is with the U.S. Copyright Office.

Infringement and Remedies

Copyright holders have exclusive rights in the work that they create. These rights arise when the work is created and continue for the length of the copyright. The federal government doesn't enforce copyrights. Authors must enforce their own rights. They can sue people who infringe on their copyright. Liability for infringement is based upon strict liability. A copyright owner can hold an infringer liable for violating a copyright even if the infringement was unwitting.

NOTE
"Piracy" refers to unauthorized copying and distribution of electronic, music, and audiovisual works.

To pursue an action for copyright infringement, a plaintiff must prove ownership of the copyright. The plaintiff also must show that the defendant has infringed on that copyright. A plaintiff usually proves ownership of a copyright by showing a copyright registration. Copyright registration is proof of the validity of the copyright.

Copyright infringement cases are very rarely simple cases of a defendant directly copying a plaintiff's work. To show that there has been an unauthorized reproduction, the plaintiff must show that the defendant had access to the copyrighted work. Access to the copyrighted work alone isn't enough to prove infringement. The plaintiff also must show that the plaintiff's and defendant's work are substantially similar.

One of the most common tests used to determine substantial similarity is "whether a lay observer would consider the works as a whole substantially similar to one another."[31] This is a fact-intensive inquiry. The court will look at all the ways in which the two works are similar. If the two works are substantially similar, then copyright infringement has occurred.

NOTE
Statutory damages are damage amounts that the law specifies. Lawmakers specify statutory damages in cases where it might be hard for a party to prove the amount of actual damages.

Remedies for copyright infringement are similar to remedies for infringements of other intellectual property rights. A court can issue an injunction, which stops the infringer from violating the copyright holder's rights. A court also can order a defendant to pay damages for violating a plaintiff's copyright. A defendant also may be liable for statutory damages under copyright law. These damages are higher for willful copyright infringement.[32]

FYI

Posting a URL to another person's copyrighted materials on your own Web page is generally not considered copyright infringement. Posting a copy of their content on your own Web page, even if you acknowledge their work, may be copyright infringement. This is because only the owner of the copyright has the right to reproduce and distribute their copyrighted materials.

The most common way for a defendant to defend against a copyright infringement case is to argue that the plaintiff's work isn't original. A defendant also can present facts that the works aren't substantially similar. Another defense in a copyright infringement case is that the use of the copyrighted work is allowed under the fair use doctrine.

Fair Use

A copyright holder has a large number of rights in his or her original work. The scope of these rights is to encourage artistic expression. However, there are some limitations on a copyright holder's exclusive rights. These limitations are a defense to copyright infringement. **Fair use** is one of the most common limitations.

The law states that fair use of a copyrighted work isn't copyright infringement.[33] The law lists a number of examples of fair use. Fair use is permitted in these situations in order to promote free speech. The examples include uses for:

- Criticism
- Comment
- News reporting
- Teaching (including multiple copies for classroom use)
- Scholarship
- Research

If portions of a copyrighted work are used for these purposes, then a defendant might have a defense against claims of copyright infringement.

The law also lists a number of factors that should be considered in determining whether a use should be considered fair use. These factors are technology neutral. They can be used to analyze the use of any type of creative work. The factors are:

- **The purpose and character of the use**—A use for nonprofit, educational, or comment purposes tends to favor fair use. A use that is for commercial or profit purposes tends to weigh against fair use.

- **The nature of the copyrighted work**—The more creative a work is, the more protection it will be afforded. Fair use tends to favor the use of facts.

- **The amount and substantiality of the work used**—Use of a small amount of a copyrighted work tends to favor fair use. However, use of a small part of a work that encompasses the substantial idea in that work weighs against fair use.

- **The effect of the use upon the potential market**—A use that has no effect on a potential market for a work tends to weigh in favor of fair use. A use of a work that has a major effect on the market is less likely to be considered fair use.

Courts weigh these factors against one another to determine whether use of a copyrighted work is fair use. If fair use is indicated, it may be a defense to a copyright infringement claim. Fair use cases are very difficult to decide. Courts must engage in a very detailed analysis to determine fair use.

In 2009, the Second Circuit Court of Appeals reviewed a fair use case.[34] In that case, a book publisher created an illustrated biography about the history of the Grateful Dead rock band. As part of the book, it included pictures of concert posters. The plaintiff owned the copyrights to the posters and sued the book publisher for copyright infringement.

The defendant argued that its use of the posters was allowed under the fair use doctrine. In reviewing the case, the Second Circuit held that the use of the copyrighted posters was fair use. It said that the use didn't exploit the copyrighted works, but was instead transformative. This means that the purpose and character of the use was different from the original use of the copyrighted works. The posters were greatly reduced in size and used to commemorate events in the band's history in a biographical fashion. As such, the use was different from the original use of the posters and could properly be considered fair use.

Fair Use for Educational Purposes

Some people believe that the use of any copyrighted work by an educator is always fair use. This isn't true. The educator must still review the fair use factors.

For example, an education professor shares one short excerpt from a copyrighted academic journal article about teaching styles with students to illustrate a lesson. This activity is probably fair use. Analysis of the fair use factors shows:

- A use in an educational setting tends to favor fair use.
- Use of a scholarly journal article that contains facts tends to favor fair use.
- Use of a small amount of a copyrighted work tends to favor fair use.
- This use likely has no effect on a potential market because it's being used in a restricted classroom setting.

The same education professor prepares a newsletter for a Web site. The professor includes a copyrighted cartoon about teaching students in the newsletter to illustrate a humorous point. This activity probably isn't fair use. The cartoon's creator must give permission for the cartoon to be included in the newsletter. Analysis of the fair use factors shows:

- A use on a Web site for entertainment purposes tends to weigh against fair use.
- Use of creative works tends to weigh against fair use. A cartoon is a very creative work.
- A use of an entire work, such as a cartoon, tends to weigh against fair use.
- Use of the work could have a major effect on the cartoonist's ability to market his or her products, especially since it's made available through the Internet. This weighs against fair use.

The rules for determining fair use can be very detailed. The U.S. Copyright Office has prepared fair use guidance for educators. You can read this guidance at *http://www.copyright.gov/circs/circ21.pdf.*

10

Intellectual
Property Law

Protecting Copyrights Online—
The Digital Millennium Copyright Act (DMCA)

In 1998, Congress passed the Digital Millennium Copyright Act (DMCA).[35] Congress created the DMCA to help protect copyrights in the digital world. It also contains provisions that help insulate Internet service providers from the actions of their customers.

DMCA Basics

The Digital Millennium Copyright Act has five titles. They are:

- **Title I**—This title implements two World Intellectual Property Organization treaties. It contains provisions about technological measures used to protect electronic copyrighted works.

- **Title II**—This title is called the Online Copyright Infringement Liability Limitation Act. It limits the liability of online service providers for copyright infringement by users.

NOTE

Many college students are aware of the DMCA because of its Title II copyright infringement provisions.

- **Title III**—This title is called the Computer Maintenance Competition Assurance Act. It allows computer technicians to make a copy of a computer program for maintenance or repair.

- **Title IV**—This title contains miscellaneous provisions.

- **Title V**—This title is called the Vessel Hull Design Protection Act. It creates a new form of IP protection for the design of vessel hulls.

Titles I, II, and III are discussed in this section.

Technology Protection Measures

Title I of the DMCA implements two World Intellectual Property Organization treaties. They're the WIPO Copyright Treaty and the WIPO Performances and Phonograms Treaty. The DMCA amended the Copyright Act (1976) to extend U.S. copyright law to creative works made by citizens in other countries. These changes were required as part of the WIPO treaties.

The WIPO treaties required two major changes. The first is that members of the treaties must prevent people from bypassing technological measures used to protect copyrighted works. Many digital products, such as DVDs, video games, electronic books, and Web sites use access controls to protect certain types of content. For example, a Web site might password protect some sections so that only registered members can get to those sections.

The technology measures and tools that some businesses use to protect their content are referred to as "digital rights management" (DRM). Many large businesses in the entertainment industry use DRM to protect their digital works.

The DMCA forbids people from accessing protected copyrighted content by bypassing these access controls. They may not tamper with content protected by technological access controls. This provision intends to protect content that's transmitted electronically from copyright infringement. In addition, a person isn't allowed to make or sell devices

that would allow other people unauthorized access
to a copyrighted work that's protected by these types of access
controls.

The DMCA also forbids the sale of devices that would allow
other people to bypass technological controls in order to copy
a copyrighted work. The DMCA doesn't prohibit people from
actually bypassing technological controls on their own to
copy a work. This is because copying might be necessary
to use parts of a work under the fair use doctrine.

NOTE

The provisions forbidding bypassing
technological measures are called
the "Circumvention of Technological
Protection Measures." You also may
hear these referred to as the DMCA
anti-circumvention measures.

There are some exceptions to these anti-circumvention measures. It may be possible
for a person to bypass technological controls that prevent unauthorized access in these
instances. Each of these exemptions has additional detailed terms. They're described only
briefly here. The exemptions include:

- Nonprofit libraries, archives, and educational institutions may bypass technology
  protection measures to make a good faith determination that they wish to obtain
  authorized access to the work.

- A person who has lawfully obtained a computer program may bypass technology
  protection measures to identify and analyze elements of the program in order
  to make sure it's compatible with other programs.

- A person may bypass technology protection measures and create tools to do
  so in order to research and identify weaknesses in encryption technologies.

- A person may bypass technology protection measures to protect children from
  certain material on the Internet.

- A person may bypass technology protection measures when those measures
  are capable of collecting or sharing personally identifying information about
  a person's online activities.

- A person may bypass technology protection measures and create tools to do so
  for testing the security of a computer system or network. The owner of the system
  must specifically authorize the testing.

Title I criminalizes the act of bypassing technological measures. A person who willfully
violates the technology protection measures for profit can be held criminally liable.
Penalties include both prison time (up to 10 years is possible) and monetary fines (up
to $1,000,000 is possible). The law makes nonprofit libraries, archives, and educational
institutions entirely exempt from its criminal liability provisions.

FYI

Title II also allows the Library of Congress to issue administrative exemptions. These exemptions
are allowed when technology protection measures substantially limit the ability of people to
make non-infringing uses of copyrighted materials. You can read the administrative exemption
rules at *http://www.copyright.gov/1201/*.

NOTE

"Online service provider" is defined by the DMCA. They're providers of online services or network access. An Internet service provider (ISP) is an online service provider.

Online Copyright Infringement

Title II of the DMCA is called the Online Copyright Infringement Liability Limitation Act. It limits the liability of an online service provider (OSP) for its customers' copyright infringement. Online service providers lobbied hard for these provisions. They were concerned that they could be held liable for their users' actions under some secondary liability legal theories. In these theories, an online service provider could be held liable for a user's actions if they knew about them and contributed to them. This was worrisome to service providers whose entire function was to provide services to customers.

DMCA exempts OSPs from copyright infringement claims that result from the conduct of their customers if certain criteria are met. If they meet these criteria, they fall into a safe harbor. If an OSP qualifies for a safe harbor exemption, only the individual infringing customer is liable for monetary damages. The OSP's service or network, through which the customer engaged in the copyright infringement, isn't liable. The DMCA provides safe harbors for common OSP activities.[36] They are:

- Transitory communications (providing network communications services)
- System caching
- Storage of information on systems or networks at the direction of users (hosting)
- Providing information location tools (search engines)

The safe harbors don't require an OSP to monitor content posted or transmitted by their users for copyright infringement. To take advantage of any of the safe harbor provisions, the OSP must develop a policy of terminating the accounts of repeat copyright offenders. OSPs also must not interfere with any technological measures that copyright owners use to protect their copyrights. OSPs must also meet additional criteria for three of the safe harbors.

Under the transitory communications safe harbor section, an OSP isn't liable for copyright infringement by its customers simply because the OSP provides digital transmissions, routing, or connections for the communicating content. To use this safe harbor, an OSP must show the following:

NOTE

The transitory communications safe harbor is commonly called the "conduit" defense. This is because the OSP is merely providing a conduit for its users to communicate. Internet service providers often rely on this safe harbor.

- Someone other than the OSP initiated the transmission of content.
- The transmission was carried out through an automated process.
- The OSP doesn't select who receives the transmitted material except as an automatic response to the request of another person.
- No copy of the transmission is retained in a manner that makes it available to other recipients.
- OSPs transmit the material through its system without modification of its content.

DMCA Takedown Notices

Under the DMCA, if a copyright owner wishes to have allegedly infringing material removed from an OSP's network, the copyright owner must send a "notice and takedown" letter to the OSP's specified agent. DMCA requires each OSP to specify an agent who will receive these notices and respond to them.

The U.S. Copyright Office maintains a list of DMCA agents. You can find this list at *http://www.copyright.gov/onlinesp/*.

A DMCA "notice and takedown letter" must be in writing and contain the following elements:[37]

- A physical or electronic signature of the copyright owner or representative
- Identification of the copyrighted work
- Identification of the infringing material that's to be removed, along with sufficient information to enable the ISP to locate it
- Contact information for the complaining party
- Statement that the complaining party has a good faith belief that the use of the copyrighted work isn't authorized by the copyright owner or the law
- Statement that the information is accurate and, that under penalty of perjury, the complaining party is authorized to act for the copyright owner

After receipt of a valid notice, the OSP must notify the user and remove or disable access to the allegedly infringing material. In the event that a user believes that the takedown is in error, the DMCA gives users an opportunity to require that the OSP reinstate the materials.

This provision protects the OSP from user-initiated communications that the OSP automatically processes. In these situations where an OSP is merely transmitting material, it won't be liable for the alleged copyright infringement of system users.

Under the information storage and information location tools safe harbor provisions, an OSP also must show that users control what material they post online. OSPs also must show that they don't have actual knowledge of users' infringing activities. OSPs must show that they don't profit from the users infringing activities. OSPs further must show that they take down or block access to infringing material when they receive proper notice from a copyright owner.

Computer Maintenance

Title III of the DMCA is called the Computer Maintenance Competition Assurance Act. It allows computer repair technicians to make temporary, limited copies of computer software while they're repairing a computer. The computer must already have a copy of the software program on it. These new copies can't be used in any manner and technicians must delete them when the repair job is over. The DMCA allows a technician to make these copies to assist in repairing the computer.

DMCA Implementation Concerns

There are a number of implementation concerns with the DMCA. Many of these concerns turn on how the law is worded. Most of them concern the provisions of DMCA Title I and Title II. Many of the issues raised will need to be litigated in order to understand the true scope of some of the DMCA's provisions.

There are many concerns about the anti-circumvention technology protection measures specified in Title I. Many scientists, educators, and industry groups are concerned that these provisions will stifle research. This is because of the criminal penalties that are attached to violating these provisions. There's already some indication that this concern isn't unreasonable.

In 2001, the U.S. Federal Bureau of Investigation (FBI) arrested a security researcher from Russia. The FBI arrested him for publishing software that bypassed access controls on e-books. This was allegedly a violation of DMCA's technology protection measures. He was arrested after making a presentation about the security issues at the Def Con conference in Las Vegas. Both the researcher and the Russian company that he worked for were charged under the DMCA. The charges against the researcher were dropped. In 2002, a jury acquitted the Russian company of charges that it violated the DMCA.

> **NOTE**
>
> To acquit means to find a person "not guilty" of the crimes with which he or she was charged.

Other complaints about these provisions center on the fact that the anti-circumvention provisions hinder fair use and, as a result, free speech. These complaints ask about what happens when DRM-protected materials enter the public domain. How can they be properly used in the public domain if there are no available tools to remove DRM protection?

There are also concerns with Title II of the DMCA. Many people argue that it places too much of a burden on OSPs in responding to "notice and takedown" letters from copyright holders. Since the OSP must act on the notice in order to maintain its safe harbor protection, it might take down material inappropriately. Taking down material in such a broad manner could hamper free speech. In 2009, Google reported that over a third of the DMCA takedown notices that it receives aren't valid copyright claims.[38]

Case Studies and Examples

The following case studies show how the concepts discussed in this chapter are used. These case studies are real-world examples of how intellectual property laws are applied.

Trade Secrets

In 2008, the U.S. government charged a design engineer with stealing trade secrets from Intel. The value of the trade secrets was estimated at $1 billion. The trade secrets were about its newest microprocessor.

The engineer worked at Intel in Massachusetts. He resigned from his job at the end of May 2008. He told Intel that he would use his accrued vacation time for two weeks until his final day at work. His employment with Intel would officially end on June 11, 2008. The engineer didn't tell Intel that he had a new job with an Intel competitor. He started his new job on June 2, 2008.

Intel heard rumors that the engineer had accepted employment with its competitor. The company began to review logs to see his network activities during his last two weeks with the company. It notified law enforcement once it discovered that the employee had accessed sensitive company documents.

The U.S. Federal Bureau of Investigations investigated the incident. Their investigation showed that the engineer remotely accessed the Intel system several times between June 8 and June 11, 2008. He downloaded highly sensitive Intel documents that contained data relating to the design of the new chip. The FBI found no evidence that he had disclosed or used the information that he downloaded from Intel.

> **NOTE**
> You can read the Department of Justice press release at *http://www.justice.gov/criminal/cybercrime/paniIndict.pdf.*

The case was still pending at the time this book was written. Many of the court documents relating to the case have been sealed to protect the information involved in the case. The case highlights that even large companies must implement access control measures to protect their secrets.

Service Provider Liability for Copyright Infringement

Napster was an online music file-sharing software program. At one point, it was the most popular peer-to-peer program in use. Napster allowed computer users to share their music collections online with other computer users. Napster freely distributed its software.

In 1999, several music companies filed a lawsuit against Napster for copyright infringement under the Digital Millennium Copyright Act. They argued that Napster users were directly infringing on their copyrights. They argued that Napster was responsible for copyright infringement on several secondary liability theories. They argued that Napster engaged in copyright infringement as well because it provided the services used by its customers to engage in copyright infringement. The case is called *A&M Records, Inc. v. Napster.* It was filed in U.S. District Court for the Northern District of California.

> **NOTE**
> The Electronic Frontier Foundation maintains a Web site regarding the Napster litigation. You can find the main court documents related to the Napster case at *http://w2.eff.org/IP/P2P/Napster/.*

Napster offered several defenses. It claimed that its activities fell within DMCA safe harbor provisions. These defenses were not successful after the district court determined that Napster failed to meet all the safe harbor requirements.

The district court held that at least some of Napster's users were engaging in activities that infringed upon the copyrights of others. It also held that Napster had knowledge of this activity. It also found that Napster provided services that its users used to engage in copyright infringement. It also found that Napster profited financially from its users' activities. Napster lost the case in district court.

Napster appealed to the Ninth Circuit U.S. Court of Appeals. The Court of Appeals upheld the district court's decision. The court ordered Napster to monitor the activities of its network. It also ordered Napster to block access to infringing material when notified by copyright owners.

Napster shut down its service in July 2001. It declared bankruptcy in 2002. In 2003, it sold all of its assets. Today, Best Buy, Inc. owns Napster. The Napster case is one of the most famous cases about service provider liability for copyright infringement under the DMCA.

CHAPTER SUMMARY

Intellectual property protection is broad. It protects a person's ownership rights in their creative ideas. It gives them the right to protect their ideas and profit from them. These rights are exclusive to the owners of intellectual property. They can take action against people who violate their IP rights.

Intellectual property protection is particularly important to think about as more content becomes available on the Internet. Intellectual property law protects ideas once they're in a physical form. When materials are published on the Web, they're in a physical form. Traditional legal concepts about IP ownership are used to protect materials published on the Internet.

KEY CONCEPTS AND TERMS

Affidavit	Patent prosecution	Servicemark
Copyrights	Patents	Strict liability
Design patents	Plant patents	Trade secrets
Fair use	Prior art	Trademarks
Intellectual property	Public domain	Utility patents

CHAPTER 10 ASSESSMENT

1. What two intellectual property methods can be used to protect computer software?

   A. Patents

   B. Trademarks

   C. Copyrights

   D. A and B

   E. A and C

2. What is strict liability?

3. A design patent can be used to protect computer software.

   A. True

   B. False

4. A utility patent has a _____-year term.

5. Which type of intellectual property protection is mentioned in the U.S. Constitution?

   A. Patents

   B. Trademarks

   C. Copyrights

   D. A and B only

   E. A and C only

6. What is the main difference between patents and trade secrets?

   A. A trade secret is public, a patent is confidential.

   B. A trade secret protects a process, a patent protects a machine.

   C. A trade secret is confidential, a patent is public.

   D. A trade secret protects a machine, a patent protects a process.

   E. None of the above

7. What are the two basic requirements to register a trademark with the U.S. Patent and Trademark Office?

8. The U.S. Patent and Trademark Office publishes the "Official Gazette" to give public notice about patents and trademarks.

   A. True

   B. False

9. What must an author do to protect his or her copyrighted works?

   A. Mark it with a ©.

   B. Register it with the U.S. Copyright Office.

   C. Nothing, copyright protection is automatic.

   D. Pay a fee to the Library of Congress.

   E. None of the above

10. Which DMCA safe harbor is called the "conduit" exception?

   A. Transitory communications safe harbor

   B. System caching safe harbor

   C. Information storage safe harbor

   D. Information location tools safe harbor

   E. None of the above

11. Which type of intellectual property protection is governed by federal and state law?

   A. Patents

   B. Copyrights

   C. Trademarks

   D. A and B only

   E. None of the above

10

Intellectual Property Law

12. What is the trademark registration period?

    A. 10 years

    B. 14 years

    C. 20 years

    D. 70 years

    E. None of the above

13. Why is it important to know who is the owner of a copyrighted work?

14. What must a person show to prove trademark infringement?

    A. Ownership of a trademark

    B. That the defendant used a similar trademark in commerce

    C. That the defendant's use of a similar trademark is likely to confuse consumers

    D. A and B only

    E. A, B, and C only

15. What is cybersquatting?

    A. When a person owns a patent but doesn't make, use, or sell their invention.

    B. When a person registers a domain name that is a registered trademark or trade name of another entity.

    C. When a person uses the copyrighted materials of another without appropriate acknowledgment.

    D. When a person publicly advertises the sensitive confidential information of a business or other entity on the Internet.

    E. None of the above

ENDNOTES

1. Internet World Stats, "Internet Usage Statistics: World Internet Users and Population Stats," September 30, 2009, *http://www.internetworldstats.com/stats.htm* (accessed March 18, 2010).

2. U.S. Constitution, Art. 1, Sec. 8, cl. 8.

3. U.S. Code, Vol. 35, Section 1-376.

4. *Diamond v. Chakrabarty*, 447 U.S. 303 (1980).

5. *Hartford v. Moore*, 181 F. 132 (S.D.N.Y. 1910).

6. U.S. Patent and Trademark Office, "The USPTO: Who We Are," *http://www.uspto.gov/about/index.jsp* (accessed March 19, 2010).

7. U.S. Patent and Trademark Office, "Patent Pendency Statistics, FY 09," *http://www.uspto.gov/patents/stats/patentpendency.jsp* (accessed March 19, 2010).

8. U.S. Code, Title 35, sec. 7.

9. U.S. Patent and Trademark Office, "Answers to the Most Frequently Asked Kids' Questions," *http://www.uspto.gov/web/offices/ac/ahrpa/opa/kids/kidprimer.html* (accessed March 19, 2010).

10. U.S. Code, Vol. 35, sec. 282.

11. U.S. Code, Vol. 35, sec 284.

12. U.S. Code, Vol. 35, sec. 285.

13. *William L. Jones et al. v. Peggy Hamilton*, Alabama Court of Civil Appeals, Opinion, January 22, 2010, available at *http://www.tradesecretsnoncompetelaw.com/uploads/file/Jones%20v%20Hamilton%20decision.pdf* (accessed March 31, 2010).

14. U.S. Code, Vol. 15, sec. 1051.

15. U.S. Code, Vol. 15, sec. 1051.

16. U.S. Patent and Trademark Office, "The USPTO: Who We Are," *http://www.uspto.gov/about/index.jsp* (accessed March 19, 2010).

17. Ibid.

18. U.S. Code, Vol. 15, sec. 1114.

19. U.S. Code, Vol. 15, sec. 1125.

20. U.S. Code, Vol. 15, sec. 1114.

21. *Toys "R" Us v. Akkaoui*, 40 U.S.P.Q.2d (BNA) 1836 (N.D. Cal. Oct. 29, 1996).

22. U.S. Code, Vol. 15, sec. 1116.

23. U.S. Code, Vol. 15, sec. 1117.

24. U.S. Code, Vol. 15, sec. 1117.

25. U.S. Code, Vol. 15, sec. 1125(d).

26. U.S. Code, Vol. 17, sec. 102(a).

27. U.S. Code, Vol. 17, sec. 101.

28. U.S. Code, Vol. 17, sec. 302.

29. U.S. Code, Vol. 17, sec. 411.

30. U.S. Copyright Office, "I've Submitted My Application, Fee, and Copy of My Work to the Copyright Office. Now What?" last revised November 5, 2009, *http://www.copyright.gov/help/faq/faq-what. html#certificate* (accessed March 19, 2010).

31. *Williams v. Crichton,* 84 F.3d 581, 590 (2nd Cir. 1996).

32. U.S. Code, Vol. 17, sec. 504.

33. U.S. Code, Vol. 17, sec. 107.

34. *Bill Graham Archives v. Dorling Kindersley Ltd.,* 448 F.3d 605 (2d Cir. 2006).

35. Digital Millennium Copyright Act, Pub. L. No. 105-304, 112 Stat. 2860 (1998) codified in scattered sections of U.S. Code Vol. 17.

36. U.S. Code, Vol. 17, sec. 512.

37. U.S. Code, Vol. 17, sec. 512.

38. *PC World,* "Google submission hammers section 92A," March 16, 2009, *http://pcworld.co.nz/ pcworld/pcw.nsf/feature/93FEDCEF6636CF90CC257 57A0072B4B7* (accessed March 22, 2010).

The Role of Contracts

CONTRACTS ARE USED TO FORM RELATIONSHIPS between parties for the sale of goods and services. People enter into contracts every day. Most of us never even think about the terms of everyday contracts or the rules governing those contracts. You enter into a contract when you buy a cup of coffee at a local coffeehouse. Many people buy things online. The terms of those purchases are governed by a contract.

This chapter discusses contract law. It's important to understand the basics of traditional contract law. You can apply those concepts to online contracts. This chapter also discusses special types of online contracts. Finally, this chapter introduces some emerging information security issues in contracting for services in cyberspace.

Chapter 11 Topics

This chapter covers the following topics and concepts:

- What general contract law principles are
- How to contract online
- What special types of contracts in cyberspace are
- How these contracts regulate behavior
- What some emerging contract law issues are
- What some case studies and examples are

Chapter 11 Goals

When you complete this chapter, you will be able to:

* Describe traditional contract law principles
* Describe the main differences between contracting on paper and contracting online
* Describe shrinkwrap, clickwrap, and browsewrap agreements
* Describe end user license agreements
* Discuss why it's important to include information security provisions in contracts

General Contracting Principles

Contracts are used everywhere. They are promises between people to sell goods or perform services. Some basic contractual principles apply to all contracts, no matter what the underlying transaction is. People use contracts to state the rules of their relationship. They determine how parties will act with one another. They recite the promises that each party makes to the other. They also help describe what happens if the parties can't complete their contract.

A mixture of common law and code law governs contract formation and performance. Many states have enacted statutes that govern certain types of contracts. One law that many states have in common is the law addressing the sale of goods. Laws governing the sale of goods are part of the Uniform Commercial Code (UCC). The National Conference of Commissioners on Uniform State Laws (NCCUSL) wrote the UCC. The NCCUSL works for uniformity in state laws. It has been in existence since 1892. Each state appoints commissioners to work on draft model laws. It took the NCCUSL 10 years to write the UCC.

The UCC is a model law that states can adopt. Every state has adopted all or parts of the UCC. Sometimes states may amend portions of the UCC when they adopt it. "Article 2" of the UCC addresses the sale of goods. A "good" is a movable object like a computer, desk, or chair. States have enacted similar laws governing the sale of goods so that commerce between the states can be predictable and uniform. This helps encourage even more commerce and business.

The UCC doesn't cover every aspect of contract law. Many parts of contract law are left to each state's common law.[1]

 NOTE

When reviewing contract laws in a particular state, it's important to study both the state's code law and common law.

> **NOTE**
>
> The American Law Institute and the NCCUSL worked together to create the Uniform Commercial Code.

Common law contracting principles also are similar among the states. The Restatement (Second) of the Law of Contracts summarizes the common law rules. The Restatement is a treatise on common law contract rules. The American Law Institute (ALI) prepares it. The ALI is a group of highly distinguished judges, lawyers, and legal scholars. They review cases on a certain type of law. They compile the principles in those cases into a series of rules. These rules are not binding authority on a court the way statutes or court rulings are. However, they do offer guidance on what the common law is.

This chapter discusses the basic rules that are applicable to all contracts. It also discusses how those rules apply to online or electronic contracts. This chapter doesn't discuss the special rules that apply to certain types of contracts such as real estate or securities transactions.

The general contract law rules are derived from the common law. It's important to keep in mind that the common law traditionally applies to contracts for services, while the Uniform Commercial Code applies to contracts for goods.

Contract Form

A contract is a legally binding agreement. It's enforceable in court. Contracts can be either oral contracts or written contracts. Oral contracts are contracts that parties don't write down. Written contracts are contracts that may have been negotiated verbally, but are then written down. An oral contract is just as enforceable as a contract that is written down. However, there are a few reasons why written contracts are best. They include:

> **NOTE**
>
> A lawyer's favorite line, "an oral contract isn't worth the paper it's written on," is attributed to Samuel Goldwyn. Goldwyn was a Hollywood producer who rose to fame in the 1920s.

- **Proof**—It's easier for a person to prove the existence of a written contract.
- **Terms**—It's easier for a person to prove the terms of a written contract.
- **Precision**—A written contract requires the parties to be more precise in defining their relationship.
- **Clarity**—A written contract is more likely to have terms that clarify what happens if a contract relationship fails.

Some types of contracts must be written down and the contracting parties must sign them. These contracts are written down to prevent fraud between the contracting parties. The rule that requires these contracts to be written down is called the **Statute of Frauds**. For example, contracts for the sale of land must be written down. Some contracts for goods that are valued over $500 also must be written down.[2] The law requires these contracts be written down and signed to provide proof of their existence.

No matter what the form of a contract, all contracts must have certain elements in order to be enforceable. Contracts must be made between parties that have the legal ability to enter into them. Parties can contract only for transactions that are legal and that don't violate basic societal principles.

Finally, the parties to the contract must show that they intended to enter into a specific transaction with specific terms. This is called mutual assent. Mutual assent is shown through the "offer" and "acceptance" process.

Capacity to Contract

The law assumes that almost anyone can enter into a contract. There are few exceptions to this rule. People who enter into contracts must be able to understand that they are negotiating for a relationship. They also must be able to understand that each party will have rights and obligations because of the parties' agreement.

A court won't find a contract enforceable if a person wasn't able to understand the consequences of entering into the contract at the time that it was formed. A person who is unable to understand the consequences of entering into a contract lacks **contractual capacity**.

The law recognizes that the following classes of people may lack contractual capacity:

> **NOTE**
> A person who lacks "contractual capacity" isn't bound by their contracts. Courts won't enforce contracts against a person who lacks contractual capacity.

- Children under the age of 18
- People who are mentally incompetent
- People who are intoxicated

In most cases, courts won't enforce contracts against people in these classes. There are special rules for contracts for necessary items such as medical care. People who lack contractual capacity can be held responsible for contracts that they enter into for necessary items. These rules are applied subjectively. Courts look at the facts and circumstances of each case. The legal representatives for both children and mentally incompetent people may approve certain types of contracts on behalf of the people that they represent.

The contractual capacity of an intoxicated person requires special review. To avoid a contract based on intoxication, a person must be so intoxicated that his or her mental capacity is limited. Courts will look at objective measures of intoxication and the actions of the party. An intoxicated person's deliberate actions, such as writing contract terms on a napkin, might be used to show that a valid contract existed.

> **NOTE**
> An intoxicated person can lack the capacity to contract through drug or alcohol use. A court can find contractual incapacity even if a person's drug or alcohol use was voluntary.

A person who is trying to avoid a contract may claim that he or she lacked the capacity to enter into the contract. If a person raises this defense, then he or she bears the burden of proving lack of contractual capacity.

Contract Legality

Some types of contracts simply aren't enforceable. This is because they are against public policy. Public policy refers to the principles that form the beliefs of a society. A contract that is contrary to those principles isn't enforceable.

NOTE

Courts won't enforce illegal contracts. An illegal contract is formed when parties try to enter into an agreement to commit a crime or other wrongdoing.

NOTE

Contracts that are unfairly burdensome are called "unconscionable." Unconscionable contracts aren't enforceable.

NOTE

In contracts for the sale of goods, the offeror is called the seller. The offeree is the buyer.

An example of an unenforceable contract is a contract for murder. It's against the law, and public policy, to murder another person. Therefore, a court will not enforce a contract where one party agreed to kill another party for a sum of money. This type of contract is called an illegal contract.

Contracts that aren't enforceable because of public policy reasons include:

- Contracts that reduce commercial competition
- Contracts to commit a crime or other wrongdoing
- Contracts that are unfairly burdensome to one party
- Contracts that discriminate based on unchangeable characteristics such as race, color, religion, or disability

Form of Offer

An **offer** is an invitation to enter into a relationship or transaction of some kind.[3] The person who makes an offer is called an **offeror**. The offeror must put enough detail in the offer so that the other party knows what he or she is agreeing to. The other party is called an **offeree**.

The offer must contain enough terms and detail to describe the underlying transaction. In a bargain for the sale of goods, an offer typically would include terms describing the quantity of goods available, as well as their price. That way, the offeree would know how much he or she gets for the contract price. These are material terms about the transaction. An offer has enough detail when the offeree knows what is part of the bargain.

To be valid, an offer must be communicated to the other person. For example, an offeror selling a couch must communicate the item to be sold, when the item is available, and the price for the item. They must communicate all of these terms in order to make a sufficient offer. An offer is valid as soon as the offeree receives it.

NOTE

Offers expire after a reasonable period of time. Courts determine what a reasonable period of time is by looking at the facts and circumstances surrounding a case.

An offeree must take action once an offer is communicated. An offer remains open until it's accepted, rejected, or retracted. An offer also can expire if too much time passes before an offeree accepts it. Sometimes offers say that they are valid only for a certain period. When that period ends, the offer expires. If an offer doesn't include a time period, then it expires after a reasonable period of time.

If an offeree doesn't agree to the terms of the offer, then it's rejected. An offeree also rejects an offer if he or she proposes terms that are different from the original offer. This is called a counteroffer. In this situation, the original offer is rejected when the counteroffer is proposed. The original offeror then has to decide whether to accept or reject the counteroffer. The parties can't go back to the original offer unless one of them proposes it again.[4]

An original offeror also can revoke an initial offer. This means that the offer is no longer available. If an offer is to be cancelled, this must be done before an offeree accepts it.

> ▶ **NOTE**
> Usually offers and counteroffers are made during the negotiation process. Verbal negotiations are very normal. Parties don't always write down the offers and counteroffers that they make during this process. Sometimes the only offers that are written down are the final, accepted offers. These end up becoming the contractual terms.

What Communications Constitute an Offer?

Courts frequently encounter questions about the types of communications that constitute an offer. The general rule is that a communication is considered an offer if an objective, reasonable person would consider it an offer.

Courts have long held that advertisements can constitute a valid offer. The *Carlill v. Carbolic Smoke Ball Company* (1892) case is one of the most cited cases in this respect. It's an old English contract law case. The Carbolic Smoke Ball was a flu and illness remedy. The manufacturer advertised in newspapers that it would pay Smoke Ball users a "reward" if they caught the flu after using the product.

The plaintiff in the case used the product and caught the flu. She asked the manufacturer to pay the "reward." The manufacturer declined. Eventually the case went to court. The English Court of Appeal held that the advertisement did indeed constitute a valid offer. It said that the plaintiff's actions in using the Carbolic Smoke Ball were a valid acceptance of that offer. The court found that the plaintiff acted reasonably in relying on the terms in the advertisement.

Not all advertisements constitute a valid offer. In *Leonard v. Pepsico, Inc.* (S.D.N.Y. 1999), the plaintiff claimed that a Pepsi television advertisement showing that "Pepsi points" could be redeemed to claim a Harrier Jet was a valid contractual offer. The plaintiff claimed he accepted the offer when he submitted Pepsi points, cash, and a claim form for the jet to Pepsi.

The court held that it was clear that Pepsi's "offer" of the Harrier Jet was a joke. It said that an objective, reasonable person wouldn't believe that the television advertisement constituted a real offer.

The best part about this case is the court's opinion. It's clear from the opinion that the judge had a sense of humor and dramatic flair. In discussing the commercial, the judge wrote, "Plaintiff's insistence that the commercial appears to be a serious offer requires the Court to explain why the commercial is funny. Explaining why a joke is funny is a daunting task...." You can read the opinion at *http://scholar.google.com/scholar_case?case=14010883517992816574&q=88+F. Supp.2d+116+(1999)&hl=en&as_sdt=2002.*

Form of Acceptance

An offer is accepted when the offeree agrees to the terms of the offeror's bargain. Traditionally, an acceptance had to have exactly the same words and terms as the original offer. This was called the **mirror image rule**. The mirror image rule meant that even a small change in terms or language between the offer and an acceptance served as a rejection of the original offer. The new terms in the acceptance then became a counteroffer. Parties had to be very careful in their negotiations to use the same terminology all the time to avoid the rule.

Today there's less emphasis on the mirror image rule. An acceptance doesn't have to be identical to an offer to be enforceable. Under the more relaxed rule, an acceptance is viewed as a counteroffer only if the terms of the acceptance change a material term in the offer. If the acceptance doesn't alter material terms, then it's enforceable. The UCC follows the relaxed mirror image rule.[5]

> **NOTE**
>
> A material term in a contract is one that is necessary to understanding the underlying transaction. Material terms include item, price, quantity, and when the item is available for delivery.

The offeree must communicate their acceptance back to the offeror. He or she must clearly communicate it to the offeror. This includes the use of words like "Yes" or "I accept." Acceptance of an offer also can be communicated through actions.

> **NOTE**
>
> An offeree's silence is not acceptance of a contract. An offeree usually has no legal obligation to respond to an offer.

The timing of the acceptance is an important consideration under the common law of contracts. When parties are in the presence of one another, acceptance is communicated instantaneously. A contract is formed when the offeror receives the acceptance. It's formed automatically because the parties are clear on the terms of the offer and of the acceptance because they're in each other's presence. There's no break in communication that might indicate that the offer has been revoked.[6]

The situation is different for delayed communications. For those communications, courts developed the **mailbox rule**. The mailbox rule means that an offer is deemed accepted for legal purposes as soon as an offeree puts a written acceptance into the mailbox. The mailbox rule developed because there was often a time lag in postal communications that could cause the parties to doubt whether a contract existed. The relationship between the parties is clear if a contract forms upon mailing the acceptance. Under the mailbox rule, an acceptance is valid as soon as it's dispatched or sent.

> **NOTE**
>
> The mailbox rule says that an acceptance is valid as soon as an offeree sends it. It applies only to acceptances. It doesn't apply to situations where the offeror revokes his offer. A revoked offer is valid once the offeree actually receives it.

If an offeror specifies that an offer must be accepted in a certain way, then the mailbox rule won't apply. The mailbox rule also doesn't apply if an offeror states that a contract doesn't form until he or she receives the acceptance. Today, many offers specifically require receipt of the acceptance before a contract is formed to avoid the application of the mailbox rule.

Meeting of the Minds

It's a basic rule of contract law that the parties to a contract must agree to its terms. To determine whether the parties really did make a contract, courts look to see if there's mutual agreement. A court studies the parties' words and actions. A court looks for evidence that both parties acted as if they had entered into a contract with one another.

The idea that contracts form when there's a meeting of the minds is a long-standing feature of American law. The United States Supreme Court held in *Baltimore & Ohio Railroad Co. v. United States* (1923) that a contract can be inferred from the conduct of the parties. This is true even if no written contract exists.

 NOTE

Mutual agreement is a contract law principle that is used to describe how the parties intend to act with respect to a contract. It's also called "mutual assent" or "meeting of the minds." One of the case studies at the end of this chapter reviews mutual assent.

Meeting of the minds is evidenced through words, such as saying "I accept" in response to an offer. It also can be shown through the actions of a party. If the parties behave in a way that suggests there's a contract, then courts likely will enforce some sort of agreement.

Consideration

In forming a contract, the parties must bargain for something of value. This is called consideration. **Consideration** is an essential contract element. It means that the parties have bargained for, and are exchanging, something of value. Every contract must be supported by consideration. If there's no consideration, the contract is not enforceable.

Consideration is reciprocal. It means that both parties are promising to do something. For example, the offeror offers to develop a Web page for $50. The offeree accepts the offer. The offeror's consideration is developing the Web page. The offeree's consideration is paying $50 for the developed Web page.

 NOTE

Consideration is an exchange of money, goods, or a promise to perform a certain action.

In the United States, courts don't usually review the value of the consideration that the parties exchange. They leave it to the parties to determine the sufficiency of their own deals. As long as a party has the capacity to contract, they are free to bargain and enter into contracts. This is true even if they enter into contracts with terms that seem unwise. Courts will only review whether the consideration was truly bargained for and whether there was a mutual exchange of promises.

Some transactions don't have consideration. If there's no consideration, there can be no contract. For example, gifts don't involve consideration. In addition, there's no consideration when value is given for a service that a person has already performed. This is called "prior consideration." Prior consideration can't be used to form a new contract.

In addition, there's no consideration when a person is already obligated to do something because of a pre-existing obligation. For instance, you can't enter into a contract with a firefighter to save your burning home because the firefighter already has an obligation to fight the fire.

Performance and Breach of Contract

NOTE

In the law, a party is discharged when he or she no longer has any responsibilities or obligations toward the other party.

A contract must be performed in order to be complete. This means that each party must fulfill his or her promises to one another. If the parties complete all of their promises to one another, then they're discharged from any further obligation.

There are three general types of contractual performance:

- **Complete performance**—A party performs all of his or her contract promises.

- **Substantial performance**—A party performs all material contract promises; non-performance of some terms results in a minor breach of contract.

- **Incomplete performance**—A party doesn't perform his or her contract promises; non-performance results in a material breach of contract.

NOTE

A **remedy** also is called legal relief. Courts grant remedies in order to enforce the rights of the parties that appear before it. A winning party is usually the party that receives a remedy.

NOTE

A **duty to mitigate** is the non-breaching party's obligation to not aggravate the harm caused by a breach. A person may not allow their damages to rise if at all possible. They must take reasonable actions to limit the amount of harm caused by the breaching party.

If one party doesn't fulfill all of their promises, then the other party may sue them for breach of contract. The non-breaching party may sue for both a minor breach of contract and a material breach of contract. Once a lawsuit is filed, a court reviews the parties' contractual performance. It then determines what remedies are available to the non-breaching party.

In contract law, a court may order a variety of legal remedies. It awards remedies depending upon the facts of the case. The available legal remedies in a contract law case include money damages, specific performance, contract rescission, and contract reformation.

The most common type of remedy in a breach of contract dispute is an award of damages. "Damages" refers to money that the court awards to the party that didn't breach the contract. For the most part, damages are used to make a party whole. They try to compensate a party and make it as if the breach never occurred. Under the law, a non-breaching party has a duty to avoid or reduce the total damages caused by the other party's breach of contract.

There are four types of money damages that can be awarded in a contract case:

- **Compensatory damages**—A money award that compensates a non-breaching party for the other party's breach. These damages place the non-breaching party in the same position he or she would have been in had the contract been fully performed. This is the most common type of damages that courts award.

- **Consequential damages**—A money award that compensates the non-breaching party for foreseeable damages that arise from circumstances outside of the contract. The non-breaching party can't mitigate these damages.

- **Liquidated damages**—A contractual grant of money damages. The parties determined the amount of damages prior to entering into the contract. The contract specifically states the amount of damages that a non-breaching party is entitled to. The contracting parties predetermine the amount of damages. Courts will approve liquidated damages as long as they're reasonable.

- **Nominal damages**—A money award to the non-breaching party even though they haven't suffered any financial loss because of a breach of contract. A nominal award recognizes that a breach occurred, but nothing more.

 NOTE

Punitive damages are damages that punish a party for bad or wrongful behavior. While punitive damages are usually available in tort law, they're generally not allowed in breach of contract cases.

NOTE

Specific performance is an equitable remedy. An equitable remedy forces a person to do (or not do) some act. Equitable remedies usually are awarded by courts only if legal remedies are inadequate. Legal remedies are requests for money damages.

Another remedy that courts can award is **specific performance**. Specific performance is a legal term that refers to situations where a court orders a party to complete their contractual duties. Courts don't usually award specific performance unless the underlying contractual transaction is unique. It's harder for courts to determine the damages amount when the underlying transaction is unique. If it's hard to determine damages, then it's more likely that a court will award specific performance.

Non-breaching parties usually don't ask for specific performance. This is because if people are forced to perform their contractual duties, they sometimes perform those duties poorly. Courts don't like to have to supervise performance to ensure that a party is performing properly. Non-breaching parties have an interest in avoiding shoddy performance.

Courts also can rescind a contract. This remedy undoes the contract. It puts the parties in the same position that they would have been in if there had been no contract at all. This remedy is often available if there's been a material breach of contract. In order to rescind a contract, the parties must return any consideration that they each received. For example, they must return the goods and money that they exchanged under the contract.

Finally, courts can reform a contract. In contract reformation, a court rewrites the contract to express the true intent of the parties to a contract. The parties are then expected to perform the contract as rewritten. Courts often use reformation to fix contracts that have obvious clerical errors. Contract reformation is an equitable remedy.

Contract Repudiation

Repudiation is a refusal to perform a contract duty. It occurs when one party either denies the existence of a contract or refuses to perform their contractual obligations. Repudiation also is called anticipatory breach of contract. Repudiation occurs when one party clearly communicates that he or she won't perform their contractual duties.

Under the common law, a non-repudiating party can react in three ways to repudiation. First, this party can immediately consider the contract terminated. That is, the party doesn't have to perform any of his or her own contractual obligations. Second, the party can wait and see if the other party decides to perform his or her obligations after all. Third, the party can immediately sue the repudiating party for breach of contract.

If one party repudiates a contract, the party who is relying on the contract bears the burden of proving that the contract is indeed valid and enforceable. Usually this is the person who files a breach of contract action. The filer must prove that there was a legitimate contract between the parties.

Another aspect of repudiation has to do with how a contract is signed. This distinction becomes important later in this chapter. Under traditional legal principles, a party to a contract can always repudiate a contract on the basis that another person forged his or her signature on the contract.

If one party claims that the signature is not authentic, then the other party has the burden of proving that the signature is authentic. He or she has to present evidence that prevents the other party from repudiating the signature. The party presents this evidence because he or she wants a court to enforce the contract.

> **NOTE**
>
> Non-repudiation becomes an important issue in online contracts because cryptography can be used to make sure that parties can't repudiate the contracts that they enter into.

In traditional contract law, contracts are negotiated face-to-face. The parties know one another and would know if a signature was forged. Sometimes contracts are signed in front of witnesses. If witnesses watch the parties signing a contract, it's harder for one party to repudiate a signature. This is a way of assuring that a party can't repudiate a signature in traditional, paper-based contracts.

Contracting Online

The rise of the Internet and e-commerce has made online contracts very common. They're used every day. A person enters into a contract when buying goods through online retailers, such as Amazon.com. They enter into auction contracts on eBay. A person agrees to terms-of-use contracts when using free wireless Internet at a local coffee shop. In many instances, you might not even be aware that you're entering into valid, enforceable contracts.

Online contracts are contracts that are entered into over the Internet or through a technological medium. There's nothing particularly special about these contracts other than the medium used to form the contract. The underlying transactions are the same for online contracts and traditional contracts.

> **NOTE**
>
> In this chapter, the term "traditional contracts" refers to written and oral contracts. "Online contracts" refers to contracts that are created through a technological communication process, such as via e-mail or the Internet.

While online contracts can make transacting business easier, they also present some unique challenges for the contracting parties and for the law. The law generally presumes that contracting parties at least know of one another prior to entering into a contract. That's not necessarily true for online contracts. When people contract over the Internet, it's unlikely that they're in the same state, geographical region, or even country. Parties that contract electronically give up certain rights when they contract online. They include:

- The contracting parties may not know the identities of one another.

- The contracting parties may have no real opportunity to bargain for the terms of their agreements.

- It may be difficult to determine the material terms of the contract if the parties exchanged multiple electronic communications.

> **NOTE**
>
> Jurisdiction is an important issue for online contracts. A complete discussion of jurisdiction is out of scope for this chapter. It's important to be aware that many online contracts contain clauses that require lawsuits about the contract to be litigated in certain places. This is an attempt by at least one party to control jurisdiction issues.

It really has become obvious that people can indeed contract through online processes. The U.S. federal government has created legislation that states, for interstate commerce, that online or electronic contracts are just as valid as traditional, paper-based contracts.[7] States also have created their own laws. Forty-seven states have adopted the Uniform Electronic Transactions Act (UETA). The UETA specifically states that its purpose is to "remove barriers to electronic commerce by validating" electronic contracts.[8]

The Validity of Online Contracts: The UETA and E-SIGN Acts

The National Conference of Commissioners on Uniform State Laws created the Uniform Electronic Transactions Act in July 1999. UETA covers business and commercial transactions. It doesn't cover transactions between private parties.

The NCCUSL created UETA for a number of purposes. One of them was to legitimize electronic contracts. UETA recognizes that parties contract electronically because of speed and other economic efficiencies. It also recognizes that some rules, like the common law Statute of Frauds, can be a barrier to electronic contracts in some circumstances. The comments to UETA make it clear that it doesn't create new rules for online contracting. Instead, it recognizes that general contract law rules and principles apply to transactions that are conducted electronically.

The main benefit of the UETA is that it specifically states that electronic contracts are enforceable. It also states that an "electronic record" satisfies any common law requirements that a contract be in writing. This helps to soften the application of a rule like the Statute of Frauds for records that might only exist in electronic form in an information system. Under the UETA, an electronic record is any record that is stored in the memory of an information system.

The UETA also requires that courts and contracting parties give an electronic signature the same effect as a handwritten signature. Under the UETA, an electronic signature is "an electronic sound, symbol, or process attached to or logically associated with an electronic record and executed or adopted by a person with the intent to sign the electronic record."[9] Clicking on an "I agree" button on a Web page is an electronic signature under the UETA definition. Typing your name at the bottom of an e-mail also can be a valid, legal signature under the UETA as long as you intend it to serve as your electronic signature.

The UETA is not a digital signature statute. It doesn't define cryptographic or technology standards for digital signatures. It does acknowledge that electronic signatures that have certain security protections may provide additional reliability about the identities of contracting parties.

Forty-seven states have enacted UETA. They have codified it within their own laws. The states that haven't enacted it have created their laws regarding electronic contracts instead.

Congress enacted the Electronic Signatures in Global and National Commerce (E-SIGN) Act in June 2000. The E-SIGN Act validates the use of electronic records and signatures in interstate commerce. Like UETA, it's designed to facilitate and promote e-commerce. It also doesn't affect fundamental contract law principles. The E-SIGN Act contains provisions that are very similar to the UETA.

Like UETA, E-SIGN is technology neutral. In fact, it forbids any state or federal statute from requiring that a specific technology be used for electronic transactions in interstate commerce.

E-SIGN specifically states that it doesn't preempt state laws based on UETA. It also doesn't preempt state laws that are similar to the UETA. State laws that are significantly different from UETA and E-SIGN are preempted by E-SIGN.

For the most part, online contracts haven't changed fundamental contract law principles. There still must be offer, acceptance, and consideration. The parties still must reach a meeting of the minds. The E-SIGN Act and UETA recognize that basic contracting principles apply to all contracts, even online ones.

Courts have acknowledged this in case law as well. The Second Circuit Court of Appeals has said, "[While] new commerce on the Internet has exposed courts to many new situations, it has not fundamentally changed the principles of contract."[10] Even though courts apply the same basic contracting principles to online contracts, they sometimes reach inconsistent results. This is particularly noticeable in early cases reviewing clickwrap contracts and current cases reviewing browsewrap contracts. How courts treat these types of cases is still evolving. They're discussed later in this chapter.

This section describes some of the ways in which online contracting is different from traditional contracting. It's important to remember that this area of law is continuing to develop.

Legal Capacity Online

The rules for contractual capacity don't change depending upon the medium. Unfortunately, in online contracting it can be very difficult for parties to determine whom they are doing business with. Courts don't enforce contracts against a person who lacks contractual capacity. Therefore, it's critical for organizations conducting business on the Internet to know who their customers are.

Businesses must be concerned about children in particular. There are laws that protect children while they're on the Internet. The Children's Online Privacy Protection Act (COPPA) requires Web sites to get parental consent before collecting personal information from children. A business would need to collect personal information in order to enter into a contract with a consumer. Therefore, COPPA can potentially apply to any business that does business on the Internet. The Federal Trade Commission (FTC) oversees COPPA. The FTC can bring enforcement actions and impose civil penalties for COPPA violations.

Studies also show that children are online more than ever before. In January 2010, a Kaiser Family Foundation study found that 64 percent of 8- to 18-year-olds use a computer for entertainment purposes each day. The same study also found that they spend almost an hour and a half a day on the computer. Seven out of 10 children in this group go online every day.[11]

Chapter 5 discusses a number of ways that Web site operators can identify children. If a business Web site can properly identify children, then it can make sure that it doesn't enter into potentially unenforceable contracts with them.

Another issue in online contracts is verifying the identity and authenticity of the contracting parties. This is a separate issue from contracting with parties that have legal capacity. Digital signatures can be used to verify the identity of contracting parties. They are discussed later in this chapter.

Form of Offer and Acceptance

A person can enter into online contracts in a number of ways. Special types of contracts, such as clickwrap contracts, are discussed in a different section of this chapter. This section discusses contracts formed through direct electronic communications. Direct electronic communications include e-mail, text messaging, and instant messaging.

In contract disputes, timing is everything. It's sometimes critical to know when a contract forms. This is usually because an offeror is arguing that he or she revoked their offer, while an offeree is arguing that he or she accepted the offer in timely fashion. A court must determine which came first: revocation or acceptance. Electronic communications can complicate the analysis of these timing issues.

General contract law principles state that when parties are communicating instantaneously, a contract forms when the offeror receives an offeree's acceptance. Communications are instantaneous when there's no break in communications between offer and acceptance. The parties are, for the most part, clear on the terms of the contract. There's no doubt about the status of the offer and acceptance. Oral communications are clearly instantaneous communications. Courts also have held that fax and telephone communications are instantaneous.

These same general contract law principles say that where there's a delay in communication, the parties must follow the mailbox rule to determine when an acceptance is valid. In these situations, unless otherwise specified in an offer, acceptance is valid once it's mailed. This is so that parties can be clear on the status of a contract when communications aren't instantaneous. Communications that take place through U.S. mail are delayed communications. These communications must follow the mailbox rule.

Both of these principles can be implicated in electronic communications. Electronic communications processes blur the line between sending and receiving communications. They can make it hard for the parties, and courts, to determine when offer and acceptance occurred.

E-mail Communications.   E-mail communications contain both nearly instantaneous and delayed communication elements. Depending upon the nature of the e-mail transmission, there may be a delay from when the message is sent to when it's received. There also may be a delay in the receiving party's actual receipt of the e-mail if the party doesn't read the e-mail at the moment when it's received.

A contracting party has the option of printing the e-mails and storing them. A chain of e-mail messages, assuming that they're not altered, can be used to demonstrate that the contracting parties achieved a meeting of the minds. Parties also can use the e-mail chain to help determine the material terms of an offer and an acceptance.

Questions about e-mail communications and timing arise if the status of the offer is called into question. Some commentators argue that the mailbox rule should apply to e-mail communications. That is, an acceptance is valid as soon as an offeree clicks on the "Send" button to e-mail their acceptance to the offeror. If an offeree receives the offeror's revocation after clicking on Send, it has no effect and the contract is formed.[12]

Other commentators argue that the mailbox rule should not apply to e-mail.[13] Since e-mail communications are nearly instantaneous, an offeror is free to revoke their offer any time before they receive the offeree's acceptance, regardless of when that acceptance is sent.

Text and Instant Messages. Sometimes electronic communications do look more like face-to-face communications. For example, text messaging and instant messaging (IM) communications are instantaneous. In this way, these communications are very much like oral conversations. Oral conversations are considered instantaneous. It can be argued that the common rules regarding instantaneous communications should apply here. That means that contracting parties can enter into enforceable contracts through text and instant messaging. The mailbox rule wouldn't apply.

Contracts made through text and instant messages suffer the same problems as oral contracts. Like oral contracts, the parties might agree to terms too quickly and then have second thoughts. The parties can easily repudiate such contracts, especially if there's no log of the conversation. It can be hard for parties to prove the existence of these contracts and their terms later when the contract is disputed. Unless a contracting party saves these messages or prints them out, it can be difficult for courts to determine the contractual terms.

Twitter and other Social Networking Sites. Consumer use of social networking sites is growing. A recent report showed that Twitter had 18.1 million unique visitors in December 2009. The same report showed Facebook had 206.9 million unique visitors in the same time.[14] Most social networking sites, including Facebook and Twitter, allow users to give periodic updates on what they're doing. The user's friends and followers can respond to the user's posts. These sites exist to facilitate online communication between parties.

> **NOTE**
> Keep in mind that the rules of evidence govern how parties use records as proof in a lawsuit. A discussion of the rules of evidence is outside of the scope of this chapter.

> **NOTE**
> By their very name, instant messages are instantaneous communications.

> **NOTE**
> Twitter limits updates to 140 characters. It calls these updates "tweets."

Since Facebook and Twitter both contain mechanisms for conversation exchange, it's entirely possible that parties can enter into a contract using these mechanisms. It will be interesting to see how courts review offer, acceptance, and mutual assent criteria using social network site postings. It might be easier to prove that a contract exists with Facebook, as Facebook pages can contain the contents of the parties' contract negotiations. It might be more difficult to prove the existence of a contract, and the contract's material terms, when it's made through a service such as Twitter.

Legal commentators continue to argue about whether the mailbox rule should apply to electronic transactions such as e-mail. Courts skirt around the issue of the exact moment that a contract forms in electronic transactions. They routinely recognize that electronic communications do create valid contracts. To do this, they review the conduct of the parties to determine if the communications and the parties' actions show an offer, acceptance, or meeting of the minds.

To ensure that online contracts are enforceable, the best course of action is for contracting parties to state when acceptance takes place. Language such as "a contract is formed when I confirm that I have received your reply" can be added to e-mail negotiations to make sure that parties understand when an enforceable contract is formed.

Existence and Enforcement

As with traditional contracts, parties to an online contract must perform their obligations to be discharged. If a party doesn't fulfill their contractual obligations, they're in breach of contract. The non-breaching party can sue them.

 NOTE

Sometimes the law comes down to common sense. Contracting parties should take steps to preserve the electronic communications that show a contract's material terms.

In the online environment, it can be difficult for a party to prove the existence of a contract. This is because there's often no hard copy of the contract in existence, such as a contract agreed to via text or instant message. It also can be difficult to prove the terms of the contract because they may have changed over time, such as through an e-mail conversation. In some ways, online communications and contracts present some of the same proof problems as oral contracts.

Contracting parties must keep a paper or electronic record of the transactions that they enter into. These records are necessary to prove the existence of a contract. They also prove its material terms and conditions. They show the date the parties entered into the contract. It's also important to save these records in case one party argues that the contract was improperly modified.

A party can save hard copies of contract terms by printing screen shots or e-mail confirmations. They also can save an electronic record of the transaction. Under the UETA, information stored in information processing systems is an electronic record. It's a valid way to memorialize a contract.

Online contracts are enforced the same way as traditional contracts. If a court hears a case about a contract dispute, it must be able to determine if there has been a valid offer, acceptance, and mutual agreement. It will review the actions of the parties in order to make this determination.

> **NOTE**
>
> The UETA specifically recognizes that agreements can be found through the actions of parties to a contract. This codifies the common law rule.

Authenticity and Non-Repudiation

There's generally no real difference between traditional contracts and online ones other than the method of entering into the contracts. The traditional legal principles and methods that courts use to resolve contract disputes can be applied to online contracts in most instances with few modifications.

One area in which there's a notable difference, however, between traditional contracts and online ones are the issues of authenticity and non-repudiation. Authenticity refers to the problem of attributing an electronic message to the person who allegedly sent it. Non-repudiation ensures that a party can't dispute the validity of their message. In the online environment, authenticity and non-repudiation can be assured with technology processes.

It's important to distinguish between repudiation and non-repudiation. Repudiation is a legal term. It refers to a party's ability to deny the existence of a contract. Non-repudiation is a technical term. It refers to a process that is used to make sure that a party can't repudiate.

Even though non-repudiation is a technical term, it can be demonstrated in non-technical ways. Assume that a traditional written contract is signed in front of witnesses. By signing the document in front of witnesses, the parties are taking steps to make sure that neither party can repudiate their signatures. The use of witnesses is a non-technical non-repudiation process.

> **NOTE**
>
> Digital signatures, digitized signatures, and electronic signatures are all different. A digital signature uses a cryptographic process to ensure authenticity and non-repudiation. A digitized signature is a digital version of a manual, handwritten signature. An electronic signature is any mark that a person uses with the intent to sign an electronic record.

Non-repudiation becomes an important issue in online contracts because cryptography can be used to make sure that parties can't repudiate the contracts that they enter into. Contracting parties can use digital signature technology, which uses a cryptographic process to create and verify electronic communications, to provide assurance of their identities. Digital signature technology also can be used to verify that the contract exists and that it's unmodified.

The law recognizes that the use of digital signature technology adds a new element to contract law analysis. Under the UETA, digital signature technology is considered a security procedure.[15] A security procedure is a procedure or process used to:

- Verify that an electronic signature belongs to a specific person
- Detect changes or errors in the information in an electronic record

The use of a security procedure strengthens reliance on an electronic communication. For information security purposes, use of a digital signature creates a presumption that the signature is valid. The party that wants to argue that the signature is invalid bears the burden of proving that it's invalid. This is different from the burden of proof for signature repudiation in traditional contracts.

In traditional contract law, the party that relies on a contract has the burden of proving that a handwritten signature is authentic. In the electronic realm, the party that wants out of a contract has the burden of proving that a digital signature is invalid. This shifting burden of proof illustrates one way in which traditional contract law principles must adjust for online contracts.

The American Bar Association recognizes that the use of digital signature technologies can have profound implications for contract law analysis. It has created digital signature guidelines to help lawyers understand the use of digital signatures. You can read about the guidelines at *http://www.abanet.org/scitech/ec/isc/dsg-tutorial.html.*

Special Types of Contracts in Cyberspace

People encounter special types of online contracts every day. When you download software over the Internet, you likely enter into a contract with the software developer regarding your use of that software. If you create a new online social networking profile, you enter into a contract with the social networking platform provider. It's fair to say that most people don't read the "terms of use" or "terms of service" documents before clicking on "I agree" in order to access an online product or service.

These types of contracts are called **contracts of adhesion**. An offeror drafts these types of contracts for its own benefit. The offeree has little opportunity to negotiate the terms of the contract. In order to use the underlying product or service, the offeree must accept all the terms of the contract. It's a "take it or leave it" contract. In this type of contract, the offeror has all of the bargaining power. The underlying question in these types of contracts is whether there's agreement between the parties over the contract terms. Do the parties truly have a meeting of the minds?

Contracts of adhesion sound bad, but they're sometimes necessary. This is especially true for e-commerce transactions. E-commerce could be substantially slowed if a merchant had to negotiate the terms of every sale with a consumer. Thus, they create form contracts for multiple uses. These forms expedite commerce.

 NOTE

In the law, boilerplate language is any standard language that a person or entity can reuse in multiple contracts with few edits.

Contracts of adhesion also are called "form" contracts or "boilerplate" contracts. This is because they're presented as standard forms. They contain standard terms that are used regardless of where the transaction takes place. These terms typically favor the offeror. For instance, they might have terms that limit a person's rights if the offeror breaches the contract. They also may require any lawsuits about the contract be filed in the offeror's home state.

Take a moment to look at the terms of service documents for common online services. You can read the Google Terms of Services document at *http://www.google.com/accounts/TOS*. The Facebook terms of service document, called "Statement of Rights and Responsibilities," is available at *http://www.facebook.com/#!/terms.php?ref=pf*.

In the online environment, end user license agreements are the most encountered contracts of adhesion. An **end user license agreement (EULA)** is a contract between the manufacturer or distributor of a piece of software or a service, and the end user of the application. It states how the software or service can be used.

EULAs are particularly important in the software context. This is because they help protect the software owner's copyright in their product. As discussed in Chapter 10, computer software can be protected by copyright laws. Software owners traditionally license their products rather than selling them. This helps them protect their copy and distribution rights. In many instances, it even gives them more control over their products than copyright law allows. The EULA specifies how consumers use software and places limitations on that use.

> **NOTE**
>
> A license is a grant of permission to use a product or service in certain situations. It's not a sale of the underlying software.

Depending on the nature of the underlying transaction, a EULA also might be called a "terms of use" or a "terms of service" agreement. A EULA is traditionally used for products like software that a user purchases or downloads. "Terms of service" is used for online services, such as search engine or social networking services. The phrase "terms of use" might be used for both products and services.

It doesn't matter what the document calls itself. It's important to understand that all of these documents try to create a contract between the software owner and the person who uses the software. This chapter uses the generic term EULA to refer to software licenses. The generic terms of service will be used to refer to contracts where the underlying transaction provides online services. There are a number of different forms of these generic contracts for software and online transactions. They include:

- Shrinkwrap contracts
- Clickwrap contracts
- Browsewrap contracts

Shrinkwrap Contracts

The term **shrinkwrap contract** almost exclusively refers to software license agreements. It specifically refers to software license agreements that are included within a box of physical-media software. This term doesn't refer to software that consumers purchase and download online.

▶ **NOTE**

Shrinkwrap licenses grew in popularity in the 1980s. Software developers used them to protect their exclusive rights granted under copyright law. They also used them to state their software warranties and to limit their liability for software failures. This helped them avoid some UCC warranty provisions.

These types of EULAs are called shrinkwrap contracts because software manufacturers put them in a software box, underneath the shrinkwrap cellophane and packaging. The consumer doesn't actually see the terms of the EULA until after they buy the software. They then become bound to the terms of the agreement when they break the shrinkwrap and open the packaging. The agreement usually creates a software license between the consumer and the software developer.

At first courts viewed these types of contracts with suspicion. They tended to interpret the terms of the contract against the software manufacturer. Courts didn't rule on whether these contracts were valid, instead, they looked at the terms in the contract. They would hold that some provisions of the contracts were unenforceable.

Today courts generally hold that shrinkwrap contracts are valid. There's an offer and acceptance, which is shown by the manufacturer offering the software for sale, and the purchaser buying and installing it. These contracts also are supported by consideration. The consideration is the exchange of a product for money, and a consumer's affirmative act of installing the software.

Courts tend to favor shrinkwrap contracts where the consumer receives the terms of the contract in multiple ways. A shrinkwrap contract is more likely to be enforceable when the agreement is printed on paper in the box and presented again to the consumer on the computer screen when the software is being installed. A shrinkwrap contract that allows a consumer to return the software without using it if they reject its terms also is more likely to be enforceable. Meeting of the minds is shown through the actions of the consumer with respect to either installing the software or returning it.

Clickwrap Contracts

▶ **NOTE**

A distinction between shrinkwrap and clickwrap contracts is that a user has an opportunity to read a clickwrap contract before purchasing a product or using a service. A user also must affirmatively agree to the contract before getting access to a product or service.

A **clickwrap contract** is a variation of the shrinkwrap contract. A clickwrap contract is usually presented to a user when they are purchasing software via the Internet. These agreements aren't used just for software purchases. Vendors use them for any type of product or service purchase that's conducted over the Internet or online.

These types of contracts usually appear on a user's computer screen before installation of a product or use of a service. They may be displayed in a separate pop-up dialogue box or on the main browser screen. A user has to click on an "I agree" or "I accept" button located on the same screen as the contract (or in the same pop-up window) before downloading and installing a product or using a service.

Enforceability of Shrinkwrap Contracts: *ProCD Inc. v. Zeidenberg*

The most famous case about shrinkwrap contracts is *ProCD Inc. v. Zeidenberg* (1996). This was the first time that a federal court of appeal looked at a shrinkwrap case. The Seventh Circuit Court of Appeals decided this case. The Seventh Circuit covers Illinois, Indiana, and Wisconsin.

ProCD sold a software product that was a searchable telephone directory database. It distributed its program and database on CD-ROM. ProCD spent more than $10 million to develop its product and to keep the database of telephone directory information current.

ProCD had both commercial use and non-commercial use versions of the product. The commercial use product was more expensive. The non-commercial use, or consumer, product was cheaper. Businesses that bought the commercial version could use it to create mailing lists of potential customers and for other marketing purposes. ProCD didn't allow this in the consumer version of the product.

ProCD had to keep businesses from buying the consumer product and using it for commercial purposes. It didn't do this through technological solutions. Instead, ProCD turned to contract law. People who bought the consumer version of the software were prohibited from using it for commercial purposes because of the license agreement that was included with the product.

The defendant, Matthew Zeidenberg, purchased the consumer version of the product. He then formed his own company and reposted the information on the Internet. He offered the information for sale at a price that was lower than ProCD's price for either its consumer or commercial product.

ProCD sued Zeidenberg. It argued that Zeidenberg breached the terms of the license agreement that was included in the ProCD software box. Zeidenberg argued that only the text written on the outside of the package containing the ProCD product was part of his contract with ProCD. He claimed that the license agreement that was inside the box was additional contract terms. He argued that they weren't enforceable under various provisions of the Uniform Commercial Code.

The district court agreed with Zeidenberg. ProCD appealed the decision of the district court to the Seventh Circuit Court of Appeals.

The Seventh Circuit held that the license agreement inside the box was an enforceable contract. In reviewing the case, the court noted that ProCD offered a full refund to a purchaser who didn't agree with the terms of the shrinkwrap contract and returned the product without using it.

One fact that also helped the court reach the decision that the shrinkwrap contract was enforceable was that Zeidenberg had multiple opportunities to read it before he installed the software. It was printed on paper inside the box, and it was displayed on the computer screen during the software installation process. Zeidenberg could not install the software without specifically clicking on an acceptance box that contained the terms of the contract. The court found that all these opportunities to read the contract put Zeidenberg on notice of it. Through his actions, he showed that he agreed with those terms. This included the term forbidding commercial use of the product.

The court's reasoning in *ProCD v. Zeidenberg* is used as the basis for validating other types of end user license agreements such as clickwrap agreements.

You can read the court's opinion *ProCD v. Zeidenberg* case at *http://caselaw.lp.findlaw.com/cgi-bin/getcase.pl?court=7th&navby=docket&no=961139*.

Courts have generally held that clickwrap contracts are enforceable. These cases are highly dependent on how the clickwrap contract is presented to the consumer. In many cases, these types of contracts are enforceable if the agreement is prominently displayed. A consumer also must affirmatively agree to the contract before receiving a product or service. Clicking on the "I agree" or "I accept" buttons is evidence of the consumer's agreement.

Browsewrap Contracts

 NOTE

A browsewrap contract is similar to a clickwrap agreement without the "click" requirement.

Browsewrap contracts describe the situation where terms of use or service documents are listed on a Web page. In these situations, a user doesn't have to make an affirmative action to accept the terms of the contract, such as clicking on a button. A browsewrap agreement assumes that a contract is entered into when a user merely visits a Web page or downloads a product.

Terms of use and terms of service documents are browsewrap contracts when they don't require a user to affirmatively agree to the terms contained in the document. They are clickwrap contracts if a user must click on a button to show their agreement with the terms.

Many popular Web pages use browsewrap contracts to display their terms of use or service provisions. For example, the CNN Web page at *www.cnn.com* has a "terms of service" link listed in small type at the bottom of their home page. Users navigate to CNN's Service Agreement when they click on that link. That agreement sets forth the terms and conditions for use of the CNN Web page. The agreement states that users who don't agree to the terms of service shouldn't access or use *CNN.com*.

Courts often are slow to find that browsewrap contracts are enforceable. One reason for this is that consumers may not know about these contracts. Terms of use or service links on Web pages are typically in very small type and located at the bottom of Web pages. Consumers aren't conditioned to look for these agreements or read them. If consumers don't know about the contract and haven't read it, how can they agree to its terms?

Courts review the facts of browsewrap cases very closely. For instance, in *Specht v. Netscape Communications Corporation* (2002), the Second Circuit Court of Appeals didn't enforce a browsewrap contract. In this case, the consumer downloaded software.

NOTE

Web sites that use browsewrap agreements will want to make sure that the embedded links to those agreements are noticeable to a consumer.

The consumer didn't have to click on any buttons to show agreement with a license prior to downloading the software. The consumer had to click on several embedded links to read the terms of the agreement. They weren't eye-catching links. The Web site didn't display the license agreement in a separate window and it didn't "pop up" at the consumer. The court held there wasn't enough notice to the consumer about the terms of the contract. It held that the contract wasn't enforceable against the consumer.

It's possible that courts will start enforcing browsewrap contracts as e-commerce and Internet use continues to grow. This is particularly true if Web pages do more to make a user aware of the browsewrap contract. For instance, a court might be more inclined to enforce a browsewrap agreement when its terms are specifically referenced during the course of a transaction.

A Missouri court recently upheld a browsewrap agreement when a user had to click on a "Submit" button that had the following language written next to it: "By submitting you agree to the Terms of Use."[16] The text included a link to the terms of use language. The court held that the user was on notice that the terms of use governed the transaction. It also found that the user had the opportunity to read those terms.

How Do These Contracts Regulate Behavior?

End user license agreements, terms of use, and terms of service agreements attempt to regulate user behavior. They state how a consumer can and can't use certain products or services. They tend to severely limit a consumer's rights and give the owner or vendor of the product or service many rights. If a consumer fails to follow the terms of these agreements, an owner can try to sue for breach of contract. If a consumer follows the terms of these contracts, then they are regulating their behavior in a manner that's most likely advantageous to the owner or vendor of the product or service.

Consumers need to take the time to read these types of agreements. They're not all created equal. It would be a mistake to think that these agreements simply govern the intellectual property rights of the owners of a product or service. While many EULAs and terms of service do this, some also have unexpected terms. Some of these terms include language that would allow the vendor to install additional software onto a consumer's computer system. The additional software could be used to learn the consumer's Internet habits in order to supply targeted advertisements. These types of contracts also can have terms about additional licensing fees or deeply buried upgrade, support, or maintenance fees.

Consumers should look for some of the following terms when reading EULAs or terms of service contracts:

- **Use**—Does the contract give the vendor the right to change the service or product whenever it wants? Does the vendor have the unilateral right to stop providing certain important features? Does the vendor have the right to investigate how the user uses the product or service to determine if there has been a violation of the contract?

- **Fees**—Does the contract have any hidden licensing fees or any hidden upgrade, support, or maintenance fees?

- **Representations and warranties**—Does acceptance of the contract mean that the consumer bears all economic risk related to downloading and using the product or service? What's the consumer's recourse if the product or service includes viruses and errors, or causes data loss or hardware/software failure? Does the contract state that use of the product or service is at the consumer's own risk? Does it state that the products are provided "as is?"

 NOTE

A consumer should exercise caution if a contract says that products or services are provided "as is" or use is at the consumers' "own risk." This means that the seller is disclaiming a number of different consumer protection warranties.

- **Advertising**—Does the contract give the vendor the right to include embedded software or spyware with the desired product or service? Does acceptance of the contract mean that the consumer consents to receiving advertising content, from either the vendor or other third parties? Is the vendor allowed to collect usage data and other statistics related to the consumer's use of the service? How is this data used?

- **Criticism**—Does the contract specifically prohibit the consumer from publicly criticizing the product or service?

- **Updates**—Does the contract state that updates are covered by the original contract? Are updates covered by a new contract that the consumer must specifically agree to?

- **Termination and breach**—Does the contract allow a consumer to stop using the product or service at any time? Can the consumer stop using the product by uninstalling and destroying software and documentation? Must the vendor destroy any consumer personal data it has collected when the contract ends?

- **Boilerplate terms**—Does the contract state that it's subject to change without notice? Does it state that the consumer specifically consents to any modifications of the contract without notice? Does it include dispute resolution terms? Does it contain jurisdiction language? Does it require that consumers file lawsuits in a certain state and county within that state?

NOTE

Terms in a contract that state that consumers must file lawsuits in a certain state or county in that state are called forum selection clauses. Contracting parties use forum selection clauses to control questions about jurisdiction. They also use them so that they can litigate lawsuits in front of a familiar court. It's the legal equivalent of "home court advantage."

Consumers must think about what they're willing to agree to in order to use a particular product or online service. They must balance their need for the use of a product or service with other contract terms that might place the consumer, or their data, at a disadvantage.

Emerging Contract Law Issues

New developments in Internet-based products and services are causing people and organizations to think more about information security. A recurring theme throughout this book is the steps that people and entities must take to protect and secure information at the same time as information is being shared more than ever before. Entities use contracts to make sure that their own data, and the personal information of their customers, is protected when it's shared.

NOTE

Third-party agreements under HIPAA are called business associate's agreements. They are discussed in Chapter 6.

Sometimes the law requires a contract. For example, both the Gramm-Leach-Bliley Act (GLBA) and the Health Insurance Portability and Accountability Act (HIPAA) require covered businesses to enter into contracts with their third-party service providers to protect data. These contracts hold the third parties accountable for the minimum levels of data privacy and information security protection that those laws require for certain types of information.

FIGURE 11-1

Basic cloud
computing diagram.

Entities also enter into these contracts voluntarily when they use new services or
buy new products. The importance of including data security terms in these contracts
continues to grow. The newest development in Internet-based products and services
that highlights information security issues is cloud computing.

Cloud Computing

The definition and limits of cloud computing are still evolving. **Cloud computing** is a type
of computing where both applications and infrastructure capabilities can be provided to
end users through the Internet. Through cloud computing, entities no longer have to own
their own computer hardware and infrastructure. They can purchase these services from
cloud service providers. They only pay for the infrastructure and applications that they
need. Figure 11-1 is a basic cloud computing diagram.

Cloud computing is not just for businesses. Individuals also use
cloud computing services. Yahoo! Mail is a cloud service. Google's
Picasa photo-sharing service is a cloud service. So is Mozy's online
computer backup service.

Cloud computing has its beginnings in the **Software as a Service
(SaaS)** model. In the SaaS model, a vendor hosts a Web-based
application and provides that application to its customers. The
customers purchase access to hosted application. The entities
access these services over the Internet. The SaaS vendor hosts
the applications and maintains the infrastructure necessary
for running the application.

> **NOTE**
>
> SaaS refers to the purchase
> of application services
> over the Internet. Cloud
> computing refers to the
> purchase of both application
> and infrastructure capabilities
> through the Internet.

> **NOTE**
>
> Gartner, Inc., is a respected company that provides internet technology advice and research. You can learn more about Gartner, Inc., at *http://www.gartner.com/technology/about.jsp.*

> **NOTE**
>
> In 2007, Dell, Inc. tried to trademark the term "cloud computing." The U.S. Patent and Trademark Office rejected the trademark because it was too generic and described services offered by many companies.

Cloud computing consumers can purchase infrastructure services such as data storage, backup facilities, and data processing. Cloud computing also includes the purchase of applications traditionally provided under the SaaS model such as e-mail services. Cloud computing is attractive to many entities. Gartner, Inc., estimates that companies spent $10 billion on cloud computing in 2009.

Many organizations believe that using cloud computing will help them save money on information technology (IT) costs. Cost savings include not spending money upfront on data centers, electricity, equipment, and physical security. It also might help save money on IT staff. Cloud computing is seen as scalable with the organization's own growth. An organization purchases only the services it needs at a fixed point in time. It can always buy more cloud services when it needs them. Buying cloud services can be faster than building the organization's own IT infrastructure.

Cloud computing leads to situations where an entity's data isn't stored on its own physical computing infrastructure. This makes information security practitioners (and lawyers) nervous. An *Information Week* survey in late 2009 showed that information security topped a list of business technology professionals' concerns about cloud computing.[17] Information security concerns about cloud computing include:

- Loss of control of data, leading to a loss of security or lessened security
- Loss of privacy of data, potentially due to aggregation with data from other cloud consumers
- Dependency on a third party for critical infrastructure and data-handling processes
- Potential security and technological defects in the cloud provider's infrastructure
- No control over the third parties that a cloud vendor might contract with
- Loss of an entity's own competence in managing IT infrastructure security

There also are legal concerns about cloud computing. Contract law governs a cloud computing relationship. Disputes over the terms of the contract could be costly to resolve. They also could take too long to resolve. A lengthy dispute about critical services could harm a business and affect its ability to operate.

FYI

A U.S. Department of Justice bulletin issued in 2009 showed that state-court contract law cases took almost two years to resolve. This statistic was for 2005, the last year for which data is available at the time of writing this book. You can read the report at *http://bjs.ojp.usdoj.gov/content/pub/pdf/cbajtsc05.pdf.*

Another legal concern about cloud computing is where data and infrastructure are located. Local law might control how entities handle data. Questions of who owns the data also could be influenced by the law of the state where data is located, assuming that the data is actually stored in the United States. Location of the data could have impact on how that data is provided in response to a public records request, subpoena, or court order. There also could be different rules for how that data must be secured. It also could affect how companies should respond to a breach of the systems used to store their data.

Information Security Terms in Contracts

Entities entering into contracts for cloud computing services need to consider a number of items from a law and information security standpoint. A cloud computing consumer will want to make sure that a cloud computing provider physically protects the cloud computing infrastructure that holds the consumer's data. A cloud computing consumer also will want to make sure that the cloud computing provider follows good information security practices and protects the security of any data on that infrastructure.

 NOTE

Since the cloud computing relationships include data, this is one time where an entity will want to make sure that it has a formal written contract with its vendors.

There are a number of information security issues to consider in any cloud computing contract. These same themes also can be considered in any contract where an entity's data might be stored, processed, transmitted, or handled by another party. It's important for both contracting parties to understand the scope of data that they must protect in a contract. The parties must think about the following:

- How data is defined
- How data is used
- How data is protected
- How the parties meet their legal and regulatory requirements

Data Definition and Use

Both parties to a contract must understand the type of data that they might transfer back and forth because of their relationship. A contract must have clear terms that define the data owned by each party. The parties also must clearly define data that must be protected.

 NOTE

A contract should define the data elements used by the parties. For instance, if personal information is transmitted between the parties, then the contract should specify what data elements are considered personal information. This definition could change depending upon the type of data transmitted between the parties.

It's also important for the parties to clearly specify in the contract how they can use any data that they share. An entity will want to make sure that its vendor, or cloud computing provider, doesn't use its data in a way that would violate its privacy policies. An entity also will want to make sure that there are limits on the vendors own use of the data. For instance, a vendor shouldn't be able to share the entity's data with other third parties without their permission. Finally, the contract should specify what happens to the data when the contract ends.

Data use terms also should specify what the parties can't do with certain types of data. For example, if credit card information is transmitted as part of a cloud computing contract, that contract should require the vendor to comply with the Payment Card Industry Data Security Standards.

General Data Protection Terms

NOTE

A minimum level of acceptable information security is called a baseline.

An entity may want to specify particular data protection terms in a contract. These terms are more specific than data use terms. For instance, an entity may want to include terms that state the specific administrative, technical, and physical safeguards that a vendor must use. When an entity includes these types of terms, they are trying to guarantee a minimum level of confidentiality, integrity, and availability.

An entity could include the following contract terms to ensure a minimum level of information security protection:

* Data transmission and encryption requirements
* Authentication and authorization mechanisms
* Intrusion detection and prevention mechanisms
* Logging and log review requirements
* Security scan and audit requirements
* Security training and awareness requirements

Contracting parties can use resources developed by the National Institute of Standards and Technology (NIST) to make sure that a contract includes the appropriate controls. The International Organization for Standardization (ISO) and the International Electrotechnical Commission (IEC) also have prepared information security controls guidance. The NIST and ISO/IEC guides are discussed in Chapter 1.

Compliance with Legal and Regulatory Requirements

NOTE

Contracts also have to include terms that help entities meet their breach notification duties in the event that a vendor's systems are compromised and the entity's data is disclosed. Breach notification laws are discussed in Chapter 9.

Sometimes laws or regulatory controls will influence the relationship covered by a contract. This happens when the data or processes used between the parties falls within the scope of a particular law. GLBA and HIPAA were already mentioned as two federal laws that pull certain types of data and relationships into their scope.

State laws also could be implicated. For example, Massachusetts and Nevada have laws that require the personal information of state residents to be encrypted in certain instances. This requirement would need to be specified in a contract in order to ensure that a vendor meets it.

Additional terms that a contract should have to address regulatory requirements include:

- GLBA language if financial data is used or transmitted between the parties
- HIPAA language if health information is used or transmitted between the parties
- Family Educational Rights and Privacy Act (FERPA) of 1974 language if student information is used or transmitted between the parties
- Language protecting the intellectual property rights of each party

An entity also will want to make sure that a contract contains terms that require the vendor to cooperate with security incident investigations. This is so the entity can meet its regulatory requirements. A contract also must have terms that require each party to assist the other with third party litigation that occurs because of the contractual relationship. For example, a contract should state that the vendor will assist the entity with any litigation against the entity that arises because of a breach of the security of the vendor's systems.

As new technologies emerge and are developed, the rules for using that technology will become very important. One way that entities can establish rules is through contractual agreements.

Case Studies and Examples

The following case studies and examples show how the concepts discussed in this chapter are used. These case studies are real-world examples of contract law issues.

Contract Formation via E-mail

Parties continue to argue about the enforceability of electronic contracts. California adopted its version of the Uniform Electronic Transactions Act in 1999. This case began before California enacted its UETA law. Would the case have even reached a U.S. Court of Appeals if California's UETA law had been in existence when this transaction began?

Stewart Lamle invented a board game called Farook. He obtained two U.S. patents for his game. In May 1996, Lamle began negotiating with toy-giant Mattel to license his game. They signed a preliminary agreement for $25,000. Under this agreement, Lamle agreed not to license the game to anyone else until after June 15, 1997.

On June 11, 1997, the parties met and discussed the terms of a licensing agreement. They agreed to terms regarding the length of the license agreement. They also agreed to geographic scope of the agreement, the percentage of royalties, and a schedule for payment of royalties. Mattel asked Lamle to draft a formal contract. It promised it would sign an agreement before January 1, 1998.

On June 26, 1997, a Mattel employee sent Lamle an e-mail with the subject line "Farook Deal." The e-mail repeated the terms agreed to at the earlier meeting. It also stated specifically that Mattel agreed in principle to the agreement and was waiting for the contract. The e-mail concluded with a closing salutation and the employee's full name. Lamle faxed a draft licensing agreement to Mattel on August 19, 1997.

FYI

States have statute of limitations rules. This means that people must bring a lawsuit for injuries that they have incurred within a certain period of time. In California, lawsuits for breach of oral contracts must be filed within two years of the date of the breach. The statute of limitations for written contracts is four years. Lamle sued Mattel exactly two years from the date that Mattel notified him that it wasn't interested in Farook. Why did Lamle sue at the two-year mark?

In August, Mattel displayed Farook at its Pre-Toy Fair. The purpose of the fair was to gauge potential interest in new toys. After the fair, Mattel decided that it wasn't interested in Farook. It notified Lamle in October.

Lamle sued for breach of contract in October 1999. He also made claims of patent infringement and intentional interference with economic relations.

The District Court for the Central District of California granted summary judgment in favor of Mattel. Summary judgment means that a court has decided that there's not a factual dispute between the parties. Lamle appealed the grant of summary judgment. The Federal Circuit Court of Appeals upheld his appeal and sent the case back to District Court.

NOTE

One of the most interesting things about this case is that Lamle represented himself *pro se*. *Pro se* means that a person isn't represented by a lawyer. Lamle represented himself throughout the whole case *pro se*. Lamle isn't a lawyer.

The District Court again granted summary judgment for Mattel. The District Court rejected Lamle's breach of contract claim. It held that no reasonable juror would believe that there was a contract between the parties. It also held that even if there was a contract, it wasn't enforceable because it wasn't in writing as required by California's Statute of Frauds. Lamle appealed again.

The Federal Circuit Court of Appeals reviewed the conduct of the parties. It held that there was a genuine question whether the parties had reached mutual agreement on contractual terms at the June 11 meeting. It held that a trial was needed and evidence should be presented on the issue of mutual assent.

The court also discussed California's Statute of Frauds. It reviewed the June 26 e-mail from the Mattel employee. It held that the name of the Mattel employee at the end of the e-mail was enough to overcome the signed writing requirements of the Statute of Frauds. It said that its ruling was consistent with other California laws that state that a typewritten name is considered a signature.

The Court also noted that if the e-mail from the Mattel employee had been sent after January 1, 2000, there would be no question at all whether the e-mail constituted a signed writing for Statute of Frauds purposes. California's version of the UETA went into effect at that time.

The Federal Circuit Court of Appeals ruling gave Lamle the right to have a jury trial on his breach of contract claim. Lamle and Mattel eventually settled their claims against one another.

You can read the Court's opinion at *http://scholar.google.com/scholar_case?case =5607112815760928119.*

Contract Dispute Statistics

The U.S. Department of Justice (DOJ) compiles statistics on court cases in state courts. One of its series is "Civil Trial Cases and Verdicts in Large Counties." This series gives statistics on cases in a national sample of urban and rural jurisdictions. The DOJ began collecting and reviewing this data in 1992.

In 2009, the DOJ issued a special study on contract cases heard in state courts.[18] The study looked at only state-court contract cases. It didn't look at contract cases tried in federal court.

> **NOTE**
>
> All of the studies in the "Civil Trial Cases and Verdicts in Large Counties" series can be read at *http:// bjs.ojp.usdoj.gov/index. cfm?ty=pbse&sid=15.*

The study found that two-out-of-three plaintiffs won their contract trials. Plaintiffs were more likely to win cases that were decided by a judge instead of a jury. The study found that juries award higher damages than judges do.

Take some time to review the Contract Bench and Jury Trials in State Courts (2005) report. What statistics surprised you?

CHAPTER SUMMARY

Contracts are used to form relationships between parties for the sale of goods and services. A mixture of common law and statutory law covers contracts. Contracts for the sale of services are usually covered by common law. Code law usually covers contracts for the sale of goods.

Electronic and online communications have created more efficient ways to enter into contracts. The traditional rules of contract law apply to contracts that are entered into online. Laws such as the Uniform Electronic Transactions Act help make sure that online contracts are enforceable in the same manner as traditional contracts.

KEY CONCEPTS AND TERMS

Browsewrap contract

Clickwrap contract

Cloud computing

Compensatory damages

Complete performance

Consequential damages

Consideration

Contract

Contracts of adhesion

Contractual capacity

Duty to mitigate

End user license agreement
(EULA)

Incomplete performance

Liquidated damages

Mailbox rule

Mirror image rule

Nominal damages

Offer

Offeree

Offeror

Remedy

Repudiation

Shrinkwrap contract

Software as a Service (SaaS)

Specific performance

Statute of Frauds

Substantial performance

CHAPTER 11 ASSESSMENT

1. Which common law rule requires an offer and acceptance to have substantially the same terms?

   A. The Statute of Frauds

   B. The mailbox rule

   C. The mirror image rule

   D. The silence rule

   E. The assurance rule

2. What is a clickwrap contract?

3. What types of damages usually aren't awarded in a contracts case?

   A. Nominal damages

   B. Punitive damages

   C. Consequential damages

   D. Compensatory damages

   E. Liquidated damages

4. The law assumes that almost all people have contractual capacity.

   A. True

   B. False

5. Instantaneous communications must follow the mailbox rule.

   A. True

   B. False

6. How do courts determine if parties really did enter into a contract?

   A. They look for contractual capacity.

   B. The look for contract legality.

   C. They review the Statute on Frauds

   D. They look for a meeting of the minds.

   E. None of the above

7. A remedy is _____.

8. Which type of online agreement are courts reluctant to enforce?

   A. Clickwrap contracts

   B. Shrinkwrap contracts

   C. Browsewrap contracts

   D. A and B only

   E. None of the above

9. What was the precursor to cloud computing?

   A. SaaS

   B. EULA

   C. SO/IEC

   D. NIST

   E. None of the above

10. What information security concerns surround cloud computing?

11. Which type of damages do the parties specifically agree to in a contract?

　A. Nominal damages
　B. Punitive damages
　C. Consequential damages
　D. Compensatory damages
　E. Liquidated damages

12. A contract to commit murder is enforceable.

　A. True
　B. False

13. What electronic signature law governs interstate commerce?

　A. UETA
　B. E-SIGN
　C. UATE
　D. COPPA
　E. GLBA

14. UETA states that electronic contracts are _____.

15. Which communications are instantaneous?

　A. Oral communications
　B. Text messages
　C. Instant messages
　D. All of the above
　E. None of the above

ENDNOTES

1. White, James J., and Robert S. Summers. *Uniform Commercial Code.* 5th ed. St. Paul, MN: West Group, 2000, page 7.

2. American Law Institute and the National Conference of Commissioners on Uniform State Laws, Uniform Commercial Code, sec. 2-201 (2004), available at *http://www.law.cornell.edu/ucc/* (accessed March 26, 2010).

3. American Law Institute, *Restatement (Second) of Contracts,* sec. 24 (1981).

4. Ibid., sec. 39.

5. Uniform Commercial Code, sec. 2-207.

6. *Restatement (Second) of Contracts,* sec. 64.

7. Electronic Signatures in Global and National Commerce Act (2000), U.S. Code Vol. 15, sec 7001 et seq (2006).

8. National Conference of Commissioners on Uniform State Laws, Uniform Electronic Transactions Act (UETA) (1999), available at *http://www.law.upenn.edu/bll/archives/ulc/fnact99/1990s/ueta99.htm* (accessed March 26, 2010).

9. Ibid., UETA sec. 2.

10. *Register.com, Inc. v. Verio, Inc.,* 356 F.3d 393, 403 (2d Cir. 2004).

11. The Henry J. Kaiser Family Foundation, "Generation M2: Media in the Lives of 8- to 18-Year-Olds," January 2010, *http://www.kff.org/entmedia/upload/8010.pdf* (accessed March 26, 2010).

12. Watnick, Valerie. "The Electronic Formation of Contracts and the Common Law 'Mailbox Rule.'" *Baylor Law Review* 56 (2004): 175.

13. Kidd, Donnie L., and William H. Daughtrey, Jr. "Adapting Contract Law to Accommodate Electronic Contracts: Overview and Suggestions." *Rutgers Computer and Technology Law Journal* 26 (2000): 215.

14. Nielsen Wire, "Led by Facebook, Twitter, Global Time Spent on Social Media Sites up 82% Year over Year," January 22, 2010, *http://blog.nielsen.com/nielsenwire/global/led-by-facebook-twitter-global-time-spent-on-social-media-sites-up-82-year-over-year/* (accessed March 26, 2010).

15. UETA, sec. 2.

16. Missouri Court of Appeals, "Opinion: *Major v. McCallister,*" No. CD29871, December 23, 2009, *http://www.courts.mo.gov/file.jsp?id=36294* (accessed March 26, 2010).

17. Korzeniowski, Paul, and Mary Jander. "Cloud Security." *InformationWeek,* November 9, 2009.

18. U.S. Department of Justice, Bureau of Justice Statistics, "Contract Bench and Jury Trials in State Courts, 2005," September 2009, *http://bjs.ojp.usdoj.gov/content/pub/pdf/cbajtsc05.pdf* (accessed March 26, 2010).

Criminal Law and
Tort Law Issues in Cyberspace

C RIMINAL LAW REFERS TO LAWS that the federal and state governments
have created to define unacceptable behavior. People who violate
acceptable levels of behavior commit crimes. Criminal law deals with crimes.
Tort law refers to wrongful acts or harm for which an individual can sue the
person who caused the harm. Tort law governs disputes between individuals.

This chapter focuses on criminal and tort law issues that are unique
to cyberspace. In particular, it focuses on how people can use computers
in cybercrime activities. It also reviews how people use computers to commit
torts. Sometimes both criminal and tort law actions can be carried out against
the same individual for the same actions.

Chapter 12 Topics

This chapter covers the following topics and concepts:

- What general criminal law concepts are
- What common criminal law issues in cyberspace are
- What general tort law concepts are
- What common tort law issues in cyberspace are
- What some case studies and examples are

Chapter 12 Goals

When you complete this chapter, you will be able to:

- Discuss common criminal law concepts
- Describe the common criminal laws used to prosecute cybercrimes
- Discuss common tort law concepts
- Describe common tort principles used in cyberspace
- Explain the difference between criminal and tort law

General Criminal Law Concepts

Cybercrimes, sometimes called computer crimes, involve situations where people use the Internet or computers as the medium for, or target of, criminal activity. Some crimes, such as computer trespass, are an extension of existing criminal laws. Computer networks facilitate these crimes. Other laws define new crimes that didn't exist before computers. The use of computers as a medium to commit crimes is growing. Criminals also target computers and the data that they contain. Consider the following:

- A federal judge sentences a computer hacker to almost five years in prison for violating the Computer Fraud and Abuse Act. He created botnets and sold access to them. Other attackers used the botnets to launch distributed denial of service (DDoS) attacks.

- A federal judge sentences a defendant to 2.5 years in prison for taking nude videos of a news reporter and posting them to the Internet. The judge also ordered the defendant to pay restitution to the victim.

- The federal government charges three members of a hacking group with hijacking the Web site of a telecommunications company. The company's users couldn't access the Web site for about 90 minutes.

- A man is charged with cyber-extortion. He attempted to extort a life insurance company by threatening to send millions of computer spam messages. He wanted to damage the reputation of the company.

Crimes are harms or wrongdoings against society. They're deviations from behavior that society, through its government, has defined as unacceptable. Some crimes don't even need individual victims. Society is the "victim" of the crime.

In simple terms, a crime is a violation of society's code of conduct. Crime and the concept of criminal law are very old. The Sumerian and Babylonian civilizations included codes of conduct in their laws in 2100 B.C.E. While these codes didn't resemble modern criminal law, they did define conduct that society decided wasn't acceptable.

The American legal system is based in large part on English common law. Chapter 3 discusses the history of the American legal system. The U.S. Constitution is the main source of law for the United States.

The Constitution presumes that U.S. citizens will behave in a lawful manner. However, it includes provisions for how the government should handle crimes in Article III. The Constitution even defines a crime. Article III, section 3, states that treason against the United States is a crime.

The U.S. Congress has passed laws regarding federal crimes since the formation of the government. Most states also have passed laws that have defined criminal offenses. Since crimes are wrongs against society, the government pursues the alleged wrongdoers. The federal government prosecutes violations of federal law. State governments prosecute violations of state laws.

> **NOTE**
>
> Federal cases are titled "United States" versus the name of the defendant. This is because the government of the United States is prosecuting the defendant for a crime. State cases are titled in the name of the state versus the name of the defendant.

Main Principles of Criminal Law

Criminal law is very different from civil law. Each system has different goals. Criminal law aims to deter wrongful behavior. It does this through a combination of punishment and rehabilitation of the offender. In contrast, civil law aims to right personal wrongs. It does this by allowing people to sue to recover monetary compensation for injuries.

> **▶ NOTE**
>
> Attorneys often specialize in different subject matter areas. This is because of legal ethics rules that require an attorney to be minimally competent. There are many areas of law. It's easier for attorneys to meet ethical competency rules by focusing their practices in certain areas.

This section focuses on substantive criminal law. Substantive law describes a person's rights and responsibilities. It defines how people should relate to one another and how they should relate to the government. Substantive law also is known as subject matter law. Criminal law is only one of many categories of substantive law. Contract law, business law, property law, and tort law are all different types of substantive law.

Substantive criminal law defines the conduct that constitutes a crime. It also establishes penalties. Governments can specify criminal penalties in the same statute that defines a crime. They also can list them in a separate penalty statute.

Type of Wrongful Conduct

Society recognizes two basic types of wrongful conduct. The first type is conduct or acts that society universally agrees are wrong, morally repugnant, or dangerous to other people. For example, almost all societies agree that murder and rape are wrong. *Mala in se* is a Latin term that defines these types of wrongful conduct. *Mala in se* means "evil in itself." It describes conduct that's inherently wrong. Crimes that are *mala in se* include murder, rape, kidnapping, robbery, theft, and arson.

Other types of conduct are *mala prohibita*. **Mala prohibita** is Latin for "wrong because it is prohibited." Society defines conduct that is *mala prohibita*. This conduct isn't inherently evil, but society prohibits it. Crimes that are *mala prohibita* include intellectual property violations (where prohibited by law, such as federal copyright offenses), traffic law violations, and tax evasion. Many types of cybercrimes are *mala prohibita*.

Crimes generally are classified into two groups, misdemeanors and felonies. The two types of crimes are usually distinguishable by the way society punishes them. **Misdemeanors** are less serious than felonies. They bear a less-severe penalty. A misdemeanor is generally punishable by no more than one year in prison.

Felonies are crimes that are more serious. They're usually punishable by more than a year in prison. The levels of felonies and misdemeanors may vary from state to state. Some states have different levels of misdemeanors and felonies. Language like "first degree" or "second degree" differentiates between different levels of crime. A state can prosecute some types of crimes as either a misdemeanor or a felony.

Elements of a Crime

Criminal law is based on the principle that a guilty mind must accompany a criminal act. Another principle is that criminal conduct harms society. In short, the American system of law holds people responsible for their actions. A government must prove the following elements to show that a crime has been committed:

- *Mens rea*
- *Actus reus*
- Causation

To prove that a crime has been committed, a government must show that a person acted with criminal intent. It must show that a person knowingly, intentionally, or recklessly engaged in criminal conduct. The Latin term **mens rea** means "guilty mind." *Mens rea* describes a person's intent to commit a crime. Someone who lacks *mens rea* can't be held responsible for a crime.

Most criminal laws have language that specifies the amount of *mens rea* that a person must have in order to be held responsible for a crime. For example, the Wisconsin first-degree murder statute states: "Whoever causes the death of another human being with intent to kill that person or another is guilty of a Class A felony."[1] The "intent to kill" portion of the statute describes the *mens rea* required to commit a crime.

Acts that are purely accidental don't meet the required mental showing for criminal prosecution. However, that doesn't mean that the government prosecutes only intentional actions. The government also can prosecute a person who acts recklessly for criminal behavior.

A showing of recklessness means that a person acted in a manner that consciously disregarded whether or not harm could result from the actions. For example, the Wisconsin first-degree reckless homicide statute states: "Whoever recklessly causes the death of another human being under circumstances which show utter disregard for human life is guilty of a Class B felony."[2] The "which show utter disregard for human life" portion of the statute describes the *mens rea* required to commit this crime.

Criminal statues don't require governments to prove damages in order to prosecute a defendant for a crime. However, governments can use the amount of harm that a defendant causes to increase the level of the crime.

The *actus reus* is the wrongful act that constitutes a crime. **Actus reus** is the Latin term for "guilty act." To be a crime, the action must be voluntary. The *actus reus* requires a physical act. For example, the U.S. Supreme Court held that a California law that punished people for being addicted to illegal drugs violated the Constitution. The California law made being "addicted" to drugs the offense, even if the person who was addicted to drugs never used or possessed drugs in the state.

NOTE

Some crimes don't require a particular mental state. For example, in most states, driving a car while under the influence of drugs or alcohol is a crime. It's a crime regardless of the mental state of the driver.

NOTE

In civil law, no showing of mental state, or *mens rea*, is required. Under civil law, wrongdoers are responsible for their actions even if they didn't intend to cause harm to another person.

In *Robinson v. California* (1962), the U.S. Supreme Court said that there were many ways that the state could make certain acts related to drug use illegal. However, simply making the status of being an addict illegal was a violation of the Constitution. The case stands for the proposition that criminal activity requires a voluntary, physical act.

A wrongful act also can include the failure to act when there's a duty to do so. For example, parents have a duty to care for their children. A state may punish a parent that fails to take care of his or her children when that failure rises to a level of criminal conduct. For instance, in March 2010 the South Korean government arrested a couple for child neglect. The government alleged that the couple's video game addiction led them to neglect their daughter. The child starved to death. Sadly, the video game that the couple was addicted to involved caring for a "virtual child" in an online game.

Jurisdiction

Courts have the ability to hear only "cases," or disputes, that are within their jurisdiction. Jurisdiction describes the types of cases that a court has the authority to hear.

Jurisdiction can be described in a number of different ways. Jurisdiction can be used to describe the function of a court. For example, trial courts generally have original jurisdiction. This is the ability to conduct trials and to hear initial disputes between parties. Appellate courts like the U.S. Supreme Court have appellate jurisdiction. They can only review decisions made by lower courts. Chapter 3 reviews this type of jurisdiction.

Jurisdiction also can describe the power of a court to hear a certain type of case and make a binding decision in that case. Courts must have the proper jurisdiction in order to make valid judgment. In order to make a valid judgment, a court must have:

* Subject matter jurisdiction
* Personal jurisdiction

Subject matter jurisdiction is the power of a court to decide certain types of cases. A court can't decide cases where it has no subject matter jurisdiction. For example, federal courts have jurisdiction only to decide cases about federal laws. This is federal question jurisdiction. They also can decide certain types of disputes between citizens of different states. This is diversity of citizenship jurisdiction. In contrast, state courts can decide only cases about state laws or actions that occurred within the geographic boundaries of the state.

FYI

In both state and federal court, jurisdiction also looks at geographical and political boundaries. If a person violates a federal law in Massachusetts, federal district courts in Massachusetts most likely have subject matter jurisdiction to decide the case. If the person violated only a state law, Massachusetts state courts would have jurisdiction to decide the case.

Personal jurisdiction refers to a court's ability to exercise power over a defendant. If a court doesn't have personal jurisdiction over a defendant, then it can't impose a sentence on that person. Personal jurisdiction is important for both criminal and civil cases. Typically, state courts can exercise personal jurisdiction over people who commit acts within the state.

For criminal law, personal jurisdiction comes into play when criminal acts are committed in a number of different states. It's also implicated when crimes affect residents in a number of different states. The U.S. Supreme Court addressed this issue in 1911. In *Strassheim v. Daily,* the Supreme Court used a "detrimental effects" test to determine if a state could exercise criminal jurisdiction over a person who committed acts outside of the state. The Court's test had three parts:

- Did the act occur outside the state?
- Did the act produce detrimental effects within the state?
- Were the acts the actual cause of detrimental effects within the state?

The test focuses on the defendant's intent. It also looks at the consequences of the defendant's actions in a particular state. Under the detrimental effects test, a state criminal court can exercise jurisdiction over a person who commits actions outside of the state if those actions cause harm within the state.

The Supreme Court's detrimental effects test used in the *Strassheim* case is a common law rule. Many states have enacted legislation that codifies the detrimental effects test. For example, Alaska law states that state courts have jurisdiction over crimes that are "commenced outside the state but consummated inside."[3]

Issues about jurisdiction aren't just questions between the states. Personal jurisdiction also can be an international issue. It's one of the main obstacles in cybercrime cases. This is because of the truly global nature of the Internet. The Council of Europe Convention on Cybercrime increases cooperation in the investigation and prosecution of cybercrimes. It went into force in 2004. Members of the convention must adopt legislation to criminalize certain types of cyber offenses and copyright infringement. They also agree to assist one another in criminal investigations. Forty-six nations have signed the Convention on Cybercrime. The United States ratified the treaty in August 2006.

> **NOTE**
>
> The United Nations discussed international cooperation to fight cybercrime at its 12th Congress on Crime Prevention in Criminal Justice in April 2010. You can view the agenda at *http://www.unodc.org/unodc/ en/crime-congress/12th-crime -congress.html.*

Jurisdictional Issues for Cybercrime Cases

Jurisdiction is a particularly challenging issue with respect to cybercrimes. Geographical boundaries don't limit computer networks. Cybercriminals can easily commit crimes that span across states and countries. This makes it difficult for law enforcement to investigate these crimes. It's particularly difficult for law enforcement to identify criminals and collect evidence across the globe. It also makes it difficult for courts to hold cybercriminals responsible for their actions.

Nigerian scams highlight the jurisdiction issues in cybercrime cases. These types of scams also are called "419 scams" or "advance fee fraud" schemes. This type of scam has been around since the early 1900s, when it was called the Spanish Prisoner Con. Today it's associated with the country of Nigeria. "4-1-9" refers to the section of the Nigerian criminal code that addresses fraud schemes.

Criminals originally conducted these scams via fax or mailed letters. They now conduct them with ease through e-mail. In a Nigerian scam, a person receives an e-mail from someone purporting to be an official of a foreign government or agency. The e-mail writer usually offers large sums of money in return for helping someone in trouble. In some cases, the e-mail claims that the Nigerian government has made it difficult for the wealthy writer to cash a large check. The writer asks the victim to advance the victim's own funds to cover the check, and to help cash it. The writer promises that the victim will get a hefty reward for his or her assistance.

A victim who advances funds soon learns that the check or underlying business transaction is fraudulent. The money advanced is lost. People operating outside the United States who send targeted e-mails to U.S. residents commit many of these types of crimes.

These cases are extremely difficult to investigate and prosecute. How would a victim in Lafayette, Indiana, be able to use the resources of local law enforcement to investigate a crime committed by a person that lives in Africa? Local police, prosecutors, and courts have limited power to investigate and prosecute these types of international cases. State subpoenas and court orders don't usually apply across international boundaries. These jurisdictional issues are becoming more common as Internet crime grows.

The Federal Trade Commission (FTC) has issued a consumer alert about Nigerian scams. You can read about it at *http://www.ftc.gov/bcp/edu/pubs/consumer/alerts/alt117.shtm*.

Criminal Procedure

Criminal procedure is the body of rules that govern how governments prosecute people for crimes. These procedural rules make sure that criminal defendants receive due process. Under "due process," a defendant in a criminal case is entitled to a fair and consistent process within the courts. The laws of criminal procedure make sure that the government safeguards the defendant's constitutional rights. They also provide the government with a method for fairly prosecuting defendants for their crimes.

FYI

A "prosecutor" is a government official who represents the government in criminal cases. They decide whether to charge a person with a crime and put on the court case against that person. "U.S. Attorneys" are federal prosecutors. States usually grant prosecutorial power to county governments. State prosecuting attorneys might be called district attorneys, county attorneys, state's attorneys, or simply county prosecutors.

Criminal procedure is discussed generally in Chapter 3. This section provides more detail on how crimes are prosecuted and punished. Most criminal procedure principles stem from the U.S. Constitution. This means that many processes are similar among the states and the federal government. However, there are some procedural rules that are unique to each jurisdiction. The description provided here is intentionally general. The process also can be different depending upon whether the crime committed is a misdemeanor or felony.

A criminal case begins when a law enforcement agency begins an investigation. Law enforcement agencies have certain rules that they must follow as they conduct their investigation. Some of these rules are discussed in Chapter 15. When law enforcement completes their investigation, they send the case to the prosecutor.

A prosecutor then reviews the case. They decide whether to bring charges against the person that law enforcement identified as the perpetrator of the crime. Prosecutors have a lot of discretion in determining whether to charge a person with a crime.

A prosecutor who decides to charge a person with a crime must file a written document in court to start the criminal process. In some states, a prosecutor may file a document called an "information." An information specifies the charges against the perpetrator of the crime. The prosecutor can exercise discretion when filing an information.

In other states, defendants have a right to a grand jury indictment. A "grand jury" is a panel of citizens who hear evidence presented by a prosecutor. The grand jury determines if there's enough evidence to bring a person to trial for a crime. The grant jury issues an "indictment" if it determines that the evidence is sufficient. An indictment is the formal written criminal charges issued by a grand jury. At this point, the perpetrator of the crime becomes a "defendant." In a criminal case, the defendant is the person accused of a crime.

FYI

The Fifth Amendment to the U.S. Constitution requires that a federal grand jury issue charges for some federal crimes. A defendant can waive the grand jury requirement. If a defendant waives the grand jury requirement, then the federal prosecutor files an information to start criminal proceedings. Federal grand juries contain between 16 and 23 people. The Federal Rules of Criminal Procedure sets this number. Grand juries conduct their deliberations in secret. You can read the Handbook for Federal Grand Jurors at *http://www.uscourts.gov/jury/grandhandbook2007.pdf*.

A criminal prosecution begins once a grand jury returns an indictment or after a prosecutor files an information. The next step in the criminal process is the "initial hearing." This is sometimes called an "arraignment." The purpose of this hearing is to begin the formal court process. At this hearing, a court must:

- Inform the defendant about the charges
- Advise the defendant about his or her legal and constitutional rights

At this point, the defendant must enter their response to the charges. This response is a "plea." A defendant can enter a plea of guilty or not guilty. In some cases, they also can enter a plea of *nolo contendere. Nolo contendere* is Latin for "I do not wish to contend." It's also called a plea of no contest. A no contest plea isn't a guilty plea. However, it has the same effect as one. Most jurisdictions have limits on how and when defendants can use this type of plea.

If a defendant enters a guilty plea, the court will set a date to sentence the defendant. In 2009, the U.S. Department of Justice issued a special study on felony sentences in state courts. That study found that 94 percent of felony defendants pleaded guilty in state court cases.[4]

 NOTE

The defendant's right to an attorney arises when a criminal proceeding begins. A defendant may voluntarily waive the right to counsel and represent himself or herself. A court must decide that a person is mentally competent in order to do this. The court also must warn the person that there are dangers to self-representation.

If the defendant enters a not guilty plea, the court sets the case for trial. The U.S. Constitution guarantees criminal defendants the right to a trial by jury. Article III of the Constitution guarantees this right. The Sixth Amendment to the Constitution clarifies the scope of the right.

Under the Sixth Amendment, criminal defendants are entitled to a court-appointed attorney if they can't afford one on their own. Courts usually only grant this request when a defendant faces a prison sentence for their crime. The Supreme Court case of *Gideon v. Wainwright* (1963) held that a court must appoint an attorney to an indigent defendant charged with a felony. The defendant must prove that he or she is indigent and can't afford an attorney. The Supreme Court in the *Gideon* case also held that a conviction is automatically reversed if a state denies a defendant the right to counsel.

After the arraignment, the prosecution and the defendant's attorneys will begin the discovery process. "Discovery" is the process where the government gives the defendant the evidence that it plans to use in the defendant's trial. U.S. Supreme Court cases have held that the government must disclose:

- Any deals that the prosecution made with a witness *(Giglio v. United States).*
- Any evidence it has that might help prove the defendant's innocence *(Brady v. Maryland).*

Courts strictly regulate the criminal discovery process. The rules for the process are clear. A court has a wide range of actions it can take against parties that fail to comply with discovery rules. A court can even dismiss the case if the prosecution fails to comply with the rules of the process. Failure to turn over evidence that might help prove the defendant's innocence can cause a conviction to be overturned.

If a criminal case goes to trial, the government bears the burden of proving that the defendant violated the law. As discussed in Chapter 3, in criminal cases the government must prove the defendant's guilt beyond a reasonable doubt. This is the highest burden of proof that a prosecutor must meet. Reasonable doubt doesn't mean that a juror is 100 percent convinced of the defendant's guilt. It does mean, however, that a juror must be fully satisfied that the prosecution has eliminated reasonable doubt about the defendant's guilt.

> **NOTE**
>
> The Sixth Amendment to the U.S. Constitution guarantees defendants a speedy trial. State criminal procedure rules include time limits for all the steps in the criminal process. In *Strunk v. United States* (1973), the U.S. Supreme Court held that a court must dismiss a criminal charge if a state violates the defendant's speedy trial rights.

The government has a high burden of proof in criminal cases because criminal punishments infringe on a person's fundamental rights. These rights include the right to liberty, property, and life. Criminal penalties can include jail time, probation, financial penalties, or even a death sentence. A court may only impose these penalties if the government meets their high burden of proof.

A criminal case ends when a jury decides that a defendant is innocent or guilty. It also ends if the jury can't reach a decision. A "hung jury" is a jury that is unable to reach a decision because the jurors disagree. A court will declare a "mistrial" if the jury can't reach a decision. In this case, the government may decide to refile the charges and prosecute the defendant again.

A defendant who is convicted may appeal. There are different rights that allow a defendant to appeal a ruling or conviction to a higher court. These rules are beyond the scope of this book.

Common Criminal Laws Used in Cyberspace

There's a great distinction between crimes that may now be committed using computers, crimes that use computers or the Internet as a medium to commit crime, and crimes where the computer is the target of the crime. The first example isn't cybercrime. For example, a person simply using a computer and printer to create a forged document commits a criminal act. It's no different than if that same person used a printing press and ink to forge the document. The crime is still a forgery. In this example, the computer is a tool used to commit the crime.

Cybercrimes are different. Cybercrimes also are called computer crimes. Cybercrimes are crimes that use computers or where the computer itself is the target of the crime. Cyberstalking, identity theft, and phishing scams are examples of crimes facilitated by computers. Denial of service (DoS) and DDoS attacks, computer viruses, and communications sabotage are examples of crimes where the computer itself is the target of the crime. The distinction between the types of crime is subtle.

Both the federal government and individual states have created a number of laws that address cybercrime. This chapter talks primarily about federal cybercrime laws. It's likely that federal laws will have the most impact on cybercrime. This is because geography or state and national borders don't matter to cybercriminals. The Internet truly blurs these lines. A criminal can easily initiate a cybercrime in one state and harm a victim in another. In addition, since cybercrime statues vary widely between the states, federal laws may end up being more comprehensive.

NOTE

It's important to remember that many states criminalize the same behavior that federal cybercrime laws address.

The Computer Fraud and Abuse Act (1984)

Congress passed the Computer Fraud and Abuse Act (CFAA) in 1984.[5] It's the first piece of federal legislation that identified computer crimes as distinct offenses. The CFAA provides both criminal and civil penalties. In enacting the CFAA, Congress chose to address computer-related offenses in a single statute. The CFAA limits federal jurisdiction to situations where cybercrime is interstate in nature or when the computers of the federal government are the target of crime.

NOTE

The Internet Crime Complaint Center (IC3) is a partnership between the U.S. Federal Bureau of Investigation (FBI) and the National White Collar Crime Center. Their 2009 "Annual Report on Internet Crime" showed that the total loss linked to online fraud was $559.7 million.[6] You can read the report at *http://www.ic3 .gov/media/annualreport/2009 _IC3Report.pdf*.

Congress amended the CFAA with the Uniting and Strengthening America by Providing Appropriate Tools Required to Intercept and Obstruct Terrorism Act (U.S.A. PATRIOT Act) in 2001. It amended the CFAA again in 2008. These amendments increased the penalties for CFAA violations. They also lowered the required damage thresholds in light of terrorism and identity theft concerns.

The CFAA criminalizes the act of causing certain types of damage to a protected computer. A protected computer is any of the following:

- A federal government computer
- A financial institution computer
- A computer used in interstate or foreign commerce

The definition of a protected computer is very broad. Under the statute, the Internet is a protected computer. The CFAA definition of "financial institution" includes those financial institutions discussed in Chapter 5 of this book.

The CFAA addresses the following types of criminal activity:

- Unauthorized access of national security information
- Unauthorized access to a government computer
- Compromising the confidentiality of a protected computer
- Unauthorized access to a protected computer with an intent to defraud
- Unauthorized access to a protected computer that causes damage

- Intentional transmission of malware, viruses, or worms that damage a protected computer
- Unauthorized trafficking of passwords or other computer access information that allows people to access other computers without authorization and with the intent to defraud
- Extortion involving threats to damage a protected computer

The CFAA doesn't just address intruders or outsider attacks on protected computers. It also takes into account that insiders may exceed the access that they have been granted in a protected computer system. Since these people already have access to these systems, their access isn't unauthorized. However, in some cases, they commit a crime if they exceed their scope of authorized access. Under the CFAA, a person exceeds authorized access when he or she accesses a computer with authorization, but uses that access to get or alter information that he or she isn't allowed to use or alter.

An insider can be charged under the CFAA with exceeding authorized access if they access national security information inappropriately. They also can be charged if they compromise the confidentiality of a protected computer, or exceed their authorization in a protected computer with intent to defraud.

Some sections of the CFAA require the government to show that the intruder caused damage. Under the CFAA, "damage" is whatever does any of the following:

- Causes loss of $5,000 or more of total damage during one year
- Modifies medical care of a person
- Causes physical injury
- Threatens public health or safety
- Damages systems used by or for government entity for administration of justice, national defense, or national security
- Causes or attempts to cause death or serious bodily injury

The federal government uses the CFAA to prosecute many different computer crimes. It used the CFAA to charge a 20-year-old University of Tennessee student with unauthorized e-mail access. In late 2008, the student accessed Vice Presidential candidate Sarah Palin's personal Yahoo! e-mail account. The student then posted her e-mail messages online. A criminal grand jury indicted the student under the CFAA and the federal Electronic Communications Privacy Act (ECPA). In April 2010, a jury convicted the student of unauthorized access to a computer and obstruction of justice.

Table 12-1 summarizes the Computer Fraud and Abuse Act provisions and potential penalties.

 NOTE

The federal government used the CFAA in 1990 to prosecute the creator of the Morris worm. This was the first prosecution under the CFAA. The Morris worm is discussed in Chapter 1.

12

Criminal Law/Tort Law
Issues in Cyberspace

TABLE 12-1 Computer Fraud and Abuse Act summary.

CRIMINAL ACTIVITY	ACTION	ADDITIONAL ELEMENTS	PENALTY
Obtaining National Security Information	Unauthorized Access Access in excess of authorized access		Felony. A defendant can receive a fine, or 10 years in prison, or both.
Trespass in a government computer	Unauthorized Access	Access must affect use of the government computer (low threshold to meet)	Misdemeanor. A defendant can receive a fine, or up to one year in prison, or both. The defendant also can be sentenced for a felony and up to 10 years in prison if he or she has a previous CFAA violation.
Compromising confidentiality of a protected computer	Unauthorized Access Access in excess of authorized access		Misdemeanor. A defendant can receive a fine, or up to one year in prison, or both. The defendant also can be sentenced for a felony and up to five years in prison if aggravating factors exist.
Access of a protected computer	Unauthorized Access Access in excess of authorized access	Intent to defraud	Misdemeanor. A defendant can receive a fine, or up to one year In prison, or both. The defendant also can be sentenced for a felony and up to 10 years in prison if he or she has a previous CFAA violation.
Access of a protected computer that causes damage	Unauthorized Access	Must cause damage: • Intentionally • Recklessly • Negligently	Different penalties depending upon *mens rea* for damage caused • **Intentional:** Felony. A defendant can receive a fine, or 10 years in prison, or both. The defendant also can receive 20 years in prison for subsequent convictions or causing damage leading to serious bodily injury. A defendant can receive life imprisonment if the offense causes or attempts to cause death. • **Reckless:** Felony. A defendant can receive a fine, or five years in prison, or both. • **Negligent:** Misdemeanor. A defendant can receive a fine, or up to one year in prison, or both.

TABLE 12-1 *continued.*

CRIMINAL ACTIVITY	ACTION	ADDITIONAL ELEMENTS	PENALTY
Transmission of malware, viruses, or worms that damage a protected computer	Intentional transmission	Must cause damage	Felony. A defendant can receive a fine, or 10 years in prison, or both.
Trafficking in passwords	Knowing, with intent to defraud	Affects interstate commerce or computer used by government	Misdemeanor. A defendant can receive a fine, or up to one year in prison, or both. The defendant also can be sentenced for a felony and up to 10 years in prison if they have a previous CFAA violation.
Threatening to damage a computer	Intent to extort	Transmits threat in interstate or foreign commerce	Felony. A defendant can receive a fine, or up to five years in prison, or both. The defendant also can be sentenced for a felony and up to 10 years in prison if he or she has a previous CFAA violation.

Computer Trespass or Intrusion

The Computer Fraud and Abuse Act is the main federal law addressing cybercrime. In addition to the CFAA, the federal government has a number of other laws that address computer trespass or intrusion. These laws generally address computers that the U.S. government owns or controls. Some laws, such as the CFAA, expand this definition to include computers used in interstate commerce.

State Laws Against Computer Trespass

It's important to keep in mind that states also may have computer trespass statutes that prohibit unauthorized access to computer systems or networks. Depending on the jurisdiction, these crimes have a variety of names. In many states, the mere act of intentionally entering a computer system or network without permission is a crime. In most jurisdictions, first-time computer trespass is a misdemeanor. The penalties for computer trespass may escalate if a person is charged and convicted of more than one offense.

Most trespass statutes only address unauthorized access into a computer system. They stop short of addressing actual computer tampering, access of information, or the injection of computer viruses or worms. These types of crimes, which are malicious in nature, typically are addressed in other statutes.

Federal law addresses fraud and related activity in connection with access devices. It outlaws the production, use, or sale of counterfeit or unauthorized access devices.[7] Access devices include any item that can be used to obtain money, goods, or things of value. They include items such as card, plate, code, account number, electronic serial number, mobile identification number, personal identification number, or other telecommunications services. A person who violates this law commits a felony. They can be imprisoned for 10 to 20 years depending upon the nature of the violation.

Theft of Information

Theft of information via computer networks is on the rise. Most of these crimes take the form of theft of personal identifying information or financial information. Financial gain is nearly always the motive for crimes such as these. Chapter 4 discusses the security and privacy of consumer financial information.

The federal Identity Theft and Assumption Deterrence Act (1998) makes identity theft a federal crime.[8] If a person violates the law, they're subject to criminal penalties of up to 15 years in prison. This period increases to 20 years in special circumstances. Violators also can be fined up to $250,000.

> **NOTE**
>
> The FTC's identity theft Web site provides useful information about preventing identity theft. You can read it at *http://www.ftc.gov/bcp/edu/microsites/idtheft/.*

This law recognizes that the victims of identity theft aren't just the businesses that grant credit. The person whose identity was stolen also is a victim. The law also requires the FTC to keep a record of identity theft complaints. The FTC must give identity theft victims educational materials to help them repair any damage to their credit and personal data.

The law makes it illegal for anyone to knowingly transfer or use another person's identification with the intent to commit a crime. Under the law, an identification document is any document made or issued by the federal or a state government. Identifying information includes information that is similar to other personal information laws discussed in this book. This information includes name, Social Security number, and driver's license number. It also includes:

- Unique biometric data, such as fingerprint, voice print, retina or iris image, or other unique physical representation
- Unique electronic identification number, address, or routing code
- Cellular telephone electronic serial number
- Any other piece of information that may be used to identify a specific person

The U.S. Secret Service, FBI, U.S. Postal Inspection Service, and Social Security Administration's Office of the Inspector General all have the power to investigate crimes committed under this law.

Interception of Communications Laws

Federal laws that address the interception of communications are discussed in Chapter 2. These laws forbid the use of eavesdropping technologies without a court order. Communications covered by the statutes include e-mail, radio communications, electronic communications, data transmission, and telephone calls. The federal Wiretap Act (1968, amended) governs real-time interception of the contents of a communication.[9]

> **NOTE**
>
> The Pen Register and Trap and Trace Statute governs access to the real-time interception of headers, logs, and other transmission information.[10]

The Electronic Communications Privacy Act (1986) governs access to stored electronic communications.[11] This includes access to the contents of the communication and the headers and other transmission information. The ECPA is an amendment to the original Wiretap Act.

The U.S.A. Patriot Act amended both the Wiretap Act and ECPA. Those amendments are discussed briefly in Chapter 2. The Patriot Act enhances law enforcement tools to intercept electronic communications to fight computer fraud and abuse offenses.

Spam and Phishing Laws

Congress created the Controlling the Assault of Non-Solicited Pornography and Marketing (CAN-SPAM) Act in 2003.[12] The act covers unsolicited commercial e-mail messages. These messages are known as spam. **Spam** is electronic junk mail. It's unsolicited e-mail that a user may receive. Spam is a nuisance to the recipient. The CAN-SPAM Act has both civil and criminal provisions.

The CAN-SPAM Act requires commercial e-mail senders to meet certain requirements. Commercial messages are messages with content that advertise or promote a product or service. The act also forbids sending sexually explicit e-mail unless it has a label or marking that identifies it as explicit.

Commercial e-mail message senders must meet the following CAN-SPAM requirements:

- Don't use false or misleading header information
- Don't use deceptive subject lines
- Identify the e-mail message as a commercial advertisement
- Include a valid physical postal address
- Inform message recipients how they can opt out of future e-mail messages
- Promptly process opt-out requests
- Monitor the actions of third parties that advertise on the sender's behalf

Each separate e-mail sent in violation of the CAN-SPAM Act is subject to penalties of up to $16,000. The FTC enforces the civil provisions of the Act. It also has promulgated rules for businesses to follow.

The CAN-SPAM Act also has criminal provisions. It includes penalties for:

- Accessing another person's computer without permission to send spam
- Using false information to register for multiple e-mail accounts or domain names
- Relaying or retransmitting spam messages through a computer in order to mislead others about the origin of the e-mail
- Harvesting e-mail addresses or generating them through a dictionary attack
- Taking advantage of open relays or open proxies without permission in order to send spam

The U.S. Department of Justice enforces the criminal provisions of the CAN-SPAM Act. Criminal penalties include fines or imprisonment of up to five years.

The first conviction under the CAN-SPAM Act occurred in 2004. In that case, the defendant searched for unprotected wireless access hot spots and exploited them to send spam messages. The spam messages advertised pornographic Web sites. Eventually the court sentenced the defendant to three year's probation and six months of home detention. He also had to pay a $10,000 fine.

Spam e-mail messages also can be phishing attempts. Phishing scams are discussed in Chapter 1. They're scams that typically take place via e-mail or instant messaging. They're a form of Internet fraud where attackers attempt to steal valuable personal information from their victims.

There's no federal anti-phishing law. However, phishing attacks can be prosecuted under a number of different federal laws. This includes many of the laws already discussed in this section. For example, if the phishing attackers are attempting to steal personal information, they may be committing identity theft. The federal Identity Theft and Assumption Deterrence Act would apply. They also may be committing computer fraud or access-device fraud. Some phishing attacks also can be prosecuted under the CAN-SPAM Act.

If a phishing attack includes malicious activity, such as spreading computer viruses, then the Computer Fraud and Abuse Act would apply. Phishing scams also can violate state laws on fraud and identity theft.

Cybersquatting

Cybersquatting is the bad-faith registration of a domain name that is a registered trademark or trade name of another entity. Cybersquatting is discussed in Chapter 10. Congress created the Anti-Cybersquatting Consumer Protection Act (ACPA) in 1999.[13] It's designed to stop people from registering domain names that are trademarks that belong to other entities.

The ACPA allows entities to sue cybersquatters. To prove their case, the plaintiff must show that the cybersquatter registered the trademark in bad faith with intent to profit from the registration. The ACPA includes nine factors that help a court determine bad faith. Those factors are:

- A person's intellectual property rights in the domain name
- Whether the domain name consists of the legal name of the person
- The person's prior use of the domain name in connection with the sale of goods or services
- The person's noncommercial or fair use of the domain name
- The person's intent to divert consumers from the mark owner's own Web site
- The person's offer to sell the domain name without having used the domain name for the sale of goods or services
- Whether the person gave false or misleading contact information when registering the domain name
- Whether the person registered multiple domain names that are identical or confusingly similar to marks owned by others
- Whether the mark incorporated in the domain name is famous and distinctive

Under the law, a plaintiff can recover damages and ask the court to issue an injunction that stops the cybersquatter from using the contested domain name. The court also can award statutory damages of up to $100,000 per violation. Courts also can award the contested domain name to the winning party.

Malicious Acts

Common malicious information security acts are discussed in Chapter 1. That chapter also discusses malicious activity such as malware, worms, viruses, and Trojan horses. For the most part, the federal government can prosecute these types of activities under the Computer Fraud and Abuse Act.

Under the CFAA, the intentional transmission of malware, viruses, or worms that damage a protected computer is a felony. Remember that for the purposes of the CFAA, almost any computer connected to the Internet is a protected computer. The government can charge people who violate this provision of the CFAA with a felony. They can be punished with up to 10 years in prison.

Well-Known Cybercrimes

This book has highlighted a number of well-known cybercrimes in each chapter. The list of what is a well-known cybercrime changes every day. The Computer Fraud and Abuse Act is the "go to" act for federal prosecution of cybercrime. It's very broad, and almost any type of Internet-related crime involving computers will fall within its scope. Prosecutors often include CFAA charges with other federal criminal charges if a computer is involved in the commission of a crime.

Some cybercrimes are popular because they were "first." For example, the Morris worm is discussed in Chapter 1. It was one of the first computer worms on the Internet. At the time, it infected and overwhelmed a number of government systems. The creator of the worm was the first person charged with violating the Computer Fraud and Abuse Act.

▷ **NOTE**

You can learn how the federal government is prosecuting cybercrime by visiting the Department of Justice Computer Crime Web page. The Web page lists notable cybercrime prosecutions. The Webpage is available at *http:// www.justice.gov/criminal/cybercrime/*.

The CFAA also was used to prosecute the creator of the Melissa virus. When it was released, the Melissa virus was one of the fastest moving and most destructive viruses. David Smith created and distributed the Melissa virus in 1999. The virus caused more than $80 million in damage. He was sentenced to 20 months in federal prison in May 2002. He also was fined $5,000.

Other cybercrimes are well known because they're the biggest. For instance, one of the hackers in the TJX Companies, Inc. case received the harshest-ever sentence for a hacking case in March 2010. The federal government had charged him with violating the CFAA, federal laws related to access device fraud, and the Identity Theft and Assumption Deterrence Act. This case is discussed in detail in Chapter 4.

The federal government has been attempting to expand the use of the CFAA. One area where it has tried to expand the reach of the CFAA is in the area of cyberbullying. In 2008, the Department of Justice indicted Lori Drew for violating the CFAA. The government argued that her activities on a social networking service exceeded her authorization in the use of a protected computer. She exceeded her authorized access by using the site in excess of the use authorized by the site's terms of service agreement. A jury found her guilty of a misdemeanor CFAA violation. That conviction was set aside in August 2009. The judge found that there were several problems in applying the CFAA to the case. The government didn't appeal the judge's reversal.

General Tort Law Concepts

▷ **NOTE**

A **tortfeasor** is a person who commits a tort. In this book, a person charged with committing a tort is called a defendant. A plaintiff is the person allegedly injured by the defendant's actions.

Tort law is discussed briefly in Chapter 2. A tort is some sort of wrongful act or harm that injures a person. A person who is injured by a tort may sue the wrongdoer for damages. The word tort is from the Latin word *tortus*, which means wrong or twisted.

In the United States, tort law has evolved from English common law. Many states give either common law or statutory recognition to most torts. When states enact tort laws, they typically are trying to expand or limit common law tort liability.

Common law tort principles are similar among the states. The American Law Institute has prepared a review of tort law similar to the review that it prepared on contract law (discussed in Chapter 11). The *Restatement (Second) of the Law of Torts* summarizes the common law tort rules.

Tort law is based on the premise that people should go about their daily business in a way that doesn't harm other people or their property. So long as people are acting reasonably, this is easy to accomplish. Tort law allows people a way to recover for their injuries if another person doesn't act reasonably.

Tort law uses the reasonable person standard to determine whether a person acts appropriately. This concept is discussed in Chapter 2. Courts use this standard to determine if a person acts reasonably in response to a particular situation. This standard determines whether conduct is tortious.

> **NOTE**
>
> Tortious conduct is wrongful conduct. It's conduct that is unreasonable given the situation.

There are three types of torts. They are:

- Strict liability torts
- Negligent torts
- Intentional torts

This section will briefly describe all three types of torts. However, you should keep in mind that most torts involving computers probably will fall under the intentional torts category.

Strict Liability Torts

Strict liability is a legal concept that means that people can be held responsible for their actions even if they didn't intend to cause harm to another person. This concept is introduced in Chapter 10. A number of areas of law apply this concept.

In tort law, a person is held liable for strict liability torts regardless of intent or negligence. Courts usually impose strict liability theories in unreasonably dangerous situations. These are situations where even a reasonable person can't prevent risk. The main reason for imposing strict liability is to discourage unreasonably risky behavior.

The classic example of a strict liability tort is when a person keeps wild animals as pets. Wild animals are inherently dangerous. Even if the owner of the animal takes reasonable precautions, there's still a risk to the public if the animal escapes. If an animal were to escape and injure a person, courts would hold the owner liable for any damages that the animal caused. Courts hold the owner liable even if the owner takes every precaution available to ensure safety.

In a tort based on strict liability, the plaintiff must show that the defendant engaged in unreasonably dangerous activities. The plaintiff also must show that he or she was harmed. The defendant bears the burden of proving that the activities were not unreasonably dangerous.

Negligence Torts

Negligence torts are based on the premise that a person is liable for any injuries or harm that are the foreseeable consequences of his or her actions. In order to prove a negligence-based tort, a plaintiff must show that:

- The defendant owed the plaintiff a duty of due care
- The defendant breached his or her duty
- The breach of duty caused the plaintiff's foreseeable injuries
- The plaintiff was damaged

Plaintiffs must prove that the defendant owed them a **duty of due care**. A duty of due care is a person's obligation to avoid acts or omissions that can harm others. The level of duty that one person owes to another is based on the reasonable person standard. The reasonable person standard is discussed in Chapter 2. It's a legal concept used to describe how an ordinary person would think and act. The plaintiff will present evidence on what a reasonable person in a similar circumstance would have done. This evidence shows the level of care that the defendant owes the plaintiff.

> **NOTE**
> The standard of care for professionals in learned occupations is important in professional malpractice cases.

There are special duty of due care rules for people in learned occupations. Learned occupations are professions where special training and skill are required. Under the law, people in these occupations are held to a higher standard of care. They are held to a standard that's reasonable for members of that profession. For example, a lawyer's duty of due care toward their clients is based on a reasonable lawyer standard. Doctors, architects, engineers, and airplane pilots are held to reasonableness standards based on their professions.

The plaintiff must show that the defendant breached a duty of due care. That is, the plaintiff must prove that the defendant's behavior fell below what a reasonable person would have done in the same situation. The plaintiff will compare the defendant's behavior against the evidence that was used to show that the defendant had a duty of due care. The plaintiff can show that the defendant breached his or her duty by showing that the defendant acted in a way that was unreasonable given the situation and the defendant's duty.

> **NOTE**
> A plaintiff also can prove a breach of duty by showing that the defendant failed to take a required action. This is called an omission.

For example, a plaintiff may be able to establish that people have a duty to keep their sidewalks free from ice in the wintertime. To prove that the defendant breached this duty, the plaintiff would present evidence that the defendant didn't shovel his or her sidewalks. The plaintiff also would have to show that the defendant's failure to keep the sidewalks clear injured the plaintiff.

The plaintiff also must show that the defendant's breach caused the plaintiff's foreseeable injuries. Often courts use the "but for" test to meet this requirement. Would the plaintiff's injuries have occurred "but for" the defendant's actions? Once it's established that the defendant caused the plaintiff's injuries, courts review whether those injuries are compensable.

The law recognizes that there are some instances where the defendant is no longer responsible for the plaintiff's injuries. This happens when the plaintiff's injuries aren't foreseeable. The famous case that explored this concept is *Palsgraf v. Long Island Railroad* (1928).[14]

In the *Palsgraf* case, a passenger was running toward a moving train. Train employees tried to help the passenger board the train. As they helped him, they bumped a package from his arms. The package contained fireworks. The fireworks exploded on the train tracks. The explosion caused a scale on the train platform to topple over. When it fell, it injured Mrs. Palsgraf. She sued the railroad for her injuries.

The Reasonable Information Security Professional

Torts based on a professional's duty to provide competent services are among the oldest negligence torts. Is an information security professional a member of a learned occupation? Will information security professionals be held to a "reasonable security professional" standard when giving advice to clients? There's some argument that this could be the case sometime in the future.

Information security as a career path continues to evolve. Many information security professionals are highly educated individuals who are experts in their fields. Most of them have certifications in various technical aspects of information security. Many computing vendors offer technology-specific security certifications for their products.

A number of independent organizations offer security-related certifications as well. The International Information Systems Security Certification Consortium (ISC)² grants certifications to many information security professionals. This organization certifies that information security professionals have varying levels of experience and knowledge in the field. You can learn about (ISC)² at *http://www.isc2.org/*.

The Global Information Assurance Certification (GIAC) program also grants information security certifications. They offer special certifications in areas such as audit, intrusion detection, and operating system security. These certifications test technical skills. Many information security professionals hold GIAC certifications. You can learn about GIAC at *http://www.giac.org/*.

Both (ISC)² and GIAC require certificate holders to follow a code of ethics. Each group has a code that defines acceptable levels of behavior for certificate holders. Both codes require certificate holders to act responsibly when giving information security advice. These organizations also require certificate holders to engage in activities that keep their information security skills up to date.

At the time of writing this book, no U.S. court has recognized a professional duty for information security professionals. Think about whether information security certifications and the ethical obligations that they sometimes require could be used to show that information security professionals are part of a learned profession. Could this change how information security professionals help their clients secure information systems?

12

Criminal Law/Tort Law
Issues in Cyberspace

The New York Court of Appeals decided the case. The court held that the plaintiff's injuries were not a foreseeable result of the actions of the railroad's employees. The court also held that the defendant had no duty to the plaintiff. The duty was owed to the passenger that the train employees were trying to help onto the train. Since there was no duty owed to the plaintiff, there could be no liability.

NOTE

In New York, the Court of Appeals is the state's highest court.

The *Palsgraf* case has come to stand for the rule that there's no duty to an unforeseen plaintiff for unforeseeable injuries. If there's no duty to this plaintiff, then there's no negligence. This is known as proximate or legal cause. It means that a plaintiff's injuries must be the natural and foreseeable results of the defendant's negligence.

Once the plaintiff proves that the defendant committed a negligent act, the plaintiff must prove damages. In a tort case, damages can be economic or non-economic. Economic damages are damages that have a monetary value. They include compensation for medical bills, lost wages, and damage to property. Non-economic damages are harder to prove. They include compensation for items such as pain and suffering, or loss of companionship.

A court awards damages in a tort case in an attempt to make a plaintiff whole. These are compensatory damages. Compensatory damages are discussed in Chapter 11. Compensatory damages try to place the plaintiff in the same position that he or she would have been in had no tortious act occurred. This is the primary goal of tort lawsuits.

A court doesn't usually award punitive damages in a negligent tort case. It may award punitive damages if the defendant's actions are grossly negligent. This doesn't happen often. Many states have placed limits on the amount of punitive damages that a court or jury can award in a tort lawsuit.

There are some defenses to negligence torts. A defendant can use these defenses to help escape or limit liability. A defendant has the burden of proving their defenses. The three most common defenses are:

- **Assumption of Risk**—The plaintiff had assumed the risk of the defendant's actions and any injuries resulting from those actions. If the defendant proves assumption of risk, he or she has no liability to the plaintiff.

- **Contributory Negligence**—The plaintiff should recover nothing because his or her own actions also contributed to his or her own injuries. If the defendant proves contributory negligence, he or she has no liability to the plaintiff. Only a few jurisdictions follow this rule because it's very harsh.

- **Comparative Negligence**—The plaintiff should recover only a *pro rata* share of damages because his or her own actions also contributed to his or her injuries. In most jurisdictions, a plaintiff less than 50 percent at fault can recover a *pro rata* share of damages based on the defendant's level of fault.

Intentional Torts

Intentional torts are torts where the defendant intended to commit the tort. Intentional torts often share many common elements with a crime. It helps to remember that civil actions address torts and criminal actions address crimes.

In a lawsuit for a tort, the person who was harmed seeks compensation from the wrongdoer. In a criminal trial, society is punishing the wrongdoer for the crimes that they committed. The same action can be both a wrong against society (a crime) and a wrong against an individual (a tort). It's entirely possible in a criminal action that the victim of a crime won't be compensated for their injuries. The victim can then bring a lawsuit against the wrongdoer for the underlying tort and recover damages. You can review the burden of proof sidebar in Chapter 3 for an example of how these two concepts work together.

The classic example of an intentional tort is battery. Battery is harmful or offensive contact with another person. The battery tort occurs when the defendant intentionally causes harmful contact with the plaintiff.

The most common defense to an intentional tort is that the plaintiff consented to the wrongful action. A defendant must prove that the plaintiff consented. A defendant can use the plaintiff's words or actions as evidence to prove consent.

Most of the torts associated with computers and cyberspace are intentional torts. These occur when the defendant uses a computer or takes some action involving a computer, intentionally to harm the plaintiff.

Civil Procedure

A plaintiff must sue a defendant in a civil lawsuit in order to recover for tort injuries. Civil procedure is the body of rules that govern how courts conduct civil cases. Civil procedure is discussed generally in Chapter 3. This section provides more detail on the civil trial process. One thing to keep in mind is that the laws of civil procedure vary from jurisdiction to jurisdiction. The federal and state governments all have different civil procedure rules. The description provided here is intentionally general.

A civil action begins when the plaintiff files their **complaint**. A complaint is a document filed with a court. A plaintiff uses a complaint to tell their story. They state how they were injured and ask the court to make them whole. A complaint must contain "a short and plain statement of the claim showing that the pleader is entitled to relief."[15] It also must show that the court has jurisdiction to hear the case. The plaintiff also must specify the relief that they demand. In a tort case, the plaintiff typically wishes to receive money damages. The damages compensate the plaintiff for their injuries.

> **NOTE**
>
> In civil procedure, the plaintiff is the party that brings the lawsuit. The defendant is the party that defends against the lawsuit. In some jurisdictions, and for some types of cases, the plaintiff could be called the petitioner. The defendant could be called the respondent.

The plaintiff must file their complaint within a certain period of time after the claimed injury. This time period is called the **statute of limitations**. For example, in Indiana, the statute of limitations for most tort actions is two years.[16] The plaintiff must sue the defendant within two years of being injured by the defendant. Not all states have the same time limits. For example, in Montana the statute of limitations for most tort actions based on negligent conduct is three years.[17]

"Service of process" refers to the procedure that delivers the complaint and a summons to the defendant. This process makes the defendant aware that the plaintiff has filed a lawsuit. There are certain formalities that must be followed in order to serve a complaint and summons on a defendant. For the most part, the complaint and summons are delivered physically to the defendant. This is to assure the court that the defendant received proper notice of the lawsuit.

The defendant must respond to the complaint after they receive it. Their response is called an **answer**. All jurisdictions have time limits that a defendant must follow when answering the complaint. Under the Federal Rules of Civil Procedure, a defendant must file their answer within 20 days after receiving the complaint.[18] A court can allow a defendant more time to answer if necessary.

> **NOTE**
>
> A defendant also can raise counterclaims in his or her answer. These are the defendant's claims against the plaintiff. They also can raise cross-claims. These are the defendant's claims against another party to hold that third party responsible for the plaintiff's injuries.

A defendant must respond to each claim in the plaintiff's complaint. They can admit or deny the claims. They also must state their defenses to each claim. The answer is the defendant's opportunity to tell their side of the story.

A defendant also can raise defenses to the plaintiff's complaint. Some of these defenses are absolute. The court must dismiss the plaintiff's lawsuit if the defendant proves the defense. For example, the defendant can question the court's jurisdiction. If the court doesn't have jurisdiction over the matter, then it must dismiss the lawsuit. A defendant also can argue that the plaintiff doesn't have a legal basis for their claim. The court must dismiss the lawsuit if there's no legal basis for the plaintiff's claim.

After the complaint and answer, the plaintiff and defendant's attorneys will begin the discovery process. This is the period of the civil lawsuit where the parties share

Electronic Discovery

For the parties in a lawsuit, electronic data can be important evidence. This is especially true since many parties and witnesses store their data in an electronic format only. The introduction of electronic-format evidence and record-keeping systems caused some problems for the legal system. These problems were acute in the discovery phase of lawsuits, where parties would engage in expensive fights over the production of electronic information.

Electronic discovery deals with information stored in an electronic format. It's also known as E-discovery. Prior to 2006, courts decided E-discovery issues on case-by-case basis under standard discovery rules. The most famous case for E-discovery issues is *Zubulake v. UBS Warburg, LLC*.[19] The U.S. District Court for the Southern District of New York decided this case.

There are actually several *Zubulake* decisions regarding electronic discovery. They stated the first real rules for parties to follow regarding electronic evidence. The rules related to the duty to preserve evidence, the duty to monitor compliance with preservation decisions, and costs of providing electronic data.

In 2006, the U.S. Supreme Court amended the Federal Rules of Civil Procedure to clarify how parties should handle E-discovery.

When a lawsuit begins, parties are obligated to preserve certain types of evidence. This includes evidence stored in an electronic format. The Federal Rules of Civil Procedure call this type of evidence "electronically stored information" (ESI). The definition is broad and is meant to include any type of information that can be stored electronically.

Parties to a lawsuit must address ESI early in the lawsuit. This is because it can be easily deleted or changed. The parties must address how discoverable ESI will be preserved. They also must address the format in which information with one another. Unlike the criminal discovery process, there are few affirmative disclosure rules in the civil discovery process. The parties must disclose their witnesses to one another. They also must provide each other with a list of documents that they have in their possession that arc related to their claims and defenses. The documents that each party must disclose include a listing of documents stored in an electronic form.

After these general disclosures, it's up to each party to ask for information that's relevant to the case. They use various procedural rules to ask each other for information and documents. The process can get very complicated. It also can get very expensive. Sometimes the parties will ask the court to intervene in the discovery process. This happens when the parties dispute whether some types of information must be disclosed.

For example, a defendant may not want to disclose trade secret information through the discovery process, even if it's relevant to the case. This is because documents filed in a court case become public records. This includes documents exchanged during the discovery process and then used as evidence at trial. The defendant doesn't want to lose trade secret protection. The defendant could lose that protection if the information is available to the public or if it's shared with the other party's legal team. In this instance, the defendant could ask the court to issue a protective order. This type of order requires the parties to keep certain information secret. It helps protect the defendant's trade secrets.

it will be shared with the other party. It can be shared in its native format, which may not be usable by the other party. It also can be shared in a reasonably useful form. If the parties don't specify how the ESI is to be shared, then a party providing ESI must notify the requesting party of the format.

In some instances, it can be hard to produce ESI for various reasons. A party doesn't have to produce ESI if it's not reasonably accessible due to undue burden or costs associated with retrieving the ESI. The party claiming that it can't produce ESI for these reasons bears the burden of proving that production is overly costly or complex.

Usually a court can sanction a party if it destroys evidence during the course of a lawsuit. This is called spoliation of evidence. It occurs when evidence in a lawsuit is inappropriately changed or destroyed. Spoliation sanctions can be severe. The Federal Rules of Civil Procedure recognize that sometimes ESI that is relevant to a case may be destroyed through the normal operations of information technology systems. The Rules provide a safe harbor to parties in these situations. The Rules state that a court may not impose sanctions on a party for failing to produce ESI that is destroyed because of the good-faith operation of information technology systems.

To fall into the safe harbor, the party must show that it took steps to preserve the ESI and acted in good faith. The duty to preserve ESI arises when a party is made aware of a legal claim or is put on notice that litigation is imminent or reasonably anticipated. Sometimes the attorney for a party might issue a preservation notice or litigation hold. These notices tell the party exactly what type of information must be preserved and for how long. Sometimes attorneys for opposing parties will send these types of notices to each other or to witnesses in order to make sure that ESI is preserved.

The American Bar Association has prepared a simple "E-Discovery Survival Guide." You can read the materials at *http://new.abanet.org/sitetation/Lists/Posts/Post.aspx?ID=33*.

After the discovery process ends, the parties either settle their lawsuits or proceed to trial. In late 2008, the U.S. Department of Justice issued a special study on civil trials in state courts. In the jurisdictions responding to the survey, only three percent of civil cases actually went to trial. The other 97 percent of cases are disposed of prior to trial. Either the parties settle the cases or the court dismisses them through other processes.[20]

If a tort case goes to trial, the plaintiff must prove all the elements of his or her claim. He or she must prove their case through a preponderance of the evidence. This is a lower standard of proof than in criminal cases. Burden of proof issues are discussed in Chapter 3.

A civil trial ends with the court or jury's decision on the case. Some civil cases are tried in front of a judge alone. These are called "bench trials." Bench trials are unusual in tort cases. The 2008 U.S. Department of Justice study on civil trials in state courts reported that juries decide nine out of ten tort cases.

Parties may appeal an adverse ruling at the trial court level. Either party may appeal a ruling to a higher court though a number of different procedural rules. These rules are outside of the scope of this book.

Common Tort Law Actions in Cyberspace

Torts are wrongful acts between individuals. Lawyers and commentators have started to use the term "cybertorts" to describe torts arising from Internet communications such as e-mail.[21] Courts are applying traditional tort law principles to areas where communications and personal interactions occur electronically. This section will briefly describe some of the ways that tort law concepts have been applied to online interactions.

Defamation

Defamation is an intentional tort. Defamation occurs when one person speaks or publishes a false statement of fact about another person that injures that person's reputation. Defamation is mentioned briefly in Chapter 2. There are two types of defamation cases. They are:

- **Libel**—Written defamation
- **Slander**—Oral defamation

The distinction between **libel** and **slander** has diminished in recent years, with "defamation" being used generally to refer to both types of cases. Defamation cases in cyberspace involving written communications are considered libel cases.

To prove defamation, a plaintiff must show all of the following:

- That the defendant made a false statement of fact
- That the defendant published the statement to third parties
- That the defendant knew or should have known that the statement was false

The defamatory statement must be more than mere opinion. For instance, in *Hammer v. Amazon.com*, the plaintiff sued Amazon.com for defamation. The plaintiff was a self-published author. An online reviewer gave the plaintiff's book a negative review. Amazon published the review. The plaintiff wanted Amazon to remove the review. Amazon refused. The court ruled that the reviewer's statements were opinion and could not support a defamation claim.[22]

 NOTE

The term **flaming** refers to contentious online debates. They're heated exchanges between online posters. They often occur on online discussion boards. People might be able to use these types of statements to support a defamation case.

The defamatory statement must be published to third parties. The publication requirement is easily satisfied when information is posted on the Internet. In fact, since many people have access to the Internet and materials posted on it, it may be easier for a plaintiff to show publication in an Internet defamation case. Information posted on the Internet may reach an audience more quickly. It also could lead to greater damage to the plaintiff.

Finally, the plaintiff must show that the defendant knew, or should have known, that the statement was false. A plaintiff shows this by presenting evidence that the defendant didn't check facts or the source of a statement.

Some types of statements are so scandalous that a court automatically presumes that defamation has occurred. These types of statements are called defamation *per se*. *Per se* is a Latin phrase that means "by itself." Types of statements considered defamation *per se* include:

- Statements that a person has a loathsome disease
- Statements that a person has committed a crime
- Statements about sexual misconduct or chastity
- Statements about professional impropriety

 NOTE

Traditionally, loathsome diseases were diseases such as leprosy and venereal disease. They are diseases that have great social stigma.

If a defamation case involves these types of statements, the plaintiffs don't have to prove all the defamation elements. They just must prove their damages.

Defamation is considered in context. A court must consider all the facts and circumstances around a case. In a traditional defamation case, the plaintiff can sue both the original maker of the defamatory statement and anyone who republishes the statement. These lines are blurred online. It makes it especially hard to determine where a defamatory statement first appears.

Internet defamation cases continue to rise. In 2009, a woman sued her former high school classmates for allegedly defamatory statements made on a Facebook Web page. The plaintiff also sued Facebook for publishing the statements. The court dismissed Facebook from the case in September 2009.

The court stated that Facebook was immune from liability under a federal law that protects internet service providers (ISPs) from statements made by users of its services. At the time this book was written, the case was still pending against the former class-mates. Information about the case, including the plaintiff's complaint, can be viewed at *http://www.citmedialaw.org/threats/finkel-v-facebook#description.*

The defendant can raise some defenses to a defamation allegation. Truth is an absolute defense to a defamation allegation. A court can't hold a defendant responsible for defamatory statements if the statements were truthful. Another defense is that the defendant acted in good faith. Statements that a defendant makes in connection with judicial or legislative proceedings have immunity from a defamation action. These types of statements are called "privileged" statements.

Internet Service Provider Liability for Torts

Congress enacted the Communications Decency Act in 1996. The U.S. Supreme Court declared many portions of this Act unconstitutional. This is because they infringed on free speech rights. One part of the Act that's still in effect is Section 230.[23]

Section 230 protects interactive computer service providers from liability for the actions of content providers. The act recognizes that "[t]he rapidly developing array of Internet and other interactive computer services available to individual Americans represent an extraordinary advance in the availability of educational and informational resources to our citizens."[24] It also recognized that Americans rely on interactive media for educational and entertainment information. In enacting the policy, Congress sought "to encourage the development of technologies which maximize user control over what information is received by individuals, families, and schools who use the Internet and other interactive computer services."[25]

Under the law, an interactive computer service is any electronic information service or system. It specifically includes a service or system that provides access to the Internet. Courts interpret this definition as broadly as possible. The act states that an interactive computer service provider may not be treated as the "publisher" or "speaker" of content posted by service users. This is a safe harbor for interactive computer service providers. It protects them from legal liability for the actions of service users. The safe harbor concept is discussed in Chapter 9.

Courts have applied this provision quite broadly to many companies who offer services over the Internet such as social networking or bulletin board posting services. For instance, courts have found that America Online, Facebook, and Craigslist are interactive service providers who fall under the section's protection.

ISPs rely on this law to insulate themselves from the actions of their customers. Section 230 specifically preempts state or local laws that would hold ISPs responsible for the acts of content providers.

One problem for online defamation cases is that it's sometimes difficult for a plaintiff to discover the identity of an online poster. This is particularly true if an anonymous poster makes defamatory statements in an online forum. Plaintiffs often have to go to court to get an ISP to turn over identifying information about an anonymous online poster.

A final item to remember is that online tort cases often involve jurisdictional issues as well. State courts can hold out-of-state defendants responsible for their actions only in limited circumstances. Most states have complicated tests for when they can exercise jurisdiction over an out-of-state defendant. These are called "long arm jurisdiction" tests. Lawyers and courts use this term because it describe situations where the "long arm of the law" can pull a defendant into a certain jurisdiction. This is the same type of problem that was discussed in the criminal law section of this chapter. These types of jurisdiction issues sometimes mean that a plaintiff must litigate their case in a state other than the state where they live.

Intentional Infliction of Emotional Distress

Intentional infliction of emotional distress (IIED) is known as the "tort of outrage." This is because it's used to address conduct that is so offensive that a reasonable person would say "Outrageous!" To prove this tort, a plaintiff must show:

- That the defendant acted intentionally or recklessly
- That the defendant's conduct was extreme and outrageous
- That the defendant's conduct caused the plaintiff severe emotional distress

The *Restatement (Second) of the Law of Torts* notes that extreme and outrageous conduct is "beyond all possible bounds of decency and to be regarded as atrocious, and utterly intolerable in a civilized community."[26] Courts have recognized that people have the right to be free from this type of behavior. Even though courts recognize this cause of action, they have held that the defendant's conduct truly must be extreme and outrageous given the circumstances. Mere bad or boorish behavior isn't enough under this tort.

 NOTE

Many states also recognize the tort of negligent infliction of emotional distress. This tort can be harder to prove because one of the elements is that the defendant owed the plaintiff a duty to act in a certain way. There's no duty requirement in IIED cases.

The landmark case recognizing this tort happened in California. In this case, the defendant won a contract for trash collection. A State Rubbish Collectors Association member previously held that contract. The defendant was not a member of the association. The association intimidated the defendant into signing a membership agreement. They threatened to hurt him and destroy his garbage truck. The plaintiffs then sued the defendant to collect on the membership agreement. The defendant argued that he was not liable under the agreement because the association had threatened him and he signed the agreement under duress. He also argued that the plaintiff's actions caused him to become severely ill and miss work.

In ruling on the case, the court said that a person has the right to live his life without "serious, intentional, and unprivileged invasions of emotional and mental tranquility."[27] The court found that the defendant could recover on his IIED claim.

IIED cases can arise through e-mail, comments made on social networking sites, and instant messaging. Since IIED cases involve interactions between a plaintiff and defendant, evidence proving the contents of the electronic communications can be very important. Like defamation cases, in most instances ISPs aren't liable for the actions of content providers that cause an IIED.

Often IIED cases involve situations where a person is using a work e-mail account or Internet access to commit the tortious activity. There are times when employers might be liable for the bad acts of employees. Employer liability for the actions of their employees is discussed briefly in Chapter 2 in the context of workplace privacy. Employers can be liable for their employees' actions when those actions take place within the scope of the employee's job. An employer also must have knowledge of the employee's tortious acts. Courts have been reluctant to hold employers responsible for the cybertorts of employees unless the employer had knowledge of its employee's actions and didn't take steps to stop them.

IIED claims also can involve claims of harassment. Some states recognize harassment as a tort, while most consider it criminal behavior. Some states also have included cyberstalking or online harassment in their criminal harassment laws. For example, Oklahoma and New York have anti-stalking laws that include online harassment as a prohibited activity.[28]

Harassment is similar to IIED in that the harasser intends to cause the plaintiff emotional distress. Harassment can include continuing to communicate with a person when they have asked that the harasser no longer talk to them. It also can include threats made against a person or their loved ones. Harassment also can include offensive sexual remarks and remarks based on characteristics such as race, national origin, religion, and gender.

Like IIED, harassment can very easily take place in the online environment. It can occur via e-mail, postings on social networking Web pages, and postings on other Web pages.

Trespass Torts

Common law recognizes trespass torts. In common law, there are two types of trespass cases: trespass on land and trespass to chattels. "Chattels" means personal property. A trespass to chattels is intentionally interfering with a person's use or possession of personal property. The defendant's use of the plaintiff's personal property must cause an injury or damage. Often this happens when the defendant harms the personal property in some way.

Courts have extended trespass to chattels cases to online situations, such as spam e-mail. The first court case holding spammers responsible for trespass to chattels was in 1997. In that case, an ISP sued a defendant for bypassing the ISP's spam-blocking controls to send spam e-mails to the ISP's customers. The defendant had changed the header information on its spam e-mails so that they could get past the filters.

The ISP argued that the spam e-mails imposed a burden on its system. It also proved that the defendant's spam messages were an intrusion to the ISP's system since they bypassed filtering controls. The U.S. District Court for the Southern District of Ohio found that the defendant's spamming activities did indeed constitute a trespass of that system.[29]

In a trespass to chattels case, the plaintiff must be able to prove that they were injured or harmed. This is the most difficult element to show in online cases. In 2003, the Intel Corporation sued an ex-employee for sending spam e-mails to over 30,000 Intel employees on multiple occasions. The California Supreme Court rejected Intel's trespass claim because it was unable to prove any damages. Intel was not able to show that the thousands of e-mails slowed its servers or caused some sort of adverse effect on its computer systems.[30]

Privacy Violations

Privacy torts are discussed in depth in Chapter 2. The four privacy torts are:

- Intrusion into seclusion
- Portrayal in a false light
- Appropriation of likeness or identity
- Public disclosure of private facts

Courts are beginning to recognize that people have a right of privacy in their electronic equipment and electronic communications. The intrusion into seclusion privacy tort is used most often in this context. For example, a plaintiff may be able to sue a defendant for accessing the plaintiff's private electronic blog without permission. However, the rise of the Internet as a communications and entertainment medium may mean that other privacy torts, such as portrayal in a false light, may grow as well.

A question that is yet to be resolved is whether people have a true right of privacy in their use of the Internet, independent of any tortious or criminal activity. A person's privacy on the Internet is somewhat limited by the logging mechanisms that ISPs and Web pages employ to make sure that systems are operating correctly. Programs used by service providers to track activity for advertising purposes also are threats to privacy. Privacy threats in cyberspace are discussed in Chapter 2.

Tort cases are firmly rooted in state laws. There may be other tort actions that a plaintiff can use to seek redress for harmful activities in cyberspace. If a plaintiff is harmed by actions in cyberspace, and has damages and injuries that they can prove, they will need to review state laws and court cases for appropriate causes of action.

Case Studies and Examples

The following case studies and examples show how the concepts discussed in this chapter are used. These case studies are real-world examples of criminal and tort law issues in cyberspace.

CAN-SPAM Act

The U.S. government first brought criminal charges under the CAN-SPAM Act in April 2004. The U.S. Postal Inspection Service, U.S. Attorneys' office, and Federal Trade Commission were involved in investigating the case.

NOTE

You can read the criminal complaint against the members of Phoenix Avatar at *http://www.ftc.gov/os/2004/04/040429phhoenixavatarcriminalcmplt.pdf*. Notice how the complaint alleges each violation of the CAN-SPAM Act.

In this case, the federal government charged the defendants with sending spam messages to sell phony diet products. The defendants operated under the name Phoenix Avatar, LLC. The defendants hid their identities in spam messages by using corporate and government computer systems and spoofing third party e-mail addresses. They used computers belonging to Ford Motor Company, computers used by the U.S. court system, and the Unisys Corporation to hide their identities. Spam that was undeliverable bounded back to the innocent third party e-mail addresses. Phoenix Avatar sent millions of spam messages this way.

One of the defendants in the case, Daniel Lin, pleaded guilty to violations of the CAN-SPAM Act in January 2006. In June 2006, the court sentenced him to three years in federal prison.

NOTE

You can read the FTC enforcement action documents at *http://www.ftc.gov/os/caselist/0423084/0423084.shtm*.

The Federal Trade Commission filed a civil enforcement action against Phoenix Avatar. The FTC brought the action for violations of both the FTC Act and the CAN-SPAM Act. The FTC Act violations were related to the defendant's sale of the phony diet products.

In March 2005, the FTC settled civil charges against Phoenix Avatar. As part of the settlement, the defendants agreed to pay a $20,000 penalty. They also agreed not to violate the CAN-SPAM Act.

Defamation

The Internet has a number of anonymous gossip Web sites. Juicy Campus was one of the first popular sites. It started in 2007 and closed down in February 2009. It allowed students to post anonymous gossip about events and people at their campuses. Juicy Campus had separate Web pages for different colleges.

Juicy Campus billed itself as a way to promote free speech on college campuses. Among its features, anonymous users could post gossip about other students, read gossip posted by other users, and vote on the "juiciest" pieces of gossip. Students ridiculed or insulted on Juicy Campus had little recourse, as the postings were anonymous. As an ISP, Juicy Campus didn't share the identities of its online posters without a court order.

Since Juicy Campus closed down, other online campus gossip Web sites have grown in popularity. One of the sites that opened when Juicy Campus shut down is CollegeACB. In its own press release, the owner of the Web site wrote: "The College ACB or College Anonymous Confession Board seeks to give students a place to vent, rant, and talk to college peers in an environment free from social constraints and about subjects that might otherwise be taboo."[31]

AutoAdmit is a similar site. It's an online law school discussion board. As on similar gossip Web sites, posts in that forum sometimes can be insulting and offensive. In 2007, two Yale Law School students sued anonymous AutoAdmit posters for defamation. The parties settled the case in 2009. The terms of the settlement were confidential. You can learn more about that case on the Citizen Media Law project Web page at *http://www. citmedialaw.org/threats/autoadmit#description*.

Think about these types of Web sites. How do they promote free speech? Are there occasions on these Web sites where one person's right to free speech infringes upon another person's right to live peacefully?

CHAPTER SUMMARY

This chapter discussed criminal and tort law issues in cyberspace. As part of the discussion, criminal and civil procedure rules were reviewed. Criminal and civil procedure refers to court processes used to conduct trials. Criminal procedure is the process governments use to hold criminals responsible for their actions. Civil procedure is the process individuals use to settle disputes with others.

The chapter also discussed substantive criminal and tort laws applicable to online activities. There are many federal laws that governments can use to help prevent and punish cybercrime. Individuals also can use traditional tort law concepts to seek redress for harm that they experience on the Internet.

KEY CONCEPTS AND TERMS

Actus reus	Libel	Slander
Answer	*Mala in se*	Spam
Complaint	*Mala prohibita*	Statute of limitations
Duty of due care	*Mens rea*	Subject matter jurisdiction
Felonies	Misdemeanor	Tortfeasor
Flaming	Personal jurisdiction	

CHAPTER 12 ASSESSMENT

1. Only the federal government prosecutes felonies.

  A. True
  B. False

2. Provide a brief definition of "crime."

3. What is *mala in se?*

  A. Conduct that a society declares is inherently wrong
  B. Conduct that society prohibits
  C. A person's criminal intent
  D. A criminal act
  E. None of the above

4. What element(s) must a government prove to show a crime has been committed?

  A. *Mens rea*
  B. *Mala prohibita*
  C. *Actus rea*
  D. A and B only
  E. A and C only

5. What type of jurisdictional issue is a concern in a cybercrime case?

  A. Original jurisdiction
  B. Subject matter jurisdiction
  C. Personal jurisdiction
  D. Appellate jurisdiction
  E. None of the above

6. The _____ guarantees a defendant the right to a speedy trial.

7. The Computer Fraud and Abuse Act applies to any unauthorized access of a computer.

  A. True
  B. False

8. Which federal laws can be used to prosecute phishing scams?

  A. The Computer Fraud and Abuse Act
  B. The Patriot Act
  C. The CAN-SPAM Act
  D. All of the above
  E. A and C only

9. Cybertorts are most likely which type of tort?

  A. Intentional torts
  B. Negligent torts
  C. Strict liability torts
  D. Crimes
  E. None of the above

10. To prove an intentional infliction of emotional distress tort, a plaintiff must show that the defendant's conduct is _____.

11. Internet service providers often have tort immunity for the actions of content providers.

  A. True
  B. False

12. What is the time period during which a plaintiff must begin their lawsuit?

  A. Statute of frauds
  B. Statute on liability
  C. Statute of limitations
  D. Pleadings statute
  E. None of the above

13. What is a defense to a defamation case?

  A. Comparative negligence
  B. Contributory negligence
  C. Assumption of risk
  D. The truth
  E. None of the above

14. The two types of defamation cases are _____.

15. What type of document must a plaintiff file to begin a civil lawsuit?

  A. Answer
  B. Discovery
  C. Motion for Summary Judgment
  D. Counter-claim
  E. Complaint

ENDNOTES

1. Wisconsin Statutes, sec. 940.01 (2009).

2. Wisconsin Statutes, sec. 940.02.

3. Alaska Statutes, title 12, sec. 12.05.010 (2009).

4. U.S. Department of Justice, Bureau of Justice Statistics, "Felony Sentences in State Courts, 2006-Statistical Tables," December 2009, *http://bjs.ojp.usdoj.gov/content/pub/pdf/fssc06st.pdf* (accessed April 2, 2010).

5. U.S. Code, Vol. 18, sec. 1030 (2006).

6. Internet Crime Complaint Center, "2009 Annual Report on Internet Crime Fraud," March 12, 2010, *http://www.ic3.gov/media/annualreport/2009_IC3Report.pdf* (accessed April 2, 2010).

7. U.S. Code, Vol. 18, sec. 1029.

8. U.S. Code, Vol. 18, sec. 1028.

9. U.S. Code, Vol. 18, sec. 2510.

10. U.S. Code, Vol. 18, sec. 3121.

11. U.S. Code, Vol. 18, sec. 2701.

12. U.S. Code, Vol. 15, sec. 7701; U.S. Code, Vol. 18, sec. 1037.

13. U.S. Code, Vol. 15, sec. 1125(d).

14. *Palsgraf v. Long Island Railroad,* 162 NE 99 (N.Y. 1928).

15. Federal Rules of Civil Procedure, Rule 8.

16. Indiana Code, 34-11-2-4.

17. Montana Code Annotated, 27-2-204(3).

18. Federal Rules of Civil Procedure, Rule 12.

19. *Zubulake v. UBS Warburg, LLC,* 2004 WL 1620866 (SD NY July 20, 2004). This was the final E-discovery decision handed down in the *Zubulake* case.

20. U.S. Department of Justice, Bureau of Justice Statistics, "Civil Bench and Jury Trials in State Courts, 2005, December 18, 2008, *http://bjs.ojp.usdoj.gov/content/pub/pdf/cbjtsc05.pdf* (accessed April 4, 2010).

21. Rustad, Michael L. *Internet Law.* St. Paul, MN: Thomson Reuters, 2009, page 143.

22. *Hammer v. Amazon.com,* 392 F. Supp. 2d 423 (E.D.N.Y 2005).

23. U.S. Code, Vol. 47, sec. 230.

24. U.S. Code, Vol. 47, sec. 230(a)(1).

25. U.S. Code, Vol. 47, sec. 230(b)(3).

26. *Restatement (Second) of the Law of Torts,* sec. 46, cmt. d.

27. *State Rubbish Collectors Association v. Siliznoff,* 240 P.2d. 282 (Ca. 1952).

28. New York Penal Code, Ch. 40, sec. 240.30; Oklahoma Statutes, Title 21, sec. 1173.

29. *CompuServe, Inc. v. Cyber Promotions, Inc.,* 962 F. Supp. 1015 (S.D. Ohio 1997).

30. Intel Corp v. Hamidi, 71 P.3d 296 (Ca. 2003).

31. CollegeACB, "College ACB Press Release," February 5, 2009, *http://collegeacb.blogspot.com/2009/02/collegeacb-press-release.html* (accessed April 7, 2010).

PART THREE

Security and Privacy in Organizations

Information Security Governance

THE CHAPTER DISCUSSES INFORMATION SECURITY GOVERNANCE. It also discusses information security policies. An organization's governance structure is an important part of its information security program. Governance focuses on the structure used to protect resources and data. This structure must provide security and support business needs. Strong governance helps create strong security programs.

Organizations use policies, standards, guidelines, and procedures to create their security program. These documents help guide employee "conduct. They're tools that organizations use in many ways. They make sure that information technology resources are secured. They also help protect an organization from legal liability.

Chapter 13 Topics

This chapter covers the following topics and concepts:

- What information security governance is
- What information security governance documents are
- What recommended information security policies are
- What some case studies and examples are

Chapter 13 Goals

When you complete this chapter, you will be able to:

- Describe the key concepts and terms associated with information security governance
- Describe the goals of different information security governance documents
- Describe the different types of policies that can be used to govern information security

A zettabyte is 1 billion terabytes. To put things in perspective, the U.S. Library of Congress has collected almost 167 terabytes of data in its Web archive project. The Web archive project is collecting and preserving snapshots of the world's Web pages. These Web pages help show the world's cultural and intellectual heritage. You can learn about that project at *http://www.loc.gov/webarchiving*.

What Is Information Security Governance?

The University of California Global Information Industry Center tries to measure information use in the United States. It defines "information" as any flow of data delivered to people. It can be in any form. The center reported that Americans consumed 3.6 zettabytes of information in 2008.[1] Our use of information is growing. For businesses, data is a valuable asset.

An organization must find ways to protect its data. It also must make sure that it can be used for business reasons. This balance is key to an organization's success. Failing to strike the right balance can harm the organization's goals. Consider the following:

- An organization can't market its products without access to customer lists.
- Customers may complain about incorrect electronic data.
- If confidential data is disclosed, an organization faces embarrassment.

An organization's executive management team is responsible for governing the organization. This means it's also responsible for information security governance. **Information security governance (ISG)** is the executive management team's responsibility to protect an organization's information assets. ISG makes protecting information assets a business decision. To do this an organization must align its information security goals to its business needs. ISG moves information security beyond technical decisions. It makes security a strategic decision.

Organizations use ISG to enhance their business. ISG makes sure that information security goals are used to meet business goals. This means that the organization uses the security goals of confidentiality, integrity, and availability in a way that makes sense for the business. ISG also makes sure that there's proper accountability and oversight for meeting these goals. The CIA triad appears in Figure 13-1.

> **NOTE**
> The security goals of confidentiality, integrity, and availability are called the CIA triad or the A-I-C triad. This term is discussed in Chapter 1.

FIGURE 13-1

The CIA triad.

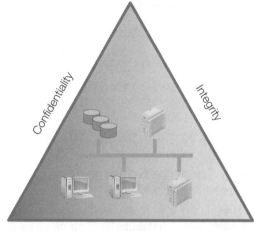

Information Security Governance Planning

Information security governance refers to executive management's responsibility to provide strategic direction, oversight, and accountability for the security of its data and information technology (IT) resources. Their main duty is to make sure that information security strategy supports business goals.

A common business goal is to make a profit. The organization must take into account many factors that affect this goal. Business drivers are forces that influence the organization's business goals. They can be internal or external. They include the people, processes, and trends.

An organization must balance business drivers to meet their goals. They do this during the business planning process. There are three types of business planning. They are:

- **Strategic planning**—This is long-term planning. It focuses on preparing new approaches and planning for new technologies. It lays the groundwork for new business directions. ISG uses strategic planning to support business objectives.

- **Tactical planning**—This is short- to medium-term planning. It allows an organization to be responsive to market conditions. It allows them to take advantage of short-term or unexpected opportunities. Tactical plans are usually six months or less in length.

- **Operational planning**—This is day-to-day planning. It focuses on the normal operations of an organization. It's responsive to daily issues.

Figure 13-2 illustrates the different types of business planning.

The organization's executive management team carries out strategic planning. This is when they determine the business's goals. Once it determines its business goals, it must figure out how information security can support these goals. It will use the same types of planning strategies to think about information security.

This is ISG planning. When planning for information security, the organization must think about:

- **Information needs**—The organization must ask how it uses data to meet its business goals. It must then think about how information security can support this. For instance, if an organization conducts most of its business on the Internet, it must think about availability and integrity. Its IT systems must hold accurate data and be ready to conduct business.

- **Regulatory requirements**—The organization must know its regulatory landscape. It must know the data protection laws that it must follow. Many of these laws are discussed in this book. Often these laws focus on protecting the confidentiality of certain types of data.

- **Risk management**—The organization must adopt a risk management approach. It must know the information security risks that it faces. It also must decide how it will respond to risk. Risk analysis is discussed in Chapter 14.

- **Security failures**—The organization must think about information security failures. It must consider the impact of a security breach, malware-infected IT resources, or unavailable data. There may be many negative impacts of an information security failure. These include lawsuits and breach notification costs. An organization will certainly lose customers after an information security incident. This affects its bottom line.

 NOTE

A 2007 survey found that companies spend about $268,000 to notify customers if they experience a data breach.[2]

An organization answers these questions to determine ISG strategic direction. It makes sure that its information security goals support its business objectives. This is the role of ISG.

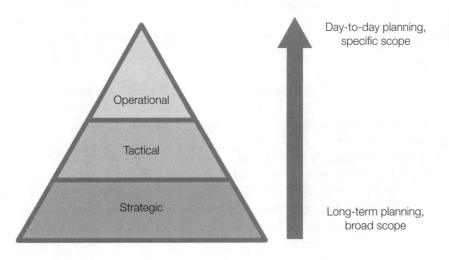

Day-to-day planning, specific scope

Long-term planning, broad scope

FIGURE 13-2

Business planning hierarchy.

Operational

Tactical

Strategic

13

Information Security Governance

Common Information Security Governance Roles

It's important to know who makes information security decisions. These decisions can be strategic, tactical, or operational. Not every organization has the same structure. This section reviews ISG roles. You will be more likely to find the roles described here in larger organizations. Smaller organizations may not fill all of these roles. They may combine many duties within one role. Non-profit and educational organizations tend to have structures with shared responsibilities.

Many different roles can make decisions about information security. The ISG roles are:

- Board of directors
- Chief information officer
- Chief information security officer
- Information security managers

The **board of directors (BOD)** runs an organization. It's an organization's top governance group. A board of directors is required by law to act with due care. It must make all of its decisions in the best interests of the organization. The BOD plans an organization's strategic direction. It also determines business goals. It makes sure that an organization uses its resources properly to meet these goals. Finally, it makes sure that an organization acts legally.

The BOD determines how information security supports business goals. It does this through strategic planning. The BOD issues high-level information security policies. It delegates tactical and operational activities to other senior managers. The main duty of a BOD is governance.

 NOTE

In March 2009, U.S. President Barak Obama appointed the first federal CIO. The federal CIO is responsible for government IT spending.

The **chief information officer (CIO)** is the organization's senior IT official. The CIO focuses on strategic IT issues. The CIO defines an organization's IT mission. It's the CIO's job to keep the BOD advised about IT issues. CIOs aren't usually involved in the day-to-day IT operations. Their duties are strategic and tactical in nature. They often delegate responsibility for information security management (ISM) to a CISO.

A CIO isn't the same as a **chief technology officer (CTO)**. A CIO is responsible for a company's internal IT systems. CIOs focus on the systems used to run the organization's business. A CIO is internally focused. A CTO develops a company's technology products. A CTO is externally focused.

The **chief information security officer (CISO)** is the organization's senior information security official. The role of the CISO is relatively new. It continues to evolve. Depending on an organization's structure, the CISO might report to the CIO. A CISO also could report to the organization's chief financial officer. CISOs are responsible for an organization's information security strategy. They also are very involved in tactical planning. They aren't generally involved in daily IT operations.

The CISO makes sure that the CIO and BOD understand information security threats. The CISO may make information security policy suggestions to the BOD. A CISO also helps determine information security safeguards. He or she delegates functional and operational tasks to other managers.

Information security managers are responsible for the functional management of an organization's information security program. They manage the operational activities. They implement the controls specified by the CISO. These managers might also:

- Create information security standards, guidelines, and procedure
- Participate in risk assessments
- Manage the security infrastructure

These roles work together. The higher-level roles make governance decisions. The lower-level roles are responsible for information security management.

Information Security Governance and Management

Information security governance and **information security management** aren't the same thing. The terms are often used interchangeably. The distinction is subtle. You should keep in mind that sometimes the difference isn't clear. Many organizations use one or both terms to refer to all ISG and ISM activities. Many activities have both ISG and ISM elements.

ISG makes sure that security is used to support business goals. It's handled by the BOD, CIO, and CISO. It offers a process for oversight and accountability. It makes sure that there's a structure in place to direct information security activities.

ISM is the visible part of ISG activities. It makes sure that ISG policies are put into practice. It's the organization's day-to-day security operations. Table 13-1 compares ISG and ISM.

ISM maintains the organization's overall security posture. ISG states what that posture must be.

TABLE 13-1 Comparison of information security governance and information security management.

INFORMATION SECURITY GOVERNANCE	INFORMATION SECURITY MANAGEMENT
Strategic and tactical	Tactical and operational
Creates policies and strategy	Implements policies and strategy
Ultimate compliance authority and oversight	Day-to-day management and authority
BOD, CIO, CISO	Information security managers (with help from CIO and CISO)

13

Information Security Governance

Creating an Information Security Governance Program

There are many resources available to help organizations create an ISG program. The International Organization for Standardization (ISO) and International Electrotechnical Commission (IEC) has created a comprehensive standard to help guide this process.[3] The standard uses the term ISM system to refer to both ISG and ISM activities.

The standard helps organizations create an ISM system. It uses a risk-based approach. It reviews how to operate, monitor, review, maintain, and improve the ISM system. It walks though each step. It discusses the processes that an organization must consider at each step.

Any organization can use this standard. It's designed to be flexible to meet an organization's needs. It can be especially helpful to organizations that have never managed information security on a strategic level. It's designed to work with the ISO/IEC security controls standard discussed in Chapter 1.

Organizations must review their ISM systems. They need to know if their ISM controls are improving security. To do this, they must measure their effectiveness. The ISO/IEC has guidance on this as well. That document is titled "ISO/IEC 27004:2009 Information Technology—Security Techniques—Information Security Management—Measurement."

This standard helps organizations review their ISM system. It helps organizations create control measurements. It also helps them analyze the measurements. The process helps organizations decide if their policies or controls need to be changed.

Information Security Governance in the Federal Government

The Federal Information Security Management Act (FISMA) is discussed in Chapter 8. Congress created FISMA to protect federal data and IT resources. U.S. federal agencies must comply with it. Federal agencies fall under the executive branch of the U.S. government. They report to the President of the United States.

FISMA requires each federal agency to develop an information security program. Each agency must name a CISO to lead the program. The program must assess the agency's information security risk. It must include plans to reduce that risk. It also must provide security awareness and training activities to employees.

Agencies must report on their FISMA compliance progress each year. They send these reports to the Government Accountability Office (GAO).

 NOTE

You can view the GAO high-risk Web site at *http://www.gao.gov/highrisk/*.

Information security is a high priority for the federal government. Since 1997, the GAO has listed information security on its list of high-risk areas. Issues are high-risk if they're vulnerable to fraud, waste, abuse, or mismanagement. The GAO publishes the list every two years.

Information Security Governance Documents

An organization's ISG documents form the basis of its information security program. They document the organization's commitment to information security. They're used to address:

- The organization's information security goals
- How the organization protects its own data
- How the organization protects the data of others
- Compliance with legal and regulatory requirements
- Employee information security responsibilities
- Consequences for failing to meet responsibilities

Organizations use policies, standards, guidelines, and procedures to create their security program. These documents are discussed briefly in Chapter 1. They work together to support information security goals. A formal policy is the highest-level governance document. Standards are the next level. Then procedures. Guidelines provide security advice. The documents move from the general (policies) to the more specific (procedure). Figure 13-3 shows how these documents work together.

In this book, these documents are collectively referred to as "ISG documents" or "policies." You should keep in mind that the term "policies" is often used in a generic way. It's used to describe the entire suite of ISG documents. It will be clear from the text when the term is used in the generic way.

> **NOTE**
> ISG documents are administrative safeguards. These safeguards are discussed in Chapter 1.

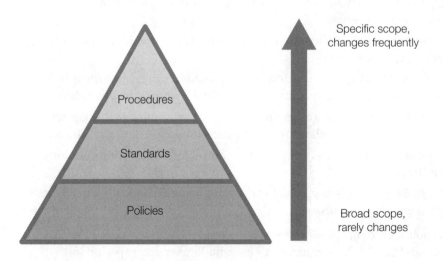

Specific scope, changes frequently

Procedures

Standards

Policies

Broad scope, rarely changes

FIGURE 13-3

Information security governance documents.

Policies

A formal **policy** is executive management's high-level statement of information security direction and goals. They're the top level of governance documents. They help minimize risk by laying out the organization's information security strategy. High-level policies are approved by an organization's BOD.

The BOD uses policies to set forth its information security goals. They also state compliance expectations. Not all organizations will have the same types of high-level policies. They're unique to each organization. Each organization develops policies by reviewing its regulatory landscape. They also must take into account the size and complexity of the organization and its IT systems. They also think about how information security can be used to meet business goals.

Policies must be drafted with care. Policy elements vary among organizations. There are some common elements to all policies. They include:

- **Policy statement**—States expected behavior, actions, or outcomes. It's a clear statement of permitted or forbidden actions.
- **Policy exclusions**—Lists situations or people who aren't covered by the policy. For the most part, there shouldn't be many exclusions in a high-level policy.
- **Policy rationale**—States the reason why the policy exists. This includes the legal or regulatory reasons for the policy. A policy might be drafted in response to information security threats.
- **Policy definitions**—Defines terms that have special meaning. Terms with common definitions don't need to be defined.
- **Who is affected by the policy**—States the people, units, or departments affected by the policy. In a high-level policy, this usually is all of the organization's employees.
- **Who must follow the policy**—Lists who must follow the policy as part of their job responsibilities.
- **Compliance language**—States how the organization will enforce the policy. It also states what happens to units and employees who fail to follow the policy.
- **Related documents**—Lists other documents that are related to the policy. Standards or procedures that support the policy should be listed in this section.
- **Policy contact**—Lists the person who is responsible for answering questions about the policy.
- **Policy history**—Lists historical data about the policy. This section should list revision and review dates.

High-level policies are concise. They're tightly worded. This is so that they're easy to understand. They list the organization's information security expectations. They don't include explanations about how to meet those expectations. Supporting documents provide that detail. Supporting documents are standards, guidelines, and procedures.

Policy documents tend to go through a lengthy development and review process. The process can be very time consuming. This is because they're high-level governance documents from executive management. They have a broad scope and address the whole organization.

Policies are rarely changed. This is because they contain language that sets forth general expectations. The broad goals stated in a policy shouldn't need to be changed often. Standards and procedures are used to provide flexibility. They're easier to change. An organization can easily update these documents in response to changing technology conditions.

Standards

Standards support high-level policies. They're just below policies in the ISG documents hierarchy. They state the activities and actions needed to meet policy goals. Standards are more specific than policies. Standards may require employees to take (or refrain from) certain actions. Standards often state a minimum level of behavior or actions that must be met to comply with a policy. This is called a **baseline**.

Standards are technology neutral. They don't refer to specific technologies or products. Instead, they refer to the safeguards and controls an organization should use to protect data and IT resources.

A number of different ISG levels can create standards. They're usually created at the CIO or CISO level. An organization's BOD isn't usually involved in creating standards. An organization usually develops standards with input from information security managers. This is because they have overall organizational responsibility for implementing information security. They're the subject matter experts in what it will take to implement the standard.

Procedures

Procedures are the lowest level of ISG documents. They're step-by-step checklists. They explain "how" to meet security goals. Organizations often tailor their procedures to a certain type of technology. They also can be limited to the activities of specific departments or end users.

Procedures usually only address single tasks. They're designed to be flexible. They change as technology changes.

Information security managers usually create procedure. Sometimes a CIO or CISO may review procedures. For the most part, however, they're department- or technology-specific documents.

Governance Documents Work Together

Policies, standards, and procedures work together to protect information security. Policies set forth the general expectation. Standards further define those expectations. Procedures tell end users how to comply with the expectation. An example might work as follows:

Policy Statement: All employee passwords to the organization's IT resources must be strong passwords.

Standard Statement: All strong passwords must have at least eight characters and have at least one number and one letter.

Procedural Statement: To change a user account password in the Microsoft Windows 7 operating system, you must do the following:

1. Open the Control Panel.
2. Double-click on User Accounts.
3. Click on Change Your Password.
4. In the Current Password text box, enter your current password.
5. In the New Password text box, enter your new password. Be sure to follow the requirements stated in the Password Standards document.
6. In the Confirm New Password text box, enter your new password again.
7. In the Type a Password Hint text box, enter a word or a phrase that can help you remember your password. Do not enter the password itself.
8. Click on Change Password.

In this example, an employee knows what the expectation is ("a strong password"), how the expectation is defined ("a strong password is eight characters and has at least one number and one letter"), and how to meet the expectation ("checklist for changing a Windows 7 account password").

Guidelines

Guidelines are the most flexible type of ISG document. Organizations can issue guidelines for a number of reasons. They issue guidelines to:

- Encourage employees to adopt good information security practices
- Educate employees about security threats and how to respond to them
- Encourage employees to take action in areas that the organization can't

An organization can use guidelines to give information security advice. They can recommend actions that an employee can apply on their own. The guidelines help employees adopt behaviors that improve information security. Sometimes they address specific kinds of employee behavior. They also might address a specific security issue. For example, an organization might create a guideline to help employees learn how to avoid social engineering attacks.

Organizations might issue guidelines to address issues that they can't control through technical measures. This is where the organization needs its employees to help it protect IT resources. They hope that they can encourage employees to take individual action.

For example, an organization may allow its employees to access its IT systems from home. It allows this because it increases productivity. It allows employees to work from home on days when they otherwise would not be working. (For example, if a parent stays home to care for a sick child.) However, the organization must safeguard its IT resources from security threats introduced by this activity. One security threat is malware that might be on an employee's home computer.

The organization has no real way to make employees use good security practices at home. It has no real authority to require employees to protect their home computers. To encourage employees to secure their home computers, the organization can issue a guideline. The guideline outlines security safeguards that employees can use at home. Following the guideline benefits employees. This is because it helps them secure their own personal data. It also helps protect the organization's IT resources. Both the employee's computer and the organization's IT resources are protected. It's a winning situation for everyone.

Creating Information Security Policies

Each type of ISG document has a different role and focus. They might be directed at different audiences. They might address similar issues from different standpoints. However, they do share some similarities. These similarities include:

- They must be easy to understand.
- They must have a well-defined scope.
- They must be regularly reviewed.
- They must be communicated to all employees.

First, the documents must be easy to read. All employees must be able to understand them. Even if the subject matter deals with legal issues, the document itself should be free from legalese. The documents shouldn't use technical jargon. The only time it's OK is when it's needed to help employees know their responsibilities. These documents must be understandable. This makes sure that employees can follow them.

Second, ISG documents must have a clear scope. They must clearly address a specific aspect of the organization's security program. Employees shouldn't have to consult many high-level documents to determine the organization's stance on a single issue.

Third, the organization must regularly review its ISG documents. Information security doesn't exist in a vacuum. Risks change. Laws change. Technology changes. An organization must respond to these changes in their security program. To do this, they must review their ISG documents on a regular basis to make sure that they're current.

Legalese Versus Plain Language

"Legalese" is an unflattering term used to describe legal writing. Legalese is language that uses too many legal phrases. It uses many Latin terms. It usually has long sentences with many commas. It's dense and hard to read. Lawyers are needed to translate documents written in legalese.

There's a growing trend in the legal profession to write documents in "plain language." This means that documents are written in the language that people use when they speak. This helps make documents more understandable. People can understand these documents faster. They also are less likely to misunderstand them.

The trend is to use plain language to write formal documents. However, legalese appears in high-level policies on a regular basis. This is because these documents are formal governance documents. An organization's legal counsel often writes them.

Legalese can make it hard to understand some very simple concepts. This is frustrating for people who need to follow the policies. Some examples of legalese and plain language follow. Are there other ways that you can make these policy statements easier to read?

Example 1—Consent

Legalese: All users of the organization's information technology resources, as a condition to the use of such resources, specifically consent to the general rights of the organization as specified herein.

Plain Language: All users of the organization's IT resources agree to the terms of this policy.

Example 2—Least Privilege

Legalese: Any access permitted hereunder shall be the minimum access required in order to protect the organization's interests.

Plain Language: Access to IT resources is limited to the minimum amount needed.

Example 3—Warranties

Legalese: The organization makes no warranties of any kind with respect to the organization's information technology resources it provides. The organization will not be responsible for damages resulting from the use of organization's information technology resources, including, but not limited to, loss of data resulting from delays, non-deliveries, missed deliveries, service interruptions caused by the negligence of an organization employee, or by any user's error or omissions. The organization specifically denies any responsibility for the accuracy or quality of information obtained through organization's information technology resources.

Plain Language: The organization provides IT resources "as is." The organization makes no promises about service level or data accuracy. The organization isn't responsible for errors. Use of IT resources is at a user's own risk.

Finally, an organization must communicate the ISG documents to its employees. Employees can't follow policies that they don't know about. Good communication makes sure that employees view ISG documents as business enablers. Organizations can communicate ISG documents to employees in a number of ways. They can use newsletters, in-person and online training, or company-wide e-mail messages.

Policy Development Process

Organizations should create a structured ISG document development process. A formal process gives many areas the opportunity to comment on a policy. This is very important for high-level policies that apply to the whole organization. A formal process also makes sure that final policies are communicated to employees. It also provides organizations with a way to make sure that policies are reviewed regularly.

In general, a policy development process should include the following steps:

1. Development
2. Stakeholder review
3. Management approval
4. Communication to employees
5. Documentation of compliance or exceptions
6. Continued awareness activities
7. Maintenance and review

The need for a new ISG document is determined in the development phase. The BOD, CIO, or CISO might decide that there's a need for a high-level policy. An information security department might suggest that there's a need for a new lower-level document. The idea for a new ISG document really can come from anywhere in an organization. This section focuses on how high-level policies are created. However, the same development process is recommended for other ISG documents as well.

Once a policy need is identified, the BOD must determine the goals of the policy. To do this, it reviews a number of areas. It looks at its use of IT resources. It reviews the data that it's legally required to protect. It considers its business objectives. An organization's CIO or CISO will give advice about information security issues. The BOD also might consider how other companies in the same industry approach a certain type of issue. After this review, the BOD establishes the policy goals.

An organization must take care when it drafts high-level policies. It must make sure that a new high-level policy doesn't conflict with any previously issued policy. Stakeholders must review the draft when it's finished.

FYI

In drafting an ISG document, it's important to be consistent. A writer should use consistent grammar, punctuation, and format. This makes the document more readable. This makes it easier for employees to understand.

At the next step, stakeholders review the ISG draft documents. **Stakeholders** are interested parties. They're employees and departments that will be affected by the new policy. They also may be subject matter experts in the underlying policy subject matter. IT resource managers also will review the document at this point. They do this to make sure that they can implement technical controls to meet the policy.

This also is the step where legal counsel, risk management, and audit will review the document. They make sure that the document meets the organization's regulatory needs. Risk management and audit departments will want to make sure that they can measure policy compliance. Legal counsel makes sure that the document helps protect the organization from legal liability. The organization may revise the policy many times during this step.

The policy must be signed when it's in final form. The BOD must always review and sign high-level information security policies. Their support is crucial for a successful information security program. They don't always sign lower-level documents. The executive with authority over certain tasks may sign lower-level documents. For example, a CIO or CISO might sign standards or guidelines. Departmental managers and supervisors sign procedures for their specific areas.

The next step is the communication step. It's one of the most critical steps in the development process. Communication is necessary to make sure that all employees know about the new policy. It helps employees know where to find resources to follow the policy. Organizations can communicate new policies in a number of different ways. Internal newsletters, memos, and company-wide e-mails can all be used to inform employees about a new policy.

As part of the process, an organization must measure policy compliance. It must know how departments act to meet policy requirements. It also must note any exceptions to compliance. An organization can show compliance by documenting the following:

NOTE

Compliance is an ongoing process. Organizations must continuously monitor compliance.

- When the ISG document was approved
- How and when it was communicated to employees
- Actions departments took to meet the responsibilities stated in the ISG document
- Deviations from the requirements in the ISG document

Sometimes departments might request an exception to a policy. They can request an exception for a number of reasons. For example, a policy might state a technical control that an IT system can't meet.

Organizations must have a formal way to review policy exception requests. The BOD must review, approve, and document each high-level policy exception request. A BOD might assign this role to an upper management official such as a CIO or CISO. Exception requests from standards and procedures might be handled by the CIO or CISO as well.

An organization must carefully consider exception requests. This is because every policy exception weakens the organization's security posture. There are two main reasons to grant a policy exception request. The first is when following the policy negatively affects the organization's business objectives. This might happen when a policy control interferes with a critical business process.

The second reason to approve an exception request is when the cost to comply with the policy is more than the cost of noncompliance. For example, an organization may grant an exception request if a particular IT resource is incapable of technically meeting a policy requirement. It might do this if buying new equipment is too expensive. In those cases, the organization still must implement controls to protect the IT resource. The policy exception request must document how an area will use compensating controls to meet the spirit of the policy.

The development process must continually educate employees about policy compliance. Ongoing security training and awareness is required to keep employees aware of their responsibilities. An organization must build regular policy awareness activities into its day-to-day routine. They can be included in other training programs, such as workplace safety programs.

Finally, an organization must review its ISG documents on a regular schedule. They must make sure the documents continue to reflect business and information security goals. Sometimes internal or external factors change so much that an organization must change its policies. At this point, it can either update its policy or withdraw it and create a new one. A BOD demonstrates due diligence and reasonable care when it regularly reviews its policies. Figure 13-4 shows the policy development process.

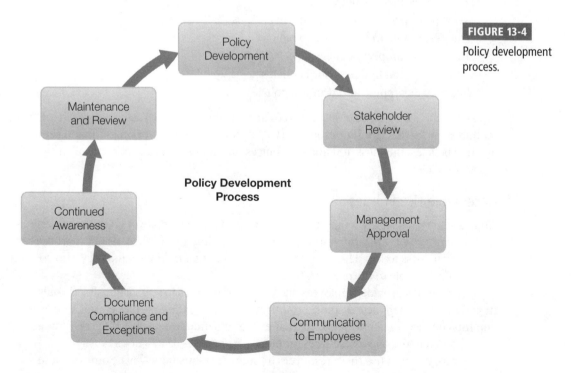

FIGURE 13-4

Policy development process.

An organization can adjust the development process if necessary. For example, it might need to create a new policy to respond to a new law. It can step that policy through the development process quickly. It can then go back and review the document once the urgent regulatory need has passed.

The process can be shortened for some ISG documents. Standards and procedures that apply to one department only may go through a shortened process. This is because there may not be as many people who need to comment on them.

An organization uses ISG documents to support its business objectives and information security goals. These policies form the basis of an information security program. They also set the tone for a culture of information security awareness.

Recommended Information Security Policies

Information security policies will vary across organizations. This is because each organization is different. They have different business goals. Their security needs aren't the same. The list of information security issues to address in a policy is endless.

All organizations face some basic security issues. They should create policies to address these issues. The basic policies that organizations should consider include:

- Acceptable use policies
- Anti-harassment policies
- Workplace privacy and monitoring policies
- Data retention and destruction policies
- Intellectual property policies
- Authentication and password policies
- Security awareness and training policies

These policies address use of IT resources and the data in those resources. Often information security and human resources (HR) departments will work together on some of these policies. Business and auditing offices might help administer some of these types of policies.

Acceptable Use Policies

An organization uses an **acceptable use policy (AUP)** to tell employees how to properly use its IT resources. Organizations should consider drafting an AUP because IT resources are valuable business assets. They're often expensive to buy and maintain. They also contain data that's valuable to the organization.

Organizations provide employees access to IT resources to support business goals. In addition to system access, most organizations give their employees e-mail accounts and Internet access. Some also give their executives mobile devices. While employees are supposed to use these resources for business purposes, that's not always the case. Employees can use these resources in many non-business ways. Some of these uses include:

- Sending and receiving personal e-mails at a work e-mail address
- Chain mail and hoax e-mail messages sent around the office
- Non-business Internet use
- Online shopping
- Accessing social networking sites during work hours
- Downloading free software (or pirated software) for non-business use
- File sharing throughout a workplace or over the Internet

Improper use of an organization's IT resources can be costly. It can result in information security compromises. It can introduce malware onto IT systems. An organization might be legally responsible for an employee's misuse of IT resources in some instances. Non-business use of IT resources can distract employees. It can lead to lost productivity.

An AUP can help prevent some of these issues. An AUP states a code of conduct. It states permitted uses of IT resources. It also lists prohibited actions. Finally, it states the consequences for violating the acceptable use rules. An AUP is one of the most important information security policy documents. It can help prevent a wide range of activities that could harm the organization's IT resources.

An AUP can address a number of concerns. They include personnel, legal, and information security issues. HR departments like AUPs because they help promote workplace productivity. They also want to make sure that employees aren't accessing or sharing objectionable electronic materials. Such behavior can cause severe disruptions in the workplace. In some instances, it also can subject the organization to liability for its employees' actions. For instance, an employer can be held responsible in some cases where an employee is using IT resources to harass other individuals. AUPs give HR departments a policy reason to terminate employees who use IT resources inappropriately.

13

Information Security
Governance

Would an AUP Help in This Situation?

The "I Love You" or "Love Bug" worm was discovered in May 2000. At the time, it was thought to be one of the largest and most destructive computer worms ever. It spread via e-mail messages with "ILOVEYOU" in the subject line. The messages included an attachment disguised as a love letter. Once a user opened the attachment (and who wouldn't open a love letter?), the worm infected the user's computer. It sent itself to everyone in the user's e-mail address book. It destroyed computer files. It also searched for sensitive information and sent it back to its creator.

At one point, industry experts estimated that the worm affected computers at more than 80 percent of U.S. businesses. Could an information security policy have helped stop the spread of the worm? What if an AUP stated that employees could not open e-mail attachments that they were not expecting? What if the consequence for opening that type of attachment included job termination? Would that have helped in this case?

Legal departments use AUPs to help an organization meet regulatory responsibilities. They also use them to help limit an organization's legal liability. For instance, an AUP can state that employees may not use unlicensed software on their computers. This helps protect the organization from copyright infringement claims. An organization protects itself in these cases by pointing to its AUP and showing that the employee violated it. If the AUP forbids the action, the legal department has evidence that the employee acted in violation of company rules. This helps create a legal defense.

Information security departments also are interested in making sure that an organization has a well-written AUP. Improper use of IT resources can have information security consequences. Employees surfing the Internet, exchanging personal e-mails, or visiting social networking sites are consuming network bandwidth. They may be using valuable network storage space for non-business content.

Their activities also could introduce malware onto the organizations IT systems. Malware could compromise data and have wide-ranging consequences. At a minimum, productivity is hampered while IT departments work to remove the malware. At its worst, the malware could transmit sensitive organizational information to external attackers. It also could expose personal indentifying information. That could trigger state breach notification laws.

AUPs also address internal employee threats. Employees can potentially use their access to IT resources to snoop or spy on the organization. They also could spy on other employees. Disgruntled employees could use their access to sabotage IT resources and data. An AUP specifically prohibits these actions. An organization can fire an employee for violating an AUP.

AUP Terms

An organization protects against these concerns by having a written AUP. Some general terms that you see in AUPs include:

- IT resources are provided for business use only.
- Employees must use IT resources and data on them for business purposes only.
- Employees must not tamper with IT resources or data on those resources.
- Employees should not access any data they don't have a business reason to see.
- No personal use of organizational IT resources is allowed.
- Don't use IT resources to circumvent security measures.
- IT resources may be monitored to ensure employee compliance.
- Use of IT resources is evidence of the employee's consent to the terms of the AUP.

AUPs may have terms about a particular type of IT resource, such as e-mail or Internet use. Some organizations include these terms in one broad AUP. Other organizations may create a separate AUP for each type of technology. Common e-mail and Internet AUP terms include:

- Don't send e-mail with sensitive organization information to external recipients.
- Don't send e-mail with sensitive organization information to internal recipients unless they have a business need to have that information.
- Don't send e-mail with offensive text, pictures, or links to offensive Web sites. Content is offensive if it's demeaning based on race, gender, national origin, disability, religion, or politics.
- Don't open e-mail attachments from unknown senders. Don't open e-mail with unexpected attachments.
- Don't click on embedded links in an e-mail from unknown senders.
- Don't download files from the Internet without permission from a business supervisor and the information security department.
- Don't use file-sharing applications or services without permission from a business supervisor and the information security department.
- Don't use IT resources to access the Internet to view offensive material.
- Don't use IT resources to access the Internet to visit social networking sites.
- Don't use IT resources for online shopping.
- Don't use IT resources to engage in activity that violates the law.

Mobile devices pose special information security threats. They're small, pocket-sized computing devices. They include cell phones, smartphones, and personal digital assistants (PDAs). Use of mobile phones is rising. A January 2010 Pew Internet & American Life Project report found that 83 percent of U.S. adults have cell phones or smartphones. Thirty-five percent of those users access the Internet from their cell phone.[4]

Many people buy their own mobile devices and use them for work purposes. Organizations sometimes give their employees mobile devices. These devices pose security threats because they can hold an organization's sensitive information. Employee's can use these devices to browse the Internet, send and receive e-mail, and view documents. The computing capacity of these devices continues to grow. They can store large amounts of data. Many of the same types of malware that infect larger IT resources also can harm these devices.

Mobile devices also are a vulnerability because of their portable nature. A person can easily lose or misplace their mobile device. They're easy to steal. A lost or stolen mobile device can put an organization's data at risk.

An AUP places controls on the use of mobile devices for business purposes. In addition to terms about e-mail and Internet use, an AUP might have specific terms about mobile devices:

- Mobile devices that are used to access organizational resources or data must be password protected.
- Mobile devices (whether provided by the organization or purchased by an employee and used for business purposes) must not store sensitive organizational information.

Organizations typically make employees aware of their AUPs when the employee begins employment. They may print it in an employee handbook. Organizations may ask employees to read the AUP. They also might ask employees to sign an acknowledgment form. It states that the employee understands and agrees to follow the rules in the AUP. The acknowledgment also might state that an employee understands the consequences for failing to follow an AUP.

Organizations should require employees to review the AUP yearly. They also must require that employees review the AUP any time it's revised. They may ask employees to sign a new acknowledgment form at that time. This helps the organization make sure that employees are aware of their responsibilities.

Enforcement

The 2007 Electronic Monitoring and Surveillance Survey found that 28 percent of employers have fired employees for e-mail abuse. The same survey said that of those employees fired for e-mail abuse, 64 percent were fired for violating company policy.[5]

An AUP must specify the consequences for violating it. Consequences for violating an AUP can include:

- Suspension of access to IT resources
- Limited access to IT resources
- Employment suspension
- Employment termination
- Referral to law enforcement

Modest AUP violations may result in suspending an employee's access to IT resources for a period of time. An organization could fire an employee for a particularly harmful AUP violation. AUP violations that amount to criminal conduct should be reported to law enforcement. For example, an organization should notify the police if an employee uses its IT resources to launch a malware attack.

It can sometimes be hard for organizations to enforce their AUPs. This is especially true if they have no technical methods to monitor compliance. Most organizations depend on employees to police their own behavior. They may have a procedure for employees to report AUP violations.

Anti-Harassment Policies

Workplace harassment is a serious issue. "Harassment" is unwanted verbal or physical conduct. It's conduct that demeans or threatens a person. Some examples include:

- Telling lewd, sexist, or racist jokes
- Making racially derogatory comments
- Making remarks about body shape, looks, or clothing
- Starting at people in a suggestive manner
- Making negative comments about a person's religious beliefs
- Threatening a person or his or her families with harm

Workplace harassment can violate federal law. This happens when the unwanted conduct is based on certain characteristics. The main law in this area is Title VII of the 1964 Civil Rights Act. It forbids workplace discrimination based on race, sex, religion, disability, and ethnicity. These are called immutable characteristics. A person can't change them.

Title VII applies to most public and private employers. Employers with 15 or more employees must follow it. The law states that employers have a duty to prevent workplace discrimination. They also have a duty to stop it if they know about it. Workplace discrimination and harassment claims are often tied together.

Workplace harassment has always been a major issue for employers. The rise in Internet and e-mail communications in the work environment adds extra complications. They introduce a new way for harassers to communicate with victims. E-mails shared among employees that have offensive, explicit, or violent content could lead to harassment claims. So could viewing offensive material from a work computer screen in a public area. Employee-downloaded screensavers on an organization's computers can be a problem if they're offensive.

These activities raise legal liability when other employees are offended or feel harassed. Employees also could make tort claims against an employer for intentional infliction of emotional distress. Some of these issues are discussed in Chapter 12.

Employers use anti-harassment policies to help limit liability for workplace harassment. Many organizations develop no-tolerance policies. They often use their AUPs to forbid offensive use of IT resources as well. Many organizations do this. However, the issue is serious enough that organizations should have a separate anti-harassment policy. In addition to forbidding in-person harassment, the policy should state that an organization's IT resources can't be used to harass others.

Anti-harassment policies should contain the following elements:

- **Definition of harassment**—It should define inappropriate conduct. This includes in-person and electronic interactions that are threatening, intimidating, or offensive in nature. Conduct is offensive if it's demeaning based on race, gender, national original, disability, religion, or politics.

- **Reporting**—The organization must give employees a way to report harassment. The reporting method must include alternatives if the alleged harasser is a victim's direct supervisor.

- **Investigation**—An organization must investigate harassment complaints. They must stop harassment when they have reasonable evidence that it's occurring.

- **No Retaliation**—The organization must make sure that it doesn't retaliate against employees who file harassment complaints. "Retaliation" is an adverse employment action made for a non-job-related reason. An organization may not take an adverse employment action against an employee who files a harassment complaint just because that employee filed a complaint.

- **Sanctions**—The policy should state the consequences for violating the policy.

 NOTE

In 2000, Dow Chemical Co. fired 74 employees for sending e-mails with pornography and violent images. It disciplined over 400 employees for similar actions. Dow had policies that prohibited employees from sending such e-mails.

Information security personnel may participate in a harassment investigation. They may investigate whether the organization's IT resources hold evidence related to the claim. Issues related to information security and forensic investigations are discussed in Chapter 15.

The law allows victims to recover damages from their harassers. They also might be able to recover damages from the harassers' employers if they failed to respond to harassment complaints. The law allows victims to receive compensatory damages. They also can receive punitive damages in some cases. The damages can be substantial.

Workplace Privacy and Monitoring Policies

Workplace privacy and monitoring issues are discussed in Chapter 2. Workplace privacy addresses an employee's privacy rights at work. It's a controversial issue. Employees don't like to have their activities monitored. It can create feelings of distrust in a workplace.

For the most part, U.S. employees have very few privacy rights in their use of an organization's IT resources. An organization may monitor an employee's work e-mail and Internet use in many instances. Monitoring is usually allowed if there's a legitimate business reason for it. Legitimate reasons to monitor e-mail and Internet access include:

- Assessing employee productivity
- Monitoring operational use of IT resources
- Monitoring policy compliance
- Monitoring the use of the organization's intellectual property
- Investigating allegations of wrongdoing
- Managing risk and protecting against legal liability

The information security department is often involved in workplace monitoring activities. This department has the knowledge and ability to carry out an organization's desire to monitor IT resource use.

Employers usually win employee legal challenges against monitoring of business e-mail and Internet use. To win these challenges, organizations must show that they had a legitimate business reason for monitoring IT resources. They also must show that they conducted the monitoring in a proper way. These issues are discussed in Chapter 2.

Does Cyber Monday Pose a Productivity Problem?

"Black Friday" is the day after the U.S. Thanksgiving holiday. It's the traditional start of the winter holiday shopping season. Stores and retailers often have sales on this day to encourage shoppers to spend money.

"Cyber Monday" is the first Monday after the holiday. It's the cyber-equivalent to Black Friday. Many retailers noticed an increase in online sales on this day. They suggested that this was because employees used their employer's computers and high-speed connections to shop online when they returned to work after the holiday. The National Retail Federation created the term in 2005 to describe this activity.[6]

In September 2009, the Information Systems Audit and Control Association (ISACA) conducted a survey on online shopping.[7] Over 1,200 U.S. consumers took part in the survey. Half of the people surveyed planned to use their work computers to shop online during the holiday season. The survey also found that employees plan to spend almost two working days shopping online.

Statistics released in 2009 suggest that more than half of all Cyber Monday purchases are made from work computers.[8]

How should an organization deal with Cyber Monday? What are the problems that it poses for productivity? What are the problems that it poses for information security?

Workplace privacy and monitoring policies are often combined together. They inform employees that:

- Their use of IT resources isn't private.
- Their use of IT resources is monitored.

Well-written policies give employees clear notice that they have no expectation of privacy in an organization's IT resources. They give an employee notice that their use of IT resources will be monitored. They also might state why an organization monitors its IT resources. Finally, they should state that an organization doesn't waive its right to monitor IT resources even if it chooses not to do so all the time.

Workplace privacy and monitoring is an area of law that continues to develop. Privacy issues are discussed in Chapter 2.

Data Retention and Destruction Policies

Data retention and destruction is a hot topic for many organizations. **Data retention policies** state how data is controlled throughout its life cycle. The data life cycle is discussed in Chapter 2. Laws and organizational policies help determine retention periods.

Data destruction policies state how data must be destroyed when it reaches the end of its life cycle. Organizations must destroy paper and electronic data when it's no longer needed. For electronic data, this means destroying it in primary and backup storage systems. For both types of data, it means destroying it in such a way that it can't be recovered. Data destruction policies are influenced by federal and state laws.

These policies help organizations cope with the large amounts of data that they use and produce. Without these policies, records management can be difficult. An organization might not know what types of data it has. It might not be able to find data when it needs it for business reasons. It might use too many resources to store data for longer than it must. Storage space for both paper and electronic data is a valuable resource.

Even if an organization has information security controls in place, data is still a vulnerability. It's vulnerable to external threats such as natural disaster or hackers. It's also vulnerable to unintentional acts committed by employees. For instance, employees can easily delete e-mails that they should keep. They also can save e-mail that should have been deleted because there was no business reason to retain it.

In order to create data retention and destruction policies for electronic data, an organization must know how its IT resources work. They also must know how to retrieve data from these systems. Finally, they must know how to remove data from these systems.

Employee awareness is critical for successful data retention and destruction policies. Employees need to be well educated on data retention requirements. They also need to know how to properly file and maintain data that the organization must retain. Finally, they need to understand proper destruction methods. This is very important to avoid accidental disclosures of either paper-based or electronic media.

Data Retention Policies

Data retention policies define the types of data that an organization has. They also address where data is stored and how it's protected. They specify how long different types of data must be retained. These policies also are called document retention policies.

NOTE

State laws might require governmental agencies to retain financial or other types of data for different lengths of time. This is to meet state auditing requirements or comply with open records laws.

Different types of data have different retention periods. This period is usually driven by a combination of federal and state laws. It's also influenced by business needs. Externally, many federal and state laws govern what organizations can do with their data. These laws also state how long certain types of data must be kept. For example, organizations that are subject to the Health Insurance Portability and Accountability Act (HIPAA) have to retain certain types of data for six years. HIPAA is discussed in Chapter 6.

Laws aren't the only factor affecting data retention. Organizations also have to think about data retention if they become involved in a lawsuit. Most federal and state courts have procedural rules that require organizations to maintain data if they're party to a lawsuit. This rule might apply even before an actual lawsuit. For example, an organization must retain paper and electronic data in situations where litigation against it is reasonably anticipated. If an organization doesn't maintain this data, it can be sanctioned by a court.

Maintaining electronic data for this purpose can be very difficult. There are special rules to follow. They're called E-discovery rules. They're discussed in Chapter 12.

In addition to legal requirements, organizations keep data for business purposes. They keep it to conduct business, market products, or to recover from a disaster. Organizations also preserve some types of data indefinitely. This might be because it has legal, fiscal, research, or historical value.

Data retention policies help an organization manage these competing concerns. A cross-functional team helps review and determine data retention requirements. This team should include experts who understand the legal requirements. Expects who know how the organization creates data should be on the team as well. The team must include experts who know the organization's IT systems. This team must understand how the organization uses data and threats to that data.

Data retention policies need to include the following elements:

- Types of organizational data
- Where that data is stored
- How that data is protected
- Legal, business, or other reason for keeping that data
- How long the data should be retained

A data retention policy must be matched with a data destruction policy. An organization must destroy data that it no longer must keep for business, archival, or historical purposes.

Data Destruction Policies

An organization creates data destruction policies to make sure that it destroys data properly. An organization's data destruction process must work hand-in-hand with a data retention policy. The data destruction policy must include the following:

- Identify data ready for destruction.
- Specify proper destruction methods for different kinds of data or storage media.
- Provide validation procedures to make sure data is properly destroyed.
- Provide consequences for improper destruction.

Legal requirements can influence an organization's data destruction policy. For example, the Gramm-Leach-Bliley Act (GLBA) requires that paper documents holding customer information be destroyed. It states that data must be destroyed in such a way that it can't be read or reconstructed. The law also requires that electronic data be destroyed or completely erased. State laws also may require organizations to destroy data in a certain way.

Data destruction policies must be consistently followed. This is important for normal maintenance reasons. It's easy to destroy data when it's done on a regular basis. Following a consistent process is critical if an organization is involved in a lawsuit. It helps protect an organization from claims that it intentionally destroyed evidence.

State Law Data Destruction Requirements

Some state laws require specific data destruction methods. Some of these laws are discussed in Chapter 9. The State of Indiana also has this type of law. All business in the state must follow the law. It requires that they properly dispose of the unredacted personal information of their customers. This information includes a customer's Social Security number or certain types of financial account information. The law applies to both paper and electronic information.

The law requires that information be disposed of in a way that makes it unreadable or unusable. It says that proper disposal methods include shredding, incinerating, mutilating, and erasing.

The state can fine a business that doesn't comply with the law. The state may impose fines that range from $500 to $10,000 per violation.

You can read Indiana's data disposal law at *http://www.in.gov/legislative/ic/code/title24/ar4/ch14.html.*

Intellectual Property Policies

Intellectual property (IP) laws protect a person or organization's ownership rights in their creative ideas. It gives them the right to protect their ideas. It gives them the right to profit from their ideas. These rights are exclusive to IP owners. They can take action against people who violate their IP rights.

Intellectual property policies are very important for most organizations. There are two main reasons why an organization should consider an IP policy. They are:

- To protect its own intellectual property
- To make sure that its employees respect the IP rights of others

Organizations have large amounts of data that they use in carrying out their business. This may include information protected by patents, copyrights, and trademarks. It also can include information protected as a trade secret. It's important to the viability of the organization. An organization must protect it. IP protections are discussed in Chapter 10.

An organization uses an IP policy to specify the IP that it owns. As in an AUP, the organization will want to state its expectations for the use of the organization's IP. An IP policy might state:

- That the organization's IP may be used only for authorized business purposes
- That the organization's IP may not be disclosed outside the organization
- Whether the IP may be removed from the building, copied onto removable media, or stored in cloud computing infrastructure
- What the rules are for using the organization's name or trademarks in correspondence

There's an information security component to protecting the organization's intellectual property. For example, an organization's electronic proprietary and trade secret data must be secured against internal misuse. It also must be secured against external attack.

The second reason for an IP policy is to make sure that an organization doesn't violate the IP rights of others. An organization can be held liable for the infringing activities of its employees. For example, an organization will want to make sure that its employees honor software licensing agreements. It will want to make sure that employees don't use software without a valid license to do so. It also must make sure that employees don't copy or distribute unauthorized copies of software. The organization also will want to make sure that employees don't share or download pirated software onto organizational computers.

Authentication and Password Policies

Authentication controls among the most basic types of information security controls that an organization can use to protect its IT resources. **Authentication** is the process where a user proves his or her identity to access an IT resource. Good authentication provides controlled access to an organization's IT resources.

The user does this by presenting credentials. **User credentials** are used to access IT resources. They usually include a user name and one of the following:

- **Something a user knows**—This includes passwords, passphrases, and personal identification numbers (PINs).
- **Something a user has**—This includes tokens, smart cards, and digital certificates.
- **Something a user is**—This includes biometric data such as a fingerprint or retina scan.

Organizations can implement authentication methods in many ways. Some ways are more complicated and expensive than others. For example, biometric authentication can be very expensive. Organizations also can choose to implement **two-factor authentication**. This type of authentication requires employees to use two different types of credentials to access IT resources.

Many organizations choose to implement passwords. This is because they can easily implement them. They also are relatively inexpensive to use. Employees generally are familiar with using passwords. Employees may be unfamiliar with other types of authentication methods, such as using biometric data.

There are a number of problems with using passwords as the only authentication method. An organization's IT resources are vulnerable if a password is compromised. A password can be compromised if an employee shares their password. It also can be compromised through a phishing or dictionary attack.

 NOTE

A dictionary attack tries to crack passwords by running through words or phrases listed in a dictionary. Strong passwords help combat dictionary attacks.

Organizations implement authentication and password policies in an attempt to reduce risk caused by password use. These policies state the user credential rules that employees must follow. Some policies state that an organization's IT department will never ask employees to share their passwords. These policies often include password creation rules.

Would You Share Your Password for Chocolate?

In 2004, a survey at a trade show in London found that more than 70 percent of the people surveyed would reveal their computer passwords to a stranger for a bar of chocolate.[9] The survey was repeated in 2007. In 2007, 64 percent of the people polled were willing to give up their passwords for chocolate. In 2008, only 21 percent of the people surveyed were willing to share their passwords.[10]

The study didn't verify whether people were sharing valid passwords. It's possible that the survey results could be influenced by chocolate lovers sharing fake passwords.

For example, they may state the number of characters that a password must have. Other common password policy statements include:

- Passwords should not be written down. If they must be written down, that paper should be stored in a secured place.
- Passwords must never be shared with anyone, including trusted colleagues, friends, or family members.
- Passwords must not contain dictionary words.
- Passwords must not include a user's name or parts of their name.
- Employees must create strong passwords that meet character and complexity requirements.
- Passwords expire after a certain period and must be changed.
- New passwords must be different from the previous password or parts of the previous password.
- Passwords may not be reused for a specified period.
- Passwords must not be inserted into e-mail messages or other forms of electronic communication.

Information security departments also can create their own policies for how passwords should be used within IT resources. For instance, they might specify that passwords should never be stored in IT resources as clear text. These policies might require that system authentication take place via encrypted channels. These also might specify that passwords can't be displayed on screens as clear-text when an employee enters it. This would help prevent shoulder surfing attacks. Where possible, passwords should expire automatically, and employees should be prompted to create new ones.

Security Awareness and Training

A recent survey asked about corporate information security policies. Two thousand people in 10 different countries took part in the survey. Seventy-five percent of the companies surveyed had information security policies. Forty percent of the employees in those companies didn't know about them. [11]

An important part of any information security program is the training and awareness component. This is because employees play a large role in meeting information security goals. Employees often view information security training as a waste of time. As one author writes, "Given a choice between dancing pigs and security, users will pick dancing pigs every time."[12]

Employee behavior can help protect data and IT resources. It also can be harmful. Employees who aren't aware of their responsibilities pose a threat. They may engage in risky online activities. These activities could harm the organization's IT resources. Their actions also could disclose data. They can subject an organization to liability. Training and awareness activities help reduce this threat.

A high-level policy lets employees know that the BOD supports training activities. An information security awareness and training policy should include the following elements:

- Why security awareness and training is important
- Who has overall responsibility for the policy
- Who provides training and awareness activities
- Which employees must take part in training activities
- How often training must take place
- What the consequences are for not participating in required training

BOD support of training activities is vital. It makes sure that employees understand that training is important. It makes employees take it seriously.

A variety of training and awareness events are necessary to reach employees. Organizations can use multiple training tools to help their employees know about security policies.

Creating an Information Security Awareness Program

Many organizations struggle with information security training and awareness. This includes the U.S. federal government. FISMA requires federal agencies to implement security awareness training. It must be part of their overall information security programs.

The National Institute of Standards and Technology (NIST) created guidance for training and awareness activities. NIST Special Publication 800-50, "Building an Information Technology Security Awareness and Training Program," was published in 2003. It steps organizations through how to design and implement a training and awareness program. It also discusses how to develop training material. Finally, it provides advice on how to review the program's effectiveness.

Any organization can use the NIST guidance to help create an information security awareness program.

Case Studies and Examples

The following case studies and examples show how the concepts discussed in this chapter are used. These case studies are real-world examples of information security governance issues.

Acceptable Use Case Study

NOTE

You can learn about the company at *http://www .autoliv.com.*

Autoliv is a seatbelt and airbag technology company. In 1998, Autoliv's employee handbook included a number of policies. It stated employee rules of conduct. It included an anti-harassment policy. It also included a computer AUP. Autoliv gave this handbook to all of its employees.

Autoliv's general rules of conduct stated:

- "Each employee is required to be familiar with these rules and with additional rules which apply to particular jobs and operations. In addition, each employee is expected to maintain conduct consistent with job efficiency and accepted standards of behavior for a business environment. Deviation from those standards may be cause for disciplinary action."

- "Disciplinary action may be taken for violation of any single rule or combination of rules, or for other improper conduct or unsatisfactory performance, and may include any of the following actions: 1) Employee discussion; 2) Notice of Caution; 3) Involuntary Suspension; 4) Termination."

Autoliv's anti-harassment policy stated that the company didn't "tolerate or permit illegal harassment or retaliation of any nature within our workforce." Its computer AUP prohibited non-business uses of company e-mail. It also prohibited "conduct that reflects unfavorably on the corporation." [13]

In 1998, Autoliv investigated employee use of its e-mail system. It investigated because of system performance issues. It found that e-mail use was causing the performance issues. It determined that the bulk of e-mail use was not business related.

In June, Autoliv sent an e-mail to all of its employees. It reminded employees about company policy. It said: "E-mail is to be used for business only. We do not wish to 'police' the e-mail system, so your cooperation would be appreciated. Please refrain from sending/receiving these types of messages as it is interfering with legitimate business e-mail."

Autoliv sent another reminder email to its employees in September 1998. This e-mail warned that an employee could be fired for AUP violations.

In January 1999, Autoliv sent another e-mail to its employees. This e-mail stated that it was a violation of the AUP to share chain letters, jokes and stories, and non-business-related announcements. It also instructed employees to delete those types of e-mails and not forward them.

A former employee complained to Autoliv that she had received harassing e-mails from two current employees. Autoliv investigated. It learned that one employee had sent

11 non-business e-mail messages. These messages included jokes, photos, and short videos that were sexually explicit. It found that another employee had sent 25 non-business e-mail messages with similar content. Autoliv immediately fired both employees.

The fired employees filed for unemployment benefits. Autoliv contested this request. A state can deny unemployment benefits if an employee is fired for "just cause." Just cause means that there's a legally sufficient reason for firing an employee. Autoliv said that it had just cause for firing the two employees.

At the unemployment hearing, the employees admitted that they had received Autoliv's handbook. They also stated that they knew about the anti-harassment policy. They said they probably had received the three e-mails about e-mail abuse. They claimed they deleted these e-mails without reading them. They argued that their firing was not "just" because they didn't know they could be fired for sending non-business e-mails.

The Utah Department of Workforce Services found that Autoliv didn't have just cause to fire the employees. This was because the employees said they didn't know that they could be fired for their behavior. They were awarded benefits. Autoliv appealed the agency's decision to the Workforce Appeals Board. It lost its appeal.

Autoliv appealed the decision to the Utah Court of Appeals. Autoliv argued again that the employees had plenty of knowledge that they could be fired for their actions. Think about the following:

* What do you think the Utah Court of Appeals decided?
* What facts support Autoliv's argument that the employees had knowledge that their conduct was unacceptable?
* What facts support the employees' argument that they didn't have knowledge that their conduct was unacceptable?
* Do you think sending offensive e-mails is a "flagrant violation of a universal standard of behavior"?
* Could Autoliv make any changes to its general rules of conduct, anti-harassment policy, or computer AUP that would make employee e-mail responsibilities clear?

The Utah Court of Appeals reversed the decision of the Workforce Appeals Board. It held that Autoliv did have just cause to fire the employees. In its opinion the court stated: "There are two ways to establish that a claimant had knowledge: 1) the employer must have provided a clear explanation of the expected behavior or a written policy regarding the same; or 2) the conduct involved is a flagrant violation of a universal standard of behavior."[14]

The court held that the employees' e-mail activities had violated a universal standard of behavior. It wrote, "We conclude that in today's workplace, the e-mail transmission of sexually explicit and offensive jokes, pictures, and videos constitutes a flagrant violation of a universal standard of behavior."[15]

You can read the court's opinion at *http://scholar.google.com/scholar_case?case=5193814440335474420&q=29+P.3d+7+&hl=en&as_sdt=800002.*

FYI

The Business Software Alliance (BSA) investigates software piracy allegations for its members. It also files IP theft lawsuits on their behalf. You can read about BSA's anti-piracy program at *http://www.bsa.org/country/Anti-Piracy.aspx.*

Intellectual Property Example

The Business Software Alliance (BSA) is a trade organization. It represents software companies. Its members include Apple, Microsoft, and Symantec. As part of its activities, BSA runs an anti-piracy program. Software piracy is copying software without permission. It's also sharing copyrighted software without permission. Software piracy is copyright infringement. It's illegal.

In 1997, BSA received a tip on its anti-piracy hotline. The tip alleged that Oriental Trading Company used unlicensed copies of software on its computers. BSA contacted the company. Oriental Trading Company then conducted an audit of its IT systems. It confirmed that there was unlicensed software on some of its systems.

Oriental Trading Company paid $525,000 to BSA to settle software piracy claims. It also agreed to delete the pirated software from its systems. It agreed to purchase legitimate replacement software. Finally, it promised to strengthen its software management policies.

The BSA has settled similar claims with other businesses. Many of the settlement agreements include terms that require the infringing companies to strengthen their IP policies. How should organizations combat software piracy? What responsibilities do employees have?

CHAPTER SUMMARY

Information security governance provides strategic direction for an information security program. Organizations must protect data in a way that supports its business goals. They use high-level policies to state their information security goals. These policies set forth employee responsibilities. An organization can address information security issues in many different policies.

Standards, guidelines, and procedures are used to support policies. They explain how employees meet policy goals. A training and awareness program is a key part of an information security program. It helps make sure that employees are aware of their duties.

KEY CONCEPTS AND TERMS

Acceptable use policy (AUP)
Authentication
Baseline
Board of directors (BOD)
Chief information officer (CIO)
Chief information security
   officer (CISO)
Chief technology officer (CTO)
Data destruction policies

Data retention policies
Guidelines
Information security
   governance
Information security
   management
Operational planning
Policy
Procedure

Stakeholders
Standards
Strategic planning
Tactical planning
Two-factor authentication
User credentials

13

Information Security
Governance

CHAPTER 13 ASSESSMENT

1. What is a policy?

  A. An overall statement of information security scope and direction

  B. A minimum threshold of information security controls that must be implemented

  C. A checklist of steps that must be completed to ensure information security

  D. A technology-dependent statement of best practices

  E. Recommended actions and operational guides

2. What is information security governance?

3. What type of policy would an organization use to forbid its employees from using organizational e-mail for personal use?

  A. Privacy policy

  B. Intellectual property policy

  C. Anti-harassment policy

  D. Acceptable use policy

  E. Monitoring policy

4. What is software piracy?

  A. Unauthorized copying of software

  B. Unauthorized distribution of software

  C. Unauthorized use of software properly purchased by an organization

  D. None of the above

  E. A and B

5. What is information security management?

6. Employer monitoring can be a normal term of employment if advance notice is given?

  A. True

  B. False

7. What is a standard?

8. Which law states requirements for federal agency information security governance?

  A. FISMA

  B. FERPA

  C. HIPAA

  D. GLBA

  E. FIPPS

9. A guideline is a list of mandatory activities that must be completed to achieve an information security goal.

  A. True

  B. False

10. Which role is the senior most information technology official in an organization?

  A. CFO

  B. CISO

  C. CTO

  D. CIO

  E. None of the above

11. What is a procedure?

12. Which management layer has overall responsibility for information security governance?

  A. CIO

  B. CISO

  C. Board of directors

  D. Employees

  E. Information security managers

13. What is the final step in the policy development process?

  A. Maintenance and review

  B. Management approval

  C. Continued awareness activities

  D. Communication to employees

  E. Stakeholder review

14. What factors drive data retention policies?

    A. Legal requirements

    B. Business need for information

    C. Historical need for information

    D. Storage space requirements

    E. All of the above

15. What is a valid reason for allowing an information security policy exception?

    A. The cost of implementing security policy is too high.

    B. The cost of compliance with the policy is more than the cost of noncompliance.

    C. It isn't technically feasible to implement the policy.

    D. End users believe that the policy makes their work harder.

    E. It's too difficult to implement the policy.

 ENDNOTES

1. The Global Information Industry Center at the University of California, San Diego, "The How Much Information? 2009 Report on American Consumers," *http://hmi.ucsd.edu/howmuchinfo.php* (accessed March 31, 2010).

2. McAfee, "Datagate: The Next Inevitable Corporate Disaster?" 2007, *http://www.mcafee. com/us/local_content/misc/dlp_datagate_research.pdf* (accessed January 22, 2010).

3. International Organization for Standardization. "ISO/IEC 27001:2005, Information Technology – SecurityTechniques – Information Security Management Systems – Requirements" (2006).

4. Rainie, Lee. "Internet, Broadband, and Cell Phone Statistics." Pew Internet & American Life Project, January 2010, *http://www.pewinternet.org/ Reports/2010/Internet-broadband-and-cell-phone -statistics.aspx* (accessed April 8, 2010).

5. American Management Association and The ePolicy Institute, "2007 Electronic Monitoring and Surveillance Survey." March 13, 2008, *http://www. amanet.org/training/articles/The-Latest-on-Workplace-Monitoring-and-Surveillance.aspx* (accessed January 22, 2010).

6. National Retail Foundation, "Cyber Monday," no date, *http://www.shop.org/cybermonday* (accessed April 8, 2010).

7. Information Systems Audit and Control Association (ISACA), "Employees Plan to Spend Nearly Two Full Work Days Shopping for the Holidays Using Work Computers," October 21, 2009, *http:// isaca.org/Template.cfm?Section=Home&CONTENT ID=52923&TEMPLATE=/ContentManagement/ ContentDisplay.cfm* (accessed January 25, 2010).

8. *comScore.com,* "Cyber Monday Online Sales Up 5 Percent vs. Year Ago to $887 Million to Match Heaviest Online Spending Day in History," December 2, 2009, *http://comscore.com/Press_Events/ Press_Releases/2009/12/Cyber_Monday_Online_ Sales_Up_5_Percent_vs._Year_Ago_to_887_Million_ to_Match_Heaviest_Online_Spending_Day_in_History* (accessed April 8, 2010).

9. BBC News, "Passwords Revealed by Sweet Deal," April 20, 2004, *http://news.bbc.co.uk/2/hi/ technology/3639679.stm* (accessed January 25, 2010).

10. The Register, "Women Love Chocolate More than Password Security," April 16, 2008, *http://www. theregister.co.uk/2008/04/16/password_security/* (accessed January 25, 2010).

11. CISCO Systems, "Data Leakage Worldwide: The Effectiveness of Security Policies," October 2008, *http://www.cisco.com/en/US/solutions/collateral/ ns170/ns896/ns895/white_paper_c11-503131.pdf* (accessed January 20, 2010).

12. McGraw, Gary and Ed Felten. *Securing Java.* New York, NY: John Wiley & Sons, Inc., 1999. Also available at *http://www.securingjava.com/* (accessed April 8, 2010). View Chapter 1, part 7.

13. *Autoliv ASP, Inc. v. Department of Workforce Services,* 29 P.3d 7 (Utah Ct. Appeals, 2001). All quoted statements are from this case.

14. Autoliv, 29 P.3d at 11.

15. Autoliv, 29 P.3d at 12-3.

Risk Analysis, Incident Response, and Contingency Planning

RISK MANAGEMENT IS AN IMPORTANT information security tool. The risk management process helps an organization understand the risks, vulnerabilities, and threats that it faces each day. It helps it understand its security posture. It also helps the organization know where to strengthen that posture. An organization can't meet its information security goals if it doesn't understand its risks. It may not be able to properly protect its resources and data.

This chapter focuses on information technology risk management. It reviews fundamental risk concepts and how they're applied. It explains how organizations use risk management to help them create their other contingency plans.

Chapter 14 Topics

This chapter covers the following topics and concepts:

- How to plan for contingencies
- What risk management is
- What incident response is
- What three types of contingency planning are
- What some special considerations are

Chapter 14 Goals

When you complete this chapter, you will be able to:

- Describe the risk assessment process
- Describe how to create an incident response plan
- Describe the business continuity planning process
- Describe how to create a disaster recovery plan
- Explain the differences between risk assessment, incident response, business continuity planning, and disaster recovery

Contingency Planning

Organizations must plan for many events. Contingency plans don't focus just on an organization's information technology (IT) assets. Instead, the field has grown to include all types of planning to make sure that an organization can continue to operate in the event of an emergency or disaster. In the last decade, the United States has seen several dramatic events that highlight the need for all types of contingency plans. The September 11 terrorist attacks of 2001. The northeastern U.S. power-grid failure in 2003. Hurricane Katrina in 2005. The H1N1 flu outbreak in 2009.

When organizations talk about contingency plans, they're talking about holistic plans. These are plans that cover the whole organization and all of its processes. They identify operations that are critical to the business's survival and recovery. Many organizations store their data and records electronically. Many of them have grown dependent on their IT resources and the automated processes those resources provide. Thus, focusing on how to protect and recover IT assets is an important contingency planning component. Some studies indicate that almost half of all companies that experience a data loss never recover.[1]

This chapter discusses contingency planning processes as they relate to IT resources. The different planning processes discussed in this chapter are:

- Incident response planning
- Disaster recovery planning
- Business continuity planning

The scope of any kind of contingency planning is very broad. This chapter focuses on only one narrow piece: planning for the security of IT resources. While all contingency plans have different goals, the foundation for these processes is the same. In order to prepare contingency plans, organizations must analyze and plan for the IT risks that they face. The risk analysis and foundation process helps an organization understand how it needs to protect its IT resources. An organization can't make any contingency plans until it understands the risks to its IT resources.

FYI

This chapter talks about risk management, incident response, and contingency planning. Risk management and contingency planning are used to protect IT resources. Incident response is a type of contingency planning that an organization uses to react to attacks against its IT infrastructure. Disaster recovery and business continuity planning are contingency plans that help an organization continue business operations following a disaster.

It's important to remember that protecting IT resources isn't the only goal of a contingency plan. It's not even the most important goal. Natural and man-made events disrupt thousands of lives each year. The most important goal of any type of contingency plan is to preserve human life. Continuing operations and restoring data are secondary goals.

Risk Management

The National Institute of Standards and Technology (NIST) says that risk management is "the process of identifying risk, assessing risk, and taking steps to reduce risk to an acceptable level."[2] **Risk management (RM)** helps an organization identify the risks that it faces. It also makes sure that organizations respond to risk in a cost-effective manner. Organizations use RM to support their business goals.

One of the main goals of RM is to protect the bottom line. When risk is realized, it negatively affects an organization's profits. RM helps an organization align its information security needs to its business goals. It makes sure that an organization spends its limited resources wisely and in ways that enhance business goals. An organization uses RM to plan for information security.

For example, an organization has a database that holds customer data. The database is critical to the organization's business. It uses the information in the database to develop products for its customers. The database also holds marketing information. The organization would be harmed if it didn't have access to this resource. Its development and marketing activities would be negatively impacted. The organization must protect this database.

A risk analysis shows that the database is at risk because system administrators don't use strong passwords. This is a vulnerability. As a result, the database is open to attack. If it's attacked, the confidentiality and availability of data on the resource are compromised. Attackers could steal this data. They also could harm the database so that the organization couldn't use it. The risk analysis shows that the vulnerability (weak passwords), together with the threat (attackers), is very critical given the organization's business.

As part of its RM function, the organization must review the potential impact of this risk. The cost of a data breach can be quite high. The organization might have to notify its customers about the breach. It also might have to report the breach to its regulatory authorities. Those agencies could fine the organization for failing to secure its data. Its customers could sue it as well. The organization could lose customers. It also faces its own operational issues if that database isn't available for a certain period.

Once the organization identifies the risk and potential impact, it can take steps to mitigate it. In this example, the organization must reduce the risk posed by weak passwords. It can require its system administrators to use strong passwords. It also can configure its systems to technically enforce password complexity requirements. Finally, it can make sure that it backs up its customer data properly. In this short example, the RM process identified a risk to a resource. It also made sure that the organization addressed that risk. The company was able to secure an important resource. As a result, it was able to protect its business operations and bottom line.

Each step in the RM process supports an organization's business goals. The most basic RM process includes the following steps:

The RM process described in this chapter is very similar to the risk management framework discussed in Chapter 8. That framework was discussed with respect to the Federal Information Security Management Act (FISMA). An organization could easily use the framework discussed in Chapter 8 to protect its IT systems.

- **Risk assessment**—Identify the threats and vulnerabilities to the organization's IT resources. Determine the impact of those threats and vulnerabilities.
- **Risk response**—Use policies and controls to respond to risk. An organization responds to risk according to its business strategy.
- **Training employees**—Train employees on known threats and vulnerabilities. Training can help avoid risk.
- **Continuously monitoring**—Monitor the organization's policies and controls for continued effectiveness. Update policies and controls that aren't effective.

Figure 14-1 shows this basic RM process.

The RM process also can help an organization with its other contingency plans. The RM process and information learned during that process can form the basis for an organization's contingency plans. In a basic sense, contingency plans are an

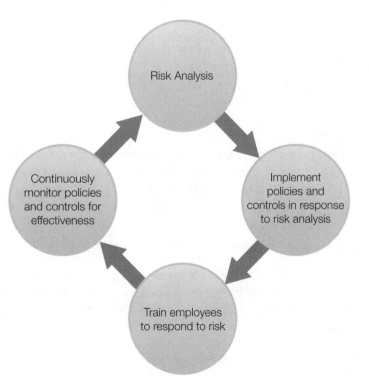

organization's response to very narrow risk assessments. For example, business continuity and disaster recovery plans are detailed contingency plans that respond to the risks of natural or man-made disasters. These risks are discovered during the RM process.

Risk Assessment Process

A **risk assessment (RA)** identifies the threats and vulnerabilities to IT resources. It reviews the probability of those threats and vulnerabilities actually happening. This is called a **realized risk**. Then the RA reviews the potential harm from a realized risk. Finally, the RA identifies policies and controls that could respond to the potential risk. Risk response is the actions taken by an organization to reduce realized risk to an acceptable level. The amount of risk that is left over after realized risk is reduced is called residual risk.

The RA is a tool for the risk management process. It provides executive management with the data that it needs to make smart decisions about information security controls.

Without a RA, the executive management team has no way to know if the controls and policies that it implements are cost effective. For example, an organization could spend a lot of money implementing a control to respond to a threat. Without a RA, the organization doesn't know whether that cost is reasonable given the cost of the underlying threat. The organization may be making a poor decision if it spends more money to respond to a risk than the actual cost of the realized risk itself. A RA helps the organization know where to spend money to correct information security risk.

There are several different methods for conducting a risk assessment. Some of them will be discussed in this chapter. In general, all methodologies have similar basic steps. The basic steps in a risk assessment are:

- Inventory assets covered by the assessment
- Identify threats and vulnerabilities
- Categorize likelihood of occurrence and potential loss
- Document where controls are needed

Risk Assessment Team

A risk assessment team must include people in a number of different roles throughout an organization. Even though the RA focuses on risks to IT systems, it's not sufficient to only include IT personnel on the team. IT personnel may not know about all of the organization's critical business processes. For the same reason, it's not enough to include

---

FYI

Many of the laws discussed in this book had risk assessment components. FISMA and the Sarbanes-Oxley Act (SOX) are two of them. The risk assessments required in these types of laws are very narrowly tailored to the systems and processes that are covered by the law. The risk assessment processes described in this chapter are more general.

only business personnel on a RA team. Business personnel may not appreciate the technology processes that support business operations. The RA team members should represent all areas involved in a business process workflow.

RA team members should include:

- **Business personnel**—These people are responsible for business process operations. They know the steps that must be completed in each business process. They also can describe how they use IT systems to accomplish their job duties.

- **IT personnel**—These people run the organization's various IT systems. This group also might include the IT system owner. These personnel understand how their IT systems work. They're responsible for maintaining those resources. They also would be responsible for implementing any changes to IT systems.

- **Information security managers**—These people run the organization's information security program. They have knowledge about information security threats and vulnerabilities. They also know how threats and vulnerabilities can be mitigated.

- **Human resources personnel**—These people understand how to deal with people issues. They can offer advice and input on how to address human-based threats and vulnerabilities. They also will be able to assist with awareness training after the RA is complete.

- **Executive management**—These people make sure that the RA team has the support and resources that it needs to complete the assessment. They can hold business units accountable for participating in the assessment. They also can make sure that the RA remains properly scoped to its original goal.

Members of the team must be objective. They must be willing to take a hard look at an organization's business objectives and processes for risk potential. They must do the same thing for IT resources. Members of the team must avoid **conflicts of interest**. In the RA context, a conflict of interest is a situation where a member's responsibilities as part of the RA team might conflict with their job responsibilities. A conflict of interest prevents the team member from meeting their RA responsibilities.

In many cases, team members are picked because they work in a certain area that is being reviewed as part of an assessment. These members are helpful in making sure that the whole RA team understands how these areas work. However, these members may not be as objective in assessing vulnerabilities, threats, and risks in their areas. These team members will have to work hard to be objective throughout the whole RA process. An organization must remove them from the RA team if they're unable to be objective.

> **NOTE**
>
> In general, a conflict of interest is any situation where a person's private interests and professional obligations collide. In these situations, independent observers might question whether a person's private interests improperly influenced his or her professional decisions.

14

Analysis, Response, Contingency Planning

Some organizations hire consultants to help with a RA. Consultants aren't employees of the organization. They help in a risk analysis by bringing objectivity to the team. They can hurt the team if they don't quickly learn how an organization's business processes and IT systems work. They also can hurt the team if they aren't respectful of an organization's culture.

A RA team is responsible for collecting information about assets and risks. It's also responsible for reporting the assessment results to an organization's executive management.

Identifying Assets, Vulnerabilities, and Threats

A risk assessment must be narrowly scoped. Otherwise, it can grow too large for the RA team to manage. If it's too large, the team will have a hard time determining the risks that the organization must address. A better practice is to conduct a focused RA. Rather than doing an assessment of the organization's whole IT infrastructure, the RA team should review one infrastructure component at a time. The team can better manage the RA and produce better overall results.

> **NOTE**
>
> Many RA projects have a project manager. This person is in charge of making sure that the RA moves forward in a timely manner. The project manager isn't necessarily a participant on the RA team. Instead, this person helps the RA team meet their project goals and final deliverables.

The scope of the RA must be clearly stated in a RA project plan. RA team members can refer back to the project plan anytime they're asked to consider a new system or process as part of the RA. If the new system or process isn't within the scope of the project plan, then the team should not consider it. Executive management must approve the project plan before the RA team begins to work.

After the organization approves the scope of the RA, the RA team must identify all the assets that are within the scope of the assessment. This inventory must include the IT resources. It also must include a listing of the personnel who run business processes that are in the scope of the RA. The inventory also must contain the data included in those processes. For instance, an organization decides to conduct a risk assessment of its e-mail infrastructure. For this assessment, the RA team must consider not only the operation of the organization's e-mail servers, but also whether employees are sending confidential data via e-mail. Depending upon how the RA team defines the project, mobile devices that send and receive e-mail could be outside of the scope of the assessment.

The RA team should consider many assets for the inventory. They include:

- Personnel
- Data
- Hardware and software
- Physical facilities
- Business process workflows
- Current controls that help safeguard any assets

It's important to identify all assets that are associated with the RA project. The RA team must list assets that are critical to business functions. They also must identify threats and vulnerabilities to those assets. Threats and vulnerabilities, and examples of each, are reviewed in Chapter 1. The RA team must identify vulnerabilities and threats in order to determine the risk to the organization's assets. For IT resources, the organization needs to know how vulnerabilities and threats might affect confidentiality, integrity, and availability.

A vulnerability is a weakness or flaw in an IT system. Information security is compromised when vulnerabilities are exploited. An exploit is a successful attack against a vulnerability. There are many different kinds of vulnerabilities, but they fall into four broad categories. They include people, process, facility, and technology vulnerabilities. Vulnerabilities can be design mistakes. They also can be configuration mistakes.

Threats are anything that can cause harm to an information system. They're successful exploits against vulnerabilities. A threat source carries out a threat or causes it to take place against a vulnerability. A threat source can be a person or a circumstance. Like vulnerabilities, threats also fall into four broad categories: human, natural, technology and operational, and physical and environmental. Threats can be deliberate or accidental.

Threat sources act upon vulnerabilities. Table 14-1 shows examples of vulnerabilities and threats.

TABLE 14-1 Examples of vulnerabilities and threats.

VULNERABILITY	THREAT SOURCE	THREAT
Data center has few physical security controls to prevent unauthorized access to data center hardware	Unauthorized users (e.g., criminals, terminated employees, curious employees)	Theft of data center hardware Theft of data on hardware Damage or destruction of hardware or data
Failure to remove user accounts in a timely manner when an employee leaves the organization	Terminated employees	Access to IT resources and theft of sensitive company data
No access controls for sensitive files stored on IT resources	Curious employees	Review of data without need to know Review of proprietary data Invasion of privacy of other employees and/or customers Unauthorized modification of data Theft of data

The RA team must put forth a good-faith effort to identify as many vulnerabilities and threats as possible. It can do this in a number of ways. For vulnerabilities that are internal to the organization, the team could interview employees in areas that are part of the assessment. The team also could send a questionnaire to a sampling of employees. The questionnaire could ask questions that are relevant to the assessment. The RA team also should review the organization's policies and procedures. The team could use automated scanning tools to look for vulnerabilities in its IT systems.

The RA team also must learn about vulnerabilities and threats that are external to the organization. They can review industry guides. They can use NIST guidance to learn more about information security issues and controls. The RA team can review information from the U.S. government and other industry experts. The SANS Institute has one of the largest collections of information security resources in the world. The team also can review known system problems listed in the National Vulnerability Database (NVD).

It's not possible for the RA team to identify every security vulnerability or threat. This is because technology changes so rapidly. For example, zero-day exploits are a type of exploit that's hard for an organization to prepare for. These exploits were discussed in Chapter 1. An organization can only prepare for zero-day exploits generally. It's hard to prepare or assess specific zero-day exploits because they're exploited so quickly after they're discovered.

Likelihood and Potential Loss

A risk is the likelihood that a threat will exploit a vulnerability and cause harm. The RA team is responsible for determining how likely it is that identified risks will occur. The team also must determine the potential loss or harm that the organization could have if the risk is realized. Likelihood and potential loss can be stated as either a qualitative measure or a quantitative measure. It depends on the risk methodology that the RA team uses.

Quantitative Risk Analysis. **Quantitative risk analysis** attempts to use real numbers to calculate risk and potential loss. The organization assigns real numbers to the value of its assets. It also assigns real values to the cost of countermeasures and controls. One of the greatest advantages of a quantitative risk assessment is that it provides an objective assessment of cost. It helps an organization understand both the cost of risk and the cost of controls. This type of RA allows management to directly compare the cost and benefits of recommended controls. One of the greatest disadvantages of quantitative risk assessments is that they're very difficult to administer.

In a quantitative risk analysis, the RA team must assign a value amount to each of the organization's assets. A number of factors shape the cost of an asset. The actual cost of the asset, as well as the cost of developing the asset, contribute to its overall cost. Asset cost also includes the costs it takes to maintain it each year. The asset's cost also might include value that is hard to measure. For example, it might be hard to value the intellectual property that goes into creating and developing an asset. It's also hard to place a value on an asset that provides an organization with its competitive edge. While quantitative risk analysis does give an organization actual money amounts for its assets, there's a subjective element to these values. This is particularly true if an asset has intangible value.

After the RA team determines the organization's vulnerabilities and threats, it must determine **exposure factor.** The exposure factor is the percentage of asset loss that is likely to be caused by an identified threat. For example, an RA team determines that an organization's data center is vulnerable to tornadoes. This is because the data center is located in the part of the midwestern United States known as "tornado alley." The RA team estimates that if a tornado struck the data center, it would be destroyed. The data center's value would be reduced to zero. The exposure factor is 100 percent.

The RA team determines that the same data center is also subject to a threat of fire. The RA team determines that if a fire were to occur, only 50 percent of the data center would be destroyed. (This is because the data center has a fire suppression system). In this scenario, the exposure factor is 50 percent. Exposure factor also is called "likelihood."

Once the RA team determines the exposure factor, it must determine **single loss expectancy (SLE)**. The SLE is the amount of money that an organization will lose if a risk is realized. It's the loss that an organization will suffer every time that risk occurs. SLE is often expressed as an equation:

> **NOTE**
>
> Exposure factor is expressed as a percentage. It can range from zero to 100 percent. An exposure factor of 100 percent means that an asset is destroyed if a specified threat occurs.

$$\text{SLE} = \text{Asset value} \times \text{Exposure}$$

In our data center example, suppose that the data center is worth $2 million. The SLE for the data center being struck by a tornado is $2 million. The SLE for the data center experiencing a fire is $1 million.

The RA team also must figure out how many times a specific risk might occur during a one-year timeframe. This is called the **annual rate of occurrence (ARO)**. An RA team can use historical data to determine this number. It also can perform research to understand the likelihood of risks within a certain area. Police departments can provide information about crime statistics. Insurance companies can provide information about how often organizations are likely to experience a serious fire or other devastating incident. ARO is expressed as a number. It can range from zero (a threat will never take place) to any number greater than zero. A risk that will happen only once a year has an ARO of one.

In our example, the RA team estimates that a fire might strike its data center once every 20 years. The ARO for that event is 1/20, or .05. The RA team estimates that a tornado might strike its data center once every 15 years. The ARO for that event is 1/15 or .067.

ARO is used to calculate **annualized loss expectancy (ALE)**. The ALE is the amount of loss that an organization can expect to have each year due to a particular risk. In a quantitative risk analysis, the ALE is the end-result number. An organization can use this number to determine how much money it should invest each year in controls to mitigate a particular risk. As a matter of good business practice, an organization shouldn't spend more than the ALE amount each year on particular risks. ALE is often expressed as an equation:

$$\text{ALE} = \text{SLE} \times \text{ARO}$$

In our example, the ALE for the tornado risk is $134,000 ($2 million $\times$ .067). The ALE tells the organization that it can afford to spend up to $134,000 per year to mitigate the potential loss caused by a tornado. The ALE for the fire risk is $50,000 ($1 million $\times$ .05). The organization can spend up to $50,000 per year to mitigate potential fire loss. Spending more on controls than the ALE amount might be unwise from a business standpoint. This is because the cost of the controls is then more than the cost of the risk. It doesn't make sense to spend more money on controls than the cost of the risk.

Organizations also can use these formulas to determine the value of a control. The value of a safeguard to the organization can be determined by comparing the ALE before implementing a control to the ALE after implementing the control. This also can be expressed as an equation:

Value of control = (ALE before safeguard) − (ALE after safeguard) − Cost of control

These equations are used in quantitative risk analysis. Many vendors have created software products that can help RA teams perform these equations.

Organizations often choose to do a quantitative RA because it computes risk in terms of money value. Sometimes executive management finds this information very helpful. It gives them concrete values upon which to measure the costs of risks and the effectiveness of controls. A quantitative risk analysis speaks the language of business: money.

Qualitative Risk Analysis.   **Qualitative risk analysis** uses scenarios and ratings systems to calculate risk and potential harm. Qualitative risk analysis doesn't assign money value to assets and risk. Instead, it uses descriptive categories to express asset criticality, risk exposure (likelihood), and risk impact.

One of the greatest advantages of this method is that it's relatively easy to use. It doesn't require RA team members to have specialized knowledge. It also doesn't require them to deduce the costs of assets, controls, and potential harm. One of the biggest disadvantages of qualitative risk assessments is that they're very subjective. The opinions of members of the RA team can affect the results of the RA.

Qualitative risk analysis is scenario-based. In this type of assessment, the RA team considers a specific vulnerability or threat. The team then considers a scenario based on them. As they walk through the scenario, they think about how the scenario will affect business operations and resources. The team will use its own experiences to determine threat likelihood. It can also use industry resources.

The RA team will create likelihood and impact categories. These categories help them classify and compare different risks. These categories are usually based on either a numeric rating system (scale of 1 to 10) or a low-medium-high standard.

Risk exposure categories classify the likelihood of certain risks. An RA team might use the following categories to determine risk exposure:

- **Low**—Events that are unlikely to happen within a year
- **Medium**—Events that are somewhat likely to happen within a year
- **High**—Events that are likely to happen within a year

Risk impact is determined the same way. Impact categories classify the harm to an organization if a risk is realized. The RA team might use the following impact categories:

- **Low**—A realized risk will have little or no effect on the organization. The organization will experience light disruption to its business processes. It will incur only low costs related to lost productivity and data. It won't experience reputational loss.
- **Medium**—A realized risk will have a moderate effect on the organization. The organization may experience moderate disruption to its business processes. It will incur moderate costs related to loss productivity and data. Its reputational loss will be moderate.
- **High**—A realized risk will have a severe effect on the organization. The organization may experience severe disruption to its business processes. It will experience high costs related to loss productivity and data. Its reputational loss will be significant.

The RA team also will need a way to compare likelihood and impact levels to determine overall risk level. The RA team will use the overall risk level to determine where the organization should apply controls. An organization won't want to implement costly controls on a system that has low exposure and impact results. However, it will want to implement controls where there's a high likelihood rating and a high impact rating. It must create a method to analyze likelihood and impact rating levels. It uses this analysis to determine the priority of issues that the organization must address. Table 14-2 shows a generic risk level matrix.

Organizations use their risk level matrix to determine the priority of the risks that they must address. Table 14-3 shows what the results of a qualitative risk analysis might look like. It uses the vulnerabilities and threats from Table 14-1. In this example, the RA team would first recommend that the organization implement controls to remove user accounts for terminated employees in a timely manner. This is because the risk level for that vulnerability is higher than the others listed in the table.

TABLE 14-2 Risk level matrix.

		LIKELIHOOD		
	RATING	**Low**	**Medium**	**High**
	Low	Low	Low–Medium	Medium–High
IMPACT	**Medium**	Low–Medium	Medium	Medium–High
	High	Medium–High	Medium–High	High

14

Analysis, Response, Contingency Planning

TABLE 14-3 Risk level outcomes.

VULNERABILITY	THREAT SOURCE	THREAT	THREAT LIKELIHOOD	THREAT IMPACT	RISK LEVEL
Data center has few physical security controls to prevent unauthorized access to data center hardware	Unauthorized users	Theft of data center hardware	Medium	High	Medium–high
Failure to remove user accounts in a timely manner when an employee leaves the organization	Disgruntled terminated employees	Theft of sensitive company data	High	High	High
No access controls for sensitive files stored on IT resources	Curious employees	Review of data without need to know	Medium	Low	Low–medium

The problem with qualitative risk assessments is that the organization has no way to determine the amount of money to spend on controls. It has no way of knowing if it's spending too much on a control relative to the actual loss it could have due to a realized risk. For some organizations, this is a significant failure of a qualitative risk analysis. This is one reason why an organization might prefer to complete a quantitative risk analysis. Table 14-4 compares the features of qualitative and quantitative risk assessments.

Document Needed Controls

The final part of an RA is to document where security controls are needed. The RA team does this by reviewing the results of its assessment. In a quantitative risk analysis, the RA team has a list of risks that it can prioritize by ALE and ARO. The RA team should review risks with high ALEs and high AROs to recommend controls.

Through a qualitative risk analysis process, the RA team has a list of risks organized by potential harm. The risk level is based on the classifications that the RA team used for risk likelihood and impact. The RA team should look at high and medium risk levels to recommend controls.

An RA team needs to suggest controls to executive management. It must identify risks that are high priorities. It also should identify controls that can mitigate or eliminate those risks. If the RA team performed a quantitative analysis, it should include a cost-benefit analysis for each of its suggested controls. If the team performed a qualitative analysis, it should show how the suggested control affects the overall risk level for a specific threat or vulnerability.

Risk Assessment Methods

There are a number of different RA processes to choose from. Some vendors offer software that organizations can use to complete RAs. This sidebar describes some of the RA methods you might hear about in the information security profession.

NIST "SP 800-30, Risk Management Guide for Information Technology Systems" is a qualitative RA method. Any type of organization can use it. It describes a nine-step RA process. You can view this NIST guide at *http://csrc.nist.gov/publications/PubsSPs.html*.

The United Kingdom's Central Computer and Telecommunications Agency (CCTA) created CRAMM (CCTA Risk Analysis and Management Method) in 1987. CRAMM has been commercialized and is sold as a software program. It's a qualitative RA method. It relies on international standards for its RA methodology. CRAMM advertises itself as an ISO/IEC 27001-compliant RA methodology. You can learn more about it at *http://www.cramm.com/*.

Carnegie Mellon University's Software Engineering Institute developed OCTAVE (Operationally Critical Threat, Asset, and Vulnerability Evaluation). OCTAVE is a qualitative RA process. It's designed to be self-directed. It allows organizations to align security operations to business strategy. You can learn about OCTAVE at *http://www.cert.org/octave/*.

Thomas Peltier developed the Facilitated Risk Analysis and Assessment Process (FRAAP) in 1993. It's a three-step process that helps organizations identify risks and threats. It's based on ISO/IEC 27001.

The Microsoft Corporation describes a risk analysis process that contains both quantitative and qualitative elements in its "Security Risk Management Guide." It created this guide in 2006. You can learn about it at *http://technet.microsoft.com/en-us/library/cc163143.aspx*.

TABLE 14-4 Qualitative and quantitative risk assessment comparison.

	QUALITATIVE RISK ASSESSMENT	QUANTITATIVE RISK ASSESSMENTS
Positive Aspects	Easy to administer	Measures the money cost of a risk
	Doesn't require formal knowledge to administer	Very objective, can be used to make cost-benefit decisions
	Calculations are simple	
	Scope of the assessment can be changed easily if necessary	
Negative Aspects	No measure of money cost of risk	Hard to administer
	Very subjective, can't be used to make cost-benefit decisions	Requires formal knowledge to administer
		Calculations are complex
		Must put effort into valuing assets (and that value may be hard to calculate)
		Very difficult to change the scope of the RA

Executive management reviews the RA team's report as it makes business decisions. It will use the report as part of its information security governance (ISG) activities. Information security governance is discussed in Chapter 13. The organization must make sure that its response to the risks identified in the RA team's report supports its business objectives. The executive management team shows due care and due diligence when it responds to issues that are raised in a risk assessment.

> **NOTE**
>
> Controls reduce the harm posed by vulnerabilities or threats. They may eliminate or reduce risk of harm. They're also called safeguards or countermeasures. Safeguards are discussed in Chapter 1.

Risk Response

Executive management must decide how an organization responds to risk. Risk response is the actions taken by executive management to reduce risk to an acceptable level. Executive management must apply the most appropriate controls to decrease its risk. The organization's risk response must be cost-effective. It also should have a limited impact on the organization's business.

Executive management must prioritize how it will respond to risks. It should respond quickly to the risks that have the greatest potential to harm business goals. Executive management must assess each risk individually. An organization won't handle all risks in the same manner.

Executive management can use a number of approaches to respond to risk. These options are discussed in Chapter 1. They are:

- **Risk avoidance**—The organization applies controls or takes other action to completely avoid a particular risk. This strategy removes all risk caused by a particular vulnerability or threat. For example, executive management could decide that the risks posed by a function in an IT system outweigh the benefit of that function. It could instruct system owners to disable that function in order to avoid the risk. The risk caused by that function is eliminated.

- **Risk mitigation**—The organization applies controls or takes other action to reduce a particular risk. This strategy doesn't eliminate all harm that could be caused by that risk. Instead, it reduces the risk to an acceptable level. The risk that is left over is called residual risk. For example, executive management could decide that the risks posted by a function in an IT system could be lessened if access to that function was limited. The organization could use access controls to limit access to that function to only a few employees. The risk caused by that function is reduced because fewer people have access to it.

- **Risk transfer**—The organization takes no action against a particular risk. Instead, it passes its risk to another entity. The other entity bears the risk of loss. Usually an organization transfers risk of loss to an insurance company. It can purchase a cyber liability insurance policy to insure against specific risks. For example, the organization could purchase insurance to cover losses due to unauthorized access to IT systems. These types of policies are called technology errors and omissions policies.

- **Risk acceptance**—The organization takes no action against the potential risk. It makes an intentional decision to do nothing. Executive management may choose this strategy if the cost of the risk is less than the cost to avoid, mitigate, or transfer the risk.

> **NOTE**
> Executive management can implement administrative, technical, or physical controls to avoid or mitigate risk.

Training Employees

The RM process includes educating employees about risk. Often employees contribute to an organization's risk. They engage in behavior that puts the organization and its data at risk. Risk can be reduced if employees understand why certain behaviors are not proper. The organization can use policies to help direct employee behavior. Risk is reduced when employees behave according to company policy.

Security awareness and training is discussed in Chapter 13. Ongoing education is an important part of any information security program. It's required to keep employees aware of their security responsibilities. An organization must include security education in its day-to-day routine.

Continuously Monitoring

Organizations must always monitor their information security risk. They also must monitor the controls that they put in place to respond to that risk. This is an ongoing process. Since technology changes quickly, executive management must be diligent reviewing its risk and response to that risk.

Many laws require organizations to continually assess their risk. For example, the Gramm-Leach-Bliley (GLBA) Safeguards Rule requires covered financial institutions to conduct RAs to identify risks to customer information as part of its information security program. Covered financial institutions must apply controls to respond to identified risks. They also must assess their current controls to make sure that they're effective. Financial institutions also must review their information security programs on a regular basis.

The Health Insurance Portability and Accountability Act (HIPAA), FISMA, and SOX also require covered organizations to conduct regular risk assessments.

> **NOTE**
> The Gramm-Leach-Bliley Act (GLBA) is discussed in Chapter 4.

Three Types of Contingency Planning

One of the most important things about conducting an RA is that it forces an organization to think "What if?" An organization must plan for the risks that it can't avoid, mitigate, accept, or transfer. It creates contingency plans to limit the financial loss it might experience due to an adverse event. Contingency plans help to minimize the length of time that services and processes are interrupted. They also help minimize customer impact due to a serious event.

The three main types of contingency plans are:

* Incident response plans
* Disaster recovery plans
* Business continuity plans

An organization creates these plans to respond to events that might negatively affect IT resources and business processes. Keep in mind that this chapter discusses these types of contingency plans from an information security perspective. These plans can have a much larger scope than just IT.

It's also important to remember that the most important goal of any type of contingency plan is to preserve human life. Other goals are secondary.

Incident Response Planning

 NOTE

Incident response is a reactive term. It describes how an organization responds to an incident. Incident handling is a proactive term. It describes how an organization manages an incident. Organizations may use both terms interchangeably.

An organization uses its **incident response (IR)** process to react to attacks against its IT infrastructure. Having an incident response process is important because it helps make sure that an organization can recover from security incidents. Organizations that are able to recover quickly from incidents are more likely to be able to continue business operations. Incident response is also called incident handling.

Incident response describes how an organization:

* Detects information security incidents
* Determines the cause of the incident
* Mitigates the damage caused by the incident
* Recovers from the incident

An **incident** is any event that involves the organization's equipment, data, or other resources. An incident must adversely affect the confidentiality, integrity, and/or availability of the organization's data and IT systems. An adverse event is an incident. The intent of the threat source does not matter. An incident includes malicious attacks. It also includes the harmful acts of well-meaning employees. Incidents are usually violations of the organization's policies, accepted security practices, or the law.

Chapter 1 reviewed many of the information security threats that an organization faces each day. Each one of these can be an incident if it adversely affects the security of an organization's resources and data. For example, Chapter 1 discussed an example where student hackers installed keystroke loggers on some computers in a university registrar's office. They gathered user name and password information from the keystroke loggers. They then used that information to change grades in the university's computer system. The university discovered the hack through logging and audit review security measures.

When the university discovered that records had been improperly modified, it would have declared an information security incident. A team would be formed to respond to the system intrusion. That team would have been responsible for determining the damage that the incident caused. They also would find the source of the incident. They also would mitigate the damage caused by the incident and recover the computer systems affected by the incident.

The student hackers' conduct was most likely a violation of the university's acceptable use policy (AUP). These types of policies are discussed in Chapter 13. Many organizations have these policies to define acceptable behaviors for the use of its IT resources. In this case, the student hackers' violated policies and also broke the law. One of the students was sentenced to seven years in prison for violating the federal Computer Fraud and Abuse Act.

> **NOTE**
> The Computer Fraud and Abuse Act is covered in Chapter 12.

Based upon what we know about this case from publicly available information, we know that the university involved did the following:

- **Detecting the incident**—The university used normal information security practices such as logging and audit review to discover that information in an IT system had been changed.

- **Determining the cause of the incident**—These same measures, and most likely computer forensic analysis, helped the university discover that the cause of the incident was student hackers who had installed a keystroke logger.

- **Mitigating the damage caused by the incident**—The university was able to restore the changed data because it made regular data backups.

- **Recovering from the incident**—The university restored data and, likely, hardened its systems to prevent this type of incident from happening again in the future.

One of the most important parts of IR is documentation. An organization must document every incident that it encounters. That way it can refer to its documentation if it encounters a similar incident in the future.

Incident Response Team

The IR team is responsible for creating the organization's IR policy and plan. This team has a different focus from the operational information security employees that will follow the IR plan and respond to incidents. Often the IR team will include many information security team members. Like an RA team, the IR planning team must include advisors from a number of departments across the organization.

The IR team will help draft the initial IR policy. It also will create the plans that define the organization's IR structure. Even though IR is often an information security responsibility, other departments may need to participate in an IR process. The information security team may have to interact with many of these departments when handling an incident.

For instance, the operational team will be involved if there's an incident involving a physical trespasser to the organization's data center. The operational team most likely will involve the organization's physical security personnel in handling the incident. This is because the incident included actual trespass onto the organization's property. IT personnel will be involved to see if any equipment has been stolen. Internal audit and legal counsel will be involved if any equipment or data are stolen. Human resources (HR) personnel could become involved if it appears that the trespasser is a former employee. Marketing and communications personnel could become involved if the facts of the incident trigger the laws that require security breach notification.

The IR team is responsible for making sure that the procedures are in place to help all of these different departments work together. They must be able to respond quickly and efficiently in the event of an incident. The operational information security team needs to know whom they can contact in each department for help. The IR team's planning puts this structure in place.

The IR planning team should include information security and IT representatives. It also should have members from physical security, HR, and internal audit. Legal counsel should be included on the team to address any legal or regulatory issues.

The IR team will help the organization create its IR policy. These policies are very specific to an organization's structure and culture. Like all information security policies, the IR policy is a statement of executive management's commitment to the IR process. The policy should state the purpose and goals of IR. It also should define what an incident is. The policy must set forth, at a high level, the organization's operational IR structure. It should define the roles and responsibilities within this structure. The IR policy also can contain information about how to measure the effectiveness of the IR process.

IR Plan Process

Once the organization approves its IR policy, the IR team can continue to define the IR plan. The IR policy contains the overall IR goals. The IR plan contains the procedural elements that are necessary to meet those policy goals. Operational information security teams will follow the IR plan to fulfill their IR job duties. In this section, the term "incident handlers" will be used to refer to the operational teams that respond to an incident.

An IR plan is specific to a particular organization. However, most IR plans have five basic parts. They are:

- Incident triage
- Investigation
- Containment or mitigation
- Recovery
- Review

> **NOTE**
> The work "triage" is most commonly associated with the medical profession. It's the process of sorting and prioritizing patient care based on the severity of a patient's condition.

The "triage" phase is the first phase in the IR process. This is the phase where a potential incident is initially assessed. It's at this point that the primary handler will verify whether an adverse event meets the definition of an incident. The primary handler is the person who is in charge of coordinating an organization's response to an information security incident. This person is often a member of the organization's information security team.

The Operational Incident Response Team

An organization often plans and coordinates IR at a high level within an organization. A cross-functional team, called the IR team, puts the IR plan into place. The responsibility for the daily operations of the IR plan often falls to an organization's information security team and other IT personnel.

There are a number of different roles involved incident response. These roles are reviewed briefly here. You may find these terms used in resources describing how to plan and implement an IR program:

- **Victim**—The person or resources that are targeted in an incident. The victim is often the organization and its IT resources and data.
- **Attacker**—The person or mechanism that caused the incident.
- **Incident reporter**—The first person or mechanism that reports an incident. The incident reporter doesn't have to be a person. An automated intrusion detection system (IDS) can be an incident reporter. A person who notices an unusual incident and reports it is also an incident reporter.
- **Primary handler**—The person who is in charge of coordinating the response to a particular incident. This person is responsible for making sure that the IR process is documented. Often this person is a member of the organization's information security department. If an organization doesn't have a dedicated information security department, this is the person with information security job duties.
- **Secondary handlers**—These are the personnel involved in investigating, responding, and recovering from an incident. Secondary handlers include technicians, analysts, and operational staff who take part in handling the incident. Legal counsel and an organization's internal auditors also can be secondary handlers. The type of secondary handlers involved in IR depends on the nature of the incident.

Not all events are incidents. The event must have an adverse effect on the confidentiality, integrity, and/or availability of an organization's IT resources or data. For example, it might be an incident if an employee mistakenly deletes a critical file needed for processing the organization's weekly payroll. The employee has compromised the availability of needed data. It might not be an incident if the employee mistakenly deleted a non-critical file. (Although, it certainly would be a business process issue.) The primary handler decides whether a reported event is actually an incident.

If an event is an incident, the primary handler must classify it. Incidents can be classified in a number of ways. They can be sorted based on threat source. An example would be whether the incident occurred due to an internal threat or an external threat. Incidents also can be sorted based upon the type of vulnerability or threat that's exploited.

Organizations may use any method for sorting incidents. Some organizations use guidance prepared by NIST.[3] The United States Computer Emergency Readiness Team (US-CERT) uses incident response categories that are based on NIST guidance. The US-CERT is the federal government's IR center. All federal agencies must report information security incidents to the US-CERT. The US-CERT's incident categories are:

- **Category 1: Unauthorized Access**—Unauthorized access is technical or physical access to an IT system without permission. An agency must report these incidents even if data isn't compromised.
- **Category 2: Denial of Service (DoS)**—Any event that prevents the normal operation of IT resources such that use of those resources is harmed.
- **Category 3: Malicious Code**—Any event that involves the use of malicious code to successfully infect, breach, or compromise IT resources. These events include viruses, worms, and Trojan horses.
- **Category 4: Improper Use**—Any event that is a violation of the agency's AUP or other related policies.
- **Category 5: Scans, Probes, and Attempted Access**— Any event where an IT resource is scanned or probed in an attempt to access or identify the agency's IT systems.
- **Category 6: Investigation**—This category is for unusual events that don't fall into one of the other categories. These incidents require more review because they're odd or potentially harmful.

The classification of an incident may change as the incident is investigated. This is because the organization learns more about the incident as the investigation progresses. Incidents also should be sorted based upon potential severity. Severity is assessed based upon the perceived level of impact to the confidentiality, integrity, and availability of an organization's IT resources or data. The severity of an incident also may change. Organizations often classify severity on a low-medium-high scale. An organization might classify severity as follows:

- **Low**—The adverse affect on the confidentiality, integrity, or availability of the organization's data or IT resources is limited. A low-impact event causes little or no damage.
- **Medium**—The adverse affect on the confidentiality, integrity, or availability of the organization's data or IT resources is moderate. A medium-impact event results in significant damage to assets.
- **High**—The adverse affect on the confidentiality, integrity, or availability of the organization's data or IT resources is severe. A high-impact event results in major damage to assets.

Classifying the nature and severity of an incident helps incident handlers know which incidents require priority handling. If the incident handlers must respond to multiple incidents, classification promotes efficiency. It also makes sure organizations respond to incidents according to the incident's potential to hurt the organization. Classification also helps incident handlers know which incidents to escalate to management.

Investigation is the second phase in the IR process. During this phase, the incident handlers learn about the incident and its source. They learn more about the impact that the incident is having on the organization. The incident handlers must find all the resources that arc affected by the incident. They also must contact other areas as needed to fully understand the scope of the incident. The IR policy and plan let the incident handlers know who they must contact.

The incident handlers must keep management informed of their IR activities. It's important that management be informed in case there are any regulatory requirements that need to be considered as the organization responds to the incident. For example, if an incident involves the disclosure of the protected health information of more than 500 people, HIPAA requires that the organization notify the Department of Health and Human Services about the disclosure. Executive management must make the final decisions about contacting third parties or the media.

It's also important during the investigation phase for the incident handlers to follow the organization's own internal policies. If handlers are investigating an incident that might be a crime, it's important that the team follow good evidentiary practices. Evidence collection issues are discussed in Chapter 15. If an incident appears to be a crime, the incident handlers must contact law enforcement according to the terms of the IR plan.

The organization must begin the containment phase almost as soon as an incident is reported. During this step, incident handlers must take steps to limit the damage caused by the incident. They will use different methods to contain an incident depending upon its nature. For example, if the incident is a self-propagating virus, incident handlers may remove an infected system from the organization's network. If the incident is a particularly authentic-looking phishing e-mail, incident handlers might issue an alert or other notification to the organization's employees. The alert would tell the employees not to respond to a phishing e-mail.

The organization repairs and recovers its IT resources and data during the recovery phase. The IT resources and data should be repaired in such a way that they're not vulnerable to the same type of incident again. This is called hardening. In addition to hardening damaged IT resources, the organization must harden resources that are similar to the damaged resources. This makes sure that similar resources aren't harmed by similar incidents.

After an IT resource is repaired, it should be tested for any additional vulnerabilities or weaknesses before it's put back into production. The recovery and repair method will depend upon the nature of the incident.

All stages in the IR process must be fully documented. The primary incident handler is responsible for making sure that each step in the process has been fully documented. This is important because the IR planning team can review the notes from the incident handlers to determine whether the IR plan worked as intended. During the review stage, both the incident handlers and the IR planning team can review the documentation to learn:

> **NOTE**
>
> As a general information security best practice, a repaired IT resource should not be tested by the same person that repairs or recovers it. This is a separation of duties best practice to make sure that vulnerabilities and weaknesses aren't overlooked.

- Dollar amount spent in handling the incident
- Dollar amount spent to prevent similar incidents in the future
- Loss of staff time in handling the incident
- How the response to the current incident compares to similar incidents in the past
- Recommendations on policy and procedural changes as a result of lessons learned from the incident

The review phase is often overlooked. This is because it's easy for an organization's employees to go back to their normal operational duties after an incident. The IR planning team must make sure that the review process is formally required by policy.

The IR process is shown in Figure 14-2. As described in this section, many of the stages overlap with one another. The lines between each stage can be indistinct at times.

Disaster Recovery and Business Continuity Planning

A 2009 AT&T study found that over one-third of the companies it interviewed had used their disaster recovery and business continuity plans to respond to an emergency. The study found that companies were likely to use their contingency plans in response to extreme weather and power outages. Almost half of the companies interviewed said that business continuity planning was a priority.[4]

> **NOTE**
>
> It helps to think of an incident as an event that an organization can deal with during its normal operations. A disaster is an event that completely disrupts those normal operations.

Disaster recovery and business continuity plans help an organization respond to a disaster. A **disaster** is a sudden, unplanned event. Disasters negatively affect the organization's critical business functions for an unknown period. The difference between a disaster and an incident is subtle. A disaster severely affects the organization's infrastructure. It interrupts critical business functions. An incident tends to refer to service failures that affect the confidentiality, integrity, and/or availability of the organization's data and IT systems. An incident may become a disaster in some situations.

Examples of disasters include natural threats and deliberate, human-made threats. Natural threats are uncontrollable events. They include earthquakes, fires, and flood. Human-made threats include sabotage and terrorist activities. Threats that can evolve into a disaster also include equipment, electrical, and communications infrastructure failure. Disasters aren't predictable. Organizations can't control these types of threats. They can take measures to try to limit the damage caused by these events. Organizations also can make plans to respond to these types of events.

FIGURE 14-2

Incident response plan phases.

Disaster recovery (DR) plans focus on how an organization recovers its IT systems after a disaster. These plans focus on IT systems only. They're the organization's immediate response to restoring critical IT resources after a devastating disaster or event. DR is largely a function of IT and is part of a larger business continuity plan.

A business continuity (BC) plan focuses on how the organization continues its business during and after a disaster. These plans tend to be more comprehensive. They cover all parts of a business, not just IT systems. These plans address the period between the disaster and a return to normal operations.

The formal distinction between DR and BC plans is eroding. This is because organizations rely on IT systems for many of their critical functions. Some organizations build their whole business model on their IT systems. Today, most organizations consider DR and BC to be the same thing. You may find the terms used interchangeably. Most references recognize that a DR plan must be part of a comprehensive BC plan.

In this book, DR and BC plans will be discussed together, unless it's necessary to differentiate between the two. If it's necessary to differentiate between the two types of plans, the distinction will be made clear in the text.

DR/BC Team

The DR/BC team is responsible for creating an organization's DR/BC policy and plans. Like the RA and IR teams, this team must include members from many areas of the organization. The people who are going to be responsible for carrying out the plan in the event of a disaster also should be included on the team.

A DR/BC plan is an organization-wide plan. Specific departments may have secondary DR/BC plans. These department-level plans must be consistent with the organization's DR/BC plan. An organization's overall DR/BC plan has a number of goals:

- Ensure that the organization's employees are safe
- Minimize the organization's amount of loss
- Recover critical business systems and infrastructure within a certain period
- Resume critical business operations within a certain period
- Repair or replace damaged facilities
- Return to normal operations

The DR/BC team will help the organization create its DR/BC policy. These policies are very specific to an organization's structure and culture.

A DR/BC team must include members from IT, HR, executive management, physical security, and legal counsel. It must include the managers or owners of critical business processes. The team also should include the employees, and their backups, who will be in charge of directing the organization's activities in a real disaster. It's important that backup personnel be included in case the people with primary DR/BC responsibilities are not available in a disaster.

One thing to keep in mind for DR/BC plans is that disasters aren't always limited to the organization. A disaster in a geographic region may mean that both the organization and its employees will be affected by it. Employees must personally respond to the same disaster. If employees must respond to the disaster at home with their own families, they may not be in a position to help the organization respond to the disaster as well.

DR/BC Plan Development

Many of the steps in the DR/BC planning process are similar to the RA and IR planning processes. Contingency planning is a part of risk management. The steps in the DR/BC planning process are:

- Develop the DR/BC policy
- Conduct a business impact analysis
- Identify threats and potential controls
- Determine recovery strategy
- Design and maintain the plan

The DR/BC team must make sure that policies and plans are in place that help the organization complete these steps. The DR/BC policy is a statement of executive management's commitment to the business continuity planning. It should state the purpose and goals of DR/BC. The policy should define DR/BC roles and responsibilities. The policy should include the organization's resource requirements for any DR/BC plan.

After a DR/BC policy is approved, the DR/BC team must conduct a **business impact analysis (BIA)**. A BIA identifies key business operations. It also identifies the resources that support those operations. The DR/BC team uses a BIA to estimate how long those critical operations and resources can be offline before the organization's entire business is negatively affected.

To complete a BIA, the DR/BC team must:

- **Identify critical business processes**—The BR/DR team must identify the organization's critical business processes. There's no master list of processes that are critical to an organization. Each organization is different. Critical processes might include payroll, attendance scheduling, and customer service activities.
- **Identify IT resources that support critical business processes**—The BR/DR team must identify the resources that support its critical business processes. Resources can include the organization's communications infrastructure. They also can include individual IT systems and components.
- **Determine how long IT resources can be offline**—The DR/BC team must identify the effect on business organizations if a resource is disrupted or damaged and a critical process can't run.
- **Determine recovery criticality**—The DR/BC team must prioritize how the organization will handle IT resources and business processes following a disaster.

A BIA closely resembles a risk assessment. Many of the same tools and techniques used in a RA are used to complete a BIA. The team can interview employees throughout the organization to learn about its many business processes. The team also could send a questionnaire to a sampling of employees. The questionnaire could ask questions about business processes and resources.

Once the DR/BC team determines the organization's critical processes and resources, it must figure out how long those processes and resources can be offline before the organization experiences irreparable harm. This period is called **maximum tolerable downtime (MTD)**. Some processes and systems are so critical that they can be down only for a few minutes before an organization suffers irreparable damage. If these processes are offline longer than the MTD, the organization might fail. Processes and systems that aren't essential to business operations may have an MTD of days or weeks.

> **NOTE**
> Some resources use the term "maximum acceptable outage" in place of MTD. The terms are the same.

The DR/BC team must determine the order in which IT resources will be handled following the disaster. It uses the results of the BIA to make this determination. If an organization must resume a business process within a short period, it will need to make sure that it can put people and processes in place to recover the process within that period. The priority list of processes and resources helps executive management make recover strategy decisions.

After the BIA is complete, the DR/BC team must identify threats and potential controls. This step is very similar to a risk assessment. In fact, the organization may have completed this exercise as part of a RA. If so, the DR/BC team can use those results at this step.

The DR/BC team must identify the threats to the organization that have disaster potential. It also must identify potential controls to respond to those threats. These controls try to reduce the possibility of the organization experiencing a disaster. If a disaster can't be avoided, these controls lessen the amount of damage to the organization.

For example, an organization's data center may be located in an area prone to tornadoes. If the organization can't move its data center, it may try to fortify it. The organization tries to make the data center more resistant to wind-related damage to protect its business processes.

Some common preventative controls that an organization can implement include:

- Fire detection and suppression systems
- Installing backup generators or uninterruptible power supplies
- Offsite storage of system backup media
- Frequent backups of critical data
- Extra equipment inventories for critical IT resources

The DR/BC team must determine a recovery strategy. It consults with executive management to do this. An organization's recovery strategy addresses the resources that it must recover after a disaster. An organization will have to consider a wide variety of recovery strategies.

An organization must prepare recovery strategies for its:

- **Critical business processes**—The organization must plan for recovering its business processes. It must understand all the workflow steps needed to complete a business process. It must know the resources and supplies needed to support these processes.
- **Facilities and supplies**—The organization must make sure that it has a plan to restore its main facility. It also must restore the utilities needed to support that facility. Utilities include telecommunications and electrical infrastructure.

Backup Site Options

It's rare when an organization experiences a disaster that forces it out of its main facility for a long time. However, the organization still must plan for this possibility. It must have a location to which it can move its operations. This is called a "backup site." An organization has several planning options for a backup site. It's important for you to know the differences between them.

A **mirrored site** is a fully operational backup site. It actively runs the organization's IT processes in parallel with the organization's main facility. A mirrored site is a redundant facility. An organization can immediately transfer all of its IT operations to the mirrored site. This site is already staffed with the organization's employees. This is the most expensive type of backup site to maintain. This type of backup site is appropriate for organizations that have a low MTD for critical processes. This type of backup site supports high availability.

A **hot site** is an operational backup site. It has all of the equipment and infrastructure that an organization needs to continue its business operations. The equipment in the hot site is fully compatible with the organization's main facility. A hot site can become operational within minutes to hours after a disaster. It's not staffed with people. It also doesn't process data in parallel with the main facility. The organization will need to bring data backups to the hot site facility. A hot site is expensive to maintain. It may be the best choice for an organization that can afford some, but not a lot, of downtime.

A **warm site** is a compromise between a hot site and a cold site. A warm site is space that contains some, but not all, of the equipment that an organization will need to continue operations in the event of a disaster. The warm site is partially prepared for operations. It has electricity and network connectivity. This type of site is more expensive than a cold site.

A **cold site** is a backup site that's little more than reserved space. It's the most inexpensive type of backup site. It doesn't have any equipment or hardware set up. It will have electrical service. It most likely won't have network connectivity. It can take weeks for an organization to get a cold site ready for business operations. An organization will have to acquire equipment and infrastructure to make the site operational.

- **Employee environment**—The organization must have plans in place for supporting its employees during a disaster. This means making sure that it has ways to communicate with employees during a disaster. The organization also must have plans in place to manage employee responsibilities until the organization can return to normal operations.

- **IT operations**—The organization must have plans in place to resume its IT operations. This means making sure that infrastructure components are in place so that business can resume. The organization will want to have contracts with its vendors so that it can get replacement equipment quickly.

- **Data recovery**—The organization must have a way to recover its data and operational information. It must have plans in place to retrieve data from offsite storage facilities. It also must have plans to retrieve paper-based information from its main facility.

A recovery strategy also must include the people that will implement it. A team with specialized skills and knowledge must head each recovery area. For example, the organization's storage administrators should serve on the team in charge of data recovery. Each team must have a leader.

Once an organization develops its DR/BC plan, it must monitor and update it in response to changing conditions. An organization must update its plan anytime its business processes or technology change. It must update the plan any time key personnel change. Organizations put contingency plans in place so that they can respond to events that adversely affect them. It's not enough to create a plan and put it away on a shelf for use "just in case."

A DR/BC plan helps an organization respond to a disaster. These plans are an important part of an organization's risk management activities. The DR/BC planning process is shown in Figure 14-3.

Testing the Plan

Organizations must test their contingency plans on a regular basis to make sure that the plan accounts for critical business functions and processes. It also should test its contingency plans to make sure that the plans don't have any deficiencies. An organization must correct plan deficiencies.

FIGURE 14-3

DR/BC planning process.

14

Analysis, Response,
Contingency Planning

Contingency plan testing has a number of objectives. They include:

- Help employees become familiar with and accept the DR/BC plan.
- Train employees how to respond during an emergency.
- Identify weaknesses or deficiencies within the plan.
- Make sure that all of the checklists and procedures needed to implement the plan are created and in place.
- Make sure that all the resources and supplies needed to implement the plan are in place and are operational.
- Make sure that all communications mechanisms work properly.
- Make sure that all DR/BC teams are able to work well together.

> **NOTE**
>
> In the DR/BC plan context, a single point of failure is a step in the plan or an assumption within the plan that is critical to the performance of the entire plan. If that step or the assumption fails, then a critical portion of the plan, or the entire plan, could fail.

Through testing, an organization can learn that it's missing key business process areas. It also can identify single points of failure within the plan and take steps to correct them. Any changes that are made to the DR/BC plan as part of the test review must be fully documented. Changes to the plan also must be communicated to all members of the organization.

There are five ways to test DR/BC plans. They also could be used to test an organization's incident response capability.

A **checklist test** is one of the most basic types of DR/BC test. In this type of test, the DR/BC team makes sure that supplies and inventory items that are needed to execute the DR/BC plan are in place. This type of test makes sure that sufficient supplies are stored at backup facilities. It also makes sure that the organization has enough reference copies of the DR/BC plan and that all copies have current information.

A **walk-through test** is often used with a checklist test. In this type of test, the DR/BC team "walks through" the entire DR/BC plan. They study each area of the plan to make sure that all of the assumptions and tasks stated in it are correct. This type of test also helps the people who are responsible for executing the DR/BC plan become very familiar with it. This type of test is sometimes called a "tabletop walk-through test" or "tabletop test" because the members of the team will sit around a table as they study the plan.

A **simulation test** is a more realistic version of a walk-through test. In this type of test, the organization role-plays a disaster scenario. The scope of these types of tests has to be carefully defined so that they don't negatively affect normal business activities. This test is designed to measure the effectiveness of employee notification procedures. Depending upon the scope of the test, it might try to measure how fast an organization can set up its backup site. It also could measure how fast an organization's vendors can provide additional equipment.

A **parallel test** is designed to test the organization's IT recovery processes. In this type of test, the organization tests its ability to recover its IT systems and its business data. The organization brings its backup sites online. It will then use historical business data to test how those systems operate. In this test, the organization tests both data processing and data recovery. During the test, the organization continues normal business operations at its main facility. The test is conducted using historical data.

A **full interruption test** is designed to test the organization's entire DR/BC plan. This test involves a scenario that destroys or severely damages the organization's main facility. The organization must transfer all business and IT functions to its backup site. In this type of test, all normal business operations stop. Operations are shut down at the main site. They must be transferred to the backup site using the processes stated in the DR/BC plan.

A full interruption test is the most expensive kind of contingency plan test. It can help the organization learn a lot about its DR/BC plan's effectiveness. However, it also has the potential to negatively affect the organization's business. If the organization can't get business operations resumed at the backup site, then the test itself can create a disaster situation for the organization. Organizations undertake these types of tests with great care.

Special Considerations

Risk management and contingency planning activities make good business sense. They help an organization prepare for threats and events that harm its ability to meet its business goals. Organizations that engage in these activities understand their information security posture. They know where they have weaknesses. They know the threats to the confidentiality, integrity, and availability of their IT resources and data.

Addressing Compliance Requirements

For many organizations, RM and contingency planning aren't just good business practices. Sometimes they are required by law. Many of the laws reviewed in this book require organization's covered by the laws to complete risk assessments and create contingency plans. Table 14-5 reviews the laws in this book that have these requirements.

TABLE 14-5 Laws with risk assessment and contingency plan requirements.

NAME OF LAW	RISK ASSESSMENT REQUIRED?	DR/BC PLAN REQUIRED?
Gramm-Leach-Bliley Act Consumer financial information	Yes	Yes
Payment Card Industry Standards* Companies that accept credit cards for payment	Yes	Yes
Health Insurance Portability and Accountability Act Protected health information	Yes	Yes
Sarbanes-Oxley Act Corporate financial information	Yes	Implied if contingency plans are indicated as an internal control required to secure financial reporting processes and systems.
Federal Information Systems Management Act Federal information systems	Yes	Yes

*The Payment Card Industry (PCI) Standards are not a law. Organizations that wish to accept credit cards for payment of goods and services must follow these standards. Banks that process credit card information enforce PCI compliance.

When to Call the Police

Children learn the basics of "when to call 9-1-1" at a very early age. Children are taught to call the police or emergency responders when:

- Someone's life is in immediate danger
- When smoke or fire is present
- When emergency medical help is needed
- When a crime is being committed

These are good rules for an organization as well. Organizations should include rules for when to call law enforcement or emergency responders in their contingency plans.

Must People Report Crime?

Under common law, in general, a person has no duty to report a crime that he or she witnesses. For purposes of the law, an organization is considered a "person." Thus, most organizations also have no obligation to report a crime that he or she witnesses.

There are some instances where people are required by law to report crimes, however. For instance, most people are required to report crimes where children or vulnerable adults are in danger. These laws require people to report suspected child abuse and neglect to law enforcement.

Some states have laws that require information technology workers to report the discovery of child pornography on computers. They must report the discovery to law enforcement. The IT worker must have discovered the pornography within the scope of his or her employment. An IT worker isn't required to search for this type of material. However, if it is discovered, he or she must report it. At the time that this book was written, seven states had these laws.

Most organizations should report any criminal activity that involves their IT resources or data. It's important to contact law enforcement right away to start investigating the crime.

Sometimes it's hard to know if a crime is committed. If the organization experiences a data breach, it's likely that a crime upon the organization was committed. Possible crimes include trespass, theft of data, theft of resources, unauthorized access, and similar crimes. These types of crimes are discussed in Chapter 12.

One of the most important reasons to promptly report crimes involving IT resources is so that forensic evidence can be collected. This type of evidence can be used to investigate computer crimes. However, this type of evidence is very volatile and must be preserved properly. Computer forensics issues are discussed in Chapter 15.

One of the things that organizations must account for in their contingency plans is the fact that communications systems will likely be overloaded in a regional disaster or emergency. It may take time to contact first responders. It may take extra time to receive their assistance. In regional natural disaster situations, people are usually discouraged from calling emergency responders unless a person's life is in immediate danger. This is to keep emergency phone lines, such as 9-1-1 trunk telephone lines, from being overloaded with calls.

Public Relations

An organization's contingency plans must consider its public relations strategy. **Public relations (PR)** is a marketing field that manages an organization's public image. It includes marketing the organization's products and services. It protects the organization's reputation and image. PR includes responding to crises that threaten that image.

An organization's PR team develops communication strategies. These strategies are used to guide communications with employees, customers, and stakeholders. Coordinating an organization's public message is sometimes difficult under normal business operations. It's more difficult in an emergency. A PR strategy for emergencies must consider:

- Who is authorized to make comments on the organization's behalf?
- Who is authorized to approve the contents of comments shared with the public?
- How often should information be shared with the public?
- How should information be shared with the public?
- How should information be shared if normal communications methods are unavailable in an emergency?

It's important that an organization have a PR strategy for emergencies. The organization must make sure that information is given to stakeholders in a reliable and organized manner. It also must make sure that reliable information is communicated to employees. An organization's reputation can suffer if it doesn't share enough information or shares it in a chaotic manner. Its reputation also can be harmed if the organization distributes conflicting information from different sources.

CHAPTER SUMMARY

This chapter reviewed risk management and contingency planning concepts. The RM process helps an organization understand the risks that it faces each day. It also helps organizations strengthen their security posture in response to threats and vulnerabilities. Many of the laws discussed in this book require organizations to use RM concepts to create information security programs.

This chapter also reviewed different types of contingency plans. An organization uses contingency plans to limit financial loss due to an adverse event. Contingency plans help minimize the length of time that an organization's services and critical processes are interrupted after an emergency.

KEY CONCEPTS AND TERMS

Annual rate of occurrence (ARO)

Annualized loss expectancy (ALE)

Business continuity (BC) plans

Business impact analysis (BIA)

Checklist test

Cold site

Conflicts of interest

Disaster

Disaster recovery (DR) plans

Exposure factor

Full interruption test

Hot site

Incident

Incident response (IR)

Maximum tolerable downtime (MTD)

Mirrored site

Parallel test

Public relations (PR)

Qualitative risk analysis

Quantitative risk analysis

Realized risk

Risk assessment (RA)

Risk management (RM)

Simulation test

Single loss expectancy (SLE)

Walk-through test

Warm site

CHAPTER 14 ASSESSMENT

1. A parallel test uses current processing data to test IT system operation.

　A. True

　B. False

2. Which item is *not* part of the risk management process?

　A. Risk analysis

　B. Risk response

　C. Continuous monitoring

　D. Training employees

　E. All of the above are parts of the risk management process

3. What does a risk assessment do?

4. Which type of contingency plan test is the least expensive?

　A. Full interruption test

　B. Parallel test

　C. Simulation test

　D. Checklist test

　E. None of the above

5. Which type of risk analysis uses real numbers to calculate risk?

　A. Quantitative

　B. Qualitative

　C. Quasi-quantitative

　D. Quasi-qualitative

　E. None of the above

6. The _____ is the percentage of asset loss that is likely to be caused by an identified threat.

7. How is annualized loss expectancy calculated?

8. What is the main benefit of a qualitative risk assessment?

　A. Measures the money cost of a risk

　B. Scope of the assessment can be easily changed

　C. Easy to administer

　D. All of the above

　E. None of the above

9. Which of the following is a qualitative risk assessment methodology?

　A. CRAMM

　B. ISO

　C. MTD

　D. BIA

　E. None of the above

10. Which risk response eliminates all risk of harm posted by a threat or vulnerability?

A. Risk transfer

B. Risk mitigation

C. Risk acceptance

D. Risk avoidance

E. None of the above

11. Which type of contingency plan reacts to attacks against an organization's IT infrastructure?

A. BC plan

B. DR plan

C. IR plan

D. A and B only

E. None of the above

12. A(n) _____ is an event that adversely affects the confidentiality, integrity, and/or availability of an organization's data and IT systems.

13. A(n) _____ is a sudden, unplanned event that negatively affects the organization's critical business functions for an unknown period.

14. Which backup site is a fully operational backup site?

A. Mirrored site

B. Hot site

C. Warm site

D. Cold site

E. None of the above

15. A business impact analysis identifies key business operations and resources.

A. True

B. False

ENDNOTES

1. HP and SCORE: Counselors to America's Small Business, "Impact on U.S. Small Business of Natural & Man-Made Disasters," 2007, *http://www.score.org/pdf/HP_Download_ImpactofDisaster.pdf* (accessed May 1, 2010).

2. National Institute of Standards and Technology, "Special Publication 800-30: Risk Management Guide for Information Technology Systems," October 2001, *http://csrc.nist.gov/publications/nistpubs/800-30/sp800-30.pdf* (accessed April 29, 2010).

3. National Institute of Standards and Technology, "SP 800-61, Rev. 1, Computer Security Incident Handling Guide," March 2008, *http://csrc.nist.gov/publications/nistpubs/800-61-rev1/SP800-61rev1.pdf* (accessed May 1, 2010).

4. AT&T, "2009 AT&T Business Continuity Study, U.S. National Results," June 1, 2009, *http://www.att.com/gen/press-room?pid=2923* (accessed May 2, 2010).

Computer Forensics and Investigations

C OMPUTER FORENSICS is the scientific process of collecting and examining data stored on, received from, or transmitted by an electronic device. It's a demanding area of study. New technologies that store data are created every day. People who choose to work in this area must constantly study these new technologies. They must learn how to collect and examine data from devices that use the new technology. Computer forensics is also a rapidly expanding profession. The U.S. Department of Labor estimates higher-than-average job growth for people in this career.[1]

This chapter introduces basic concepts about computer forensics. It also discusses the role of the computer forensic examiner. Finally, it reviews legal issues surrounding how digital evidence is gathered and used.

Chapter 15 Topics

This chapter covers the following topics and concepts:

- What computer forensics is
- What a computer forensic examiner does
- What the general rules for collecting, handling, and using digital evidence are
- What some legal issues regarding the seizure of digital evidence are

Chapter 15 Goals

When you complete this chapter, you will be able to:

- Define computer forensics
- Explain the role of a computer forensic examiner
- Explain why digital evidence must be carefully handled
- Describe why chain of custody is important
- Explain the laws that affect the collection of digital evidence
- Describe concerns regarding the admissibility of digital evidence

What Is Computer Forensics?

Computer forensics is a relatively new scientific process for examining data stored on, received, or transmitted by electronic devices. The data is examined to find evidence about an event or crime. Law enforcement uses computer forensics to investigate almost any type of crime. Consider the following:

- Illinois state prosecutors used cell phone records and data gathered by computer forensic examiners to convict a defendant of murdering two people. The defendant used his computer to search "hire a hit man." He also searched for directions from his home to the victims' home. The case was unique because almost no physical evidence existed to link the defendant to the murders. A judge sentenced him to life in prison.
- A Hong Kong shipping company pleaded guilty to violating U.S. pollution laws. It was fined $10 million. A ship operated by the company ran into the San Francisco Bay Bridge. It spilled more than 50,000 gallons of fuel into the San Francisco Bay. Computer forensic examiners found that someone on the ship altered its computerized navigation charts after the crash.
- A Missouri jury convicted a defendant of possessing child pornography. Digital evidence was used to convict him. Computer forensic examiners found pornographic images on his computer. A judge sentenced the defendant to 35 years in prison.

NOTE
The word forensics is from the Latin word *forensis,* which means "belonging to the forum." It refers to the types of arguments used in a court or public forum to prove or disprove past theories or arguments.

Computer forensics has many different names. It's also called system or digital forensics, computer forensic analysis, computer examination, data recovery, and inforensics (information forensics). These terms are used interchangeably. This book uses the term "computer forensics."

Computer forensic examiners use specialized software and tools to collect and study data stored on various electronic devices. The evidence collected is called **digital evidence** or just electronic evidence. Computer forensics includes all the steps through which this evidence is collected, preserved, analyzed, documented, and presented. The goal of computer forensics is to find evidence that helps investigators analyze an event or incident.

Computer forensic examiners study and collect electronic data for many reasons. They don't just investigate crimes. Other computer forensics uses include:

- **Individuals**—People may hire computer forensic examiners to find evidence to support tort claims. They can find digital evidence about sexual harassment or discrimination. Examiners also can uncover evidence for any type of civil litigation. They also can find evidence to support a criminal defense case.

- **Military**—The military uses computer forensics to gather intelligence information to support its operations. It also uses computer forensics to prepare for and respond to cyberattacks.

- **Organizations**—Organizations use computer forensics the same ways that individuals use it. Computer forensic examiners also can investigate employee wrongdoing. They can look for embezzlement or theft of intellectual property (IP). They also can look for unauthorized use of information technology (IT) resources. They can look into attempts to harm an organization's IT resources. An organization's incident response (IR) program can include forensic activities. Incident response is discussed in Chapter 14.

- **Colleges and universities**—Many colleges and universities offer programs in computer forensics. Some may have forensic research programs. They also use computer forensics for IR.

- **Data recovery firms**—Data recovery firms use computer forensics to rescue data for their clients. They also advise clients how to keep data safe from loss.

Most electronic devices hold some type of data. Computer forensics can study any of them. Potential sources of digital evidence include:

- **Computer systems**—This includes laptop and desktop computers, and servers. It also includes the hardware and software that the system uses. This category also includes peripheral devices that can be attached to computer systems. These devices enhance the user experience. They may include keyboards, microphones, Web cameras, and memory card readers.

- **Storage devices**—This includes internal and external hard drives. It also includes removable media such as floppy disks, Zip disks, compact discs (CDs), digital versatile discs (DVDs), thumb flash drives, and memory cards.

- **Mobile devices**—This includes cell phones and smart phones. It also includes personal digital assistants (PDAs) and pagers. Global positioning system (GPS) devices hold data as well. Digital and video cameras, and audio and video multimedia devices also fall into this category.

- **Networking equipment**—This includes network hubs, routers, servers, switches, and power supplies. Networking equipment can be wired or wireless.
- **Other potential sources**—Many office devices have data storage ability. This includes copiers and fax machines, answering machines, printers, and scanners. Entertainment devices store data as well. They include digital video recorders (DVRs), digital audio recorders, and video game systems. Surveillance equipment is included in this category. This category includes any device not already mentioned that can store data.

Our dependence on electronic devices to live our lives continues to grow. As a result, computer forensics as a special area of study also grows. Computer forensics is a fast-growing profession. Computer forensic examiners aren't always experts in collecting data from every possible type of electronic device. They often focus on certain types of devices. In addition, most computer forensic examiners focus their skills in specific areas. The three main areas of computer forensics are:

- Media analysis
- Code analysis
- Network analysis

Media analysis focuses on collecting and examining data stored on physical media. This includes computer systems and storage devices. It also includes mobile devices. When people think about computer forensics, they most often think about media analysis. This type of analysis discovers normal and deleted data. It also finds encrypted, hidden, and password-protected data. This chapter focuses mostly on media analysis concepts. These concepts apply to other types of computer forensic analysis as well.

Code analysis focuses on reviewing programming code. It's also called malware forensics. This area looks for malicious code or signatures. The need for code analysis continues to grow. In 2009, antivirus vendor Symantec created 2,895,802 new malicious code signatures for its products. This is a 71 percent increase from 2008.[2]

Network analysis focuses on collecting and examining network traffic. An examiner reviews transaction logs and uses real-time monitoring to find evidence. Organizations often use this type of analysis to investigate incidents.

Some computer forensic examiners also might have specialties within these three major categories. For example, some examiners might specialize in e-mail forensics. E-mail forensics includes a combination of media and network analysis. It's used to find the sender, recipient, date, time, location information, and contents of e-mail messages. As technology advances, it's not unusual to find examiners with very specialized skills. Figure 15-1 shows different computer forensic categories.

What Is the Role of a Computer Forensic Examiner?

Computer forensics is a fairly new field. It's only a few decades old. It's growing quickly. In 1984, the U.S. Federal Bureau of Investigation (FBI) began creating software programs to collect computer evidence. In 1990, the International Association of Computer

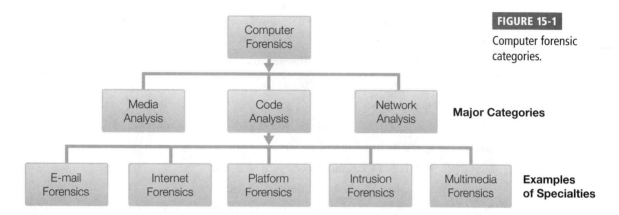

FIGURE 15-1

Computer forensic categories.

Investigative Specialists (IACIS) was formed. The IACIS is the oldest computer forensic professional group. It was the first group to use the phrase "computer forensics."

The first international conference on computer forensics was held in 1993. In 1995, the International Organization on Computer Evidence (IOCE) was formed. The IOCE creates guiding principles for computer forensic examiners.

Computer forensic examiners find evidence on electronic devices. They collect it for both civil and criminal cases. They must collect this evidence in a scientific manner, regardless of the underlying case. They also must have a full understanding of various technologies, hardware, and software. An examiner helps answer who, what, where, when, why, and how.

> ▶ **NOTE**
> The scientific method is a way to answer questions in a repeatable and verifiable way. It's a formal method of investigation.

A computer forensic examiner must have the following traits:

- A sound knowledge of computing technologies
- Use of the scientific method to conduct repeatable and verifiable examinations
- Understanding of the laws of evidence and legal procedure
- Access to computer forensic tools and the skill to use them
- Outstanding record-keeping skills

No matter how careful they are, people always leave traces of their activities when they interact with other people and with their surroundings. This is a basic tenet of forensic science. It's known as **Locard's exchange principle**. It applies to the digital world and the physical world. If people attempt to steal electronic information or delete incriminating files, they leave electronic traces of their activities. For example, log information can document these activities. A computer forensic examiner needs to know how to find this trace evidence material. This evidence is used to help prove a person's actions in a computer system.

> ▶ **NOTE**
> Dr. Edmund Locard was a forensics pioneer. He lived from 1877 to 1966. He argued that scientific methods should be applied to criminal investigations. He believed that when people or objects interact, they transfer physical evidence to one another. Forensic scientists recover that evidence. They study and learn from it.

Computer forensic examiners do more than turn on a computer and search through files. They must perform complex data recovery procedures. In particular, they must:

- Protect the data on any electronic device.
- Avoid deleting, damaging, or altering data in any way on any electronic device.
- Make exact copies of electronic data without altering the original device.
- Discover normal, deleted, password-protected, hidden, and encrypted files.
- Study data to create timelines of electronic activity.
- Identify files and data that may be relevant to a case.
- Fully document all evidence-collection activities.
- Provide expert testimony on the steps taken to recover digital evidence.

Computer forensic examiners must have special skills. They have skills beyond those of the traditional information security professional. The law requires that computer forensic examiners be competent at what they do. Examiners can show that they are competent by earning advanced degrees. They also can become certified. Since the profession is still new, there are many computer forensic certifications to choose from. Both independent organizations and vendors offer them.

States and courts struggle with how to make sure computer forensic examinations are done only by competent examiners. Courts rely on legal principles and trial rules to screen examiners before they testify. States create laws that govern the activities of these examiners. Often, computer forensic examiners are governed under the broad terms of a state's private detective laws.

Many states regulate private detectives and investigators. They require a private detective to have a state-issued license before he or she can conduct investigations. These laws were created before computer forensics existed as a separate field. The broad language of these laws can pull computer forensic examiners within the scope of these regulated professions. This isn't unusual. Even the U.S. Department of Labor includes computer forensic examiners within the private detective profession.

At the time this book was written, four states appear to require computer forensic examiners to have a private detective license. They are Illinois,[3] Michigan,[4] Oregon,[5] and Texas.[6] In Texas, the law is interpreted very broadly. It actually includes computer technicians and computer repair personnel within the scope of its law.

Some states don't include computer forensic examiners within their private detective licensing laws. Delaware,[7] North Carolina,[8] and Virginia[9] are examples. North Carolina law states that any person who performs computer forensic services in order to collect evidence isn't a private investigator. The North Carolina law also excludes examiners who provide expert testimony. It also excludes any person who engages in network or system vulnerability testing.

In 2009, the American Bar Association (ABA) issued a report on computer forensic examiners. The ABA asked states to stop requiring computer forensic examiners to get a private detective license. It said that the role of private detectives is different from that of computer forensic examiners. It also stated that courts have broad discretion to make sure that digital evidence used in trials is reliable. Since the courts have that discretion, the ABA argued that there's no need to license computer forensic examiners.

Computer Forensic Examiner Certifications

There are many independent and vendor-specific computer forensic credentials. An examiner must weigh which credential best suits his or her career path. Popular vendor-neutral credentials include:

- **Certified Computer Examiner (CCE)**—The International Society of Forensic Computer Examiners (ISFCE) offers the CCE. The ISFCE has offered the CCE since 2003. It's a vendor-neutral certification. CCE holders have basic knowledge of forensic examination procedures. You can learn more at *http://www.isfce.com/*.

- **Certified Computer Forensics Examiner (CCFE)**—The Information Assurance Certification Review Board (IACRB) offers the CCFE. It's also vendor neutral. CCFE candidates must take a written exam and a practical application test. There are nine subject-matter areas in the CCFE exam. You can learn more at *http://www .iacertification.org/index.htm*.

- **Certified Forensic Computer Examiner (CFCE)**—The International Association of Computer Investigative Specialists (IACIS) offers the CFCE. Only law enforcement personnel may earn it. It's vendor neutral. CFCE candidates must pass an intensive practical exam. You can learn more at *http://www.iacis.com/*.

- **GIAC Certified Forensic Analyst (GCFA)**—The Global Information Assurance Certification (GIAC) program offers the GCFA. Like the CCE and CCFE, this certification also tests practical knowledge. It's vendor neutral. You can learn about GIAC at *http://www.giac.org/*.

Some forensic software vendors offer certifications for their products. EnCase is a popular forensic tool sold by Guidance Software. It offers the EnCase Certified Examiner (EnCE) credential. The EnCE exam has a written section and a practical section. The practical section covers use of the EnCase forensics program. You can learn more at *http://www .guidancesoftware.com/computer-forensics-training-ence-certification.htm*.

Another software vendor that offers a certification is AccessData. AccessData offers a product known as the Forensic Toolkit. The product is better known as FTK. AccessData offers the AccessData Certified Examiner (ACE) credential. It tests knowledge of the FTK tool. The ACE exam is a multiple-choice test. You can learn more at *http://www.accessdata .com/acePreparation.html*.

Collecting, Handling, and Using Digital Evidence

 NOTE

Computer forensic examiners should always collect digital evidence in a reliable (forensically sound) manner. The nature of the underlying investigation doesn't matter. The examiner should always use a reliable and repeatable process.

Computer forensic examiners find evidence on electronic devices. They use this evidence to help reconstruct past events or activities. They use the evidence to gain a better understanding of a crime or event. It can be used to show possession and use of digital data. This section discusses how computer forensic examiners collect digital evidence. It focuses on how this evidence is collected in a criminal investigation. You need to keep in mind that almost the same process will be used in a civil investigation. An organization's IR process also will be similar.

A computer can play one of three roles in computer crime. This concept was discussed in Chapter 12. A computer, or any electronic device, can be used to commit a crime. Cyberstalking, identity theft, and phishing scams are examples of crimes facilitated by computers. The computer also can be the target of a crime. Denial of service (DoS) and distributed denial of service (DDoS) attacks, computer viruses, and communications sabotage are examples of crimes where the computer itself is the target of the crime. Finally, the computer can be a witness to a crime. In each case, the computer or electronic device will hold information about the underlying crime or event. If the computer forensic examiner knows how the computer was used, he or she will be able to tailor the examination to that use.

The examiner must gather evidence in a way that makes it admissible in court. Evidence is only useful if it's admissible. To be admissible, evidence must be collected in a lawful way. It also must be collected in a scientific manner. For digital evidence, this means that a computer forensic examiner conducts a repeatable and verifiable examination of an electronic device. The examiner must use established practices and procedures. The examiner also must be able to explain the results of his or her work to a client, judge, or jury in a clear way.

FYI

It's important that evidence used in a court case be admissible. A judge or jury can consider only admissible evidence when they decide cases. Evidence that is invalid for some reason is called inadmissible evidence. Inadmissible evidence can't be presented to a judge or jury. A judge or jury who accidentally hears about that evidence cannot consider it later in deliberations. Admissible evidence is good evidence. Inadmissible evidence is bad evidence.

The Investigative Process

Different law enforcement agencies and organizations may use different investigative processes. The process used can depend on the type of case. It also can depend on the urgency of the case. The process also can depend on the agency or organization that performs the investigation. In general, the investigative process has the following steps:

- Identification
- Preservation
- Collection
- Examination
- Presentation

Identification

During the identification step, the computer forensic examiner learns about the crime, event, or activity that is being investigated. He or she must identify the types of electronic devices that may be involved. The examiner must prepare to conduct the investigation. The examiner must make sure that he or she has all the tools needed to conduct the investigation.

A computer forensic examiner's approach to a case may depend heavily on its facts and circumstances. For example, the examiner may have to collect evidence on-site if seizing the devices and taking them back to a lab isn't possible. This might happen in cases where evidence is located on an organization's business computers. Seizing the computers may not be possible if the computers are instrumental to the organization's business. This might be the case if the computers belong to a witness and not to a criminal suspect.

Preservation

During the preservation step, computer forensic examiners must secure the crime scene and any electronic devices. This means that they must make sure that no one tampers with the scene or electronic devices. This is to make sure that suspects and witnesses don't have a chance to access, destroy, or modify digital evidence. Examiners also must make sure that no one can access electronic devices remotely once they are seized. All of these actions make sure that potential digital evidence can't be altered. This step is very important because once digital evidence is altered, it's difficult, if not impossible, to reverse the results.

Computer forensic examiners also should learn about the operation of the electronic devices they will be examining. They will want to gather information from people at the scene to learn how the devices are used. They should try to learn logon names and passwords for access to the devices. They also should try to discover the type of Internet access used by each electronic device and programs used on each device. It's also important for examiners to know if devices are encrypted, or if they are equipped with software that could destroy evidence.

Chain of Custody

A **chain of custody** is an important evidentiary concept. Courts and attorneys use a chain of custody document to help prove that evidence is admissible. A chain of custody document shows who obtained evidence, where and when it was obtained, who secured it, and who had control or possession of it. It's used to prove that evidence is reliable.

Evidence is reliable when it's not destroyed, changed, or altered. It can't be modified after it's originally collected. A court may find that evidence isn't admissible in court if its chain of custody is poorly documented or incomplete. A chain of custody protects the integrity of evidence.

A chain of custody documents how evidence is collected, used, and handled throughout the lifetime of a particular case. It's a journal that records every interaction that a person or object has with the evidence.

This step also includes documenting the crime scene. Examiners must record the location of all electronic devices. They also should note whether the device is on or off. They should record the condition of all devices. Examiners also should record the content of any display screens before electronic devices are moved. The crime scene can be documented using video, photos, and written notes. The documentation created at this step is important for creating a chain of custody.

Collection

The collection step also is known as the "bag and tag" step. During this step, computer forensic examiners must collect the electronic devices. These devices require special collection, packaging, and transportation in order to preserve potential evidence. For example, in most instances, a cell phone must be kept powered on in order to preserve data stored on the device. However, it must be protected from any calls or text messages that could change the data on it. The cell phone must be packaged and transported in a special evidence bag once it's collected. These special evidence bags are called Faraday bags. They keep a cell phone shielded from incoming calls or from connecting to wireless networks. This is so that data stored on it can't be changed by an incoming call or wireless network connection. A computer forensic examiner also must make sure that the collected cell phone has an additional power supply to maintain evidence that could be lost if its battery runs out. Examiners will collect electronic devices in different ways depending upon the device and its power status. They will follow different rules for devices that are on and devices that are off.

During this step, examiners must be aware of other evidence that could be on electronic devices. A keyboard or mouse could contain fingerprints or other physical evidence related to the case. Computer forensic examiners must work with other forensic technicians. They must make sure that this type of physical evidence isn't destroyed.

FYI

Slack space is the space between the end of a data file and the end of the disk space that is allocated to store it. Data doesn't always fill the whole space that's allocated to it. Residual information can be left over when a smaller file is written into space that used to be occupied by a larger file. This leftover data may be located in the slack space. Computer forensic examiners look at the slack space because it might contain meaningful data.

As a practical matter, examiners must document how all electronic devices are configured. The cables and peripheral devices that are hooked up to each computer will need to be tagged. Examiners also must collect any manuals or other materials about the electronic devices that are located near the crime scene.

Examination

During the examination step, computer forensic examiners will want to make duplicate images of any electronic storage media. This is called "imaging." One thing to remember is that a **forensic duplicate image** is not the same as a file copy or system backup copy. It's an exact copy of the storage media. It includes deleted files, slack space, and areas of the storage media that a normal file copy would not include. A duplicate image is a bit-by-bit copy of the original storage media.

Computer forensic examiners use special tools called "write blockers" to create digital images. These tools keep examiners from altering the original storage media. Write blockers can be either hardware- or software-based. They work somewhat like a one-way flow valve in plumbing. Most examiners will make two or more duplicate images of the original storage media. One copy is a working copy that they will use to look for evidence. The other is a control copy that can be used if something goes wrong with the first copy.

A duplicate image must be verified against the original storage media. This makes sure that the duplicate image is identical to the original. It makes sure that nothing has changed on the original media or the image. Examiners verify the images using a cryptographic equation called an "algorithm." They will apply the algorithm to the original media to create a hash. A "hash" is the value that is the result of the cryptographic equation on the image. The examiner will apply the same algorithm to the duplicate image to create another hash.

The examiner can prove that the duplicate image accurately represents the original media if the hashes are the same. If the hashes are different, the images are not the same. Different hashes mean that the imaging process was faulty or some sort of change took place between the original media and the duplicate image. Hashes are used to measure the integrity of the original media and the forensic duplicate. If the hashes don't match, then the data has changed somehow.

> ▶ **NOTE**
> The output of a hashing algorithm is sometimes called a "checksum."

15

Computer Forensics and Investigations

Can a Person Be Compelled to Provide His or Her Encryption Key or Password?

Many information security professionals advise their clients to encrypt data. This helps protect the data in the event that the client experiences a security breach. In cases where the electronic devices are seized for evidence, encryption can be a problem for a computer forensic examiner. Can the government compel a data owner to provide an encryption key or password? What happens if the data owner is a suspect in the case? Does requiring a suspect to provide an encryption key or password violate the person's Fifth Amendment self-incrimination protections? The Fifth Amendment is discussed in Chapter 2. It's most famous for its "right to remain silent."

The U.S. Supreme Court has held that the Fifth Amendment protects communications that are compelled, testimonial, and incriminating in nature.[10] Testimonial communications are communications that provide facts or assertions. The heart of the issue is whether providing a password is testimonial. A defendant can potentially incriminate himself or herself if compelled to disclose a key or password to decrypt data on an electronic device.

Case law in this area is just beginning to develop. One case suggests that requiring a defendant to provide a password may not raise a self-incrimination issue. In December 2006, Sebastien Boucher entered the United States from Canada. His car was searched at the border. He had a laptop in his car, and border officers searched the laptop with Boucher's permission. The laptop contained files that appeared to be child pornography. Boucher said that he sometimes visited adult Web sites and that occasionally he downloaded adult pornography. He said those downloads sometimes include child pornography and that he always deleted it as soon as he found it. The officers arrested Boucher and seized the laptop. They turned the laptop off.

The government later got a search warrant to search the laptop. The computer forensic examiner could not examine the hard drive because it was encrypted. He could not break the encryption code. The government asked for a grand jury subpoena to force Boucher to share the password, enter it on the laptop in front of the grand jury, or produce an unencrypted copy

Computer forensic examiners need to know how to collect two very different types of data. **Persistent data** is stored on a hard drive or other storage media. It's preserved when an electronic device is turned off. **Volatile data** is stored in memory. Volatile data exists in registries, the cache, and random access memory (RAM). It also is the connections that one electronic device might have with another while both devices are powered on. Volatile data is lost when an electronic device is turned off. Examiners must know when this data must be collected and how to do it.

Computer forensic examiners search for relevant information on the duplicate image. They have checklists of items that they review and look for. In general, they might look at:

- File access history (when were files created, edited, and last accessed)
- File download history

of the hard drive. Boucher argued that all of those options violated his Fifth Amendment rights. A magistrate judge said that Boucher didn't have to provide the password or unencrypted copy. The government appealed.

The U.S. District Court for the District of Vermont reversed the magistrate's ruling. He directed Boucher to provide an unencrypted version of the hard drive. The judge said that because Boucher showed unencrypted data to the border officers, the government knew that the incriminating data existed. Therefore, Boucher was not giving testimony. Since he wasn't giving testimony, he wasn't incriminating himself by providing the password or unencrypted data. The government already knew incriminating data existed and was located on the hard drive. Since Boucher already admitted that the laptop was his, he isn't further incriminating himself by providing the requested password or data.[11]

Another case reached a different result. This case was decided in March 2010 in the U.S. District Court for the Eastern District of Michigan. The facts are slightly different. In this case, a grand jury had indicted a defendant for receiving child pornography by computer. The government still needed to collect evidence about the crimes. The government asked for a subpoena requiring the defendant to provide all passwords to his computer. The judge in this case said that the government was seeking testimony from the defendant when it asked him for his computer passwords. In this case, it appears that the government didn't know the extent of the potentially incriminating information on the defendant's computer. Therefore, requiring the defendant to share passwords is seeking testimony from him because the government will use his password to gather information that incriminates him.[12]

The case law on this issue is new. You can expect judges to continue to define the scope of the Fifth Amendment in these situations. Since this is an area of federal constitutional law, the U.S. Supreme Court has the power to make a decision on the issue. It can do this if a case is appealed to it.

- Internet browsing history
- Attempts to delete or conceal files or other data
- E-mail communications
- Instant message or Internet chat logs
- Image files
- Files containing address books or other contact information
- Documents containing financial or medical information

Examiners produce a report of files or data that might be relevant to the investigation. They must use examination procedures that are auditable. That means that an independent party can verify and repeat all of the same steps and receive the same results.

Presentation

Computer forensic examiners must be able to report on their findings. They must be able to describe how they gathered digital evidence. They often have to explain how they collected this evidence if a case goes to trial. Examiners are usually considered expert witnesses when they testify in a court case. Expert witness testimony is governed by the Federal Rules of Evidence. Expert witnesses must show that their activities followed a scientific methodology. A court assesses this process to make sure that evidence offered at trial is reliable.

The test for measuring the reliability of a scientific methodology is called the Daubert test. It was first discussed in a U.S. Supreme Court case called *Daubert v. Merrell Dow Pharmaceuticals.*[13] This test is important to computer forensics. It comes into play because of the tools that examiners use to collect digital evidence. An expert witness is a person. The software tools used by examiners can't be expert witnesses. Thus, examiners must testify on behalf of the tools.

The use of a tool must satisfy the Daubert test to show that the digital evidence gathered by the tool is reliable. The Daubert test asks the following questions to determine reliability:

- Has the tool been tested?
- Is there a known error rate for the tool?
- Has the tool been peer reviewed?
- Is the tool accepted in the relevant scientific community?

The examiner will testify about how the tool works. The examiner also will testify about his or her qualifications as a computer forensic examiner. Finally, the examiner will testify about the process the examiner used to collect the digital evidence. The court will use the Daubert test to decide whether to admit the evidence collected by the examiner.

Guiding Principles for Forensic Examination

Computer forensic examiners all follow some common principles. The International Organization on Computer Evidence has created the most well-known set of principles. They were created in 1999. They are:

- Examiners should not change digital evidence after they seize it.
- If original digital evidence must be accessed, the person accessing it must be competent.
- All digital evidence handling must be fully documented and available for review.
- Each person who handles digital evidence is responsible for it while it's in his or her possession.
- Any agency that handles digital evidence must comply with these principles.[14]

The IOCE is an international group of law enforcement agencies. These agencies exchange information about computer forensic issues. They all agree to follow the IOCE principles.

These principles are followed in different forms by other organizations. For example, the Certified Computer Examiner (CCE) credential requires CCE holders to follow a code of ethics. That code of ethics has terms that are similar to the IOCE principles.

The American Academy of Forensic Sciences

The American Academy of Forensic Sciences (AAFS) recognizes computer forensics as a scientific discipline. The AAFS is one of the most well-known professional organizations for forensic scientists. It has members from many different forensic disciplines. Its goals are to promote integrity and advance cooperation in the forensic sciences.

The AAFS has different sections for different areas. It created a digital and multimedia sciences section in February 2008. The digital and multimedia sciences section was the first new AAFS section in 28 years. The section started with 42 members in 2008. By 2010, it had grown to 66 members. Members must show active participation in computer forensic activities. All AAFS members have ethical rules that they must follow.

You can learn more about the AAFS at *http://www.aafs.org.*

Legal Issues Involving Digital Evidence

There are special rules for collecting and handling digital evidence. However, the process for obtaining the electronic devices and the evidence on them in the first place must follow established legal principles. The law asks two basic questions about evidence:

- Did the person or organization that collected the evidence have the legal authority to do so?
- Is the evidence admissible in court?

Legal principles and statutes are used to address the first question. Many of the laws that address electronic evidence gathering are discussed in Chapter 2 of this book. These laws focus on the situations where a private entity or the government can collect information about a person.

Court rules and case law are used to address the second question. As discussed in Chapter 3, both the federal government and state governments have trial court rules for civil and criminal proceedings. In addition to these rules, federal and state courts have evidentiary rules. Evidentiary rules govern how parties introduce evidence at trials. This book uses the Federal Rules of Evidence to illustrate admissibility requirements. Many states have evidence rules based on the Federal Rules of Evidence.

One thing to keep in mind as you review this section is that there are differences between how law enforcement and private entities conduct investigations. Law enforcement agencies have very specific rules that they must follow when they collect evidence. This is because a law enforcement agency is acting on behalf of a government. They are agents of either the federal or a state government. In the United States, a government can't take some actions against its citizens without proper authority. This is part of our "checks and balances" system of government. For example, unless special circumstances exist, law enforcement must get permission from a court to monitor a person's telephone conversations.

The Evidence Silver Platter Doctrine

The difference between the government's ability to collect evidence of a crime and a private entity's ability to collect evidence about that same activity is an interesting area of study. It's also a complicated area of study. The resolution of many court cases depends on these differences. Sometimes laws create special rules for law enforcement and private entities.

The Electronic Communications Privacy Act (ECPA) sets out the rules for access, use, disclosure, and interception of stored electronic communications. Electronic communications include telephone, cell phones, computers, e-mail, faxes, and texting. Under the ECPA, no one may access the contents of these communications unless it's allowed somewhere else in the ECPA. The law has different rules for the government and for private entities.

The ECPA has strict rules for the government. The government can't access any stored electronic communications without a search warrant. To get a search warrant, the government must prove to a court that it has probable cause to believe that criminal activity is taking place. The stored communications must hold evidence of the criminal activity. If the government can't prove probable cause, then it can't access these communications.

The ECPA has different rules for private entities. Private entities may access stored communications within their ordinary course of business. To use this exception, the private entity must have a legitimate business interest for accessing these communications. They also must show that the access occurred on equipment provided by a communications service provider. The ECPA also allows private entities to access employee communications if the employee gives consent. The private entity must be able to prove that it provided notice of access to its employees and that the employees consented to it.

Sometimes private entities find evidence of criminal activity. The ECPA allows most types of private entities to lawfully disclose this evidence to law enforcement agencies. This evidence often is very useful to a criminal investigation. Sometimes a prosecutor will want to use this evidence at a criminal trial. The evidence rule known as the "silver platter doctrine" applies in these cases. This rule is called the silver platter doctrine because the private entity gives admissible evidence to law enforcement "on a silver platter." Law enforcement didn't need a search warrant to access the evidence because it didn't collect it or direct its collection.

The silver platter doctrine allows the admission of evidence lawfully collected by a private entity. The evidence collected by the private entity must be collected and documented properly. To take advantage of the silver platter doctrine, the government must show that the private entity isn't affiliated with law enforcement or a government (state or federal). The private entity must not be collecting the evidence under the direction of law enforcement or a government. The private entity also can't be an Internet service provider (ISP). There are special rules under the ECPA for ISPs.

The rules are different for private entities. Private entities are individuals and organizations that aren't related to a governmental agency. As long as a private entity is acting within the rule of law, it may take certain actions to protect its own interests. This is why an employer may monitor an employee's telephone conversations when the employee is using the employer's telephone equipment. This is discussed in Chapter 2. A private entity generally has the right under the law to monitor and collect data about its own IT resources in order to protect them.

Authority to Collect Evidence

There are many laws that define the government's ability to monitor and collect data about individuals. As discussed in Chapters 2 and 3, the most basic protections afforded to U.S. citizens stem from the Constitution. The Fourth Amendment protects citizens from an intrusive government.

Other laws further define how the government can collect and monitor data. These laws affect the activities of computer forensic examiners. The Electronic Communications Privacy Act, the Wiretap Act, and the Pen Register and Trap and Trace Statute are discussed in this section.

The Fourth Amendment and Search Warrants

The Fourth Amendment protects people from unreasonable government search and seizure. A "search" happens when a person's reasonable expectation of privacy in a place or thing is compromised. A "seizure" happens when the government interferes with a person's property. Interference includes taking the property or using it in such a way that the person who owns it can't use it.

The Fourth Amendment states that the government may not search or seize areas and things in which a person has a reasonable expectation of privacy. If a person has a reasonable expectation of privacy in a place or item, then the government must get a search warrant before searching it or taking it. Under the Fourth Amendment, the "government" includes law enforcement. This section uses the terms government and law enforcement interchangeably.

FYI

The Fourth Amendment applies to federal government actions only. Most state governments have state constitutional protections that are similar to the Fourth Amendment. The Fourth Amendment doesn't apply to private individuals or entities that conduct searches or seizures. The private individual or entity must act alone and without government direction. The Fourth Amendment may apply when a private individual or entity follows government directions in conducting a search.

▶ **NOTE**

A search warrant is a court order. A judge issues a search warrant after the government proves that it has probable cause to believe that criminal activity is taking place. Probable cause is a burden of proof. Different burdens of proof are discussed in Chapter 3.

Several court cases have held that people have a reasonable expectation of privacy in their personal computers and mobile devices. The U.S. Court of Appeals for the Ninth Circuit has found that a person has a reasonable expectation of privacy in a personal computer. That case is called *United States v. Heckenkamp*.[15] Other courts have held that people have a reasonable expectation of privacy in data stored on personal pagers.[16] To search these devices, law enforcement must get a search warrant.

To get a search warrant, law enforcement must specify the criminal activity that is being investigated. It must describe where the search will take place. It also must list the items that will be searched. Finally, law enforcement must state the evidence that they expect to find. They also must state how that evidence relates to the criminal activity that is being investigated.

If law enforcement conducts a search without a valid warrant, then any evidence that it finds isn't admissible in court. This means that a judge won't allow the government to use that evidence to prove its case. Although the rule is strict, there are some exceptions. Court-recognized exceptions to the Fourth Amendment's search warrant requirements include:

- **Consent**—Law enforcement can search places and items if the person in control of them freely consents to the search. For example, a person can allow law enforcement to search his or her home, car, or computer. A person's consent must be free and voluntary. If law enforcement finds evidence of criminal activity during a voluntary search, it's admissible in court. Cases reviewing this exception often focus on whether a person's consent really was free and voluntary.

- **Plain view doctrine**—Law enforcement doesn't need a warrant to search and seize evidence that is in an officer's "plain view." The officer must be able to see the evidence from a place where the officer has a right to be. This exception is often used to seize drugs or other contraband. For example, a police officer can seize drug paraphernalia that he or she sees in a car if the officer can plainly see the items in the car's back seat while standing on a public street.

- **Exigent circumstances**—Law enforcement is allowed to make a warrantless search and seizure in emergency circumstances. This exception applies if public safety would be harmed or evidence would be destroyed if law enforcement took the time to go to court to get a warrant. This exception also is called the "emergency" exception. Law enforcement often seizes drugs and weapons using this exception. Court cases reviewing this exception focus on whether a true emergency existed at the time the search or seizure took place.

- **Search incident to a lawful arrest**—Law enforcement doesn't need a warrant to search for weapons or contraband on the body of an arrested person. In some cases, law enforcement may make a brief visual inspection of the area where a person is arrested to make sure that no accomplices are hiding nearby. Law enforcement officers are allowed to make these warrantless searches in order to protect their own safety. They also can use this exception to make sure that critical evidence isn't destroyed during the arrest process. Courts strictly construe this exception to make sure that it's not abused. This exception also is called the "protective sweep" exception.

- **Inventory search**—Law enforcement may conduct inventory searches without a warrant when they arrest a suspect. These searches are allowed when they're made for a non-investigative purpose. For example, if a suspect has a laptop computer when he or she is arrested, law enforcement may seize the computer for safekeeping while the suspect is in custody. This helps protect law enforcement from claims that they lost or stole a suspect's property. For the exception to apply, the law enforcement agency must have standard policies and procedures for conducting inventory searches. They also must document the search. Court cases reviewing this exception focus on whether law enforcement was following a documented policy for inventory searches. They review whether the inventory search was a ploy to hide a more thorough search for evidence.

One important thing to keep in mind is that the Fourth Amendment search warrant exceptions allow for the seizure of the media containing the digital evidence. Law enforcement can seize the physical media only. If they want to conduct a forensic examination of that media, they must get a warrant to do so. The search warrant must authorize the forensic examination. Unless emergency circumstances exist, the secondary search warrant ensures that any digital evidence collected from the media will be admissible in court. Computer forensic examiners must make sure there's a valid search warrant for any electronic devices that they collect. They also must make sure that the warrant allows them to search the data on the device.

Federal Laws Regarding Electronic Data Collection

Three main federal laws govern the collection of electronic communications data. These laws cover many different communications. They include e-mail, radio and electronic communications, data transmissions, and telephone calls. Computer forensic examiners often study these communications when they investigate cases or events. An examiner must make sure that his or her actions follow the law.

These laws forbid the use of eavesdropping technologies. This means that the government, individuals, and private entities can't use certain technologies to snoop on electronic communications. The only time use of these technologies is allowed is when the law says it's allowed. Usually this is when the law allows an exception or if an entity has a court order. The three laws are:

NOTE

Keep in mind that states also might have laws governing the collection of electronic communications evidence. You must always review both federal and state laws when considering a legal issue.

- The Electronic Communications Privacy Act[17]
- The Wiretap Act[18]
- The Pen Register and Trap and Trace Statute[19]

The Electronic Communications Privacy Act.   The Electronic Communications Privacy Act governs the use, disclosure, and interception of stored electronic communications. It was first passed in 1986. Congress has amended it several times. The ECPA governs access to the contents of stored communications, as well as access to transmission data about the communications. Transmission data includes header and log data. The ECPA doesn't apply to real-time collection of electronic communications.

The ECPA is a complicated statute. Under the ECPA, no one may access the contents of these communications unless it's allowed somewhere else in the ECPA. There are different rules for the government and for private entities. The government can't access any stored electronic communications without a search warrant. If it accesses them without a warrant, any evidence that it discovers won't be admissible. There are several exceptions to the ECPA for private entities. Some of these exceptions were part of the Uniting and Strengthening America by Providing Appropriate Tools Required to Intercept and Obstruct Terrorism Act (U.S.A. PATRIOT Act). Congress passed the Patriot Act in 2001. It modified parts of the ECPA. These changes are discussed in Chapter 2. Under the ECPA, a private entity may voluntarily disclose the contents of stored communications to law enforcement. Law enforcement doesn't need a search warrant if the private entity discloses the information voluntarily. (This is the application of the silver platter doctrine.) As long as the evidence was collected and documented properly, it will likely be admissible.

Private entity voluntary disclosure is permitted under the ECPA as long as the private entity isn't an ISP. If it's an ISP, then additional conditions must be met. These conditions prevent ISPs from having to monitor all communications across their networks. They also prevent ISPs from snooping on their subscribers. They also help ISPs maintain their safe harbor protections under U.S. intellectual property laws. These laws are discussed in Chapter 10.

If an ISP wishes to disclose the contents of a communication to law enforcement, the disclosure must fall under a permitted ECPA exception. There are six permitted exceptions. If the disclosure doesn't fall under one, then it may not be admissible in court. The permitted exceptions that allow disclosure are:

- The disclosure is made with the consent of the sender or receiver of the communication.
- The disclosure is related to the ISP's services or is made to protect the ISP's rights.
- The ISP inadvertently received the contents of the communication and the contents appear to be related to criminal activity.

- The ISP reasonably believes that disclosure is required to prevent an emergency involving immediate danger of death or serious bodily injury.
- U.S. child protection laws require the disclosure.
- The disclosure is made in response to a court order.

The Wiretap Act.   The ECPA applies to access to and disclosure of stored communications only. The federal Wiretap Act governs real-time interception of the contents of an electronic communication. The act doesn't apply to transmission information. It applies to anyone who intentionally intercepts or tries to intercept any wire, oral, or electronic communication. The act forbids the real-time interception of these communications. Communications covered by the act include e-mail, radio communications, data transmissions, and telephone calls.

> **NOTE**
> The Wiretap Act also is known as "Title III." This is because it was first passed as Title III of the Omnibus Crime Control and Safe Streets Act of 1968.

Under the Wiretap Act, no one is allowed to install wiretaps on telephones to intercept telephonic communications. The Act also forbids using network sniffers to intercept Internet traffic or other computer-based communications. There are exceptions to the Wiretap Act. The exceptions are similar to those allowed under the ECPA. They allow interception of real-time communications. For example, law enforcement can install telephone wiretaps or network sniffers if it has a court order to do so.

There are three main exceptions to the federal Wiretap Act for private entities. Private entities can use these exceptions to monitor content on their own communications systems. These exceptions are:

- The Consent Exception
- The Provider Exception
- The Trespasser Exception

A private entity may monitor content on its own communications systems when one of the parties to the communication consents to the monitoring. This is the consent exception. One way that entities gather consent is by using network banners. A **network banner** is a warning banner that provides notice of legal rights to the users of computer networks. These banners are displayed when a computer user logs onto a network or visits an entity's home page.

These banners have many purposes. They're used to show consent to monitoring under the Wiretap Act or consent to access under the ECPA. They're also used to eliminate a user's Fourth Amendment reasonable expectation of privacy in a computer network. They also may be used to inform a user of the terms of use for the computer network. Typically, these banners inform the user that use of the network (after viewing the banner) is proof that the user consents to network monitoring and the terms of use. This method of gathering consent is discussed in Chapter 2. Terms of use issues are discussed in Chapter 11.

A private entity can monitor its communications systems to protect its "rights or property." This is called the provider exception. Monitoring under this exception must be reasonable. It must be done in the ordinary course of business. This exception belongs only to the private entity. The entity may disclose evidence of business-related wrong-doing on its systems to law enforcement. This exception isn't a general exception. The law doesn't allow a private entity to gather evidence of crime unrelated to it and turn that evidence over to law enforcement.

Court cases about the provider exception have upheld it in a number of situations. For example, an entity's system administrators can use this exception to monitor a hacker's communications within its network. They may do this to prevent damage to the entity's network.[20] The entity can give any evidence collected from the monitoring to law enforcement. This is because hacking into a computer network is illegal.

> **NOTE**
>
> Under the Wiretap Act, a computer trespasser is a person who uses a computer system without permission. A computer trespasser has no relationship at all with the private entity.

The trespasser exception was created in 2001. This exception recognizes that there might be times when private entities don't have the expertise needed to track or monitor system intruders. Since they don't have the skills to track system intruders, the provider exception isn't helpful to them. The trespasser exception allows the entity to ask the government to help in these situations. The government can assist the entity in intercepting the communications of a computer trespasser.

The following conditions must be met in order to use this exception:

- Law enforcement must get the consent of the private entity.
- The interception must be legal.
- The interception must be part of a legitimate investigation.
- The interception must not monitor communications of anyone other than the trespasser.

If these conditions are met, then law enforcement may help a private entity monitor a computer trespasser. Law enforcement doesn't need a court order to take advantage of this exception.

> **NOTE**
>
> **Pen register devices** monitor outgoing transmission data. They record dialing, routing, signaling, or address information. **Trap and trace devices** monitor incoming transmission data. They capture incoming electronic signals that identify the origin of a communication.

The Pen Register and Trap and Trace Statute. The Wiretap Act governs real-time interception of the contents of a communication. It doesn't apply to transmission information. The Pen Register and Trap and Trace Statute governs real-time monitoring of this type of data. Transmission information includes headers, logs, network routing, and other transmission data. This law doesn't apply to communications content.

Under the Pen Register and Trap and Trace Statute, no one is allowed to use pen register or trap and trace devices to intercept electronic communications transmission data. Like the Wiretap Act, some exceptions allow the use of these devices. For example, the law allows law enforcement to install pen register or trap and trace devices if they have a court order to do so.

There are three exceptions to the Pen Register and Trap and Trace Statute for private entities. Private entities can use these exceptions to use pen register or trap and trace devices on their own communications systems. The exceptions are:

- A private entity may use pen register or trap and trace devices if necessary to operate, maintain, or test its communication services. It also may use these devices to protect its property rights. (This is similar to the provider exception under the Wiretap Act.)

- A private entity may use pen register or trap and trace devices to protect the entity from fraudulent, unlawful, or abusive use of service. It would use these devices to prove the existence of a fraudulent, unlawful, or abusive electronic communication.

- A private entity may use pen register or trap and trace devices when the user of the electronic communications service consents.

These three laws, in addition to the provisions of the Fourth Amendment, govern the collection of electronic communications evidence. Computer forensic examiners must make sure that their evidence collection activities comply with these laws. The examiner's credibility is damaged if the examiner doesn't follow the law. If the examiner doesn't follow the law, any evidence that he or she gathered might not be admissible.

Admissibility of Evidence

Even if evidence is lawfully collected, it still must be admissible. At the federal level, the main guidance regarding the submission of evidence at trial is the Federal Rules of Evidence (FRE). The FRE apply to use of evidence at federal trials. Many states also have rules of evidence. Often these rules are based on the federal rules. One thing to keep in mind whenever you are reviewing evidence is that you need to understand whether you must follow state rules or federal rules.

Under the FRE, relevant evidence is admissible unless some other rule or law says that it's not. Admissible evidence is evidence that the judge and jury can consider when they deliberate about a case. Evidence can be either inculpatory or exculpatory. Inculpatory evidence supports or confirms a given theory. Exculpatory evidence rebuts or contradicts a given theory.

Computer forensic examiners are hired to find digital evidence. There are two basic types of digital evidence:

> **NOTE**
>
> In criminal cases, defense attorneys want to present exculpatory evidence. They want to rebut the prosecution's case. The prosecution is interested in presenting inculpatory evidence to support their case.

- **Computer-generated records**—These records and logs are the output of computer programs. They are created automatically by a computer program or process, even if a person initiates that program or process.

- **Records created by people and stored electronically**—These records are created by people. They just happen to be in a digital form. This kind of evidence includes files, pictures, images, spreadsheets, and other documents created by a person. It also can include Internet browsing history.

> ### The Fruit of the Poisonous Tree Doctrine
>
> The fruit of the poisonous tree doctrine is a long-standing legal doctrine, whose name stems from a biblical passage.[21] The doctrine has been in place since 1920.[22] The U.S. Supreme Court first used the term "fruit of the poisonous tree" in 1939.[23] The doctrine prevents the government from using illegally gathered evidence at a criminal trial. It also prevents the government from using any legally gathered evidence that it obtained because of the illegally gathered evidence.
>
> This doctrine is used to keep the government from violating people's constitutional rights. If the government were allowed to use illegally gathered evidence at trial, the protections granted by the Fourth Amendment would be meaningless.
>
> Under the fruit of the poisonous tree doctrine, the poisonous tree is evidence that's seized illegally. The fruit of the poisonous tree is evidence that is later gathered because of knowledge gained through the first illegal act. Neither the tree, nor its fruit, can be used at a trial.

The rules of evidence apply to digital evidence in the same way that they apply to traditional types of evidence. This section focuses on issues that are important for digital evidence. In order to be admissible, digital evidence must be:

- Lawfully gathered
- Relevant
- Authentic and reliable

Evidence is lawfully gathered if it's collected in accordance with the law. The main laws that govern the collection of electronic evidence are discussed earlier in this section. Evidence that isn't gathered lawfully is tainted with illegality. This means that it can't be used in court. It also means that any subsequent evidence gathered as a result of the illegally obtained evidence also can't be used in court. In the law, this is known as the **fruit of the poisonous tree doctrine**. This doctrine primarily applies to criminal cases.

Evidence is admissible only if it's relevant. Another name for relevant evidence is **probative evidence**. Probative evidence proves or disproves a legal element in a case. If evidence isn't probative, then it can be excluded from a trial. The FRE say that evidence is relevant if it makes "the existence of any fact that is of consequence to the determination of the action more probable or less probable than it would be without the evidence."[24] Evidence can be inculpatory or exculpatory.

Relevance can occasionally be a problem for digital evidence. This is because it's sometimes hard for judges and juries to understand very technical information. They might not understand why the evidence is relevant. This is where a good computer forensic examiner can help. The examiner can help explain the technical information in everyday language. The examiner can help show how the evidence is relevant to the case. The party that wants to introduce digital evidence must show how it's relevant.

Evidence is admissible if it's authentic.[25] This means that the party introducing the evidence must show that the evidence is what it says it is. For example, suppose a party wishes to produce a printout of an electronic document and use it to prove an element in the case. Before being able to use the document, the party must show that the document was stored in a computer system. The party also must show that the document hasn't been altered, manipulated, or damaged since it was created.

Reliability is closely related to authenticity. It's often questioned in digital evidence issues. The reliability of digital evidence can be suspect if the program used to find the evidence has significant flaws. If the output of a program can change because of these flaws, then it's not reliable. If it's not reliable, then the information that the output represents may not be authentic.

Sometimes reliability is implicated at the forensic examination level. If a computer forensic examiner uses a new tool or program to conduct a forensic examination, the reliability of that tool must be demonstrated. The Daubert test is used to satisfy the court that new forensic tools are reliable. If the tool is reliable, then the court is more likely to admit the digital evidence.

The Hearsay Rule

There are other rules that may apply when courts consider the admissibility of digital evidence. The hearsay rule[26] is often implicated with respect to computer records and digital evidence. The hearsay rule is a very complicated evidentiary rule with numerous exceptions. Sometimes even the most experienced attorneys can be confused by the hearsay rule and its many exceptions.

Hearsay is any out-of-court statement that is made by a person that is offered to prove some issue in a case. Hearsay statements are statements made by people. They aren't usually made under oath. Hearsay statements are sometimes offered by parties at trial when there are no direct witnesses available to testify. Gossip is a common example of hearsay. Statements that a news reporter makes when he or she reports on events from an anonymous source are hearsay. Hearsay isn't admissible unless a specific exception applies.

Trial Court Objections

Trial attorneys often make hearsay objections. An **objection** is a formal protest made to a judge. An attorney usually makes an objection if the opposing party is asking questions that are inappropriate or violate a court rule.

If the judge agrees with the attorney who made the objection, the court will sustain the objection. This means that the objection is correct. In this case, the attorney who originally asked a question must not ask it or must rephrase it. If the judge doesn't agree with the attorney who made the objection, the court will overrule it. This means that the original objection wasn't correct. When a judge overrules an objection, he or she is allowing the original line of questioning to continue.

Records recovered from a computer can be hearsay. It depends on how they were created originally. Many courts have held that computer-generated records aren't hearsay. Computer-generated records are the logs and output of computer programs. These records are created without human intervention. Some courts have said that computer-generated information isn't a statement of a person and can't be hearsay.[27] If the records aren't hearsay, then they're admissible.

Computer records that might be hearsay contain assertions by people. These types of records include documents and files, bookkeeping records, and records of transactions that are entered by people (and not through an electronic process). For these types of documents, a party must show that the document is admissible due to a hearsay exception. The party also must show that the document is authentic.

Some courts allow computer records to be admitted over a hearsay objection if they're created in the ordinary course of business. Records created in the ordinary course of business are often admissible, even if the hearsay objection would otherwise apply.[28] The theory is that records created as part of a business process tend to be reliable. This is because the records are created repeatedly.

The Best Evidence Rule

The Federal Rules of Evidence require that original documents be used at trial.[29] This is called the best evidence rule. The rule requires that original documents, pictures, and recordings be used at trial. This is to make sure that evidence is reliable and authentic.

This rule can create an interesting problem for digital evidence. In its original form, digital evidence is almost never in a format that a person can read and understand. The original form of digital evidence would be particularly unhelpful at a trial. It would not be usable. However, any printout that represents digital evidence would not meet the best evidence rule.

The Federal Rules of Evidence have made an exception for this quirk of digital evidence since 1972. The rule states that an accurate printout of computerized data is an "original" for purposes of the best evidence rule.[30] The Federal Rules of Evidence acknowledge that it's practical to address computerized evidence in this way.[31]
Any other result would not make sense.

CHAPTER SUMMARY

Computer forensics is the scientific process of collecting and examining data stored on electronic devices. The data is examined to find evidence about an event or crime. Evidence found on electronic devices is called digital evidence. Like traditional forms of evidence, digital evidence is subject to rules that govern how it can be used later. If digital evidence isn't properly collected, it can't be used in court.

Computer forensic examiners collect digital evidence using special programs and tools. They must collect the evidence carefully to make sure that it's not changed. Examiners often have special skills. They must have a thorough knowledge of computing technologies. They also must understand the scientific method. Finally, examiners must be familiar with the law and evidence rules.

KEY CONCEPTS AND TERMS

Chain of custody	Hearsay	Persistent data
Code analysis	Locard's exchange principle	Probative evidence
Computer forensics	Media analysis	Trap and trace devices
Digital evidence	Network analysis	Volatile data
Forensic duplicate image	Network banner	
Fruit of the poisonous tree doctrine	Objection	
	Pen register devices	

CHAPTER 15 ASSESSMENT

1. A system backup copy is considered a forensic duplicate image.

A. True
B. False

2. What is an exception to the Fourth Amendment's search warrant requirement?

A. Consent
B. Plain view doctrine
C. Inventory search
D. All of the above
E. None of the above

3. Which principle is a basic assumption of forensic science?

A. The silver platter doctrine
B. Exigent circumstances
C. Locard's exchange principle
D. The Daubert test
E. None of the above

4. What are the three main electronic communications eavesdropping laws?

5. What is another common term for computer forensics?

6. Which type of computer forensics focuses on examining programming code?

A. Media analysis
B. Malware forensics
C. Internet forensics
D. Network analysis
E. None of the above

7. Which forensic certification is only available to law enforcement personnel?

A. CCE
B. GCFA
C. CCFE
D. EnCE
E. None of the above

8. A computer can play one of _____ roles in a crime.

9. Which investigative step includes "bag and tag?"

A. Identification
B. Preservation
C. Collection
D. Examination
E. None of the above

10. Which investigative step includes interviewing persons of interest for information about electronic devices?

A. Identification
B. Preservation
C. Collection
D. Presentation
E. None of the above

11. Which organization created the most well-known guiding principles for computer forensic examiners?

A. IOCE
B. ISO/IEC
C. ISFCE
D. IACRB
E. None of the above

12. What is volatile data?

13. Which law governs the collection of real-time transmission data?

A. The Electronic Communications Privacy Act
B. The Wiretap Act
C. The Pen Register and Trap and Trace Statute
D. The Fourth Amendment
E. None of the above

14. A trap and trace device monitors incoming transmission data.

A. True
B. False

15. A forensic duplicate image is a _____.

ENDNOTES

1. U.S. Department of Labor, Bureau of Labor Statistics, "Private Detectives and Investigators," Occupational Outlook Handbook, 2010-11 ed., *http://www.bls.gov/oco/ocos157.htm* (accessed May 12, 2010).

2. Symantec, "Internet Security Threat Report, Trends for 2009, Volume XV," April 2010, page 47, *http://eval.symantec.com/mktginfo/enterprise/white_papers/b-whitepaper_internet_security_threat_report_xv_04-2010.en-us.pdf* (accessed May 10, 2010).

3. Illinois Compiled Statutes, chapter 225, sec. 447, art. 5-10.

4. Michigan Compiled Laws, chapter 338.822.

5. Oregon Revised Statutes, chapter 703.401, 703.405, 703.407, 703.411.

6. Texas Occupations Code Annotated, sec. 1702.104.

7. Delaware Code, title 24, sec. 1301.

8. North Carolina General Statutes, chapter 74C, sec. 3.

9. Virginia Code, title 9.1, sec. 140.

10. *Fisher v. United States,* 425 U.S. 391 (1976).

11. *In re Boucher,* 2009 WL 424718 (D. Vt., February 19, 2009).

12. *U.S. v. Kirschner,* 2010 U.S. Dist. Lexis 30603. (E.D. Mich., March 30, 2010).

13. *Daubert v. Merrell Dow Pharmaceuticals, Inc.,* 509 U.S. 579 (1993).

14. International Organization on Computer Evidence, "Principles," 1999, *http://www.ioce.org/core.php?ID=5* (accessed May 15, 2010).

15. *United States v. Heckenkamp,* 482 F.3d 1142, 1146 (9th Cir. 2007).

16. *United States v. Al-Marri,* 230 F. Supp 2d 535, 541 (S.D.N.Y. 2002).

17. U.S. Code, Vol. 18, sec. 2701-2712 (2006).

18. U.S. Code, Vol. 18, sec. 2510-22.

19. U.S. Code, Vol. 18, sec. 3121-27.

20. *United States v. Mullins,* 992 F.2d 1472 (9th Cir. 1993).

21. Matt. 7:17-20 (Contemporary English Version).

22. *Silverthorne Lumber Co. v. United States,* 251 U.S. 385 (1920).

23. *Nardone v. United States,* 308 U.S. 338 (1939).

24. Federal Rules of Evidence, Rule 401.

25. Federal Rules of Evidence, Rule 901.

26. Federal Rules of Evidence, Rule 801.

27. See *United States v. Washington,* 498 F.3d 225, 230-31 (4th Cir. 2007) (holding that printed results from a computerized test weren't the statement of a person and aren't excluded as hearsay); *United States v. Hamilton,* 413 F.3d 1138, 1142-43 (10th Cir. 2005) (holding that computer-generated header information isn't hearsay).

28. Federal Rules of Evidence, Rule 803(6).

29. Federal Rules of Evidence, Rule 1002.

30. Federal Rules of Evidence, Rule 1001(3).

31. Federal Rules of Evidence, Rule 1001(3), Advisory Committee Notes (1972).

Answer Key

CHAPTER 1 Information Security Overview

1. C   2. E   3. D   4. C   5. A   6. Logical control   7. C   8. D   9. A   10. E
11. D   12. B   13. C   14. E   15. A

CHAPTER 2 Privacy Overview

1. A   2. E   3. C   4. A   5. D   6. D   7. 8   8. B   9. A   10. B   11. A
12. A legitimate business reason   13. D   14. B   15. C

CHAPTER 3 The American Legal System

1. E   2. B   3. A   4. D   5. C   6. A   7. Stare decisis   8. D   9. E   10. A
11. Congress   12. D   13. 9   14. C   15. 94

CHAPTER 4 Security and Privacy of Consumer Financial Information

1. D   2. B   3. A   4. B   5. C   6. Social engineering   7. A   8. E
9. National Bank Act of 1864   10. B   11. C   12. B   13. 12   14. B   15. C

CHAPTER 5 Security and Privacy of Information Belonging to Children and Educational Records

1. B   2. A   3. B   4. 13   5. D   6. B   7. CIPA   8. Technical protection
measure (TPM)   9. B   10. A   11. C   12. A   13. B   14. B   15. A

CHAPTER 6 Security and Privacy of Health Information

1. Reasonable and appropriate   2. D   3. 60   4. 12   5. D   6. An organization
that performs a health care activity on behalf of a covered entity   7. C   8. B
9. 30   10. D   11. A   12. B   13. C   14. E   15. Unsecured

CHAPTER 7 Corporate Information Security and Privacy Regulation

1. A   2. A   3. To protect shareholders and investors from financial fraud.
SOX also was designed to restore investor faith in American stock markets.
4. C   5. E   6. Internal controls are the processes and procedures that a company
uses to provide reasonable assurance that its financial reports are reliable.
7. D   8. C   9. B   10. C   11. B   12. D   13. Provides management with
reasonable assurance that: 1) financial reports, records, and data are accurately
maintained; 2) transactions are prepared according to GAAP rules and are
properly recorded; and 3) unauthorized acquisition or use of data or assets
that could affect financial statements will be prevented or detected in a timely
manner.   14. C   15. B

CHAPTER 8   Federal Government Information Security and Privacy Regulations

1. A   2. A government agency must state what information is to be collected; why the information is being collected; the intended use of the information; how the agency will share the information; whether people have the opportunity to consent to specific uses of the information; how the information will be secured; and whether the information collected will be a system of records as defined by the Privacy Act of 1974.   3. C   4. B   5. E   6. US-CERT   7. B   8. D   9. CyberScope   10. B   11. A   12. B   13. B   14. E   15. D

CHAPTER 9   State Laws Protecting Citizen Information and Breach Notification Laws

1. A   2. 2003   3. D   4. A legal concept that protects an entity from liability if it follows the law   5. B   6. D   7. C   8. A person must be able to easily understand it   9. E   10. C   11. D   12. A legal concept that describes a person's right to sue another for harm that the latter caused   13. A   14. D   15. B

CHAPTER 10   Intellectual Property Law

1. E   2. A legal concept that means that people can be held responsible for their actions even if they didn't intend to cause harm to another person.   3. B   4. 20   5. E   6. C   7. A person or business must use the trademark in interstate commerce, and the trademark must be distinctive   8. A   9. C   10. A   11. C   12. A   13. It's important to know the ownership of a copyrighted work in order to determine the length of copyright protection.   14. E   15. B

CHAPTER 11   The Role of Contracts

1. C   2. An agreement where the complete terms of the agreement are presented on a computer screen, usually in the form of a pop-up window. A user must take an affirmative action to accept the terms of the agreement.   3. B   4. A   5. B   6. D   7. Legal relief granted by a court   8. C   9. A   10. Loss of control of data, loss of privacy of data, third-party dependency for critical infrastructure, potential security and technology defects, lack of control over third parties, loss of an entity's own competence in IT infrastructure security.   11. E   12. B   13. B   14. Enforceable   15. D

CHAPTER 12   Criminal Law and Tort Law Issues in Cyberspace

1. B   2. Crimes are wrongdoings against society.   3. A   4. E   5. C   6. The Sixth Amendment to the U.S. Constitution   7. B   8. E   9. A   10. Extreme and outrageous   11. A   12. C   13. D   14. Libel and slander   15. E

CHAPTER 13 Information Security Governance

1. A   2. Executive management providing strategic direction, oversight, and accountability for an organization's data and IT resources.   3. D
4. E   5. Middle management providing day-to-day guidance and oversight for an organization's information and information resources.   6. A
7. A list of mandatory activities that must be completed to achieve an information security goal   8. A   9. B   10. D   11. A checklist of actions that should be performed to achieve a certain goal   12. C   13. A   14. E   15. B

CHAPTER 14 Risk Analysis, Incident Response, and Contingency Planning

1. B   2. E   3. A risk assessment identifies the threats and vulnerabilities to IT resources.   4. D   5. A   6. Exposure factor   7. The annualized loss expectancy (ALE) is the amount of loss that an organization can expect to have each year due to a particular risk. ALE is often expressed as the equation: ALE = SLE × ARO. SLE is single loss expectancy. ARO is annual rate of occurrence.   8. C   9. A   10. D   11. C   12. Incident   13. Disaster
14. A   15. A

CHAPTER 15 Computer Forensics and Investigations

1. B   2. D   3. C   4. The Electronic Communications Privacy Act; the Wiretap Act; the Pen Register and Trap and Trace Statute.   5. Computer forensics also is known as system forensics, digital forensics, computer forensic analysis, computer examination, data recovery, and inforensics (information forensics). These terms are used interchangeably.   6. B   7. E   8. Three   9. C   10. B
11. A   12. Data stored in the memory of an electronic device. Volatile data is lost when the electronic device is turned off.   13. C   14. B   15. Bit-by-bit copy

Standard Acronyms

3DES	triple data encryption standard		**DMZ**	demilitarized zone
ACD	automatic call distributor		**DoS**	denial of service
AES	Advanced Encryption Standard		**DPI**	deep packet inspection
ANSI	American National Standards Institute		**DRP**	disaster recovery plan
AP	access point		**DSL**	digital subscriber line
API	application programming interface		**DSS**	Digital Signature Standard
B2B	business to business		**DSU**	data service unit
B2C	business to consumer		**EDI**	Electronic Data Interchange
BBB	Better Business Bureau		**EIDE**	Enhanced IDE
BCP	business continuity planning		**FACTA**	Fair and Accurate Credit Transactions Act
C2C	consumer to consumer		**FAR**	false acceptance rate
CA	certificate authority		**FBI**	Federal Bureau of Investigation
CAP	Certification and Accreditation Professional		**FDIC**	Federal Deposit Insurance Corporation
			FEP	front-end processor
CAUCE	Coalition Against Unsolicited Commercial Email		**FRCP**	Federal Rules of Civil Procedure
			FRR	false rejection rate
CCC	CERT Coordination Center		**FTC**	Federal Trade Commission
CCNA	Cisco Certified Network Associate		**FTP**	file transfer protocol
CERT	Computer Emergency Response Team		**GIAC**	Global Information Assurance Certification
CFE	Certified Fraud Examiner			
CISA	Certified Information Systems Auditor		**GLBA**	Gramm-Leach-Bliley Act
CISM	Certified Information Security Manager		**HIDS**	host-based intrusion detection system
CISSP	Certified Information System Security Professional		**HIPAA**	Health Insurance Portability and Accountability Act
CMIP	common management information protocol		**HIPS**	host-based intrusion prevention system
			HTTP	hypertext transfer protocol
COPPA	Children's Online Privacy Protection		**HTTPS**	HTTP over Secure Socket Layer
CRC	cyclic redundancy check		**HTML**	hypertext markup language
CSI	Computer Security Institute		**IAB**	Internet Activities Board
CTI	Computer Telephony Integration		**IDEA**	International Data Encryption Algorithm
DBMS	database management system		**IDPS**	intrusion detection and prevention
DDoS	distributed denial of service		**IDS**	intrusion detection system
DES	Data Encryption Standard			

IEEE	Institute of Electrical and Electronics Engineers	**SAN**	storage area network
IETF	Internet Engineering Task Force	**SANCP**	Security Analyst Network Connection Profiler
InfoSec	information security	**SANS**	SysAdmin, Audit, Network, Security
IPS	intrusion prevention system	**SAP**	service access point
IPSec	IP Security	**SCSI**	small computer system interface
IPv4	Internet protocol version 4	**SET**	Secure electronic transaction
IPv6	Internet protocol version 6	**SGC**	server-gated cryptography
IRS	Internal Revenue Service	**SHA**	Secure Hash Algorithm
(ISC)²	International Information System Security Certification Consortium	**S-HTTP**	secure HTTP
ISO	International Organization for Standardization	**SLA**	service level agreement
		SMFA	specific management functional area
ISP	Internet service provider	**SNMP**	simple network management protocol
ISS	Internet security systems	**SOX**	Sarbanes-Oxley Act of 2002 (also Sarbox)
ITRC	Identity Theft Resource Center	**SSA**	Social Security Administration
IVR	interactive voice response	**SSCP**	Systems Security Certified Practitioner
LAN	local area network	**SSL**	Secure Socket Layer
MAN	metropolitan area network	**SSO**	single system sign-on
MD5	Message Digest 5	**STP**	shielded twisted cable
modem	modulator demodulator	**TCP/IP**	Transmission Control Protocol/Internet Protocol
NFIC	National Fraud Information Center	**TCSEC**	Trusted Computer System Evaluation Criteria
NIDS	network intrusion detection system		
NIPS	network intrusion prevention system	**TFTP**	Trivial File Transfer Protocol
NIST	National Institute of Standards and Technology	**TNI**	Trusted Network Interpretation
		UDP	User Datagram Protocol
NMS	network management system	**UPS**	uninterruptible power supply
OS	operating system	**UTP**	unshielded twisted cable
OSI	open system interconnection	**VLAN**	virtual local area network
PBX	private branch exchange	**VOIP**	Voice over Internet Protocol
PCI	Payment Card Industry	**VPN**	virtual private network
PGP	Pretty Good Privacy	**WAN**	wide area network
PKI	public-key infrastructure	**WLAN**	wireless local area network
RAID	redundant array of independent disks	**WNIC**	wireless network interface card
RFC	Request for Comments	**W3C**	World Wide Web Consortium
RSA	Rivest, Shamir, and Adleman (algorithm)	**WWW**	World Wide Web

Law and Case Citations

U.S. Federal Laws

Administrative Procedure Act (1946), U.S. Code Vol. 5, sec. 500–596 (2006).

Anti-Cybersquatting Consumer Protection Act (1999), U.S. Code Vol. 15, sec. 1125(d) (1999).

American Inventor's Protection Act (1999), Pub. L. No. 106-113, 113 Stat. 1501 (1999).

American Recovery and Reinvestment Act (2009), Pub. L. No. 111-5, 123 Stat. 115 (2009).

Banking Act of 1933 (also called the Glass-Stegall Act), Pub. L. No. 73-66, 48 Stat. 162, codified as amended throughout U.S. Code Vol. 12 (2006).

Banking Act of 1935, Pub. L. No. 74-305, 49 Stat. 684, codified as amended throughout U.S. Code Vol. 12 (2006).

Bank Holding Act (1956), Pub. L. No. 84-511, 70 Stat. 133, U.S. Code Vol. 12 sec. 1841 *et seq.* (2006).

Bank Secrecy Act (1970), U.S. Code Vol. 12 sec. 1829b; Vol. 12 sec. 1951–1959; and Vol. 31 sec. 5311 *et seq.* (2006).

Cable Communications Policy Act of 1984, U.S. Code Vol. 4, sec. § 551 (2006).

Census Confidentiality Rules, U.S. Code Vol. 13, sec. 9 (2006).

Children's Internet Protection Act (2000) Pub. L. No. 106-554, 114 Stat. 2763A-335, codified in scattered sections of U.S. Code (2006).

Children's Online Privacy Protection Act (1998), U.S. Code Vol. 15, sec. 6501 (2006).

Civil Rights Act (1964), U.S. Code Vol. 42, sec. 1971 *et seq.* (1988).

Communications Decency Act (1996), Pub. L. No. 104-104, 110 Stat. 56 (1996).

Computer Fraud and Abuse Act (1984), U.S. Code Vol. 18, sec. 1030 (2006).

Computer Security Act of 1987, Pub. L. No. 100-235, 101 Stat. 1724 (1987).

Consolidated Omnibus Budget Reconciliation Act (1986), Pub. L. No. 99-272, 100 Stat. 82 (1986).

Controlling the Assault of Non-Solicited Pornography and Marketing Act (2003), U.S. Code Vol. 15, sec. 7701 *et seq.* (2003).

Copyright Act (1976), U.S. Code Vol. 17, sec. 101 *et seq.* (2006).

Digital Millennium Copyright Act (1998), Pub. L. No. 105-304, 112 Stat. 2860, codified in scattered sections of U.S. Code Vol. 17 (2006).

Driver's Privacy Protection Act of 1994, U.S. Code Vol. 18, sec. 2721 (2006).

Drug Abuse Prevention, Treatment, and Rehabilitation Act (1980), U.S. Code Vol. 21, sec. 1175 (2006).

E-Government Act, Pub. Law No. 107-347, U.S. Code Vol. 44 (various sections) (2006).

Electronic Communications Privacy Act, U.S. Code Vol. 18, sec. 2701 (2006).

Electronic Signatures in Global and National Commerce Act (2000), U.S. Code Vol. 15, sec 7001 *et seq.* (2006).

Fair and Accurate Credit Transaction Act (2003), Pub L. 108-159, 117 Stat. 1952, made amendments to the Fair Credit Reporting Act of 1970.

Fair Credit Reporting Act (1970), U.S. Code Vol. 15, sec. 1681 *et seq.* (2006).

Family Educational Rights and Privacy Act (1974), U. S. Code Vol. 20, sec. 1232g (2006).

Federal Credit Union Act (1934), U.S. Code Vol. 12, sec. 1751 *et seq.* (2006).

Federal Information Security Management Act, Title III of the E-Government Act of 2002, U.S. Code Vol. 44, sec. 3541 *et seq.* (2006).

Federal Reserve Act (1913), Pub. L. No 63-43, 38 Stat. 251, codified as amended throughout U.S. Code Vol. 12 (2006).

Federal Trade Commission Act (1914), U.S. Code Vol. 15, sec. 41-58 (2006).

Financial Institutions Regulatory and Interest Rate Control Act (1978), Pub. L. No. 95-630, 92 Stat. 3641, codified as amended in scattered sections of U.S. Code (2006).

Financial Institutions Reform, Recovery and Enforcement Act (1989), Pub. L. No. 101-73, 103 Stat. 183, codified as amended in scattered sections of U.S. Code (2006).

Financial Services Regulatory Relief Act (2006), Pub. L. No. 109-351, 120 Stat. 1966 (2006).

Freedom of Information Act, U.S. Code Vol. 5, sec. 552 (2006).

Genetic Information Nondiscrimination Act (2008), Pub. L. No. 110-233, 122 Stat. 881 (2008).

Gramm Leach Bliley Act (1999), U.S. Code Vol. 15, sec. 6801, *et seq.* (2006).

Health Insurance Portability and Accountability Act (1996), U.S. Code Vol. 42, sec. 1320d (2006).

Health Information Technology for Economic and Clinical Health Act (2009), Pub. L. No. 111-5, 123 Stat. 226 (2009).

Identity Theft and Assumption Deterrence Act (1998), U.S. Code Vol. 18, sec. 1028 (2006).

Lanham Act (1946), U.S. Code Vol. 15, sec. 1051 *et seq.* (2006).

Mail Privacy Statute, U.S. Code Vol. 39, sec. 3623 (2006).

National Bank Act (1864), 13 Stat. 99 (1864), current version at U.S. Code Vol. 12 sec. 21-216b (2006).

Patent Act (1952), U.S. Code Vol. 35, sec. 1-376.

Pen Register and Trap and Trace Statute, U.S. Code Vol. 18, sec. 3121 *et seq.*

Plant Variety Protection Act (1970), U.S. Code Vol. 7, sec. 2421, 2422, 2541 (2006).

Privacy Act of 1974, U.S. Code Vol. 5, sec. 552a (2006).

Public Company Accounting Reform and Investor Protection Act (2002), also called Sarbanes-Oxley Act (2002), Pub. L. No. 107-204, 116 Stat. 745, codified as amended in scattered sections of U.S. Code Vol. 15 (2006).

Securities and Exchange Act of 1934, U.S. Code, Vol. 15, sec 78a *et seq.* (2006).

Uniting and Strengthening America by Providing Appropriate Tools Required to Intercept and Obstruct Terrorism Act (2001), Pub. L. No. 107-56, 115 Stat. 272 (Oct. 26, 2001), codified at various sections of the U.S. Code.

Veterans Affairs Information Security Act, Title IX of the Veterans Benefits, Health Care, and Information Technology Act (2006), U.S. Code Vol. 38, sec. 5722 *et seq.* (2006).

Wiretap statutes, U.S. Code Vol.18, sec. 2510; U.S. Code Vol. 47, sec. 605 (2006).

(U.S. regulations and state laws are cited in the text and endnotes of each chapter.)

Court Rules

U.S. Supreme Court, *Federal Rules of Civil Procedure*, http://www.uscourts.gov/uscourts/RulesAndPolicies/rules/CV2008.pdf (accessed February 14, 2010).

U.S. Supreme Court, *Federal Rules of Criminal Procedure*, http://www.uscourts.gov/uscourts/RulesAndPolicies/rules/CR2008.pdf (accessed February 14, 2010).

U.S. Supreme Court, *Federal Rules of Evidence*, http://www.uscourts.gov/uscourts/RulesAndPolicies/rules/EV2008.pdf (accessed May 11, 2010).

Indiana Supreme Court, *Indiana Rules of Trial Procedure*, http://www.in.gov/judiciary/rules/trial_proc/index.html#_Toc244662873 (accessed February 14, 2010).

Court Cases

Autoliv ASP, Inc. v. Department of Workforce Services, 29 P.3d 7 (Utah Ct. Appeals, 2001).
Utah Court of Appeals held that the transmission of sexually explicit and offensive jokes, pictures, and videos constitutes a flagrant violation of a universal standard of behavior.

Baltimore & Ohio Railroad Co. v. United States, 261 U.S. 592 (1923).
The U.S. Supreme Court held that mutual assent can be determined from the conduct of the parties, even if there's no express, written contract.

Bill Graham Archives v. Dorling Kindersley Ltd., 448 F.3d 605 (2d Cir. 2006).
The Second Circuit Court of Appeals held that reduced versions of copyrighted posters used in an illustrated book were fair use.

Brady v. Maryland, 373 U.S. 83 (1963).
The U.S. Supreme Court held that the prosecution has a duty to disclose any evidence that it has that might help prove the defendant's innocence.

Brown v. Board of Education, 347 U.S. 483 (1954).
The U.S. Supreme Court overruled Plessy v. Ferguson. It held that separate but equal practices are inherently unequal and violate the U.S. Constitution.

Burnet v. Coronado Oil & Gas Co., 285 U.S. 393 (1932).
The U.S. Supreme Court recognizes the value of precedent in deciding cases.

Carlill v. Carbolic Smoke Ball Company, 1 QB 256; Court of Appeal (1892).
English court case that held that an advertisement could constitute a valid offer.

City of Ontario v. Quon, 529 F.3d 892 (9th Cir. 2009) *cert. granted* December 14, 2009.
In December 2009, the U.S. Supreme Court agreed to hear a case about employee privacy rights on employer-provided equipment. The Supreme Court agreed to review a ruling by the Ninth Circuit Court of Appeals that held that reading text messages sent on devices provided by the employer violated the worker's privacy rights.

CompuServe, Inc. v. Cyber Promotions, Inc., 962 F.Supp. 1015 (S.D. Ohio 1997).

The first court case holding that spammers could be liable for the tort of trespass to chattels.

Claridge v. RockYou, Inc., United States District Court Northern District of California, C 09 6032 BZ (2009).

An Indiana man sued RockYou. The lawsuit claims that RockYou stored personal data in an unencrypted database and failed to take reasonable steps to secure that personal information.

Daubert v. Merrell Dow Pharmaceuticals, Inc., 509 U.S. 579 (1993).

The U.S. Supreme Court case that set forth the test for admitting scientific expert witness testimony.

Deal v. Spears, 980 F.2d. 1153 (8th Cir. 1992).

Eighth Circuit Court of Appeals found that a recorder purchased at a consumer electronics store and connected to an extension phone line didn't qualify as ordinary telephone equipment.

Diamond v. Chakrabarty, 447 U.S. 303 (1980).

The U.S. Supreme Court held that patentable subject matter is "anything under the sun that is made by man."

Free Enterprise Fund and Beckstead and Watts v. Public Company Accounting Oversight Board, 537 F.3d 667 (Fed. Cir, 2008).

Court case challenging the constitutionality of the Public Company Accounting Oversight Board. The case was on appeal to the U.S. Supreme Court at the time this book was written.

Fisher v. United States, 425 U.S. 391 (1976).

The U.S. Supreme Court held that the Fifth Amendment protects communications that are compelled, testimonial, and incriminating in nature.

Gideon v. Wainwright, 372 U.S. 335 (1963).

The U.S. Supreme Court held that a state must appoint counsel to an indigent defendant who has been charged with a felony. Denial of the Sixth Amendment right to counsel at trial results in an automatic reversal of any conviction.

Giglio v. United States, 405 U.S. 150 (1972).

The U.S. Supreme Court held that the prosecution has a duty to disclose to the defendant any deals that it makes with witnesses.

Griswold v. Connecticut, 381 U.S. 479 (1965).

First U.S. Supreme Court decision to articulate a Constitutional right to privacy.

Hammer v. Arizona, 392 F. Supp. 2d 423 (E.D.N.Y 2005).

The District Court for the Eastern District of New York held that a defamatory statement is more than mere opinion.

Hartford v. Moore, 181 F. 132 (S.D.N.Y. 1910).

The District Court for the Southern District of New York recognized that an invention that seems obvious after it's created may actually meet the non-obvious requirement for patentability.

In re Boucher, 2009 WL 424718 (D. Vt., February 19, 2009).

The District Court for the District of Vermont held that it's not a violation of the Fifth Amendment to require a defendant to provide an unencrypted version of his hard drive.

Intel Corp v. Hamidi, 71 P.3d 296 (Ca. 2003).

> The California Supreme Court held that the plaintiff didn't sustain any damages in a trespass to chattels spam case. As such, the plaintiff could not recover damages.

Jacobellis v. Ohio, 378 U.S. 184 (1964).

> The U.S. Supreme Court stated that the First Amendment doesn't protect pornography or obscenity. The famous line, "I know it when I see it," is from the majority decision in this case.

Jones v. Hamilton, Alabama Court of Civil Appeals, Opinion, January 22, 2010, available at http://www.tradesecretsnoncompetelaw.com/uploads/file/Jones%20v%20Hamilton%20 decision.pdf (accessed March 31, 2010).

> The Alabama Court of Appeals held that information left in the back seat of a vehicle that was accessible to many employees was not properly protected as a trade secret.

Katz v. United States, 389 U.S. 347 (1967).

> The U.S. Supreme Court held that the Fourth Amendment of the U.S. Constitution protects a person's right to privacy.

Lamle v. Mattel, Inc., 394 F.3d 1355 (Fed. Cir. 2005).

> The Federal Circuit Court of Appeals held that an e-mail outlining contract terms is a signed writing under the California Statute of Frauds.

Leonard v. Pepsico, Inc., 88 F.Supp.2d 116 (S.D.N.Y. 1999), aff'd 210 F.3d 88 (2d Cir. 2000).

> Second Circuit Court of Appeals case that held an advertisement was a valid contractual offer only if a reasonable person considered it to be an offer.

Major v. McCallister, Missouri Court of Appeals, No. CD29871 (December 23, 2009).

> The Missouri Court of Appeals held that a browsewrap contract was enforceable where the user was put on notice in many ways that the terms of the contract applied to the service provided on a Web site.

Miller v. California, 413 U.S. 15 (1973).

> The U.S. Supreme Court created a three-part test for identifying materials as obscene.

Nardone v. United States, 308 U.S. 338 (1939).

> The U.S. Supreme Court first uses the term "fruit of the poisonous tree" to describe evidence that is inadmissible at court because it's collected illegally.

Owasso Independent School District No. I-011 v. Falvo, 534 U.S. 426 (2002).

> The U.S. Supreme Court held that the practice of peer grading doesn't violate the Family Educational Rights and Privacy Act (FERPA).

Palsgraf v. Long Island Railroad, 162 NE 99 (N.Y. 1928).

> The New York Court of Appeals held that there's no duty to an unforeseen plaintiff for unforeseeable injuries.

Pavesich v. New England Life Ins. Co., 50 S.E. 68 (Ga. 1905).

> First state case to specifically recognize a right to privacy in a state constitution.

Pemberton v. Bethlehem Steel Corp., 502 A.2d 1101 (Md. App.), cert. denied, 508 A.2d 488 (Md.), cert. denied, 107 S.Ct. 571 (1986).

> Maryland Court of Appeals held that the publication of a mug shot isn't a privacy violation because the photograph is part of the public record.

People v. Weaver, 12 N.Y.3d 433 (N.Y. 2009).

New York's highest court held that police officers need a warrant in order to place a tracking device on a suspect's car.

Plessy v. Ferguson, 163 U.S. 537 (1896).

The U.S. Supreme Court legalized racial, separate but equal, segregation practices. The Court stated that these practices didn't violate the U.S. Constitution.

ProCD Inc. v. Zeidenberg, 86 F.3d 1447 (1996).

The Seventh Circuit Court of Appeals upheld a shrinkwrap contract where users had the opportunity to return software for a full refund if they didn't agree to the terms in the contract.

Register.com, Inc. v. Verio, Inc., 356 F.3d 393, 403 (2d Cir. 2004).

The Second Circuit Court of Appeals has said recognized that e-commerce hasn't changed the fundamental principles of contract law.

Robinson v. California, 370 U.S. 660 (1962).

The U.S. Supreme Court said that a state statute could not criminalize the status of being an addict. Criminal behavior is evidenced by a specific action, not status.

Schifano v. Greene County Greyhound Park, Inc., 624 So.2d 178 (Ala. 1993).

Alabama Supreme Court case held that people can't state a claim for false light when they are in a public place.

Silverthorne Lumber Co. v. United States, 251 U.S. 385 (1920).

The U.S. Supreme Court first articulated a doctrine that says that evidence is inadmissible at court if it's illegally collected.

Smith v. Maryland, 422 U.S. 735 (1979).

The U.S. Supreme Court found that there's no right of privacy in the routing information of electronic communications.

Specht v. Netscape Communications Corporation, 306 F.3d 17 (2002).

The Second Circuit Court of Appeals didn't enforce terms of a browsewrap contract where those terms were located on a submerged Web page.

State Rubbish Collectors Association v. Siliznoff, 240 P.2d. 282 (Ca. 1952).

Landmark case that recognized a cause of action for intentional infliction of emotional distress.

State v. Smith, Slip Opinion No. 2009-Ohio-6426 (Oh. 2009).

The Supreme Court of Ohio found that individuals have a reasonable expectation of privacy in their cell phones.

State v. Sveum, 769 N.W.2d 53 (Wis. Ct. App. 2009).

Wisconsin Court of Appeals held that police didn't need a warrant to attach a tracking unit to a suspect's car.

Strassheim v. Daily, 221 U.S. 280 (1911).

The U.S. Supreme Court used the detrimental effects test to determine if a state could exercise criminal jurisdiction over a person that committed acts outside of the state.

Strunk v. United States, 412 U.S. 434 (1973).

The U.S. Supreme Court held that a criminal charge must be dismissed if the defendant's speedy trial rights are violated.

Toys "R" Us v. Akkaoui, 40 U.S.P.Q.2d (BNA) 1836 (N.D. Cal. Oct. 29, 1996).

The District Court for the Northern District of California ordered an adult website to stop using its domain name because it cast a famous trademark in an unflattering light.

United States v. Al-Marri, 230 F. Supp 2d 535, 541 (S.D.N.Y. 2002).

The District Court for the Southern District of New York held that people have a reasonable expectation of privacy in data stored on personal pagers.

United States v. American Library Association, 539 U.S. 194 (2003).

The U.S. Supreme Court upheld the constitutionality of the Children's Internet Protection Act (CIPA).

United States v. Barrows, 481 F.3d 1246 (10th Cir. 2007).

Tenth Circuit Court of Appeals held that an employee didn't have a reasonable expectation of privacy in his personal computer when he took no steps to protect his computer.

United States v. Heckenkamp, 482 F.3d 1142, 1146 (9th Cir. 2007).

The Ninth Circuit Court of Appeals held that person has a reasonable expectation of privacy in a personal computer.

U.S. v. Kirschner, 2010 U.S. Dist. Lexis 30603 (E.D. Mich., March 30, 2010).

This District Court for the Eastern District of Michigan held that it is a violation of the Fifth Amendment to require a defendant to provide the password to his computer.

United States v. Miami University; Ohio State University, 294 F.3d 797 (6th Cir. 2002).

The Sixth Circuit Court of Appeals held that disciplinary records are records that are protected by Family Educational Rights and Privacy Act (FERPA). A student's consent is required prior to releasing the records.

United States v. Mullins, 992 F.2d 1472 (9th Cir. 1993).

The Ninth Circuit Court of Appeals held that the Wiretap Act's provider exception can be used by system administrators to track a hacker throughout an entity's computer network in order to prevent damage to the network.

United States v. White, 401 U.S. 745 (1971).

The U.S. Supreme Court found there's no right of privacy in information that's voluntarily disclosed to another person.

Whalen v. Roe, 429 U.S. 589 (1977).

The U.S. Supreme Court specifically recognized a right of "informational privacy."

Wheaten v. Peters, 33 U.S. 591 (1834).

The U.S. Supreme Court first acknowledged that a person has an interest in being "let alone."

White v. Samsung Electronics of America, Inc., 989 F.2d 1512 (9th Cir. 1992).

A Ninth Circuit Court of Appeals case where a game show host argued successfully that being a host on a popular game show was her identity, and that a business misappropriated her identity.

Williams v. Crichton, 84 F.3d 581, 590 (2d Cir. 1996).

The Second Circuit Court of Appeals stated a test used for determining "substantial similarity" between copyrighted works.

Zubulake v. UBS Warburg, LLC, 2004 WL 1620866 (SD NY July 20, 2004).

A series of decisions in the District Court for the Southern District of New York that helped define the limits of electronic discovery.

The Constitution of the United States of America

We the People of the United States, in Order to form a more perfect Union, establish Justice, insure domestic Tranquility, provide for the common defence, promote the general Welfare, and secure the Blessings of Liberty to ourselves and our Posterity, do ordain and establish this Constitution for the United States of America.

Article. I.

Section. 1.

All legislative Powers herein granted shall be vested in a Congress of the United States, which shall consist of a Senate and House of Representatives.

Section. 2.

The House of Representatives shall be composed of Members chosen every second Year by the People of the several States, and the Electors in each State shall have the Qualifications requisite for Electors of the most numerous Branch of the State Legislature.

No Person shall be a Representative who shall not have attained to the Age of twenty five Years, and been seven Years a Citizen of the United States, and who shall not, when elected, be an Inhabitant of that State in which he shall be chosen.

Representatives and direct Taxes shall be apportioned among the several States which may be included within this Union, according to their respective Numbers, which shall be determined by adding to the whole Number of free Persons, including those bound to Service for a Term of Years, and excluding Indians not taxed, three fifths of all other Persons. The actual Enumeration shall be made within three Years after the first Meeting of the Congress of the United States, and within every subsequent Term of ten Years, in such Manner as they shall by Law direct. The Number of Representatives shall not exceed one for every thirty Thousand, but each State shall have at Least one Representative; and until such enumeration shall be made, the State of New Hampshire shall be entitled to chuse three, Massachusetts eight, Rhode-Island and Providence Plantations one, Connecticut five, New-York six, New Jersey four, Pennsylvania eight, Delaware one, Maryland six, Virginia ten, North Carolina five, South Carolina five, and Georgia three.

When vacancies happen in the Representation from any State, the Executive Authority thereof shall issue Writs of Election to fill such Vacancies.

The House of Representatives shall chuse their Speaker and other Officers; and shall have the sole Power of Impeachment.

Section. 3.

The Senate of the United States shall be composed of two Senators from each State, chosen by the Legislature thereof for six Years; and each Senator shall have one Vote.

Immediately after they shall be assembled in Consequence of the first Election, they shall be divided as equally as may be into three Classes. The Seats of the Senators of the first Class shall be vacated at the Expiration of the second Year, of the second Class at the Expiration of the fourth Year, and of the third Class at the Expiration of the sixth Year, so that one third may be chosen every second Year; and if Vacancies happen by Resignation, or otherwise, during the Recess of the Legislature of any State, the Executive thereof may make temporary Appointments until the next Meeting of the Legislature, which shall then fill such Vacancies.

The text of the U.S. Constitution is in its original form. Spelling, punctuation, and capitalization are the same as in the original document.

No Person shall be a Senator who shall not have attained to the Age of thirty Years, and been nine Years a Citizen of the United States, and who shall not, when elected, be an Inhabitant of that State for which he shall be chosen.

The Vice President of the United States shall be President of the Senate, but shall have no Vote, unless they be equally divided.

The Senate shall chuse their other Officers, and also a President pro tempore, in the Absence of the Vice President, or when he shall exercise the Office of President of the United States.

The Senate shall have the sole Power to try all Impeachments. When sitting for that Purpose, they shall be on Oath or Affirmation. When the President of the United States is tried, the Chief Justice shall preside: And no Person shall be convicted without the Concurrence of two thirds of the Members present.

Judgment in Cases of Impeachment shall not extend further than to removal from Office, and disqualification to hold and enjoy any Office of honor, Trust or Profit under the United States: but the Party convicted shall nevertheless be liable and subject to Indictment, Trial, Judgment and Punishment, according to Law.

Section. 4.

The Times, Places and Manner of holding Elections for Senators and Representatives, shall be prescribed in each State by the Legislature thereof; but the Congress may at any time by Law make or alter such Regulations, except as to the Places of chusing Senators.

The Congress shall assemble at least once in every Year, and such Meeting shall be on the first Monday in December, unless they shall by Law appoint a different Day.

Section. 5.

Each House shall be the Judge of the Elections, Returns and Qualifications of its own Members, and a Majority of each shall constitute a Quorum to do Business; but a smaller Number may adjourn from day to day, and may be authorized to compel the Attendance of absent Members, in such Manner, and under such Penalties as each House may provide.

Each House may determine the Rules of its Proceedings, punish its Members for disorderly Behaviour, and, with the Concurrence of two thirds, expel a Member.

Each House shall keep a Journal of its Proceedings, and from time to time publish the same, excepting such Parts as may in their Judgment require Secrecy; and the Yeas and Nays of the Members of either House on any question shall, at the Desire of one fifth of those Present, be entered on the Journal.

Neither House, during the Session of Congress, shall, without the Consent of the other, adjourn for more than three days, nor to any other Place than that in which the two Houses shall be sitting.

Section. 6.

The Senators and Representatives shall receive a Compensation for their Services, to be ascertained by Law, and paid out of the Treasury of the United States. They shall in all Cases, except Treason, Felony and Breach of the Peace, be privileged from Arrest during their Attendance at the Session of their respective Houses, and in going to and returning from the same; and for any Speech or Debate in either House, they shall not be questioned in any other Place.

No Senator or Representative shall, during the Time for which he was elected, be appointed to any civil Office under the Authority of the United States, which shall have been created, or the Emoluments whereof shall have been encreased during such time; and no Person holding any Office under the United States, shall be a Member of either House during his Continuance in Office.

Section. 7.

All Bills for raising Revenue shall originate in the House of Representatives; but the Senate may propose or concur with Amendments as on other Bills.

Every Bill which shall have passed the House of Representatives and the Senate, shall, before it become a Law, be presented to the President of the United States: If he approve he shall sign it, but if not he shall return it, with his Objections to that House in which it shall have originated, who shall enter the Objections at large on their

Journal, and proceed to reconsider it. If after such Reconsideration two thirds of that House shall agree to pass the Bill, it shall be sent, together with the Objections, to the other House, by which it shall likewise be reconsidered, and if approved by two thirds of that House, it shall become a Law. But in all such Cases the Votes of both Houses shall be determined by yeas and Nays, and the Names of the Persons voting for and against the Bill shall be entered on the Journal of each House respectively. If any Bill shall not be returned by the President within ten Days (Sundays excepted) after it shall have been presented to him, the Same shall be a Law, in like Manner as if he had signed it, unless the Congress by their Adjournment prevent its Return, in which Case it shall not be a Law.

Every Order, Resolution, or Vote to which the Concurrence of the Senate and House of Representatives may be necessary (except on a question of Adjournment) shall be presented to the President of the United States; and before the Same shall take Effect, shall be approved by him, or being disapproved by him, shall be repassed by two thirds of the Senate and House of Representatives, according to the Rules and Limitations prescribed in the Case of a Bill.

Section. 8.

The Congress shall have Power To lay and collect Taxes, Duties, Imposts and Excises, to pay the Debts and provide for the common Defence and general Welfare of the United States; but all Duties, Imposts and Excises shall be uniform throughout the United States;

To borrow Money on the credit of the United States;

To regulate Commerce with foreign Nations, and among the several States, and with the Indian Tribes;

To establish an uniform Rule of Naturalization, and uniform Laws on the subject of Bankruptcies throughout the United States;

To coin Money, regulate the Value thereof, and of foreign Coin, and fix the Standard of Weights and Measures;

To provide for the Punishment of counterfeiting the Securities and current Coin of the United States;

To establish Post Offices and post Roads;

To promote the Progress of Science and useful Arts, by securing for limited Times to Authors and Inventors the exclusive Right to their respective Writings and Discoveries;

To constitute Tribunals inferior to the supreme Court;

To define and punish Piracies and Felonies committed on the high Seas, and Offences against the Law of Nations;

To declare War, grant Letters of Marque and Reprisal, and make Rules concerning Captures on Land and Water;

To raise and support Armies, but no Appropriation of Money to that Use shall be for a longer Term than two Years;

To provide and maintain a Navy;

To make Rules for the Government and Regulation of the land and naval Forces;

To provide for calling forth the Militia to execute the Laws of the Union, suppress Insurrections and repel Invasions;

To provide for organizing, arming, and disciplining, the Militia, and for governing such Part of them as may be employed in the Service of the United States, reserving to the States respectively, the Appointment of the Officers, and the Authority of training the Militia according to the discipline prescribed by Congress;

To exercise exclusive Legislation in all Cases whatsoever, over such District (not exceeding ten Miles square) as may, by Cession of particular States, and the Acceptance of Congress, become the Seat of the Government of the United States, and to exercise like Authority over all Places purchased by the Consent of the Legislature of the State in which the Same shall be, for the Erection of Forts, Magazines, Arsenals, dock-Yards, and other needful Buildings;—And

To make all Laws which shall be necessary and proper for carrying into Execution the foregoing Powers, and all other Powers vested by this Constitution in the Government of the United States, or in any Department or Officer thereof.

Section. 9.

The Migration or Importation of such Persons as any of the States now existing shall think proper to admit, shall not be prohibited by the Congress prior to the Year one thousand eight hundred and eight, but a Tax or duty may be imposed on such Importation, not exceeding ten dollars for each Person.

The Privilege of the Writ of Habeas Corpus shall not be suspended, unless when in Cases of Rebellion or Invasion the public Safety may require it.

No Bill of Attainder or ex post facto Law shall be passed.

No Capitation, or other direct, Tax shall be laid, unless in Proportion to the Census or enumeration herein before directed to be taken.

No Tax or Duty shall be laid on Articles exported from any State.

No Preference shall be given by any Regulation of Commerce or Revenue to the Ports of one State over those of another; nor shall Vessels bound to, or from, one State, be obliged to enter, clear, or pay Duties in another.

No Money shall be drawn from the Treasury, but in Consequence of Appropriations made by Law; and a regular Statement and Account of the Receipts and Expenditures of all public Money shall be published from time to time.

No Title of Nobility shall be granted by the United States: And no Person holding any Office of Profit or Trust under them, shall, without the Consent of the Congress, accept of any present, Emolument, Office, or Title, of any kind whatever, from any King, Prince, or foreign State.

Section. 10.

No State shall enter into any Treaty, Alliance, or Confederation; grant Letters of Marque and Reprisal; coin Money; emit Bills of Credit; make any Thing but gold and silver Coin a Tender in Payment of Debts; pass any Bill of Attainder, ex post facto Law, or Law impairing the Obligation of Contracts, or grant any Title of Nobility.

No State shall, without the Consent of the Congress, lay any Imposts or Duties on Imports or Exports, except what may be absolutely necessary for executing it's inspection Laws: and the net Produce of all Duties and Imposts, laid by any State on Imports or Exports, shall be for the Use of the Treasury of the United States; and all such Laws shall be subject to the Revision and Controul of the Congress.

No State shall, without the Consent of Congress, lay any Duty of Tonnage, keep Troops, or Ships of War in time of Peace, enter into any Agreement or Compact with another State, or with a foreign Power, or engage in War, unless actually invaded, or in such imminent Danger as will not admit of delay.

Article. II.

Section. 1.

The executive Power shall be vested in a President of the United States of America. He shall hold his Office during the Term of four Years, and, together with the Vice President, chosen for the same Term, be elected, as follows:

Each State shall appoint, in such Manner as the Legislature thereof may direct, a Number of Electors, equal to the whole Number of Senators and Representatives to which the State may be entitled in the Congress: but no Senator or Representative, or Person holding an Office of Trust or Profit under the United States, shall be appointed an Elector.

The Electors shall meet in their respective States, and vote by Ballot for two Persons, of whom one at least shall not be an Inhabitant of the same State with themselves. And they shall make a List of all the Persons voted for, and of the Number of Votes for each; which List they shall sign and certify, and transmit sealed to the Seat of the Government of the United States, directed to the President of the Senate. The President of the Senate shall, in the Presence of the Senate and House of Representatives, open all the Certificates, and the Votes shall then be counted. The Person having the greatest Number of Votes shall be the President, if such Number be a Majority of the whole Number of Electors appointed; and if there be more than one who have such Majority, and have an equal Number of Votes, then the House of Representatives shall immediately chuse by Ballot one of them for President; and if no Person have a Majority, then from the five highest on the List the said House shall in like Manner chuse the President. But in chusing the President, the Votes shall be taken by States, the Representation from each State having one Vote; A quorum for this purpose shall consist of a Member or Members from two thirds of the States, and a Majority of all the States shall be necessary to a Choice. In every Case, after the Choice of the President, the Person having the greatest Number of Votes of the Electors shall be the Vice President. But if there should remain two or more who have equal Votes, the Senate shall chuse from them by Ballot the Vice President.

The Congress may determine the Time of chusing the Electors, and the Day on which they shall give their Votes; which Day shall be the same throughout the United States.

No Person except a natural born Citizen, or a Citizen of the United States, at the time of the Adoption of this Constitution, shall be eligible to the Office of President; neither shall any Person be eligible to that Office who shall not have attained to the Age of thirty five Years, and been fourteen Years a Resident within the United States.

In Case of the Removal of the President from Office, or of his Death, Resignation, or Inability to discharge the Powers and Duties of the said Office, the Same shall devolve on the Vice President, and the Congress may by Law provide for the Case of Removal, Death, Resignation or Inability, both of the President and Vice President, declaring what Officer shall then act as President, and such Officer shall act accordingly, until the Disability be removed, or a President shall be elected.

The President shall, at stated Times, receive for his Services, a Compensation, which shall neither be increased nor diminished during the Period for which he shall have been elected, and he shall not receive within that Period any other Emolument from the United States, or any of them.

Before he enter on the Execution of his Office, he shall take the following Oath or Affirmation:— "I do solemnly swear (or affirm) that I will faithfully execute the Office of President of the United States, and will to the best of my Ability, preserve, protect and defend the Constitution of the United States."

Section. 2.

The President shall be Commander in Chief of the Army and Navy of the United States, and of the Militia of the several States, when called into the actual Service of the United States; he may require the Opinion, in writing, of the principal Officer in each of the executive Departments, upon any Subject relating to the Duties of their respective Offices, and he shall have Power to grant Reprieves and Pardons for Offences against the United States, except in Cases of Impeachment.

He shall have Power, by and with the Advice and Consent of the Senate, to make Treaties, provided two thirds of the Senators present concur; and he shall nominate, and by and with the Advice and Consent of the Senate, shall appoint Ambassadors, other public Ministers and Consuls, Judges of the supreme Court, and all other Officers of the United States, whose Appointments are not herein otherwise provided for, and which shall be established by Law: but the Congress may by Law vest the Appointment of such inferior Officers, as they think proper, in the President alone, in the Courts of Law, or in the Heads of Departments.

The President shall have Power to fill up all Vacancies that may happen during the Recess of the Senate, by granting Commissions which shall expire at the End of their next Session.

Section. 3.

He shall from time to time give to the Congress Information of the State of the Union, and recommend to their Consideration such Measures as he shall judge necessary and expedient; he may, on extraordinary Occasions, convene both Houses, or either of them, and in Case of Disagreement between them, with Respect to the Time of Adjournment, he may adjourn them to such Time as he shall think proper; he shall receive Ambassadors and other public Ministers; he shall take Care that the Laws be faithfully executed, and shall Commission all the Officers of the United States.

Section. 4.

The President, Vice President and all civil Officers of the United States, shall be removed from Office on Impeachment for, and Conviction of, Treason, Bribery, or other high Crimes and Misdemeanors.

D

The U.S. Constitution

Article III.

Section. 1.

The judicial Power of the United States shall be vested in one supreme Court, and in such inferior Courts as the Congress may from time to time ordain and establish. The Judges, both of the supreme and inferior Courts, shall hold their Offices during good Behaviour, and shall, at stated Times, receive for their Services a Compensation, which shall not be diminished during their Continuance in Office.

Section. 2.

The judicial Power shall extend to all Cases, in Law and Equity, arising under this Constitution, the Laws of the United States, and Treaties made, or which shall be made, under their Authority;—to all Cases affecting Ambassadors, other public Ministers and Consuls;—to all Cases of admiralty and maritime Jurisdiction;—to Controversies to which the United States shall be a Party;—to Controversies between two or more States;—between a State and Citizens of another State,—between Citizens of different States,—between Citizens of the same State claiming Lands under Grants of different States, and between a State, or the Citizens thereof, and foreign States, Citizens or Subjects.

In all Cases affecting Ambassadors, other public Ministers and Consuls, and those in which a State shall be Party, the supreme Court shall have original Jurisdiction. In all the other Cases before mentioned, the supreme Court shall have appellate Jurisdiction, both as to Law and Fact, with such Exceptions, and under such Regulations as the Congress shall make.

The Trial of all Crimes, except in Cases of Impeachment, shall be by Jury; and such Trial shall be held in the State where the said Crimes shall have been committed; but when not committed within any State, the Trial shall be at such Place or Places as the Congress may by Law have directed.

Section. 3.

Treason against the United States, shall consist only in levying War against them, or in adhering to their Enemies, giving them Aid and Comfort. No Person shall be convicted of Treason unless on the Testimony of two Witnesses to the same overt Act, or on Confession in open Court.

The Congress shall have Power to declare the Punishment of Treason, but no Attainder of Treason shall work Corruption of Blood, or Forfeiture except during the Life of the Person attainted.

Article. IV.

Section. 1.

Full Faith and Credit shall be given in each State to the public Acts, Records, and judicial Proceedings of every other State. And the Congress may by general Laws prescribe the Manner in which such Acts, Records and Proceedings shall be proved, and the Effect thereof.

Section. 2.

The Citizens of each State shall be entitled to all Privileges and Immunities of Citizens in the several States.

A Person charged in any State with Treason, Felony, or other Crime, who shall flee from Justice, and be found in another State, shall on Demand of the executive Authority of the State from which he fled, be delivered up, to be removed to the State having Jurisdiction of the Crime.

No Person held to Service or Labour in one State, under the Laws thereof, escaping into another, shall, in Consequence of any Law or Regulation therein, be discharged from such Service or Labour, but shall be delivered up on Claim of the Party to whom such Service or Labour may be due.

Section. 3.

New States may be admitted by the Congress into this Union; but no new State shall be formed or erected within the Jurisdiction of any other State; nor any State be formed by the Junction of two or more States, or Parts of States, without the Consent of the Legislatures of the States concerned as well as of the Congress.

The Congress shall have Power to dispose of and make all needful Rules and Regulations respecting the Territory or other Property belonging to the United States; and nothing in this Constitution shall be so construed as to Prejudice any Claims of the United States, or of any particular State.

Section. 4.

The United States shall guarantee to every State in this Union a Republican Form of Government, and shall protect each of them against Invasion; and on Application of the Legislature, or of the Executive (when the Legislature cannot be convened), against domestic Violence.

Article. V.

The Congress, whenever two thirds of both Houses shall deem it necessary, shall propose Amendments to this Constitution, or, on the Application of the Legislatures of two thirds of the several States, shall call a Convention for proposing Amendments, which, in either Case, shall be valid to all Intents and Purposes, as Part of this Constitution, when ratified by the Legislatures of three fourths of the several States, or by Conventions in three fourths thereof, as the one or the other Mode of Ratification may be proposed by the Congress; Provided that no Amendment which may be made prior to the Year One thousand eight hundred and eight shall in any Manner affect the first and fourth Clauses in the Ninth Section of the first Article; and that no State, without its Consent, shall be deprived of its equal Suffrage in the Senate.

Article. VI.

All Debts contracted and Engagements entered into, before the Adoption of this Constitution, shall be as valid against the United States under this Constitution, as under the Confederation.

This Constitution, and the Laws of the United States which shall be made in Pursuance thereof; and all Treaties made, or which shall be made, under the Authority of the United States, shall be the supreme Law of the Land; and the Judges in every State shall be bound thereby, any Thing in the Constitution or Laws of any State to the Contrary notwithstanding.

The Senators and Representatives before mentioned, and the Members of the several State Legislatures, and all executive and judicial Officers, both of the United States and of the several States, shall be bound by Oath or Affirmation, to support this Constitution; but no religious Test shall ever be required as a Qualification to any Office or public Trust under the United States.

Article. VII.

The Ratification of the Conventions of nine States, shall be sufficient for the Establishment of this Constitution between the States so ratifying the Same.

Amendments to the Constitution of the United States of America.

Amendment I (1791)

Congress shall make no law respecting an establishment of religion, or prohibiting the free exercise thereof; or abridging the freedom of speech, or of the press; or the right of the people peaceably to assemble, and to petition the Government for a redress of grievances.

Amendment II (1791)

A well regulated Militia, being necessary to the security of a free State, the right of the people to keep and bear Arms, shall not be infringed.

Amendment III (1791)

No Soldier shall, in time of peace be quartered in any house, without the consent of the Owner, nor in time of war, but in a manner to be prescribed by law.

Amendment IV (1791)

The right of the people to be secure in their persons, houses, papers, and effects, against unreasonable searches and seizures, shall not be violated, and no Warrants shall issue, but upon probable cause, supported by Oath or affirmation, and particularly describing the place to be searched, and the persons or things to be seized.

Amendment V (1791)

No person shall be held to answer for a capital, or otherwise infamous crime, unless on a presentment or indictment of a Grand Jury, except in cases arising in the land or naval forces, or in the Militia, when in actual service in time of War or public danger; nor shall any person be subject for the same offence to be twice put in jeopardy of life or limb; nor shall be compelled in any criminal case to be a witness against himself, nor be deprived of life, liberty, or property, without due process of law; nor shall private property be taken for public use, without just compensation.

Amendment VI (1791)

In all criminal prosecutions, the accused shall enjoy the right to a speedy and public trial, by an impartial jury of the State and district wherein the crime shall have been committed, which district shall have been previously ascertained by law, and to be informed of the nature and cause of the accusation; to be confronted with the witnesses against him; to have compulsory process for obtaining witnesses in his favor, and to have the Assistance of Counsel for his defence.

Amendment VII (1791)

In Suits at common law, where the value in controversy shall exceed twenty dollars, the right of trial by jury shall be preserved, and no fact tried by a jury, shall be otherwise re-examined in any Court of the United States, than according to the rules of the common law.

Amendment VIII (1791)

Excessive bail shall not be required, nor excessive fines imposed, nor cruel and unusual punishments inflicted.

Amendment IX (1791)

The enumeration in the Constitution, of certain rights, shall not be construed to deny or disparage others retained by the people.

Amendment X (1791)

The powers not delegated to the United States by the Constitution, nor prohibited by it to the States, are reserved to the States respectively, or to the people.

Amendment XI (1795)

The Judicial power of the United States shall not be construed to extend to any suit in law or equity, commenced or prosecuted against one of the United States by Citizens of another State, or by Citizens or Subjects of any Foreign State.

Note: Article III, section 2, of the Constitution was modified by amendment 11.

Amendment XII (1804)

The Electors shall meet in their respective states and vote by ballot for President and Vice-President, one of whom, at least, shall not be an inhabitant of the same state with themselves; they shall name in their ballots the person voted for as President, and in distinct ballots the person voted for as Vice-President, and they shall make distinct lists of all persons voted for as President, and of all persons voted for as Vice-President, and of the number of votes for each, which lists they shall sign and certify, and transmit sealed to the seat of the government of the United States, directed to the President of the Senate; — the President of the Senate shall, in the presence of the Senate and House of Representatives, open all the certificates and the votes shall then be counted; — The person having the greatest number of votes for President, shall be the President, if such number be a majority of the whole number of Electors appointed; and if no person have such majority, then from the persons having the highest numbers not exceeding three on the list of those voted for as President, the House of Representatives shall choose immediately, by ballot, the President. But in choosing the President, the votes shall be taken by states, the representation from each state having one vote; a quorum for this purpose shall consist of a member or members from two-thirds of the states, and a majority of all the states shall be necessary to a choice. And if the House of Representatives shall not choose a President whenever the right of choice shall devolve upon them, before the fourth day of March next following, then the Vice-President shall act as President, as in case of the death or other constitutional disability of the President. The person having the greatest number of votes as Vice-President, shall be the Vice-President, if such number be a majority of the whole number of Electors appointed, and if no person have a majority, then from the two highest numbers on the list, the Senate shall choose the Vice-President; a quorum for the purpose shall consist of two-thirds of the whole number of Senators, and a majority of the whole number shall be necessary to a choice. But no person constitutionally ineligible to the office of President shall be eligible to that of Vice-President of the United States.

Note: A portion of Article II, section 1 of the Constitution was superseded by the 12th amendment.

Amendment XIII (1865)

Section 1.

Neither slavery nor involuntary servitude, except as a punishment for crime whereof the party shall have been duly convicted, shall exist within the United States, or any place subject to their jurisdiction.

Section 2.

Congress shall have power to enforce this article by appropriate legislation.

Note: A portion of Article IV, section 2, of the Constitution was superseded by the 13th amendment.

Amendment XIV (1868)

Section 1.

All persons born or naturalized in the United States, and subject to the jurisdiction thereof, are citizens of the United States and of the State wherein they reside. No State shall make or enforce any law which shall abridge the privileges or immunities of citizens of the United States; nor shall any State deprive any person of life, liberty, or property, without due process of law; nor deny to any person within its jurisdiction the equal protection of the laws.

Section 2.

Representatives shall be apportioned among the several States according to their respective numbers, counting the whole number of persons in each State, excluding Indians not taxed. But when the right to vote at any election for the choice of electors for President and Vice-President of the United States, Representatives in Congress, the Executive and Judicial officers of a State, or the members of the Legislature thereof, is denied to any of the male inhabitants of such State, being twenty-one years of age, and citizens of the United States, or in any way abridged, except for participation in rebellion, or other crime, the basis of representation therein shall be reduced in the proportion which the number of such male citizens shall bear to the whole number of male citizens twenty-one years of age in such State.

Section 3.

No person shall be a Senator or Representative in Congress, or elector of President and Vice-President, or hold any office, civil or military, under the United States, or under any State, who, having previously taken an oath, as a member of Congress, or as an officer of the United States, or as a member of any State legislature, or as an executive or judicial officer of any State, to support the Constitution of the United States, shall have engaged in insurrection or rebellion against the same, or given aid or comfort to the enemies thereof. But Congress may by a vote of two-thirds of each House, remove such disability.

Section 4.

The validity of the public debt of the United States, authorized by law, including debts incurred for payment of pensions and bounties for services in suppressing insurrection or rebellion, shall not be questioned. But neither the United States nor any State shall assume or pay any debt or obligation incurred in aid of insurrection or rebellion against the United States, or any claim for the loss or emancipation of any slave; but all such debts, obligations and claims shall be held illegal and void.

Section 5.

The Congress shall have the power to enforce, by appropriate legislation, the provisions of this article.

Note: Article I, section 2, of the Constitution was modified by section 2 of the 14th amendment.

Amendment XV (1870)

Section 1.

The right of citizens of the United States to vote shall not be denied or abridged by the United States or by any State on account of race, color, or previous condition of servitude—

Section 2.

The Congress shall have the power to enforce this article by appropriate legislation.

Amendment XVI (1913)

The Congress shall have power to lay and collect taxes on incomes, from whatever source derived, without apportionment among the several States, and without regard to any census or enumeration.

Note: Article I, section 9, of the Constitution was modified by amendment 16.

D

The U.S. Constitution

Amendment XVII (1913)

The Senate of the United States shall be composed of two Senators from each State, elected by the people thereof, for six years; and each Senator shall have one vote. The electors in each State shall have the qualifications requisite for electors of the most numerous branch of the State legislatures.

When vacancies happen in the representation of any State in the Senate, the executive authority of such State shall issue writs of election to fill such vacancies: Provided, That the legislature of any State may empower the executive thereof to make temporary appointments until the people fill the vacancies by election as the legislature may direct.

This amendment shall not be so construed as to affect the election or term of any Senator chosen before it becomes valid as part of the Constitution.

Note: Article I, section 3, of the Constitution was modified by the 17th amendment.

Amendment XVIII (1919)

Section 1.

After one year from the ratification of this article the manufacture, sale, or transportation of intoxicating liquors within, the importation thereof into, or the exportation thereof from the United States and all territory subject to the jurisdiction thereof for beverage purposes is hereby prohibited.

Section 2.

The Congress and the several States shall have concurrent power to enforce this article by appropriate legislation.

Section 3.

This article shall be inoperative unless it shall have been ratified as an amendment to the Constitution by the legislatures of the several States, as provided in the Constitution, within seven years from the date of the submission hereof to the States by the Congress.

Note: This amendment was repealed by amendment 21.

Amendment XIX (1920)

The right of citizens of the United States to vote shall not be denied or abridged by the United States or by any State on account of sex.

Congress shall have power to enforce this article by appropriate legislation.

Amendment XX (1933)

Section 1.

The terms of the President and the Vice President shall end at noon on the 20th day of January, and the terms of Senators and Representatives at noon on the 3d day of January, of the years in which such terms would have ended if this article had not been ratified; and the terms of their successors shall then begin.

Section 2.

The Congress shall assemble at least once in every year, and such meeting shall begin at noon on the 3d day of January, unless they shall by law appoint a different day.

Section 3.

If, at the time fixed for the beginning of the term of the President, the President elect shall have died, the Vice President elect shall become President. If a President shall not have been chosen before the time fixed for the beginning of his term, or if the President elect shall have failed to qualify, then the Vice President elect shall act as President until a President shall have qualified; and the Congress may by law provide for the case wherein neither a President elect nor a Vice President shall have qualified, declaring who shall then act as President, or the manner in which one who is to act shall be selected, and such person shall act accordingly until a President or Vice President shall have qualified.

Section 4.

The Congress may by law provide for the case of the death of any of the persons from whom the House of Representatives may choose a President whenever the right of choice shall have devolved upon them, and for the case of the death of any of the persons from whom the Senate may choose a Vice President whenever the right of choice shall have devolved upon them.

Section 5.

Sections 1 and 2 shall take effect on the 15th day of October following the ratification of this article.

Section 6.

This article shall be inoperative unless it shall have been ratified as an amendment to the Constitution by the legislatures of three-fourths of the several States within seven years from the date of its submission.

Note: Article I, section 4, of the Constitution was modified by section 2 of this amendment. In addition, a portion of the 12th amendment was superseded by section 3.

Amendment XXI (1933)

Section 1.

The eighteenth article of amendment to the Constitution of the United States is hereby repealed.

Section 2.

The transportation or importation into any State, Territory, or Possession of the United States for delivery or use therein of intoxicating liquors, in violation of the laws thereof, is hereby prohibited.

Section 3.

This article shall be inoperative unless it shall have been ratified as an amendment to the Constitution by conventions in the several States, as provided in the Constitution, within seven years from the date of the submission hereof to the States by the Congress.

Amendment XXII (1951)

Section 1.

No person shall be elected to the office of the President more than twice, and no person who has held the office of President, or acted as President, for more than two years of a term to which some other person was elected President shall be elected to the office of President more than once. But this Article shall not apply to any person holding the office of President when this Article was proposed by Congress, and shall not prevent any person who may be holding the office of President, or acting as President, during the term within which this Article becomes operative from holding the office of President or acting as President during the remainder of such term.

Section 2.

This article shall be inoperative unless it shall have been ratified as an amendment to the Constitution by the legislatures of three-fourths of the several States within seven years from the date of its submission to the States by the Congress.

Amendment XXIII (1961)

Section 1.

The District constituting the seat of Government of the United States shall appoint in such manner as Congress may direct:

A number of electors of President and Vice President equal to the whole number of Senators and Representatives in Congress to which the District would be entitled if it were a State, but in no event more than the least populous State; they shall be in addition to those appointed by the States, but they shall be considered, for the purposes of the election of President and Vice President, to be electors appointed by a State; and they shall meet in the District and perform such duties as provided by the twelfth article of amendment.

Section 2.

The Congress shall have power to enforce this article by appropriate legislation.

Amendment XXIV (1964)

Section 1.

The right of citizens of the United States to vote in any primary or other election for President or Vice President, for electors for President or Vice President, or for Senator or Representative in Congress, shall not be denied or abridged by the United States or any State by reason of failure to pay poll tax or other tax.

Section 2.

The Congress shall have power to enforce this article by appropriate legislation.

Amendment XXV (1967)

Section 1.

In case of the removal of the President from office or of his death or resignation, the Vice President shall become President.

D

The U.S. Constitution

Section 2.

Whenever there is a vacancy in the office of the Vice President, the President shall nominate a Vice President who shall take office upon confirmation by a majority vote of both Houses of Congress.

Section 3.

Whenever the President transmits to the President pro tempore of the Senate and the Speaker of the House of Representatives his written declaration that he is unable to discharge the powers and duties of his office, and until he transmits to them a written declaration to the contrary, such powers and duties shall be discharged by the Vice President as Acting President.

Section 4.

Whenever the Vice President and a majority of either the principal officers of the executive departments or of such other body as Congress may by law provide, transmit to the President pro tempore of the Senate and the Speaker of the House of Representatives their written declaration that the President is unable to discharge the powers and duties of his office, the Vice President shall immediately assume the powers and duties of the office as Acting President.

Thereafter, when the President transmits to the President pro tempore of the Senate and the Speaker of the House of Representatives his written declaration that no inability exists, he shall resume the powers and duties of his office unless the Vice President and a majority of either the principal officers of the executive department or of such other body as Congress may by law provide, transmit within four days to the President pro tempore of the Senate and the Speaker of the House of Representatives their written declaration that

the President is unable to discharge the powers and duties of his office. Thereupon Congress shall decide the issue, assembling within forty-eight hours for that purpose if not in session. If the Congress, within twenty-one days after receipt of the latter written declaration, or, if Congress is not in session, within twenty-one days after Congress is required to assemble, determines by two-thirds vote of both Houses that the President is unable to discharge the powers and duties of his office, the Vice President shall continue to discharge the same as Acting President; otherwise, the President shall resume the powers and duties of his office.

Note: Article II, section 1, of the Constitution was affected by the 25th amendment.

Amendment XXVI (1971)

Section 1.

The right of citizens of the United States, who are eighteen years of age or older, to vote shall not be denied or abridged by the United States or by any State on account of age.

Section 2.

The Congress shall have power to enforce this article by appropriate legislation.

Note: Amendment 14, section 2, of the Constitution was modified by section 1 of the 26th amendment.

Amendment XXVII (1992)

No law, varying the compensation for the services of the Senators and Representatives, shall take effect, until an election of representatives shall have intervened.

Source: http://www.archives.gov/exhibits/charters/constitution_transcript.html

Glossary of Key Terms

A

Acceptable use policy (AUP) | States the proper use an organization's information technology resources.

Actus reus | A Latin term used to describe a crime. It means "guilty act."

Administrative procedure | Sets forth the process under which administrative agencies make and enforce rules.

Administrative safeguards | Management and regulatory controls. These safeguards are usually policies, standards, guidelines, and procedures. They also can be the laws an organization must follow.

Adware | Software that displays advertising banners, re-directs a user to Web sites, and conducts advertising on a user's computer. Adware also displays pop-up advertisements.

Affidavit | A sworn written statement.

Annual rate of occurrence (ARO) | How many times a threat might affect an organization during a one-year time frame.

Annualized loss expectancy (ALE) | The amount of loss that an organization can expect to have each year due to a particular risk. ALE is often expressed as the equation: ALE = SLE × ARO. SLE is single loss expectancy. ARO is annual rate of occurrence.

Answer | A defendant's response to the plaintiff's complaint.

Appellate jurisdiction | The power of a court to review a decision made by a lower court. It also is called statutory law.

Audit | An evaluation and verification that certain objectives are met.

Authentication | The process through which a user proves his or her identity to access an information technology resource.

Authorization | A written consent that allows protected health information (PHI) to be shared. Patients sign consents. These documents are required for many purposes. This term is defined by the Health Insurance Portability and Accountability Act.

Availability | The security goal of ensuring that you can access information systems and their data when you need them. They must be available in a dependable and timely manner.

B

Baseline | A minimum level of behavior or action that must be met in order to comply with a governance document. Baselines are often specified in standards.

Beyond a reasonable doubt | The standard of proof in a criminal case.

Biometric data | Data about a person's physical or behavioral traits used to identify a particular person. Biometric data is unique because it can't be changed.

Blog | A personal online journal. Also called a Weblog.

Board of directors (BOD) | An organization's governing body. It plans an organization's strategic direction. A board of directors is required by law to act with due care and in the best interests of the organization.

Breach notification law | A law that requires that state residents be notified if an entity experiences a security breach that compromises their personal data.

Browsewrap contract | An agreement where the complete terms of the agreement are presented on a Web page. A user doesn't have to take any affirmative action to accept the terms of the agreement other than to use the Web page.

Business associates | An organization that performs a health care activity on behalf of a covered entity. This term is defined by the Health Insurance Portability and Accountability Act.

Business continuity (BC) plans | Plans that address the recovery of an organization's business processes and functions in the event of a disaster. Business continuity plans tend to be comprehensive business plans for returning an organization to normal operating conditions.

Business impact analysis (BIA) | A process that identifies key business operations and the resources used to support those processes. A business impact analysis also identifies maximum tolerable downtime for critical business functions.

C

Chain of custody | Documentation that shows how evidence is collected, used, and handled throughout the lifetime of a case. A chain of custody document shows who obtained evidence, where and when it was obtained, who secured it, and who had control or possession of it.

Checklist test | A basic type of disaster recovery and business continuity test that checks to make sure that supplies and inventory items needed for an organization's business recovery are on hand.

Chief information officer (CIO) | An organization's senior information technology official. This role focuses on developing an organizations own IT resources.

Chief information security officer (CISO) | An organization's senior information security official.

Chief technology officer (CTO) | An organization's most senior technology official. This role focuses on developing an organization's technology products.

Civil procedure | Sets forth the procedures and processes that courts use to conduct civil trials.

Clickstream | The data trail that an Internet user creates while browsing. A clickstream is a record of the pages that a computer user visits when navigating on a particular Web site.

Clickwrap contract | An agreement where the complete terms of the agreement are presented on a computer screen, usually in the form of a pop-up window. A user must take an affirmative action to accept the terms of the agreement.

Cloud computing | A type of computing where both applications and infrastructure capabilities can be provided to end users through the Internet.

Code analysis | A category of computer forensics that focuses on examining programming code for malicious code or signatures. Code analysis also is known as malware forensics.

Code law | Law that is enacted by legislatures.

Cold site | A backup site for disaster recovery and business continuity planning purposes that is little more than reserved space. A cold site doesn't have any hardware or equipment ready for business operations. It will have electrical service, but most likely won't have network connectivity. It can take weeks to months for an organization to ready a cold site for business operations.

Common law | A body of law that is developed because of legal tradition and court cases. The U.S. common law is a body of law that was inherited from England.

Compensatory damages | A money award that compensates a non-breaching party for the other party's breach. These damages place the non-breaching party in the same position they would have been in had the contract been fully performed.

Competitive edge | The designs, blueprints, or plans that make an organization's product or service unique.

Complaint | The first document filed in a civil case. A plaintiff files it and it states the plaintiff's cause of action against a defendant.

Complete performance | Contractual performance where a party to a contract satisfies all of his or her promises.

Compliance | The action of following applicable laws and rules and regulations.

Computer forensics | The scientific process of collecting and examining data that is stored on or received or transmitted by an electronic device. Computer forensics also is called system forensics, digital forensics, computer forensic analysis, computer examination, data recovery, or inforensics.

Concurrent jurisdiction | Jurisdiction that is shared by several different courts.

Confidentiality | The security goal of ensuring that only authorized persons can access information systems and their data.

Conflict of interest | Any situation where a person's private interests and professional obligations collide. Independent observers might question whether a person's private interests improperly influence his or her professional decisions.

Consequential damages | A money award that compensates the non-breaching party for foreseeable damages that arise from circumstances outside of the contract.

Consideration | The mutual exchange of value between contracting parties. Consideration can be expressed as an exchange of money, goods, or a promise to perform a certain action.

Consumer goods | Items that an individual purchases for personal, family, or household use.

Consumer services | Services that an individual purchases for personal, family, or household use.

Contract | A legally binding agreement that is enforceable in court.

Contract of adhesion | A contract where one party has very little bargaining power. A contract of adhesion is a "take it or leave it" contract.

Contractual capacity | A legal term that refers to the ability of a party to enter into a contract.

Control | Any protective action that reduces information security risks. These actions may eliminate or lessen vulnerabilities, control threats, or reduce risk. Safeguards is another term for controls.

Cookie | A small string of code that a Web site stores on a user's computer. Web sites use cookies to remember specific information about visitors to the site.

Copyrights | Used to protect books, art, music, videos, computer programs, and other creative works.

Covered entity | Health plans, health care clearinghouses, any health care provider that transmits certain types of health information in electronic form. These entities must follow the HIPAA Security and Privacy Rules. This term is defined by the Health Insurance Portability and Accountability Act.

Criminal procedure | Sets forth the procedures and processes that courts follow in criminal law cases.

Cryptography | The science and practice of hiding information so that unauthorized persons can't read it.

D

Data destruction policies | State how data is to be destroyed when it reaches the end of its life cycle.

Data retention policies | State how data is to be controlled throughout its life cycle.

Deceptive trade practices | Any commercial practice that uses false or misleading claims to get customers to buy a product or service.

Defamation | A tort that involves maliciously saying false things about another person.

Denial of service (DoS) attack | Attack that disrupts information systems so that they're no longer available to users.

Design patents | Issued to protect new and original ornamental designs for manufactured objects.

Digital evidence | Evidence collected from an electronic device.

Disaster | A sudden, unplanned event that negatively affects the organization's critical business functions for an unknown period.

Disaster recovery (DR) plans | Plans that address the recovery of an organization's information technology systems in the event of a disaster.

Disclosure controls | A term used in the Sarbanes-Oxley Act. It refers to processes and procedures that a company uses to make sure that it makes timely disclosures to the U.S. Securities and Exchange Commission.

Disclosure | Refers to how a covered entity shares PHI with other organizations that may not be affiliated with it. This term is defined by the Health Insurance Portability and Accountability Act.

Discovery | The legal process used to gather evidence in a lawsuit.

Diversity of citizenship jurisdiction | Refers to the power of federal courts to hear disputes between citizens of different states only when they are above a certain dollar amount.

Dividend | Represents a shareholder's portion of the company's earnings.

Docket | The official schedule of a court and the events in the cases pending before a court. Many courts publish their dockets online.

Due process | The principle that ensures all parties in a case are entitled to a fair and consistent process within the courts.

Dumpster diving | Looking through discarded trash for personal information.

Duty of due care | A person's obligation to avoid acts or omissions that can harm others.

Duty to mitigate | A non-breaching party's obligation not to aggravate the harm caused by a breach.

E

Electronic protected health information (EPHI) | Patient health information that is computer based. It is PHI stored electronically. This term is defined by the Health Insurance Portability and Accountability Act.

End user license agreement (EULA) | A contract between the manufacturer or distributor of a piece of software or a service and the end user.

Exploit | A successful attack against a vulnerability.

Exposure factor | The percentage of asset loss that is likely to be caused by an identified threat or vulnerability.

External attacker | An attacker that has no current relationship with the organization they're attacking.

F

Fair information practice principles | Guidelines used to help describe how personal information should be collected and used.

Fair use | A copyright law concept that some use of copyrighted works in limited ways isn't copyright infringement.

Federal question jurisdiction | Refers to the power of federal courts to hear only disputes about federal laws or constitutional issues.

Felonies | The greater of two types of crimes. Felonies are more serious than misdemeanors. They're generally punishable by more than one year in prison.

Flaming | A series of insulting communications between Internet users. Flaming often occurs on online discussion boards.

Forensic duplicate image | An exact copy of an electronic media storage device. A bit-by-bit copy includes deleted files, slack space, and areas of the storage device that a normal file copy would not include.

Form 8-K | A report that a public company must file with the U.S. Securities and Exchange Commission. A company must file it within four days of experiencing a major event that affects shareholders and investors.

Form 10-K | A report that a public company must file with the U.S. Securities and Exchange Commission at the end of its fiscal year. It's a detailed and comprehensive report on the company's financial condition.

Form 10-Q | A report that a public company must file with the U.S. Securities and Exchange Commission at the end of each fiscal quarter. It's a report on the company's financial condition at the end of its first three quarters in a fiscal year.

Fruit of the poisonous tree doctrine | A legal doctrine that states that evidence that isn't gathered lawfully is tainted with illegality. Illegally gathered evidence can't be used in court. In addition, any subsequent evidence gathered as a result of the illegally obtained evidence can't be used in court either.

Full interruption test | A disaster recovery and business continuity test where an organization stops all of its normal business operations and transfers those operations to its backup site. This is the most comprehensive form of disaster recovery and business continuity plan testing. It also is the most expensive.

G

Global positioning system (GPS) | A navigation technology that uses satellites above the earth to compute the location of a GPS receiver.

Guidelines | Recommended actions and operational guides to users, IT staff, operations staff, and others when a specific standard doesn't apply.

H

Hearsay | Any out-of-court statement made by a person that is offered to prove some issue in a case. Gossip is a common example of hearsay.

Hot site | An operational backup site for disaster recovery and business continuity planning purposes. It has equipment and infrastructure that is fully compatible with an organization's main facility. It's not staffed with people. A hot site can become operational within minutes to hours after a disaster.

I

Identity theft | A crime that takes place when a person's personally identifiable information is used without permission in order to commit other crimes.

Incident | An event that adversely affects the confidentiality, integrity, and/or availability of an organization's data and information technology systems.

Incident response (IR) | A contingency plan that helps an organization respond to attacks against an organization's information technology infrastructure.

Incomplete performance | Contractual performance where a party to a contract doesn't perform his or her contractual promises.

Information security | The study and practice of protecting information. The main goal of information security is to protect its confidentiality, integrity, and availability.

Information security governance | Executive management's responsibility to provide strategic direction, oversight, and accountability for an organization's information and information systems resources.

Information security management | How an organization manages its day-to-day security activities. It makes sure that the policies dictated by the executive management team as part of its governance function are properly implemented.

Information | Intelligence, knowledge, and data. You can store information in paper or electronic form.

Inspector general (IG) | A federal government official who independently evaluates the performance of federal agencies. Inspector generals are independent officials.

Integrity | The security goal of ensuring that no changes are made to information systems and their data without permission.

Intellectual property | The area of law that protects a person's creative ideas, inventions, and innovations. It's protected by patents, trade secrets, trademarks, and copyright.

Internal attacker | An attacker that has a current relationship with the organization he or she is attacking. It can be an angry employee.

Internal controls | A term used in the Sarbanes-Oxley Act. It refers to the processes and procedures that a company uses to provide reasonable assurance that its financial reports are reliable.

J

Judicial review | A court's review of any issue. For federal courts, this refers to the authority of a court to declare actions unconstitutional.

Jurisdiction | The power of a court to hear a particular type of case. It also refers to the power of a court to hear cases involving people in a geographical area. For instance, a state court has the power to decide cases raised by citizens of that state.

L

Least privilege | A rule that systems should run with the lowest level of permissions needed to complete tasks. This means users should have the least amount of access needed to do their jobs.

Legislative history | The materials generated while creating laws. It includes committee reports and hearings. It also includes transcripts of debate and reports issued by legislatures. The legislative history is reviewed to help determine what a legislature intended when it created a law.

Libel | Written defamation.

Liquidated damages | A contractual grant of money damages that the parties determined prior to entering into a contract.

Locard's exchange principle | A basic assumption in forensic science that states that people always leave traces of their activities when they interact with other people or with other objects.

M

Mailbox rule | A common law rule that states that an acceptance is valid as soon as an offeree places it in the mail.

Mala in se | A Latin term used to describe conduct that is inherently wrong. It means "evil in itself."

Mala prohibita | A Latin term used to describe conduct that society prohibits. It means "wrong because it is prohibited."

Malware | A term that refers to any software that performs harmful, unauthorized, or unknown activity. The word malware combines the words malicious and software.

Mantrap | A physical security safeguard that controls entry into a protected area. This entry method has two sets of doors on either end of a small room. When a person enters a mantrap through one set of doors, that first set must close before the second set can open. Often a person entering a facility via a mantrap must present different credentials at each set of doors to gain access.

Maximum tolerable downtime (MTD) | The amount of time that critical business processes and resources can be offline before an organization begins to experience irreparable business harm.

Media analysis | A category of computer forensics that focuses on collecting and examining data stored on physical media.

Medical identity theft | A specialized type of identity theft. A crime that takes place when a person's personally identifiable health information is used without permission in order receive medical services or goods.

Mens rea | A Latin term used to describe the state of mind of a criminal. It means "guilty mind."

Minimum necessary rule | A rule that covered entities may only disclose the amount of PHI absolutely necessary to carry out a particular function. This term is defined by the Health Insurance Portability and Accountability Act.

Mirror image rule | A common law rule that states that an offer and acceptance must contain identical terms.

Mirrored site | A fully operational backup site for disaster recovery and business continuity planning purposes. This site actively runs an organization's information technology functions in parallel with the organization's mail processing facility. It's fully staffed. It has all necessary data and equipment to continue business operations.

Misdemeanor | The lesser of two types of crimes. Misdemeanors are less serious than felonies. They're generally punishable by no more than one year in prison.

N

National security systems | Information technology systems that hold military, defense, and intelligence information.

Need to know | A rule that users should have access to only the information they need to do their jobs.

Network analysis | A category of computer forensics that focuses on capturing and examining network traffic. It includes reviewing transaction logs and using real-time monitoring to identify and locate evidence.

Network banner | A warning banner that provides notice of legal rights to users of computer networks. They're generally displayed as a computer user logs into a network or on an entity's home page.

Nominal damages | A money award to the non-breaching party even though he or she hasn't suffered any financial loss because of a breach of contract.

Nonpublic personal information (NPI) | Any personally identifiable financial information that a consumer provides to a financial institution. This term is defined by the Gramm-Leach-Bliley Act.

O

Objection | A formal protect made by an attorney to a trial court judge. An attorney usually makes an objection if the opposing party is asking questions or submitting evidence that is inappropriate or violates a trial court rule.

Offer | An invitation made by an offeror to an offeree to enter into a contract.

Offeree | A person who receives an offer.

Offeror | A person who makes an offer.

Online profiling | The practice of tracking a user's actions on the Internet in order to create a profile of that user. The profile can be used to direct targeted advertising toward a particular user.

Operational planning | Day-to-day business planning.

Original jurisdiction | The authority of a court to hear a dispute between parties in the first instance, rather than on appeal.

P

Parallel test | A disaster recovery and business continuity test where an organization tests its ability to recover its information technology systems and its business data. In this type of test, the organization brings its backup recovery sites online. It will then use historical business data to test the operations of those systems.

Parental control | Software that allows a parent to control a child's activity on a computer. Parental controls can be used to restrict access to certain content, such as violent games, or to specific Web sites. They also can restrict the times a child can use a computer.

Patch | A piece of software or code that fixes a program's security vulnerabilities. Patches are available for many types of software, including operating systems.

Patent prosecution | The actions that the U.S. Patent and Trademark Office must complete in order to reject a patent application or issue a patent.

Patents | Used to protect inventions like machines, processes, designs, and specialized plants.

Pen register devices | Devices that monitor outgoing transmission data. They record dialing, routing, signaling, or address information.

Persistent data | Data that is stored on a hard drive or other storage media. It's preserved when an electronic device is turned off.

Personal jurisdiction | A court's ability to exercise power over a defendant.

Physical safeguard | Controls keep unauthorized individuals out of a building or other controlled areas. You can also use them to keep unauthorized individuals from using an information system. Examples include key-card access to buildings, fences, and intrusion monitoring systems.

Plant patents | Issued to protect inventions or discoveries of new varieties of plants that are reproduced asexually.

Pleadings | Documents filed in a court case.

Policy | An organization's high-level statement of information security direction and goals. Policies are the highest level governance document.

Pop-up advertisements | Advertisements that open a new Web browser window to display the advertisement.

Precedent | This doctrine means that courts will look at prior cases to determine the appropriate resolution for new cases.

Preemption | Legal concept that means that a higher ranking law will exclude or preempt a lower ranking law on the same subject.

Preponderance of the evidence | The standard of proof in a civil case. It means that it's more probable than not that an action (or wrong) took place.

Pretexting | Obtaining unauthorized access to a customer's sensitive financial information through false or misleading actions. Also called social engineering.

Prior art | Evidence of public knowledge about an invention that existed prior to a claimed invention or discovery date.

Privacy | A person's right to have control of his or her own personal data. The person has the right to specify how that data is collected, used, and shared.

Privacy impact assessment (PIA) | A review of how a federal agency's IT systems process personal information. The E-Government Act of 2002 requires federal agencies to conduct these assessments.

Private cause of action | A legal concept that describes a person's right to sue another for harm that the latter caused.

Privately held company | A company held by a small group of private investors.

Probative evidence | Probative evidence is evidence that proves or disproves a legal element in a case. If evidence isn't probative, then it can be excluded from a trial. Probative evidence also is known as relevant evidence.

Procedural law | Branches of law that deal with processes that courts use to decide cases.

Procedure | Detailed step-by-step tasks, or checklists, that should be performed to achieve a certain goal or task. Procedures are the lowest level governance document.

Protected health information (PHI) | Any individually identifiable information about the past, present, or future health of a person. It includes mental and physical health data. This term is defined by the Health Insurance Portability and Accountability Act.

Proxy server | A server that accepts Internet requests and retrieves the data. The proxy server can filter content to ensure that users view only acceptable content. Libraries and schools use proxy servers to comply with the Children's Internet Protection Act (CIPA).

Public company | A publicly traded company owned by a number of different investors. Investors own a percentage of the company through stock purchases. The stock of a public company is traded on a stock exchange.

Public domain | Refers to the collection of works that are free for public use. It includes works where the copyright has expired. It also includes some government works.

Public employees | Employees that work for the federal or state government.

Public records | Records required by law to be made available to the public. These types of records are made or filed by a governmental entity.

Public relations (PR) | A marketing field that manages an organization's public image.

Q

Qualitative risk analysis | A risk analysis method that uses scenarios and ratings systems to calculate risk and potential harm. Unlike quantitative risk analysis, qualitative risk analysis doesn't attempt to assign money value to assets and risk.

Quantitative risk analysis | A risk analysis method that uses real money costs and values to determine the potential monetary impact of threats and vulnerabilities.

R

Radio Frequency Identification (RFID) | A wireless technology that uses radio waves to transmit data to a receiver.

Realized risk | The loss that an organization has when a potential threat actually occurs.

Reasonable person standard | A legal concept used to describe an ordinary person. This fictitious ordinary person is used to represent how an average person would think and act.

Record | Any information about a person that a federal agency maintains. This term is defined in the Privacy Act of 1974.

Red Flag | Any pattern, practice, or activity that may indicate identity theft. This term is defined by the Fair and Accurate Credit Transaction Act of 2003.

Remedy | Legal relief that a court grants to an injured party.

Repudiation | A refusal to perform a contract duty.

Residual risk | The amount of risk left over after safeguards lessen a vulnerability or threat.

Risk acceptance | A business decision to accept an assessed risk and take no action against it.

Risk assessment (RA) | A process for identifying threats and vulnerabilities that an organization faces. Risk assessments can be quantitative, qualitative, or a combination of both.

Risk avoidance | A business decision to apply safeguards to avoid a negative impact.

Risk management (RM) | The process that an organization uses to identify risks, assess them, and reduce them to an acceptable level.

Risk mitigation | A business decision to apply safeguards to lessen a negative impact.

Risk transfer | A business decision to transfer risk to a third party to avoid that risk.

Risk | The chance, or probability, that a threat can exploit a vulnerability. The concept of risk includes an understanding that an exploited vulnerability has a negative business impact.

S

Safe harbor | A legal concept that protects an entity from liability if it follows the law.

Safeguard | Any protective action that reduces information security risks. They may eliminate or lesson vulnerabilities, control threats, or reduce risk. Safeguards also are called controls.

Seal program | A program administered by a trusted organization that verifies that another organization meets recognized privacy practices.

Search engine | A program that retrieves files and data from a computer network. Search engines are used to search the Internet for information.

Securities | The general term used to describe financial instruments that are traded on a stock exchange. Stocks and bonds are securities.

Security breach | Any compromise of a computer system that results in the loss of personally identifiable information.

Separation of duties | A rule that two or more employees must split critical task functions. Thus, no one employee knows all of the steps required to complete the critical task.

Servicemark | Used to protect words, logos, symbols, or slogans that identify a service.

Shoulder surfing | Looking over the shoulder of another person to obtain sensitive information. The attacker doesn't have permission to see it. This term usually describes an attack in which a person tries to learn sensitive information by viewing keystrokes on a monitor or keyboard.

Shrinkwrap contract | A software licensing agreement where the complete terms of the agreement are in a box containing the physical-media software.

Simulation test | A disaster recovery and business continuity test where an organization role-plays a specific disaster scenario. This type of test doesn't interrupt normal business operations and activities.

Single loss expectancy (SLE) | The amount of money that an organization stands to lose every time a specified risk is realized.

Single point of failure | In an information system, a piece of hardware or application critical to the entire system's functioning. If that single item fails,

then a critical portion or the entire system could fail. For networks, single points of failure could be firewalls, routers, switches, or hubs.

Slander | Oral defamation.

Social engineering | An attack that relies on human interaction. They often involve tricking other people to break security procedures so the attacker can gain information about computer systems. This type of attack isn't technical.

Social networking sites | Web site applications that allow users to post information about themselves.

Software as a Service (SaaS) | Commerce model where a vendor hosts a Web-based application and provides that application to its customers through the Internet.

Spam | Unsolicited e-mail. Spam is usually advertising or promotional e-mail.

Specific performance | A legal term that refers to situations where a court orders a party to complete their contractual duties.

Stakeholders | People that are affected by a policy, standard, guideline, or procedure. They're people who have an interest in a policy document.

Standards | Mandatory activities, actions, or rules that must be met in order to achieve policy goals. Standards are usually technology neutral.

Statute of frauds | A common law rule that states that certain types of contracts must be in writing and signed by the contracting parties.

Statute of limitations | The time period stated by law during which a plaintiff must take legal action against a wrongdoer. If a plaintiff doesn't take legal action within the stated time, they're forever barred from bringing that action in the future.

Strategic planning | Long-term business planning.

Strict liability | A legal concept that means that a person can be held responsible for their actions even if they didn't intend to cause harm to another person.

Subject matter jurisdiction | The power of a court to decide certain types of cases.

Substantial performance | Contractual performance where a party to a contract satisfies all of his or her material promises. Substantial performance doesn't meet all contract terms, non-performance of some terms may result in a minor breach of contract.

Substantive law | Branches of law that deal with particular legal subject matter, arranged by type. Property law, contract law, and tort law are all substantive areas of law.

System of records notice (SORN) | A federal agency's notice about agency record-keeping systems that can retrieve records through the use of a personal identifier. The Privacy Act of 1974 requires federal agencies to provide these notices.

T

Tactical planning | Short- to medium-term business planning.

Technical safeguard | Controls implemented in an information system's hardware and software. Technical controls include passwords, access control mechanisms, and automated logging. They improve the system's security.

Technology protection measure (TPM) | Technology used to filter objectionable content. CIPA requires the use of a TPM to protect children from objectionable content.

Threat | Any danger that takes advantage of a vulnerability. Threats are unintentional or intentional.

Tort | A wrongful act or harm for which a civil action can be brought. Tort law governs disputes between individuals.

Tortfeasor | A person who commits a tort.

Trade secrets | Used to protect formulas, processes, and methods that give a business a competitive edge.

Trademarks | Used to protect words, logos, symbols, or slogans that identify a product or service.

Trap and trace devices | Devices that monitor incoming transmission data. They capture incoming electronic signals that identify the originating transmission data.

Two-factor authentication | A method of authentication that requires a user to prove their identity in two or more ways.

U

Unfair trade practices | Any commercial practices that a consumer can't avoid and that cause injury.

Use | How a covered entity shares or handles PHI within its organization. This term is defined by the Health Insurance Portability and Accountability Act.

User credentials | Pieces of information used to access information technology resources. User credentials include passwords, personal identification numbers (PINs), tokens, smart cards, and biometric data.

Utility patents | Issued to protect inventions and discoveries such as machines, manufactured products, processes, and compositions of matter. They're the most common type of patent.

V

Volatile data | Data that is stored in the memory of an electronic device. It's lost when an electronic device is turned off.

Vulnerability | A weakness or flaw in an information system. Exploiting a vulnerability harms information security. You reduce them by applying security safeguards.

W

Walk-through test | A basic type of disaster recovery and business continuity test that reviews a disaster recovery/business continuity plan to make sure that all of the assumptions and tasks stated in the plan are correct. This type of test is sometimes called a tabletop walk-through test or tabletop test.

Warm site | A partially equipped backup site for disaster recovery and business continuity planning purposes. A warm site is space that contains some, but not all, of the equipment and infrastructure that an organization needs to continue operations in the event of a disaster. It's partially prepared for operations and has electricity and network connectivity.

Web beacon | A small, invisible electronic file that is placed on a Web page or in an e-mail message. Also called a "Web bug."

Window of vulnerability | The period between discovering a vulnerability and reducing or eliminating it.

Workplace privacy | Privacy issues encountered in the workplace. Hiring and firing practices and daily performance practices all have potential privacy concerns.

Z

Zero-day vulnerability | A vulnerability exploited shortly after it's discovered. The attacker exploits it before the vendor releases a patch.

References

Albion Research Ltd. "Risky Thinking—On Risk Assessment, Risk Management, and Business Continuity," 2010. http://www.riskythinking.com/ (accessed May 4, 2010).

American Bar Association. "Report to the House of Delegates, Section of Science and Technology Law," July 16, 2008. http://www.abanet.org/leadership/2008/annual/recommendations/ThreeHundredOne.doc (accessed May 11, 2010).

Anderson, Ross. *Security Engineering: A Guide to Building Dependable Distributed Systems*. New York: John Wiley & Sons, Inc., 2001.

Bonfield, Lloyd. *American Law and the American Legal System*. St. Paul, MN: Thomson/West, 2006.

Brinson, J. Dianne, et al. *Analyzing E-Commerce and Internet Law*. Upper Saddle River, NJ: Prentice-Hall, Inc., 2001.

Calder, Alan, and Steve Watkins. *International IT Governance: An Executive Guide to ISO 17799/ISO 27001*. London: Kogan Page Ltd (2006).

Cannon, J.C. *Privacy: What Developers and IT Professionals Should Know*. Boston: Addison-Wesley, 2005.

Carter, Patricia I. *HIPAA Compliance Handbook, 2010*. Frederick, MD: Aspen Publishers, 2010.

CERT Coordination Center. *Handbook for Computer Security Incident Response Teams (CSIRTs)*. 2nd ed. April 2003. http://www.cert.org/csirts/ (accessed May 1, 2010).

Cohen, Cynthia F., and Murray E. Cohen. "On-Duty and Off-Duty: Employee Right to Privacy and Employer's Right to Control in the Private Sector," 19 *Employer Responsibility and Rights Journal* 235 (2007).

Congressional Research Service. "Computer Security: A Summary of Selected Federal Laws, Executive Orders, and Presidential Directives," April 16, 2004. http://fas.org/irp/crs/RL32357.pdf (accessed April 24, 2010).

Duranske, Benjamin Tyson. *Virtual Law: Navigating the Legal Landscape of Virtual Worlds*. Chicago: American Bar Association, 2008.

Federal Communications Commission. "Children's Internet Protection Act (CIPA)," http://www.fcc.gov/cgb/consumerfacts/cipa.html (accessed February 16, 2010).

Federal Trade Commission. "Children's Online Privacy Protection Act of 1998" (n.d.). http://www.ftc.gov/ogc/coppa1.htm (accessed March 5, 2010).

———. "COPPA Compliance Checklist" (n.d.) http://www.ftc.gov/bcp/edu/ microsites/coppa/checklist.htm (accessed March 5, 2010).

———. "Fighting Fraud With the Red Flags Rule, A How-To Guide for Business," March 2009. http://www.ftc.gov/bcp/edu/pubs/business/idtheft/bus23.pdf (accessed February 1, 2010).

———. *Privacy of Consumer Financial Information* ("Financial Privacy Rule"), Code of Federal Regulations, Title 16, sec. 313, May 24, 2000.

———. "Protecting Kids' Privacy," January 2009. http://www.ftc.gov/ bcp/edu/pubs/consumer/tech/tec08.shtm (accessed March 5, 2010).

———. *Standards for Insuring the Security Confidentiality, Integrity and Protection of Customer Records and Information* ("Safeguards Rule"), Code of Federal Regulations, Title 16, sec. 314, May 23, 2002.

———. "Young Investor Website Settles FTC Charges,," May 6, 1999). http://www.ftc.gov/opa/1999/05/younginvestor.shtm (accessed March 5, 2010).

Feinman, Jay M. *Law 101: Everything You Need to Know About the American Legal System.* New York: Oxford University Press, Inc., 2006.

Ferrara, Gerald R., et al. *Cyberlaw: Your Rights in Cyberspace.* Cincinnati, OH: Thomson Learning, 2001.

Gallegos, Frederick. "Computer Forensics: An Overview," ISACA Control Journal 6 (2005). http://www.isaca.org/Content/NavigationMenu/Students_and_Educators/IT_Audit_Basics/Computer_Forensics_An_Overview.htm (accessed May 10, 2010).

Grama, Joanna, and Scott Ksander. "Recent Indiana Legislation Hopes to Stem Release of Personally Identifying Information," 50 Res Gestae, Volume 4, December 2006; reprinted in *Indiana Civil Litigation Review*, Vol. III, No. 2, Fall–Winter (2006).

H.R. Rep. No. 107-787, pt.1, at 54 (2002), as reprinted in 2002 U.S.C.C.A.N. 1880, 1889. http://frwebgate.access.gpo.gov/cgi-bin/getdoc.cgi?dbname=107_cong_ reports&docid=f:hr787p1.107.pdf (accessed April 21, 2010).

Harshbarger, William G., Jr. information technology security engineer, Purdue University. Interview by author. West Lafayette, Indiana, April 14, 2010.

Hirsch, Eric Donald, Joseph F. Kett, and James S. Trefil. *The New Dictionary of Cultural Literacy.* 3rd ed. New York: Houghton Mifflin Co., 2002.

House of Representatives Committee on Oversight and Government Reform. "Federal Information Security: Current Challenges and Future Policy Considerations," March 24, 2010. http://oversight.house.gov/index.php?option=com_content&task=view&id=4855&Itemid=28 (accessed April 21, 2010).

Hutchins, John P. ed. *U.S. Data Breach Notification Law: State by State.* Chicago: American Bar Association, 2007.

International Organization for Standardization. "ISO/IEC 27001:2005—Information Technology—Security Techniques—Information Security Management Systems—Requirements," 2006.

———. "ISO/IEC 27002: 2005, Information Technology—Security Techniques—Code of Practice for Information Security Management," July 2007.

Internet Crime Complaint Center. "2009 Annual Report on Internet Crime Fraud," March 12, 2010. http://www.ic3.gov/media/annualreport/2009_IC3Report.pdf (accessed April 2, 2010).

Internet Free Expression Alliance. "TITLE XVII—Children's Internet Protection," (n.d.). http://ifea.net/cipa.pdf (accessed March 14, 2010),

IT Governance Institute, "IT Control Objectives for Sarbanes-Oxley: The Role of IT in the Design and Implementation of Internal Control Over Financial Reporting, Second Edition," September 2006. http://www.isaca.org/AMTemplate.cfm?Section=Deliverables&Template=/MembersOnly.cfm&ContentFileID=19363 (accessed April 15, 2010).

Kidd, Donnie L., and William H. Daughtrey, Jr. "Adapting Contract Law to Accommodate Electronic Contracts: Overview and Suggestions." *Rutgers Computer and Technology Law Journal* 26 (2000): 215.

Kraft, Betsy Harvey. *Sensational Trials of the 20th Century*. New York: Scholastic Press, 1998.

Kroger, John R. Convictions: *A Prosecutor's Battles Against Mafia Killers, Drug Kingpins, and Enron Thieves*. New York: Farrar, Straus, and Giroux, 2008.

Ksander, Scott L., chief information security officer, Purdue University. Interview by author. West Lafayette, Indiana, April 14, 2010.

LaFave, Wayne, and Jerold H. Israel. *Criminal Procedure*. 2nd ed. St. Paul, MN: West Publishing Co., 1992.

Landoll, Douglas J., *The Security Risk Assessment Handbook*. Boca Raton, FL: Auerbach Publications, 2006.

"Legislative History of Major FERPA Provisions." (U.S. Department of Education, February 11, 2004). http://www2.ed.gov/policy/gen/guid/fpco/ferpa/leg-history.html (accessed February 16, 2010).

Lonardo, Thomas, Doug White, and Alan Rea. "To License or Not to License Revisited: An Examination of State Statutes Regarding Private Investigators and Digital Examiners," *The Journal of Digital Forensics, Security and Law* 4, no. 3 (2009): Reprint. http://www.jdfsl .org/ subscriptions/JDFSL-V4N3-Lonardo.pdf (accessed May 10, 2010).

Microsoft Corporation. "Security Risk Management Guide," March 16, 2006. http://technet .microsoft.com/en-us/library/cc163143.aspx (accessed May 1, 2010).

Moeller, Robert R. *Sarbanes-Oxley Internal Controls*. Hoboken, NJ: John Wiley & Sons, Inc., 2008.

National Institute of Standards and Technology (NIST). "Special Publication 800-53 (Rev. 3): Recommended Security Controls for Federal Information Systems and Organizations," August 2009.

———. "FISMA Detailed Overview," April 13, 2010. http://csrc.nist.gov/groups/SMA/fisma/ overview.html (accessed April 17, 2010).

———. "Special Publication 800-30, Risk Management Guide for Information Technology Systems," October 2001. http://csrc.nist.gov/publications/nistpubs/800-30/sp800-30.pdf (accessed April 29, 2010).

———. "Special Publication 800-34, Contingency Planning Guide for Information Technology Systems," June 2002. http://csrc.nist.gov/publications/nistpubs/800-34/sp800-34.pdf (accessed May 2, 2010).

Obama, Barack, president of the United States. Remarks "On Securing Our Nation's Cyber Infrastructure," May 29, 2009. http://www.whitehouse.gov/the_press_office/Remarks-by -the-President-on-Securing-Our-Nations-Cyber-Infrastructure/ (accessed April 21, 2010).

Organization for Economic Cooperation and Development. "OECD Guidelines on the Protection of Privacy and Transborder Flows of Personal Data," September 1980. http://www.oecd.org/ document/18/0,3343,en_2649_34255_1815186_1_1_1_1,00.html (accessed February 6, 2010).

Patrick, Walter F. "Creating an Information Systems Security Policy" (SANS Institute, 2001). http://www.sans.org/reading_room/whitepapers/policyissues/creating_an_information _systems_security_policy_534 (accessed January 21, 2010).

Peltier, Thomas R. *Information Security Risk Analysis*. Boca Raton, FL: Taylor & Francis Group, LLC, 2005.

Prosser, William L., et al. *Prosser and Keeton on the Law of Torts*. 5th ed. St. Paul, MN: West Pub. Co., 1984.

Rudolph, Kaie. Personal communication and unpublished manuscript on computer forensics. West Lafayette, Indiana, May 10, 2010.

Rustad, Michael L. *Internet Law*. St. Paul, MN: Thomson Reuters, 2009.

Scheb, John M., and John M. Scheb II. *An Introduction to the American Legal System*. Albany. NY: Delmar, 2002.

Soma, John T., and Stephen D. Rynerson. *Privacy Law*. St. Paul, MN: Thomson/West, 2008.

Sprague, Robert, and Corey Ciocchetti. "Preserving Identities: Protecting Personal Identifying Information Through Enhanced Privacy Policies and Laws." *Albany Law Journal of Science and Technology* 19 (2009): 91.

Stewart, James Michael, Ed Tittel, and Mike Chapple. CISSP: *Certified Information Systems Security Professional Study Guide*. 4th ed. Alameda, CA: Sybex, 2008.

Stim, Richard. *Intellectual Property: Patents, Trademarks, and Copyrights*. Albany, NY: Delmar, 2001.

Swire, Peter P., and Sol Bermann. *Information Privacy, Official Reference for the Certified Information Privacy Professional (CIPP)*. York, ME: International Association of Privacy Professionals, 2007.

Tasker, Ty, and Daryn Pakcyk. "Cyber-Surfing on the High Seas of Legalese: Law and Technology of Internet Agreements." *Albany Law Journal of Science and Technology* 18 (2008): 79.

Taylor, Laura. FISMA: *Certification & Accreditation Handbook*. Rockland, MA: Syngress Publishing, Inc., 2007.

Thomas, Daphyne Saunders and Karen A. Forcht, "Legal Methods of Using Computer Forensics Techniques for Computer Crime Analysis and Investigation," *Issues in Information Systems* V, No. 2 (2004): 692. http://www.iacis.org/iis/2004_iis/PDFfiles/ThomasForcht .pdf (accessed May 12, 2010).

Tipton, Harold, and Kevin Henry, eds. *Official (ISC)² Guide to the CISSP CBK*. Boca Raton, FL: Auerbach Publications, 2007.

Tipton, Harold, and Micki Krause, eds. *Information Security Management Handbook*. 5th ed. Boca Raton, FL: Auerbach Publications, 2004.

U.S. Copyright Office. "Copyright Basics," Circular 1, last revised October 2008. http:// www .copyright.gov/circs/circ1.pdf (accessed March 21, 2010).

———. "Reproduction of Copyrighted Works by Educators and Librarians," Circular 21, last revised November 2009. http://www.copyright.gov/circs/circ21.pdf (accessed March 21, 2010).

U.S. Department of Health and Human Services. "Breach Notification Rule," 2009. http:// www .hhs.gov/ocr/privacy/hipaa/administrative/breachnotificationrule/index.html (accessed March 6, 2010).

———. "HIPAA Security Information Series," 2003. http://www.hhs.gov/ocr/privacy/hipaa/ administrative/securityrule/securityruleguidance.html (accessed March 5, 2010).

————. "OCR Privacy Brief: Summary of the HIPAA Privacy Rule," May 2003. http://www.hhs
.gov/ocr/privacy/hipaa/understanding/summary/privacysummary.pdf (accessed March 3,
2010).

U.S. Department of Health, Education, and Welfare. "Records, Computers and the Rights
of Citizens: Report of the Secretary's Advisory Committee on Automated Personal Data
Systems," July 1973. http://aspe.hhs.gov/datacncl/1973privacy/c3.htm (accessed
February 6, 2010).

U.S. Department of Justice. "Searching and Seizing Computers and Obtaining Electronic Evidence
in Criminal Investigations." 3rd ed. September 2009. http://www.justice.gov/criminal/
cybercrime/ssmanual/index.html (accessed May 14, 2010).

U.S. Department of Justice and Federal Bureau of Investigation. "Regional Computer Forensics
Laboratory, RCFL Annual Report for Fiscal Year 2009," 2009. http://www.rcfl.gov/
downloads/documents/RCFL_Nat_Annual09.pdf (accessed May 12, 2010).

U.S. Department of Justice, Computer Crime and Intellectual Property Section. "Prosecuting
Computer Crimes," February 2007. http://www.justice.gov/criminal/cybercrime/ccmanual/
index.html (accessed April 2, 2010).

U.S. Department of Justice, National Institute of Justice. "Electronic Crime Scene Investigation:
A Guide for First Responders," 2nd ed., April 2008. http://www.ncjrs.gov/pdffiles1/
nij/219941.pdf (accessed May 10, 2010).

————. "Forensic Examination of Digital Evidence: A Guide for Law Enforcement," April 2004.
http://www.ncjrs.gov/pdffiles1/nij/199408.pdf (accessed May 10, 2010).

————. "Investigations Involving the Internet and Computer Networks," January 2007. http://
www.ncjrs.gov/pdffiles1/nij/210798.pdf (accessed May 10, 2010).

U.S. Executive Branch. "The National Strategy to Secure Cyberspace," February 2003. http://
www.us-cert.gov/reading_room/cyberspace_strategy.pdf (accessed April 24, 2010).

U.S. Government Accountability Office. "Cybersecurity: Progress Made but Challenges Remain
in Defining and Coordinating the Comprehensive National Initiative," GAO-10-338, March 5,
2010. http://www.gao.gov/products/GAO-10-338 (accessed April 23, 2010).

————. "Information Security: Concerted Response Needed to Resolve Persistent Weaknesses,"
March 24, 2010. http://www.gao.gov/new.items/d10536t.pdf (accessed April 23, 2010).

U.S. Office of Management and Budget. "Fiscal Year 2009 Report to Congress on the
Implementation of the Federal Information Security Management Act of 2002," March
2010. http://www.whitehouse.gov/omb/assets/egov_docs/FY09_FISMA.pdf (accessed
April 21, 2010).

————. "Memo M-03-22: OMB Guidance for Implementing the Privacy Protections of the
E-Government Act of 2002," September 26, 2003. http://www.whitehouse.gov/omb/
memoranda_m03-22/#15 (accessed April 25, 2010).

————. "Memo M-10-15: FY 2010 Reporting Instructions for the Federal Information
Security Management Act and Agency Privacy Management," April 21, 2010. http://www
.whitehouse. gov/omb/assets/memoranda_2010/m10-15.pdf (accessed April 23, 2010).

U.S. Patent and Trademark Office. "A Guide to Filing a Design Patent Application," n.d. http://
www.uspto.gov/patents/resources/types/index.jsp (accessed March 19, 2010).

————. "A Guide to Filing A Non-Provisional (Utility) Patent Application," n.d. http://www
.uspto.gov/patents/resources/types/utility.jsp (accessed March 19, 2010).

———. "General Information About 35 U.S.C. 161 Plant Patents," n.d. http://www.uspto.gov/web/offices/pac/plant/ (accessed March 19, 2010).

———. "Trademark Basics," n.d. http://www.uspto.gov/trademarks/basics/index.jsp (accessed March 21, 2010).

U.S. Securities and Exchange Commission. "Commission Statement on Implementation of Internal Control Reporting Requirements," May 16, 2005. http://www.sec.gov/news/press/2005-74.htm (accessed April 14, 2010).

———. "Staff Statement on Management's Report on Internal Control Over Financial Reporting," May 16, 2005. http://www.sec.gov/info/accountants/stafficreporting.htm (accessed April 15, 2010).

Warren, Samuel, and Louis Brandeis. "The Right to Privacy," 4 *Harvard Law Review* 193 (1890).

Watnick, Valerie. "The Electronic Formation of Contracts and the Common Law 'Mailbox Rule.'" *Baylor Law Review* 56 (2004): 175.

Welytok, Jill Gilbert. *Sarbanes-Oxley for Dummies*. Hoboken, NJ: Wiley Publishing Inc., 2008.

Whitcomb, Carrie Morgan, "An Historical Perspective of Digital Evidence: A Forensic Scientist's Point of View," *International Journal of Digital Evidence* 1, Issue 1 (2002): Reprint. http://www.utica.edu/academic/institutes/ecii/publications/articles/9C4E695B-0B78-1059-3432402909E27BB4.pdf (accessed May 12, 2010).

White, James J., and Robert S. Summers. *Uniform Commercial Code*. 5th ed. St. Paul, MN: West Group, 2000.

Winter, Cory S. "The Rap on Clickwrap: How Procedural Unconscionability Is Threatening the E-Commerce Marketplace." *Widener Law Journal* 18 (2008): 249.

Wood, Charles Cresson. *Information Security Policies Made Easy*. 8th ed. Houston: Pentasafe Security Technologies, Inc., 2001.

Wu, Stephen S., ed. *A Guide to HIPAA Security and the Law*. Chicago: American Bar Association Publishing, 2007.

Index